ISSUES FOR DEBATE IN ENVIRONMENTAL MANAGEMENT

SELECTIONS FROM CQ RESEARCHER

$SAGE

Los Angeles | London | New Delhi
Singapore | Washington DC

For information:

 SAGE Publications, Inc.
2455 Teller Road
Thousand Oaks, California 91320
E-mail: order@sagepub.com

SAGE Publications Ltd.
1 Oliver's Yard
55 City Road
London EC1Y 1SP
United Kingdom

SAGE Publications India Pvt. Ltd.
B 1/I 1 Mohan Cooperative Industrial Area
Mathura Road, New Delhi 110 044
India

SAGE Publications Asia-Pacific Pte. Ltd.
33 Pekin Street #02-01
Far East Square
Singapore 048763

Printed in the United States of America

Library of Congress Cataloging-in-Publication Data

Issues for debate in environmental management: selections from CQ researcher.
    p. cm.
ISBN 978-1-4129-7877-4 (pbk.)
    1. Environmentalism—Economic aspects. 2. Industries—Environmental aspects. 3. Environmental policy—Economic aspects. I. CQ researcher.

HC79.E5I86 2010
333.7—dc22   2009029558

This book is printed on acid-free paper.

09   10   11   12   13   10   9   8   7   6   5   4   3   2   1

Acquisitions Editor:	Lisa Cuevas Shaw
Editorial Assistant:	MaryAnn Vail
Production Editor:	Laureen Gleason
Typesetter:	C&M Digitals (P) Ltd.
Cover Designer:	Candice Harman
Marketing Manager:	Christy Guilbault

Contents

Annotated Contents

The New Environmentalism:
Can New Business Policies Save the Environment?

Concern about the environment is intensifying, but new efforts to reduce pollution and save energy differ from past environmental movements. Unable to get much satisfaction from the Republican-dominated federal government, environmental activists have set their sights on businesses — trying to influence corporate behavior and even forming partnerships with companies to confront environmental challenges. A growing number of businesses — including Wal-Mart, the world's biggest retailer — are concluding that saving the environment is good for the bottom line. But some conservative critics charge that such actions actually dilute companies' primary purpose — to increase shareholder value. Meanwhile, in the absence of federal action, state and local governments are instituting policies aimed at weaning industry from fossil fuels. And some environmentalists are even rethinking nuclear power.

Curbing Climate Change: Is the World Doing Enough?

The scientific consensus on global warming is sobering: It's real, it's happening now and carbon-dioxide emissions caused by the burning of fossil fuels are almost certainly responsible. Predicting what the exact effects will be on humanity and the planet's living resources is trickier, but a growing body of evidence suggests they will be profound. The international community generally—and the European Union in particular—take the threat very seriously, and most wealthy industrial nations have adopted mandatory limits on carbon emissions under the 2005 Kyoto

Protocol. The United States—the world's largest carbon emitter—has refused to sign the protocol or adopt mandatory limits, and is seen by other nations as obstructing progress on the issue. Kyoto expires in 2012, and world governments are working on a successor agreement. Many experts say the effort will fail without active U.S. leadership and the participation of major developing-world polluters such as China and India, with potentially dire consequences.

Confronting Warming: Can States and Localities Prevent Climate Change?

Growing concern about climate change has led states and cities to adopt new policies to try to conserve energy and reduce emissions of carbon dioxide and other greenhouse gases. California recently adopted new rules that aim to reduce such gases by 30 percent by 2020, while a cap on carbon emissions in the Northeast took effect Jan. 1, 2009. But critics say the efforts are more symbolic than substantive, pushing real sacrifices far off into the future. Many business groups, meanwhile, complain that the new rules will increase the cost of energy and hurt the economy—despite current promises that a "Green New Deal" can create jobs. The Obama administration promises to be far more aggressive in addressing global warming than the skeptical Bush White House. Even though the issue is coming to the fore in Washington, states and cities that have filled the policy vacuum in recent years pledge to stay vigilant in addressing the issue.

Reducing Your Carbon Footprint: Can Individual Actions Reduce Global Warming?

As climate change rises closer to the top of the government's policy agenda—and an economic crisis intensifies—more and more consumers are trying to change their behavior so they pollute and consume less. To reduce their individual "carbon footprints," many are cutting gasoline and home-heating consumption, choosing locally grown food and recycling. While such actions are important in curbing global warming, the extent to which consumers can reduce or reverse broad-scale environmental damage is open to debate. Moreover, well-intentioned personal actions can have unintended consequences that cancel out positive effects. To have the greatest impact, corporate and government policy must lead the way, many environmental advocates say.

Carbon Trading: Will It Reduce Global Warming?

Carbon emissions trading—the buying and selling of permits to emit greenhouse gases caused by burning fossil fuels—is becoming a top strategy for reducing pollution that causes global climate change. Some $60 billion in permits were traded worldwide in 2007, a number expected to grow much larger if the next U.S. administration follows through on pledges to reduce America's carbon emissions. Advocates say carbon trading is the best way to generate big investments in low-carbon energy alternatives and control the cost of cutting emissions. But carbon trading schemes in Europe and developing countries have a mixed record. Some industries are resisting carbon regulations, and programs intended to help developing countries onto a clean energy path have bypassed many poor nations, which are the most vulnerable to the impacts of climate change. Some experts argue that there are simpler, more direct ways to put a price on carbon emissions, such as taxes. Others say curbing climate change will require both taxes and trading, plus massive government investments in low-carbon energy technologies.

Race for the Arctic: Who Owns the Region's Undiscovered Oil and Gas?

With oil prices soaring, revelations that the Arctic could contain up to 22 percent of the world's undiscovered oil and gas have given extra impetus to an international race to claim the region's $1 trillion in oil and other riches. Russia kick-started the race last summer when it stunned the world by planting its flag on the North Pole seabed—two miles below the Arctic Ocean. Global warming has dramatically shrunk the ice covering the ocean, raising the prospect of new, shorter transcontinental shipping routes and spurring the United States, Canada, Russia, Denmark and Norway to begin gathering data to prove they own large swaths of offshore Arctic territory. But environmentalists warn that tougher international rules are needed—possibly an Arctic treaty—to prevent energy exploration from exacerbating global warming and damaging the fragile region. The Inuit and other indigenous groups also fear their concerns will be ignored in the dash to extract riches from the region.

Future of Recycling: Is a Zero-Waste Society Achievable?

Three-quarters of all Americans recycle at home, making recycling one of the nation's most popular environmental activities. Skeptics argue that recycling does little to help the environment and often costs more than burying waste in landfills, but rising energy prices and concerns about climate change are strengthening the supporters' case. Making new goods from scrap metal, glass or paper uses less energy and generates fewer greenhouse gases than extracting and processing virgin materials. Today the U.S. recycles more than 30 percent of its municipal solid waste, and advocates say that figure could be much higher. Diverting more waste from landfills, however, will involve finding ways to handle new materials such as food scraps. Meanwhile, a growing stream of junked computers, televisions and other electronic trash—much of it containing toxic materials—is forcing manufacturers to take responsibility for disposing of their products.

Buying Green: Does It Really Help the Environment?

Americans will spend an estimated $500 billion this year on products and services that claim to be good for the environment because they contain non-toxic ingredients or produce little pollution and waste. While some shoppers buy green to help save the planet, others are concerned about personal health and safety. Whatever their motives, eco-consumers are reshaping U.S. markets. To attract socially conscious buyers, manufacturers are designing new, green products and packaging, altering production processes and using sustainable materials. But some of these products may be wastes of money. Federal regulators are reviewing green labeling claims to see whether they mislead consumers, while some critics say that government mandates promoting environmentally preferable products distort markets and raise prices. Even if green marketing delivers on its pledges, many environmentalists say that sustainability is not a matter of buying green but of buying less.

Regulating Toxic Chemicals: Do We Know Enough About Chemical Risks?

Chemicals are integral to many everyday products, from electronics and toys to building materials and household goods. But environmental, health and consumer advocates say the agencies responsible for protecting Americans from exposure to harmful chemicals are allowing too many dangerous substances into the market without testing them for toxicity. Some goods, such as medicines, are tested for safety before they can be sold, but many common products do not go through premarket safety screening. Many concerns focus on infants and young children, who are especially sensitive to toxic hazards. Chemical manufacturers say the existing regulatory system works effectively and can be tightened to address new concerns, but critics argue that a precautionary approach—which would require producers to show that materials are safe before they can be marketed—would protect consumers more fully.

Coal's Comeback: Can Coal Become a Clean Energy Source?

Many Americans regard coal as a high-polluting fuel of the past, but today the U.S. is on the verge of a new coal energy boom. Coal-burning power plants generate half the nation's electricity, and that share could grow. More than 150 new coal power plants are planned or under construction, but critics oppose many of them. Coal is cheap and plentiful compared to other fuels, but it also produces air pollutants that contribute to acid rain, smog and climate change and cause thousands of deaths every year. Supporters say technology can make coal a pollution-free energy source in coming decades and that coal could even be used to make liquid fuels as a substitute for oil. But environmental and health advocates argue that the damaging impacts from mining, transporting and burning coal cancel out its value as an energy source. As Congress and the states debate proposals to combat global warming, regulators and businesses weigh coal's energy benefits against its health and environmental liabilities.

Ecotourism: Does It Help or Hurt Fragile Lands and Cultures?

In the booming global travel business, ecotourism is among the fastest-growing segments. Costa Rica and Belize have built national identities around their celebrated environmental allure, while parts of the world once all but inaccessible—from Antarctica to the Galapagos Islands to Mount Everest—are now featured in travel guides, just like Manhattan, Rome and other less exotic destinations. Advocates see ecotourism as a powerful yet environmentally benign tool for sustainable economic development in even the poorest nations. But as the trend expands, critics see threats to the very flora and fauna tourists flock to visit. Moreover, traditional subsistence cultures may be obliterated by the ecotourism onslaught, replaced by service jobs that pay native peoples poverty wages. Meanwhile, tour promoters are using the increasingly popular "green" label to lure visitors to places unable to withstand large numbers of tourists.

Rebuilding New Orleans: Should Flood-Prone Areas Be Redeveloped?

Five months after Hurricane Katrina flooded most of New Orleans, some 80 percent of the "Crescent City" remains unrepaired. Damage is estimated at $35 billion. Most schools and businesses are still closed, and two-thirds of the 460,000 residents have moved out. How many will return remains troublingly uncertain. Municipal leaders only this month began setting up a process to decide which of the city's 73 neighborhoods can be resettled and which would be left uninhabited to soak up future floodwaters. Questions about who will help the city's poorer residents—many of them African-American—hang over the city, along with concern about how much of New Orleans' storied popular culture will survive. Meanwhile, as a new hurricane season approaches, efforts to repair and strengthen the protective system of levees, canals and pumps lag behind schedule.

Protecting Wetlands: Is the Government Doing Enough?

The nation's millions of acres of wetlands are valuable natural resources. Ponds, lakes, swamps, bogs, bays and marine estuaries not only shelter countless fish, birds and animals but also filter pollutants from water and soak up floodwaters. Since the United States was settled, more than half of its wetlands have been lost, and crucial areas like Louisiana's coast and the Florida Everglades are eroding daily. Although the U.S. is now gaining more wetlands every year than it is losing, scientists say too many acres of crucially needed wetlands are still being lost. For several decades national policy has called for protecting wetlands, but the powerful construction, energy and agriculture industries say current environmental regulations make projects too expensive. Conservationists,

sportsmen and many state officials argue that stronger regulations are still urgently needed. Meanwhile, recent Supreme Court decisions have intensified debate over how broadly the federal government can oversee activities affecting wetlands.

Looming Water Crisis: Is the World Running Out of Water?

In the past decade drought has marched across much of the globe, hitting China, the Mediterranean, southeast Australia and the U.S. Sun Belt. The amount of water used by humans has tripled since 1950, and irrigated cropland has doubled. About one-fifth of the world's population lacks sufficient water, a figure that could reach 40 percent by 2025 by some estimates, in part because of growing world economies. In the poorest societies more than a billion people lack access to clean water, and dirty water kills 5,000 children—enough to fill 12 jumbo jets—every day. By century's end drought is expected to spread across half the Earth's land surface due to climate change, causing hunger and higher food prices. The United Nations says it would cost an extra $10 billion or more annually to provide clean water and sanitation for all. Some recommend privatizing water supplies, while others suggest that charging more for water to encourage conservation would help to avoid future crises.

Oceans in Crisis: Can the Loss of Ocean Biodiversity Be Halted?

The world's oceans are in a dire state. Large predatory species are being decimated—including sharks, whales, tuna, grouper, cod, halibut, swordfish and marlin—and replaced by species with less commercial and nutritive value. In fact, a growing body of evidence suggests that the world's marine ecosystems have been altered so dramatically they are undergoing evolution in reverse, returning to a time when algae and jellyfish dominated the seas. The crisis is having an increasingly profound effect on humans. Fishing cultures from Newfoundland to West Africa are vanishing, and toxic algal blooms have closed beaches and recreational areas from Florida to the Black Sea. The damage is being caused by overfishing, climate change and destruction of habitat due to coastal development and pollution. Scientists and policy makers widely agree that a broad-based approach known as ecosystem-based management would help restore the oceans' productivity, but significant research and strong international cooperation are needed to bring about such a shift.

Biofuels Boom: Can Ethanol Satisfy America's Thirst for Foreign Oil?

Energy companies across the Midwest are building new plants to convert locally grown corn into ethanol. The construction spurt is the most visible evidence of expanded interest in renewable fuels, which politicians increasingly believe can begin to wean America from its voracious appetite for foreign oil. Ethanol, the only renewable fuel being produced in the United States in any significant quantity, is being aggressively promoted as a key ingredient in the quest for energy security. But before competing head-to-head with gasoline, it will have to overcome major hurdles. Not only is it more expensive to produce, but some studies say it takes more energy to process corn into ethanol than the fuel delivers. Experts believe a more viable long-term ethanol source could be switchgrass or other so-called cellulosic biomass. The current biofuels boom also bodes well for other renewables, including biodiesel, which has achieved popularity in Europe.

Fish Farming: Is It Safe for Humans and the Environment?

Global demand for fish products has doubled since the 1950s and is still rising. Today more than 40 percent of the world's seafood comes not from wild catches but from land-based and offshore farms. With many wild fisheries already overharvested throughout the world, aquaculture is an important food source—especially for poor countries—and has made seafood more abundant and affordable. But some fish farms pollute surrounding waters, and escaped farm fish compete with wild stocks and spread diseases. Moreover, raising carnivorous fish can use up more fish protein for feed than it produces, further stressing wild fisheries. There are also growing concerns about whether imported seafood is safe to eat and whether the United States regulates fish imports strictly enough. Congress is considering legislation to expand ocean aquaculture, but many fish and marine experts urge caution, saying we know little about the potential impact on the oceans.

Preface

Can new business policies save the environment? Will carbon trading reduce global warming? Is a zero-waste society achievable? These questions—and many more—are at the heart of environmental management and issues of sustainability. How can instructors best engage students with these crucial issues? We feel that students need objective, yet provocative examinations of these issues to understand how they affect citizens, managers and organizations today and will for years to come. This collection aims to promote in-depth discussion, facilitate further research and help readers formulate their own positions on crucial issues. Get your students talking both inside and outside the classroom about *Issues for Debate in Environmental Management*.

This first edition includes seventeen up-to-date reports by *CQ Researcher*, an award-winning weekly policy brief that brings complicated issues down to earth. Each report chronicles and analyzes executive, legislative and judicial activities at all levels of government.

CQ RESEARCHER

CQ Researcher was founded in 1923 as *Editorial Research Reports* and was sold primarily to newspapers as a research tool. The magazine was renamed and redesigned in 1991 as *CQ Researcher*. Today, students are its primary audience. While still used by hundreds of journalists and newspapers, many of which reprint portions of the reports, the *Researcher's* main subscribers are now high school, college and public libraries. In 2002, *Researcher* won the

American Bar Association's coveted Silver Gavel award for magazine excellence for a series of nine reports on civil liberties and other legal issues.

Researcher staff writers—all highly experienced journalists—sometimes compare the experience of writing a *Researcher* report to drafting a college term paper. Indeed, there are many similarities. Each report is as long as many term papers—about 11,000 words—and is written by one person without any significant outside help. One of the key differences is that writers interview leading experts, scholars and government officials for each issue.

Like students, staff writers begin the creative process by choosing a topic. Working with the *Researcher's* editors, the writer identifies a controversial subject that has important public policy implications. After a topic is selected, the writer embarks on one to two weeks of intense research. Newspaper and magazine articles are clipped or downloaded, books are ordered and information is gathered from a wide variety of sources, including interest groups, universities and the government. Once the writers are well informed, they develop a detailed outline, and begin the interview process. Each report requires a minimum of ten to fifteen interviews with academics, officials, lobbyists and people working in the field. Only after all interviews are completed does the writing begin.

CHAPTER FORMAT

Each issue of *CQ Researcher*, and therefore each selection in this book, is structured in the same way. Each begins with an overview, which briefly summarizes the areas that will be explored in greater detail in the rest of the chapter. The next section chronicles important and current debates on the topic under discussion and is structured around a number of key questions, such as "Is going 'green' good for the corporate bottom line?" or "Can the industrial world switch from fossil fuels to other forms of energy?" These questions are usually the subject of much debate among practitioners and scholars in the field. Hence, the answers presented are never conclusive but detail the range of opinion on the topic.

Next, the "Background" section provides a history of the issue being examined. This retrospective covers important legislative measures, executive actions and court decisions that illustrate how current policy has evolved. Then the "Current Situation" section examines contemporary policy issues, legislation under consideration and legal action being taken. Each selection concludes with an "Outlook" section, which addresses possible regulation, court rulings and initiatives from Capitol Hill and the White House over the next five to ten years.

Each report contains features that augment the main text: two to three sidebars that examine issues related to the topic at hand, a pro versus con debate between two experts, a chronology of key dates and events and an annotated bibliography detailing major sources used by the writer.

ACKNOWLEDGMENTS

We wish to thank many people for helping to make this collection a reality. Tom Colin, managing editor of *CQ Researcher*, gave us his enthusiastic support and cooperation as we developed this edition. He and his talented staff of editors and writers have amassed a first-class library of *Researcher* reports, and we are fortunate to have access to that rich cache. We also wish to thank our colleagues at CQ Press, a division of SAGE and a leading publisher of books, directories, research publications and Web products on U.S. government, world affairs and communications. They have forged the way in making these readers a useful resource for instruction across a range of undergraduate and graduate courses.

Some readers may be learning about *CQ Researcher* for the first time. We expect that many readers will want regular access to this excellent weekly research tool. For subscription information or a no-obligation free trial of *CQ Researcher*, please contact CQ Press at www.cqpress.com or toll-free at 1-866-4CQ-PRESS (1-866-427-7737).

We hope that you will be pleased by this edition of *Issues for Debate in Environmental Management.* We welcome your feedback and suggestions for future editions. Please direct comments to Lisa Cuevas Shaw, Executive Editor, SAGE Publications, 2455 Teller Road, Thousand Oaks, CA 91320, or lisa.shaw@sagepub.com.

—The Editors of SAGE

Contributors

Brian Beary—a freelance journalist based in Washington, D.C.—specializes in European Union (EU) affairs and is the U.S. correspondent for *Europolitics,* the EU-affairs daily newspaper. Originally from Dublin, Ireland, he worked in the European Parliament for Irish MEP Pat "The Cope" Gallagher in 2000 and at the EU Commission's Eurobarometer unit on public opinion analysis. A fluent French speaker, he appears regularly as a guest international-relations expert on television and radio programs. Beary also writes for the *European Parliament Magazine* and the *Irish Examiner* daily newspaper. His last report for *CQ Global Researcher* was "Race for the Arctic."

Peter Behr recently retired from *The Washington Post,* where he was the principal reporter on energy issues and served as business editor from 1987–1992. A former Nieman Fellow at Harvard University, Behr worked at the Woodrow Wilson Center for Scholars and is working on a book about the history of the U.S. electric power grid.

Adriel Bettelheim is deputy editor for social policy at *CQ Weekly,* where he previously covered science and technology. He is the author of *Aging in America A to Z* (CQ Press, 2001) and was a member of the *CQ Researcher* team that won the 1999 Society of Professional Journalists Award for Excellence for a 10-part series on health care. He has a bachelor's degree in chemistry from Case Western Reserve University.

Thomas J. Billitteri is a freelance journalist in Fairfield, Pennsylvania, who has more than 30 years' experience covering business, nonprofit institutions and related topics for newspapers and other publications. He has written previously for *CQ Researcher* on teacher education, parental rights and mental-health policy. He holds a BA in English and an MA in journalism from Indiana University.

Rachel S. Cox is a freelance writer in Washington, D.C. She has written for *Historic Preservation* magazine and other publications. She graduated in English from Harvard College.

Alan Greenblatt is a staff writer for Congressional Quarterly's *Governing* magazine. He previously covered elections and military and agricultural policy for *CQ Weekly.* He was awarded the National Press Club's Sandy Hume Memorial Award for political reporting. He holds a bachelor's degree from San Francisco State University and a master's degree in English literature from the University of Virginia.

Peter Katel is a veteran journalist who previously served as Latin America bureau chief for *Time* magazine, in Mexico City, and as a Miami-based correspondent for *Newsweek* and the *Miami Herald's* Spanish language edition *El Nuevo Herald.* He also worked as a reporter in New Mexico for 11 years and wrote for several nongovernmental organizations, including International Social Service and the World Bank. He has won several awards, including the Interamerican Press Association's Bartolome Mitre Award. He is a graduate of the University of New Mexico in University Studies.

Tom Price is a Washington-based freelance journalist and a contributing writer for *CQ Researcher.* Previously he was a correspondent in the Cox Newspapers Washington Bureau, and chief politics writer for the *Dayton Daily News* and *The Journal Herald.* He is author, with Tony Hall, of *Changing the Face of Hunger: One Man's Story of How Liberals, Conservatives, Democrats, Republicans and People of Faith are Joining Forces to Help the Hungry, the Poor, and the Oppressed.* He also writes two Washington guidebooks, *Washington, D.C., for Dummies,* and the *Irreverent Guide to Washington, D.C.* His work has appeared in *The New York Times, Time, Rolling Stone* and other periodicals. He earned a bachelor of science in journalism at Ohio University.

Jennifer Weeks is a *CQ Researcher* contributing writer in Watertown, Massachusetts, who specializes in energy and environmental issues. She has written for *The Washington Post, The Boston Globe Magazine* and other publications, and has 15 years' experience as a public-policy analyst, lobbyist and congressional staffer. She has an AB degree from Williams College and master's degrees from the University of North Carolina and Harvard.

Colin Woodard has reported from more than 40 foreign countries on six continents and lived in Eastern Europe for more than four years. He is the author of *Ocean's End: Travels Through Endangered Seas,* a narrative, nonfiction account of the deterioration of the world's oceans. He also writes for *The Christian Science Monitor* and *The Chronicle of Higher Education.* His previous *CQ Global Researcher* report was on climate change.

The New Environmentalism

1

Can New Business Policies Save the Environment?

Tom Price

Huge windows reduce energy bills at the experimental Wal-Mart Supercenter that opened in Aurora, Colo., in November 2005. The eco-friendly store uses recycled materials for construction and solar and wind power to supplement standard power sources. Wal-Mart and many other businesses are jumping on the conservation bandwagon, joining environmental groups they once fought with.

From *CQ Researcher*, December 1, 2006.

Across the globe, evidence abounds of a rising concern for protecting the planet.

But the new concern about the environment is not your father's environmental movement. Corporate executives, investors, conservative Christians, labor unions and others not traditionally associated with the cause have joined the intensifying campaign to save the Earth. There's even a handful of environmentalists who are promoting nuclear power.

- Environmental Defense, a leading advocacy group, hires a director of corporate partnerships and begins helping businesses "go green." Among the many fruits of these collaborations: fuel-efficient hybrid FedEx delivery trucks, reusable UPS shipping envelopes and measures to cut greenhouse-gas emissions at DuPont facilities that saved the company $325 million in one year.[1]

- The National Association of Evangelicals — known for conservative politics — proclaims a "sacred responsibility to steward the Earth," urging governments to "encourage fuel efficiency, reduce pollution, encourage sustainable use of natural resources and provide for the proper care of wildlife and their natural habitats."[2]

- British chemist and environmentalist James Lovelock — famous for arguing that Earth acts as a self-sustaining organism — says building more nuclear power plants is "the only green solution" to the threat of global warming.[3]

In the burgeoning, new environmental movement, a growing number of people are perceiving threats to the environment,

1

Public Support for Environment Is Up

Support for the environment is up after taking a big dip beginning in 2000. Pro-environment respondents outnumbered pro-economy respondents by 17 percentage points in 2005 and 15 points this year.

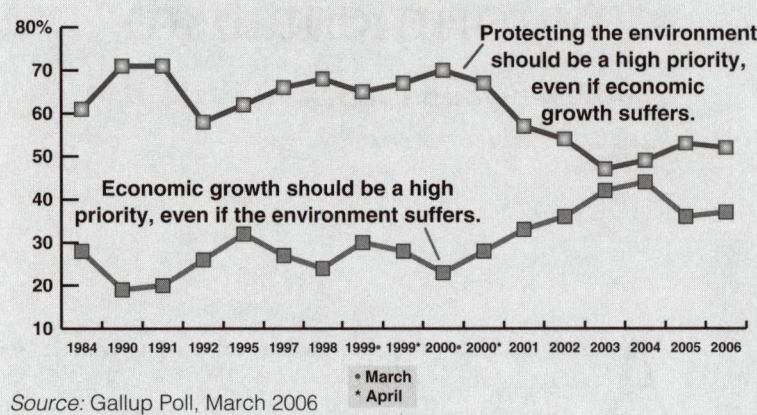

Percentages of Americans who agree with the following statements:

Source: Gallup Poll, March 2006

businesses are jumping on the conservation bandwagon and environmentalists are joining hands with groups they once crossed swords with.

"We're seeing the environmental movement getting deeper and broader at the same time," says Rainforest Action Network Executive Director Michael Brune. "We're seeing an increase in straight-up, old-school, traditional grassroots activists wanting to get involved. We're also seeing genuine interest from the business community, evangelicals, labor and other non-traditional allies."

In the words of Oklahoma State University sociology Professor Riley Dunlap, who has studied public opinion about the environment for 40 years and is the Gallup Organization's environmental scholar, "These local government initiatives, state initiatives, corporate initiatives represent a different kind of environmentalism."

The broadening consensus has been spurred mainly by concerns that global warming poses a real and potentially catastrophic threat to life on Earth but that a conservative federal government refuses to act.

"There's undoubtedly a buzz about global warming that wasn't there a year ago," says David Yarnold, executive vice president of Environmental Defense. "The sense of urgency has grown. And the more people learn about climate change, the more they want to know what they can do."

In a July poll by the Pew Research Center, 70 percent of Americans said there is "solid evidence" for global warming, and 74 percent said it constitutes a serious or somewhat serious problem. In a measure of public confusion about the topic and what should be done, however, 59 percent who believed in global warming thought human activity is the cause, while 30 percent blamed natural climate patterns.[4]

In another poll last January, Pew found that nearly 60 percent of Americans wanted the federal government to make energy and the environment top priorities, the highest percentage since 2001.[5] A Harris Poll last year found three-quarters of Americans feel "protecting the environment is so important that requirements and standards cannot be too high, and continuing environmental improvements must be made regardless of cost."[6]

Despite public support, "there's been an appalling vacuum of leadership coming from within the [Washington] Beltway — on both sides of the aisle," Brune says. "The current administration and [Republican-controlled] Congress can't be accused of being environmental leaders, but even most Democrats haven't been stepping up and showing an appropriate level of response to the environmental threats we face."

In the absence of action in Washington, he adds, "You're seeing a lot of others trying to show leadership."

Although environmentalists were heartened by the Democratic capture of Congress in the November 2006 elections, they're not expecting revolutionary changes in federal policies. President George W. Bush has two more years in office, Democrats hold only a slim majority in the Senate and not all Democrats are environmentalists. For instance, Rep. John D. Dingell, D-Mich. — the presumptive chair of the Energy and Commerce Committee, whose district includes Detroit — has opposed raising automobile gas-mileage requirements.

The most that U.S. Greenpeace Executive Director John Passacantando expects out of the Democrats are "some baby steps." So environmentalists aren't about to change the strategy they've developed since Republicans seized control of Congress in 1994: influencing corporations and state and local governments.

Environmental Defense presents itself to businesses essentially as a consulting firm, offering advice on how they can increase profits by adopting green business practices. The more aggressive Rainforest Action Network (RAN) also enters partnerships — but usually only after businesses succumb to public protests.

"We're not as confrontational as some other groups," says Gwen Ruta, Environmental Defense's corporate partnership director. "We've had pretty good success in going to companies in the spirit of cooperation and saying, 'This is what we want to do.' "

RAN usually stages public demonstrations to "get on the radar screen," says Ilyse Hogue, who manages the organization's campaign to promote green banking, or socially responsible investing. Once a bank agrees to work with her organization, she says, "the intellectual capital at these institutions is so vast that it's fun to participate in the dialogue. These are very bright people who just never really looked at these issues."

Investors also are pressuring companies to adopt green business practices, using tactics such as proposing policy resolutions at shareholders' meetings or investing only in corporations with positive environmental records. How-to guides to shareholder activism have been published both by Friends of the Earth and a partnership of the As You Sow Foundation and Rockefeller Philanthropy Advisors.[7]

"Not to engage the private sector is to miss a huge opportunity to have a positive impact on global warming," says Rockefeller Senior Vice President Doug Bauer.

Some investors band together to increase their clout. Through the Carbon Disclosure Project, for instance, major global investors each year ask about 2,000 companies — including the world's largest 500 — to reveal their impact on greenhouse-gas emissions. In 2006, 225 investors with $31.5 trillion in assets made the request — up from 143 investors the year before. Nearly three-quarters of the largest 500 companies responded this year, up from just under 50 percent in 2005.[8]

The project aims to spur companies to reduce emissions after they've compiled the information needed for

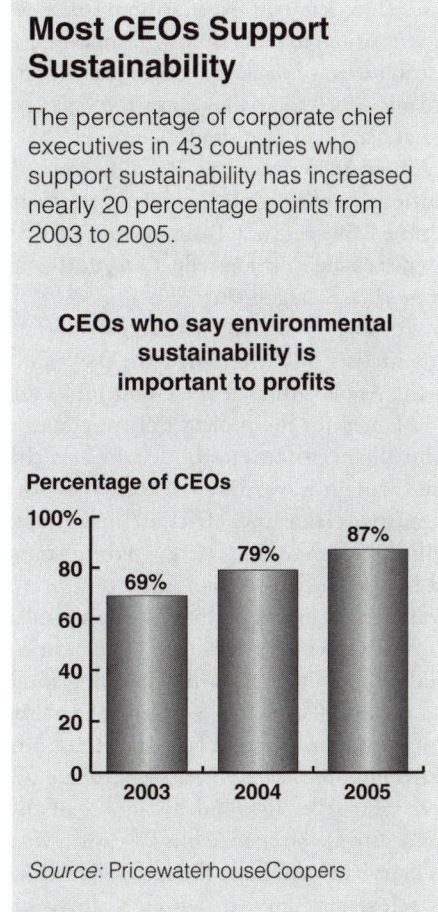

Most CEOs Support Sustainability

The percentage of corporate chief executives in 43 countries who support sustainability has increased nearly 20 percentage points from 2003 to 2005.

CEOs who say environmental sustainability is important to profits

Percentage of CEOs

- 2003: 69%
- 2004: 79%
- 2005: 87%

Source: PricewaterhouseCoopers

the report. Wal-Mart's experience indicates that's happening. In preparing its report, Wal-Mart discovered that refrigerants used in its grocery stores caused more of the company's "greenhouse-gas footprint" than its truck fleet did. Wal-Mart said it is acting on that discovery. (*See sidebar, p. 6.*)

Complaining that the federal government is not acting effectively, cities and states are adopting their own environmental-protection programs — forcing nationwide companies to cope with a patchwork of environmental regulations.

Nearly half the states are requiring that power plants use at least some renewable fuels, and California just mandated cuts in motor vehicles' carbon dioxide emissions. If that law withstands the auto industry's challenges, other states are prepared to act. Meanwhile, just as they did in striving to reduce acid rain, Northeastern states are establishing a consortium to set limits on greenhouse-gas emissions, distribute emission allowances to plants and permit cleaner plants to sell their allowances to dirtier facilities. Western states are crafting a similar agreement.[9]

Gov. Arnold Schwarzenegger, R-Calif., reached across the Atlantic to explore global-warming strategies with British Prime Minister Tony Blair. Former President Bill Clinton is discussing emission-reduction efforts with leaders of the world's 22 largest cities.[10]

Labor unions — which in the past clashed with environmentalists — have joined the new movement through the Apollo Alliance for Good Jobs and Clean Energy.[11] Named for the project that put man on the moon, the alliance promotes both jobs and the environment through government incentives for high-mileage autos, clean and efficient manufacturing, green buildings, renewable energy, public transportation and hydrogen-fuel technology.[12]

Environmentalism has become such a popular topic that it turned former Vice President Al Gore into a best-selling author and movie star while inspiring a real movie star — Leonardo DiCaprio — to try to take environmentalism to television. Gore's book about the threat of global warming, *An Inconvenient Truth*, made *The New York Times* best-seller list, and his movie of the same name was a surprise box-office hit. DiCaprio is teaming up with "Survivor" producer Craig Piligian to create a "reality" television show in which a down-and-out American town gets re-made into a healthy green community. DiCaprio and Piligian are shopping the concept, tentatively titled "E-topia," to networks and sponsors. Instead of just upgrading a wardrobe or a room, as other such shows do, "E-topia" will "take an American town that has been destroyed and bring it back to its former glory and then some," Piligian said. "This town will be reborn as the prototype for the future."[13]

As activists and business executives confront environmental challenges, here are some of the questions they're trying to answer:

Is going "green" good for the corporate bottom line?

A growing number of companies are adopting environmental-protection policies they say are good for business. Some conservative critics contend, however, that such actions actually dilute companies' primary — some say only — purpose: to increase shareholder value.

Corporate executives say they implement green practices for a variety of reasons: to attract more customers, cut costs, drive up the value of their companies' stock, recruit and retain high-quality employees and assure their companies' long-term health.

"Increasingly, suppliers and customers are demanding greater devotion to the environment," says Douglas Pinkham, president of the Public Affairs Council, the professional association for public affairs officers. Employees prefer environmentally friendly corporations because "nobody wants to work for a company that's known as an environmental pirate."

But companies are not going green "just because it helps their reputation," Pinkham adds. "Companies are saying we can make a buck by being environmentally sustainable."

And that goes beyond short-term profit-and-loss calculations, says business consultant Margery Kraus. "I heard an executive comment once that you can't have a successful business in a failed world," explains Kraus, head of APCO Worldwide, an international consulting firm. "I think that says it all." (See "At Issue," p. 18.)

According to Oklahoma State's Dunlap, American businesses are beginning to practice "what people in Europe call ecological modernization."

"You don't hear much talk about business vs. environment there," Dunlap explains. "They've adopted the approach that what's good for the environment is good for the economy, and I think we're seeing America kind of struggling to do the same.

"In the old days, it was easy to blame industry for 'greenwashing,' " or trying to appear more environmentally active than they really are. "But I'm increasingly convinced that we're seeing industries realize they have to integrate environmental concerns into their bottom line if they're to be successful."

A 2005 PricewaterhouseCoopers survey of chief executives in 43 countries found 87 percent saying environmental sustainability is important to company profits. That represented a rapid rise from 79 percent in 2004 and 69 percent in 2003.[14] (See graph, p. 3.)

Cost-saving is the most obvious benefit of greening a business. As Wal-Mart Chief Executive Lee Scott put it, when a company doesn't recycle, "We pay twice — once to get it, once to have it taken away."[15]

Wal-Mart expects to save $2.4 million a year by shrinking packaging for one private-label toy line, $26 million by cutting delivery-truck idle time and $28 million by recycling plastic in its stores. For really big savings, the giant retailer plans to reduce its stores' energy use by 30 percent and cut its trucks' fuel consumption by 25 percent in three years and 50 percent within 10 years.[16]

DuPont has already saved more than $3 billion by cutting energy use by 7 percent.[17] FedEx is deploying hybrid trucks that reduce fuel costs by more than a third.[18] PNC Financial Services Group is building green bank branches that use 45 percent less energy than standard structures.[19]

General Electric is betting billions that environmentalism sells as well as saves. In mid-2005, the global conglomerate launched its "Ecomagination" initiative to develop products and services that address environmental challenges. GE Chairman and CEO Jeff Immelt announced the company will produce improved technology in solar energy, hybrid locomotives, fuel cells, low-emission aircraft engines, light and strong materials, efficient lighting and water purification.

GE will invest $1.5 billion in research and development in those technologies by 2010 — up from $700 million in 2004 — "and we plan to make money doing it," Immelt said. Moreover, the company intends to double its revenues in those areas, from $10 billion in 2004 to at least $20 billion in 2010 and substantially more later.[20]

Potlatch Corp. Public Affairs Vice President Mark Benson isn't as precise about his forest-products company's future earnings, but he agrees it makes sense to prepare for a green marketplace. Potlatch seeks to distinguish itself from competitors by complying with all of the American Forest and Paper Association's environmental guidelines and then earning certification from the environmental movement's Forest Stewardship Council as well. As a result, Benson says, "we've positioned ourselves so, if that [green] market takes off, we're going to be there to serve it."

Retailers are discovering that "dedication to the environment makes them more attractive to consumers — especially if they're trying to appeal to an upscale audience," Pinkham says. Potlatch's policies also may make it more attractive to green investors, a group that is growing in numbers and influence, Benson says.

Assets devoted to so-called socially responsible investing (SRI) — of which green investing is a part — have grown slightly faster than other kinds of investing over the last decade, according to the Social Investment Forum, the SRI industry's trade association. SRI investments now represent 9.4 percent of all professionally managed assets tracked in Nelson Information's *Directory of Investment Managers.*[21]

Among SRI investors, 37 percent consider companies' environmental records when making investment decisions, the forum reported. Many also attempt to influence corporate environmental policy by introducing resolutions at shareholders' meetings.

Investors are proposing a growing number of resolutions, according to a report from the As You Sow Foundation and Rockefeller Philanthropy Advisors. Investors' proposals have addressed the environment more than any other issue in recent years, the report said, and the number of environmental resolutions proposed has increased faster than most other topics.[22]

But not everyone is bullish on green business.

Jerry Taylor, a senior fellow at the libertarian Cato Institute, suggests that talk of consumers' and companies' concern about the environment is overblown. "Public demands have always been for bigger and bigger and bigger homes," he notes. "How do you square that with the rise of environmentalism? And if consumers are looking at more fuel-efficient cars, I think that has more to do with the price of gas than anything else." If gas prices drop, Americans might go right back to their big SUVs, he says.

Businesses may find conservation economical now, he adds, but if energy prices drop, companies might find it less expensive to use more energy than to buy energy-efficient equipment, he says. Competition could force companies to enlarge packaging to catch consumers' eyes, he says, even if that uses more materials.

While executives contend they adopt green policies to boost the bottom line, Competitive Enterprise Institute President Fred Smith Jr. charged the policies usually are intended "to appease [a business's] critics, to apologize for past mistakes, to bribe its opponents."

"The modern firm solves one — but only one — of the major problems of mankind: the creation of wealth," Smith said. "That wealth then allows individuals in their various roles the opportunity to protect values they care about."[23]

Wal-Mart Sets Ambitious 'Green' Goals

Wal-Mart, the world's largest retailer, wants to be the greenest as well. President and Chief Executive Officer Lee Scott laid out the corporation's ambitious long-term goals a year ago: to use only renewable energy, to create no waste and to sell products that "sustain our resources and environment."

He also established specific short-term goals:

- increase truck fuel efficiency by 25 percent in three years and 100 percent in 10;
- cut store energy consumption by 30 percent and reduce facility greenhouse-gas emissions by 20 percent in seven years;
- reduce solid waste at stores by 25 percent in three years;
- establish a program within 18 months that gives preference to suppliers that "aggressively" reduce their greenhouse-gas emissions, and
- increase sales of organic food and other environmentally friendly products.

"Environmental problems are *our* problems," Scott told employees at the company's Bentonville, Ark., headquarters. Solving them is good for humanity, he said, and it's good for business.[1]

During 2005, Wal-Mart opened two experimental stores — in McKinney, Texas, and Aurora, Colo. — to test green technology.

Highly efficient light-emitting diodes — or LEDs — illuminate exterior signs and interior display cases. Heating systems burn cooking oil and motor oil from the stores' restaurants and auto repair shops. Heat is recovered from refrigerators and freezers, and solar collectors and wind turbines supply electricity. Doors were installed on refrigerated cases that usually are left open, and their lights brighten and dim as shoppers open and close the doors. The restrooms have water-conserving sinks, and the men's rooms use waterless urinals. Countertops are made with recycled glass and concrete.

Outside, drought-tolerant vegetation cuts the water needed for irrigation. Food waste is composted and sold. Roads are paved with recycled materials, and concrete is mixed with fly ash from burned coal and slag from steel production.[2]

Some of the innovations were immediate hits, the company reported in a one-year review, while others "still need to be refined." Some of the earliest successes — the lighting, landscaping, sinks and urinals — will begin showing up in other Wal-Marts in 2007. The company hopes the other innovations will prove themselves over the next two years.

"Due to our size and scope, we are uniquely positioned to have great success and impact in the world, perhaps like no company before us," Scott said.

Seemingly small changes, when Wal-Mart makes them, can save millions of dollars.

Because its truck fleet travels a billion miles a year, for instance, raising fuel efficiency by just one mile per gallon would save the company more than $52 million annually at current fuel prices, Scott said. Meeting his goal of doubling efficiency by 2015 would jump that savings to $310 million.

If the company could sell one compact fluorescent light bulb to each of the 100-plus million shoppers who walk into Wal-Mart stores every week, those customers' electric bills would drop a collective $3 billion. If the company succeeds in encouraging green practices by its 60,000 suppliers and 1.3 million employees, environmental benefits will ripple around the world.[3]

Known primarily for its low prices, Wal-Mart confronts a stiff challenge in selling green products that often cost more than their non-green counterparts.

Is more federal action needed to encourage energy efficiency?

Almost everyone agrees Americans would be better off if they used energy more efficiently. Even those who don't fear global warming see benefits in reducing U.S. dependence on energy sources from unstable regions of the world, such as the Middle East. Most also agree that only federal action could spur significant gains in efficiency.

But there is disagreement over whether the desire for efficiency warrants government intervention and which measures would be most effective. Most environmental organizations advocate government mandates. Many businesses prefer incentives for voluntary action.

"We cannot solve these issues without the active participation of the federal government," says the Rainforest Action Network's Brune.

"We've seen that if a green product costs the same, it's a runaway success," Vice President Andrew Ruben says. "If it costs a little more, it can be successful. Above that, we've got to do things in a smarter way" to try to bring the price down. The company's goal is to price organic products no more than 10 percent above their conventional counterparts.

Environmentalists and organic-farming advocates give Wal-Mart's plan mixed reactions.

The company has consulted with the World Wildlife Fund, the Natural Resources Defense Council, Greenpeace and other environmental organizations. Environmental Defense, another Wal-Mart advisor, opened a Bentonville office so it could dispatch a representative to corporate headquarters at a moment's call.

Describing Wal-Mart's impact on the U.S. economy as "almost beyond calculation," Environmental Defense Executive Vice President David Yarnold said he and his colleagues "really believe that Wal-Mart can create a race to the top for environmental benefits."[4]

The Sierra Club refused to work with Wal-Mart because of concern about its labor policies, but Executive Director Carl Pope said Wal-Mart managers "deserve the chance to show that their business model is compatible with high standards, not just low prices."[5]

Nu Wexler, a spokesman for Wal-Mart Watch — which was created to challenge the company's business practices — said his organization is "encouraged by Wal-Mart's new environmental initiatives because they could, if implemented, change the way American businesses approach environmental sustainability."[6]

The Cornucopia Institute, an advocate for small organic farms, attacked the company for purchasing from "industrial-scale factory farms" and from China. Pressure to cut prices could destroy family farms and reduce some of the environmental benefits of organic farming, said Mark Kastel, Cornucopia's senior farm-policy analyst.

"Food shipped around the world — burning fossil fuels and undercutting our domestic farmers — does not meet the consumer's traditional definition of what is truly organic," Kastel said.[7]

Ronnie Cummins, national director of the Organic Consumers Association, questioned the authenticity of organic food grown in China, where "organic standards are dubious, and farm-labor exploitation is the norm."[8]

Wal-Mart replied that it would not compromise organic standards.[9] In addition, a spokesman said, "whenever possible, as with all fresh merchandise, we try to purchase fresh organic products from local suppliers for distribution to stores in their areas. This is good for the surrounding communities and helps to generate savings on distribution costs that we can pass on to our customers."[10]

---

[1] Lee Scott, presentation to Wal-Mart employees, Bentonville, Ark., Oct. 24, 2005; www.walmartstores.com/Files/21st%20Century%20 Leadership.pdf.

[2] "Experimental Wal-Mart Stores One Year Later," Wal-Mart; www.walmartfacts.com/FactSheets/11132006_Experimental_Stores.pdf.

[3] Marc Gunther, "The Green Machine," *Fortune*, Aug. 7, 2006. p. 42. Michael Barbaro, "Wal-Mart Effort on Health and Environment Is Seen," *The New York Times*, June 22, 2006, p. 2.

[4] "Environmental Defense Will Add Staff Position in Bentonville, Arkansas," Environmental Defense, July 12, 2006; www.environmentaldefense.org/pressrelease.cfm?ContentID=5322.

[5] Abigail Goldman, "Wal-Mart goes 'green,' " *Los Angeles Times*, Nov. 13, 2006.

[6] *Ibid.*

[7] Mark Kastel, "Wal-Mart Declares War on Organic Farmers, the Cornucopia Institute, Sept. 28, 2006; www.cornucopia.org/WalMart_ News_Release.pdf.

[8] Ronnie Cummins, "Open Letter to Wal-Mart," the Organic Consumers Association, July 4, 2006; www.organicconsumers.org/2006/article_1009.cfm.

[9] Tom Daykin, "Wal-Mart threatens farmers, report says," *The Milwaukee Journal Sentinel*, Sept. 28, 2006.

[10] Mya Frazier, "Critics' latest beef with Wal-Mart is . . . organics?" *Advertising Age*, Oct. 16, 2006, p. 47.

"There is no substitute for having clear national goals," Sierra Club spokesman Eric Antebi agrees. "It's great to have over 300 mayors doing their part. It's critical that states are taking the lead. But there are still too many gaps."

"There are some places where voluntary business actions will offer the greatest opportunities," says Denis Hayes, president and CEO of the Bullitt Foundation, and one of the key organizers of the first Earth Day. "But it's nice to have a regulatory basement beneath which you're not allowed to sink."

U.S. energy consumption is like a giant ocean liner that can't change direction quickly, says Americans for Balanced Energy Choices Executive Director Joe Lucas. "We don't want draconian measures," says Lucas, whose advocacy group is funded by coal producers and

The Rainforest Action Network's Jumpstart Ford campaign urges Ford and other corporations to reduce their dependence on oil. The campaign claims Ford has the worst fleetwide fuel efficiency and the highest average vehicle greenhouse-gas emissions of major U.S. automakers.

consumers. "Don't force the ocean liner to do a U-turn immediately."

The federal government should continue to fund efforts to develop technologies that burn coal more efficiently and with fewer emissions, he says. And the government should offer incentives for farmers and foresters to adopt practices that absorb more greenhouse gases from the atmosphere.

Similarly, the auto industry opposes higher fuel-efficiency standards but favors tax breaks for those who buy fuel-efficient cars. "Competition among the automakers will drive this process far better and with fewer disruptions to the marketplace than any regulations that can be adopted," said Frederick Webber, president and CEO of the Alliance of Automobile Manufacturers.[24]

American businesses and individuals have become much more energy efficient since the emergence of the modern environmental movement and the 1973 Arab oil embargo. Today coal emits 70 percent less pollution per unit of energy produced than it did 30 years ago, Lucas says. Compared with the growth in gross domestic product, the United States puts a declining amount of greenhouse gases into the air, he adds.

America's new cars and light trucks average about 24 miles per gallon now, up from 15 in 1975. The typical refrigerator uses less than half as much electricity as its counterpart in 1972.[25]

Population growth, economic expansion and consumer tastes, however, have driven total energy consumption up by a third since 1973, and it is expected to jump another 30 percent by 2025.[26] Americans burned 75 percent more coal in 2005 than in 1980, and the coal industry says consumption will increase more than 30 percent over the next two decades.[27]

This doesn't surprise Joel Schwartz, a visiting fellow at the American Enterprise Institute (AEI), who doubts the need for, or effectiveness of, government regulations. "When you make things more efficiently," he explains, "you free up resources to make something else. Pound for pound, cars are more energy efficient now. Because of consumer demand, the efficiency benefits have gone into creating bigger cars that get about the same fuel economy."

If the United States did import less oil, Schwartz adds, "it would get used somewhere else. Developing countries would use that energy."

Nevertheless, environmentalists want the federal government to impose tougher restrictions on the use of fossil fuels. Cars began getting better gas mileage after federal corporate average fuel economy (CAFE) standards were enacted in 1975, they note. But the standard for passenger cars has not been raised since 1990, and the average fuel efficiency of cars and light trucks has actually declined since 1987. Over the last two decades, the auto industry has focused technology on getting heavier vehicles to run faster, and the growing American population has driven more miles.

The Union of Concerned Scientists wants CAFE standards increased to more than 40 miles per gallon (mpg) by 2015 and 55 mpg by 2025. Boosting mileage standards would not require U.S. auto companies to reinvent the wheel, the organization contends. For instance, Ford could apply existing technology to boost the Explorer SUV's fuel efficiency to 36 miles per gallon from 21.[28]

Environmental organizations also want restrictions on greenhouse-gas emissions, which are not regulated because they are not legally classified as pollutants under the Clean Air Act.[29] One often-advocated plan would assign every company an emissions allowance and let those that emit less sell their excess allowance to others. This so-called "cap-and-trade" scheme has been used successfully to reduce the sulfur emissions that cause acid rain.

Sens. John R. McCain, R-Ariz., and Joseph I. Lieberman, D-Conn., introduced legislation to do that in early 2005, and Maryland Republican Rep. Wayne T. Gilchrest did the same in the House. Neither bill got out of committee.

Recently some conservatives, concerned about U.S. reliance on imported oil, have suggested raising taxes on fossil fuels. "That's the way to get consumption down," said Alan Greenspan, former chairman of the Federal Reserve Board. "It's a national-security issue." Joining him have been such prominent conservative economists as Gregory Mankiw, former chairman of President Bush's Council of Economic Advisors, and Andrew Samwick, the council's former chief economist.[30]

While he doesn't agree that it's needed, Schwartz says a tax would be the most effective way to curb fossil-fuel use, as long as it were combined with other tax cuts so it didn't depress the economy.

Can the industrial world switch from fossil fuels to other forms of energy?

Environmentalists argue the only way to stop global warming is to stop burning fossil fuels. But switching from coal and oil is no easy task, and alternative energy sources have their own drawbacks — including damage to the environment.

"No energy source is perfect," says David Hamilton, director of the Sierra Club's global warming and energy program, using words echoed by Lucas, the coal-industry advocate.

For Hamilton, that means accepting the shortcomings of alternative fuels in the near term while conducting the research and development needed to make them work over the long haul. For Lucas, it means environmentalists have to accept that fossil fuels will be the world's primary energy source for the foreseeable future.

Eliminating coal and oil is "a pipe dream," that could occur only in "science-fiction land," Lucas says. "For the next 30 to 50 to 100 years, folks are going to have little choice but to use coal."

Currently, nearly 80 percent of the world's energy comes from burning fossil fuels.[31] In the United States, it's 86 percent.[32] Coal produces 52 percent of the electricity consumed in the United States,[33] and oil powers nearly all U.S. transportation.[34]

The coal producers and their customers project that America will continue to get a majority of its electricity from coal in 2025. They also say they will steadily reduce coal emissions during that time and will begin building "ultra-low-emissions plants" in the decade following 2025. Those plants could eliminate more than 99 percent of sulfur, nitrogen oxide and particulate emissions, along with 95 percent of mercury, they say. They also aim to be able to capture and sequester carbon dioxide, fossil fuels' primary contributor to global warming.[35]

The Rainforest Action Network's Brune acknowledges that "we have massive amounts of coal in the United States and around the world. If we want to extract every bit of fossil fuel, we could go for a couple hundred more years. But the planet wouldn't be able to survive."

Industry has not proven that it can capture and sequester greenhouse gases on a commercial scale, he says, and coal mining itself does terrible damage to the environment.

Even if factories could capture greenhouse gases in the future, Hamilton says, "scientists say we need to actually reduce emissions now, not just get on a path to reducing emissions in 10 years."

That would require a variety of methods for conserving and switching to alternative sources of energy, environmentalists say. "There is no silver bullet," Sierra Club spokesman Antebi says. "I heard someone say that you need silver buckshot.

"We're going to need to make our cars go further on a gallon of gas," he continued. "We're going to need solar and wind power and biofuels. We're going to need to design our buildings to operate more efficiently. We're going to need to clean up our power plants and use new technologies to reduce their impact on global warming."

Wind power has been the fastest-growing U.S. source of energy, jumping by 160 percent from 2000 to 2005. But it accounts for less than two-tenths of a percent of American energy consumption.[36] And it is not without its problems.

Jesse Ausubel, director of Rockefeller University's human-environment program, terms wind one of environmentalism's "false gods." To replace a typical, traditional power plant, he said, a windmill farm would have to cover 300 square miles. Other environmentalists oppose windmill farms because they endanger birds and can clutter the landscape.[37]

Similarly, U.S. use of ethanol — a fuel made from corn and other plants — increased by 145 percent from 2000 to 2005. Like wind power, however, it supplies a tiny fraction of America's energy — about a third of a percent.[38] Spurred by government incentives, annual ethanol production may more than double from 4.5 billion gallons now to more than 10 billion by 2010.[39] But that still would represent less than 1 percent of U.S. energy sources, and ethanol, too, carries environmental baggage. (*See sidebar, p. 12.*)

Despite problems posed by some alternative-energy sources, Hamilton says, "we're going to need almost every tool in the shed for a while.

"Scientists are saying we won't have the luxury to go back and stop global warming if we reach some of these biological tipping points," he continues. "We need to solve this problem now, and if we do we will then have the opportunity to make technological improvements later.

"You can always take the wind turbines down because some people think they're ugly. You can't take the carbon dioxide out of the air — it stays there for 200 years."

Many environmentalists place hope in solar energy, even though it currently produces less than a tenth of a percent of U.S. power. A handful of environmentalists are calling for more use of nuclear power. A growing number of environmental organizations are acknowledging that nuclear shouldn't be rejected out of hand. But most argue that nuclear's downsides will not be overcome in the foreseeable future.

Pro-nuclear environmentalists, such as British scientist Lovelock, contend it offers the only realistic alternative to fossil fuels. Other alternatives are "largely gestures," Lovelock said. "If it makes people feel good to shove up a windmill or put a solar panel on their roof, great, do it.

It'll help a little bit, but it's no answer at all to the problem."[40]

Bruce Babbitt — Clinton administration Interior secretary and one-time head of the League of Conservation Voters — described nuclear power as "the lesser [evil] of the only two alternatives that are on the table right now. One is to fry this planet with continuing use and burning of fossil fuels, and the other is to try to make nuclear power work."[41]

Environmentalists can't "just say 'no way, no how,' " Environmental Defense's Yarnold says. "That's one reason some people look at a caricature of environmentalists and say, 'There they go again.' "

But he also says the nuclear industry must answer tough questions about reactor safety, waste disposal and weapons proliferation before new plants should be opened.

The industry might be able to address some concerns about safety, the Bullitt Foundation's Hayes says, "but the one I can't think of any way to make progress on is nuclear proliferation. I'm pretty terrified of a world in which 60 countries have nuclear stockpiles, and if they all have nuclear power I can't think of any way to avoid that."

BACKGROUND

Early Warnings

American environmentalists can trace their roots to distinguished writers — and some obscure bureaucrats — of the mid-19th century.[42]

Students still read Henry David Thoreau's *Walden* (published in 1854) and his other paeans to nature. In 1857, after the discovery of the California redwoods, poet James Russell Lowell proposed establishing a society for the protection of trees.

But even earlier, the U.S. commissioner of patents warned in 1849 about "the folly and shortsightedness" of wasting timber and slaughtering buffalo. Other commissioners of patents and of agriculture issued similar warnings about environmental destruction throughout the 1850s and '60s.

Congress had gotten the message by 1864, when it gave Yosemite Valley to California to establish a state park. Eight years later, it made Yellowstone the world's first national park.

CHRONOLOGY

1870-1900 *Environmentalists organize, and Congress begins to act.*

1870 Congress passes law to protect Alaska wildlife.

1872 Yellowstone becomes world's first national park.

1891 Congress empowers president to create national forests.

1900-1969 *Teddy Roosevelt leads crusade to protect the environment. Modern environmental movement is born.*

1901 President Theodore Roosevelt makes conservation a priority.

1906 Congress passes Antiquities Act; Roosevelt creates the first national monuments — Devil's Tower in Wyoming and Petrified Forest in Arizona.

1916 National Park Service created.

1962 Writer and biologist Rachel Carson warns of the dangers of pesticides in her landmark book *Silent Spring*.

1970-1979 *Modern environmental movement soars into prominence; Congress responds with landmark laws.*

1970 Some 20 million Americans celebrate first Earth Day. . . . Clean Air Act passed. . . . Environmental Protection Agency created.

1972 Clean Water Act passed; DDT is banned.

1973 Endangered Species Act passed.

1974 Safe Water Drinking Act enacted.

1975 Fuel-economy and tailpipe-emission standards are established.

1980-1987 *Environmental activism slows, but Congress passes significant legislation, and international agreements target global environmental challenges.*

1980 Superfund created to clean hazardous-waste sites. . . . Landmark Alaska Lands legislation sets aside more than 100 million acres, doubling U.S. parks and refuge acreage

1987 Two-dozen nations agree to phase out chlorofluorocarbons, which damage Earth's ozone layer.

1990-1999 *Climate change becomes top global environmental issue.*

1992 U.N. convention calls for greenhouse-gas reductions.

1994 Republican takeover of Congress diminishes environmentalists' power in federal government.

1995 Attack on acid rain launched.

1997 Kyoto Protocol mandates greenhouse-gas reductions; U.S. fails to ratify.

2000-2006 *Republican control of Congress and White House further weakens environmentalists' voice. Environmentalists increase efforts to influence business. More businesses go "green."*

2000 Republican George W. Bush wins White House; GOP holds Congress. . . . Thirty-five institutional investors with several trillion dollars in assets launch Carbon Disclosure Project to pressure corporations to address global warming.

2001 Vermont Sen. James Jeffords, an environmentalist, leaves Republican Party mid-year, giving Democrats control of Senate.

2002 GOP regains control of Senate.

2006 Environmentalists celebrate Democratic capture of Congress but don't expect great success while Bush occupies White House and Senate is nearly evenly divided. . . . Carbon Disclosure Project grows to 225 investors with $31.5 trillion in assets. . . . Tyson Foods warns meat prices to rise because ethanol production is driving up cost of corn.

The Promise — and Problems — of Ethanol

For environmentalists, ethanol wields a double-edged sword. It replaces oil-based fuels, reducing emissions of greenhouse gases and other pollutants. But it poses its own threats.

Tyson Foods, the world's largest meat processor, recently underscored one ethanol worry — that increased production of ethanol, almost all from corn, will drive up the price of that widely used grain. Rising corn prices will lead to higher chicken, beef and pork prices in 2007, the company announced in November.

"The American consumer is making a choice here," Tyson President and CEO Richard Bond said. "This is either corn for feed or corn for fuel. That's what's causing this."[1]

Critics also worry that devoting more land to expanded corn production could damage the environment by increasing harmful runoff of pesticides and fertilizers and by discouraging the preservation of land for conservation reserves, wetlands, wildlife preserves and wilderness.[2] According to Friends of the Earth, corn requires nearly six times more fertilizer and pesticide than most crops.[3]

Ethanol enjoys substantial government subsidies, in no small part because of farm-state lawmakers whose constituents grow corn. Ethanol production consumed about 14 percent of U.S.-grown corn in 2005 and was projected to run as high as 19 percent this year. America's entire corn crop would supply just 3.7 percent of the energy demanded by the U.S. transportation sector, however, researchers at the Polytechnic University of New York estimated.[4]

Corn ethanol contains less energy than gasoline, so an ethanol-fueled vehicle gets lower fuel efficiency. *Consumer Reports* magazine compared gasoline with an ethanol fuel burned in a Chevy Tahoe sport utility vehicle, a so-called "flexible fuel" model that can run on gasoline or a mixture of up to 85 percent ethanol and 15 percent gas. The ethanol blend delivered 27 percent lower gas mileage.[5]

According to a team of researchers from the University of California at Berkeley, corn ethanol can make a real, but relatively small, contribution to reducing greenhouse-gas emissions. They compared the energy in the ethanol with the fossil fuels used to make it — powering farm machinery and production equipment, for instance. The ethanol contained 20 percent more energy than was used to make it, and it reduced greenhouse-gas emissions by 13 percent.[6]

Most modern cars can run on a 10 percent ethanol blend, and about a third of U.S. motor fuel uses that mixture to reduce pollution. But only about 5 million of America's 230 million passenger vehicles can run on 85-percent ethanol, called E85, and many of them are gas-guzzlers like the Tahoe.[7] The United States had 70 percent more E85-dispensing service stations in August than it did at the beginning of last year, but that's still just 850 of 169,000 stations nationwide.[8]

Ethanol proponents hope other crops will prove to be more efficient energy sources.

Ethanol from sugarcane has eight times the energy of corn ethanol.[9] It delivers 40 percent of Brazil's automobile fuel, costs less than half as much as gasoline there and helps to generate electricity as well.[10] But the United States doesn't have much land suitable for the crop. In addition, federal laws keep sugar prices artificially high and restrict imports of cheaper sugar from overseas.[11]

Entrepreneurs and scientists are trying to produce ethanol from more economical plant matter, such as farm waste, municipal trash, grass, leaves and wood. Corn ethanol is made from the corn's starch. Ethanol also can be made — with greater difficulty — from cellulose, which is the main component of plant-cell walls.

Not only can cellulosic ethanol be made from more materials, it also can reduce greenhouse-gas emissions by

---

During the 1870s, Congress passed legislation to protect fur-bearing animals in Alaska, fisheries in the Atlantic Ocean and Eastern lakes and trees on government lands. Environmental organizations also began to sink roots. Botanists and horticulturalists created the American Forestry Association (now known as American Forests), and New Englanders founded the Appalachian Mountain Club.

The 1890s also proved to be "green." Congress established Sequoia and General Grant (now part of Kings Canyon) national parks, and brought Yosemite back under federal control. Congress also gave the president power to create national forests, and President Benjamin Harrison issued a proclamation that created the first national wildlife refuge, in Alaska. In the private sector, John Muir and some friends on the West Coast founded

67 to 89 percent, according to the U.S. Energy Department's Argonne National Laboratory.[12]

The economies of tropical and subtropical countries, with year-round growing seasons, could benefit from the growing demand for sugarcane ethanol. "The risk," Earth Policy Institute President Lester Brown warned, "is that economic pressures to clear land for expanding sugarcane production . . . in the Brazilian cerrado and Amazon basin . . . will pose a major threat to plant and animal diversity."[13]

The Rainforest Action Network is "very concerned about biofuel's impact on rain forests," Network Executive Director Michael Brune says. Ethanol can contribute to reducing fossil-fuel consumption, he says, but only as part of a comprehensive approach that includes more efficient motor-vehicle engines and clean generation of electricity.

"If we replaced gas-guzzling internal-combustion engines with a similar engine that uses biofuel, we'll just be replacing one problem with another," Brune says. "If we use more advanced auto technology and 'green' the electricity grid, then the impact of an appropriate use of biofuels would be revolutionary."

More Corn Used for Ethanol

Nearly 20 percent of the corn grown in the United States this year — a five-percentage-point increase over 2005 — was used for ethanol production. If the nation's entire corn crop were used for ethanol, it would supply just 3.7 percent of the energy needed for transportation alone.

Percentage of U.S. Corn Used for Ethanol Production

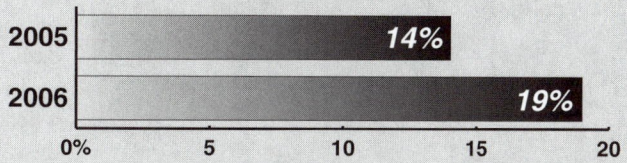

Source: Polytechnic University of New York

[1] Marcus Kabel, "Tyson Foods Sees Higher Meat Prices," The Associated Press, Nov. 13, 2006.

[2] Brad Knickerbocker, "Why the Next Congress Will Be 'Greener,' But Only by a Few Shades," *The Christian Science Monitor*, Nov. 15, 2006, p. 2.

[3] Mike Nixon, "Skepticism Rides along with Gasoline Ethanol Requirement," *St. Louis Daily Record*, July 15, 2006.

[4] Adriel Bettelheim, "Biofuels Boom," *CQ Researcher*, Sept. 29, 2006, pp. 793-816.

[5] "The Ethanol Myth," *Consumer Reports*, October 2006, p. 15.

[6] Elizabeth Douglass, "Report Challenges Claims about Ethanol," *Los Angeles Times*, Jan. 27, 2006, p. C2.

[7] Elizabeth Douglass, "A Future Without Oil?" *Los Angeles Times*, April 16, 2006, p. C1; "Annual Vehicle Distance Traveled in Miles and Related Data 2004," Federal Highway Administration, www.fhwa.dot.gov/policy/ohim/hs04/htm/vm1.htm.

[8] Alexei Barrionuevo, "An Alternative Fuel Is Scarce, Even in the Farm Belt," *The New York Times*, Aug. 31, 2006, p. C1.

[9] Jerry Taylor and Peter Van Doren, "California's Global Warming Dodge," *The Arizona Republic*, May 7, 2006.

[10] Marla Dickerson, "Homegrown Fuel Supply Helps Brazil Breathe Easy," *Los Angeles Times*, June 15, 2005, p. 1.

[11] "Sugar's sweet deal," *Sarasota Herald-Tribune*, Aug. 15, 2006, p. A10.

[12] Barbara McClellan, "Biofuel Crossroads," *Ward's Auto World*, Nov. 1, 2006, p. 30.

[13] Lester R. Brown, "Rescuing a Planet Under Stress," *The Futurist*, July 1, 2006, p. 18.

the Sierra Club to preserve wilderness. Back East, creation of the Massachusetts Audubon Society touched off the Audubon movement, which led to the National Association of Audubon Societies in 1905.

President Theodore Roosevelt (1901-1909), an avid outdoorsman, doubled the acreage in national parks and established 53 wildlife sanctuaries. Following congressional passage of the American Antiquities Act in 1906,

Roosevelt created the first national monuments — Devil's Tower in Wyoming and Petrified Forest in Arizona. The early-20th century also spawned Western opposition to federal environmental-protection activities, notably when Western business and government representatives met at the Denver Public Lands Convention and demanded that federal lands be turned over to the states.

Getty Images/Sandy Huffaker

The Kumeyaay wind farm on the Campo Indian Reservation serves 30,000 customers in San Diego. Wind power is the fastest-growing U.S. source of energy but accounts for less than two-tenths of a percent of American energy consumption. Replacing a typical, traditional power plant with wind power would require a 300-square-mile wind farm, according to one expert.

While most early 20th-century environmentalism focused on preserving pristine nature, public officials also began to take note of a growing side effect of urbanization — pollution of waters near big cities. Congress responded in 1910 by passing legislation that restricted dumping refuse into Lake Michigan in or near Chicago.

In something of a harbinger of current partnerships between environmental organizations and businesses, conservationists and sportsmen found allies within railroads and travel agencies. Together, they promoted creation of a federal bureau to look after the national parks. Congress responded in 1916 by establishing the National Park Service.

Three years later, supporters of the parks founded the National Parks Association (which was renamed the National Parks and Conservation Association in 1970). The organization sought to build public backing for the parks through educational activities and by encouraging Americans to visit.

The roaring '20s became better known for environmental exploitation than environmental protection, as Congress opened federal lands to mining and drilling for small fees, authorized federal hydroelectric projects and set the U.S. Army Corps of Engineers to dredging and damming inland waters.

In the 1930s, the Great Depression was worsened when poor agricultural practices contributed to massive dust storms that turned formerly bountiful farmland on the Plains into the Dust Bowl. In efforts to fight the Depression, President Franklin D. Roosevelt's New Deal policies created the Civilian Conservation Corps, through which unemployed workers planted trees, built roads, erected fire towers and carried out other public works.

The environmental costs of industrialization commanded increasing attention during the 1930s, '40s and '50s. Offshore oil drilling began. Smog episodes in St. Louis led to the nation's first smoke-control ordinance. Los Angeles established the first air-pollution control bureau. California adopted the first automobile-emissions standards. Congress passed laws — that would be strengthened after the '60s — to address water and air pollution.

The political and counter-culture ferment of the 1960s spurred interest in environmentalism that emphasized personal responsibility. This manifested itself in movements to encourage recycling, organic gardening and farming, cooperatives and purchases of "green" products.

Mimicking the violent political activists of the era, a few organizations and individuals began engaging in "ecoterrorism," destroying property that they viewed as encroaching on nature and setting booby traps to threaten loggers. Their legacy included trials and guilty pleas this year from alleged members of the Earth Liberation Front and Animal Liberation Front who were charged with firebombing ranger stations, corrals, lumber mill offices, ski resorts, slaughterhouses and federal plant-inspection facilities throughout the West between 1996 and 2001.[43]

Era of Activism

Taking an entirely different tack, biologist Rachel Carson wrote *Silent Spring*, highlighting the dangers posed by DDT and other pesticides and foreshadowing the coming era of massive environmental activism.

That era was kicked off by the first Earth Day, on April 22, 1970. The event was conceived by Democratic Sen. Gaylord Nelson of Wisconsin as a way to "shake up the political establishment and force this issue onto the national agenda."[44] He modeled it after the teach-ins that built opposition to the Vietnam War on college campuses, and it succeeded beyond his wildest dreams.

An estimated 20 million Americans — including 10 million students from 2,000 colleges and 1,000 high schools — participated in a wide variety of activities throughout the country. There were marches, rallies, songfests, mock funerals for the internal-combustion engine, mock trials of polluters, trash pickup drives and protests against aircraft noise and polluting companies. New York City closed Fifth Avenue for Earth Day events. Congress shut down because so many members were out participating. Earth Day speakers ranged from famed anthropologist Margaret Mead to liberal Sen. Edward M. Kennedy, D-Mass., to conservative Sen. Barry Goldwater, R-Ariz., to Nixon administration Cabinet officers.[45]

At the same time, according to organizer Hayes, Attorney General John R. Mitchell ordered the FBI to investigate the organizers of Earth Day.[46] In addition, a Georgia gubernatorial candidate called Earth Day a communist plot because it was held on Russian revolutionary Vladimir Lenin's birthday, and the Daughters of the American Revolution denounced it as "subversive."[47]

But lawmakers heard loud and clear that Earth Day was above all an expression of national will. Later in 1970, Congress passed the Clean Air Act, and President Richard M. Nixon established the Environmental Protection Agency. These were followed in subsequent years by a flood of landmark laws, including the Clean Water Act, the Endangered Species Act, the Marine Mammal Protection Act, the Safe Drinking Water Act, the Toxic Substances Control Act, the Resource Conservation and Recovery Act to regulate hazardous waste, fuel-economy standards, tailpipe-emission and lead-paint restrictions, bans on DDT, the phasing out of leaded gasoline, PCBs and ozone-destroying chlorofluorocarbons and a U.S.-Canada agreement to clean up the polluted Great Lakes.

The '70s also witnessed the birth of Green political parties, which eventually wielded significant influence in Europe but not in the United States. While the first Green parties were organized in New Zealand and Australia, the first Green Party candidate won election to a national legislature in Switzerland, in 1979. Green parties contributed to some of the movements that overthrew communist regimes in former Soviet-bloc countries. The German Green Party joined the governing coalition in 1998, and its leader served as foreign minister. Greens also have been mayors of Dublin, Rome and other major European cities.

In the United States, although Congress passed environmental legislation at a slower pace in the 1980s and '90s, some of the new laws were highly significant. The Superfund program began to clean up hazardous-waste sites in the '80s, for example, and the attack on acid rain began in the following decade.

Global warming has been the world's top environmental issue since the 1990s. Most — though not all — scientists believe that fossil-fuel emissions are causing the planet to heat up. Scientists can't make specific predictions about how much or how fast. Worst-case scenarios are truly catastrophic, forecasting drought, famine, floods, animal and plant extinctions, destruction of island and coastal communities — even massive human death.

The 1992 U.N. Framework Convention on Climate Change called on industrialized nations to reduce their emissions of "greenhouse gases," which are released when coal, oil and other fossil fuels are burned. The reduction was voluntary, however, and countries soon realized that the convention's goal — to stabilize emissions at 1990 levels by 2000 — would not be met.

The Kyoto Protocol, negotiated in 1997, set mandatory emissions reductions. But the United States — the world's largest greenhouse-gas emitter — has refused to ratify it, arguing that compliance would damage the economy. Critics warn that countries that have ratified may not meet the cuts because they aren't making sufficient changes in their consumption of fossil fuels. And rapidly industrializing countries — notably China and India — are expected to make major increases in their emissions.

CURRENT SITUATION

Democrats Take Over

Environmentalists celebrated the Democratic takeover of Congress on Nov. 7, 2006, and can point to growing signs of public support for environmental protection. But many environmental leaders remain focused on businesses for solutions to environmental problems, especially global warming.

Meanwhile, environmental groups are reporting recent increases in membership and financial contributions. The Sierra Club now has 800,000 members, a one-third rise in the last four years.[48] Between 2003 and 2006, membership jumped from 400,000 to 550,000 in the Natural Resources Defense Council and from 300,000 to 400,000 at Environmental Defense. Both reported substantial budget hikes as well.[49]

Overall, giving to environmental organizations increased by 7 percent from 2003 to 2004 and by 16.4 percent the next year — greater growth in both years than any other category of nonprofit organization tracked by the Giving USA Foundation.[50]

The Gallup Organization reports that the percentage of Americans who worry about the environment "a great deal" or "a fair amount" increased from 62 to 77 percent between 2004 and 2006. Since 1984, Gallup has asked Americans to choose between two sides in a mock debate: whether "protection of the environment should be given priority, even at the risk of curbing economic growth," or "economic growth should be given priority, even if the environment suffers to some extent." (*See graph, p. 2.*)

The pro-environment side has always prevailed, usually by a large margin. After falling precipitously during the early years of the Bush administration — from a 43-percentage-point pro-environment margin in 2000 to 5 percentage points in 2003 and 2004 — the pro-environment gap began widening again. Pro-environment respondents outnumbered pro-economy respondents by 17 percent in 2005 and 15 percent this year.[51]

Despite such positive signs, environmental activists don't expect major legislation to work its way through the House and Senate and survive presidential vetoes during the next two years. They also believe businesses are essential to the solutions, with or without government action.

Democratic congressional leaders tend to be more supportive of environmentalists' positions than Republicans.

But Democrats didn't win large enough majorities to override vetoes or break GOP filibusters in the Senate. Indeed, the agenda Democratic leaders announced for the opening days of the next Congress, in 2007, does not include environmental legislation.

The loss of Republican power means environmentalists won't have to battle attempts to roll back environmental protections, such as California Rep. Richard Pombo's efforts to weaken the Endangered Species Act, sell national park land in Alaska, open the Arctic National Wildlife Refuge to oil drilling and increase drilling off the nation's coasts. Pombo, who chaired the House Resources Committee, was defeated.

Individual representatives and senators will introduce environmental bills, including some to address global warming. But, said Sierra Club Executive Director Carl Pope, "I don't think we're going to see, at a national level, major progress, because Bush is still going to be there."[52]

Environmentalists "can't wait for the federal government, which is why you're seeing all these other players take the first steps," Sierra Club spokesman Antebi says.

Focus on Business

Environmentalists are drawing more sympathy from corporate executives, Public Affairs Council President Pinkham says, because "we've reached a tipping point where most business people agree that global warming is an issue that can't be ignored. Even companies with doubts are coming to realize you can't sit on the sidelines."

Environmental organizations are working with companies on a wide range of environmental challenges. Some relationships are cooperative, others confrontational. Environmentalists seek to apply pressure by winning support from companies' customers, employees and investors. They also appeal to executives' sense of social responsibility.

"We attempt to appeal to the most core, basic values that remind us that we're all human, that we all need to live on a healthy Earth together, and that some of us have far more decision-making power than others," says the Rainforest Action Network's Hogue. "If you're the CEO of a major bank or a government official or a logging executive, you are a human being first, and you don't want to do anything that you can't explain in good faith to your children and grandchildren."

In addition to its partnerships with FedEx, UPS and DuPont, Environmental Defense has struck agreements with numerous firms, including Wegmans Food Markets and Bon Appétit Management Company on implementing health and environmental standards for farmed salmon, McDonald's on reducing antibiotics in chicken, Compass Group food services on limiting antibiotics in pork and chicken, Bristol-Myers Squibb on incorporating environmental considerations into pharmaceutical development and packaging, and with other companies on other topics.

Having negotiated accords on environmentally friendly lending policies with Citigroup, JPMorgan Chase and Goldman Sachs, the Rainforest Action Network (RAN) now is running campaigns against Wells Fargo's investments in oil, coal, logging and mining operations. Among RAN's other campaigns to change corporate policies, it's pressing for revisions in Weyerhaeuser's logging practices and for increases in the fuel-efficiency of Ford vehicles.

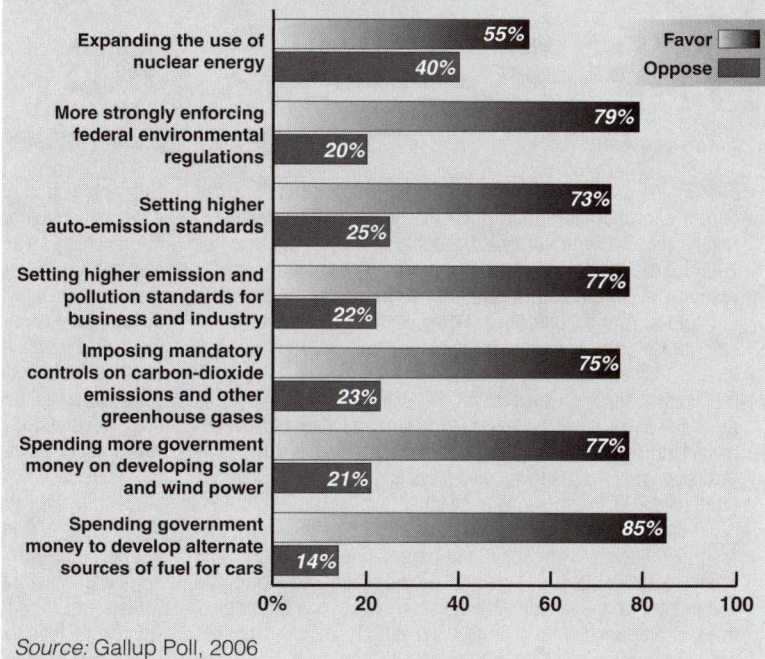

Public Strongly Favors Action on Environment

Americans strongly favor environmental initiatives by both industry and government to cut pollution and increase energy efficiency.

Do you generally favor or oppose:

	Favor	Oppose
Expanding the use of nuclear energy	55%	40%
More strongly enforcing federal environmental regulations	79%	20%
Setting higher auto-emission standards	73%	25%
Setting higher emission and pollution standards for business and industry	77%	22%
Imposing mandatory controls on carbon-dioxide emissions and other greenhouse gases	75%	23%
Spending more government money on developing solar and wind power	77%	21%
Spending government money to develop alternate sources of fuel for cars	85%	14%

Source: Gallup Poll, 2006

"You're seeing tremendous leadership from the private sector right now," Environmental Defense's Yarnold says. But environmentalists continue to press for government action because "businesses alone can't solve the global-warming problem."

Environmental groups want the federal government to require companies to meet environmental standards and to help them do so. New regulations are needed, environmentalists argue, not only to force recalcitrant companies to act but also to encourage corporations that want to act but can't afford to do more than their competitors.

"Many corporations, especially those active in international areas, are realizing they need to be more environmental and more progressive to stay competitive in the international arena," Oklahoma State University's Dunlap says. "A lot of American firms are caught in a bit of a dilemma. In some ways, they like having an administration that seems friendly to the market and keeping regulations minimal. On the other hand, they're not

getting the incentives and the regulatory push to stay on the cutting edge."

Brune, of the Rainforest Action Network, describes companies that are "trying to lead by example and trying to pressure the government to wake up and step up to the plate."

The Sierra Club's Hamilton says he knows corporate executives "who have almost begged Congress to tell them what to do to reduce emissions, so they know how to plan for it. But companies are reluctant to take action on their own for fear of losing competitive advantage, because they don't know what is going to be required of them" when Congress finally does act.

"Businesses crave certainty," Yarnold explains. "Global businesses in particular crave certainty. To be operating in one regulatory environment in Europe and another in the United States is crazy. It's not good for business." Conflicts in state laws also will increase

Are businesses better equipped than governments to address 21st-century environmental challenges?

YES
Margery Kraus
President and CEO,
APCO Worldwide*

Written for *CQ Researcher*, November 2006

There is no doubt the environment is on people's minds: Used hybrid cars can fetch more than the original sticker price at resale; the *Oxford American Dictionary*'s word of the year for 2006 is "carbon neutral." However hip it may be, environmental responsibility is more than just the "flavor of the month," it is our future. And businesses not only can be the most efficient catalyst for creating a more sustainable planet but they also are increasingly expected to play that role.

A recent study conducted by APCO Worldwide reveals that the American public holds businesses to a higher standard on environmental issues than it does the U.S. government. There is a belief that business is less encumbered by politics and bureaucracy and has more resources to act and influence others to do so.

Today's progressive companies already know they have this responsibility and embrace it. Big corporations are larger than many nations. Major companies' global reach and standards allow them to directly impact environments beyond the boundaries of any one country. As they expand globally, businesses are able to build factories with proven technologies that often exceed the requirements of local governments.

Corporations have a tremendous opportunity to influence individual behavior. Employees can be offered incentives to use public transportation, recycle and contribute time to community environmental efforts. More broadly, businesses can sway consumer bases to adopt environmentally responsible behavior.

Finally, an increased number of businesses see sustainable products as a new part of their business. They are engineering or re-engineering those products to be recyclable and to incorporate recycled materials; they are employing clean production processes to create less waste and pollution.

Down the road, these forward-looking businesses will have a healthy, sustainable work force, clean water and quality of life that will enable them to have good employees and more consumers. Their ultimate incentive: You can't run a successful business in a failed world.

Obviously, safeguarding our environment is best accomplished by governments, businesses and individuals working together. However, businesses, especially multinational corporations, are well-positioned to take decisive leadership and have the infrastructure and resources to achieve measurable results — and consumers are expecting nothing less.

* The public-relations and strategic-communications firm represents many of the world's largest corporations.

NO
Michael Brune
Executive Director,
Rainforest Action Network

Written for *CQ Researcher*, November 2006

Businesses and governments both have a vital role to play in addressing environmental challenges. We are beginning to see strong policies from a select number of high-profile businesses on issues such as forest protection and climate change. Meanwhile, state and local governments are responding to widespread public support for environmental protection, compensating for a disturbing lack of leadership in the White House and Congress.

One test for either businesses or governments is to determine to which constituency they are the most loyal. Most companies are guided by the old business axiom, "The customer is always right." These businesses realize that not only do consumers want to do business with companies that exhibit strong environmental values but also their own employees want to feel good about their employer's environmental record. Indeed, it is this view that has helped Home Depot, Lowe's, FedEx Kinko's and others to work with Rainforest Action Network to help protect endangered forests, and for Citigroup, Bank of America, JPMorgan Chase and Goldman Sachs to take principled stands on climate change and forest protection.

Conversely, many officials in Washington are stuck in the past, guarding the status quo. Within the last few years, the federal government has failed to enact, protect or enforce strong environmental policies, as evidenced by the attempted rollback of the Forest Service's "Roadless Rule" and the gutting of the Clean Water Act. Our politicians have fallen into the trap of believing they must choose between prosperity and the environment. Consequently, neither political party has stood up to the corporations whose policies are destabilizing and devastating our environment.

By leveraging public opinion and consumer choice to publicly stigmatize companies that refuse to adopt responsible environmental policies, environmental organizations are able to positively influence corporations' policies. This tactic strengthens marketplace democracy and empowers the consumer. It also has created significant progress and dramatic successes for environmental preservation. It gives consumers the ability to influence companies, stepping in where government has failed.

The reality is there is a new voice of business that shows how it is possible to do well by doing good, earning profits while upholding environmental principles. These businesses have shown a strong interest in working with government to meet the pressing environmental challenges of the 21st century. It's time for officials in Congress and the White House to listen and get to work.

pressure for federal legislation, says Robert Brulle, an associate professor of sociology and environmental science at Drexel University, who is researching the 21st-century history of the environmental movement.

Environmentalists' top legislative goals are the cap-and-trading scheme for greenhouse gases and significant increases in vehicle fuel-economy standards. California Democrat Barbara Boxer, in line to chair the Senate Environment and Public Works Committee, said she plans "to roll out a pretty in-depth set of hearings on global warming. It isn't going to help any business, it isn't going to help anybody, if we do nothing" about the issue, she insisted.

Sen. McCain said he and Sen. Lieberman will re-introduce their global-warming bill and "absolutely" will push for a floor vote. McCain, a potential 2008 presidential candidate, also expressed optimism that President Bush would sign the legislation before he leaves the White House in January 2009.

"I think the president is coming around," McCain said. "He made a statement recently where he said that climate change is a significant issue. To tell you the truth, I'm worried more about [other] people in the administration than the president himself."[53]

In the past, Bush has said he agrees that human activity has contributed to climate change, but he has consistently rejected the idea of imposing mandatory curbs on carbon-dioxide emissions. Bush also has resisted calls to impose tougher standards on vehicle fuel economy, household appliances and building insulation — measures that could sharply reduce America's oil consumption.

Those Bush positions — plus opposition from other GOP lawmakers — lead other legislators to suggest that action is less likely than McCain predicts.

California Democrat Henry A. Waxman, incoming chair of the House Government Reform Committee, said environmentalists need to understand that "President Bush would veto any bill that ever got to him."[54] Oklahoma Republican James M. Inhofe, outgoing chair of the Senate Environment and Public Works Committee, expressed confidence that he can round up the 41 votes needed to sustain a filibuster against global-warming legislation.

Inhofe said he is seeing "an awakening" to his argument that harmful global warming is a myth. "People are realizing that [environmentalists] are saying things that are just flat not true," Inhofe said.[55]

Gov. Arnold Schwarzenegger, R-Calif., discusses his environmental initiatives as New York City Mayor Michael Bloomberg looks on at fuel-cell maker Bloom Energy in Sunnyvale, Calif., on Sept. 21, 2006. The mayor announced he is launching a citywide greenhouse-gas inventory and appointing an environmental advisory board. California just mandated cuts in motor vehicles' carbon-dioxide emissions.

Boxer, Inhofe's successor, acknowledged that passing legislation will be difficult. "Maybe I want to take the ball 50 yards," she said, "but I can take it only 30."[56]

OUTLOOK
Entrepreneurs in Spotlight

Environmentalists are counting on entrepreneurs to produce a future green world. Once governments impose restrictions on greenhouse-gas emissions, leaders of environmental organizations say, entrepreneurs will supply the technology that makes the restrictions work.

"It's going to look much the way it did during the information-technology gold rush at the advent of the Internet Age," Greenpeace Executive Director Passacantando says. "A whole new generation of entrepreneurs is going to lead us into the new era, and eventually we will have an economy that's built on low carbon-dioxide emissions or no carbon-dioxide emissions."

Environmental Defense's Yarnold sees hope in different pro-environment precedents — such as the restrictions on emissions that cause acid rain and deplete the ozone layer.

"Things were invented," he says. "Processes were created. People rise to the challenge. Investments get made. It creates economic activity. It creates jobs.

"Will there be solar panels made with nanotechnology? Are there chemical compounds that are better at conducting electricity than the materials we now have? I don't know. But I do know the circumstances under which those will be carried out. Efficient markets find low-cost, highly efficient solutions, and that's what will happen if the government puts a hard cap on carbon dioxide."

As Passacantando puts it, the choice of technologies "is not going to be Greenpeace's pick. It's going to be the entrepreneurs.'"

Environmentalists are most optimistic about conservation and renewable energies such as solar and wind.

"We have enough sunlight hitting the state of California every day to fulfill the country's energy needs," Oklahoma State's Brune says. "Enough wind flows through the Midwest to fulfill the country's energy needs. Both forms of energy are clean, create more jobs and have no greenhouse-gas emissions. Neither creates the environmental legacy of nuclear waste or the national-security problems associated with nuclear plants."

Some environmentalists acknowledge the possibility that new technology could make coal, oil and nuclear energy acceptable as well.

"There's great hope in low-carbon coal," Yarnold says, "and nuclear has to be on the table." Before new nuclear plants can be built, he adds, the industry must prove it can dispose of waste safely and prevent nuclear materials from being turned into weapons — obstacles that many environmentalists believe are insurmountable. Others caution that the transition away from fossil fuels won't be so simple. Envisioned solutions can be double-edged swords: windmill farms that deface the landscape and injure birds that fly too close; hydropower projects that dam waterways and injure fish; agriculture-based fuels that levy their own environmental costs and drive up the cost of food.

Critics from the left and the right warn against succumbing to pressure to take actions that don't really provide long-term solutions.

"You'll probably find that promises to do something about global warming will become more popular over time," the Cato Institute's Taylor says. "Politicians will make those promises, and voters will embrace politicians who make those promises. But the public doesn't seem to

be willing to pay anything to reduce greenhouse gases. So politicians are going to find it's popular to propose programs but not popular to impose programs with costs, and I don't think greenhouse gases will be reduced much at all."

While Europe appears to be ahead of the United States in protecting the environment, Drexel University's Brulle says, Europe really is practicing "simulation of environmentalism. We have symbolic responses. But, when you look at carbon-dioxide emissions in Europe, they have not significantly gone down."

Brulle fears the United States will follow the same path. "We're not going to just stop using coal any more than we're going to destroy the economy of West Virginia," he says. Neither are Americans about to abandon a consumer culture that requires ever-higher energy consumption, he says.

"The way to reduce greenhouse-gas emissions now is to conserve big time, but I don't see any political will to do that," Brulle says. That leaves increased use of nuclear power as the only alternative for the foreseeable future, he argues.

"The question," he says, "is which is the worst poison. One will be absolutely fatal — climate change. One might be fatal, but is not always fatal — nuclear power.

"I'm not a fan of nuclear power, by any means. But, given the alternative of destroying the global eco-system for thousands of years, we have to seriously consider putting nuclear power into the mix."

NOTES

1. "Corporate Innovation: Changing the Way Business Thinks About the Environment," Environmental Defense; environmentaldefense.org/corporate_innovation.cfm. See also Jia Lynn Yang, "It's Not Easy Being Green — But Big Business Is Trying," *Fortune*, Aug. 7, 2006.

2. "For the Health of the Nation: An Evangelical Call to Civic Responsibility," National Association of Evangelicals, Oct. 7, 2004; www.nae.net/images/civic_responsibility2.pdf.

3. Elizabeth Keenan, "Plugging Into Nuclear," *Time*, June 19, 2006, p. 46; Andrew C. Revkin, "Updating Prescriptions for Avoiding Worldwide Catastrophe,"

The New York Times, Sept. 12, 2006, p. F2. For background, see Marcia Clemmitt, "Climate Change," *CQ Researcher*, Jan. 27, 2006, pp. 73-96.

4. Accessed at people-press.org/reports/display .php3?ReportID=280.

5. Accessed at www.pewtrusts.com/pdf/pew_research_ economy_012506.pdf.

6. Accessed at www.harrisinteractive.com/harris_poll/ index.asp?PID=607.

7. Accessed at www.foe.org/camps/intl/corpacct/wall-street/handbook/index.html and rockpa.org/ wp-content/uploads/2006/06/Power%20of%20 Proxy.pdf.

8. The Carbon Disclosure Project, "The $31.5 Trillion Question: Is Your Company Prepared for Climate Change?" www.cdproject.net/viewrelease.asp?id=8/.

9. Juliet Eilperin, "Cities, States Aren't Waiting For U.S. Action on Climate," *The Washington Post*, Aug. 11, 2006, p. A1.

10. *Ibid*. See also Karen Matthews, "States To Lower Greenhouse Gas Emissions," The Associated Press, Oct. 16, 2006.

11. Accessed at www.apolloalliance.org.

12. Accessed at www.apolloalliance.org/strategy_ center/a_bold_energy_and_jobs_policy/ten_point_ plan.cfm. For background on hydrogen, see Mary H. Cooper, "Alternative Fuels," *CQ Researcher*, Feb. 25, 2005, pp. 173-196.

13. Michael Schneider, "Leo's Green Builds Skein," *Daily Variety*, Oct. 17, 2006, p. 1.

14. Karen Krebsbach, "The Green Revolution: Are Banks Sacrificing Profits for Activists' Principles?" *US Banker*, Feb. 6, 2005.

15. Marc Gunther, "The Green Machine," *Fortune*, Aug. 7, 2006, p. 42.

16. *Ibid*.

17. Yang, *op. cit*.

18. Accessed at fedex.com/us/about/responsibility/ environment/hybridelectricvehicle.html?link=4.

19. Steven Mufson, "As Power Bills Soar, Companies Embrace 'Green' Buildings," *The Washington Post*, Aug. 5, 2006, p. A1.

20. General Electric, press release, "GE Launches Ecomagination to Develop Environmental Technologies"; http://home.businesswire.com/portal/ site/ge/index.jsp?ndmViewId=news_view&ndmConf igId=1002373&newsId=20050509005663&newsLa ng=en&ndmConfigId=1002373 &vnsId=681.

21. "2005 Report on Socially Responsible Investing Trends in the United States," Social Investment Forum, Jan. 24, 2006; www.socialinvest.org/areas/ research/trends/sri_trends_report_2005.pdf.

22. "Proxy Season Preview — Spring 2006," As You Sow Foundation and Rockefeller Philanthropy Advisors; www.asyousow.org/publications/2006_proxy_ preview.pdf.

23. Carol Hymowitz, moderator, "Corporate Social Concerns: Are They Good Citizenship, Or a Rip-Off for Investors?" *The Wall Street Journal Online*, Dec. 6, 2005; http://online .wsj.com/public/article/SB113355105439712626 .html?mod=todays_free_feature.

24. Testimony before U.S. House Energy and Commerce Committee, May 2, 2006.

25. Barbara Mantel, "Energy Efficiency," *CQ Researcher*, May 19, 2006, pp. 433-456.

26. *Ibid*.

27. The Coal Based Generation Stakeholders Group, "A Vision for Achieving Ultra-Low Emissions from Coal-Fueled Electric Generation," January 2005; www .nma.org/pdf/coal_vision.pdf.

28. Mantel, *op. cit*.

29. *Ibid*.

30. Daniel Gross, "Raise the Gasoline Tax? Funny, It Doesn't Sound Republican," *The New York Times*, Oct. 8, 2006.

31. Worldwatch Institute, *Vital Signs 2006-2007* (2006), p. 32.

32. U.S. Energy Department, "Annual Energy Review 2005," Energy Information Administration, July 27, 2006, Table 1.3; www.eia.doe.gov/emeu/aer/pdf/ pages/sec1_9.pdf.

33. *Ibid*., Table 8.4a; www.eia.doe.gov/emeu/aer/pdf/ pages/sec8_17.pdf.

34. *Ibid*., Table 2.1e; www.eia.doe.gov/emeu/aer/pdf/ pages/sec2_8.pdf.

35. The Coal Based Generation Stakeholders Group, *op. cit.*

36. "Annual Energy Review 2005," *op. cit.*, Table 1.3.

37. Peter Schwartz and Spencer Reiss, "Nuclear Now! How Clean, Green Atomic Energy Can Stop Global Warming," *Wired*, February 2005.

38. U.S. Energy Department, *op. cit.*, Table 10.1; www.eia.doe.gov/emeu/aer/pdf/pages/sec10_3.pdf.

39. Adriel Bettelheim, "Biofuels Boom," *CQ Researcher*, Sept. 29, 2006, pp. 793-816.

40. Revkin, *op. cit.*, p. 2.

41. Frank Clifford, "Alarmed by 'Cycle of Anti-Environmentalism,' *Los Angeles Times*, Nov. 15, 2005, p. B2.

42. Unless otherwise noted, this "Background" section is based on "The Evolution of the Conservation Movement," Library of Congress; lcweb2.loc.gov/ammem/amrvhtml/conshome.html; Lorraine Elliott, "Environmentalism," *Encyclopaedia Britannica*, 2006; www.britannica.com/eb/article-224631; *History of the Environmental Movement*, Glen Canyon Institute; www.glencanyon.org/library/movementhistory.php; "History," U.S. Environmental Protection Agency; epa.gov/history/index.htm; Tom Arrandale, "National Parks Under Pressure," *CQ Researcher*, Oct. 6, 2006, pp. 817-840; Mary H. Cooper, "Environmental Movement at 25," *CQ Researcher*, March 31, 1995, pp. 273-296, and William Kovarik, "Environmental History Timeline," www.radford.edu/~wkovarik/envhist.

43. The Associated Press, "3 Plead Guilty to Ecoterror Charges," *Los Angeles Times*, July 21, 2006, p. A19.

44. "History of Earth Day," Earth Day Network; www.earthday.org/resources/history.aspx.

45. Beverly Beyette, "Earth Observance: The Day Politics Stood Still," *Los Angeles Times*, May 23, 1985, p. 5-1. Joanne Omang, " 'Sun Day,' Slated in May," *The Washington Post*, Sept. 19, 1977, p. A20.

46. Beyette, *op. cit.*

47. The Associated Press, April 23, 1970 (Lenin's birthday); Dan Eggen, "Earth Day: From Radical to Mainstream," *The Washington Post*, April 22, 2000, p. B1 (Daughters of the American Revolution).

48. Jerry Adler, "Going Green," *Newsweek*, July 17, 2006, p. 42.

49. *Encyclopedia of Associations*, 2003 and 2006.

50. *Giving USA 2006: The Annual Report on Philanthropy for the Year 2005*, published by the Giving USA Foundation.

51. The Gallup Organization, 2006.

52. Bettina Boxall, "Conservationist Clout," *Los Angeles Times*, Nov. 9, 2006. p. 27.

53. Darren Samuelsohn, "Sen. McCain Pledges Push for 'Long-Overdue' Emissions Bill," *Environment and Energy Daily*, Nov. 17, 2006.

54. *Ibid.*

55. *Ibid.*

56. Charles Babington, "Party Shift May Make Warming a Hill Priority," *The Washington Post*, Nov. 18, 2006, p. A6.

BIBLIOGRAPHY

Books

Bailey, Ronald, ed., *Global Warming and Other Eco Myths: How the Environmental Movement Uses False Science to Scare Us to Death*, Prima Publishing, 2002.
In this collection of essays the writers argue that many warnings about threats to the environment are way overblown.

Gore, Al, *An Inconvenient Truth: The Planetary Emergency of Global Warming and What We Can Do About It*, Rodale Books, 2006.
Former Vice President Al Gore urges action on global warming in this book written to accompany his surprisingly popular movie of the same name.

Savitz, Andrew W., and Karl Weber, *The Triple Bottom Line: How Today's Best-Run Companies Are Achieving Economic, Social and Environmental Success — and How You Can Too*, Jossey-Bass, 2006.
A business consultant and a freelance writer offer practical advice on how companies can profit from responding to environmental and other public needs.

Articles

Adler, Jerry, "Going Green," *Newsweek*, July 17, 2006, p. 42.
Adler looks at how individual Americans are taking action to protect the environment.

Gunther, Marc, "The Green Machine," *Fortune*, Aug. 7, 2006, p. 42.
Gunther reports on Wal-Mart's ambitious plans to become the world's greenest retailer and increase profits at the same time.

Holstein, William J., "Saving the Earth, And Saving Money," *The New York Times*, Aug. 13, 2006, p. 9.
Gwen Ruta, director of corporate partnerships for Environmental Defense, explains how her organization works with businesses.

Hymowitz, Carol, moderator, "Corporate Social Concerns: Are They Good Citizenship, Or a Rip-Off for Investors?" *The Wall Street Journal Online*, Dec. 6, 2005. Available online at http://online.wsj.com/public/article/SB113355105439712626.html?mod=todays_free_feature.
Debaters about corporations' environmental responsibility included Benjamin Heineman Jr., then senior vice president of GE; Ilyse Hogue, director of the Rainforest Action Network's Global Finance Campaign; and Fred Smith Jr., president and founder of the Competitive Enterprise Institute.

Pollan, Michael, "Mass Natural," *The New York Times*, June 4, 2006, p. 15.
Pollan fears Wal-Mart's plan to become an organic grocer and its massive purchasing power and lust for low prices will hurt organic farmers and consumers.

Schwartz, Peter, and Spencer Reiss, "Nuclear Now! How Clean, Green Atomic Energy Can Stop Global Warming," *Wired*, February 2005.
The authors argue that nuclear power can end global warming and the other environmental degradations associated with extracting and burning coal and oil.

Reports and Studies

Coal Based Generation Stakeholders Group, "A Vision for Achieving Ultra-Low Emissions from Coal-Fueled Electric Generation," January 2005; www.nma.org/pdf/coal_vision.pdf.
The coal industry and its customers tell how they plan to meet America's energy and environmental needs by cleaning up their acts.

Friends of the Earth, "Confronting Companies Using Shareholder Power: A Handbook on Socially-Oriented Shareholder Activism;" www.foe.org/camps/intl/corpacct/wallstreet/handbook/index.html.
The environmental organization urges corporate shareholders to press their companies to adopt environmentally friendly practices.

Hayward, Steven F., "Index of Leading Environmental Indicators 2006," *American Enterprise Institute*, 2006; www.aei.org/books/bookID.854/book_detail.asp.
The think tank's annual analysis of environmental statistics contends Earth is in much better shape than leading environmental organizations say.

National Association of Evangelicals, "For the Health of the Nation: An Evangelical Call to Civic Responsibility," Oct. 7, 2004; www.nae.net/images/civic_responsibility2.pdf.
Conservative religious leaders admonish believers that faith requires acting to relieve social ills and to protect the environment.

Price, Tom, "Activists in the Boardroom: How Advocacy Groups Seek to Shape Corporate Behavior," *Foundation for Public Affairs*, 2006.
The author examines how advocacy organizations influence companies' policies through both confrontation and cooperation.

Worldwatch Institute, *State of the World 2006: A Worldwatch Institute Report on Progress Toward a Sustainable Society, W. W. Norton*, 2006.
The environmental group reports on developments important to environmental protection and sustainability, including renewable alternatives to oil and the special challenges posed by rapid economic development in China and India.

For More Information

American Enterprise Institute, 1150 17th St., N.W., Washington, DC 20036; (202) 862-5800; www.aei.org. Conservative think tank that studies environmental and other issues.

Bullitt Foundation, 1212 Minor Ave., Seattle, WA 98101-2825; (206) 343-0807; www.bullitt.org. Philanthropic organization working to protect, restore and maintain the natural environment of the Pacific Northwest.

Cato Institute, 1000 Massachusetts Ave., N.W., Washington, DC 20001; www.cato.org. Libertarian think tank that questions environmental-protection measures that interfere with free markets.

Ecomagination, ge.ecomagination.com. Web site where General Electric explains its plans to profit from making environmentally friendly products.

Environmental Defense, 257 Park Ave. South, New York, NY 10010; (212) 505-2100; www.environmentaldefense.org. The advocacy group forms partnerships with corporations to promote environmentally friendly business practices.

League of Conservation Voters, 1920 L St., N.W., Suite 800, Washington, DC 20036; www.lcv.org. Advocacy group that reports on government officials' actions on environmental issues.

Natural Resources Defense Council, 40 West 20th St., New York, NY 10011; www.nrdc.org. Advocacy group that studies and acts on a wide range of environmental issues, with special focus on wildlife and wilderness areas.

Pew Center on Global Climate Change, 2101 Wilson Blvd., Suite 550, Arlington, VA 22201; (703) 516-4146; www.pewclimate.org. Funded by Pew Charitable Trusts.

Rainforest Action Network, 221 Pine St., 5th Floor, San Francisco, CA 94104; (415) 398-4404; www.ran.org. The activist group protests corporate practices that harm the environment and helps design pro-environment business practices.

Resources for the Future, 1616 P St., N.W., Washington, DC 20036; www.rff.org. Independent scholarly organization that analyzes energy, environment and natural-resources issues.

Rockefeller Philanthropy Advisors, 37 Madison Ave., 37th Floor, New York, NY 10022; (212) 812-4330; www.rockpa.org. Studies and offers advice about shareholder activism by nonprofit organizations.

Sierra Club, 85 Second St., Second Floor, San Francisco, CA 94105; www.sierraclub.org. Founded in 1892 to protect wilderness but now active on many environmental issues.

Social Investment Forum, 1612 K St., N.W., Suite 650, Washington, DC 20006; (202) 872-5319; www.socialinvest.org. The socially responsible investing industry's trade association.

Wal-Mart Sustainability, www.walmartfacts.com/featuredtopics/?id=1. Web site where Wal-Mart showcases its efforts to become environmentally friendly.

Worldwatch Institute, 1776 Massachusetts Ave., N.W., Washington, DC 20036; (202) 452-1999; www.worldwatch.org. Studies environmental and economic trends.

2

Curbing Climate Change

Is the World Doing Enough?

Colin Woodard

In front of the U.S. Embassy in London, the "Statue of Taking Liberties" holds the torch of protest against the U.S. withdrawal from the Kyoto Protocol, which places limits on greenhouse gases created by burning fossil fuels.

Newsmakers/Sion Touhig

From *CQ Global Researcher*, February 2007.

From the shores of Jokulsarlon Lagoon, the view of Iceland's ice cap is breathtaking: A vast dome of snow and ice, 3,000 feet tall, smothers the jagged mountains; a glacier spills the 12 miles down to the water's edge.

More stunning is how fast it's all vanishing.

A century ago there was no lagoon, and this spot was under 100 feet of glacial ice. The glacier, the Breidamerkurjokull, extended to within 250 yards of the ocean. Now the Atlantic is more than two miles away from the glacier's massive, miles-wide snout, which stands in an expanding lake of its own melt water. Jokulsarlon — "glacier lake" in Icelandic — is now more than 350 feet deep and has more than doubled its size in the past 15 years, threatening to wash out Iceland's principal highway.

In the 250 miles between the lake and Reykjavik, Iceland's capital, the highway passes by another dozen glaciers, all of them steadily retreating back up the valleys they once filled. Stand on their snouts and you hear cracking, moans and the gurgle of the many streams of water pouring from their insides, feeding unruly brown rivers that rush toward the sea. As they retreat, a new landscape scrolls out from underneath, places that haven't seen the light of day since medieval times.

Iceland is losing its ice, and it's not alone. Greenland's 10,000-year-old ice sheet is retreating at a rate that has astonished scientists who study it. Arctic Ocean sea ice has shrunk by 6 percent since 1978, while the average thickness has declined by 40 percent in recent decades, threatening polar bears, seals and the Inuit people who hunt them. (*See sidebar, p. 35.*)

Japanese activists and advocates for now-endangered polar bears cheer the signing of the Kyoto Protocol in 2005, requiring cuts in carbon emissions. The treaty has the support of 169 nations; only Australia and the United States, among industrialized nations, refused to join.

In Antarctica enormous floating ice shelves have disintegrated, and many of the glaciers that empty the West Antarctic ice sheet have picked up speed, raising the possibility that a large portion of the southern ice cap may break up, which would quickly raise world sea levels by 20 feet.

Mid-latitude glaciers are vanishing as well. All appear to be the result of significant increases in average temperatures: 0.6 degrees Celsius (1.1 degrees Fahrenheit) globally and 1.6 degrees Celsius in the Arctic during the 20th century.[1]

Iceland's president, Olafur Ragnar Grimsson, has invited fellow world leaders to come to Iceland and bear witness. "Nowhere in the world can you see traces of climate change as clearly as in the North," he said. "It's an important mission."[2]

The vast majority of the world's scientists are now convinced that the warming of the past 50 years has largely come from greenhouse gas emissions, mostly created by the burning of fossil fuels. The "greenhouse effect" is how the Earth retains much of its warmth from the sun, as certain gases in the atmosphere trap some of the radiation reflected off the planet's surface and warm the planet.

Greenhouse gases (GHG) occur naturally in the atmosphere and include water vapor, carbon dioxide, methane, nitrous oxide and ozone. But human activity has been boosting the concentrations of some of them,

most notoriously the carbon dioxide (CO_2), which is released by burning fossil fuels. The overproduction of man-made gases has been blamed for much of the excess retention of heat in the atmosphere that has contributed to global warming.

"Everything we're seeing in the Arctic is 100 percent consistent with that," says Robert Corell, a senior fellow at the American Meteorological Society in Washington, D.C., who oversaw the Arctic Climate Impact Assessment, a four-year study involving 300 scientists from around the world.

A climate study conducted by the U.N. Intergovernmental Panel on Climate Change (IPCC), released on Feb. 2, 2007, flatly states that the climate-change debate is over.[3] "Feb. 2 will be remembered as the date when uncertainty was removed as to whether humans had anything to do with climate change on this planet," said IPCC Executive Director Achim Steiner. "The evidence is on the table."

Made up of more than 1,000 scientists from 113 countries, the IPCC said new research over the last six years shows with 90 percent certainty that human-generated greenhouse gases have caused most of the rise in global temperatures over the past half-century. "Warming of the climate system is unequivocal," said the IPCC's "Summary for Policymakers" — one of four reports scheduled for release this year.[4] The IPCC generally is considered a cautious body because all participating governments must sign off on its conclusions.

"We know the climate is changing and that we have a 10- or 20-year window to address it," says Hermann Ott, a climate expert at Germany's Wuppertal Institute. "It's very urgent that we act at both the national and international level pretty soon."

The industrial powers, which produce most of the world's pollutants, are in the best position to act. And it has been the 27 nations of the European Union (EU) that have spearheaded efforts to reduce greenhouse gas emissions. They have acted in large part because of widespread public concern — sparked by recent climactic extremes witnessed in their home countries.

Europe was hit with a devastating summer heat wave in 2003 that killed 25,000 people; roads buckled in Germany and water levels on the Danube plunged to record lows, forcing a suspension of the Budapest-Vienna hovercraft service and allowing illegal migrants to wade between Romania and Bulgaria. The year before, torrential rains triggered devastating floods across Central Europe, causing $15 billion in damages. Last winter many Austrian ski resorts were unable to open in December because it was not cold enough to make snow.[5]

European leaders are so convinced of the seriousness of global warming that — in a dramatic announcement on March 9 — they unilaterally committed themselves to more than double the amount of greenhouse gases they had promised earlier to scour from their emissions.[6]

Yet skeptics remain, even in Europe. Henrik Svensmark, a weather scientist at the Danish National Space Center, for instance, believes that changes in the sun's magnetic field — and the corresponding impact on cosmic rays — not greenhouse gas emissions, may be the key to global warming.[7]

Habibullo Abdussamatov, head of the research laboratory at Pulkovo Astronomical Observatory in St. Petersburg, Russia, takes a similar non-mainstream position.[8]

That global warming exists is not new to the Inuit. The Inuit Circumpolar Conference, which represents 150,000 people living in the High Arctic, recently filed a protest with the Inter-American Commission on Human Rights, charging that U.S. greenhouse gases are destroying their homes and livelihoods. (*See sidebar, p. 35.*)

And residents of low-lying Pacific island nations fear their entire countries may be eliminated as melting ice causes oceans to rise.[9] (*See sidebar, p. 30.*)

"We are frightened and worried. And we cannot think of another Tuvalu to move to . . . if nothing is done urgently and we are forced out of our islands," Tuvalu Ambassador Enele Sosene Sopoaga told the U.N. General Assembly last fall.[10]

Climate experts in the United States and abroad say they expect the United States to become more aggressive about climate change after the 2008 presidential election, regardless of which party wins. They cite many factors, including the Republican defeats in the 2006 midterm elections, muscular action by state and city governments

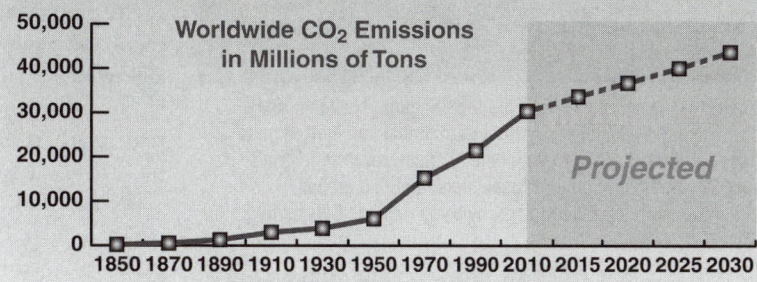

Global Carbon Dioxide Emissions: 1850-2030

For most of human history, carbon-dioxide emissions were irrelevant to climate. But only decades after the dawn of the Industrial Age, the accumulation of carbon dioxide generated by the burning of fossil fuels began to noticeably change the lower atmosphere. Now carbon emissions threaten to spiral past our ability to control their effects on global warming.

Worldwide CO_2 Emissions in Millions of Tons

Projected

1850 1870 1890 1910 1930 1950 1970 1990 2010 2015 2020 2025 2030

Source: "Climate Change 101: International Action," Pew Center on Global Climate Change

to reduce emissions and increasing pressure for substantive action from corporate and religious leaders such as Boeing, General Electric, BP, the U.S. Conference of Catholic Bishops and the Baptist General Convention of Texas.[11]

"The rest of us are waiting to see when and how the U.S. will re-engage in climate issues, says Harald Winkler, principal scientific officer at the University of Cape Town Energy Research Center in South Africa. "The large, carbon-emitting developing countries aren't going to make a move until the U.S. federal government moves."

Uncertainty over U.S. action has complicated international efforts to develop a successor to the Kyoto Protocol, the international agreement that expires in 2012, under which 41 of the world's industrialized countries — but not the United States — agreed to reduce their greenhouse gas emissions. Experts say that significantly reducing global GHG emissions hinges not only on U.S. participation but also participation by large developing countries like China, India and Brazil.[12] China, where the economy has been growing at more than 9 percent a year for more than two decades, is expected to surpass the United States as the world's largest carbon emitter in 2009.[13]

Critics of Kyoto — led by the United States — say the protocol has little hope of significantly reducing emissions as long as China and India are exempt. But

A rush-hour cloud of pollution drapes Bangkok, Thailand, on Feb. 2, 2007, the day that a report by the International Panel on Climate Change (IPCC) asserted that climate changes very likely have been caused by human burning of fossil fuels, and that global temperatures are expected to rise by three degrees Celsius by 2100.

these countries say they are lifting tens of millions out of poverty and that they should not be penalized for pursuing the same heavily polluting development path the rich industrial nations followed.

To address the challenge of global warming, many argue, the international community must find a mechanism by which rich nations help poorer ones adopt clean energy and transportation technologies and adapt to the effects of a changing climate.

As the world's leaders grapple with climate change, here are some of the questions being debated:

Are all countries doing their part to control global warming?

The short answer is no, although most are doing far more than the United States.

To date, 169 countries have signed the Kyoto Protocol, including every industrial nation except Australia and the United States. Kyoto, which went into effect in 2005, has been a polarizing agreement. Its supporters call it only a baby step toward confronting climate change; its detractors — most of whom now agree that global warming is real — say it already has slowed economic growth without making a meaningful reduction in greenhouse gas emissions.

Under the agreement, the 41 wealthy countries agreed to collectively reduce their emissions 5.2 percent below 1990 levels by 2012. The EU committed to an overall 8 percent reduction, Japan and Canada to 6 percent. But few

countries appear on target to meet their commitments. As of 2004, Canada's emissions had increased 26.6 percent over 1990 levels, and Japan's by 6.5 percent; European Union (EU) emissions had decreased by just 0.6 percent.

Within the EU, Great Britain reduced its emissions by 14.3 percent and Germany by 17.3 percent, but those gains were offset by substantial increases in Greece (26.6 percent), Portugal (41 percent) and Spain (49 percent).[14]

In their March 9 announcement of new emission-reduction goals, however, EU leaders agreed to unilaterally reduce their overall emissions to 20 percent of 1990 levels within 13 years and use renewable sources for one-fifth of their electric power. They also vowed to use biofuels in 10 percent of road vehicles by 2020.[15]

French President Jacques Chirac called the decision to make unilateral reductions one of the "great moments in European history." And in a clear challenge to the United States, China and India, German Chancellor Angela Merkel said the EU's 27 members would commit to a 30 percent reduction if other countries followed suit. The plan will be presented to President Bush and other world leaders in June.[16]

Why has the United States been so cool to Kyoto? Some American critics see the treaty as a misguided piece of "one-worldism" that will wreck the U.S. economy. Others argue that it doesn't really matter, that following Kyoto guidelines is unlikely to have a significant effect on global warming, primarily because new mega-economies such as China, India and Brazil have not signed on to control their emissions.

Thomas H. Wigley, a senior scientist at the National Center for Atmospheric Research in Boulder, Colo., estimated that even if the United States had joined Kyoto and all countries met and stuck to their targets, warming in 2100 would be reduced by a mere 8 percent. Wigley is against Kyoto, but only because he advocates a far stronger commitment to reducing gases.

Many around the world saw the hesitation of the United States as self-serving. "Of course, the consensus is that the president is paying his dues to Big Oil and Big Metal for supporting his election," wrote Scottish columnist Charles Fletcher, "and of course that is, to us, outrageous. But money is unsentimental. The fight against global warming and pollution should be equally clear-eyed in its assessment of what just happened."

In Fletcher's eyes, "What happened was that the American president was honest and spoke plainly, and we should start dealing with it. He said: 'I will not accept anything that will harm our economy and hurt our American workers.' "[17]

Kyoto's proponents argue that it has been an essential first step and has yielded benefits simply by focusing attention on the need to reduce emissions. "It is only the first battle in the war against climate change," says Tony Juniper, vice chair of the Amsterdam-based Friends of the Earth International, since "the commitments made by governments under Kyoto do not go anywhere near far enough."[18]

Unfortunately, nobody knows exactly what "far enough" is. Scientists do know that since the Industrial Revolution, greenhouse gas concentrations in Earth's atmosphere have increased from 280 parts per million (ppm) of carbon dioxide to 379 in 2005, while the world has warmed by more than 0.6 degrees Celsius. A British government study suggests that if current emissions trends hold, the concentration will reach 550 ppm by 2035 and likely increase average temperatures by another 2 degrees C. While 2 degrees may not sound like much, average temperatures during the last Ice Age were only 5 degrees Celsius lower than they are today.[19]

"At Kyoto, the countries of the world sat down and talked about what reductions they could manage," says Alex Evans, a senior policy associate at the Center on International Cooperation (CIC) at New York University. "Now we need to ask

Bangladesh Faces Catastrophic Flooding

Thirty million residents of Bangladesh would lose their homes if the sea level rises three feet at the end of the century, which some experts predict (gray line on map, top panel). Pedicabs slosh through flooded streets in Dhaka (bottom panel). The low-lying, densely populated region of the Indian subcontinent lies mostly in the Ganges River delta and is vulnerable to sea-level rises that may be caused by melting polar glaciers.

Sources: ESRI and UNEP

Pacific Islanders' Sinking Feeling

Tiny nations face inundation

People in the Republic of the Marshall Islands have a lot to lose if global warming causes the seas to rise as much as scientists think they could. Their entire nation would cease to exist.

The Marshallese live on 1,100 islands spread across three-quarters of a million square miles of the central Pacific Ocean. Most of the islands are small, so small that if you added them all together, you would have a parcel of land no bigger than the District of Columbia.

A few are no more than a couple hundred yards wide, and their average elevation is just seven feet above sea level. They're arranged in 29 sandy, ring-shaped chains called atolls. Stand most anywhere on Majuro Atoll, the capital and home to one-third of the country's 58,000 people, and you can hear the surf crashing on either side of you.[1]

Small island states are among the most vulnerable to climate change. Many of them will not be able to adapt by retreating from the coastal zone. There isn't anywhere else to go. The International Panel on Climate Change (IPCC) notes that land lost to sea-level rise and associated effects "is likely to be of a magnitude that would disrupt virtually all economic and social sectors in these countries."[2]

Understandably, the governments of places like the Bahamas, Fiji and the Federated States of Micronesia have been among the most vocal critics of the U.S. and other governments that have opposed aggressive action on climate change.

Atoll nations like Kiribati, the Maldives, Tuvalu and the Marshall Islands are doubly vulnerable because they are literally built on the backs of reef-building corals that formed the islands and today protect them from storms. According to a study by the Tyndall Centre for Climate Change Research in the United Kingdom, the predicted increase in sea-surface temperatures can be expected to damage and kill the relevant corals through bleaching, preventing them from keeping pace with rising seas.[3]

Signs of erosion are everywhere on Majuro. Beaches have vanished, seawalls have been battered down and chunks of the main road have been swept away by the sea. At a cemetery in the middle of town, islanders have to keep reburying their relatives because the sea keeps uncovering their coffins during storms. There are no rivers in the Marshall Islands; people rely on a thin "lens" of fresh groundwater for drinking and irrigation, but more and more of those lenses are becoming contaminated with brine.

On Majuro, some of those changes may be the result of poorly conceived developments and the mining of lagoon sand for use in construction, acknowledges Holly Barker, a senior adviser to the Marshallese ambassador to the United States "It's true that on Majuro there are some human impacts, but we see exactly the same effects on the outer islands, where people are still living sustainably off the land and there is no industry whatsoever," says Barker, who previously lived on remote Mille Atoll as a Peace Corps volunteer.

ourselves what level of risk we are actually prepared to tolerate."

One of the most important accomplishments of the European Union is the creation of the Emission Trading Scheme (ETS), which is based on the premise that the free market is the most cost-effective way to reduce carbon emissions. First, member governments assigned binding carbon-emission quotas to large polluters, effectively creating an artificial "shortage" in polluting rights. Then an emissions commodity market was set up. Companies needing to emit more carbon dioxide could buy credits from those producing less, or from developing nations, who could use the money on U.N.-certified projects that cut or absorb emissions.

The system has its downsides, such as sharp increases in electricity prices as utilities pass the cost of buying credits on to consumers. In Germany, for instance, off-peak prices for electricity doubled in just two years, largely because much of the power there comes from burning coal, which produces more greenhouse gases than other fossil fuels.

"ETS has had its share of problems, but it has been a really very valuable learning experience," says Eileen Claussen, president of the Pew Center on Global Climate Change. "They've figured out how to make it work well and have gotten a lot of private-sector players invested in the new carbon-trading market. It's definitely part of the way forward for the rest of us."[20]

"On Mille there are these huge gun turrets that the Japanese built 100 yards inshore during World War II so that U.S. vessels coming in wouldn't see them. Now they're standing out in the water."

A 1992 study of Majuro Atoll by the National Oceanic and Atmospheric Administration (NOAA) determined that if sea levels rise by three feet, the atoll will cease to exist. Defending the atoll from a 50-year storm event would be impossible in such a case, and NOAA has issued a sober policy recommendation: "Full retreat of the entire population of Majuro Atoll and the Marshall Islands must be considered in planning for worst-case [sea-rise] and climate-change scenarios."[4]

"For the Marshall Islands, climate change is an issue of sovereignty," Barker says. "The Marshallese have extremely low carbon emissions. Other countries' lifestyle habits don't give them the right to take away a nation. Where will the Marshallese go? Will they still have a voice at the United Nations? Will they cease to be a nation?"

In 2001, Tuvalu, another Pacific atoll nation, convinced New Zealand to take an annual quota of refugees, so as to allow an orderly evacuation of the nation. "While New Zealand responded positively in the true Pacific way of helping one's neighbors, Australia on the other hand has slammed the door in our face," Paani Laupepa of the Tuvalu Ministry of Natural Resources, said at the time.

He also had sharp words for the United States, saying that its refusal to ratify the Kyoto Protocol had "effectively denied future generations of Tuvaluan their fundamental freedom to live where our ancestors have lived for thousands of years."[5]

Should it come to that, the most likely refuge for the Marshallese would be the United States, which governed the islands for more than 40 years after World War II under a

Children of the Marshall Islands in the South Pacific may lose their world if the oceans rise even a few feet. The islands are spread across low-lying atolls. Refugees from the Marshalls are already immigrating to New Zealand as the global temperature rises.

Mieco Beach Yacht Club

mandate from the United Nations. The U.S. Postal Service still delivers the mail within the country, and Marshallese serve in the U.S. military in relatively large numbers.

[1] The author has reported on climate change from the Marshall Islands in both 1997 and 1999. For a full report see Colin Woodard, *Ocean's End* (2000), pp. 163-189.

[2] International Panel on Climate Change, "Climate Change 2001," Section 17.2.2.1.

[3] Jon Barnett and Neil Adger, *Climate Dangers and Atoll Countries*, Tyndall Centre, October 2001, p. 4.

[4] P. Holthus, *et al.*, "Vulnerability Assessment of Accelerated Sea-level Rise, Case Study: Majuro Atoll, Marshall Islands, Apia, Western Samoa," South Pacific Regional Environment Program, 1992.

[5] "Pacific islanders flee rising seas," BBC, Oct. 9, 2001, 20:29 GMT.

Denmark has become a global leader in developing technologies and policies to reduce greenhouse gas emissions. Its government supports the wind-energy industry, which now provides a quarter of Denmark's electricity and supplies the majority of wind turbines in use elsewhere in the world. Wind turbines dot the countryside like giant pinwheels, while huge offshore wind farms capture the stiff winds in the Baltic and North seas.

Authorities in the Danish capital, Copenhagen, have deployed 2,000 bicycles in public locations around the city, which can be borrowed for free; a heavy sales tax on automobiles discourages their purchase. The country is home to the world's largest solar-powered district heating station — a 12-megawatt facility on the island of

Aero — and hundreds of special plants that process kitchen and farm wastes into fertilizers and clean-burning methane fuels.

"Planning for the environment has always been popular in Denmark," explains Christian Matthiessen, a geographer at the University of Copenhagen. "We're an agricultural nation where nobody lives more than 30 miles from the sea. The environment has always played a role for everybody."[21]

Tiny Iceland, population 280,000, intends to go even further by withdrawing from the carbon economy altogether. In 1998 the government committed itself to using the island's enormous geothermal resources to charge hydrogen fuel cells, whose only waste product is water vapor. Cells would then be used to power cars, boats and other energy needs that can't be directly met by geothermal and hydro resources.

"Our vision is that when we have transformed Iceland into a hydrogen economy, then we are completely independent of imported fossil fuel," says the father of the plan, Bragi Arnason of the University of Reykjavik. "There will be no greenhouse gas emissions from our fuel."[22]

But Iceland and Denmark are tiny nations, and it is clear that meaningful reductions of global emissions would have to include not only the United States but also China, India and other rapidly industrializing nations.

Between 1990 and 2004, U.S. annual greenhouse gas emissions increased by 16 percent, the equivalent of the total combined annual emissions of Great Britain, the Netherlands and Finland. India's emissions increased by about 60 percent and China's by roughly 70 percent.[23]

"China's environmental issues are no longer just China's issues," says Jianguo Liu, who holds the Rachel Carson Chair in Sustainability at Michigan State University and is a guest professor of the Chinese Academy of Sciences. "They've become global issues."

Should rich nations assist poor ones in fighting global warming?

As the world decides what to do after Kyoto expires, perhaps the paramount question has become how to fairly and effectively engage the developing world. Most critical will be working out a compromise under which rich countries agree to help poor ones reduce their emissions and adapt to the disasters and dislocations expected to follow the ongoing change in climate.

Rich countries are likely to help poorer ones with emissions reductions because it is in their own interest to do so, at least with regard to the largest polluters. "Basically there is no way that we can force China and India to contribute to mitigating climate change," says Ott of the Wuppertal Institute. "They're saying, 'we are developing the way we learned it from you, and when we reach your level of wealth, we'll start caring about the climate, just as you did.' " For this reason, many experts say rich countries will need to help developing ones help themselves.

Various developing countries require different sets of expectations, argues Ott, who convened a series of meetings with experts from developing countries to try to find equitable solutions. In short, he says, newly industrialized countries, such as South Korea and Taiwan, should be reducing emissions without outside support, while rich countries should help rapidly industrializing nations such as China, India and Brazil with investments that will put them on a cleaner path. Other nations with little culpability for the problem and even fewer resources to confront it, such as Liberia and Bangladesh, shouldn't be expected to do much on their own.

"Most of the additional greenhouse gases in the atmosphere today are due to the past industrialization of the developed countries, so they must take the lead in combating climate change," says Winkler of the University of Cape Town. "We all need to be doing something, but each of us will be doing different things based on what we are responsible for and what we are capable of, given our situation."

Assistance could yield considerable benefits. China alone expects to build more than 500 new power plants in the next five years. Left to its own devices, China would build conventional plants that would be used for decades. If the outside world were to help transfer the latest pollution-control technology, the growth in China's emissions would be considerably slower.

"Give them a chance to develop, but by leapfrogging over that phase with bad windows, bad air conditioners, dirty coal plants and the internal combustion engine," says Stephen Schneider, co-director of Stanford University's Center for Environmental Science and Policy. Such technology transfers would also provide a cost-effective means for Western companies to earn credits under an ETS.

Building a high-tech, low-emissions plant in India, for example, where labor and material costs are low, would be far cheaper than replacing an existing high-emissions plant in, say, Indiana. "For the planet, a ton of carbon in Beijing is the same as a ton of carbon in Boston or Brussels," Schneider notes. "So everyone wins."

Western companies are reluctant to deploy new technologies to many developing countries, largely because of the poor state of intellectual-property protection in the Third World. "You don't want to give up a more efficient technology if it is just going to be copied, because then, what do you have left?" says C. S. Kiang, dean of the College of Environmental Sciences at Peking

University in Beijing. Part of the solution, he says, would be to give recipient countries ownership of some subset of the deployed technology. "China's never had intellectual property of its own before, but once they own some they will respect it," he says, creating a "win-win situation" for both parties and the environment.

While the ETS gives Western countries incentives to help rapidly developing parts of the world, they have fewer incentives to help poor countries adapt. Building Dutch-style defenses to protect densely populated, low-lying areas of Bangladesh from rising seas and stronger storms, for example, would cost billions of dollars, with little or no financial return for rich countries. The argument, therefore, is a moral one.

The expected impacts of global warming — more frequent and severe floods, droughts, heat waves and storms — are expected to fall most heavily on poor nations. An estimated 97 percent of deaths related to natural disasters occur in developing countries, which generally have poorer sanitation, flood control and health-care infrastructure.[24]

Even when Hurricane Katrina hit New Orleans, the poor suffered the most. "People with resources can move and rebuild and start new lives in the event of hurricanes or other disasters," says the Pew Center's Claussen. "But poor people often have nowhere else to go, nowhere else to turn, no resources to make the changes in their lives that will protect them from this global problem." In this respect, she suggests, the world is like New Orleans writ large.[25]

A draft IPCC report offers stark predictions — based on new research — on the coming effects of global warming, especially on poor people. Leaked to The Associated Press in March, the report — the second of four IPCC studies being issued this year — predicts that hundreds of millions of Africans and tens of millions of Latin Americans could face water shortages within 20 years, and more than 1 billion people in Asia could face water shortages by 2050.

While some regions may produce more food thanks to a longer growing season, that will be only temporary, the report said. By 2080, between 200 million and 600 million people could face starvation, water shortages could threaten 1.1 to 3.2 billion people and about 100 million people could be flooded each year, according to the report.[26]

Wind turbines harness the stiff winds on the Baltic Sea, in the channel between Denmark and Sweden. More than 20 percent of Denmark's electricity is generated by wind, an alternative to the burning of fossil fuels, blamed for global warming.

CQ Press/Priit Vesilind

Will reducing greenhouse gases harm the global economy?

Despite some bravado, virtually everyone agrees that a lot of money will have to be spent if the world is to see a substantial reduction in greenhouse gas emissions. The biggest disagreements lie in whether the cost of mitigating climate change is greater or lower than the cost of the damages expected to be wrought by global warming.

Myron Ebell, director of global warming policy at the Competitive Enterprise Institute, a Washington think tank that received funding from Exxon Mobil, says global warming is too expensive to be worth addressing. Until recently, Ebell maintained global warming wasn't taking place.[27] Now he concedes it's real but that achieving meaningful emissions reductions will cost hundreds of trillions of dollars. That's far more than even rich countries can afford, he says, and, in any case, considerably less than the cost of simply adapting to the new situation.

"By far the best strategy at present is to build resiliencies in societies so they are better able to handle environmental challenges," Ebell argues. "Rather than promoting policies that would impoverish the world by putting it on an energy-starvation diet, [one] should be advocating policies that lead

CHRONOLOGY

1800s-1920s *Scientists sound early warnings about climate change.*

1886 Swedish chemist Svante Arrhenius theorizes that carbon dioxide (CO_2) buildup caused by industrialization will warm the atmosphere.

1924 American physicist Alfred Lotka predicts that humans will double atmospheric CO_2 in 500 years.

1950s *Concern about greenhouse gases (GHG) grows.*

1954 Embryo ecologist G. Evelyn Hutchinson of Yale University predicts deforestation will increase CO_2 levels.

1957 Climate-science pioneer David Keeling of the Scripps Institution begins monitoring CO_2 levels and finds them rising yearly.

1970s-1980s *Scientists predict sharp rises in temperatures and sea levels.*

1979 First World Climate Conference in Geneva, Switzerland, calls on governments to prevent human-caused climate changes. . . . National Academy of Sciences warns a "wait and see" attitude may mean "waiting until it is too late."

1985 Scientific conference in Villach, Austria, predicts sharp rise in global temperatures and sea levels and calls for treaty to limit CO_2.

1988 U.N. establishes Intergovernmental Panel on Climate Change (IPCC).

1990s *Kyoto Protocol sets global goals for reducing use of fossil fuels.*

1990 Pope John Paul II declares the greenhouse effect has reached "crisis proportions."

1992 At summit in Rio de Janeiro 154 nations sign U.N. Framework Convention on Climate Change pledging to reduce GHG emissions to 1990 levels by 2000.

1994 Fearing catastrophic flooding, the Alliance of Small Islands States asks for a 20 percent cut in global GHG emissions by 2005. . . . Climate-change convention becomes effective, with 184 signatories.

1997 Climate convention signatories meet in Kyoto, Japan; adopt legally binding goals to cut greenhouse emissions to 5.2 percent below 1990 levels by 2012. . . . GOP-controlled U.S. Senate vows not to ratify resulting Kyoto Protocol.

1998 Despite the Senate action, Clinton administration signs treaty on Nov. 12.

2000s-Present *U.S. backs away from Kyoto treaty. Antarctic glaciers begin to crumble; heat wave hits Europe.*

2001 President George W. Bush repudiates Kyoto Protocol, reneging on campaign pledges. . . . National Academy of Sciences and 18 foreign counterparts say it's "evident" human activities contribute to climate change.

2002 Antarctica's gigantic Larsen-B ice shelf disintegrates. . . . Bush recommends tax incentives for companies to voluntarily reduce GHG emissions.

2003 Heat wave kills thousands in Europe.

2004 Swiss reinsurance company says global warming could cause $150 billion in yearly damages. . . . Scientists report unexpectedly rapid warming of the Arctic region and predict half of its sea ice will disappear by 2010.

2005 Kyoto Protocol takes effect on Feb. 16 after ratification by Russia; U.S. and Australia are only industrialized non-participants.

2007 On Feb. 2 the IPCC declares with 90 percent certainty that human activity causes global warming. On March 9 European leaders agree unilaterally to cut overall greenhouse emissions to 20 percent below 1990 levels by 2020. Leaked IPCC draft says water shortages will affect hundreds of millions of Africans and tens of millions of Latin Americans within 20 years and more than 1 billion Asians by 2050. By 2080, millions more could face starvation, and up to 3 billion could face water shortages.

Inuit Confront Hard Reality

Melting Arctic ice is changing ancient ways

Like the residents of tropical Pacific atolls, the Inuit people of the High Arctic have a lot to lose from climate change. For them, however, profoundly disruptive changes are already underway.

Some parts of the Arctic — in Alaska, Western Canada and Eastern Russia — have warmed by 4 to 7 degrees Fahrenheit in the past 50 years, a single lifetime — causing the destruction of Inuit villages along with the sea ice that once protected them from winter storms. Ice and permafrost are no longer reliable, causing hunting deaths and damage to roads, infrastructure and forests.[1]

"Climate change isn't some abstract discussion or theory for us, it's a harsh and stark reality we live with every day," says Patricia Cochran, the Anchorage-based chair of the Inuit Circumpolar Conference (ICC), which represents 150,000 Inuit living in Greenland, Canada, Russia and Alaska. "Members of our community are dying because of extreme changes in sea and river ice conditions that are making it difficult for our people to hunt, trap, fish and snowmobile, which are critical activities for us."

Inuit elders report that weather, and the location and characteristics of plant and animal species, are becoming increasingly unpredictable. Seals and other important game species that forage near the sea ice edge are in trouble, with serious economic consequences for Inuit hunting communities.

The village of Shishmaref, Alaska, was forced to move off an island because of erosion caused by powerful winter storms. Many others are not able to store meat the traditional way — burying it in the permafrost — because the Earth is no longer reliably cold enough.[2]

Inuit leaders spent years trying to get developed countries to act to curb their emissions, but their efforts in climate change summits were complicated by the fact that they, unlike small island states, do not have a nation-state and, therefore, no seat at the table. Shelia Watt-Cloutier of Iqaluit, Canada, attended the 2003 climate change summit in Milan but couldn't get anyone to pay attention.

"I couldn't even get our Canadian negotiators to express our views on the plenary floor," recalls Watt-Cloutier, the past chair of the ICC. "We ended up asking Samoa" — a small island state — "to say something about the Arctic and, thankfully, they did."

The Inuits' relationship with both Canada and small island states has since developed, but Inuit leaders have been discouraged by the world's failure to act forcefully to reduce greenhouse

An Inuit woman from Igloolik hunts for seal in the melting ice of the Foxe Basin, near Canada's Baffin Island.

CQ Press/Priit Vesilind

gas emissions. In December 2005 they took a radical step, filing an official legal petition with the Inter-American Commission on Human Rights (IACHR), charging the United States with violating their human rights by not cutting emissions.

"This was not an act of aggression or anger, it was a gift of generosity from our hunters who see what is happening," Watt-Cloutier says. "It's meant to educate and inform and, yes, add pressure to the United States and other countries around the world to do the right thing."

In November 2006, the Washington-based IACHR responded to the 163-page petition with a short letter saying "it will not be possible to process your petition at present." The petition did not provide sufficient evidence to allow proper evaluation.

"I was shocked," Watt-Cloutier says. "It wasn't a ruling, it was sort of an ambiguous response." The Inuit plan to continue to draw attention to the situation in the Arctic, at the IACHR and elsewhere, for as long as it takes.

---

[1] Petition to the Inter-American Commission on Human Rights: Violations resulting from global warming caused by the United States, Dec. 7, 2005, pp. 33-37.

[2] *Ibid.*

to wealthier and more creative societies . . . free markets, private property and the rule of law."[28]

Sir Nicolas Stern, former chief economist of the World Bank and head of Britain's Government Economic Service, dismisses the concern about cost. Stern directed a 700-page study on climate change for the British government that was released in October 2006. It concluded that failure to act could wind up costing the world as much as 20 percent of its annual income — $7 trillion — while greenhouse gas emissions could be brought under meaningful control for an annual cost of just 1 percent of global gross domestic product, or about $350 billion.

"Costs of mitigation," the Stern Review reads, "are small relative to the costs and risks of the climate change that will be avoided."[29]

Left to business as usual, the study says, greenhouse gas concentrations in the atmosphere could reach more than triple their pre-industrial level by century's end, potentially causing "a radical change in the physical geography of the world," including sudden shifts in the pattern of monsoon rains in Asia, drying out of the Amazon rain forest and the destruction of ice caps with an attendant rise in sea levels that would threaten the homes of 1 in 20 humans.

Far-northern nations such as Sweden, Russia and Canada will see net economic benefits through higher crop yields and lowered heating requirements.[30]

Benefits will include, among other things, "new Arctic shipping routes, a boom in trade with Russia, corn instead of wheat on the Prairies, golf instead of skiing in Ontario, Chardonnay instead of ice wine in Niagara, lower heating bills and fewer deaths due to pneumonia," writes Jacqueline Thorp in Toronto's *Financial Post.*[31]

But much of the rest of the world will see net losses from floods, extreme weather events and changes in environmental conditions. Even for Canada, there could be a grim tradeoff: Rising waters will inundate low-lying farmland in Canada's Maritime Provinces as well as in the Fraser River delta on the west coast, displacing millions of acres and hundreds of communities. Warmer temperatures will force farmers to plant new kinds of crops and allow the in-migration of warm-weather diseases such as Hantavirus, West Nile virus, chytrid fungus, dengue fever and Lyme disease.[32]

The Stern Review suggests governments should enact measures that:

- Set up and expand ETS schemes that, in effect, put a price on greenhouse gas emissions;
- Encourage the development and adoption of renewable-energy technologies, and
- Establish energy-efficiency standards for buildings and appliances.

The report cautions that funds will still have to be spent to adapt to the changing climate — an estimated $15 billion to $50 billion a year among the 24 relatively wealthy nations that comprise the Organization for Economic Cooperation and Development (OECD) alone — but many of these investments represent infrastructure that will provide tangible benefits unrelated to climate change.[33]

If the world does decide to take substantive action, is there money to be made from the technological revolution that would follow? "In general, it's hard to see an economic upside to responding to global warming," says Raymond J. Kopp, a senior fellow at Resources for the Future in Washington. "But some companies will definitely be able to take advantage of this. It all depends on how you are positioned." Companies committed to the status quo, he notes, stand to lose ground to competitors that have a head start in adapting to a carbon-constrained world.

For example, Toyota has jumped to the head of the pack in developing low-emission cars. Its Prius, a gas-electric hybrid, is the market leader. In the United States, the dominant automobile market in the world, Toyota has had difficulty keeping up with demand for the mid-size Prius, which gets 45-50 miles to the gallon with substantially less emission than comparable conventional vehicles. Ironically, Toyota developed the Prius in an effort to catch up to General Motors (GM), which had invested billions in low-emission vehicles. But GM soon turned to large sport utility vehicles instead and is now losing sales to Toyota's more fuel-efficient cars.

In 2004, Toyota had a sales goal of 28,000 cars in the United States; instead it has sold at a rate of 110,000 annually, and the company expects to sell nearly 300,000 this year, once a new North American assembly line allows dealers to keep them in stock. It also sells well in Europe and Japan. "Many thought the Prius would get things started and fade away," says Toyota spokesman John Hanson. "Instead it has become an icon for what a hybrid is, and demand continues to increase."

Similarly, British energy giant BP, which supports efforts to curtail greenhouse gas emissions, is better positioned for a low-carbon future than Exxon Mobil, which opposes such action. BP is investing $8 billion over the next decade in solar, combined-cycle gas turbines, hydrogen and wind technologies.

"We think the political commitment to renewables around the world will grow, and we'll have more of the answers than our competitors will," Chris Mottershead, BP's adviser on energy and the environment, told *The Economist.* "We're happier with our position than we were three years ago, because the world seems more inclined to change."[34]

Billionaire CNN founder Ted Turner is also bearish on the economic opportunities offered by global warming. "The greatest fortunes in the history of the world will be made in this new energy business," Turner told the World Affairs Council in February in Houston, center of the U.S. oil business.

BACKGROUND

Complex Problem

Earth's climate has alternated between hot and cold, glacial and inter-glacial, for millions of years, a fact that gives comfort to those who downplay the dramatic warming of the last few decades. They note that climate is affected by numerous factors, including latitude, elevation and proximity to the ocean, and is periodically disrupted by such anomalies as El Niño, the periodic rise in sea temperatures in the eastern Pacific.

As early as the 1890s, however, scientists speculated that the build-up of carbon dioxide in the atmosphere might be another cause of climate change. The process has been called the "greenhouse effect" although garden greenhouses work on different principles. The greenhouse effect is an increase in the temperature of the planet as radiant energy from sunlight is trapped in the atmosphere by carbon dioxide and other gases, collectively called "greenhouse gases." This dynamic keeps the surface of the planet warm, even when turned toward the cold void of space.

A global-warming problem exists because humans have been increasing the natural level of CO_2 by burning fossil fuels for power, heat and transportation and have added other greenhouse gases such as methane (from refineries and animal feedlots) and chlorofluorocarbons (from refrigeration and air conditioners). There is now the equivalent of 60 percent more CO_2 in the atmosphere than before the Industrial Revolution.[35]

Unfortunately, nobody knows exactly how the world's climate will behave as greenhouse gases increase. Although scientists feel confident of the general trend — more severe weather events, melting polar ice and changing sea levels and currents — knowing exactly how, when and where the changes will occur remains a matter of educated guesswork.

Meanwhile, scientists continue to study the problem. The United Nations Intergovernmental Panel on Climate Change has updated its predictions on the causes and consequences of climate change in 1995, 2000 and in February 2007. The latest update predicts that greenhouse gas emissions will cause the Earth to warm by 2 to 4.5 degrees Celsius by the end of the century, causing further reduction of winter snowfall and polar sea ice, stronger hurricanes and typhoons and an increase in the frequency of heat waves and other extreme weather events. Sea levels could rise by one to two feet.

Arctic Ice Is Shrinking

The ice cap that usually covers the seas surrounding the North Pole is quickly receding, at the rate of 9 percent each decade. Since 1979, when ice filled out the area inside the gray outline, it has withdrawn from the north shore of Alaska and the coastline of Siberia.

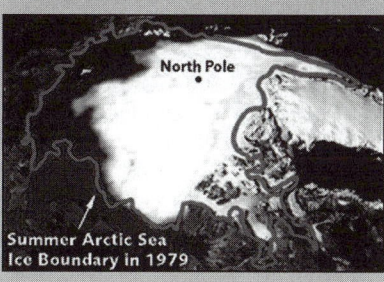

North Pole

Summer Arctic Sea Ice Boundary in 1979

Sources: NASA and Natural Resources Defense Council

Newsmakers/Michel Porro

Environmental activists stack sandbags for a symbolic dike in The Hague, Netherlands, one of the lowest countries in the world. Knowing their vulnerability, the Dutch plan to spend as much as $25 billion to upgrade their dike system in preparation for possible rises in sea-level elevations.

Bitter Debate

Countries have reacted in very different ways to such predictions. Europeans, by and large, have taken the threat seriously and invested accordingly. The United States has generally taken a wait-and-see approach, fearful of slowing economic growth. The current Republican administration, in particular, has been reluctant to take action until science can report with certainty that climate change is an imminent danger. Yet scientists warn that it is nearly impossible to provide certainty before it's too late for governments to take meaningful action. President George W. Bush also strongly believes that new technologies will solve the problem if the free market is allowed to respond on its own.

But political and scientific pressures convinced the president to address the issue in his State of the Union message in January 2007. Bush said that new energy technology would "help us to confront the serious challenge of global climate change." That was enough to encourage a raft of optimism from industries ready to ramp up alternative-energy projects. And the White House itself claimed that the president's new technology proposals will stop the projected growth in carbon-dioxide emissions from cars, light trucks and SUVs within 10 years.[36]

The first international attempt to regulate greenhouse gases — the 1992 U.N. Framework Convention on Climate Change — sought to stabilize emissions at 1990 levels through voluntary measures. The United States ratified the agreement, and ultimately 189 nations signed on to it. Unfortunately, it became clear within a few years that voluntary pledges were not going to work. This led to the 1997 Kyoto Protocol, which featured legally binding cuts in emissions.

While the United States was deeply involved in creating the treaty — and signed it during the Clinton administration — the Republican-controlled Congress did not ratify it, in large part because it did not require emissions cuts from China and India. In March 2001, shortly after his inauguration, Bush repudiated the protocol on the grounds that it would hurt the U.S. economy, reneging on campaign pledges to require cuts in greenhouse gas emissions if elected.

Instead, he came out a year later with a plan offering tax incentives to get companies to voluntarily cut their emissions by 18 percent over 10 years. The scheme backfired; emissions increased steeply, discrediting the notion that voluntary targets could address the problem.[37]

Other countries, notably the Netherlands, began preparing for the effects of climate change. With a quarter of its territory below sea level and much of the rest vulnerable to flooding, the country had little choice. The Dutch plan to spend an extra $10 billion to $25 billion to upgrade their vast network of dikes, pumping stations and sea defenses.

"It's better to be safe than sorry when you live below sea level," notes Peter C.G. Glas, director of inland water systems at Delft Hydraulics, which designed and built much of the dike infrastructure.[38]

While the U.S. government dithered over improving the flood defenses of New Orleans, which is also largely below sea level, the Dutch were busy strengthening sea walls and modifying a large dam at the mouth of the Zuider Sea against a future sea-level rise.

The real threat to the Netherlands from global warming, however, isn't rising seas but surging rivers, Dutch experts say, because the country straddles the flood-prone Rhine River delta. Climate models suggest that rainfall in northern Europe could increase by 5 to 10 percent, while melting Alpine glaciers could increase the flow of rivers.

Over the centuries, ever-higher dikes have been constructed to keep the river contained, but they've been proving less and less adequate with time. In 1995 the Rhine nearly breached the defenses, and with some dikes

20 feet high, failure would have caused catastrophic flooding.

The prospect of worsening floods has prompted the Dutch to change tactics. Instead of building higher levees, the government plans to allow the rivers to flood certain areas when necessary. Some 220,000 acres of land will be surrendered to the rivers by 2050, creating a natural flood zone of marshlands and forest. An additional 62,000 acres will be made into pastures, from which livestock will be evacuated during floods.

Because the Netherlands is so densely populated, sacrificing all that land won't be easy, and engineers are trying to minimize the dislocations. Dura Vermeer, a Dutch construction company, has designed giant floating greenhouses, commercial buildings and even towns that can be deployed in the new sacrifice zones. Such planning is expected to be a growth industry.

"This could be the future for many countries," says Jeroen van der Sommen of the Delft-based Netherlands Water Partnership, which promotes the country's water know-how abroad.

Rapid Meltdown

Recent events — notably thawing in both polar regions — lead many scientists to fear far greater climate disruptions than even the IPCC has predicted.

One of the most dramatic events was the 2002 collapse of Antarctica's Larsen-B ice shelf, a 10,000-year-old, 650-foot-thick expanse of floating ice the size of Rhode Island. Pedro Skvarca, a glaciologist with the Argentine Antarctic Institute, flew over the shelf's seaward edge as it decomposed.

"The surface of the ice shelf was almost totally covered by melt ponds and lakes, and waterfalls were spilling over the top," he recalls. Bits and pieces of the shelf had broken off, filling the Weddell Sea with bergs and slush. Two weeks later almost the entire shelf was gone. "It was

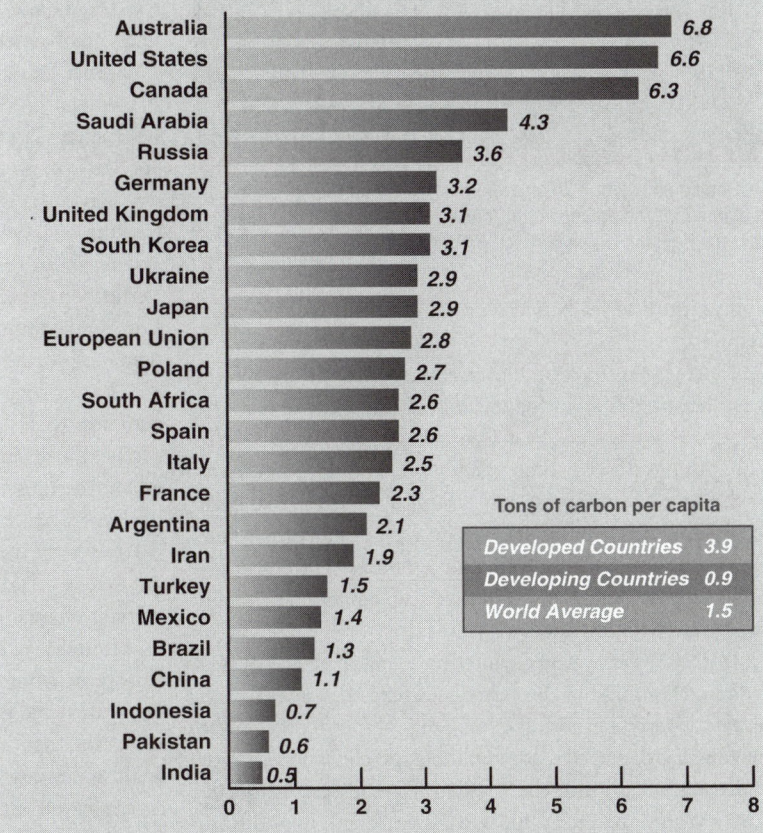

Top 25 Greenhouse-Gas Emitters

Australia emits 6.8 tons of carbon per year for every member of its 20 million population — the world's highest per-capita emissions rate. The United States is a close second, at 6.6 tons of carbon per capita — or about 1.9 billion tons. China, India and other rapidly developing nations have far lower emissions rates.

Country	Tons of carbon per capita
Australia	6.8
United States	6.6
Canada	6.3
Saudi Arabia	4.3
Russia	3.6
Germany	3.2
United Kingdom	3.1
South Korea	3.1
Ukraine	2.9
Japan	2.9
European Union	2.8
Poland	2.7
South Africa	2.6
Spain	2.6
Italy	2.5
France	2.3
Argentina	2.1
Iran	1.9
Turkey	1.5
Mexico	1.4
Brazil	1.3
China	1.1
Indonesia	0.7
Pakistan	0.6
India	0.5

Tons of carbon per capita

Developed Countries	3.9
Developing Countries	0.9
World Average	1.5

Source: Kevin Baumert, et al., "Climate Data: Insights and Observations," Pew Center on Global Climate Change, November 2004

unbelievable to see how fast it had broken up," Skvarca says. "The coastline hadn't changed for more than 9,000 years and then it changed completely in just a few weeks."

Scientists say the collapse will likely have worldwide effects. The collapse of Larsen-B as well as the smaller Larsen-A and Wordie ice shelves was caused by a steep increase in summertime temperatures in the Antarctic Peninsula region. With the ice shelves gone, the far larger glaciers and ice sheets behind them have begun

The famed snows of Kilimanjaro are nearly gone. Global warming is blamed for the meltdown on Africa's highest peak, which lies near the Equator in Kenya.

sliding into the sea between two and six times faster than before.

"The glaciers took off like race horses after the ice shelves were removed," says Ted Scambos, lead scientist at the National Snow and Ice Data Center in Boulder, Colo. "We're seeing things that we didn't think glaciers could do in terms of the speed of their response." Similar changes have been recorded in the Amundsen Sea in West Antarctica, where glaciers drain the West Antarctic Ice Sheet, a precariously balanced portion of the southern ice cap containing enough ice to raise world sea levels by 20 feet.[39]

In the Arctic, warmer winter temperatures have caused the rapid thinning of the Greenland Ice Sheet, a reduction of Arctic Sea ice and the thawing of permafrost. The thawing has damaged roads, buildings, pipelines and airports in Russia and shrunk the Alaskan ice-road season to 100 days a year, down from 300 just 30 years ago. In addition, melting permafrost releases carbon dioxide trapped underneath, adding to atmospheric CO_2 levels and speeding up global warming even faster than expected.

The loss of sea ice is leaving polar bears with fewer places to hunt, and in late 2006 the Bush administration placed them on the endangered species list.[40]

CURRENT SITUATION

Frustration in Europe

In Europe there is increasing impatience with the United States, not only because Washington has failed to regulate greenhouse gas emissions but also because that failure has put European industry at a competitive disadvantage. "Right now, the EU is on its way, but the U.S. and the rest of the world are still in the station," says Kopp of Resources for the Future. "At the end of the day, EU nations are in a global economy, so they can't run too far ahead of the U.S. or they will disadvantage their economy too much and run into political problems. They need U.S. involvement."

Some European countries are tired of waiting. In November 2006 the EU's high-level group on competitiveness, energy and the environment proposed introducing a "border" tax on products imported from countries that have not signed the Kyoto Protocol. The measure, which has the backing of French Prime Minister Dominique de Villepin and EU Vice President for Enterprise and Industry Gunter Verheugen, of Germany, aims to even the playing field for European industries, which have incurred the costs of participating in the European emissions trading scheme.[41]

"It's an idea that's gaining momentum, but it's also very controversial," says John Hontelez, secretary-general of the European Environmental Bureau in Brussels. "If you are serious about Europe taking the lead and fulfilling its Kyoto obligations, a border-tax adjustment is one of the few easy ways to ensure you do not simply become a hostage of those countries that don't see that fighting climate change is necessary."

Hontelez, who heads a federation of more than 140 European environmental organizations, favors enacting a tax against the United States and Australia, the only other industrial nation to reject the Kyoto Protocol, but not against developing countries like China. "The U.S. and Australia are really acting irresponsibly toward the global population," he says.

But EU Trade Commissioner Peter Mandelson, of Great Britain, opposes the proposal. "Not participating in the Kyoto process is not illegal," he said in a December 2006 speech. "Collective responsibility will only be fostered by policies of dialogue, incentive and cooperation" rather than "coercive measures."

It is also unclear if the measure would be allowed under World Trade Organization (WTO) rules, which prevent foreign products from being treated differently than domestic ones.[42]

But Hontelez says the EU should consider the measure regardless of what the WTO allows. "I don't think trade

Should a trade tax be imposed on the U.S. and other countries that don't sign the Kyoto Protocol?

YES
John Hontelez
Secretary-General, European Environmental Bureau, Brussels, Belgium

Written for *CQ Global Researcher*, January 2007

If we are serious about Europe taking the lead and fulfilling its Kyoto obligations, border tax adjustments based on carbon emissions are one of the few easy ways to ensure we do not simply become a hostage of those countries that don't see that fighting climate change is necessary.

I am very much in favor of taking measures with the United States and Australia, two countries that should have accepted Kyoto and are really acting irresponsibly toward the global population.

But you can't use this tax in the same way for products from China and India and so on because these countries haven't made or violated Kyoto Protocol commitments, and in 1997 it was quite right not to require them to make the same commitments as developed nations.

The tax would increase the possibilities for the European Union (EU) to achieve greater greenhouse gas reductions without damaging important parts of our industry. It would also show the outside world that the EU is very serious about climate policies, even understanding that it is very difficult, in practice, to measure the CO_2 inputs of the products that are being considered.

For example, if you use aluminum for cans or pipes that are produced in Europe, the cost includes the CO_2 emissions right that this company has had to buy. So the price includes their payment down on the mechanisms to reduce CO_2 emissions, while the products outside the EU aren't including that cost. A border tax adjustment would prevent that. You ensure that all the EU aluminum products are not wiped out simply for the reason that other countries are not reducing CO_2.

The money generated from this tax would probably go to a kind of export support for products that are leaving the EU. It's not what I would like to have happen, but for the sake of compromise, I suppose the money has to go both ways.

The refusal of the U.S. administration to implement Kyoto has a devastating effect because now we see what the fast-developing countries like China, India and Brazil are doing, and of course we should not put the same restrictions on them. Nevertheless, it is an issue, of course.

But as long as the U.S. is not joining in the effort, these countries will have all the reasons in the world to say: Why should we limit our economic development and start controlling emissions when the world is refusing to take part? That's the message the U.S. sends to the rest of the world.

NO
Peter Mendelson
Trade Commissioner, European Union

From Speech to EU, Brussels, Dec. 18, 2006

We in the developed world are responsible for 80 percent of historical carbon emissions. We have an historical environmental debt, as well as a self-interest in our own survival, which both mean we must lead in finding solutions.

Our leadership is necessary. But it is not enough. China will become the biggest emitter of CO_2 in or around 2010. A billion Indians will not be far behind. And assuming that countries like China, India and Brazil continue to move towards Western levels of economic growth, we are confronted with the urgent challenge of greening that growth.

I see three essential parts to the political challenge we face. The first is public education to build a constituency for difficult change and break current patterns of behavior. The second challenge is greater efficiency in the way we use energy. We also need to help China, India and others dramatically to improve their energy efficiency. The third outstanding challenge is to lower greenhouse gas emissions.

But it is also essential to establish that economic growth — and the trade that drives it — are not inherently at odds with sustainable climate policy. Economic growth is what gives us the resources to manage the human impact on the environment at the local level. But growth's impact on the environment will have to change. Efficiency gains can help. But we have to do more than stabilize our impact — we need to reverse it. We will not achieve this without a global shift to renewable-energy sources and green technologies. And here trade policy has an important role.

There is one trade-policy response to climate change about which I have serious doubts. That is the idea of a specific "climate" tariff [or "border" tax] on countries that have not ratified the Kyoto Protocol. This would be highly problematic under current WTO [World Trade Organization] rules. I also suspect it would not be good politics.

Not participating in the Kyoto process is not illegal. Nor is it a subsidy under WTO rules.

How would we choose what goods to target? China has ratified Kyoto but has no Kyoto targets because of its developing-country status. The U.S. has not ratified, but states like California have ambitious climate-change policies.

Above all, dealing with climate change is an international challenge. It requires international cooperation. Coercive policies will harm this. Collective responsibility will only be fostered by policies of dialogue, incentive and cooperation.

Carbon Dioxide Emissions of Major Economies

Despite Kyoto Treaty carbon-reduction goals established by 169 nations in 2005, major economic powers have largely failed to reduce carbon emissions. The United States, not a signatory to the treaty, shows a steady rise, while EU and Japanese emissions have flattened out. Emerging giant China presents the most precipitous climb in emissions as it industrializes.

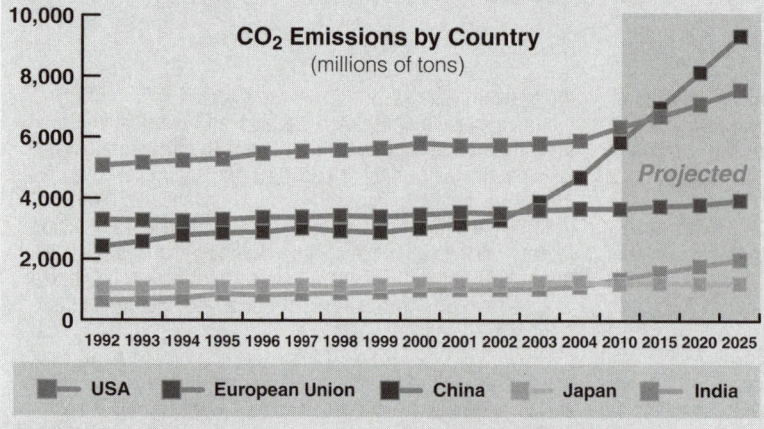

CO_2 Emissions by Country
(millions of tons)

Source: "Climate Change 101: International Action," Pew Center on Global Climate Change

has a higher moral standing than fighting for sustainable development and against climate change," he explains. "It's irresponsible not to act because we have some trade rules."

China's Efficiency Drive

While China's government has resisted mandatory CO_2 reductions, it is extremely concerned about reducing pollution and increasing energy efficiency. The primary motivation is economic: If current trends continue, the combined costs of acid rain, dirty air and rampant energy consumption could slow the country's phenomenal growth.

To meet energy demands, China builds a new power plant every week, on average. That's enough additional capacity every year to power a country the size of England. Since 70 percent of China's electricity comes from burning coal, the effect on the environment is baleful. Sulfur-dioxide pollution — another by-product of burning coal — contributes to 400,000 premature deaths a year and produces the acid rain that now falls on a third of China, damaging lakes, forests and crops. If coal-consumption trends continue, officials worry pollution effects will become untenable.[43]

"If China wants to continue to grow, they need more energy, and one way to deal with that is with greater energy efficiency," says Kiang of Peking University, noting that the country uses energy only a tenth as efficiently as Japan. "China wants to do something to improve its energy efficiency, and in the end that will improve the climate-change situation even though it was not the original target."

Under its 11th five-year plan, issued in 2006, the Chinese government has set some of the world's most aggressive efficiency targets, including a 20 percent cut in energy use per unit of gross domestic product (GDP) by 2010. New regulations include automobile fuel-efficiency standards that are higher than those in the United States and construction codes that encourage the use of insulated windows and efficient lighting.

In addition, China intends to generate 16 percent of its energy from renewable sources by 2020. State-owned utilities are building wind farms. In Dunhuang, the construction of a 100-megawatt solar-generating plant — one of the world's largest — should prevent 400,000 tons of greenhouse gas emissions each year.[44]

"The government pays more attention to climate change now because it is expected to have a huge impact on water resources," says Liu of Michigan State and the Chinese Academy of Sciences. "Water shortages are already a serious problem in northern China, while southern China is afflicted by flooding. In the long term, the government will be very interested and willing to reduce emissions of greenhouse gases."

"The government is fully aware of the possible impacts of climate change on China," says Kiang. "But the climate-change issue hasn't reached the general public" in large part because of the small number of non-governmental organizations, the sector that focused attention on the issue in the West.

For now, at least, the government rejects international calls for mandatory greenhouse gas cuts, citing fairness.

"You cannot tell people who are struggling to earn enough to eat that they need to reduce their emissions," said Lu Xuedu, deputy director general of China's Office of Global Environmental Affairs, in October 2006.[45]

Son of Kyoto

Delegates to a climate change summit in Nairobi, Kenya, in 2006 sought to construct a successor agreement to the Kyoto Protocol but were handicapped by the non-participation of the United States, the world's largest emitter of man-made greenhouse gases.

"We're living in this two-track world at the moment," says Winkler of the University of Cape Town. "We're expected to build on the architecture of the Kyoto Protocol, but without U.S. participation, we can't expect any engagement from the big developing countries."

Delegates were unable to reach agreement on a timetable for future emission cuts or other key elements, and many expressed frustration with the U.S. policy articulated by Undersecretary of State Paula J. Dobriansky, who maintained that the best way to address climate change was through voluntary international partnerships "that are integrated with economic growth."[46]

China indicated it was not ready to adopt mandatory cuts, while India's environment minister said it was "surreal" to expect his country to slash emissions when its per capita emissions are so much lower than those of the developed world and so many of its people live in poverty.

The Bush administration's newest climate policy is centered not on the Kyoto process but on the new Asia-Pacific Partnership on Clean Development, which promotes the development of clean-energy technologies by the private sector. Created in July 2006, the initiative involves the United States, Australia, China, India, South Korea and Japan and features no mandatory emissions limits. Administration officials say it is a "growth-oriented strategy" that "enables investment in the technologies and practices we need to address these important issues."[47]

"The fairness and effectiveness of this proposal will be superior to the Kyoto Protocol," said Australian Prime Minister John Howard. "It demonstrates the very strong commitment of Australia to reducing greenhouse gas emissions, according to an understanding that it's fair in Australia and not something that will destroy Australian jobs and unfairly penalize Australian industries."[48]

For Schneider of Stanford's Center for Environmental Science and Policy, the most revealing element of the Bush administration plan was the amount it pledged to invest in the project: $50 million — less than the cost of a single clean-energy power plant. "That number is off by a factor of a hundred," he says. "They put up nothing. This is purely cover. If they truly have a climate policy they had better make some real investments, many billions a year."

OUTLOOK

Will the U.S. Act?

The future direction of international climate policy clearly is tied to domestic U.S. politics. Advocates for robust action say meaningful progress can only occur if and when the United States engages with the issue. They are encouraged, however, by growing signs that opinion in Washington is shifting toward action.

Former Vice President Al Gore's Academy Award-winning documentary on global warming, "An Inconvenient Truth," has focused public opinion on the issue, and the takeover of Congress by the Democrats increases prospects for congressional action on climate change. New House Speaker Nancy Pelosi appointed a Select Committee on Energy Independence and Global Warming to recommend legislation.

"[House] debate on global warming has been stifled for 12 years," said Pelosi, a California Democrat. "We can't wait any longer."[49]

In the Senate, global-warming naysayer James M. Inhofe, R-Okla., was replaced as chairman of the Senate Environment and Public Works Committee by Barbara Boxer, another California Democrat and a strong advocate of climate action. At least four climate-change measures have been introduced in the Senate so far in 2007, mostly to establish a carbon-emission trading system.

"Things are moving right now at an incredibly quick pace," said Antonia Herzog, a scientist with the Natural Resources Defense Council. But even if both chambers were to pass legislation this year, it is unclear whether Bush would sign such a measure.[50]

Pushing for action in Congress is an unlikely alliance of environmentalists, evangelical Christians and large companies seeking to burnish their good-citizen images and get a consistent national policy to replace the growing patchwork of state carbon-emission limits. In January the United States Climate Action Partnership (USCAP) — a coalition of nearly a dozen energy companies and environmental activists — called for action to "slow, stop and reverse the growth of greenhouse gas emissions over the shortest period of time reasonably achievable."[51]

A wide range of religious leaders — from the Ecumenical Patriarch of the Christian Orthodox churches, Bartholomew I, to the more than 60 Jewish, Catholic, evangelical and mainstream protestant organizations in the National Religious Partnership for the Environment — are also pushing for action on global warming.

"Climate change was seen early on as the preeminent environmental challenge for people of faith," explains partnership Executive Director Paul Gorman. "It's deep religious insight and conviction that's moved this thing along."[52]

Meanwhile, many states have taken the issue into their own hands, creating regional emissions-trading schemes for power plants in the Northeast and in West Coast states.

Five Western governors announced on Feb. 26 that they would set limits on their emissions. Even in conservative Texas, the previously anti-global-warming power company TXU has agreed to be sold to a private investor group that plans to halt the building of coal-fired power plants and adopt green strategies.

Arnold Schwarzenegger, the Republican governor of California, said in June 2006 that the global-warming debate is over. "We know the science, we see the threat, and the time for action is now," he said, adding that his state would be "the leader in the fight against global warming."[53]

International observers hope that there will be major progress at the federal level in the United States after the 2008 presidential elections. "I see the U.S. leading in not very long," says Ott at the Wuppertal Institute in Germany. "The EU is very timid and cautious as an actor on the world stage. The U.S. often takes a long time to act, but when it does, it does it in full-scale. That gung-ho, 'we can do it' mentality would be helpful."

NOTES

1. Intergovernmental Panel on Climate Change, "Climate Change 2007: The Physical Science Basis — Summary for Policy Makers," Feb. 2, 2007; www.ipcc-wg2.org (global temperature increases); Arctic Climate Impact Assessment, "Impacts of a Warming Arctic," 2004, p. 23 (Arctic temperature increases).

2. "Iceland's president says the world should look to icebound North for global change help," The Associated Press, Sept. 20, 2006.

3. Elisabeth Rosenthal and Andrew C. Revkin, "Science Panel Calls Global Warming 'Unequivocal,' " *The New York Times online*, Feb. 3, 2007; www.nytimes.com.

4. Juliet Eilperin, "Humans Faulted For Global Warming; International Panel Of Climate Scientists Sounds Dire Alarm," *The Washington Post*, Feb. 3, 2007, p. A1; also see IPCC, "Climate Change 2007," *op. cit.*

5. See Colin Woodard, "Europe's scorching summer," *E Magazine*, Jan. 1, 2004; Dean Calbreath, "Changes in climate pose greatest challenge for insurers, say experts from around world," *San Diego Union-Tribune*, April 23, 2004, and "Lack of snow in Europe has skiers down," Reuters, Dec. 12, 2006.

6. Dan Bilefsky, "Europe Sets Ambitious Limits on Greenhouse Gases, and Challenges Others to Match It," *The New York Times*, March 10, 2007, p. A5.

7. Quoted by Lawrence Soloman, "The Deniers — Part VI," *National Post Online*, Canada, Feb. 2, 2007.

8. *Ibid.*

9. Interview, John Hontelez, January 2007; Interview, Shelia Watt-Cloutier, December 2006; Colin Woodard, *Ocean's End: Travels through Endangered Seas* (2000), pp. 163-189.

10. Quoted in States News Service, Sept. 27, 2006.

11. Interviews with Philip Gorman, August 2005; Eileen Claussen, August 2005. For background see Tom Price, "The New Environmentalism," *CQ Researcher*, Dec. 1, 2006, pp. 985-1008.

12. For background see Marcia Clemmitt, "Climate Change," *CQ Researcher*, Jan. 27, 2006, pp. 73-96.

13. *The Economist Pocket World in Figures* (2007), pp. 32-33; Keith Bradsher, "China to pass U.S. in 2009 in Emissions," *The New York Times*, Nov. 7, 2006, p. C1.

14. U.N. Framework Convention on Climate Change, "Report on the Implementation on its 25th Session," 2006, p. 12.

15. Bilefsky, *op. cit.*

16. *Ibid.*

17. Charlie Fletcher, *Scotland on Sunday*, Edinburgh, April 1, 2001.

18. Quoted in Tony Juniper, "A crucial first step," *The Guardian Unlimited*, Feb. 16, 2005.

19. "Stern Review on the Economics of Climate Change," HM Treasury, Oct. 30, 2006, pp. iii-iv; www.hm-treasury.gov.uk/about/about_index.cfm.

20. "Selling Hot Air," *The Economist*, Sept. 9, 2006, Survey on Climate Change, pp. 17-19.

21. Colin Woodard, "Europe: Planning Ahead," in *Feeling the Heat: Dispatches from the Frontlines of Climate Change* (2004), pp. 31-32; www.awea.org/faq/wwt_potential.

22. Quoted in "Hydrogen Economy," BBC Newsnight, Aug. 21, 2002; Asgeir Sigfusson, "Iceland: Pioneering the Hydrogen Economy," *Foreign Service Journal*, December 2003, pp. 62-65.

23. U.N. Framework, *op. cit.*, p. 12; Subodh Sharma, *et al.*, "Greenhouse Gas Emissions from India: A Perspective," *Current Science,* Vol. 90, No. 3, February 2006, p. 328.

24. *Ibid.*

25. Eileen Clausen, "Climate change: the state of the question and the search for the answer," speech given at St. Johns University, Oct. 5, 2006.

26. Seth Borenstein, "Draft of new international climate report warns of droughts, starvation, disease," The Associated Press, March 10, 2007.

27. Marlo Lewis, "The Snowe-Rockefeller Road to Kyoto," *American Spectator*, Nov. 3, 2006; Clemmitt, *op. cit.*, p. 80.

28. Myron Ebell, Letter to the Editor, *The Financial Times*, Sept. 28, 2005, p. 14.

29. Stern Review, *op. cit.*, pp. viii-x; Gaby Hinsliff, "The price of failing to act on climate change," *The Observer* (London), Oct. 29, 2006, p. 1.

30. Stern Review, *op. cit.*, pp. iv-x.

31. Jacqueline Thorpe, *Financial Post*; Canada.com, Jan. 27, 2007.

32. Canadian Institute for Climate Studies, Canada Impact, "Implications for Canada of recent IPCC Assessment Reports," prepared by the Canadian Climate Program Board and Canadian Global Change Program Board, Aug. 28, 1998.

33. *Ibid*, pp. xviii-xi.

34. "A Coat of Green," *The Economist*, Survey on Climate Change, *op. cit.*, p. 20.

35. Stern Review, *op. cit.*, p. iii.

36. Alhouse, Peter, "Bush's address tackles energy and climate, Jan. 24, 2007, NewScientist.com news service, at http://environment.newscientist.com/channel/earth/dn11020-bushs-address-tackles-energy-and-climate.html.

37. Eric Pianin, "Bush Unveils Global Warming Plan; President's Approach Focuses on New Technology, Incentives for Industry," *The Washington Post*, Feb. 15, 2002, p. A9.

38. The author reported this section during a 2001 assignment in the Netherlands, published in Woodard (2004), *op. cit.*, pp. 25-30.

39. Stefan Lovegren, "Warming to Cause Catastrophic Rise in Sea Level?" National Geographic News, April 26, 2004.

40. Juliet Eilperin, "US Wants Polar Bears Listed as Threatened," *The Washington Post*, Dec. 27, 2006, p. A1.

41. Andrew Bounds, "EU Trade Chief to Reject 'Green' Tax Plan," *The Financial Times*, Dec. 17, 2006.

42. For a discussion, see Bill Curry, "French PM Wants to Hit Canada with Carbon Tax," *Globe & Mail* (Toronto), Nov. 15, 2006, p. A1.

43. Keith Bradsher and David Barboza, "The Cost of Coal," *The New York Times*, June 11, 2006, p. 1; "Anti-hero," *The Economist*, Survey of Climate Change, *op. cit.*, pp. 18-19.

44. "China to build one of the world's biggest solar power stations," Agence France-Presse, Nov. 21, 2006.

45. Quoted in Bradsher, *op. cit.*

46. Jeffrey Gettleman and Andrew C. Revkin, "Big Conference on Warming Ends, Achieving Modest Results," *The New York Times*, Nov. 17, 2006.

47. "US defends climate change policy ahead of Sydney conference," US Fed News, Jan. 7, 2006; testimony

by James L Connaughton, Chairman, White House Council on Environmental Quality, CQ Congressional Testimony, Sept. 20, 2006.

48. "U.S. agrees to climate deal with Asia," BBC News Online, July 28, 2005.

49. Quoted in Manu Raju, "House Creates Global Warming Panel, Despite Skepticism in Both Parties," *CQ Today*, March 8, 2007.

50. Quoted in Karoun Demirjian, "Taking climate legislation to the Hill; 4 major bills battle for Congress' support," *Chicago Tribune*, March 8, 2007, p. C4.

51. Marie Horrigan, "Prioritizing Global Warming," CQPolitics.com, Feb. 23, 2007.

52. For background, see Colin Woodard, "Changes in the Air," *Trust*, spring 2006, pp. 18-25.

53. Quoted in Miguel Bustillo, "Gov. Vows Attack on Global Warming," *Los Angeles Times*, June 2, 2005, p. B1.

BIBLIOGRAPHY

Books

Flannery, Tim, *The Weather Makers: How man is changing the climate and what it means for life on Earth, Atlantic Monthly Press,* **2006.**
An Australian scientist describes the evidence for climate change, the disturbances it is causing to coral reefs, polar bears and other creatures, and the efforts some coal and oil companies have made to delay or prevent political action on the issue.

Kolbert, Elizabeth, *Field Notes from a Catastrophe: Man, Nature, and Climate Change, Bloomsbury,* **2006.**
A reporter for the *New Yorker* provides a readable account of how climate change is affecting the planet, with first-hand accounts from Iceland, Alaska and Greenland.

Michaels, Patrick J., *Meltdown: The Predictable Distortion of Global Warming by Scientists, Politicians, and the Media, Cato Institute,* **2004.**
A prominent climate-change skeptic from the University of Virginia argues that global warming has been hyped by scientists, activists and the media.

Motovalli, Jim (ed.), *Feeling the Heat: Dispatches from the Frontlines of Climate Change, Routledge,* **2004.**

The editor of *E: The Environmental Magazine* dispatched a group of reporters to report on the effects of climate change worldwide.

Woodard, Colin, *Ocean's End: Travels Through Endangered Seas, Basic Books,* **2000.**
Author Woodard describes the collapse of marine ecosystems and the potential link to climate change, including accounts of his travels to the Antarctic Peninsula — where glaciers and ice sheets are collapsing — to the Marshall Islands — whose people fear they will lose their country to rising seas — and to flood-ravaged New Orleans.

Articles

Calvin, William H., "The Great Climate Flip-flop," *Atlantic Monthly,* **January 1998.**
A professor of evolutionary biology at the University of Washington examines concerns that global warming could slow or stop the Gulf Stream and other ocean currents, possibly triggering the sudden onset of an Ice Age.

Easterbrook, Gregg, "Case Closed: The Debate about Global Warming is Over," *Issues in Governance Studies,* **June 2006.**
A Brookings Institution scholar summarizes scientific thinking on climate change and argues that reducing emissions will be easier and more affordable than commonly thought.

Oreskes, Naomi, "The Scientific Consensus on Climate Change," *Science,* **Dec. 3, 2004, p. 1686.**
A professor of history and science studies at the University of California, San Diego, refutes the popular notion that scientists disagree on whether or not global warming is happening.

Sharma, Subdoh, et al., "Greenhouse gas emissions from India: A perspective," *Current Science,* **Feb. 10, 2006, p. 326.**
A professor of optics at the S.N. Bose Centre for Basic Sciences in Calcutta discusses current and projected trends in India's greenhouse-gas emissions described by three Indian scientists.

Reports and Studies

"Climate Change 2007," International Panel on Climate Change, *IPCC,* **Feb. 2, 2007, available online.**
The U.N. panel provides the latest official scientific assessment of the causes and likely effects of climate

change; additional reports will follow throughout the year, including region-by-region impact assessments.

"Impacts of a Warming Arctic," *Arctic Climate Impact Assessment,* Nov. 24, 2004, available online.
A 140-page report synthesizes the findings of an international team of scientists charged with studying global warming in the Arctic. It predicts dire consequences for the entire region, including the disappearance of Arctic sea ice and the continued decay of the Greenland ice sheet.

"South-north dialogue on equity in the greenhouse: a proposal for an adequate and equitable global climate agreement," *Deutsche Gessellschaft fur Technische Zusammenarbeit (GTZ),* May 2004, available online.
Leading climate-policy experts from both developed and developing countries discuss creating an equitable framework for future climate-change negotiations. In German.

Barnett, Jon, and Neal Adger, "Climate Dangers and Atoll Countries," *Tyndall Centre Working Paper No. 9,* October 2001, available online.
A British think tank summarizes the risks facing low-lying atoll nations from rising sea levels and extreme weather events associated with climate change.

Stern, Nicolas, et al., "Stern review on the Economics of Climate Change," *H.M. Treasury Office,* updated January 2007, available online.
An independent review commissioned by the British government argues that addressing climate change would be far less costly than the economic damages expected from allowing greenhouse-gas emissions to continue unabated.

For More Information

American Meteorological Society, 45 Beacon St., Boston, MA 02108; (617) 227-2425; www.ametsoc.org. Promotes the development and dissemination of information on atmospheric and related sciences.

Arctic Climate Impact Assessment, University of Alaska — Fairbanks, P.O. Box 747740, Fairbanks, AK 99775; www .acia.uaf.edu. International project of the Arctic Council and International Arctic Science Committee for evaluating knowledge on climate variability, climate change and increased ultraviolet radiation.

Intergovernmental Panel on Climate Change, 7bis Avenue de la Paix, C.P. 2300, CH-1211 Geneva 2, Switzerland; (+41)-22-730-8208; www.ipcc.ch. U.N.-sponsored organization of scientists who assess findings on global warming.

Inuit Circumpolar Conference, 170 Laurier Ave. W., Suite 504, Ottawa, Ontario, Canada K1P 5V5; (613) 563-2642; inuitcircumpolar.com. International non-governmental organization representing 150,000 Inuit of Alaska, Canada, Greenland and Russia.

Pew Center on Global Climate Change, 2101 Wilson Blvd., Suite 550, Arlington, VA 22201; (703) 516-4146; www .pewclimate.org. Nonprofit organization that issues information and promotes policy discussion of global warming.

Resources for the Future, 1616 P St., N.W., Washington, DC 20036; (202) 328-5000; www.rff.org. Non-partisan think tank conducting independent research on environmental, energy and natural resource issues.

U.N. Environment Programme, United Nations Ave., Gigiri, P.O. Box 30552, 00100, Nairobi, Kenya; (254-20) 7621234; www.unep.org. Voice for the environment in the U.N. system.

Wuppertal Institute for Climate, Environment and Energy, Döppersberg 19, 42103 Wuppertal, Germany; +49 (0)202/2492-0; www.wupperinst.org. German research organization working towards sustainable development.

Confronting Warming

3

Can States and Localities Prevent Climate Change?

Alan Greenblatt

John Coleman concentrates on cutting energy use for the city of Fayetteville, Ark., as if his job depended on it. In fact, it does.

"I got the City Council to let me hire this person based on the promise that we would reduce our energy consumption to more than cover his or her salary," recalls Fayetteville Mayor Dan Coody.

Coleman has found easy pickings all over town — even at City Hall: inefficient thermostats, wasteful light-bulbs, computers that are left on all night. In 2007, Fayetteville budgeted $1.9 million for utility costs, but thanks to Coleman ended up spending about $180,000 less than that. "You just barely covered my salary," Coleman joked at an end-of-year meeting. "I get to stick around for another year."[1]

Actually, they more than covered his salary of $57,000. Coleman is one of dozens of so-called sustainability directors now employed by cities around the country. (Coody got the idea from a similar program in Seattle.) By switching police departments from paper tickets to electronic ones, or looking for dramatic savings by putting municipal utilities on an energy diet, these environmental specialists are helping city officials like Coody make good on their promise to cut down on emissions that cause global warming.

Scientists say a buildup of six types of heat-trapping gases in the Earth's atmosphere are beginning to cause potentially dramatic climate changes, such as planetary warming, melting ice caps, rising sea levels and intensified droughts, floods and hurricanes. The gases — called "greenhouse" gases (GHG) because they act as a greenhouse by

Solar panels cover the Staples Center arena in Los Angeles. As a national leader in anti-pollution and energy-saving efforts, California adopted the first statewide "green" building code and vehicle fuel-efficiency standards.

From *CQ Researcher*, January 9, 2009.

49

Many States Set Energy-Efficiency Standards

Energy efficiency standards are in place in 21 states, including all the Northeast states except New Hampshire and Rhode Island. Some standards encourage greater efficiency in generation, transmission and use of electricity and natural gas. Others require utilities to generate a fixed percentage of their power from renewable sources such as wind and solar.

States With Energy-Efficiency Standards
(As of August 2008)

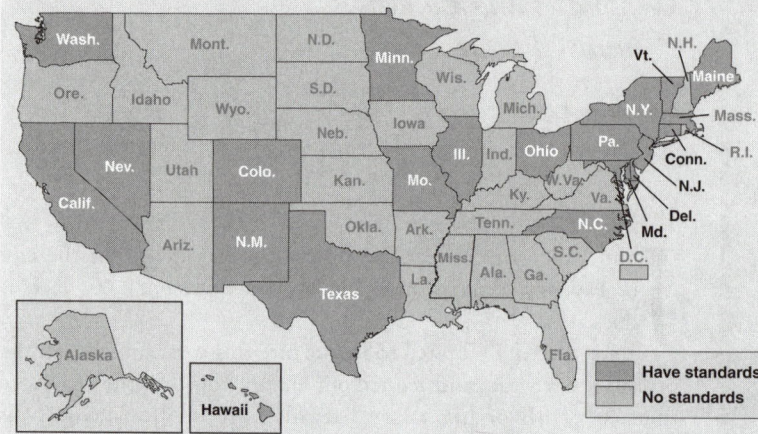

Sources: World Resources Institute; Environmental Protection Agency

During the Bush years, global warming became an increasingly pressing topic — yet growing public concern never translated into serious policy breakthroughs in Washington. While Congress and the White House slept, however, state and local governments throughout the country have come up with their own methods for limiting pollutants that scientists believe are contributing to climate change.

"I was one of many Americans who were outraged when my country would not sign the Kyoto Protocol," says Minneapolis Mayor R. T. Rybak. "The federal government dropped the ball on a critical environmental issue."

Cities are not only tightening their own energy belts but increasingly issuing new rules, such as stricter building codes, to make sure that residents and businesses cut back as well.

Among states, California has been leading the way. A 2006 law imposed the first statewide cap on carbon emissions. California also adopted the first statewide green-building code last summer, and the state has long been the leader in setting fuel-efficiency standards for vehicles.[3]

Numerous states — but not all — have engaged in other serious efforts to address climate change. About half the states, for instance, require utilities to generate a significant share of their power from renewable, non-carbon-based sources such as wind and solar. And many states are encouraging greater use of biofuels, such as ethanol. Groups of states in the Northeast, Upper Midwest and interior West have formed regional compacts to create "cap-and-trade" systems.

Under cap and trade, large polluters such as power plants are issued permits for each ton of carbon they emit. Companies that reduce the amount of pollution they spew are able to sell, or "trade," permits they don't need.

"States have been tripping all over themselves to show national leadership on this issue," says Barry G. Rabe, a professor of environmental policy at the University of

retaining the sun's heat in Earth's atmosphere — are emitted when carbon-based fossil fuels like oil, coal and natural gas are burned. Under the 1997 Kyoto Protocol, industrialized countries were asked to reduce their GHG emissions — often referred to as "carbon" emissions because carbon dioxide (CO_2) is the most abundant greenhouse gas — by 5.2 percent below 1990 levels by 2012. The U.S. reduction target was set at 7 percent.*

Although the U.S. government is not bound by the treaty, hundreds of mayors, including Coody, have pledged to abide by the protocol, even though it was never ratified by the Senate and has been explicitly rejected by President George W. Bush. But local officials believe it still provides a good guidepost for their own efforts in the fight against climate change.[2]

---

* The six types of greenhouse gases are carbon dioxide, methane, nitrous oxide, hydrofluorocarbons, perfluorocarbons and sulfur hexafluoride.

Michigan. "California, I would argue, has made as heavy an investment in time and treasury into climate change as any government on Earth, including the European Union."

President-elect Barack Obama has said he will approve a waiver for California and 19 other states to regulate greenhouse gas emissions from vehicles. California passed a law in 2002 to do just that, and it has been widely imitated by other states. But states have not been able to enforce the policy absent a waiver from the Environmental Protection Agency (EPA), which the Bush White House has blocked.[4]

Obama has promised to do more than just sign off on state actions, though. "When I am president, any governor who's willing to promote clean energy will have a partner in the White House," Obama said in a videotaped address to state leaders gathered at a climate change summit in California in November. "Any company that's willing to invest in clean energy will have an ally in Washington. And any nation that's willing to join the cause of combating climate change will have an ally in the United States of America."[5]

As a candidate, Obama pledged to pursue a national cap-and-trade system to limit carbon emissions. Prominent supporters of cap and trade now hold key committee posts in Congress, including Henry A. Waxman, the new chair of the House Energy and Commerce Committee, and Barbara Boxer, chair of the Senate Environment and Public Works Committee. Both are California Democrats.

But attempts to pass cap-and-trade legislation have failed four times over the last five years, and it's not clear the outcome will be different this year or next. Even if federal lawmakers do act, so much momentum has built up in this area among state and local leaders that it's unlikely they'll suddenly concede the issue to Washington.

At the November climate change summit, California Republican Gov. Arnold Schwarzenegger and leaders of more than a dozen other states and provinces from other countries pledged to work together to slash greenhouse gas emissions. Fighting global warming, Schwarzenegger declared, couldn't be just a matter of national policy but must go "province by province."[6]

Not everyone has climbed on board the limited-carbon bandwagon, however. In November, Gov. Rick Perry, R-Texas, argued strongly against a national cap-and-trade policy, warning that it would "cripple the Texas energy sector, irreparably damaging both the state and national economies and severely impacting national oil and gas supplies."[7]

And not everyone who supports limiting greenhouse gases believes state and local efforts are effective. "Carbon dioxide is a naturally occurring gas that is fairly well blended in the atmosphere around the world," says Myron Ebell, director of energy and global warming policy at the Competitive Enterprise Institute, a free-enterprise advocacy group. "If California does something and China and India don't, then what we do is virtually useless."

Ebell and other critics also argue that the efforts undertaken thus far may have been good public relations but are not effective at reducing carbon emissions. Often, public officials have done little more than pledge to reduce emissions or increase use of alternative fuels at some distant date in the future. In a way, Ebell suggests, their actions have been reminiscent of a famous prayer of Saint Augustine: "Give me chastity and continence, but not yet."

But the policies pursued by state and local leaders have been evolving rapidly. A decade ago, few people thought they even had a role in addressing an issue that was global in scope. State and local laws, however, have quickly changed from being mainly symbolic to having real teeth, with penalties for noncompliance for entities ranging from utilities to developers, all in the span of a few short years.

As state and local leaders continue to contemplate ways of addressing climate change, here are some of the issues they are debating:

Should states regulate carbon emissions?

In the absence of federal action, states are making ambitious efforts to cut down on carbon usage. In the last few years, they have sought to regulate auto tailpipe emissions, required utilities to generate significant shares of their power from renewable energy sources and denied permits to coal-fired power plants. (*See sidebar, p. 62.*)

Several states in the Northeast, West and Midwest have formed regional compacts to create cap-and-trade systems, setting limits on emissions from major polluters. A few have even set overall limits on carbon emissions on a statewide basis. California led the way in 2006 with a law that would reduce the state's total carbon emissions to 1990 levels by 2020.

"The political will to do something about climate change has grown substantially," says Patrick Hogan, a

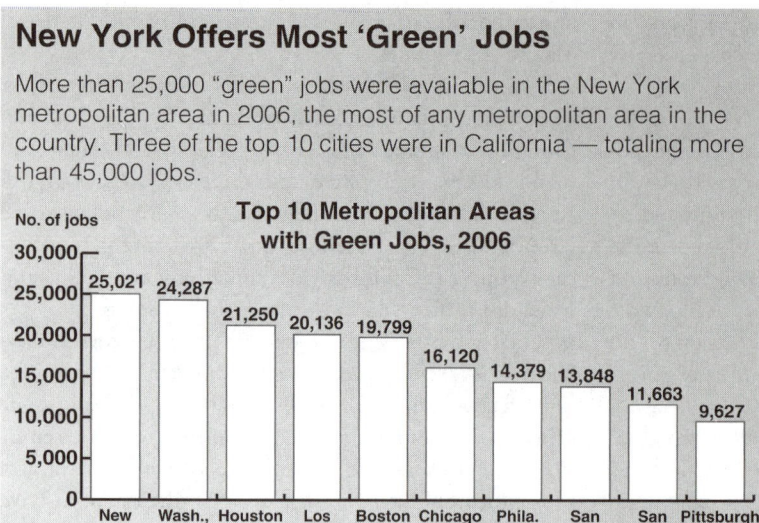

New York Offers Most 'Green' Jobs

More than 25,000 "green" jobs were available in the New York metropolitan area in 2006, the most of any metropolitan area in the country. Three of the top 10 cities were in California — totaling more than 45,000 jobs.

Top 10 Metropolitan Areas with Green Jobs, 2006

No. of jobs

Metropolitan Area	No. of jobs
New York	25,021
Wash., DC	24,287
Houston	21,250
Los Angeles	20,136
Boston	19,799
Chicago	16,120
Phila.	14,379
San Francisco	13,848
San Diego	11,663
Pittsburgh	9,627

Source: "Current and Potential Green Jobs in the U.S. Economy," Global Insight, October 2008

regional policy coordinator at the Pew Center on Global Climate Change. "An important thing to bear in mind is that several actions that states are taking, like renewable energy portfolio standards, will deliver economic and environmental benefits beyond anything related to climate change."

But not everyone applauds the state action. There was considerable internal debate within the Bush administration about granting California a waiver to regulate tailpipe emissions — a regulatory course more than a dozen other states stand ready to follow. California's tailpipe law has also been the subject of several lawsuits.

Despite a Supreme Court decision that appeared to bolster California's argument and advice from some Environmental Protection Agency officials to grant the waiver, the White House was concerned that a waiver could lead states to impose varying fuel-economy standards that would create a burden for the automobile industry.[8]

The incoming Obama administration is expected to approve the waiver for California and the other states. But even if that argument is about to be settled, there are endless debates about whether state actions will help or hurt their economies.

Margo Thorning, senior vice president of the American Council for Capital Formation, a Washington think tank, argues that the various state actions necessarily will increase energy costs. "Over the past 15 years, I've participated in or seen many of the analyses of the economic impact of reducing greenhouse gases," she says. "In every case there is a slower economy and less overall employment, even though new green jobs are created. The reason that happens is that renewables are more expensive."

Ebell, at the Competitive Enterprise Institute, agrees that state efforts on climate change will lead to higher energy costs and that various industries will look to Washington to create a single standard rather than having to satisfy a patchwork quilt of competing regulations.

Some of the state requirements are not realistic anyway, argues Rabe, the University of Michigan professor. He notes that California set a renewable-energy standard for utilities of 20 percent by 2010, which the state clearly won't meet. (It's at 11 percent now.) Legislators this year debated raising the standard to 33 percent by 2020. Rabe calls it "hubris" to create ever-tougher but elusive standards for the future.

"State regulators and state legislatures are putting a lot of pressure onto utilities to invest in alternative energy like windmills that are very expensive but are not viable power, by which I mean they're not available at times of peak demand," Ebell says.

But John Cahill, an attorney who helped design the Regional Greenhouse Gas Initiative, the Northeast's cap-and-trade program, as an aide to former Republican New York Gov. George E. Pataki, says complaints that such programs could hurt the economy are missing the point.

"The fact is that carbon is having a long-term impact on our country's and the world's natural resources," Cahill says. "What we're trying to do with cap and trade is capture the cost of our emissions, rather than making future generations pay for it."

And Ron Burke, Midwest climate change director at the Union of Concerned Scientists, says states and localities are trying to "get ahead of trends" that point to lower usage of carbon in the future, whether due to declining oil supplies or environmental concerns.

"Every city and state that does a greenhouse gas inventory gets a step ahead," Burke says. "They'll be better prepared to deal with a low-carbon economy in the future."

Burke also argues that state efforts to require utilities to turn to renewable energy sources is part of a long tradition of environmental activism. He notes that California's law seeking to regulate tailpipe emissions is in keeping with the state's historic role in promoting more efficient cars.

Due to its smog problems, the state was granted special status under the Clean Air Act of 1970 to set air-quality standards that are stricter than federal limits. California's subsequent standards have often been adopted by other states, and thus by carmakers.

"If not for California's leadership, I think it's fair to say that cars wouldn't be as clean today as they are," Burke says. "We would have suffered through more bad air days over the last 30 years."

Can local governments prevent global warming?

Seattle Mayor Greg Nickels still recalls his concern as he looked out over the Cascade Mountains during the winter of 2005. The snowpack his city relies on for both drinking water and hydroelectric power had just about failed to materialize.

"At that point, it was sort of an 'Aha' moment," he says. "Climate change went from being an esoteric issue affecting someone else in the near future to hitting us here, now."

Nickels has since spearheaded an effort among local officials to abide by the Kyoto Protocol, even though it hasn't been ratified by the U.S. Senate. More than 900 mayors have signed on from cities that are home to a total of more than 81 million Americans, according to the U.S. Conference of Mayors. "We as mayors recognize the threat of hurricanes, drought and the lack of snowpacks" that have been linked to global warming, Nickels says. "It's our obligation to take action."

But there are limits on what local officials can do. They lack the authority to regulate the dominant sources of greenhouse gas emissions — power plants and vehicles. The mayors' efforts, as a result, have mostly been

Minneapolis Mayor R. T. Rybak says people thought he was "flaky" when he replaced the city's gas-guzzling Ford Crown Victoria with a Prius like the one above. "I was not considered as flaky by the time I switched from a Prius to a plug-in," he adds. Many cities are not only tightening their own energy belts but increasingly issuing new rules to force residents and businesses to cut back as well.

Getty Images/David Paul Morris

small-bore affairs. Many local officials lack the ability even to measure their cities' total emission levels, let alone reduce them.

In many instances, their actions appear more symbolic than substantive. Critics say it's going to take more than door-to-door promotion of new lightbulbs, to cite one Minneapolis initiative, or replacing inefficient streetlights, to prevent global warming.

"Virtually all of the actions that have been taken at the local level are symbolic," says Ebell, of the Competitive Enterprise Institute. "They are meant to gain immediate public approval for the current incumbent and put all the responsibility for achieving those future goals on some future officeholder."

Even some environmentalists concede that the mayors' efforts, while obviously well-intentioned, won't put a serious dent in carbon emissions as yet.

"It's a mixed bag," says Teri Shore, a campaign director with Friends of the Earth in San Francisco. "You've got a lot of cities and counties that have signed up and set goals, but the harder part comes with actually implementing those goals."

The University of Michigan's Rabe notes that because of the lack of standardized emissions reporting, it's hard to know whose efforts have been successful and which haven't. For example, it was only in September that

Chicago put forward models of the first city-specific climate-change projections.

At that time, Chicago Mayor Richard M. Daley announced a plan to reduce the city's greenhouse gas emissions by 25 percent in 2020, compared with 1990 levels, through tougher building codes, improved transportation, reduced industrial pollution and use of clean and renewable energy sources.

"We can't solve the world's climate change problem in Chicago," Daley said, "but we can do our part."[9]

Chicago had already drawn praise for its green rooftops program, which boasts plantings on more than 200 buildings, including City Hall and the Target and Apple stores. But not even the cities that have been most ambitious about trying to meet their reduction targets have succeeded. Promises by big-city mayors to plant a million trees each have run into obstacles such as cost and lack of usable land. And New York City Mayor Michael Bloomberg's plan to charge cars a "congestion pricing" fee for driving into parts of Manhattan was rejected by the state legislature in April.

"Every locality is really good about talking about the virtues of their programs, but I don't think we've seen careful analysis and scrutiny about what works and doesn't," Rabe says. "What you have is a lot of self-celebration and claiming of success."

But Rabe notes that the municipal experiments are just

Midwest Has Most Wind Potential

North Dakota has the potential to produce more than 1.2 trillion kilowatt hours of wind energy annually — more than any other state. Most of the 20 states with the greatest potential are in the West and Midwest.

States With the Most Wind Energy Potential
(in billions of kilowatt hours annually)

North Dakota	1,210
Texas	1,190
Kansas	1,070
South Dakota	1,030
Montana	1,020
Nebraska	868
Wyoming	747
Oklahoma	725
Minnesota	657
Iowa	551
Colorado	481
New Mexico	435
Idaho	73
Michigan	65
New York	62
Illinois	61
California	59
Wisconsin	58
Maine	56
Missouri	52

Source: "Current and Potential Green Jobs in the U.S. Economy," Global Insight, October 2008

getting under way. And Shore says that cities are trying to remake themselves into "green incubators" and engaging in a friendly competition to find the best ways of limiting their local carbon "footprints."

"Having hundreds of cities across the country doing a test-run of innovations is a good thing," says Kathleen Casey Ridihalgh, a Sierra Club regional representative in Seattle. "It kind of gives us a huge pilot test of what we need to do at the federal level."

Toward this end, mayors are reducing municipal electricity use, planting thousands if not millions of trees, promoting car and bike sharing and purchasing more environmentally friendly vehicle fleets themselves — and, in New York, requiring cabbies to do the same.[10]

"People thought I was flaky when I took office and got rid of the city's Crown Victoria that was getting 10 miles per gallon and replaced it with a Prius," says Minneapolis Mayor Rybak. "I was not considered as flaky by the time I switched from a Prius to a plug-in."

James Brainard, the mayor of Carmel, Ind., and co-chair of a climate change task force for the U.S. Conference of Mayors, says that local officials can have an enormous impact due to their influence over building codes and transportation planning. He points out that metropolitan areas since World War II have been designed around automobile driving.

Cutting down on vehicle miles traveled, or VMT, has become a top goal of environmental activists and land-use planners. "Mayors are the ones who decide how planning and zoning are going to take place," Brainard says. "We have to train our planning commissioners and others to insist on good city design where one is not forced to drive from place to place."

Even a prominent advocate of local action such as Seattle's Nickels concedes federal action will be necessary not only to meet the Kyoto standards but also to surpass them. But cities can still have considerable influence over transportation and land-use planning.

Perhaps as important, cities have helped spark and keep alive a dialogue about translating concerns about climate change into tangible action. "Mayor Nickels getting various mayors to sign off on climate change predates what we did at the state level," says Terry Tamminen, who served as an energy and environment adviser to California Gov. Schwarzenegger. "It's a great way to stimulate action at the next level of government."

Should state and local governments do more to prepare for the consequences of climate change?

While she was still running for vice president, Gov. Sarah Palin, R-Alaska, said during a September interview with Katie Couric of CBS News that she wasn't "going to solely blame all of man's activities" for climate change, arguing that "the world's weather patterns are cyclical."

"But," she added, "[it] kind of doesn't matter at this point, as we debate what caused it. The point is, it's real, we need to do something about it."[11]

Palin received some criticism during the campaign for these remarks and others that suggested she denied a link between human activity and global warming. How could she address the problem, critics asked, if she wouldn't examine the underlying cause?

New Jobs Accompany 'Green' Strategies

Many new jobs are expected to be created if certain "green" economic initiatives — such as retrofitting buildings and harnessing wind and solar power — are launched. Many of the jobs are engineering-related, but blue-collar jobs would be created as well.

Potential 'Green' Investments and Jobs

Building Retrofitting — Electricians, heating/air conditioning installers, carpenters, construction equipment operators, roofers, insulation workers, carpenter helpers, industrial truck drivers, construction managers, building inspectors

Mass Transit/Freight Rail — Civil engineers, rail track layers, electricians, welders, metal fabricators, engine assemblers, bus drivers, dispatchers, locomotive engineers, railroad conductors

Smart Grid — Computer software engineers, electrical engineers, electrical equipment assemblers, electrical equipment technicians, machinists, team assemblers, construction laborers, operating engineers, electrical power line installers and repairers

Wind Power — Environmental engineers, iron and steel workers, millwrights, sheet metal workers, machinists, electrical equipment assemblers, construction equipment operators, industrial truck drivers, industrial production managers, first-line production supervisors

Solar Power — Electrical engineers, electricians, industrial machinery mechanics, welders, metal fabricators, electrical equipment assemblers, construction equipment operators, installation helpers, laborers, construction managers

Advanced Biofuels — Chemical engineers, chemists, chemical equipment operators, chemical technicians, mixing and blending machine operators, agricultural workers, industrial truck drivers, farm product purchasers, agricultural and forestry supervisors, agricultural inspectors

Source: Robert Pollin, et al., "Green Recovery: A Program to Create Good Jobs and Start Building a Low-Carbon Economy," Center for American Progress, Sept. 2008

That argument aside, Palin's stance — skepticism about global warming's roots but acceptance of it as real — reflects an increasingly important part of the larger debate: If climate change is already having real impacts — and will continue to do so, even if efforts to reduce greenhouse gas emissions succeed — how should governments begin to adapt to the resulting problems, such as flooding, coastal erosion and species loss? Should they, for example, build higher seawalls to offset rising sea levels?

"Alaska has been thinking about adaptation certainly more than it has been thinking about reducing emissions, and that's because it's on the front lines of climate change," says Hogan of the Pew climate change center.

Up until the last year or two, most environmentalists dismissed talk about adaptation. Their concern seemed to be that shifting the policy debate away from efforts to prevent climate change by cutting down on carbon emissions amounted to Palin-style denials that human activity causes global warming.

They also felt that planning for the effects brought about by climate change was defeatist. "It was seen as a potential smokescreen behind which high-emission countries could hide so they wouldn't have to make binding agreements to reduce," said Nathan Hultman, a professor of science, technology and international affairs at Georgetown University.[12]

The notion that adaptation is just a smokescreen seems to be changing. The Intergovernmental Panel on Climate Change, which shared the 2007 Nobel Peace Prize with former Vice President Al Gore, has been stressing the importance of adaptation in recent reports, while a group of scientists published an article in *Nature* in 2007 called "Lifting the Taboo on Adaptation."[13]

There are still advocates who argue that discussion about how to adapt to climate shifts amounts to a distraction from the larger project of reducing emissions. "There are people out there working on adaptation, but I have to say the overwhelming effort is to try to reduce our emissions," says Tom Adams, president of the California League of Conservation Voters. "At this point, some fairly significant climate impacts are inevitable, but a lot of us feel that this is a genuine planetary emergency, and it's imperative that we cut emissions."

Cahill, the former aide to New York Gov. Pataki, makes a similar point. "My concern is about using adaptation as a diversion program from a national cap-and-trade program," he says. "I would just be wary of something talking about adaptation without national cap and trade."

Still, Cahill and other environmentalists recognize that, even if all carbon emissions ceased tomorrow, changes are already occurring, and there is already enough carbon dioxide in the air to guarantee more changes to come. For that reason, policy makers are increasingly concerned about how to plan for the changes.

Not surprisingly, the issue has drawn the most attention in areas along coastlines, such as Maryland and Oregon. But because climate change will manifest itself differently in different locales, adaptation questions are drawing attention all over. For instance, Republican Gov. James Douglas of Vermont has been working with the state university to begin crafting plans to help the forestry and farming industries cope with climate change's local effects.

And Seattle Mayor Nickels' concerns about diminishing snowpack are increasingly shared in the Puget Sound area. In parts of the nearby Cascade Range, snowpack has declined by as much as 60 percent. In response, King County, which includes Seattle, has begun planning backwards from 2050, formulating plans to adapt to climate change effects seen as likely to occur even if carbon emissions are significantly cut between now and then.

Officials expect coastal-erosion problems associated with rising sea levels, health effects such as new infectious diseases and heat stroke, increasing numbers of forest fires and ecological issues affecting salmon. In 2007, the county council agreed to a tax inspired by such looming dangers, part of County Executive Ron Sims' $335 million plan to bolster river levees and reduce flood risks.

The county is now building climate-change risks into all of its long-term planning and policy development. "We're learning to define ourselves not in 2009 terms but in 2050 terms," Sims said. "We're making decisions based on something that has not occurred yet."[14]

Like most environmentalists, Burke of the Union of Concerned Scientists says that both responses to climate change — reduction of carbon emissions, or "mitigation," and adaptation — are important.

Still, he says, "If you had to argue one versus the other, which I don't think is really helpful, I think mitigation is a higher priority given the urgency with which we need to create these reductions.

"You see that reflected in how most cities and states are going about their planning," Burke continues. "They're definitely doing the mitigation piece first and then moving onto adaptation."

Relatively few jurisdictions have turned full-scale attention to adaptation and planning questions. Even normally proactive California has barely paid attention to adaptation issues, according to a recent study, and is unprepared for flooding, coastal erosion and loss of wildlife habitat predicted to occur in coming decades due to higher temperatures.[15] Last Nov. 14, Gov. Schwarzenegger issued an executive order to identify the state's biggest vulnerabilities to rising sea levels and draft an "adaptation strategy."[16]

States and local governments face a practical challenge when it comes to crafting adaptation plans. Much of the science in this area has been, not surprisingly, global in scope. Thus, planning for climate change's local impacts will require experts to "downscale" large-scale data to make them applicable and useful for communities.

But Sims argues that it's imperative for states, cities and counties to accept the need to make decisions based on scientific modeling rather than historical experience.

"With all the discussion we've had on global warming, I am stunned that people haven't realized that it's actually going to occur," he says. "The ice caps are melting now. They're not going to refreeze next year because we reduce our emissions. We're going to live in that world. So plan for it."

BACKGROUND

States Take Charge

Climate change has become such a hot issue among state and local officials that it's worth remembering they have taken it seriously only for a few years. "We're still very much at the embryonic stage of dealing with climate change in this country," says Cahill, the former aide to Gov. Pataki. "But at the same time, the train has left the station."

Although environmentalists deride President Bush for not squarely addressing global warming, the Clinton administration's record was not notably better. Congress rejected President Bill Clinton's 1993 proposal to impose a tax on energy, and the Senate passed a unanimous resolution in 1997 that it would reject the Kyoto Protocol if it harmed the U.S. economy.

At first, states expressed skepticism about Kyoto, with 16 passing legislation opposing its ratification in 1998 and 1999. Most were resolutions simply stating an

California state Sen. Fran Pavley sponsored legislation in 2002 to regulate tailpipe emissions. In 2006, another law she authored called for reductions in industrial carbon dioxide emissions from power plants, oil refineries and other plants by 25 percent by 2020. The law includes penalties for noncompliance.

opinion, but some states forbade their agencies from any unilateral steps to reduce greenhouse gases.[17]

But it soon became clear that many states were eager to address the problem of global warming, particularly after Bush's formal rejection of Kyoto in 2001. "Ironically . . . American states may be emerging as international leaders at the very time the national government continues to be portrayed as an international laggard on global climate change," the University of Michigan's Rabe wrote in 2004.[18]

Most initial state-level efforts were largely symbolic, lacking specific mandates or resources. As early as 1989, New Jersey Gov. Thomas Kean, a Republican, signed an executive order instructing all state agencies to take the lead in reducing greenhouse gases.

But New Jersey and other states soon put real teeth into their efforts. In 2001, Massachusetts Gov. Jane Swift, also a Republican, issued a rule limiting a variety

CHRONOLOGY

1980s-1990s *Despite growing scientific concern, U.S. officials make mostly symbolic efforts to address global warming.*

1988 The United Nations and the World Meteorological Organization create the International Panel on Climate Change (IPCC) to assess scientific information related to global warming.

1989 New Jersey Gov. Thomas Kean directs state agencies to start cutting greenhouse gas emissions (GHG).

1990 Amendments to the Clean Air Act introduce states to emissions trading.

1992 Delegates to World Environmental Summit in Rio de Janeiro adopt U.N. Framework Convention on Climate Change, calling on industrialized nations to voluntarily reduce emissions to 1990 levels by 2000.

1997 The Kyoto Protocol is adopted in Kyoto, Japan, on Dec. 11, committing industrialized countries to cut GHG emissions by an average of 5 percent below 1990 levels by 2012. The treaty goes into effect in 2005; 183 countries have ratified it so far, but not the United States. The Clinton administration signed it in 1997, but the Senate had voted unanimously in July to oppose any treaty that would harm the U.S. economy and exempt developing countries.

1998-1999 Sixteen states pass legislation and resolutions critical of the Kyoto treaty and GHG reduction efforts.

1999 A law deregulating electricity in Texas includes a provision promoting renewable energy, sparking large-scale efforts to harvest wind energy in the state.

2000s *Federal inaction spurs local action to cut GHGs.*

2002 California regulates GHG emissions from vehicles.

2005 Governors from seven Northeastern states form Regional Greenhouse Gas Initiative to create a cap-and-trade system limiting emissions. . . . U.S. Conference of Mayors encourages cities to abide by Kyoto Protocol emission limits.

2006 California enacts first statewide cap on carbon emissions as part of a landmark global warming law. . . . Washington is first major U.S. city to mandate green construction for all large private buildings.

2007 In response to a case brought by Massachusetts and other states, Supreme Court rules Environmental Protection Agency can regulate carbon dioxide as a pollutant. . . . Regulator in Kansas denies permits for two 700-megawatt power plants due to GHG pollution concerns.

2008 April 7: New York State Assembly kills a plan by Mayor Michael Bloomberg to charge drivers an $8 "congestion pricing" fee for entering parts of Manhattan. . . . April 22: Los Angeles City Council approves ordinance requiring developers to meet tougher environmental building standards. . . . June 6: Senate rejects a vote to consider federal greenhouse gas legislation that includes a national cap-and-trade system. . . . July 18: California Building Standards Commission approves first statewide "green building codes," requiring greater energy efficiency in both commercial and residential properties. . . . Sept. 18: Chicago Mayor Richard M. Daley announces a plan to reduce GHG emissions by 25 percent by 2020, compared with 1990 levels, through tougher building codes and improved transportation. . . . Sept. 30: California Gov. Arnold Schwarzenegger signs bill that will award increased state and federal transportation funds to regions that encourage dense development. . . . Nov. 19: Governors of Illinois, Wisconsin and California sign agreement with counterparts in Indonesia and Brazil to address forestry issues pertaining to global warming. . . . Canada reverses course and expresses support for a North American cap-and-trade system. . . . Dec. 8: Local government groups urge Congress and the incoming Obama administration to devote $10 billion to their efforts to create green jobs and promote energy efficiency as part of an economic stimulus plan. . . . Dec. 11: California Air Resources Board moves to implement the state's 2006 global warming law, approving a plan to cut emissions 25 percent by 2020.

2009 Jan. 1: Northeast's multistate limits on carbon emissions take effect. . . . March 3: Los Angeles voters will decide whether to require Department of Water and Power to install solar collectors on roofs of government, commercial and industrial buildings by 2014.

of pollutants from six major power plants, including the nation's first carbon dioxide standards. "The new, tough standards will help ensure older power plants in Massachusetts do not contribute to regional air pollution, acid rain and global warming," Swift said.[19] Her action was soon copied in New Hampshire.

But California quickly emerged as the leader among states in addressing the issue. As the only state allowed to set air pollution controls stricter than those mandated by federal law (thanks to a provision in the Clean Air Act), California is an almost constant environmental battlefield. There was strong pressure from environmental forces to move on the issue of greenhouse gases at the start of this decade, with both the legislature and governor's mansion in Democratic hands for the first time in two decades.

California lawmakers responded in 2002, enacting a measure to regulate tailpipe emissions — greenhouse gases released from vehicles — which in 1999 accounted for 37 percent of carbon dioxide emissions in the state.[20]

The idea came from Bluewater Network, a San Francisco environmental group that has since become part of Friends of the Earth, a global organization. They found their sponsor in then-state Rep. Fran Pavley, a Democratic freshman willing to take on the fight when more prominent legislators were avoiding it. "We were happy at that point to find any progressive author, because we knew it would be a difficult bill," said Bluewater Executive Director Russell Long.

The legislation survived a committee challenge and was ready to reach the floor by the middle of 2001, but Pavley held off on a vote until 2002 so she could broaden her backing. Car makers and oil companies spent an estimated $5 million attempting to sink it, and she was ardently attacked by talk-radio hosts for impinging on the freedom of Californians to drive SUVs and other large vehicles.

Pavley responded with polls demonstrating overwhelming popular support for the bill, even among SUV owners. She also got help from water-quality districts, religious leaders, technology executives from Silicon Valley and celebrities such as Paul Newman, Tom Hanks and former President Clinton, who called wavering lawmakers. Her bill's progress was helped immeasurably, however, by legislative leaders who showed the former civics teacher some parliamentary tricks to ensure its passage.

Her law required the state's Air Resources Board to adopt "cost-effective" and "reasonable" restrictions on carbon dioxide emissions from cars and light trucks by 2005, with automakers having until 2009 to comply. Not surprisingly, carmakers have fought the law through numerous court challenges.

A total of 19 other states have since enacted laws saying they will abide by California's rules once they are approved, but the Bush administration has refused to grant California the necessary waiver.

"All we asked for was permission to enforce, because the rules were all in place," California Air Resources Board spokesman Stanley Young said in a recent interview. "We've been ready for two years on Pavley. The rules were fully fleshed out. They were formally adopted back in 2005, and we're ready to move on them as soon as we get the green light."

Pavley was back in 2006 with another piece of legislation designed to address global warming. The measure to address stationary sources of pollution aims to reduce industrial carbon dioxide emissions by 25 percent by 2020. It affects not only power plants but also other polluters such as oil refineries and cement plants.

The legislation was the first in the nation to require a cap-and-trade system. It also served to codify limits on future greenhouse gas emissions that Schwarzenegger had outlined in 2005. The 2006 law represented the first imposition of statewide, enforceable limits on GHG emissions that include penalties for noncompliance.

States Challenge the EPA

States have been exploring numerous other avenues toward curbing emissions in recent years. In 2007, first Western and then Midwestern states joined together in regional compacts meant to mirror and build on the Northeast's Regional Greenhouse Gas Initiative, which aims to set up cap-and-trade systems to limit emissions. Various states have taken steps to encourage use of high-efficiency vehicles, either through purchases for their own fleets or tax incentives for individuals to purchase them. States such as New Mexico, New Jersey and Minnesota have recently crafted and adopted plans for reducing their overall greenhouse gas emissions.

'Green' Jobs Counted on to Revive Economy

But critic says stimulus program won't help.

In October, Progressive Insurance announced the winner of its $10 million Automotive X Prize, a competition to encourage students to develop designs for safe, low-emission, "production capable" cars. Among the finalists were engineering students from West Philadelphia High School.

"Our team has built four cars, including a hybrid Jeep that gets double the mileage it's supposed to get," said Lawrence Jones-Mahoney, 18. "If we can do it as high school students, why can't the major auto companies?"[1]

Amid the nation's current economic doldrums, many people see green manufacturing projects as a hopeful sign. Investment in alternative energy and more efficient automobiles and buildings was high and growing rapidly over the past year, at least until the price of oil began to drop.

Many still are counting on "green collar" jobs to revive the economy, restoring the manufacturing sector in places where it's long been in decline. "American cities have suffered more than anyone from the loss of manufacturing jobs," says Minneapolis Mayor R. T. Rybak. "Cities have become the green incubators for America."

Every month seems to see another study released suggesting that there will be an explosion of investment and job creation in the green sector. The Center for American Progress estimates that a government-funded $100 billion green stimulus package would create 2 million jobs in the next two years for engineers, machinists, construction workers and others.[2]

The Apollo Alliance, a coalition of business, labor and environmental groups, estimates that a $300 billion investment over 10 years will create 3.3 million jobs in renewable energy, hybrid cars and infrastructure replacement.[3] The U.S. Conference of Mayors forecasts 4.2 million green jobs

by 2038 and suggests that cities and towns prepare to compete for them.[4]

"Everything that is good for global warming is good for jobs," says Van Jones, author of the 2008 book *The Green Collar Economy.* "Buildings do not weatherize themselves, wind turbines do not construct themselves, solar panels do not install themselves. Real people are going to have to get up in the morning and do these things."

This is one of the central premises of *New York Times* columnist Thomas Friedman's 2008 bestselling book, *Hot, Flat and Crowded* — that energy-technology jobs will serve as a cornerstone of economic revival in this country, in large part because they mostly cannot be done by workers overseas.

President-elect Barack Obama has pledged to make green jobs and manufacturing a centerpiece of any economic-stimulus package. "President-elect Obama did a great job on the campaign trail [communicating] that this is an opportunity, an economic opportunity for America, and that if we miss it, other countries in the world will be way ahead of us," Kansas Gov. Kathleen Sebelius, a Democrat, said at a November climate-change summit in California. "Jobs are clearly part of this."[5]

For all the apparent promise, however, the interest in green technology has not yet translated either into mass employment or a huge economic windfall. "People are talking about this in the future, but it's not happening today," says Eric Crawford, president of Greenman Alliance, a Milwaukee-based recruiting firm. "Everyone wants a green job," but the demand for such jobs totally outstrips the supply.

And government investment in clean technology has not always reaped large dividends. Under New Jersey's

But environmentalists and state officials alike have been hoping the federal government would take action. In the face of its reluctance to regulate greenhouse gas emissions, several environmental groups as early as 1999 had petitioned the EPA to use its authority under the Clean Air Act to regulate the gases. The agency denied it had such authority and also argued that the link between greenhouse gases and climate change was not firmly established.

Massachusetts and 11 other states appealed the EPA's denial. In April 2007, the Supreme Court ruled, 5-4, in the states' favor, noting that they had standing to bring such a case due to the "risk of catastrophic harm" they faced as sovereign entities. Justice John Paul Stevens wrote that the EPA had provided "no reasonable explanation for its refusal to decide whether greenhouse gases cause or contribute to climate change." In his dissent, Chief Justice

energy master plan, solar power should account for more than 2 percent of the Garden State's electricity by 2020. But solar systems now generate only 0.07 percent of current energy needs.

That's despite the fact that the state has already handed out more than $170 million in rebates to encourage their installation. To meet its 2020 goal, the state would have to spend $11 billion more. "We need to do things differently because ratepayers can't keep paying for rebates indefinitely," says Jeanne M. Fox, president of New Jersey's Board of Public Utilities.[6]

About half the states require utilities to generate a portion of their power from renewable sources, such as wind and solar. Above, wind turbines near Palm Springs, Calif.

clean up the environment. In a column published in *The New York Times* just after the November election, former Vice President Al Gore called for large governmental investments in clean energy as the optimum way to address climate change — a shift from his traditional focus on increased regulation of carbon pollution.[7]

"With his op-ed, Gore has reversed the longstanding green-lobby prioritization of regulation first and investment second," wrote Michael Shellenberger and Ted Nordhaus for *The New Republic Online*.[8]

"This idea that we're going to have a massive environmental WPA — it's not going to help the economy, it's going to hurt the economy," says Myron Ebell, director of energy and global warming policy at the Competitive Enterprise Institute, referring to the Depression-era jobs program, the Works Progress Administration.

Putting government money into green energy would not create great economic returns, Ebell suggests, because — at least so far — renewable energy is more expensive than dirty fuels such as coal. It also means directing dollars away from other fields entirely, he says.

"I believe just on a very simple analysis that there is no question it will take net jobs out of the economy and it will be a net economic harm," Ebell says.

Even if Ebell's right, however, the goal of green investment is not only to stimulate the economy but also to help

[1] Jim Motavalli, "Upstart Team Eyes the X Prize," *The New York Times*, Sept. 7, 2008, p. AU6.

[2] Robert Pollin, *et al.*, "Green Recovery: A Program to Create Good Jobs and Start Building a Low-Carbon Economy," Center for American Progress, September 2008.

[3] "The New Apollo Program: Clean Energy, Good Jobs," The Apollo Alliance, September 2008.

[4] "Current and Potential Green Jobs in the U.S. Economy," *Global Insight*, October 2008.

[5] "Governors Say Climate Change Programs Can Aid Economic Recovery," *Carbon Control News*, Nov. 24, 2008.

[6] Anthony DePalma, "New Jersey Dealing With Solar Policy's Success," *The New York Times*, June 25, 2008, p. B1.

[7] Al Gore, "The Climate for Change," *The New York Times*, Nov. 9, 2008, p. WK10.

[8] Michael Shellenberger and Ted Nordhaus, "A New Inconvenient Truth," *The New Republic Online*, Nov. 17, 2008, www.tnr.com/politics/story.html?id=971eed4b-1dc8-4afd-a8fe-193c373286ac.

John G. Roberts Jr. argued that it was an issue better decided by Congress and the executive branch.[21]

But the court's majority determined that carbon dioxide was indeed an air pollutant under the federal Clean Air Act, and that law gives California the authority to regulate any such pollutant, as long as the state can get a waiver from the EPA. Other states are then allowed to follow California's rules.

The Supreme Court decision set the political stage for Congress to set a new mileage standard for cars and light trucks. In December 2007 President Bush signed into law requirements that a car manufacturer's entire fleet average 35 miles per gallon by 2020.

But just hours after that bill was signed, EPA Administrator Stephen L. Johnson dashed hopes that the *Massachusetts v. EPA* decision would lead the agency to

Kansas Regulator Blocks Coal-Fired Plants

Project is among 60 canceled in 2008 to protect environment.

Many people would be surprised to find Kansas at the epicenter of a nationwide environmental debate. Yet the decision by Rod Bremby, secretary of the Kansas Department of Health and Environment (KDHE), to block a pair of massive coal-fired power plants has set off one of the nation's fiercest political and legal environmental battles.

Several other states have blocked coal-fired plants over the past year, but Bremby is the only regulator to have done so strictly out of concern for climate change and without getting specific statutory cover from the legislature. "To approve the permit didn't seem a reasonable option, given that carbon dioxide is a pollutant," he said in an interview, "and we're talking about 11 million tons of carbon."

Bremby delayed making his coal-plant decision until after the U.S. Supreme Court's ruling in a case (*Massachusetts v. EPA*) brought in 2007 by Massachusetts and other states seeking to force the federal Environmental Protection Agency to regulate greenhouse gases.

The states' victory — along with an opinion from the Kansas attorney general that Bremby had the authority to block the permit — allowed him to overrule his own staff and refuse Sunflower Electric Power Corp.'s application to build its $3.6 billion power-plant project outside Holcomb.

The project is one of roughly 60 coal-fired plants canceled over the past year due to environmental concerns. Florida Gov. Charlie Crist asked a utility to cancel two projects in his state. The Texas energy giant TXU Corp. has shelved eight out of 11 planned coal plants, investing heavily in wind energy instead. Only three out of 10 plants once planned for southern Illinois remain active.[1] Nowadays, wherever a coal-fired plant is proposed, the Sierra Club or an allied group steps forward with a lawsuit to block it.[2]

"There have been other decisions in which state public utility commissions or environmental regulators have blocked construction or operation of coal-fired plants on the basis of climate change," says Robert Glicksman, a University of Kansas law professor, "but those have been based on legislation designed to minimize pollution or used climate change coupled with other factors."

In Washington state, for instance, the legislature in 2007 limited the amount of greenhouse gases coal plants could emit. To obtain construction permits, energy companies must show they can capture or sequester any carbon dioxide above strict limits.

Because Kansas lacks such legislation, and despite the attorney general's opinion, many critics say Bremby overstepped his authority. Kansas law gives the secretary authority to block emissions found to endanger health or the environment. But that power, according to the health department's own testimony, applies only to emergencies, says Jay Emler, who chairs the state Senate Utilities Committee.

Legislators — their attention focused by a million-dollar lobbying campaign by Sunflower and its allies — voted

approve California's waiver application for enforcement of the Pavley bill. "The Bush administration is moving forward with a clear national solution, not a confusing patchwork of state rules, to reduce America's climate footprint from vehicles," Johnson said in a statement. Congress has since investigated the circumstances surrounding Johnson's decision.[22]

CURRENT SITUATION

Limiting Land Use

American governors are now working with partners from around the world, as well as with each other, to combat environmental threats. On Nov. 19, governors from 13 states and regional leaders from four other nations signed a declaration to work together to combat global warming. The statement was the capstone of a climate summit organized by California's Schwarzenegger.

Under a separate agreement, Illinois, California and Wisconsin pledged to work with the governors of six provinces within Indonesia and Brazil to help slow tropical deforestation and land degradation through joint projects and incentive programs.

"When California passed its global warming law two years ago, we were out there on an island, so we started forming partnerships everywhere we could," Schwarzenegger said.[23]

three times to ban Bremby's department from regulating greenhouse gases. Each time, Democratic Gov. Kathleen Sebelius sided with Bremby and vetoed their efforts. The legislature came close to overriding her, but fell short.

The battle is now left to the state and federal courts, which are weighing a half-dozen lawsuits. Environmentalists, needless to say, are delighted by the outcome so far, believing that delays, and their concomitant costs, can only serve to move power generation away from coal. "Each time you step back and reassess the politics and economics of coal," says Bob Eye, a Sierra Club attorney and former KDHE counsel, "things are more difficult for the coal-plant proponents."

Plant advocates, of course, make exactly the opposite argument, saying the protracted fighting will simply cause Sunflower to look to friendlier states. Uncertainty about permitting — as well as the state's general regulatory climate — has caused problems for the business community, which put energy costs at the top of its list of concerns in a Kansas Chamber of Commerce survey last fall. "We've heard people saying that because of what happened last session they feel that the state has hung a big 'We're not open for business' sign out," said Kent Eckles, the chamber's vice president for government affairs.[3]

U.S. House Select Committee on Energy Independence and Global Warming

Action by Rod Bremby ignited fierce battle in Kansas.

"His decision, which I say is nothing but a political decision, has had a disastrous effect on the economy of Kansas," says Sen. Emler, "and will until it's rectified."

Bremby and his allies have pointed out that Sunflower was the only applicant not to receive a clean-air permit, out of more than 3,100 applications received during the six years Sebelius has been governor. But the issue is expected to be front and center again during the upcoming legislative session.

"I anticipate a full-blown debate until we get this fixed," says Senate President Steve Morris, who strongly supports Sunflower's project.

Then again, Bremby always suspected he couldn't win many friends with his decision. "We knew going in that we were in a no-win situation," he says, "There would be litigation either way we went."

---

[1] Michael Hawthorne, "How Coal Got a Dirty Name," *Chicago Tribune*, July 9, 2008, p. 1.

[2] Judy Pasternak, "Coal at Heart of Climate Battle," *Los Angeles Times*, April 14, 2008, p. A1.

[3] Jeannine Koranda, "Climate Cleanup Costs Could Trickle Down," *The Wichita Eagle*, Nov. 10, 2008, p. A1.

On Dec. 11, the California Air Resources Board approved a set of regulations designed to implement the state's 2006 greenhouse gas law. It aims to reduce carbon emissions to 1990 levels by 2020, which would amount to a 25 percent cut. The plan will allow businesses to buy and sell emission credits, impose fees on water use and require utilities to generate a full third of their power from renewable sources — about three times as much as they do currently.

California estimates that about 30 percent of its greenhouse gas emissions come from cars. The new vehicle regulations would account for 18 percent of the state's overall reduction goal, according to the new state plan. The air board's plan also includes a "feebate" proposal,

which would give rebates to people buying fuel-efficient cars, while adding fees to the purchase of gas-guzzlers.[24]

The Air Resources Board will almost certainly have to revisit some of these issues in response to a major land-use bill Schwarzenegger signed last September, known as SB 375, which directed the board to come up with regional greenhouse gas reduction targets by September 2010. The next step under the law calls for regional planning boards to rewrite their master plans in ways that seek to meet those targets. The ones that come closest will be rewarded with extra federal and state transportation dollars.

The best way to meet the standards, argues Adams at the California League of Conservation Voters, is to cut

The rooftop garden atop Chicago's City Hall is one of about 200 such green roofs in the city. Mayor Richard M. Daley announced in 2008 the first city-specific climate-change projections in the nation along with plans to reduce greenhouse gas emissions by 25 percent in 2020, compared with 1990 levels.

down on sprawl. He points out that the number of miles traveled per vehicle is still growing at one-and-a-half times the rate of population growth. It's only by creating more compact and energy-efficient communities, Adams believes, that the state's long-term environmental goals can be achieved.

It's no surprise that environmentalists backed SB 375, but it also had the support of home builders, who liked the prospect of more predictability in the zoning process. One of the bill's main goals is inducing localities to coordinate their major planning tasks — transportation, land use and housing. Few have been able to do that up to now.

In addition, SB 375 provides relief from certain air-quality standards that had, perversely, discouraged developers from undertaking "infill" projects that use small plots of undeveloped land within existing communities. "Builders thrive on certainty, knowing what the rules are," says Tim Coyle, a senior vice president at the California Building Industry Association. Local governments also supported the law. Although it provides incentives and creates a policy-making framework, it doesn't create specific mandates for any individual regions.

SB 375 will take years to implement, but it already has received lots of attention from other states. "It's really a very important piece of legislation," says Peter Kasabach, executive director of New Jersey Future, a smart-growth group. "How we develop our land is going to impact our greenhouse-gas targets.

"A lot of folks think that if we drive hybrids or change our lightbulbs, we'd be OK," he says. "But a significant amount of our greenhouse gas targets will be met by how we get around and reduce vehicle miles traveled."

Green Building

The number of local governments attempting to shrink their carbon footprints continues to grow, with more than 900 mayors having signed a pledge to bring their cities in line with the Kyoto Protocol's carbon reduction targets.

In 2007, Congress authorized up to $2 billion a year in block grants for state and local programs designed to save energy. "If we reflect back on the mayors' initiative, it was such a powerful vehicle to establish the voice of local action," says Michelle Wyman, executive director of the American affiliate of the international group ICLEI-Local Governments for Sustainability. "There's increasing sentiment that local climate action is where the real work is being done in the United States."

In September, Chicago Mayor Daley unveiled what *The New York Times* described as "perhaps the most aggressive plan of any major American city to reduce heat-trapping gases."[25] The plan, which aims to cut Chicago's carbon output by 25 percent by 2020, focuses on tougher building codes.

Green building codes have drawn the most attention among local governments seeking to cut back on carbon. Buildings account for 40 to 50 percent of a city's energy demands. They use a fourth of the drinking water and produce 35 percent of the solid waste, mostly in the form of construction materials. And buildings make up anywhere from 30 to 70 percent of municipal carbon emissions, according to the American Institute of Architects (AIA).

Many cities have received grants from former President Clinton's foundation to rewrite their codes, but far more are pursuing such strategies on their own. In November, more than 25,000 local officials attended the "Greenbuild" conference in Boston sponsored by the U.S. Green Building Council.[26]

The trend has exploded in recent years. From 2003 to 2007, the number of cities with green building programs grew by 418 percent, from 22 to 92, according to the AIA. By mid-2008, 14 percent of municipalities with populations of more than 50,000 had adopted such programs, with many more cities planning programs soon.

Can "green" jobs revive the U.S. economy?

YES

Bracken Hendricks
Senior Fellow, Center for American Progress

Benjamin Goldstein
*Research Associate,
Center for American Progress*

From "A Strategy for Green Recovery," Nov. 10, 2008

There is a growing consensus in Washington and on Main Streets across the country that the economy needs a jump-start. There are compelling reasons why the infrastructure and work-force components of the economic stimulus and recovery package should be "green."

Confronting the mounting energy and global warming crises represents an extraordinary opportunity to reinvigorate the economy through investment in clean, sustainable, low-carbon energy sources. Investment in new, clean technologies and improving energy efficiency can drive immediate spending into some of the hardest-hit sectors of the economy, such as construction and manufacturing, and can ensure that this infusion flows directly into job creation and domestic investment. Further, smart policies for energy efficiency can reduce household utility bills and free up income for consumer spending.

There are many ways that government spending can boost the economy and create jobs as part of a stimulus and recovery program. Yet dollars directed toward renewable energy and energy efficiency would result in more jobs than spending in most other areas, including, for example, rebates for increasing household consumption, which was the primary aim of the $168 billion stimulus program last April. "Green" investments, on average, create more than twice as many jobs per dollar invested as traditional, fossil fuel-based generating technologies by redirecting money previously spent on wasted energy and imported fuel toward advanced technology, modern infrastructure and skilled labor.

Green investments also pave the road for sustained economic recovery. Larger, capital-intensive, green infrastructure projects such as renewable-energy generating facilities may take two years to get fully up and running but will be good job creators with a dependable economic-multiplier effect. About 22 percent of total household expenditures go to imports. But only about 9 percent of a green infrastructure investment program purchases imports. This is another critical advantage of a green economic-recovery program: Investments are focused primarily on increasing domestic productive capacity, improving national infrastructure and making the entire economy more efficient over the long term.

Confronting energy and climate challenges will require a sustained commitment and long-term policy framework. But near-term green investments can immediately stimulate the economy, create millions of good jobs and put a solid down payment on the low-carbon future vital for our economic growth.

NO

Margo Thorning
*Senior Vice President and
Chief Economist, American
Council for Capital Formation*

Written for *CQ Researcher*, January 2009

The U.S. economy has slowed markedly in recent months, prompting some to suggest putting even more taxpayer dollars into subsidized renewable energy in the United States. Advocates claim lots of new "green collar" jobs would be created, and the threat of global warming would be lessened. Both claims are unlikely to be realized.

Despite many years of tax credits and taxpayer-funded research and development, most forms of renewable energy are still not competitive with electricity generated by coal, natural gas or nuclear power. Wind-powered electricity is estimated to cost as much as 50 percent more than coal-fired generation, and solar generation up to 700 percent more.

Both wind and solar must be backed up by conventional generation capacity, which adds greatly to their cost, because the wind does not always blow, and the sun is available only 12 hours a day. Furthermore, renewable resources are often geographically remote, and building transmission lines to large metropolitan areas is expensive.

Proposals like that of the Center for American Progress to invest $100 billion-$200 billion of taxpayer money in green infrastructure are based on the flawed premise that raising the price of conventional energy through a tax on carbon emissions and using the money to pay for more expensive renewable energy will promote economic recovery. In fact, substituting higher-cost energy for lower-cost conventional energy will slow U.S. economic and job growth.

A study by the American Council for Capital Formation and the National Association of Manufacturers shows that if the U.S. had adopted the Senate's Lieberman-Warner global warming bill last year, overall U.S. employment would have been reduced by 850,000 to 1,860,000 jobs in 2014. This figure includes gains from new green jobs. The high energy prices required to curb greenhouse gas emissions cause net job loss even after taking into account increased employment in renewable energy.

What's more, a recent EPA report concluded that even if the United States achieved the emission-reduction targets in the Lieberman-Warner bill, it would make virtually no difference in global greenhouse gas concentrations unless developing countries also adopt stringent reduction targets.

Although renewable energy has a role to play in the U.S. economy, the Obama administration should consider policies to promote U.S. energy supplies of all types and avoid unrealistic climate change policies.

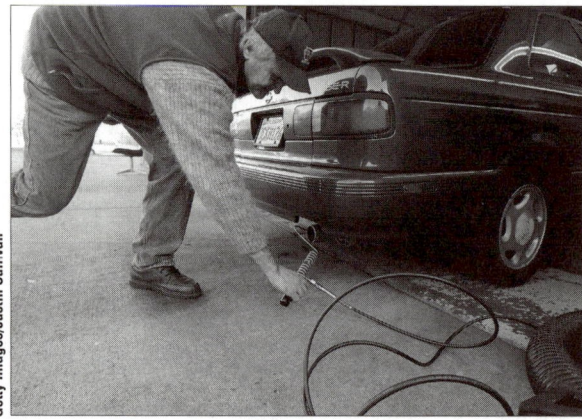

A motorist in San Rafael, Calif., checks his tailpipe exhaust level. California passed a law in 2002 to regulate tailpipe emissions, and 19 other states followed suit. The Bush White House has blocked the other states from enforcing their laws, but President-elect Barack Obama has said he will approve a waiver allowing enforcement.

By and large, cities' green building programs are based on the standards of the council's rating system, known as LEED (Leader in Energy and Environmental Design). To encourage developers to build green, cities are offering tax incentives, reductions in permit fees and access to grants for projects that meet certain environmental benchmarks. Some cities offer bonus density allowances — a green building project might be exempt from height restrictions, for example. But the most popular incentive by far is expedited permitting for green projects. Cities can implement such a policy at virtually no cost to themselves, which has proven extremely attractive.

Some cities are going further and actually requiring energy-efficient construction through their building codes. Washington, D.C., in 2006 became the first major U.S. city to mandate green construction for all private buildings of at least 50,000 square feet, beginning in 2012. But in 2007, Boston became the first city actually to implement a green requirement for private construction and renovation projects.

Since then, a handful of other cities have adopted similar mandates. San Francisco last August adopted the strictest codes of any U.S. city so far, requiring green standards for any residential buildings taller than 75 feet and commercial buildings of more than 5,000 square feet.

Last July, California became the first state to require certain environmental standards in its statewide building code.

Cap-and-Trade

In September, 10 Northeastern states concluded their first auction selling the right to emit carbon dioxide from power plants. The idea, as explained by the plan's architect, former Pataki aide Cahill, is to translate everyone's awareness that carbon emissions have a price into an actual cost.

Cap-and-trade auctions have taken place for years as a means of reducing acid-rain-causing sulfur dioxide, and the European Union runs a cap-and-trade program for carbon. But the Northeastern effort — known as the Regional Greenhouse Gas Initiative, or RGGI (pronounced "Reggie") — was the first CO_2 auction in the United States.

RGGI, which went into force on Jan. 1, places an overall regional limit on the amount of carbon that power plants can emit. The cap-and-trade plan is the central mechanism for regulating and limiting carbon emissions. Each utility has a permit for each ton of carbon it is allowed to emit — and the number of permits will steadily shrink over time. Utilities that emit less than their quota can sell their excess permits. (That's the "trade" part of cap and trade.)

The Northeastern states aren't the only ones interested in such an approach. In the West, seven states and four Canadian provinces are developing a similar regime, with negotiators having drawn up a blueprint for their governors in September. In the Midwest, six other states are working on a regional carbon-trading program. Florida is developing its own program, although it may join forces either with the Western effort or RGGI.

The history of RGGI, in particular, includes many touch-and-go moments when states dropped out of or rejoined the program. But the effort has stayed afloat based on the hope that once carbon emissions carry a price, utilities will burn less coal, oil and natural gas because it's in their economic interest, while carbon-free alternatives will become comparatively more attractive.

Not everyone agrees that such a scenario will play out. Wind power, for instance, is already heavily subsidized yet still can't compete on price with coal. And the region-by-region approach that's now in place leaves plenty of opportunities open for undermining the system.

In the Northeast, for example, it would be easy enough for a big industrial customer in New York, which is part of RGGI, to look for cheaper power generated by coal plants in Pennsylvania or Ohio, which are not part of the initiative. If that occurs, said Kenneth Pokalsky, a regulatory analyst for the Business Council of New York State, "We'll have the worst of both worlds: higher energy costs in New York to implement a program that has no discernible impact on worldwide greenhouse gas emissions."[27]

Nevertheless, hoping to build on the RGGI model and benefit from lessons learned there and from the troubled European model, the system being developed in the West is even bolder. The Western Climate Initiative is targeting not just carbon dioxide but five other greenhouse gases as well. And the WCI isn't limiting its scope to power plants. Instead, it's trying to bring all major industries, transportation fuels and residential furnaces, stoves and hot-water heaters into its system.

Such an ambitious approach may represent the logical evolution of cap and trade, but it nonetheless has made business groups, local governments and unions nervous about the potential impact on their costs and the economy. Officials involved in WCI are tweaking their plans, looking at giving away a good share of emission allowances rather than auctioning them off. They're also seeking other ways to protect entities that would be affected if the system takes effect.

Focus on Renewables

Even as the regional cap-and-trade systems get under way, more than half the states are trying to cut down on coal as a share of their power sources individually. Twenty-seven states now require utilities to rely on renewable sources such as wind and solar to generate a significant share of electricity — up to 25 percent in future years. That's nearly twice as many states as had renewable portfolio standards in place just five years ago.

"It's an important step in the process of weaning ourselves from foreign oil," said Rhode Island state Sen. David E. Bates, who helped push through legislation in 2004 that requires a 20 percent renewable energy portfolio in his state by 2020. "We provided incentives for companies to produce renewable energy. We also took great pains to make it a workable formula. You can't tell a national grid to produce green energy in 20 years without making sure the energy is available."[28]

Meeting the required targets remains quite a challenge, however, especially in coal-dependent regions such as the South and Midwest. Coal generates about half the nation's electricity.

Joe Manchin, the governor of West Virginia, has touted wind energy but noted in a recent interview that his state's coal production is key for the entire Eastern Seaboard. "Economists and scientists . . . will tell you that coal is going to be the primary factor that's going to power this nation and most of the world for the next 30 to 50 years."[29]

According to the American Wind Energy Association, wind energy capacity has been growing rapidly, with wind turbines installed in 2008 capable of generating 7,500 megawatts of additional electricity. That's up from 5,249 megawatts installed in 2007. But 7,500 megawatts is still only enough electricity to power about 2 million homes.[30]

OUTLOOK

Will Washington Help?

If California has been a leader in state-level efforts to prevent climate change, two Californians are likely to have a profound effect on the national response to the issue. Sen. Barbara Boxer, who chairs the Senate Environment and Public Works Committee, has pledged to introduce legislation to create a national cap-and-trade program in this Congress. Henry A. Waxman, another California Democrat, will be Boxer's counterpart in the House, having ousted legendary Rep. John D. Dingell, D-Mich., as chairman of the Energy and Commerce Committee in November.

Dingell, who has been in Congress for a half-century and had been the panel's top Democrat since 1981, represents the Detroit area and has been a leading champion of the auto industry in Congress. His replacement by Waxman was widely seen as a signal that House Democrats will favor a more aggressive approach on climate change.

President-elect Obama, for his part, has also promised to make climate change a priority — a switch from the outgoing Bush administration. Obama is expected to approve the EPA waiver to allow California and 19 other states to regulate greenhouse gas emissions from vehicles.

But even if new leadership in Washington appears ready to tackle an issue long left to states and localities, does that mean national policy will trump the efforts of lower levels of government?

A lot will depend, of course, on what form congressional action will take. Plenty of people are skeptical, despite the changed circumstances in Washington, that Congress will actually act on cap and trade or any equally ambitious responses to global warming. There has been a lot of talk that caution will remain a watchword, given the fragile state of the economy. Further regulation may be seen as more than the economy — and the tottering auto sector in particular — can bear.

"Yes, there will be concerns about the current economic climate," says former Pataki aide Cahill, who helped design the Regional Greenhouse Gas Initiative (RGGI). "But it will take several years to develop the regulatory framework to go ahead and implement a national cap and trade. We all have enough confidence in the economy that it won't still be where it is now."

But the Competitive Enterprise Institute's Ebell points out that a Senate vote to consider last year's major climate-change legislation received only 48 votes — far short of the 60 needed under Senate rules to formally consider the bill. Although Democrats picked up seven seats in the November elections, some of them replaced Republicans who had voted in favor of the bill.

"I think there will be somewhat more enthusiasm for cap and trade in the 111th Congress than in the 110th," Ebell says, "but I don't know that it will translate into actual legislation."

If Congress does manage to overcome its own procedural hurdles and economic concerns to move major greenhouse gas legislation, one of the biggest challenges for lawmakers will be how to balance competing desires among states. Some, such as California, Massachusetts and New Jersey, will want to be rewarded for their pioneering efforts. Others in the South and Midwest, though, will not want to be penalized for not having acted sooner. It will be tough to create a national system that balances those different interests.

Rabe, the University of Michigan policy professor, says Congress has only recently taken into account the role that states and localities are playing. He says states will lobby to ensure that any federal system allows them maximum flexibility to set their own courses, while demanding that any money generated by a cap-and-trade system be shared generously with them. "States and localities are going to want it both ways," Rabe says.

But the fact that states and localities will be very much part of the national debate demonstrates how well-established their role in addressing climate change has already become. They may have gotten into the game due mainly to federal inaction. Still, many observers predict that states, cities and counties will continue to address this challenge even if Congress and the White House agree on climate change legislation.

"Even if we get federal climate change legislation — or when we get it — that doesn't eliminate the need for states and cities to have their own strategies, their own plans," says the Union of Concerned Scientists' Burke.

Given the growing understanding that global warming is misnamed — that climate change will play out very differently around the world, with some regions heating up and others cooling down and some getting drier while others get wetter — states and localities should continue their work, suggests Hogan at the Pew Center on Global Climate Change.

"There should be a substantial role for the states," Hogan says. "The history of environmental regulation teaches us that the states do some things well, and the feds do some things well.

"Environmental goals are typically best achieved when all levels of government are doing their part."

NOTES

1. Ellen Perlman, "Mister Sustainability," *Governing*, April 2008, p. 36.

2. For background, see the following *CQ Researcher* reports: Marcia Clemmitt, "Climate Change," Jan. 27, 2006, pp. 73-96; Mary H. Cooper, "Global Warming Treaty," Jan. 26, 2001, pp. 41-64; Mary H. Cooper, "Alternative Fuels," Feb. 25, 2005, pp. 173-196, and Thomas J. Billitteri, "Reducing Your Carbon Footprint," Dec. 5, 2008, pp. 985-1008; and the following *CQ Global Researcher* reports: Colin Woodard, "Curbing Climate Change," February 2007, pp. 27-50, and Jennifer Weeks, "Carbon Trading," November 2008, pp. 295-320.

3. Michael Grunwald, "Arnold Schwarzenegger," *Time*, Oct. 6, 2008, p. 60.

4. For background, see Mary H. Cooper, "Bush and the Environment," *CQ Researcher*, Oct. 25, 2002, pp. 865-896.

5. Samantha Young, "Schwarzenegger Opens Climate Summit With Obama," The Associated Press, Nov. 19, 2008.

6. Margot Roosevelt, "California Offers to Lead on Climate Change Fight," *Los Angeles Times*, Nov. 20, 2008, p. A22.

7. Kate Galbraith, "Texas Worries About a Carbon Cap," *The New York Times Green Inc. Blog*, http://greeninc.blogs.nytimes.com/2008/12/04/texas-worries-about-a-carbon-cap/, Dec. 4, 2008.

8. Juliet Eilperin, "Ex-EPA Official Says White House Pulled Rank," *The Washington Post*, July 23, 2008, p. A4. The case is *Massachusetts v. EPA.*

9. Dirk Johnson, "Chicago Unveils Multifaceted Plan to Curb Emissions of Heat-Trapping Gases," *The New York Times*, Sept. 19, 2008, p. A13.

10. Alan Greenblatt, "Cities vs. Carbon," *CQ Weekly*, Nov. 19, 2007, p. 3474.

11. Alec MacGillis, "Palin Gives Beliefs, Demurs on Policies," *The Washington Post*, Oct. 1, 2008, p. A7.

12. Alan Zarembo and Thomas H. Maugh II, "U.N. Says It's Time to Adapt to Warming," *Los Angeles Times*, Nov. 17, 2007, p. A1.

13. Roger Pielke Jr., *et al.*, "Lifting the Taboo on Adaptation," *Nature*, Feb. 8, 2007, p. 445.

14. Christopher Swope, "Local Warming," *Governing*, December 2007, p. 25.

15. Louise Bedsworth and Ellen Hanak, "Preparing California for a Changing Climate," Public Policy Institute of California, November 2008.

16. Chris Bowman, "California Bulks Up Defenses Against Tide of Global Warming," *The Sacramento Bee*, Nov. 24, 2008, p. A1.

17. Barry G. Rabe, *Statehouse and Greenhouse* (2004), p. 20.

18. *Ibid.*, p. xiv.

19. *Ibid.*, p. 77.

20. Alan Greenblatt, "Fran Pavley: Legislative Prodigy," *Governing*, September 2002, p. 80.

21. Linda Greenhouse, "Justices Say EPA Has Power to Act on Harmful Gases," *The New York Times*, April 8, 2007, p. A1.

22. John M. Broder and Felicity Barringer, "EPA Says 17 States Can't Set Greenhouse Gas Rules for Cars," *The New York Times*, Dec. 20, 2007, p. A1.

23. John M. Broder, "Obama Affirms Climate Change Goals," *The New York Times*, Nov. 19, 2008, p. A4, www.nytimes.com/2008/11/19/us/politics/19climate.html.

24. Michael Gardner, "Emissions Plan Calls for Tougher Rules, Fees," *The San Diego Union-Tribune*, Nov. 21, 2008, p. A1.

25. Dirk Johnson, "Chicago Unveils Multifaceted Plan to Curb Emissions of Heat-Trapping Gases," *The New York Times*, Sept. 19, 2008, p. A13.

26. David Beard, "At Least 25,000 at Greenbuild Conference in Boston," *The Boston Globe Greenblog*, Nov. 19, 2008, www.boston.com/lifestyle/green/greenblog/2008/11/at_least_25000_at_greenbuild_c.html.

27. Tom Arrandale, "Carbon Goes to Market," *Governing*, September 2008, p. 26.

28. Chelsea Waugaman, "Voltage Charge," *Governing*, November 2005, p. 76.

29. Mannix Porterfield, "Manchin Wants Aggressive Renewable Energy Policy," Beckley [West Virginia] *Register-Herald*, Oct. 20, 2008.

30. Dirk Lammers, "US Wind Energy Adds 1,400 MW of Capacity," The Associated Press, Oct. 22, 2008.

BIBLIOGRAPHY

Books

Linstroth, Tommy, and Ryan Bell, *Local Action: The New Paradigm in Climate Change Policy,* **University of Vermont Press, 2007.**
An environmental consultant and a planner use case studies to illustrate how local governments are fighting global warming.

Rabe, Barry G., *Statehouse and Greenhouse: The Emerging Politics of American Climate Change Policy,* **Brookings Institution Press, 2004.**

A political scientist explains how states came to be lead actors in the fight against climate change and what their initial strategies were.

Articles

Arrandale, Tom, "Carbon Goes to Market," *Governing*, September 2008, p. 26.
Many states, especially those in the Northeast, are moving ahead with regional cap-and-trade systems to cut down on carbon emissions.

Davidson, Paul, "Utilities Shrink the Role of Coal," *USA Today*, Sept. 22, 2008, p. 4B.
Power companies are shifting away from coal-fired electricity amid increased regulatory hurdles due to global warming concerns.

Gerstenzang, James, and Janet Wilson, "White House Puts Warming Threats on Back Burner," *Los Angeles Times*, July 12, 2008, p. A1.
The Bush administration rejects the Environmental Protection Agency's conclusions about global warming threats.

Gore, Al, "The Climate for Change," *The New York Times*, Nov. 9, 2008, p. WK10.
The former vice president emphasizes the need for direct government investments in clean energy technology.

Johnson, Dirk, "Chicago Unveils Multifaceted Plan to Curb Emissions of Heat-Trapping Gases," *The New York Times*, Sept. 19, 2008, p. A13.
Following 18 months of research, Chicago Mayor Richard M. Daley releases a plan to reduce greenhouse gas emissions by 25 percent by 2020.

McGreevey, Patrick, and Margot Roosevelt, "Sprawl Measure OKd, Smog Bill Dies," *Los Angeles Times*, Oct. 1, 2008, p. B1.
The California legislature has approved a bill that rewards communities that take urban sprawl and global warming into account in their development planning.

Perlman, Ellen, "Mr. Sustainability," *Governing*, April 2008, p. 36.
The new sustainability coordinator in Fayetteville, Ark., is succeeding in his efforts to get city departments to cut down on energy usage.

Roosevelt, Margot, "California Offers to Lead on Climate Change Fight," *Los Angeles Times*, Nov. 20, 2008, p. A22.
Led by California, a dozen U.S. states have agreed with counterparts in five countries overseas to reduce greenhouse gas emissions.

Swope, Christopher, "Local Warming," *Governing*, December 2007, p. 25.
Many communities throughout the country, particularly those in the Seattle area, are starting to plan for the consequences of climate change.

Reports and Studies

"Analysis of the Lieberman-Warner Climate Security Act (S. 2191)," *American Council for Capital Formation, National Association of Manufacturers*, March 2008, www.accf.org/pdf/NAM/fullstudy031208.pdf.
Examining a congressional cap-and-trade proposal, a study underwritten by two business groups finds that it would severely undermine economic growth.

Aulisi, Andrew, *et al.*, "Climate Policy in the State Laboratory: How States Influence Federal Regulation and the Implications for Climate Change Policy in the United States," *World Resources Institute*, August 2007, pdf.wri.org/climate_policy_in_the_state_laboratory.pdf.
An environmental organization provides a report on states' aggressive climate change policies, with particular attention to those in California and the Northeast's Regional Greenhouse Gas Initiative.

Bedsworth, Louise, and Ellen Hanak, "Preparing California for a Changing Climate," *Public Policy Institute of California*, November 2008, www.ppic.org/content/pubs/report/R_1108LBR.pdf.
A leading think tank finds that California is not prepared to cope with global warming.

Pollin, Robert, *et al.*, "Green Recovery: A Program to Create Good Jobs and Start Building a Low-Carbon Economy," *Center for American Progress*, September 2008, www.americanprogress.org/issues/2008/09/pdf/green_recovery.pdf.
Economists at the University of Massachusetts find that a $100 billion initiative would both lower greenhouse gas emissions and provide an economic stimulus for the country.

For More Information

American Council for Capital Formation, 1750 K St., N.W., Suite 400, Washington, DC 20006; (202) 293-5811; www.accf.org. A business research group that promotes economic growth and "cost effective environmental policies."

Climate Change Division, U.S. Environmental Protection Agency, 1200 Pennsylvania Ave., N.W., Washington, DC 20460; (202) 343-9990; www.epa.gov/climatechange. Provides comprehensive information about science, health effects, regulations and policies concerning global warming.

Climate Communities, 1130 Connecticut Ave., N.W., Suite 300, Washington, DC 20036; (202) 261-6011; www .climatecommunities.us. A national coalition of cities and counties that lobbies and educates federal policy makers in support of local efforts to address climate change.

Competitive Enterprise Institute, 1899 L St., N.W., 12th Floor, Washington, DC 20036; (202) 340-4034; www.cei .org. A think tank and advocacy organization that promotes free enterprise and limited government.

Environmental Council of the States, 444 N. Capitol St., N.W., Suite 445, Washington, DC 20001; (202) 624-3660; www.ecos.org. The association of state environmental agencies, provides a clearinghouse of information for members and lobbies federal authorities.

Heartland Institute, 19 S. LaSalle St., Suite 903, Chicago, IL 60603; (312) 377-4000; www.globalwarmingheartland .org. A conservative think tank that presents conferences and issues publications skeptical about the role of humans in causing climate change.

ICLEI-Local Governments for Sustainability, 436 14th St., Suite 1520, Oakland, CA 94612; (510) 844-0699; www .iclei.org/us. An international organization that provides grants and technical assistance to local governments seeking to increase energy efficiency.

Mayors Climate Protection Center, U.S. Conference of Mayors, 1620 I St., N.W., Washington, DC 20006; (202) 861-6700; http://usmayors.org/climateprotection. Provides assistance to mayors attempting to reduce greenhouse gas emissions.

Pew Center on Global Climate Change, 2010 Wilson Blvd., Suite 1550, Arlington, VA 22201; (703) 516-4146; www.pewclimate.org. Supports and disseminates research related to climate change.

U.S. Climate Change Science Program, 1717 Pennsylvania Ave., N.W., Washington, DC 20006; (202) 223-6262; www .climatescience.gov. Integrates research on climate change performed by 13 federal agencies.

Reducing Your Carbon Footprint

Can Individual Actions Reduce Global Warming?

Thomas J. Billitteri

Early-bird shoppers crowd into a Best Buy store in Los Angeles at 5 a.m. on Nov. 28 for post-Thanksgiving bargains. Concern about climate change, coupled with the nation's economic woes, is causing many Americans to ratchet back on their consumption of goods and services. But many environmentalists say government must also do its part to reduce carbon emissions by enacting tough, environmentally friendly policies.

From *CQ Researcher*, December 5, 2008.

W hen Karen Larson, a mother of two in Madbury, N.H., took the "New Hampshire Carbon Challenge" she couldn't believe the results.[1]

The statewide effort to help residents reduce their environmental impact includes an online calculator to help consumers measure their "carbon footprint" — the amount of carbon dioxide (CO_2) created by their activities and consumption patterns. Carbon dioxide is the main greenhouse gas (GHG) that scientists believe leads to global warming.[2]

The calculator showed that Larson could save $700 a year and cut her carbon footprint by some 4,400 pounds by taking such actions as replacing her lightbulbs with compact fluorescents, cutting back on showers by a few minutes, putting electronics on power strips that she turned off when not in use, lowering her furnace a few degrees and getting an annual tune-up on her heating system.

"It blew my mind when I finished and it told me how much money per year I could save," Larson says. But the financial savings were only a "side benefit" to a larger objective, she adds. "The main goal was to find out how to be more earth-friendly and not use so many resources."

From voluntary actions like Larson's to emerging federal policies promoted by President-elect Barack Obama, more and more attention is shifting to the impact consumers have on the environment and how individuals can lower the amount of carbon dioxide emitted by the production, transportation, use and disposal of the goods and services they consume.

Studies show the amount of CO_2 emitted by individuals can rival that of industry and commerce. For example:

- American consumers control — directly or indirectly — about two-thirds of the nation's greenhouse-gas emissions, compared to 43 percent for consumers elsewhere.[3] Passenger cars account for 17 percent of U.S. emissions, as do residential buildings and appliances.[4]
- Transportation accounts for a third of carbon output in the United States, 80 percent of it from highway travel.[5]
- The average home creates more pollution than the average car, according to the Environmental Protection Agency (EPA).[6] If every U.S. home replaced a single incandescent lightbulb with a compact fluorescent, it would prevent the equivalent of the GHG emissions from more than 800,000 cars.[7]

"Individual actions can make a significant difference," says Bill Burtis, communications manager for Clean Air-Cool Planet, an environmental group in Portsmouth, N.H. "We're not going to be able to solve the problem without a concerted and unified effort at reaching individuals and changing behavior in residential sectors, whether it's the compact fluorescent lightbulb or changing our use of two-cycle, highly polluting gas-powered lawn equipment."

However, environmental advocates argue that while individual carbon-fighting actions are important, putting too much attention on voluntary actions by individuals can undermine efforts to pass mandatory government policies to control emissions.

"Every time an activist or politician hectors the public to voluntarily reach for a new bulb or spend extra on a Prius, ExxonMobil heaves a big sigh of relief," Mike Tidwell, director of the Chesapeake Climate Action Network, a grassroots group in Takoma Park, Md., wrote last year.[8]

"While . . . we have a moral responsibility to do what we can as individuals, we just don't have enough time to win this battle one household at a time," he wrote. "We must change our laws. I'd rather have 100,000 Americans phoning their U.S. senators twice per week demanding a prompt phase-out of inefficient automobile engines and lightbulbs than 1 million Americans willing to 'eat their vegetables' and voluntarily fill up their driveway and houses with the right stuff."

Nonetheless, experts say concern about climate change, coupled with worries about the faltering economy, are prompting more and more consumers to make environmentally friendly choices. An ABC News/Planet Green/Stanford University poll in July found that 71 percent of respondents said they were trying to reduce their carbon footprint, mainly by driving less, using less electricity and recycling. A fourth of them said saving money was their primary goal, a third said improving the environment was their chief aim and 41 percent said they were motivated by a combination of the two. (*See graph, p. 78.*)[9]

And according to a Harris Poll last spring, more than 60 percent of respondents said they had cut their home energy use to offset their carbon footprint or reduce their emissions, and 43 percent said they'd bought more energy-efficient appliances.[10]

But such findings should be viewed warily, say public opinion researchers. Soaring energy prices, reflected last summer in $4-per-gallon gasoline prices, are likely a stronger motivator for many Americans to cut their carbon appetites than concern about climate change, they say. And only about one in 10 respondents to the Harris Poll said they had ever calculated their personal or household carbon footprint, and more than one in four said they were doing nothing to reduce emissions.

"Experience suggests that we should be somewhat skeptical of claims people make about doing the 'right thing,' " Harris noted in an analysis of its poll results. While the polling company found it "encouraging" that so many Americans feel it is important to reduce their carbon emissions, U.S. energy consumption keeps rising, leading Harris to conclude that "whatever actions people are taking are probably modest ones."[11]

The trend toward larger homes, for instance, spurs greater energy use and higher personal carbon output. The average size of a new single-family home in the United States more than doubled from 1950 to 2005 — from 983 square feet to 2,434 — while the average number of occupants fell 22 percent between 1950 and 2000.[12] Between 1990 and 2006, residential carbon dioxide emissions jumped 26 percent, outpacing the 20 percent growth in population.[13]

For many consumers — even those committed to improving the environment — cutting back on carbon isn't always easy. For one thing, figuring out one's environmental footprint can be a challenge. Should a footprint consist only of carbon-based fossil fuels, such as those that run most cars and power plants, or should it also include non-carbon-based greenhouse gases like nitrous oxide emitted by fertilizers? Should it include methane gas released by landfills and from the digestive tracts of cattle? How should people measure their share of emissions stemming from the manufacture and transportation of consumer goods? And how does one best measure his share of emissions stemming from travel in airplanes or trains?

"Despite its ubiquitous appearance, there seems to be no clear definition of [carbon footprint] and there is still some confusion [over] what it actually means and measures," noted a research firm in Great Britain, where studies on climate change and consumers' environmental choices have been robust for years.[14]

Consumers also must figure out which actions actually help the environment and which only seem to. For example, in a list of 10 "green heresies," *Wired* pointed out that conventional agriculture can be more environmentally friendly than organic farming. "Organic produce *can* be good for the climate, but not if it's grown in energy-dependent hothouses and travels long distances to get to your fridge," the magazine noted.[15]

And of course, the geographic realities of American life — homes and jobs separated by miles — can thwart the good intentions of even the most environmentally conscious consumer.

Big Metro Areas Have Smaller Carbon Footprints

Big-city areas like Los Angeles emit less carbon per capita than smaller areas like Knoxville, Tenn., in large part because urban areas have high-density development patterns or depend on low-polluting mass transit.

Highest and Lowest Carbon Emissions in Metro Areas

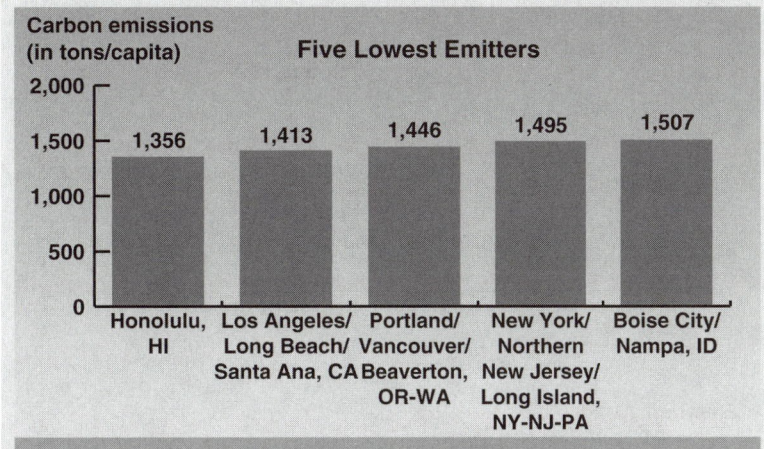

Carbon emissions (in tons/capita) — **Five Lowest Emitters**

Honolulu, HI	Los Angeles/ Long Beach/ Santa Ana, CA	Portland/ Vancouver/ Beaverton, OR-WA	New York/ Northern New Jersey/ Long Island, NY-NJ-PA	Boise City/ Nampa, ID
1,356	1,413	1,446	1,495	1,507

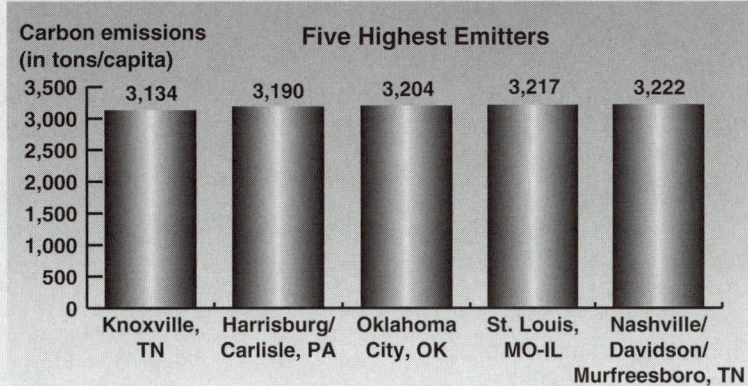

Carbon emissions (in tons/capita) — **Five Highest Emitters**

Knoxville, TN	Harrisburg/ Carlisle, PA	Oklahoma City, OK	St. Louis, MO-IL	Nashville/ Davidson/ Murfreesboro, TN
3,134	3,190	3,204	3,217	3,222

Source: "Shrinking the Carbon Footprint of Metropolitan America," Brookings Institution, May 2008

"When we don't live close to where we work, there's not much choice in the matter," says Duane T. Wegener, a professor of psychological sciences at Purdue University who studies the social aspects of energy policy. The ways most cities are built "tie us into a particular level of energy use, and there's not a lot of control over it."

As consumers and policy makers continue to seek ways to reduce harmful, globe-warming pollutants, here are some of the questions they are asking:

Home Heating and Cooling Emit Most Carbon

Space heating and cooling alone account for more than a third of all the energy used in residential buildings in the United States and more than 450 million metric tons of carbon dioxide.

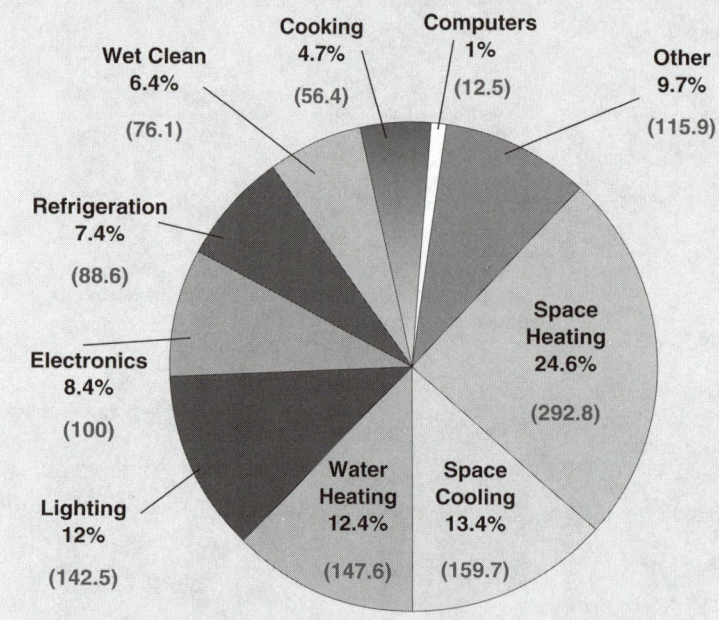

Carbon Dioxide Emissions From Residential Energy Use
(by percentage and in million metric tons)

Wet Clean 6.4% (76.1)
Cooking 4.7% (56.4)
Computers 1% (12.5)
Other 9.7% (115.9)
Refrigeration 7.4% (88.6)
Electronics 8.4% (100)
Lighting 12% (142.5)
Water Heating 12.4% (147.6)
Space Cooling 13.4% (159.7)
Space Heating 24.6% (292.8)

Source: "Buildings Energy Data Book," U.S. Department of Energy, November 2008

Are measures of individual carbon emissions valid?

Measuring one's carbon footprint is both art and science.

A growing number of agencies and organizations — from the federal Environmental Protection Agency to the nonprofit Nature Conservancy to the Berkeley Institute of the Environment at the University of California — offer online calculators intended to help people measure their greenhouse-gas emissions.

The calculators gauge the environmental impact of various activities, from heating and lighting a home to flying across the country, and guide consumers on how to reduce their carbon output. But the calculators vary widely in their detail and conclusions.

Air travel, a significant emission source, is a case in point. Calculating a per-passenger carbon footprint is a highly complex task that must take into account such factors as aircraft type, weather conditions, the number of landings and takeoffs along a given route and whether an aircraft flies with a full or partial load.

In June the Montreal-based United Nations International Civil Aviation Organization (ICAO) introduced a carbon calculator that "responds to the wish of many travelers for a reliable and authoritative method to estimate the carbon footprint of a flight," said Robert Kobeh González, president of the ICAO Council.[16]

But the calculator can produce misleading data, according to an official of a company that produces fuel data and supplied the aircraft-performance model used for the ICAO's estimates of airline emissions.

"Producing a single number is crude," Dimitri Simos, a director at Lissys Limited, said. "If you go from Heathrow [airport in London] to Athens, ICAO gives 217 kilograms [478 pounds] of CO_2 [per person]. That hides huge variations. Fly in a full [Boeing] B767 and it's nearer to 160 kg [352 pounds] per person, or in a half-empty [Airbus] A340 it's more like 360 kg [793 pounds]."[17]

While carbon calculators help make people more aware of their individual environmental impact, Daniel Kammen, a professor in the energy and resources group at UC Berkeley, told the *Chicago Tribune* that "the downside is that the methodology is being worked on as we speak."[18]

Still, many see the calculators as useful. Elise L. Amel, director of environmental studies and associate professor of industrial and organizational psychology at the University of St. Thomas in Minneapolis, says that while most carbon calculators are "not very fine-grained," they still serve a valuable purpose.

"Usually the options for somebody's response [to a calculator's questions] don't necessarily perfectly match any one individual situation," she says. Most calculators "use general categories" and give a "rough estimate . . . so it's no wonder they all give you a little something different. But I don't think they should be used to necessarily diagnose each minute activity that you should adjust. They're just to get people aware that, 'Wow, we're using resources at a rate that's really hard to replace.'"

Making people think about their carbon footprint — and doing something about it — is the idea behind the New Hampshire Carbon Challenge and its calculator.[19]

The challenge, which has been online for a year, enables New England residents to measure their carbon footprints, set goals for reducing their emissions and pledge action. Households that take the challenge can be linked to other households through organizations such as churches, schools, civic group and businesses to show the collective action of residents' individual efforts.

So far, about 1,000 households in New Hampshire and Massachusetts have taken the challenge, and thousands more have used the calculator and other Web-based tools developed by the challenge, says Denise Blaha, the organization's codirector. People who have taken the challenge have reduced their home and vehicle energy use by an average of 17 percent, saving roughly $850 annually in fuel and electricity costs, she says. More than 5 million pounds of CO_2 have been pledged for reduction as a result of the challenge, with an energy cost saving of $700,000, she says.

"Households have really been the overlooked sector," Blaha says. "Most of our actions are very, very concrete, real-world and simple to make: changing lightbulbs, putting electronic devices on power strips and turning down your thermostat."

Still, while swapping energy-hogging lightbulbs for miserly compact fluorescents may be simple, some efforts at environmental responsibility can be maddeningly complex.

For example, some consumers try to factor in "food miles" — the distance food travels from farm to table — into their carbon-footprint calculations. Conventional wisdom says food travels an average of 1,500 miles from

farm to plate, Jane Black, a *Washington Post* food writer, noted in the online journal *Slate*.[20] But, she wrote, the ubiquitous figure is based on a university study of how far 33 fruits and vegetables grown in the United States traveled to a Chicago produce market. That figure, though it perhaps raises consumers' awareness of the environmental issues involved in food choices, oversimplifies the complex and global nature of the food industry, Black argued.

"If we all think in food miles, the answer is obvious: Buy local. But new studies show that in some cases it can actually be more environmentally responsible to produce food far from home."

Black cited a 2006 report from Lincoln University in New Zealand, which concluded that it was four times more energy efficient for people in London to purchase New Zealand lamb, which feeds on grass, than grain-fed lamb from England.

She also noted that Tesco, the British grocery giant, has begun adding carbon labels to its products. The labels — which reveal how much carbon was emitted by an item's production, transportation and consumption — are now on an initial 20 products, including orange juice and detergent.[21]

But, Black wrote, "Like food miles, these new numbers raise as many questions as they answer."

Should government do more to encourage individuals to reduce their carbon footprints?

While individuals can do much to reduce their carbon consumption and conserve precious resources, environmental advocates say policy makers should provide more incentives to further those efforts.

"Government needs to take a holistic approach to the whole carbon footprint issue," says Eric Carlson, founder and president of Carbonfund.org, a nonprofit organization in Silver Spring, Md., that sells "carbon offsets" — certificates that consumers and businesses can purchase voluntarily to help compensate for their own carbon footprints. The certificates are used to subsidize "green" efforts such as renewable-energy, reforestation and energy-efficiency projects.

Carlson says the federal government has a number of piecemeal consumer programs that provide incentives for greater energy efficiency, such as tax credits for home insulation and the purchase of hybrid cars.

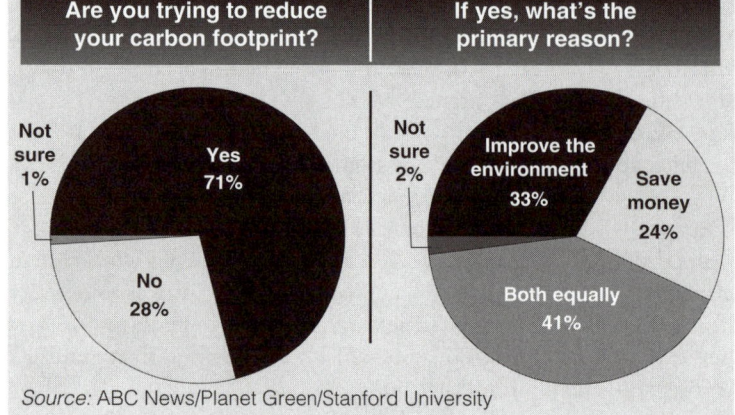

Americans Seeking to Reduce Footprint

More than 70 percent of Americans say they are trying to reduce their carbon footprints. Of those, a third say they want to improve the environment, while a quarter are seeking to save money.

Are you trying to reduce your carbon footprint?

Not sure 1%
Yes 71%
No 28%

If yes, what's the primary reason?

Not sure 2%
Improve the environment 33%
Save money 24%
Both equally 41%

Source: ABC News/Planet Green/Stanford University

But he says Washington should adopt much broader policies aimed at encouraging business and consumers to transition from carbon-emitting energy to green power.

He suggests that the government adopt a "cap-and-trade" climate policy that would set limits on how much carbon dioxide energy producers, utilities or manufacturers could emit. (*See "Current Situation," p. 88.*) The European Union and a handful of other countries have adopted similar carbon-trading systems since 2005.[22] Companies that emit less than allowable amounts could sell their excess "rights to pollute" to others. In some versions of the scheme the rights are auctioned to companies, and the auction revenue is returned to taxpayers or used for renewable-energy development.

Legislation sponsored by Sens. Joseph I. Lieberman, I-Conn., and John W. Warner, R-Va., featured a cap-and-trade system, but the Senate rejected it earlier this year. President-elect Obama favors such a system.

Some have argued that cap-and-trade plans could raise energy costs, squeeze consumers and hurt the economy more than help the environment. Cap-and-trade bills are "nothing short of government re-engineering of the American economy," wrote Ben Lieberman, a policy analyst at the conservative Heritage Foundation.[23]

Yet others say the approach would be good for the environment, partly because it would tend to make goods and services created and transported in carbon-intensive ways more expensive and lower the relative price of items produced in less carbon-intensive ways. Producers and consumers would have incentives to make more environmentally friendly choices.

Including the cost of carbon emissions in the price of goods and services would give consumers an idea of the carbon intensity of the items they buy and motivate them to make greener choices, says Eric Haxthausen, director of U.S. climate change policy for the Nature Conservancy.

He gives the example of buying fruit in a grocery store. "There's a lot of emphasis on buying local," he says. "It's tricky, but the beauty of the cap-and-trade approach is that it's all worked out through the pricing system. You don't have to calculate whether this fruit was shipped on an ocean-going vessel" and therefore had a bigger carbon footprint to reach the grocery shelf than fruit grown closer to home. The price "would distinguish between a high and low" footprint.

Consumers need more information about the environmental consequences of the goods and services they use, according to Rep. Brian Baird, D-Wash., chairman of the House Subcommittee on Research and Science Education. For instance, he told the panel at a hearing last year, households consume more than a third of the energy used in the United States each year, 60 percent of which is used at home. Yet consumers typically lack the information they need to factor energy use into purchases and behaviors, he continued, and both government and industry have "fallen far short in providing the needed information to the public in a way that will result in behavior changes."[24]

At the hearing — on how the social sciences can help solve the nation's energy problems — John A. "Skip" Laitner, senior economist for technology policy at the American Council for an Energy-Efficient Economy, said more funding was needed "to expand our understanding of the social dynamics of energy consumption, energy conservation and energy efficiency." (*See sidebar, p. 84.*) Funding for non-economic social-science research on energy consumption has fallen sharply since the 1980s, he said.[25]

Advocates also say part of the answer to shrinking individual environmental footprints is for government authorities, including those on the state level, to adopt stronger energy-efficiency building standards for such things as thermal insulation and heating and cooling systems. While such codes are "unsexy," Carlson says, they are highly effective in cutting energy consumption and reducing carbon emissions.

Many environmental advocates also call for a wider array of subsidies and tax incentives for energy-efficient appliances and alternative-energy equipment.

California is widely viewed as one the states most determined to promote energy efficiency and clean-energy technology. For example, under a 10-year "Go Solar California" rebate program, the state plans to inject more than $3 billion into financial incentives for Californians to adopt solar energy. The money, which comes from utility bills, is expected to pay for about 3,000 megawatts of new solar energy.[26]

But the program has sparked controversy in some quarters, as the *San Francisco Chronicle* noted last summer. The rebates are aimed at cutting solar prices over time by creating a big and competitive solar industry in the state, the newspaper said, but "solar remains far more expensive than many other forms of power generation."

Moreover, a consumer watchdog group complained that wealthy companies or homeowners have received too many of the rebates, the *Chronicle* reported. Mark Toney, executive director of The Utility Reform Network, said "subsidies should go to the most needy, not the most wealthy."[27]

A spokesman for the California Public Utilities Commission said in mid-November that a program to direct some solar-rebate money to low-income housing was in "the talking stage."

Efforts Focus on Home Energy Use

Nearly two-thirds of Americans are reducing home energy usage, including 43 percent who have bought more energy-efficient appliances, according to a recent survey. Nevertheless, more than a quarter are doing nothing to offset their carbon footprints.

Which of the following have you done in an attempt to offset your carbon footprint or reduce your emissions?

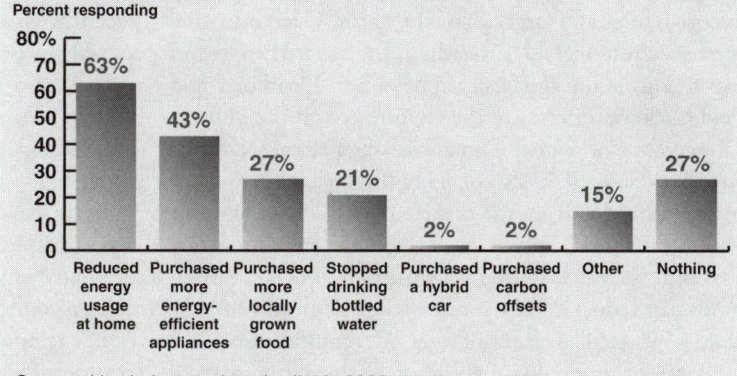

Percent responding

Reduced energy usage at home	Purchased more energy-efficient appliances	Purchased more locally grown food	Stopped drinking bottled water	Purchased a hybrid car	Purchased carbon offsets	Other	Nothing
63%	43%	27%	21%	2%	2%	15%	27%

Source: Harris Interactive, April 18, 2008

Can individual action significantly reduce global climate change?

In September the nonprofit Pew Center on Global Climate Change and the Alcoa aluminum company foundation kicked off a partnership aimed at encouraging the company's U.S. employees and their local communities to reduce their energy consumption and shrink their carbon footprints.

Pew and Alcoa initially are rolling out the program at nine of the company's 120 U.S. locations, with plans to expand it. The Make an Impact program, modeled after a similar Alcoa effort in Australia, includes an interactive Web site that offers a carbon calculator and other tools to help employees cut their energy bills and emissions.

Concern about energy efficiency and climate change "is a huge focus inside our business, and this is about translating that into a tool that can be used to increase awareness and actions on climate change" among Alcoa's employees and their communities, says Libby Archell, director of communications for the Alcoa Foundation.

Katie Mandes, vice president of communications at the Pew center, says efforts focused on individuals can make a significant difference in curbing greenhouse-gas emissions. "Are individuals going to be able to solve this problem? No," she says. "But is there a role for individuals? Yes. . . . It's got to be an across-the-board change."

Individuals and households can play a larger role in cutting energy use and emissions than many consumers realize. "U.S. households account for about 38 percent of national carbon emissions through their direct actions, a level of emissions greater than that of any entire country except China and larger than the entire U.S. industrial sector," wrote Gerald T. Gardner, professor emeritus of psychology at the University of Michigan-Dearborn, and Paul C. Stern, director of the Committee on the Human Dimensions of Global Climate Change at the National Research Council.[28] "By changing their selection and use of household and motor-vehicle technologies without waiting for new technologies to appear, making major economic sacrifices or losing a sense of well-being, households can reduce energy consumption by almost 30 percent — about 11 percent of total U.S. consumption."

A study by graduate students at the University of Michigan's School of Natural Resources and Environment a decade ago underscored how cost-effective changes in construction methods and other choices can reduce residential energy consumption.

A conventionally built 2,450-square-foot home in Ann Arbor, Mich., had a global-warming potential equal to 1,013 metric tons of CO_2 over its life span — from construction to use and, ultimately, to demolition — with 92 percent of that occurring during the home's use phase. An energy-efficient home, meanwhile, had a global-warming potential of only 374 metric tons of CO_2 — 67 percent of it occurring in the home's use phase. And although the energy-efficient home cost about 10 percent more than the conventional home, over its lifespan the more efficient home wound up costing about the same as the less efficient one.[29]

And at today's energy prices, the life-cycle costs are substantially lower for the efficient house, according to Gregory Keoleian, codirector of the Center for Sustainable Systems at the University of Michigan.

Refrigeration accounts for 8 percent of average U.S. residential energy consumption.[30] A separate study by the center found that households can save significant costs and energy by replacing refrigerators made before 1995.

Though many consumers still use old energy-hungry appliances, many others own units carrying the government's "Energy Star" label denoting energy efficiency. Last year alone, the joint program between the Environmental Protection Agency and Energy Department helped Americans save enough energy to avoid greenhouse-gas emissions equivalent to the output of 27 million cars while saving $16 billion on utilities.[31]

Even so, the program has drawn some criticism recently. *Consumer Reports* magazine in October questioned the Energy Star label on several refrigerator models and said the program's qualifying standards are lax and its testing procedures dated. Moreover, the article pointed out, the program allows companies to test their own products, with the government relying on manufacturers to evaluate appliances made by competitors and to report suspicious claims about energy use.[32]

Many environmentalists say that while individual carbon-reducing actions, including purchasing energy-efficient appliances, are important in fighting GHG emissions, government action is crucial.

"We need fundamental change and strong policy to drive those changes," says Joe Loper, vice president of policy and research at the Alliance to Save Energy, an advocacy group in Washington. "If I take all those actions and reduce my footprint and no one else does it, it's not going to matter."

Tidwell, of the Chesapeake Climate Action Network, says living a low-carbon lifestyle is good, but "if that becomes the dominant core of our response to climate change, then we fail. We might as well do nothing.

"Instead of wagging our finger at Aunt Betty and telling her she needs to change all her lightbulbs, what we need to do is pass laws in this country so the next time Aunt Betty goes to buy lightbulbs, there are only energy-efficient lightbulbs. You do that with . . . statutory changes that send the right clean-energy market signals to the economy."

In fact, Congress and the Bush administration did take a step in that direction last year with passage of an energy bill that, among other things, requires that traditional incandescent lightbulbs be phased out in favor of more-efficient ones by 2020.[33] But Tidwell asks, "Why wait 12 years?"

He compares the effort to fight GHG emissions to the 1960s-era battle for civil rights, noting that the government didn't rely on voluntary action to curb racial discrimination but instead banned it outright. "When it comes to climate change, we have to start thinking of this as the moral and economic immediate crisis that it is," he says. With that in mind, he adds, "you quickly begin to realize that we have to set strict energy standards that are fair but mandatory."

"We don't have time to green our neighborhoods one house at a time. Nature has chosen its own deadline."

BACKGROUND

Environmental Awakening

Concern about society's impact on the environment has deep historical roots. In ancient Rome, garbage, sewage and the detritus of the metal-working and tanning industries polluted the water and air, turning the fetid atmosphere into what the Romans sometimes called *gravioris caeli* — "heavy heaven."[34]

In the 18th and 19th centuries, economists and political philosophers such as John Stuart Mill worried about the impact of population growth, industrialization and urbanization on food supplies, resources and natural beauty.

In 20th-century America, environmentalism and conservationism grew deep roots, nurtured by the preservation of lands for parks and monuments under Presidents Theodore Roosevelt (1901-1909) and William Howard Taft (1909-1913) and the formation of the Civilian Conservation Corps under President Franklin D. Roosevelt (1933-1945).[35] The Corps put hundreds of thousands of unemployed young adults, mostly men, to work planting trees, developing lakes and ponds, building logging roads, improving campgrounds and performing other tasks.

In the early 1960s, Rachel Carson, an environmental writer and marine biologist with the U.S. Fish and Wildlife Service, became what many regard as the chief catalyst of the modern environmental movement with publication of her 1962 book *Silent Spring*, which described the threats that the pesticide DDT posed to the environment and food chain. In an earlier work, *The Sea Around Us*, published in 1951, she presciently warned of a "startling alteration of climate" and "evidence that the top of the world is growing warmer."[36]

Other environmental milestones in the second half of the 20th century reinforced the idea that choices made not only by government and industry but also by individuals could have a profound influence on climate change, the sustainability of natural resources and, ultimately, the future of the human race. On the first Earth Day, April 22, 1970, millions of Americans participated in rallies and forums that helped thrust environmental concerns onto the political stage.

"It was on that day that Americans made it clear that they understood and were deeply concerned over the deterioration of our environment and the mindless dissipation of our resources," Earth Day's founder, the late Sen. Gaylord Nelson, D-Wis., wrote on the event's 10th anniversary. "That day left a permanent impact on the politics of America."[37]

Throughout the 1970s, a tide of environmental legislation flowed from Washington, including the Clean Air Act of 1970, Endangered Species Act of 1973 and Clean Water Act of 1977. Also, the Environmental Protection Agency was formed in the early 1970s under the Republican administration of President Richard M. Nixon.

But environmentalism was not always as durable as the millions who gathered on Earth Day 1970 had hoped. In the 1980s, for example, the Reagan administration drew heavy criticism for the actions of Interior Secretary James G. Watt and EPA Administrator Anne Gorsuch, both of whom resigned under fire.

Still, the 1980s saw a growing awareness of the consequences of both individual and industrial behavior on the global climate. For example, the Montreal Protocol, an international treaty that the Reagan administration and scores of other governments signed, called for the elimination of ozone-depleting chemicals called chlorofluorocarbons, found in such items as air conditioners and consumer aerosol products.

But getting a handle on carbon emissions has been a much tougher task. Richard A. Benedick, the Reagan administration's chief representative in the Montreal Protocol talks, noted in *The New York Times* in 2005 that tackling carbon dioxide emissions was different than phasing out chlorofluorocarbons, which the newspaper noted were produced by only a small number of companies in a few countries.[38]

"Carbon dioxide is generated by activities as varied as surfing the Web, driving a car, burning wood or flying to Montreal," *Times* environmental reporter Andrew C. Revkin pointed out. "Its production is woven into the fabric of an industrial society, and, for now, economic growth is inconceivable without it."[39]

'Planetary Emergency'

By the late 1990s and early 2000s the scientific community widely agreed that carbon dioxide and other greenhouse gases spelled a global climate catastrophe in the making. But many consumers and policy makers seemed to ignore warnings of catastrophic climate change. Domestic energy use continued to soar at the turn of the 21st century, gas-gulping sport-utility vehicles crowded the highways and conservative pundits belittled the notion that human activity was altering the climate in perilous ways.

In 2001 the Bush administration backed away from the Kyoto Protocol, an international treaty setting targets for industrialized nations to reduce their greenhouse-gas emissions, which the Clinton administration signed but never sent to the Senate for ratification. President George W. Bush complained that the treaty would damage the U.S. economy and that it didn't require developing countries to cut emissions.[40]

Still, other voices have persisted in raising alarms about climate change, none so urgently as former Vice President Al Gore. In a celebrated 2006 documentary film and book — *An Inconvenient Truth* — Gore warned of global peril stemming from rising greenhouse-gas emissions. "Not only does human-caused global warming exist," Gore wrote, "but it is also growing more and more dangerous, and at a pace that has now made it a planetary emergency."[41]

While industry and governments are key targets of Gore's message, individual Americans increasingly are hearing it too — sometimes from unlikely sources, including religious leaders. The Vatican announced this year that "polluting the environment" was among seven new sins requiring repentance.[42] And in March, 44 Southern Baptist leaders, including the current president of the conservative Southern Baptist Convention and two past presidents, signed a declaration supporting stronger action on climate change.[43] The year before, the convention had questioned the notion that humans are mainly responsibile for global warming.

While individual action is widely viewed as important to protecting the environment, many still question how much impact consumers can have on GHG emissions through their daily choices. Research offers competing views.

In a 2007 study provocatively titled "The Carbon Cost of Christmas," European researchers concluded that in the United Kingdom total consumption and spending on food, travel, lighting and gifts over three days of festivities — Christmas Eve, Christmas Day and the traditional U.K. holiday of Boxing Day — could result in as much as 650 kilograms [1,433 pounds] of CO_2 emissions per person — 5.5 percent of Britons' total annual carbon footprint and equivalent to the weight of 1,000 Christmas puddings.[44]

The researchers said consumers could cut their carbon emissions by more than 60 percent by taking such steps as cutting out unwanted gifts, buying "low-carbon" presents such as recycled wine glasses, reusing Christmas cards or using the phone or e-mail to send greetings, composting vegetable peelings when cooking Christmas dinner and reducing holiday lighting.

"In this time of seasonal goodwill, we should all spare a thought for the planet," they wrote.

But another study by researchers at the Massachusetts Institute of Technology pointed to "very significant limits" that voluntary lifestyle choices can have on energy use and carbon emissions. The researchers — MIT students under the direction of Timothy Gutowski, a professor of mechanical engineering — studied 18 different lifestyles ranging from that of a Buddhist monk, a retiree and a 5-year-old to a coma patient, pro golfer and investment banker. They found that even the most constrained lifestyle has an environmental impact far larger than the global average and that none of the lifestyles — including the most modest, that of a homeless person — ever resulted in CO_2 emissions below 8.5 metric tons annually, according to Gutowski.[45]

"The takeaway [from the study] is that we have a very energy-intensive system" that limits how much voluntary actions by individuals can affect climate change, Gutowski says. Still, he says, "I wouldn't want to say people shouldn't take voluntary action. It's a complicated path. Groups may take voluntary action, government agencies notice and then take actions that change the system."

Even so, individuals can sometimes innocently make matters worse by trying to be "green." An example is

CHRONOLOGY

1890-1960 *Conservation movement emerges, nurtured by government action, including passage of Air Quality Act in 1967.*

1970s *Under pressure from environmentalists, Congress enacts landmark anti-pollution measures.*

1970 Millions gather for Earth Day on April 22. . . . Congress establishes Environmental Protection Agency and expands Clean Air Act.

1972 Government bans DDT.

1973 Endangered Species Act enacted.

1974 Safe Drinking Water Act enacted.

1978 New York State Department of Health declares public health emergency at Love Canal hazardous waste landfill site.

1979 Accident at Three Mile Island in Pennsylvania, the most serious in the history of U.S. commercial nuclear power plants, leads the Nuclear Regulatory Commission to tighten oversight.

1980s-1990s *Concern about greenhouse gas (GHG) emissions and climate change grows worldwide.*

1983 Interior Secretary James Watt and EPA chief Anne Gorsuch resign amid environmentalists' criticism.

1987 Twenty-four nations initially sign Montreal Protocol, pledging to phase out ozone-depleting chemicals; 169 other countries eventually sign on.

1988 NASA scientist James Hansen warns Congress that global warming is occurring.

1989 Oil tanker *Exxon Valdez* runs aground, contaminating more than 1,000 miles of Alaskan coastline and killing hundreds of thousands of birds and other wildlife in the biggest U.S. oil spill in history.

1992 First international pledge to reduce greenhouse-gas emissions emerges from Earth Summit in Rio de Janeiro, Brazil.

1997 Kyoto Protocol limiting GHG emissions is approved, but wealthy nations are allowed to meet obligations by purchasing "offset" projects in developing countries. United States signs but does not ratify the agreement.

1998 U.S. Green Building Council starts Leadership in Energy and Environmental Design (LEED) program to rate energy-efficient buildings.

2000-Present *Bush administration relaxes strict environmental controls. President-elect Barack Obama pledges to make environmental issues a central focus.*

2001 President George W. Bush reneges on campaign pledge and rejects controls on greenhouse emissions.

2005 Kyoto Protocol takes effect. . . . Members of European Union begin trading carbon credits.

2006 "An Inconvenient Truth," a documentary film featuring former Vice President Al Gore, focuses national attention on global warming.

2007 Federal Trade Commission begins review of environmental marketing guidelines to include carbon offsets, renewable energy certificates and other so-called green products.

2008 British supermarket giant Tesco begins to print "green scores" on some items to show their environmental impact. . . . Senate rejects global warming bill that features a cap-and-trade system on greenhouse gas emissions. . . . Alcoa Aluminum Co. and Pew Center on Global Climate Change form partnership to help Alcoa employees and their communities reduce their carbon footprints. . . . President-elect Barack Obama says his presidency will "mark a new chapter in America's leadership on climate change." He pledges to develop a two-year economic-stimulus plan to save or create 2.5 million jobs, including "green" jobs in alternative energy and environmental technology.

Using Psychology to Influence Consumers' Behavior

Peer pressure proves potent.

Policy makers and environmentalists aren't the only ones trying to figure out how to coax consumers to shrink their carbon appetites. So too are psychologists.

Last summer the American Psychological Association formed a task force to address the role that psychology can play in helping individuals embrace environmentally sustainable practices and cope with the consequences of climate change.

"There hasn't been as much focus on the psychological impacts [of climate change], and we have reason to believe they'll be very serious," says task force member Susan Clayton, a professor of psychology and chair of environmental studies at the College of Wooster in Ohio.

If people have less access to "green, natural, healthy settings," she says, the result could be increased stress and aggression and diminished social interaction. Climate change also could lead to increased competition for dwindling resources such as food and water, sparking social conflict, she says.

When it comes to influencing individual behavior, Clayton says it is "more effective to change the structure of the situation" than trying to change people's minds through preaching.

That might mean providing recycling bins to households, not simply lecturing them on the merits of recycling. Letting consumers know how many of their neighbors are replacing their lightbulbs with compact fluorescents also can be effective, she says. "Social norms matter a lot. . . . Peer pressure never goes away" as an effective catalyst for influencing behavior, she says.

And, Clayton adds, providing the means for feedback on individual behavior — say, putting separate electric meters in apartment houses so tenants can monitor their individual power usage — can give consumers an incentive to conserve.

"Psychologists are increasingly becoming involved in helping alleviate environmental problems," according to Douglas Vakoch, an associate professor in the department of clinical psychology at the California Institute of Integral Studies in San Francisco.

"Most people recognize [that] we face a severe environmental crisis, but it's hard to deal with that head-on because many people feel helpless to do anything about it. . . . Psychologists are very experienced in dealing with denial and in helping to frame messages in ways that people can hear the bad news without being paralyzed by it."

Vakoch says policy experts and government leaders can learn from the psychology field. "The most important lesson . . . is that there is no 'one size fits all' solution to environmental problems," he says. "To create effective public policies, leaders need to recognize that different people are willing to adopt

consumers' efforts to recycle old computers and other electronic items, which contain a toxic brew of chemicals, heavy metals and plastics such as mercury, lead and polyvinyl chloride.

In November the CBS News program "60 Minutes" followed recycled computer parts from Denver to Guiyu, China, which reporter Scott Pelley described as "one of the most toxic places on Earth . . . a town where the blood of the children is laced with lead." In Guiyu, computer parts are stripped, melted down and recycled by impoverished Chinese risking their health and lives for $8 a day.[46]

"This is really the dirty, little secret of the electronic age," said Jim Puckett, founder of the Seattle-based Basel Action Network, a watchdog group named for a treaty intended to keep wealthy nations from exporting toxic waste to poor countries.[47]

One way to keep harmful products from adding toxins to the environment is to produce them in an environmentally conscious way in the first place. Forrester Research Inc. found in a survey of 5,000 U.S. adults that 12 percent were willing to pay more for electronics that consume less energy or are made by an environmentally friendly manufacturer.[48]

In addition, computer manufacturers have been creating products that are more energy efficient than past models, companies are creating software to help older computers use less energy and some are making new models out of recycled materials, *The Wall Street Journal* reported.[49]

Katharine Kaplan, a product manager in the Energy Star program, said computer makers have sought to improve energy efficiency for years and that "the newer focus has been on toxins and recycling."[50]

more environmentally sound behaviors for different reasons. What's compelling for one person will fail for another."

Psychological research has helped shed light on individuals' understanding of environmental issues and their willingness to make changes in their personal consumption habits.

For example, Stanford University psychologist Jon Krosnick found that as people's knowledge about climate change grew, the more concerned about it they became, though political affiliation and trust in science were also important factors.

The link between knowledge about climate change and concern about it "was especially true for respondents who described themselves as Democrats and those who said they trusted scientists," Krosnick told the annual convention of the American Psychological Association in August. "But for Republicans and those who had little trust in scientists, more knowledge did not mean there was more concern."[1]

In another study, Robert B. Cialdini, a professor of psychology and marketing at Arizona State University, found that a small change in message cards asking guests at an upscale Phoenix hotel to reuse their towels had huge potential environmental consequences.

One card exhorted residents to "Help Save the Environment" and was followed by information stressing respect for nature, Cialdini told a House subcommittee last year.[2] Another card stated "Help Save Resources for Future Generations," followed by information stressing the importance of saving energy for the future. A third card asked guests to "Partner With Us to Help Save the Environment," followed by information urging them to cooperate with the hotel in preservation efforts. A fourth card, Cialdini noted, said "Join Your Fellow Citizens in Helping to Save the Environment," followed by information that the majority of hotel guests reuse their towels when asked.

The outcome was striking, he said. Compared with the first three messages, the final one — based on a "social norm," or the perception of what most others were doing — increased the reuse of towels by an average of 34 percent, Cialdini said.

Not everyone in the psychological field agrees that trying to change consumer habits can ever do enough to make a significant difference in nationwide or worldwide carbon emissions or climate change. But many believe the effort is worthwhile.

"There's a huge debate going on among psychologists over whether it's just futile to even bother talking about individual behavior" or whether action by policy makers and corporations is the key to solving the nation's environmental problems, says Elise L. Amel, director of environmental studies and associate professor of industrial and organizational psychology at the University of St. Thomas in Minneapolis.

"I think it's got to be both. This is such a crucial problem coming so quickly that we can't leave any stone unturned."

---

[1] "Climate Change, Global Warming, Among Environmental Concerns Discussed at Psychology Meeting," press release, American Psychological Association, Aug. 15, 2008.

[2] Robert B. Cialdini, testimony to the Subcommittee on Research and Science Education, House Committee on Science and Technology, Sept. 25, 2007.

But corporate efforts to make their products and services green — and to induce consumers to sign on to those efforts — can be challenging. For instance, in Britain, critics say carbon labels on retail goods often confuse consumers or give them information they don't want.[51]

Forum for the Future, a London think tank, expressed concern this year about giving consumers information without proper context. "Only a handful of our focus group participants associated carbon emissions [and climate change] with what they buy in the shops," the group stated in a report. "The majority knew that carbon emissions are linked with cars, airplanes and factories. They made that connection because they can 'see' the emissions, which makes them easy to interpret as being 'bad for the environment.' However, the link between products and climate change was less intuitive to them."[52]

In the United States, most companies are willing to embrace only "incremental change" on carbon labeling, Joel Makower, a sustainability consultant and cofounder and executive editor of Greener World Media Inc., in Oakland, Calif., told *The Christian Science Monitor.*[53]

Wal-Mart, the world's biggest retailer, kicked off a broad sustainability strategy in 2005 aimed at reducing the company's environmental impact. But Matt Kisler, the company's senior vice president of sustainability, told *The Monitor* that he has doubts about current carbon-labeling methodologies and customers' ability to link carbon with consumer goods. "I'm not sure the consumer will ever make a purchase based on the carbon footprint, especially the mass consumer," he told the newspaper.[54]

Green goods can indeed be a tough sell, but some analysts say a more concerted effort by business is

How to Shrink Your Carbon Footprint

Driving habits and home energy use are key factors.

Here are several ways environmentalists, behaviorists and climate scientists say individual consumers can shrink their own carbon footprints:

Alter driving habits. Use of private motor vehicles accounted for more than 38 percent of total U.S. energy use in 2005, according to calculations by Gerald T. Gardner, professor emeritus of psychology at the University of Michigan-Dearborn, and Paul C. Stern, director of the Committee on the Human Dimensions of Global Climate Change at the National Research Council.[1]

Carpooling to work with another person can potentially save as much as 4.2 percent of individual and household energy consumption, they estimated. Other savings can come from avoiding sudden accelerations and stops (up to 3.2 percent); combining errand trips to a half of current mileage (up to 2.7 percent); cutting speeds from 70 to 60 miles per hour (up to 2.4 percent) and getting frequent tune-ups (3.9 percent).

Buying a car that gets an average of 30.7 miles per gallon rather than 20 can save an estimated 13.5 percent of household energy use, the authors estimated.

Reduce home energy consumption. Home space heating accounts for 34 percent of a typical homeowner's utility bill, according to the U.S. Department of Energy. Appliances and lighting account for the same proportion, followed by water heating (13 percent), electricity for air conditioning (11 percent) and refrigeration (8 percent).[2]

Residential buildings not only soak up money for utilities but also emit carbon dioxide. Heating accounts for 25 percent of CO_2 emissions, according to the Energy Department, followed by cooling (13.4 percent), water heating (12.4 percent), lighting (12 percent) and electronics, including color televisions (8.4 percent). Refrigerators and freezers account for more than 7 percent or residential carbon emissions.[3]

Gardner and Stern estimated that replacing 85 percent of all incandescent bulbs with compact fluorescents of equal brightness would reduce total individual and household energy consumption in the United States by 4 percent. Turning down the heat from 72 to 68 degrees during the day and to 65 degrees at night, and turning up the air conditioning from 73 to 78 degrees, would save 3.4 percent of energy consumption, they estimated.[4]

Many other steps can reduce a consumer's energy consumption — and carbon footprint — as well. For example, a home-energy checklist assembled by the American Council for an Energy-Efficient Economy suggests turning down the water-heater temperature to 120 degrees, cleaning or replacing furnace and air-conditioner filters, caulking leaky windows, improving attic and wall insulation and replacing inefficient appliances, among other tips.[5]

Downsize and scale back on consumption. Bigger homes typically use more energy, emit more carbon dioxide and produce more waste (which winds up in methane-emitting landfills) than smaller homes. Bigger cars tend to use more fuel. Bigger consumption patterns, from purchases of furniture, food and electronics to car and airplane travel, add to consumers' emissions.

The median size of a new single-family home rose more than 60 percent between 1970 to 2006, according to data from the National Association of Home Builders, and in 2006 nearly a fourth of new homes contained 3,000 square feet or more. Also that year, more than a fourth of the new homes had three or more bathrooms and about one in five had garage space for three or more cars.[6]

Know that geography can matter. Researchers at the Brookings Institution, a think tank in Washington, found that the carbon footprints of the nation's 100 largest metropolitan areas vary significantly and that development patterns and the availability of rail transit play a key role in the differences.

needed to guide consumers on the merits of environmentally friendly items.

A report by McKinsey & Co. consultants this fall cited a 2007 consumer survey by the trade publication *Chain Store Age*, which found that only 25 percent of respondents reported having bought a green product other than organic foods or energy-efficient lighting. The McKinsey researchers also noted that most green items have small market shares. For instance, green laundry detergent and household cleaners account for less than 2 percent of U.S. sales.[55]

"[R]egions with high density, compact development and rail transit offer a more energy- and carbon-efficient lifestyle than sprawling, auto-centric areas," Brookings said. In addition, it said, while carbon output from urban centers continues to grow, the carbon footprint of a resident of a large metro area is 14 percent smaller than that of the average American and has grown in recent years by only half as much.[7]

Beware of "greenwashing." Along with an avalanche of "green" products and information on how to cut personal carbon emissions has come a steady tide of "greenwashing" — what TerraChoice Environmental Marketing Inc., based in Philadelphia, calls "the act of misleading consumers regarding the environmental practices of a company or the environmental benefits of a product or service."[8]

In a paper titled "The 'Six Sins of Greenwashing,'" the firm said it surveyed six "category-leading big-box stores" and identified 1,018 consumer products making 1,753 environmental claims. Of the total products examined, it said, "all but one made claims that are demonstrably false or that risk misleading intended audiences."[9]

Based on the survey, the firm identified what it said were six patterns of greenwashing:

- **The Sin of the Hidden Trade-Off** — Basing the suggestion that a product is "green" on only one environmental attribute without paying attention to other factors that may be more important, such as impacts on global warming, energy or water use or deforestation. An example is paper marketed as having recycled content without attention to the air, water and global-warming impact of its manufacture.
- **The Sin of No Proof** — Making an environmental claim that can't easily be backed up by supporting information or a reliable third-party certification.
- **The Sin of Vagueness** — Making poorly defined claims or ones that are so broad that consumers are likely to misunderstand the true meaning. An example is claiming a product is "chemical free." "[N]othing is free of chemicals," TerraChoice said. "Water is a chemical. All plants, animals and humans are made of chemicals as are all of our products."
- **The Sin of Irrelevance** — Making claims that might be true but are unimportant or not helpful. The most common example concerns chlorofluorocarbons, a key factor in depletion of the ozone layer, TerraChoice said. "Since CFCs have been legally banned for almost 30 years, there are no products that are manufactured with it."
- **The Sin of the Lesser of Two Evils** — Claims that, while they may be true within a product category, can distract consumers from the category's broader environmental impact. Organic cigarettes are an example, TerraChoice said.
- **The Sin of Fibbing** — Making false claims, such as saying a detergent is packaged in "100% recycled paper" but whose container is made of plastic.

[1] Gerald T. Gardner and Paul C. Stern, "The Short List: The Most Effective Actions U.S. Households Can Take to Curb Climate Change," *Environment*, September/October, 2008.

[2] "Your Home's Energy Use," U.S. Department of Energy, www1.eere.energy.gov/consumer/tips/home_energy.html.

[3] "2008 Buildings Energy Data Book," U.S. Department of Energy, http://buildingsdatabook.eren.doe.gov/.

[4] Gardner and Stern, *op. cit.*, http://buildingsdatabook.eere.energy.gov/TableView.aspx?table=2.4.3.

[5] "Home Energy Checklist for Action," American Council for an Energy-Efficient Economy, www.aceee.org/consumerguide/checklist.htm.

[6] "Selected Characteristics of New Housing," National Association of Home Builders, April 3, 2008, www.nahb.org/page.aspx/category/sectionID=130.

[7] "Brookings Institution Ranks Nation's 100 Largest Metro Areas for Carbon Footprint," press release, Brookings Institution, May 29, 2008, www.brookings.edu/~/media/Files/rc/papers/2008/05_carbon_foot print_sarzynski/pressrelease.pdf. The report is by Marilyn A. Brown, Frank Southworth and Andrea Sarzynski, "Shrinking the Carbon Footprint of Metropolitan America," Brookings Institution, May 8, 2008, www.brookings.edu/reports/2008/05_carbon_footprint_sarzyn ski.aspx.

[8] "The 'Six Sins of Greenwashing,'" TerraChoice Environmental Marketing Inc., November 2007.

[9] *Ibid.*

"Consumers in the United States and other developed countries have…done little to lighten their carbon footprint," the McKinsey consultants wrote. "Some of this lag between talking and walking could reflect insincerity, laziness or posturing. But much more of it stems from the failure of business to educate consumers about the benefits of green products and to create and market compelling ones."[56]

Patagonia, the clothing and outdoor-gear retailer, tracks the environmental footprint of more than a dozen of its products and shares both the good and bad on its Web site, though it warns that its environmental examinations are "partial and preliminary."[57]

For example, a down jacket's footprint, from origin of the fiber to the garment's distribution, spans more than 20,000 miles, touching California, Hungary, Japan, China and Nevada. The jacket's manufacture and transportation created nearly seven pounds of CO_2 emissions and enough energy to burn an 18-watt compact fluorescent bulb continuously for 22 days, according to Patagonia.[58]

The jacket uses "high-quality goose down . . . [that] comes from humanely raised geese," and the garment's light shell is made from recycled polyester, Patagonia says. But the zipper is treated with a substance "that contains perfluorooctanoic acid (PFOA), a synthetic chemical that is now persistent in the environment."

Says Patagonia, "We're investigating alternatives to the use of PFOA in water repellents — and looking for ways to recycle down garments."[59]

CURRENT SITUATION

Creating Incentives

Beginning in 2009 buyers of the fuel-sipping Honda Civic hybrid will no longer receive one of the most popular incentives for going green: a tax credit.[60]

Tax incentives on hybrids phase out after an automaker sells 60,000 of them, a benchmark Honda reached in 2007 and that Toyota — maker of the hybrid Prius — hit in 2006. With gas prices having fallen sharply since peaking at $4-plus per gallon last summer, "it's getting a lot more expensive to be an environmentally conscious driver," *The Wall Street Journal* noted in an article about dwindling tax incentives on hybrid cars.[61]

Even so, the tax code remains one of the most powerful tools in the environmental-policy arsenal.

Consumers have long received tax breaks on everything from hybrid cars to energy-efficient appliances and home weatherization. The Emergency Economic Stabilization Act of 2008 — the so-called bailout bill passed this fall to deal with the rapidly deteriorating economy — included, extended or amended several such incentives as well as others aimed at businesses and public utilities.[62] For example, the measure included tax breaks for solar systems

to generate electricity or heat hot water, energy-efficient home improvements and even bicycle commuting.[63]

As legislators and policy analysts contemplate how climate change and energy consumption are likely to unfold in coming decades, they are weighing other ideas to reduce carbon emissions.

"The most efficient approaches to reducing emissions involve giving businesses and individuals an incentive to curb activities that produce CO_2 emissions, rather than adopting a 'command-and-control' approach in which the government would mandate how much individual entities could emit or what technologies they should use," the Congressional Budget Office said in a report on policy options for reducing carbon-dioxide emissions.[64]

Cap-and-trade systems, which can be structured in a variety of ways, provide such incentives. They allow companies that emit CO_2 and other polluting gases to buy (or are allocated) emission credits that allow them to continue emitting a certain amount of the pollutant. Companies emitting less can save their allowances for the future or sell them at a profit to other companies.

So-called "cap-and-dividend" or "cap-and-cash-back" schemes also have been suggested. Entrepreneur and writer Peter Barnes, the author of *Who Owns the Sky?* and *Climate Solutions: A Citizens Guide*, described the idea this way: The caps would be placed "upstream — that is, on the small number of companies that bring carbon into the economy. An upstream cap could be administered without monitoring smokestacks, without a large bureaucracy and without favoring some companies over others. . . . If carbon doesn't come into the economy, it can't go out."

Caps would be auctioned rather than given away free, and the revenue would go to taxpayers to help offset the higher price of fuel and other carbon-intensive products.[65]

"This can be done through yearly tax credits, or better yet through monthly cash dividends wired … to people's bank accounts or debit cards."

Because that income would be taxed, the government would recoup about 25 percent of the money and could use it "as it sees fit," Barnes wrote. "More importantly, ordinary families would get the lion's share of the auction revenue, and get it in a way that rewards conservation. Since everyone would get the same amount back, those

Will President-elect Obama's clean energy plan work?

YES
Bracken Hendricks
Senior Fellow, Center for American Progress

NO
Kenneth P. Green
Resident Scholar, American Enterprise Institute

Written for *CQ Researcher*, December 2008

Written for *CQ Researcher*, December 2008

Barack Obama is not yet sworn in as president, and it is far too early to know the details of his policies, let alone their effectiveness. Yet it is clear from the recent election campaign that the energy road map the president-elect and Democrats in Congress have laid out will move the nation forward. After years of inaction and obstruction from the White House, it is time for leadership. We must place clean energy center stage in America's economic renewal.

Clean energy means jobs and hundreds of billions in investment. The country faces a collapsing housing market, record unemployment and a fiscal crisis that hurts communities. New demand for goods and services from an energy transition can stimulate the economy. Retrofitting millions of homes for energy efficiency will put construction workers back on the job. Rebuilding our infrastructure for transit, alternative fuels and a renewable electricity grid will jump-start local economies. And retooling industry to serve the growing market for a new generation of cars and clean technology is our best hope for restoring manufacturing jobs.

A recent study by the Center for American Progress showed that investing $100 billion in smart incentives for energy efficiency and renewable energy would create 2 million jobs. These "green" jobs are in familiar professions in manufacturing and construction, driven by new technology and innovation. Clean and efficient energy investments have more local content and are harder to outsource, and they redirect spending from wasted energy into skilled labor. As a result, they create more jobs at better wages.

Climate solutions also mean fixing broken markets. Inaction in the face of global warming is not costless. Global warming is the biggest market failure the world has ever known, and if left unchecked will cost the economy trillions of dollars in lost productivity. We need smart policies that cap emissions and help businesses respond to the real costs of waste and pollution. Designed properly, smart climate policies can cut energy bills, increase consumer choice and create new markets and desperately needed demand for the ingenuity of American companies and workers.

We cannot drill our way out of our oil dependence, and we cannot deny our way to a stable climate. Barack Obama and congressional leaders instead have offered a vision that invests in innovation, that faces tough challenges squarely and that finds opportunity in crisis. This is real leadership. It is long overdue, and it will put America back to work.

Barack Obama campaigned on an energy agenda of greenhouse-gas pricing, vehicle-efficiency standards and a fleet of plug-in hybrid cars. His plan is supposed to increase energy independence, lower greenhouse-gas emissions and create 5 million "green" energy jobs. Will it work? It's doubtful.

Obama's proposed cap-and-trade program, which would reduce greenhouse-gas emissions 80 percent by 2050, is 10 percent more stringent than the variation (S 2191) proposed by Sens. John Warner and Joseph Lieberman that was killed in 2007. The Congressional Budget Office estimated their proposal would cost $1.2 trillion from 2009-2018. The Environmental Protection Agency projected it would raise gas prices by $0.53 per gallon and hike electricity prices 44 percent in 2030. Economists at CRA International estimated the Warner-Lieberman proposal would result in a loss of 4 million jobs by 2015, growing to 7 million by 2050. In the face of a global financial crisis and a long, deep recession, passage of such a plan is both unlikely and undesirable.

The Obama plan also calls for reducing oil imports by tightening vehicle fuel-economy standards and subsidizing a fleet of 1 million plug-in hybrid vehicles. But there's a problem here: U.S. automakers are teetering on the brink of bankruptcy, Americans are strapped for cash, and plug-in hybrids are considerably more expensive than currently available cars. The National Renewable Energy Laboratory estimates the additional costs of plug-in hybrid vehicles that slightly outperform conventional hybrids at between $3,000 and $7,000. For the really fuel efficient ones, the laboratory estimates a premium of $12,000-$18,000.

Hybrids also cost more to insure. Are Americans going to shell out that kind of cash in a recession? I don't think so. Government fleets might buy some, but even they are strapped for cash and will have to cut costs elsewhere to afford plug-in hybrids.

As for creating green jobs, "job creation" is simply a myth. Governments do not create private-sector jobs, or wealth. They can only curtail jobs in one way (through taxation or regulation) and generate other jobs with subsidies and incentives. But since they impose costs in "managing" such programs — and because the market has already rejected the goods that the government is pushing (or there would be no need for intervention) — there are invariably fewer jobs and less wealth creation at the end of the day.

Markets create jobs, as markets create wealth: All the government can do is move it about to suit its priorities.

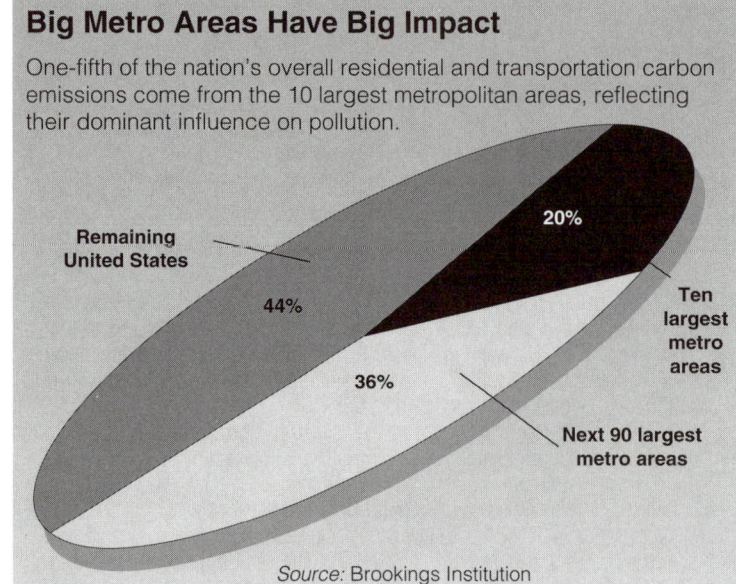

Big Metro Areas Have Big Impact

One-fifth of the nation's overall residential and transportation carbon emissions come from the 10 largest metropolitan areas, reflecting their dominant influence on pollution.

Remaining United States — 44%

20% — Ten largest metro areas

36% — Next 90 largest metro areas

Source: Brookings Institution

who use the most carbon would lose, and those who use the least would gain — their dividends would exceed what they pay in higher prices."

The approach would benefit low-income families because they use less energy than wealthier ones and would pay little if any tax on their dividends, Barnes argued.

Barnes wrote that while a carbon cap would raise fuel prices "for years to come," the cap-and-dividend approach would protect families' finances "by permanently linking dividends to carbon prices. As carbon prices rise, so — automatically — do dividends. If voters scream about rising fuel prices . . . politicians can truthfully say, 'How you fare is up to you. If you guzzle, you lose; if you conserve, you gain.'"

The Chesapeake Climate Action Network's Tidwell favors the cap-and-dividend idea and says that while it would lead to higher prices for fossil-based fuels, it would create an incentive for industry and consumers to conserve and switch to alternative forms of energy. The cap-and-dividend approach, he argues, would "lead to more energy-efficient cars, the discontinued use of energy-inefficient lightbulbs, and it will overnight [provide an incentive for] energy audits for homes, weatherization" and other carbon-reducing actions.

"Let's let the invisible hand of [economist] Adam Smith take over, but first we make carbon fuels more expensive as they come out of the ground and give the money back to all Americans in a way that protects the poor, so it's fair and effective and market-driven."

Roger W. Stephenson, executive vice president for programs at Clean Air-Cool Planet, says his group also favors an approach that generates dividends, but rather than sending a check to individuals, he says it would be better to recycle the revenue through the tax system for such purposes as reducing payroll taxes, corporate tax rates and other business and consumer taxes and modifying the earned-income tax credit for low-income working people. Some money could also be used for social services, such as giving a "carbon boost to the food-stamp program" to help compensate poor people who are outside the tax system but nonetheless affected by higher energy costs.

"We have to be sure that non-taxpayers are taken into account — the bottom quintile of the population — people who don't pay taxes but who can be affected disproportionately" by a carbon-capping system, he says.

While the cost of the emission allowances would raise consumers' energy prices, Stephenson says, the government could limit the auction price of the credits to avoid extremes in consumers' utility bills.

Stephenson says in addition to a carbon-cap regime, new technology and greater energy efficiency — especially in transportation — also are needed to solve the climate-change problem. "Transport is 30 percent or more of emissions," he noted. "We cannot and are not going to stop driving. Therefore technology and efficiency solutions are essential."

Obama's Plan

President-elect Obama's energy plan calls for a wide range of efforts to reduce the carbon footprints of both industry and consumers, including an "economy-wide cap-and-trade program" aimed at cutting greenhouse-gas emissions by 80 percent by 2050. Under the plan, all pollution credits would be auctioned and the proceeds used for investments in "clean" energy, habitat protection and "rebates and other transition relief for families."[66]

The Obama plan also calls for other energy- and carbon-cutting efforts, including weatherizing at least a million low-income homes annually for the next decade, cutting electricity demand 15 percent from projected levels by 2020, putting a million plug-in hybrid cars on the road by 2015 and requiring a fourth of the nation's electricity to be generated by renewable sources by 2025.[67]

Obama even wants the federal government to practice what he is preaching. He has said he would transform the White House fleet to plug-in vehicles within a year of his inauguration "as security permits" and ensure that half of the new vehicles the government purchases are plug-ins and battery-powered cars by 2012, according to *The New York Times*.[68]

In mid-November Jason Grumet, the Obama campaign's chief energy and environment adviser, told a conference on carbon trading that Obama "will move quickly on climate change" but offered no specifics.[69]

Obama said during his campaign that spending $150 billion over the next decade to increase energy efficiency would help to create 5 million "green-collar" jobs in such industries as insulation installation, wind-turbine production and construction of energy-efficient buildings.[70] But some policy experts have questioned the job-creation number and underlying assumptions behind it, and the numbers have even been debated by the president-elect's own advisers.[71] "U.S. automakers are teetering on the brink of bankruptcy, Americans are strapped for cash and plug-in hybrids are considerably more expensive than currently available cars," according to Kenneth P. Green, resident scholar at the American Enterprise Institute. "As for creating green jobs," he continues, " 'job creation' is simply a myth." (*See "At Issue," page 89.*)

While many details of Obama's energy plan remain to be fleshed out, he is wasting no time in making climate change and cutting CO_2 emissions a priority. In November, in a four-minute video message to the Governors' Global Climate Summit, he said his presidency would "mark a new chapter in America's leadership on climate change."[72] Separately, he also pledged to develop a two-year economic-stimulus plan to save or create 2.5 million jobs, including "green" jobs in alternative energy.

"I promise you this: When I am president, any governor who's willing to promote clean energy will have a partner in the White House," Obama told the climate summit.

"Any company that's willing to invest in clean energy will have an ally in Washington. And any nation that's willing to join the cause of combating climate change will have an ally in the United States of America."[73]

Fred Krupp, president of the Environmental Defense Fund, said Obama was "clearly rejecting the timid, business-as-usual approach" to climate and energy issues.[74]

Eileen Claussen, president of the Pew Center on Global Climate Change, said in a statement that the president-elect's remarks were "exactly the kind of leadership the country and the world have been waiting for . . . . We urge the bipartisan leadership in Congress to work closely with the new president to quickly enact an economy-wide cap-and-trade system."

As policy makers in Washington turn their attention toward shaping a new energy strategy, concerns about a global climate catastrophe stemming from carbon-dioxide and other GHG emissions have never been stronger. Greenhouse-gas emissions from developed nations rose 2.3 percent between 2000 and 2006, according to the United Nations Framework Convention on Climate Change.[75] And individuals, as well as industry, are the source of those emissions.

The U.N. also reported in November that a poisonous, brownish haze of carbon dust from cars, coal-fired power plants, wood-burning stoves and other sources was blocking out sunlight in Asia and other continents, altering weather patterns and making people sick.[76] The thick, atmospheric blanket sprawls from the Arabian Peninsula to the Yellow Sea, goes past North and South Korea and Japan in the spring, and sometimes drifts to California.[77]

"We used to think of this brown cloud as a regional problem, but now we realize its impact is much greater," said Professor Veerabhadran Ramanathan, the leader of the U.N. scientific panel. "When we see the smog one day and not the next, it just means it's blown somewhere else."[78]

Achim Steiner, executive director of the U.N. Environment Program in Beijing, said, "The imperative to act has never been clearer."[79]

OUTLOOK

Economic Imperatives

Several developments could lead to significant changes — both positive and negative — in how consumers use energy and leave their carbon imprints on the environment.

One is the financial crisis. In the short term, many consumers are feeling pressured financially to lower their thermostats, forgo vacations and take other steps to conserve money — all of which help reduce carbon emissions.

In its annual Thanksgiving survey, AAA said the number of Americans planning to travel by car, plane, bus or train was down 1.4 percent from last year's record and marked the first decline since 2002. Air travel was expected to fall by 7.2 percent, the group said.[80]

The nation's economic woes also are causing consumers — even the wealthiest ones — to ratchet back on consumption of goods and services. "People are saying, 'We are going to save money, and we are going to save the environment,'" said Wendy Liebmann, chief executive of WSL Strategic Retail, a consulting firm in New York.[81]

But the economic slowdown could also drive up consumers' carbon emissions. With state and federal budgets under severe pressure, less money may be available for everything from tax credits for energy-saving home retrofitting to subsidies for mass-transit services.

In November, financial pressure stemming from the credit crisis propelled officials from 11 major transit agencies — including those in New York, Boston, Washington, Los Angeles and Chicago — to seek help from Congress to avoid cuts in bus and subway service for millions of riders.[82]

In New York, the Metropolitan Transportation Authority called for raising fare and toll revenues by 23 percent in 2009 because of a huge budget gap, and it also drafted proposals for service reductions.[83]

Such moves would likely put more cars on the road and lead to greater emissions.

In the longer term, the incoming Obama administration could make dramatic changes to U.S. energy policy that would affect not only industry but consumers as well.

"Few challenges facing America, and the world, are more urgent than combating climate change," Obama told the governors' climate summit.[84]

Still unknown is whether Congress will pass a climate bill and how such legislation might be structured to provide incentives for consumers to lower their carbon emissions. "I think we have to wait and see" what Congress and the Obama administration do on energy policy, says Haxthausen of the Nature Conservancy.

"A reasonable conjecture is that [the administration] would want to get out in front of this issue, whether with legislation or a set of principles. In both houses of Congress, members are ready to work on this issue. They'll probably be looking to the administration for signals."

NOTES

1. See New Hampshire Carbon Challenge, http:// carbonchallenge.sr.unh.edu/.

2. For background, see Marcia Clemmitt, "Climate Change," *CQ Researcher*, Jan. 27, 2006, pp. 73-96; and Colin Woodard, "Curbing Climate Change," *CQ Global Researcher*, February 2007, pp. 27-50.

3. Jeffrey Ball, "A Big Sum of Small Differences," *The Wall Street Journal*, Oct. 2, 2008.

4. *Ibid.*

5. Marilyn A. Brown, Frank Southworth and Andrea Sarzynski, "Shrinking the Carbon Footprint of Metropolitan America," Brookings Institution, May 2008, p. 8, www.brookings.edu/reports/2008/05_carbon_footprint_sarzynski.aspx.

6. "What's your EnviroQ? Answer Page," Environmental Protection Agency, www.epa.gov/epahome/enviroq/index.htm.

7. "Compact Fluorescent Light Bulbs," www.energystar.gov/index.cfm?c=cfls.pr_cfls.

8. Mike Tidwell, "Consider Using the N-Word Less," *Grist*, Sept. 4, 2007, http://grist.org/feature/2007/09/04/change_redux/index.html.

9. Gary Langer, "Fuel Costs Boost Conservation Efforts; 7 in 10 Reducing 'Carbon Foot-print,'" ABC News, Aug. 9, 2008, http://abcnews.go.com/PollingUnit/story?id=5525064&page=1.

10. Harris Interactive, "For Earth Day: Two-thirds of Americans Believe Humans are Contributing to Increased Temperatures," The Harris Poll #44, April 18, 2008, www.harrisinteractive.com/harris_poll/index.asp?PID=898.

11. *Ibid.*

12. Center for Sustainable Systems, University of Michigan, "Residential Buildings," http://css.snre.umich.edu/css_doc/CSS01-08.pdf.

13. *Ibid.*

14. Thomas Wiedmann and Jan Minx, "A Definition of 'Carbon Footprint,'" *ISA* [UK] *Research & Consulting*, June 2007, www.isa-research.co.uk/docs/ISA-UK_Report_07-01_carbon_footprint.pdf.

15. Joanna Pearlstein, "Surprise! Conventional Agriculture Can Be Easier on the Planet," in "Inconvenient Truths: Get Ready to Rethink What It Means to Be Green," *Wired*, May 19, 2008, www.wired.com/science/planetearth/magazine/16-06/ff_heresies_intro.

16. "Universal, Neutral and Transparent Method for Estimating the Carbon Footprint of a Flight," press release, International Civil Aviation Organization, June 18, 2008, www.icao.int/icao/en/nr/2008/PIO200803_e.pdf.

17. Gerard Wynn, "Critics [say] air travel carbon offsetting too crude," Reuters, Aug. 21, 2008, www.reuters.com/article/environmentNews/idUSLK20281120080821.

18. Tim DeChant, "Calculating footprint often uses fuzzy math; Results vary, but give idea of environmental impact," *Chicago Tribune*, Aug. 10, 2008, p. 1.

19. The New England Carbon Estimator is at http://carbonchallenge.sr.unh.edu/calculator.jsp.

20. Jane Black, "What's in a Number?" *Slate*, Sept. 17, 2008, www.slate.com/id/2200202/.

21. See Eric Marx, "Are you ready to go on a carbon diet?" *The Christian Science Monitor*, Nov. 10, 2008, www.csmonitor.com/2008/1110/p13s01-wmgn.html.

22. For background, see Jennifer Weeks, "Carbon Trading," *CQ Global Researcher*, November 2008, pp. 295-320.

23. Ben Lieberman, "Beware of Cap and Trade Climate Bills," *Web Memo No. 1723*, Heritage Foundation, Dec. 6, 2007, www.heritage.org/Research/Economy/wm1723.cfm.

24. Opening Statement of Chairman Brian Baird before the Subcommittee on Research and Science Education, House Committee on Science and Technology, Sept. 25, 2007, http://science.house.gov/publications/OpeningStatement.aspx?OSID=1293.

25. Testimony of John A. "Skip" Laitner before the Subcommittee on Research and Science Education, House Committee on Science and Technology, Sept.

25, 2007, p. 11, http://science.house. gov/publications/Testimony.aspx?TID=7922.

26. David R. Baker, "State rebates lead more people to go solar," *San Francisco Chronicle*, July 15, 2008, www.sfgate.com/cgi-bin/article.cgi?f=/c/a/2008/07/14/BUNL11OVEF.DTL.

27. Quoted in *ibid.*

28. Gerald T. Gardner and Paul C. Stern, "The Short List: The Most Effective Actions U.S. Households Can Take to Curb Climate Change," *Environment*, September/October 2008, www.environmentmagazine.org/Archives/Back%20Issues/September-October%202008/gardner-stern-full.html.

29. Steven Blanchard and Peter Reppe, "Life Cycle Analysis of a Residential Home in Michigan," University of Michigan Center for Sustainable Systems, September 1998, www.umich.edu/~nppcpub/research/lcahome/homelca.PDF. The project was submitted in partial fulfillment of requirements for the degree of master of science in natural resources.

30. "Residential Buildings," Center for Sustainable Systems, University of Michigan, http://css.snre.umich.edu/css_doc/CSS01-08.pdf.

31. "About Energy Star," www.energystar.gov/index.cfm?c=about.ab_index.

32. "Energy Star has lost some luster," *Consumer Reports*, October 2008, p. 24.

33. Paul Davidson, "A new twist for light bulbs that conserve energy," *USA Today*, April 22, 2008, p. 10B, www.usatoday.com/money/industries/energy/environment/2008-04-21-light-bulbs_N.htm.

34. Environmental timeline, Radford University, www.runet.edu/~wkovarik/envhist/about.html.

35. Jennifer Weeks, "Buying Green," *CQ Researcher*, Feb. 29, 2008, pp. 193-216.

36. Rachel Carson, *The Sea Around Us*, Illustrated Commemorative Edition, (Oxford University Press, 2003), pp. 223, 225.

37. Gaylord Nelson, "Earth Day '70: What It Meant," *EPA Journal*, April 1980, www.epa.gov/history/topics/earthday/02.htm.

38. Andrew C. Revkin, "On Climate Change, a Change of Thinking," *The New York Times*, Dec. 4, 2005.

39. *Ibid.*

40. "Q&A: The Kyoto Protocol," BBC News, Feb. 16, 2005, http://news.bbc.co.uk/2/hi/science/nature/4269921.stm.

41. Al Gore, *An Inconvenient Truth* (2006), p. 8.

42. Daniel Stone, "The Green Pope," *Newsweek*, April 17, 2008, www.newsweek.com/id/132523.

43. Neela Banerjee, "Southern Baptists Back a Shift on Climate Change," *The New York Times*, March 10, 2008, www.nytimes.com/2008/03/10/us/10baptist.html?scp=1&sq=southern%20baptists%20back%20a%20shift&st=cse.

44. Gary Haq, Anne Owen, Elena Dawkins and John Barrett, "The Carbon Cost of Christmas," Stockholm Environment Institute, 2007, www.climatetalk.org.uk/downloads/CarbonCostofChristmas2007.pdf.

45. Timothy Gutowski, *et al.*, "Environmental Life Style Analysis," IEEE International Symposium on Electronics and the Environment, May 19-20, 2008. All other authors were graduate or undergraduate students at the Massachusetts Institute of Technology during the 2007 spring term.

46. "Following The Trail Of Toxic E-Waste," "60 Minutes," CBS News, Nov. 9, 2008, www.cbsnews.com/stories/2008/11/06/60minutes/main4579229.shtml.

47. *Ibid.*

48. Joseph De Avila, "PC Movement: How Green Is Your Computer?" *The Wall Street Journal*, Sept. 4, 2008, http://online.wsj.com/article/SB122048465164497063.html.

49. *Ibid.*

50. *Ibid.*

51. Marx, *op. cit.*

52. *Ibid.*

53. *Ibid.*

54. *Ibid.*

55. Sheila M. J. Bonini and Jeremy M. Oppenheim, "Helping 'green' products grow," *The McKinsey Quarterly*, October 2008.

56. *Ibid.*

57. "Environmentalism: Leading the Examined Life," *Patagonia*, www.patagonia.com/web/us/contribution/patagonia.go?assetid=23429&ln=267. See also www.patagonia.com/web/us/footprint/index.jsp.

58. *Ibid.*

59. www.patagonia.com/web/us/footprint/index.jsp.

60. Mike Spector, "The Incentives to Buy Hybrids Are Dwindling," *The Wall Street Journal*, Nov. 6, 2008, http://online.wsj.com/article/SB122593537581103821.html.

61. *Ibid.*

62. U.S. Department of Energy, "Consumer Energy Tax Incentives," www.energy.gov/taxbreaks.htm. See also, "P.L. 110-343/The Emergency Economic Stabilization Act of 2008: Energy Tax Incentives," www.energy.gov/media/HR_1424.pdf.

63. Ashlea Ebeling, "The Green Tax Gusher," *Forbes*, Nov. 24, 2008, p. 150.

64. "Policy Options for Reducing CO2 Emissions," Congressional Budget Office, February 2008, p. vii, www.cbo.gov/ftpdocs/89xx/doc8934/02-12-Carbon.pdf.

65. Peter Barnes, "Obama's 'number 1 priority,'" Reuters, http://blogs.reuters.com/great-debate/2008/11/11/obamas-number-1-priority/.

66. "New Energy for America," http://my.barackobama.com/page/content/newenergy_more#emissions.

67. *Ibid.*

68. Jim Motavalli, "The Candidates' Clean Car Plans," *The New York Times*, Oct. 23, 2008, http://wheels.blogs.nytimes.com/2008/10/23/the-candidates-clean-car-plans/.

69. Deborah Zabarenko, "Obama will act quickly on climate change: adviser," Reuters, Nov. 12, 2008, www.reuters.com/article/environmentNews/idUSTRE4AB84K20081112?feedType=RSS&feedName=environmentNews.

70. Jeffrey Ball, "Does Green Energy Add 5 Million Jobs? Pitch Is Potent; Numbers Are Squishy," *The Wall Street Journal*, Nov. 7, 2008, p. A13.

71. *Ibid.*

72. The Associated Press, "Obama Promises Leadership on Climate Change," *The New York Times*, Nov. 18, 2008, www.nytimes.com/aponline/washington/AP-Obama-Climate-Change.html?sq=climate%20summit&st=nyt&scp=2&pagewanted=print.

73. Quoted in *ibid.*

74. *Ibid.*

75. Richard Black, "Obama vows climate 'engagement,'" BBC News, Nov. 18, 2008, http://news.bbc.co.uk/2/hi/science/nature/7736321.stm.

76. Andrew Jacob, "Report Sees New Pollution Threat," *The New York Times*, Nov. 14, 2008, www.nytimes.com/2008/11/14/world/14cloud.html?hp.

77. *Ibid.*

78. *Ibid.*

79. *Ibid.*

80. Oren Dorell and Alan Levin, "Economy sets travel back a bit for holiday," *USA Today*, Nov. 18, 2008, www.usatoday.com/travel/news/2008-11-18-aaa-holiday-travel-forecast_N.htm.

81. Jennifer Saranow, "Luxury Consumers Scrimp for Sake of Planet, and Because It's Cheaper," *The Wall Street Journal*, Nov. 4, 2008, http://online.wsj.com/article/SB122575617614495083.html.

82. Lena H. Sun, "U.S. Transit Agencies Ask Congress for Help in Averting Service Cuts," *The Washington Post*, Nov. 19, 2008, p. 2D, www.washingtonpost.com/wp-dyn/content/article/2008/11/18/AR2008111803174_pf.html.

83. William Neuman, "M.T.A. Said to Plan 23% Increase in Fare and Toll Revenue," *The New York Times*, Nov. 19, 2008, www.nytimes.com/2008/11/19/nyregion/19transit.html.

84. Juliet Eilperin, "Obama Addresses Climate Summit," *The Washington Post*, www.washingtonpost.com/wp-dyn/content/article/2008/11/18/AR2008111803286.html.

BIBLIOGRAPHY

Books

Barnes, Peter, *Climate Solutions: A Citizens Guide*, Chelsea Green Publishing, 2008.
An entrepreneur and writer blames global warming on market failure and misplaced government priorities.

Brower, Michael, and Warren Leon, *The Consumer's Guide to Effective Environmental Choices*, Three Rivers Press, 1999.
Though nearly a decade old, this book by veteran environmental experts helps consumers determine what impact their decisions will have on the environment, backed by research from the Union of Concerned Scientists.

Gore, Al, *An Inconvenient Truth*, Rodale, 2006.
The former vice president and Nobel Peace Prize winner argues that exploding population growth and a technology revolution have transformed the relationship between humans and the Earth.

Articles

Ball, Jeffrey, "Six Products, Six Carbon Footprints," *The Wall Street Journal*, Oct. 6, 2008, http://online.wsj.com/article/SB122304950601802565.html.
Companies calculate the carbon footprints of their products in different ways, making it hard for consumers to compare goods.

Bonini, Sheila M., and Jeremy M. Oppenheim, "Helping 'green' products grow," *The McKinsey Quarterly*, October 2008.
Two consultants contend that the failure of business to educate consumers about green products has helped discourage them from doing more to reduce their carbon footprints.

Ebeling, Ashlea, "The Green Tax Gusher," *Forbes*, Nov. 24, 2008, www.forbes.com/forbes/2008/1124/150.html.
As part of this fall's $700 billion bailout bill, Congress enacted a new round of tax breaks that benefit consumers who embrace energy-saving home improvements and alternative energy.

El Nasser, Haya, " 'Green' efforts embrace poor," *USA Today*, Nov. 23, 2008, www.usatoday.com/news/nation/2008-11-23-green-poor_N.htm.
Cities and community groups are trying to help low-income households reduce their energy consumption.

Gardner, Gerald T., and Paul C. Stern, "The Short List: The Most Effective Actions U.S. Households Can Take to Curb Climate Change," *Environment*, www.environmentmagazine.org/Archives/Back%20Issues/September-October%202008/gardner-stern-full.html.
A professor emeritus of psychology and the director of the National Research Council's Committee on the Human Dimensions of Global Climate Change argue that households often lack accurate and accessible information on how to reduce carbon emissions and mitigate climate change.

Knight, Matthew, "Carbon dioxide levels already a danger," CNN, www.cnn.com/2008/TECH/science/11/21/climate.danger.zone/index.html.
International scientists — led by James Hansen, director of NASA's Goddard Institute for Space Studies — conclude

that carbon dioxide concentrations in Earth's atmosphere are in the danger zone, threatening food shortages, more intense storms and other calamities.

Specter, Michael, "Big Foot," *The New Yorker*, Feb. 25, 2008.
An excessive carbon footprint is the modern equivalent of a scarlet letter, but calculating one's environmental impact of modern life "can be dazzlingly complex," the writer says.

Wald, Matthew L., "For Carbon Emissions, a Goal of Less Than Zero," *The New York Times*, March 26, 2008, www.nytimes.com/2008/03/26/business/businessspecial 2/26negative.html?scp=14&sq=carbon&st=cse.
Researchers around the world are searching for so-called carbon-negative technologies that remove carbon dioxide from the atmosphere.

Reports and Studies

"Policy Options for Reducing CO₂ Emissions," Congressional Budget Office, February 2008, www

.cbo.gov/ftpdocs/89xx/doc8934/02-12-Carbon.pdf.
The congressional agency analyzes incentive-based options for reducing greenhouse-gas emissions, especially carbon dioxide.

Brown, Marilyn A., Frank Southworth and Andrea Sarzynski, "Shrinking the Carbon Footprint of Metropolitan America," Brookings Institution, May 2008, www.brookings.edu/reports/2008/~/media/ Files/rc/reports/2008/05_carbon_footprint_sarzynski/ carbonfootprint_report.pdf.
The researchers quantify transportation and residential carbon emissions for the 100-largest U.S. metropolitan areas.

Haq, Gary, Anne Owen, Elena Dawkins and John Barrett, "The Carbon Cost of Christmas," Stockholm Environment Institute, 2007, www.climatetalk.org .uk/downloads/CarbonCostofChristmas2007.pdf.
Three days of Christmas festivities could result in 650 kilograms (1,433 pounds) of carbon dioxide emissions per person, according to the United Kingdom-based researchers.

For More Information

Alliance to Save Energy, 1850 M St., N.W., Suite 600, Washington, DC 20036; (202) 857-0666; www.ase.org. Group that promotes energy efficiency worldwide.

American Council for an Energy-Efficient Economy, 529 14th St., N.W., Suite 600, Washington, DC 20045-1000; (202) 507-4000; www.aceee.org. Fosters energy efficiency to promote economic prosperity and environmental protection.

Carbonfund.org, 1320 Fenwick Lane, Suite 206, Silver Spring, MD 20910; (240) 247-0630; www.carbonfund.org. Provides certified carbon offsets to help individuals, businesses and organizations reduce their carbon footprints.

Chesapeake Climate Action Network, P.O. Box 11138, Takoma Park, MD 20912; (240) 396-1981; www .chesapeakeclimate.org. Grassroots group that fights global warming in Maryland, Virginia and Washington, D.C.

Clean Air-Cool Planet, 100 Market St., Suite 204, Portsmouth, NH 03801; (603) 422-6464; www .cleanair-coolplanet.org. Nonprofit organization that

partners with businesses, colleges and communities in the Northeast to reduce carbon emissions.

Energy Star, US EPA, Energy Star Hotline (6202J), 1200 Pennsylvania Ave., N.W., Washington, DC 20460; (888) 782-7937; www.energystar.gov. Environmental Protection Agency and Department of Energy program promoting energy-efficient products.

Nature Conservancy, 4245 North Fairfax Dr., Suite 100, Arlington, VA 22203-1606; (703) 841-5300; www .nature.org. Conservation organization that works worldwide to protect ecologically sensitive land and water.

New Hampshire Carbon Challenge, 8 College Road, CSRC, Morse Hall, Durham, NH 03824; (603) 862-3128; http://carbonchallenge.sr.unh.edu. Works to help households and communities reduce their energy consumption.

Pew Center on Global Climate Change, 2101 Wilson Blvd., Suite 550, Arlington, VA 22201; (703) 516-4146; www.pewclimate.org. Seeks new approaches to dealing with climate change.

Carbon Trading

5

Will It Reduce Global Warming?

Jennifer Weeks

A worker pours chemicals into a vat of molasses used to make ethanol in Simbhaoli, Uttar Pradeshi, India. Replacing gasoline with ethanol in cars can reduce emissions of carbon-based "greenhouse gases" (GHGs), created by burning fossil fuels, which contribute to climate change. Projects in developing countries that produce such alternative fuels are part of an international carbon trading scheme that allows polluters in industrialized countries to "offset" some of their GHG emissions by buying pollution credits from companies in developing countries.

From *CQ Global Researcher*, November 2008.

It's little wonder that Tirumala temple in Tirupati, in the south Indian state of Andhra Pradesh, prepares 30,000 meals for visiting Hindu pilgrims daily. The shrine is among the busiest religious pilgrimage sites in the world. In years past, cooks fired up pollution-spewing diesel generators to power their stoves to boil water in massive cauldrons. But today there's a new, clean energy source: the sun. Curved solar collectors heat water up to 280 degrees Centigrade, creating steam to cook foods such as rice, lentils and vegetables.[1]

"With most businesses, the first question is of economics," says engineer Deepak Gadhia, whose company built the system. "But spiritual organizations look at larger issues. They want energy that is spiritually positive."[2]

In fact, the temple does quite well financially, too, and so do many other temples, schools and government offices throughout India that use energy-saving systems built by Gadhia and his wife. The energy they save enables them to amass credits that can be used in a process called "carbon trading" — buying and selling rights to emit greenhouse gases.

Two years ago, the energy-saving systems at those sites were approved as carbon credit sources under the Kyoto Protocol.[3] The international agreement is designed to stem global warming, and — among other things — allows some developing countries to profit from projects that reduce emissions of greenhouse gases (GHGs) that cause climate change. (*See sidebar, p. 102.*)

Under the protocol, most of the world's wealthy countries agreed to reduce their GHG emissions by fixed percentages between 2008 and 2012, mainly by reducing energy use and switching to

Which Countries Emit the Most Carbon Dioxide?

Australia and major oil producing countries like the United States, Norway, Russia, Canada, Saudi Arabia, Kuwait and other Gulf states emit the most carbon dioxide (CO_2) per capita. Carbon dioxide is the most abundant greenhouse gas — one of several blamed for causing global warming.

Carbon Dioxide Emissions Per Capita, 2004
(in metric tons*)

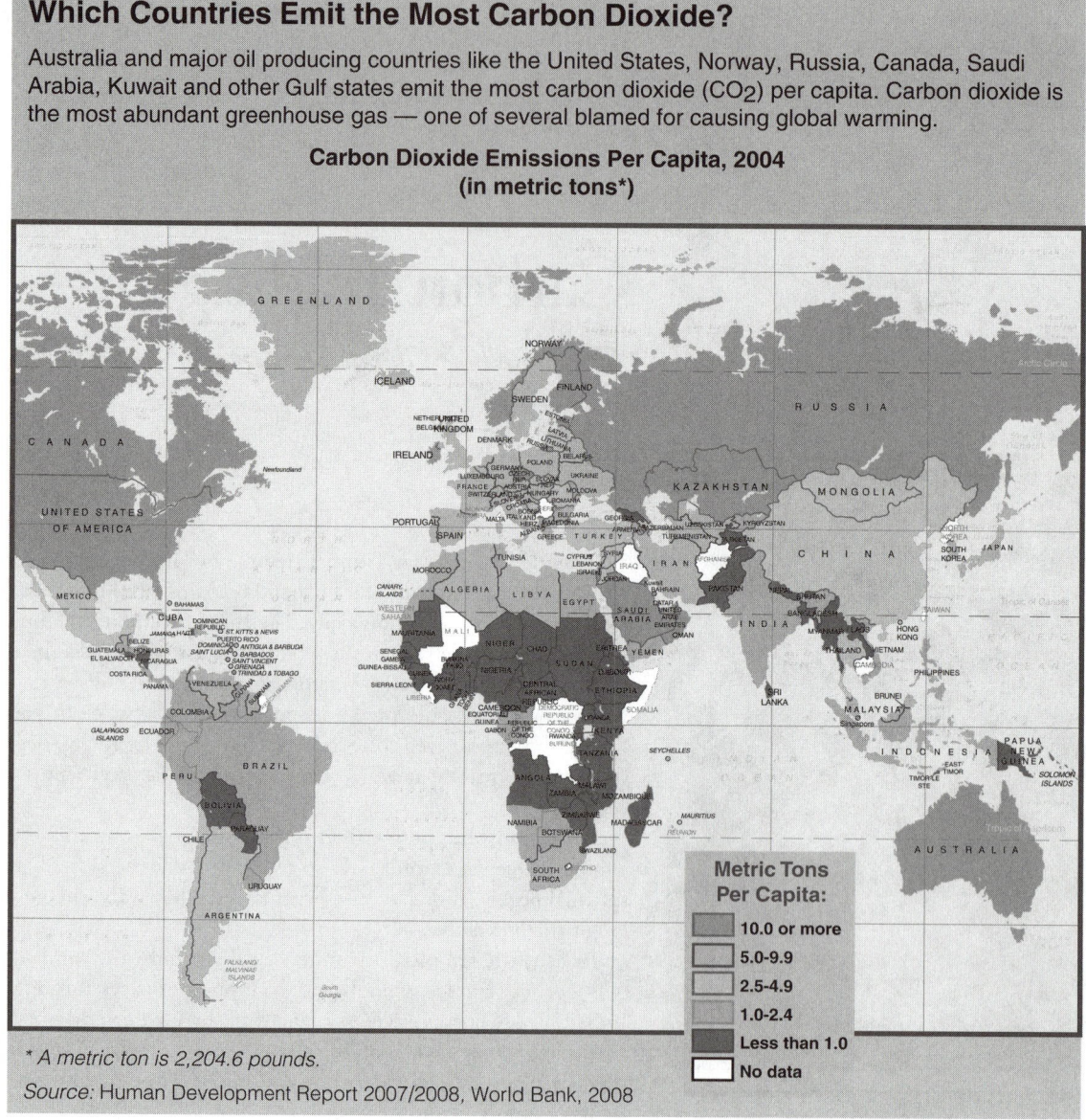

Metric Tons Per Capita:
- 10.0 or more
- 5.0-9.9
- 2.5-4.9
- 1.0-2.4
- Less than 1.0
- No data

A metric ton is 2,204.6 pounds.

Source: Human Development Report 2007/2008, World Bank, 2008

low-carbon fuels. But if they can't reach the required reductions, rich nations can also "offset" some of their GHG emissions by buying credits from energy-saving projects — like the Gadhia solar cookers — in developing countries.

If U.N. officials certify that those projects reduce GHG emissions beyond levels that would have occurred otherwise, they can sell "certified emission reductions," each representing one avoided metric ton of carbon dioxide (CO_2). Companies in industrialized nations buy these credits to help reach their GHG reduction targets.

Virtually all scientists agree that human use of carbon-based fossil fuels such as oil, coal and natural gas is raising concentrations of heat-trapping gases in the atmosphere to the highest levels in at least 650,000 years.[4] The gases are called "greenhouse" gases because their heat-trapping properties warm the Earth's surface, much as the glass walls of a greenhouse retain the sun's heat. Unless countries sharply reduce their GHG emissions by mid-century, the buildup of greenhouse gases — often referred to as "carbon" emissions since carbon dioxide (CO_2) is by far the most abundant GHG in Earth's atmosphere — could cause dramatic planetary warming. Climate scientists predict that higher temperatures will cause melting of the polar ice caps, rising sea levels and more intense droughts, floods and hurricanes.[5]

The Kyoto Protocol, which was signed in 1997 and went into effect in 2005, requires major industrialized countries (except for the United States, which failed to ratify the agreement) to reduce their GHG emissions, on average, by 5.2 percent below 1990 levels.[6] Members of the European Union vowed to reduce their emissions even farther — to 8 percent below 1990 levels by 2012. At the same time, the EU launched the world's largest mandatory carbon emissions trading system, in which governments cap national emissions and allow polluters to buy and sell permits to emit carbon dioxide. Australia, Canada and Japan are developing their own emission reduction systems, which will likely include some form of carbon trading.

Global interest in carbon trading is part of a gradual movement toward market-based environmental policies — strategies that give polluters economic incentives to clean up instead of simply telling them how much pollution they can release and what kinds of controls to install. The approach makes sense because climate change is what scholars refer to as a "commons problem" — in which a resource (in this case, Earth's atmosphere) is held in common by everyone. Individual polluters profit more by using and degrading a common resource than by cleaning it up while their competitors continue polluting.

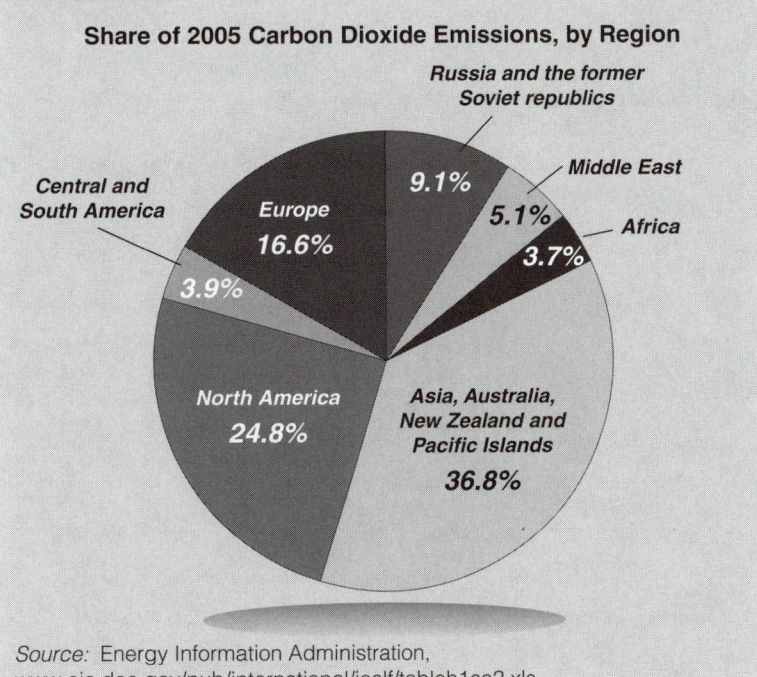

Most Emissions Come From Asia, North America

Nearly two-thirds of the world's carbon dioxide emissions — the main pollutant blamed for global warming — came from Asia and North America in 2005.

Share of 2005 Carbon Dioxide Emissions, by Region

- Russia and the former Soviet republics — 9.1%
- Middle East — 5.1%
- Africa — 3.7%
- Asia, Australia, New Zealand and Pacific Islands — 36.8%
- North America — 24.8%
- Central and South America — 3.9%
- Europe — 16.6%

Source: Energy Information Administration, www.eia.doe.gov/pub/international/iealf/tableh1co2.xls

"The rational man finds that his share of the cost of the wastes he discharges into the commons is less than the cost of purifying his wastes before releasing them," wrote biologist Garrett Hardin in a famous 1968 essay that identified commons problems as a central challenge for modern societies. "Since this is true for everyone, we are locked into a system of 'fouling our own nest,' so long as we behave only as independent, rational, free-enterprisers."[7]

Climate experts agree that one of the best ways around the commons problem is to "put a price on carbon" by making factories, power plants and other large GHG sources pay for their emissions. Hitting them in the pocketbook gives them more incentive to clean up — for example, by imposing a tax so that every source pays for its own GHG emissions at some set rate per ton.

However, an alternative approach — trading emission allotments — has become increasingly popular in

Europe Leads the World in Carbon Trading

The European Union accounted for 70 percent of the €40 billion ($60 billion) spent worldwide to buy carbon emission allowances in 2007. The Clean Development Mechanism, which allows companies in industrialized countries to buy emission credits from companies in the developing world, accounted for 29 percent.

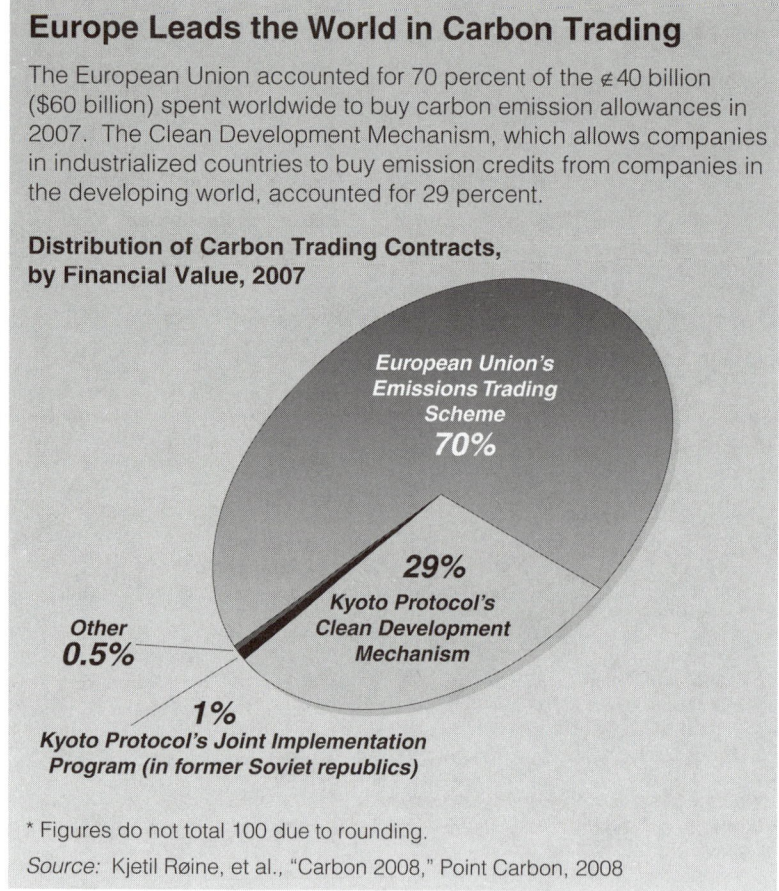

Distribution of Carbon Trading Contracts, by Financial Value, 2007

European Union's Emissions Trading Scheme **70%**

29% *Kyoto Protocol's Clean Development Mechanism*

Other **0.5%**

1% *Kyoto Protocol's Joint Implementation Program (in former Soviet republics)*

* Figures do not total 100 due to rounding.

Source: Kjetil Røine, et al., "Carbon 2008," Point Carbon, 2008

them decide how, it will stimulate research and development into a wide range of new, clean technologies. "It puts an infrastructure in place that releases capital for long-term investments," Hasselknippe explains.

Global carbon markets have grown quickly since the Kyoto Protocol entered into force in 2005. The total value of international carbon trades increased more than 80 percent between 2006 and 2007, from €22 billion ($33 billion) to €40 billion ($60 billion).[8] The market is expected to grow still larger as Europe lowers its cap on GHG emissions, and new trading systems gear up in some U.S. states and in other countries.[9]

Moreover, public support is growing for the U.S. government to act on climate change. President George W. Bush rejected the Kyoto treaty shortly after taking office in 2001, claiming that capping GHG emissions would harm the U.S. economy. But since then 23 states have joined regional carbon trading schemes, and the United States is widely expected to participate in a post-Kyoto agreement to limit GHG emissions after 2012.[10] Many U.S. political leaders, including both major presidential candidates, say the United States should create a cap-and-trade system similar to Europe's to cut GHG emissions in the United States far below 1990 levels by 2050.[11]

Ironically, several market-based elements were included in the Kyoto agreement at U.S. insistence in hope of convincing the United States to sign on to the treaty. They included two programs that let companies in industrialized countries offset some emissions by investing in carbon reduction projects elsewhere. The Clean Development Mechanism (CDM) paves the way for projects in developing countries, such as Gadhia's steam cookers at the temples in India, while Joint Implementation (JI) supports projects in other industrialized countries, mainly former Soviet satellite countries that are transitioning to market economies.

recent decades. It is usually enacted through so-called cap-and-trade policies, in which regulators set an overall cap on emissions and then issue quotas that limit how much pollution each company can release. If a company wants or needs to emit more than its allowance, it must buy permits from cleaner companies that don't need all their allotments. Over time, regulators can lower a country's cap to further reduce total pollution.

Advocates say carbon emissions trading encourages companies to use clean fuels and technologies because firms that reduce their own emissions can then sell their unneeded allowances. "The carbon market gives companies an incentive to reduce emissions so they can make money," says Henrik Hasselknippe, global carbon services director for Point Carbon, an international market research firm in Oslo, Norway. Moreover, he predicts, since carbon trading tells companies to limit their emissions but lets

However, offset projects are controversial for several reasons. First, companies in industrialized countries can emit more carbon than is allowed under their countries' total allowable levels under the Kyoto Protocol by buying credits from developing countries, which have no emission caps. In effect, offsets allow industrialized countries to outsource reductions to places where they can be done more cheaply.

Supporters say offsets are primarily designed to lower the cost of meeting Kyoto targets, and that it shouldn't matter where reductions take place because a ton of CO_2 causes the same amount of warming whether it's released in Germany or Malaysia. But others worry that if rich countries rely on offsets too heavily, they will have little incentive to reduce fossil fuel use or develop cleaner technologies. Ultimately, they argue, developing countries will refuse to make deep cuts in their own emissions if they see little change in rich countries.

"The developed world is responsible for the majority of greenhouse gas emissions," the World Wildlife Fund warned in 2007. "If the [European Union] is to maintain its status as a major player in global climate change negotiations, then it must put its own back yard in order first and ensure that Europe is placed firmly on a path towards a low carbon economy."[12]

Moreover, say critics, offset projects sometimes credit "anyway tons" — reductions from projects that would have gone forward anyway, even without extra revenue from selling emission reductions. Reductions are supposed to be "additional" to business as usual, but that concept can be hard to prove.

As governments, corporations and advocacy groups weigh the pros and cons of carbon trading, here are some issues they are debating:

Are current trading systems working?

Global carbon markets are booming, but some experts question whether carbon trading systems are making emission reductions affordable or reducing GHG emissions at all.

Two markets dominated world carbon trading through 2007. The European Union's Emissions Trading Scheme (EU ETS) accounted for 70 percent of trades by value, followed by the Clean Development Mechanism, which accounted for 29 percent. Joint Implementation projects and all other carbon trading forums generated less than 2 percent.

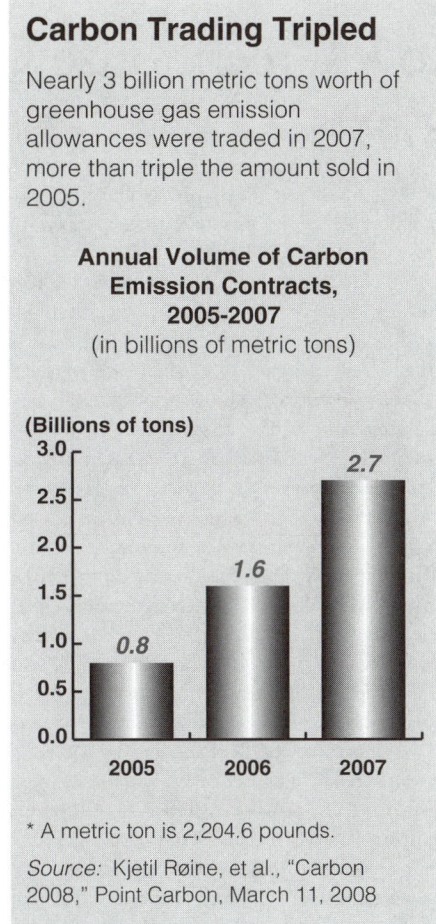

Carbon Trading Tripled

Nearly 3 billion metric tons worth of greenhouse gas emission allowances were traded in 2007, more than triple the amount sold in 2005.

Annual Volume of Carbon Emission Contracts, 2005-2007
(in billions of metric tons)

(Billions of tons)

Year	Value
2005	0.8
2006	1.6
2007	2.7

* A metric ton is 2,204.6 pounds.

Source: Kjetil Røine, et al., "Carbon 2008," Point Carbon, March 11, 2008

During its trial phase from 2005 through 2007, the EU ETS produced mixed results. Carbon allowances initially traded for €20-30 (about $30-$45) per ton of CO_2, but in April 2006 the Czech Republic, Estonia, the Netherlands, Switzerland and France announced that their 2005 GHG emissions had been lower than expected. Demand for allowances fell sharply. Share prices plunged to €10-15 ($15-23) within a few days. And prices for allowances that were valid only for the trial period — and hence not usable after 2007 — fell to almost zero in early 2007. Allowances then stabilized at €15-25 ($23-38) for the second trading period.[13]

Some observers called the price gyrations a sign that the ETS was failing. Open Europe, a London think tank, charged that ETS had failed to provide either a "workable

How Greenhouse Gases Are Measured

When discussing greenhouse gas (GHG) emissions, businesses and government agencies often use shorthand terms, like "carbon" or "carbon dioxide," to refer to the various gases emitted when carbon-based fuels are burned.

The Kyoto Protocol and other schemes to regulate greenhouse gases cover six major types of emissions that remain in the atmosphere for a significant time, trapping heat that is reflected back to Earth, which warms the planet's surface. Most are caused by various human activities.

Climate scientists have assigned each gas a global warming potential (GWP), based on its heat-trapping properties. A GWP value measures the impact a gas has on the climate over a given time period (usually 100 years) compared to the heat-producing impact of a ton of carbon dioxide (CO_2) — the most abundant greenhouse gas. For example, methane's GWP value is 25, which means that a ton of methane released into the atmosphere will cause as much warming as 25 tons of CO_2 over a 100-year period.[1] Thus, the higher the GWP, the more global warming the gas causes.

Carbon trading schemes allow emitters to trade allowances to release some or all of the six types of gases, whichever are covered by a particular system. For example, under the Kyoto Protocol, so-called Clean Development Mechanism (CDM) projects in developing countries can generate credits that they can then sell abroad by reducing their own emissions from any of the six GHG categories. Each credit certifies that the project has reduced greenhouse gas emissions by the equivalent of one metric ton (2,205 pounds) of carbon dioxide per year.

Under the European Union's Emissions Trading System (EU ETS), an electric power company in Italy might buy credits to cover excess CO_2 emissions created by its coal- or oil-fired power plants. These credits could come from

Types of Greenhouse Gases

GHG Categories	GWP Value*	Major Sources
Carbon dioxide (CO_2)	1	Fossil fuel combustion, deforestation
Methane (CH_4)	25	Landfills, rice paddies, digestive tracts of cattle and sheep
Nitrous oxide (N_2O)	298	Fertilizer, animal waste
Hydrofluorocarbons (HFCs)	Varies (up to 14,800)	Semiconductor manufacturing and other industrial processes
Perfluorocarbons (PFCs)	Varies (up to 12,200)	Same as HFCs, plus aluminum smelting
Sulfur hexafluoride (SF_6)	22,800	Electrical transmission systems, magnesium and aluminum production

* Global warming potential

Source: U.S. Environmental Protection Agency

CDM projects that reduced other GHG emissions through such actions as collecting methane emissions from landfills or reducing hydrofluorocarbon leakage at aluminum-smelting plants. Using the GWP values for these gases, project owners can calculate how many tons of CO_2 equivalent the project releases or avoids, and then sell the reduction credits easily across international borders.

---

[1] U.S. Environmental Protection Agency, "Inventory of U.S. Greenhouse Gas Emissions and Sinks: Fast Facts," April 2008.

market in carbon" or reduced emissions.[14] Others said market volatility was not surprising for the trial phase of a new system without historical data to guide it.

"Since companies had not previously been required to track and disclose emissions, there were no hard numbers on which to base allocations," wrote Annie Petsonk, an attorney for the New York-based Environmental Defense Fund. "So companies were asked how much they'd need to emit, and naturally they said, 'A lot!'

When emissions data became available and companies saw that cutting emissions was easier than they anticipated, the price of allowances plummeted."[15]

In a detailed assessment, Massachusetts Institute of Technology (MIT) economists A. Denny Ellerman and Paul Joskow pointed out that ETS was not intended to deliver big emissions cuts during its trial run, and that estimating emissions for any given year is difficult because weather patterns and fuel prices affect fossil fuel use.

Similar fluctuations occurred when the United States launched a trading program for sulfur dioxide (SO_2) allowances in the late 1990s, they noted, and as in the SO_2 program, ETS allowance prices settled down once policy makers had some real emissions data to work with.[16]

In its second trading period, which runs from 2008 through 2012, the EU's total emissions cap is 6.5 percent below the 2005 level. "Leaders learned their lesson after they over-allocated allowances in Phase I, and the cap is more stringent now. They have definitely done a better job in Phase 2," says Anja Kollmuss, an analyst at the Stockholm Environment Institute (SEI).

EU leaders now are grappling with new challenges for Phase 3, which starts in 2013, including bringing more emitters under the pollution cap. Currently the ETS only covers six sectors — energy, iron and steel, cement, glass, ceramics and pulp and paper — which produce about 45 percent of EU emissions. The European Parliament voted in July 2008 to include aviation emissions, beginning in 2012, and EU government ministers formally approved the policy in October over industry resistance.[17] Airlines assert that their industry has been hit hard by high oil prices and that the EU does not have legal authority to regulate emissions from flights, regardless of where airlines are based. (*See "At Issue," p. 115.*) European leaders also propose to include emissions from petrochemicals, aluminum and ammonia production in Phase 3.

Another critique points up flaws in both the ETS and CDM systems. In a 2007 report, the World Wildlife Fund warned that many EU countries might allow emitters to use offset credits from CDM and JI projects to meet most or all of their Phase 2 EU emission limits. Because they are not buying allowances from other EU sources, that would mean they aren't really cutting carbon among EU emitters.[18]

That prospect raises two problems, says Kollmuss. First, the Kyoto Protocol and EU directives say offsets should be "supplemental" to direct reductions. "When emitters can use a high fraction of offset credits, some sectors may not have to actually cut their emissions at all," she says.

Second, some offsets fail the "additionality" test, critics say, which occurs when the GHG reductions they produce are not additional to what would have happened anyway. For example, if local law already requires landfill owners to collect methane emissions instead of venting them into the air, they should not be able to market that action as a CDM project and sell the emission credits to a company in an industrialized country. Conversely, they say, if there is no clear financial reason to carry out a project unless it can produce CDM credits that can be sold, then the project is probably additional.

"Additionality is a simple concept, but it often comes down to subjective decisions," says Kollmuss. "And it's very easily fudged."

As one example, Stanford University law professors Michael Wara and David Victor pointed out in a 2008 paper that nearly all new renewable and gas-fired power plants in China are applying for CDM credits, even though China's energy sector is growing rapidly and the Chinese government has asked companies to invest in non-coal energy sources. Given these trends, they contend, China would probably be moving toward lower-carbon fuels even without CDM credits for new power plants. "[I]n practice, much of the current CDM market does not reflect actual reductions in emissions, and that trend is poised to get worse," the authors argued.[19]

Such controversies have spurred development of an entirely new industry of consultants and third-party certifiers who screen and verify claims from "green" development projects and help buyers find high-quality offset sources. (*See sidebar, p. 110.*)

U.N. officials acknowledge that additionality is a key challenge but argue that the CDM has effective rules for measuring it. They also point out that that the CDM has generated three times more funding for climate-friendly technology transfers to developing countries than direct foreign aid programs.

"Has the Kyoto Protocol's Clean Development Mechanism met the goal for which it was designed?" Yvo de Boer, executive secretary of the U.N. Framework Convention on Climate Change, asked in October. "In my view, the answer is yes."[20]

The EU has barred using reforestation projects in developing countries as offsets because regulators say reductions from these projects are hard to measure and can be quickly reversed (for example, if a forest plantation burns down). Ironically, developing countries without large industrial sectors would have a better chance of earning money through the CDM if the EU accepted forestry credits, since farming and forestry projects are among their best options for slowing climate change.

Carbon marketers generally see the CDM as an important tool despite its flaws. "CDM has the strictest review and approval process for emission reduction projects in the world," says Point Carbon's Hasselknippe. "Some offset projects in North America [where companies are experimenting with emission reductions and trading] are even more questionable than CDM projects. Without a regulated market, anything goes."

Are there better ways to cut emissions?

Creating carbon markets and trading carbon emission allowances is the best way to speed the transition to a low-carbon world, say proponents, because it puts a limit on carbon pollution and creates big profit incentives for cutting emissions. But critics see it as a complicated scheme that isn't guaranteed to deliver innovative energy solutions. Instead, some say, carbon taxes would be a simpler and more direct way to slow climate change.

Both approaches make polluters pay for carbon emissions, which spurs investments in cleaner technologies — with one important difference. In cap-and-trade schemes regulators specify how much pollution can be emitted, but they can't predict exactly how much allowances will cost once trading starts. Many factors, including weather, economic conditions and the discovery of new technologies influence fossil fuel use, which can drive demand for carbon allowances either up or down.

Economists can model what allowance prices may look like, but experience can be quite different from predictions, as the U.S. acid rain trading program of the 1990s (*see p. 112*) and the trial phase of EU ETS both showed.

Carbon taxes, on the other hand, charge polluters a set rate for each ton of greenhouse gases released, so there are no surprises about compliance costs. Regulators can't be sure, however, how taxes will affect pollution levels because they don't know how businesses will handle those costs. Some companies may pay taxes on their emissions and pass the expense on to consumers, while others clean up their operations to avoid the extra charge. In other words, carbon taxes offer more certainty for businesses, but cap-and-trade systems provide more certainty that the environment will improve.

"A tax doesn't put any legal limits on how much pollution can be released, so it's like a blind bet," says Fred Krupp, president of the Environmental Defense Fund

(EDF). "You know what the ante is, but not what the payoff will be. Only a cap guarantees results."

Norway has achieved mixed results since it imposed a $65-per-ton carbon tax on oil and gas companies in 1991. The tax prompted StatoilHydro, one of Norway's largest energy companies, to sharply cut its carbon emissions, largely by pumping them into an undersea reservoir. Today the firm is one of the world's few companies doing large-scale geologic storage of CO_2 emissions.[21]

But StatoilHydro also has expanded drilling operations since the tax was levied. So, even though the company is more carbon efficient than many other big energy producers, its net emissions have increased as world demand for oil has grown. Today Norway's total GHG emissions are 15 percent higher than in 1991. Norway still has the tax in place, but it also has joined the EU ETS, even though it is not an EU member.

Cap-and-trade supporters also argue that carbon trading generates larger investments in new technologies than taxes do, because polluters can turn emissions into income by cleaning them up and selling their unneeded allowances. "A tax creates no such market and, so, fails to enlist the full range of human potential in a struggle where every bit of creativity is needed," writes Krupp.[22] But many energy experts say a whole suite of measures is needed to commercialize new energy technologies and that the process shouldn't be left up to market forces. Rather, they argue, a combination of big governmental investments and other measures like tax credits and clean energy targets are needed to help ensure that clean technologies are put to use.

"Emissions trading won't do much to stimulate investment in research and development of technologies that may be able to deliver deep cuts in emissions in the future," says Chris Riedy, research director at the CAP Institute for Sustainable Futures at the University of Technology in Sydney, Australia. "Markets are very good at meeting short-term goals but not so good at looking many years ahead."

Australia is developing a national carbon trading plan, Riedy notes, but it also has established a national target to generate 20 percent of its energy from renewable fuels by 2020. "That will ensure that renewable energy is developed over time until it can establish itself in the market," says Riedy. "We need to give the industry some long-term certainty."

The challenge is even larger in fast-growing countries like China, India and Brazil, which are just now industrializing and have not yet accepted binding caps on GHG emissions. As those countries raise their living standards over the next several decades, they will account for a rising share of world energy consumption. It is crucial to help those countries move onto clean energy pathways in order to slow climate change.

For instance, carbon trading could become an important option for China at some point, says Yang Fuqiang, chief representative in Beijing for the U.S.-based Energy Foundation. "China is now the top CO_2 emitter in the world, and we expect that its emissions will be much larger by 2030, perhaps as much as 20 percent of world emissions," he says. "If carbon becomes a commodity that is traded in the market, and China is the biggest source, trading can help China make more cuts because businesses will see value in carbon."

But several things must happen before carbon trading becomes a useful tool for cutting Chinese GHG emissions, Yang continues. First, Beijing must make a political commitment to reducing emissions. Then the Chinese government must fund development of clean energy sources. Carbon trading will not work, however, without a strong legal system to ensure trades are protected and penalties enforced if partners violate the rules.

"China's legal systems aren't strong enough for carbon trading yet," says Yang.

Does carbon trading help developing countries?

Global climate change policy has been complicated by the need to create strategies that enable countries to share the burdens fairly. Because developed nations got rich from fossil-fueled growth and produced most of the human-driven warming that has occurred to date, the framers of the Kyoto Protocol decided that developed countries should make the deepest GHG emissions cuts. However, large developing countries like China and India are rapidly becoming the world's biggest carbon sources, so it is also crucial to limit their emissions while allowing their citizens to enjoy rising standards of living, say climate experts.

"[W]e need to provide resources to see that the developing countries don't get hooked onto the same path of development that we have," said Rajendra K. Pachauri,

AFP/Getty Images/Frederic J. Brown

China's booming growth has made it one of the world's top emitters of carbon dioxide, the most abundant greenhouse gas (GHG). Advocates of carbon trading say that if China were to set formal limits on its GHG emissions, polluters would have an incentive to cut emissions in order to trade their allowances for cash.

chairman of the Intergovernmental Panel on Climate Change (IPCC), which advises governments on climate science.[23]

The Clean Development Mechanism was designed as a first step to help poor countries grow while reducing their emissions. But critics argue that CDM projects primarily benefit the rich nations that sponsor them and that some actually damage the environment in the host countries.

For instance, the environmental advocacy group International Rivers charged in a 2007 report that awarding carbon reduction credits to numerous hydropower projects resulted in "blindly subsidizing the destruction of rivers, while the dams it supports are helping destroy the environmental integrity of the CDM." The study contended that the CDM has few standards to block projects that harm nearby ecosystems and that many hydropower projects applying for CDM credit would clearly be built in any case. As examples it cited a 60-megawatt dam in Kenya that started construction in 1999 (before the CDM was established) and an 880-megawatt dam in Brazil that applied for CDM validation six months after it began generating power in May 2007.[24]

Funding is not the only yardstick, replies U.N. spokesman David Abbass. "A company might have the ability to undertake an emission-reduction improvement, but not the incentive," he says. "If CDM was a motivating factor, then the project could potentially qualify, regardless of when construction was begun. In most hydro projects, CDM is providing incentives for efficiency improvements such as installing more efficient turbines. Such a decision could be undertaken after dam construction has begun or even after the dam has entered operation."

Forest carbon credits are also controversial. Under the CDM program, carbon credits can be granted for planting trees on formerly forested land that is either being reforested or used for other purposes. Many early CDM forestry projects were commercial tree plantations that were popular because planting swathes of fast-growing tree species absorbs large quantities of carbon. But opponents complained that such projects sometimes ended up clearing large areas of native forest, expelling local populations and damaging the environment.

"The fact that eucalyptus absorbs carbon dioxide to grow . . . can never be used to justify the environmental, social, economic and cultural damage that has occurred in places where large-scale monoculture tree plantations have been implemented in our country," wrote 53 unions and nonprofits in 2003 opposing a tree plantation proposed by a company called Plantar in the Brazilian state of Minas Gerais. The project ultimately was approved by the CDM board after three tries, not for absorbing carbon into the trees but for using a low-carbon process to turn those trees into charcoal.[25]

"The CDM is riven with fraud, just like other government-to-government aid programs, and it doesn't save any carbon," says Michael Northcott, a divinity professor at Scotland's Edinburgh University who views carbon trading as a route by which governments can avoid imposing hard limits on GHG emissions. Citing projects like the Plantar venture, Northcott writes, "The new global carbon market is not incentivizing real reductions in emissions. But it has created tremendous, new trading opportunities and new opportunities for fraud and injustice."[26]

Now, however, awarding credits for forest protection is gaining new support from tropical countries and conservation experts, who say forests can soak up carbon emissions, protect biodiversity and provide economic benefits to developing nations. Advocates are proposing some new approaches to make this method more rigorous. For example, avoided emissions would be measured at the national level instead of project by project, so it would be harder for a host country to claim credit for saving one forest while it cut down others.[27]

Advocates say the new approach would reward countries that preserve their forests instead of cutting them down and then seeking carbon credits for new tree plantations. "Central African countries consider that their efforts made in managing forests deserve to be recognized and supported, because they are positive for climate," the 15-member Coalition of Rainforest Nations contended in 2007.[28] More than 300 national leaders, research institutes and conservation groups have signed a policy statement urging governments to include tropical forests in global carbon markets.[29]

As negotiations on a post-Kyoto climate treaty proceed, CDM officials say the program needs to be scaled up. "Carbon markets and market-based mechanisms, like the [CDM], are essential for achieving the large shifts in investment required . . . to put the world on a clean path to development," said the U.N.'s de Boer.[30]

For the long term, some experts are thinking beyond the CDM model. "The CDM only lets developing countries trade credits if they prove additionality project-by-project, which is a nightmare. It's cumbersome, it leads to endless arguments and small countries have been squeezed out by big projects in China, India and Brazil," says EDF's Krupp. "We should . . . offer all developing nations technical assistance and more generous emissions targets if they agree to cap their emissions quickly. We need a global system where everyone agrees to a cap that's fair, given their level of development."

Even CDM advocates agree that benefits have been spread unequally up to now. About three-quarters of all CDM projects to date are located in China, Brazil, India and South Korea.[31] Many poor regions like sub-Saharan Africa, which are extremely vulnerable to the negative impacts of climate change, have seen little benefit from carbon trading.

"So far, the poorest developing countries have been bypassed — and there have been limited benefits for broad-based sustainable development" from carbon trading, the U.N. Development Programme observed in its 2007/2008 *Human Development Report.* "Marginal women farmers in Burkina Faso or Ethiopia are not well placed to negotiate with carbon brokers in the City of London."

However, the report noted, new approaches, such as "bundling" many small, rural projects together for CDM credit, could help poor countries participate.[32] Under a 2006 initiative called the Nairobi Framework, the U.N. is working to channel CDM projects to countries in sub-Saharan Africa. In 2008 the U.N. Environment Programme estimated that CDM projects in Africa could generate nearly $1 billion worth of credits by 2012.[33]

BACKGROUND

Who Pays for Pollution?

The fledgling global carbon trading industry represents the intersection of two complex debates that stretch back for more than a century. Scientists have worked since the early 1800s to understand how Earth's climate systems function and whether human actions affect them. And for nearly as long, economists who study the environment have sought cost-effective ways to control pollution.

Climate science has been international from its earliest days. In 1859 Irish physicist John Tyndall showed that certain gases in the atmosphere absorbed heat. Svante Arrhenius, a Swedish chemist, built on this idea with his calculation in 1896 that doubling the quantity of CO_2 in the atmosphere would raise Earth's average by 5 to 6 degrees Centigrade. Other researchers have shown that natural processes also influence climate cycles. For example, in 1860, Scottish physicist James Croll theorized that regular variations in Earth's orbit could trigger ice ages. Eighty years later Milutin Milankovic, a Serbian geophysicist, calculated these variations more precisely and developed a theory of glacial periods, now known as Milankovic cycles.

Other environmental issues were more urgent in the early 1900s. Air and water in industrialized countries were already heavily polluted from factory operations and urban growth, but governments had little power to respond. In Britain and the United States the nuisance doctrine — an historic concept of English common law — held that people should not use their property in ways that infringed heavily on their neighbors and that injured parties could sue those responsible for noise, odors and toxic discharges. Noxious facilities such as metal smelters were frequent early targets for nuisance lawsuits in the United States.

Indonesian environmental activists at the U.N. climate change conference in Bali, Indonesia, last December demonstrate against a proposal to award carbon credits to tropical countries that join the Reducing Emissions From Deforestation and Degradation (REDD) program. The protesters say the Indonesian government can't handle the delicate and complicated carbon trading scheme and that the program will benefit developed countries and large corporations at the expense of indigenous communities. Delegates agreed to include forest conservation in future discussions on a new global warming treaty.

However, nuisance law was ineffective at controlling harmful discharges and emissions from large-scale industrial production. With pollution coming from many sources, it was hard to prove direct connections between discharges and impacts. Moreover, by the early 1900s, U.S. courts had come to view pollution as an unavoidable result of economic activity. Rather than shutting down dirty factories, they generally weighed harms against benefits and compensated plaintiffs for serious damages while allowing polluters to keep operating.[34]

Governments then developed new approaches, like zoning, which established rules for using large areas of land. City and state agencies enforced a growing body of public health laws barring practices such as dumping untreated waste into waterways. In 1920, British economist Arthur Pigou proposed a new option: pollution taxes. Pollution, he argued, was a "negative externality" — a production cost that polluters did not have to pay for. If

CHRONOLOGY

1900s-1960s *As scientists study Earth's climate, experts debate controlling pollution efficiently.*

1920 British economist Arthur Pigou suggests taxing polluters for the indirect costs of their emissions.

1945 Researchers start developing models to test atmospheric behavior.

1957 American geochemist Charles David Keeling begins measuring atmospheric carbon dioxide (CO_2) levels in Hawaii, where readings are not skewed by pollution.

1960 British economist Ronald Coase proposes tradable emission allowances.

1970s-1980s *Scientists warn that humans may be causing global warming. Stricter pollution controls are enacted.*

1970 Congress creates Environmental Protection Agency, expands Clean Air Act.

1972 First major global environmental conference — held in Stockholm, Sweden — spurs creation of United Nations Environment Programme.

1976 Scientists identify deforestation as a major cause of climate change.

1980 U.S. President Ronald Reagan's election signals a backlash against technology-specific regulations.

1987 Montreal Protocol sets international limits on ozone-destroying gases.

1988 U.N. creates Intergovernmental Panel on Climate Change (IPCC) to provide expert views on global warming.

1990 IPCC says global temperatures are rising and likely to keep increasing. . . . U.S. adopts emissions trading to reduce acid rain.

1990s *Governments pledge to tackle climate change, but worry about costs.*

1992 The United States and over 150 nations pledge to cut greenhouse gas (GHG) emissions below 1990 levels by 2000.

1995 IPCC finds that global warming has a "human-driven" signature.

1997 Kyoto Protocol is adopted after intense negotiations, requiring developed countries to cut GHG emissions 5.2 percent, on average, below 1990 levels by 2012. U.S. Senate refuses to ratify it until developing nations also are required to make cuts.

2000s-Present *Carbon emissions trading begins, primarily in Europe. Support grows in United States for action to reduce GHGs.*

2001 IPCC says major global warming is "very likely."

2002 Clean Development Mechanism (CDM) — which allows industrialized countries to partly fulfill their carbon-reduction commitments by purchasing GHG reductions in developing countries — begins.

2003 Chicago Climate Exchange launches voluntary GHG trading system for selected U.S. companies and nonprofits.

2005 Kyoto Protocol enters into force with only the United States and Australia as non-participating developed countries. . . . EU Emissions Trading Scheme begins trials. . . . Seven Northeastern states agree to form GHG cap-and-trade system for electric power plants.

2006 EU carbon allowance prices plummet after emissions are lower than expected. . . . Global carbon trading reaches $30 billion, triple the previous year's level. . . . California promises to cut CO_2 emissions 25 percent by 2020 and to start trading emissions in 2012.

2007 IPCC says climate warming is mostly due to human activities. . . . Australia joins Kyoto Protocol. . . . Three more states join Northeastern cap-and-trade system. . . . 180 countries agree to negotiate a post-Kyoto climate change treaty.

2008 EU emissions trading scheme enters Phase 2, with tighter caps. . . . U.N. proposes stricter standards for CDM projects.

manufacturers were taxed for their pollution they would have an incentive to pollute less, according to the theory.

Economists generally agreed with Pigou's approach, but environmental regulation did not gain a serious foothold until after World War II. Economic growth expanded worldwide in the 1950s and '60s, first in the United States and then in post-war Western Europe and Japan. Governments began to limit industrial pollution, but instead of taxing it they applied so-called command-and-control standards, which told polluters how much pollution they could release and often specified what kind of technologies had to be used to clean up their operations. The same standards applied to all producers, whether their operations were relatively clean or dirty. As a result, these laws imposed much larger costs on some sources than on others.

In 1960 University of Chicago economist Ronald Coase proposed a way to control pollution with lower total costs to society. If rights to pollute could be bought and sold, he argued, polluters could bargain and find an efficient way to distribute those rights. Other economists took up his idea and called for government regulators to limit total quantities of pollutants and then create markets for pollution rights.

"[N]o person, or agency, has to set the price — it is set by the competition among buyers and sellers of rights," wrote Canadian economist John Dales in 1968.[35] This approach was more effective, proponents contended, because producers (who knew more about their own costs and production methods than regulators) could decide who would clean up and find the best ways to do it.

International Cooperation

By the 1960s, protecting the environment was a national political issue in many industrialized countries. Social Democrat Willy Brandt campaigned for chancellor in West German in 1961 with a promise to clean up air pollution. Japanese activists began suing large polluters in the mid-1960s, pressuring regulators and industrialists into adopting tighter controls. In 1970 two versions of Earth Day were launched: an international celebration on the date of the spring equinox, formally endorsed by the United Nations, and a U.S. observance on April 22 that drew millions of Americans to rallies and teach-ins.

National governments began setting standards for air and water quality, waste management and land conservation. Then a 1972 international conference on the environment, held in Stockholm, set lofty goals for international cooperation and led to the formation of the United Nations Environment Programme. The conferees declared that most environmental problems in the developing world were caused by poverty and underdevelopment, and that rich countries should try to reduce the gap between rich and poor countries.[36]

Meanwhile, international cooperation was growing in the field of climate science. In the 1950s and '60s, international research groups in the United States, England, Mexico and elsewhere developed circulation models to simulate climate processes and began testing theories about how the system might change in response to natural or manmade events. French, Danish, Swiss, Russian and U.S. scientists drilled into ice sheets in Greenland and Antarctica and analyzed air bubbles trapped thousands of years earlier to determine how the atmosphere's composition had changed over time. A growing body of climate studies showed that many processes shaped global climate patterns, and that human actions could disrupt the system.

In 1976, frustrated with the slow pace of pollution reductions under the Clean Air Act, U.S. policymakers began experimenting with market-based measures. As a first step, companies were permitted to build new factories in polluted areas if they bought credits from nearby sources that had reduced emissions below legal limits. In 1977 Congress amended the act to allow policies like banking credits (saving them for use or sale in the future). In 1982 the Environmental Protection Agency (EPA) used a trading program to phase out lead from gasoline. Refiners were issued tradable lead credits that they could sell if they were already blending unleaded gasoline or use while retooling their plants. Lead, which had been outlawed from U.S. gasoline, was finally eliminated by 1987.

Other nations also tried market-based environmental policies, primarily pollution taxes. Many European countries — including West Germany, the Netherlands, Czechoslovakia and Hungary — taxed water pollution discharges to help fund sewage treatment and bring water quality up to healthy standards.[37] France and Japan imposed charges for air pollution emissions. China also

Nonprofit Auditors Keep Projects 'Honest'

Gold Standard projects provide jobs, help the environment.

Power outages and voltage fluctuations once plagued the Honduran city of La Esperanza, and many rural residents in the surrounding countryside had no electricity at all.

Now a small hydroelectric project on the nearby Intibuca River reliably produces 13.5 megawatts of electricity — enough to power 11,000 households for a year — while avoiding 37,000 tons of annual carbon dioxide emissions from diesel generators previously used to produce electricity. And because it is a so-called run-of-river project, it generates electricity without damming the river.

The La Esperanza Hydroelectric Project is the first to be certified as reducing greenhouse gas (GHG) emissions under the Kyoto Protocol's Clean Development Mechanism (CDM). The CDM allows Third World developers whose projects reduce carbon emissions to sell "emission credits" — equal to the emissions they avoid — to polluting companies in industrialized countries.

The project also will provide a variety of other sustainable benefits in the community, such as reducing local residents' use of carbon-consuming trees for fuel, encouraging reforestation and providing reliable jobs and technical skills for the dam construction, maintenance and operating staffs, providing running water for households near the project and engaging more women in work and community life.

How can La Esperanza's developers prove their facility will provide all those benefits? The project is being evaluated by Gold Standard, an independent, nonprofit organization in Basel, Switzerland. Founded by the World Wildlife Fund and other nongovernmental organizations and funded by public and private donors, Gold Standard accredits high-quality CDM projects that benefit the local community and cut carbon emissions. Gold Standard approval gives carbon-credit buyers extra assurance that the carbon credits they are purchasing come from measurable GHG reductions that have clearly benefited the host countries where they were carried out.

Nonprofits like Gold Standard have emerged to provide extra certification for carbon offset projects because of concerns that private verification companies, which are paid by project developers, have a financial incentive to certify that the projects they are auditing reduce carbon emissions just to get them approved. And the CDM Executive Board, which reviews CDM applications, does not have enough staff to verify all of the information submitted by auditors.

"Right now, good auditors get their projects approved, but that shouldn't be the only incentive," says Stanford University law professor Michael Wara. The CDM board has "done the best it can, but it's in an untenable situation," he contends, because it is understaffed and facing a growing demand for offset credits.

---

adopted air and water pollution taxes in the early 1980s, although these levies were quite low, and a large share of the funds were distributed back to pollution sources as subsidies.[38]

Then, in an important milestone for global environmental cooperation, 23 nations signed the Montreal Protocol in 1987, agreeing to restrict production and use of industrial chemicals that were damaging Earth's protective ozone layer. Over the next decade, as science showed that damage was still occurring, more nations joined, and members amended the agreement to eliminate the substances completely. Several nations used allowance trading systems to phase out domestic use of ozone-depleting chemicals, including the United States, Canada, Mexico and Singapore.

The protocol established some other important precedents: It relied on expert advice from scientists, forced governments to act in time to prevent serious environmental harm and required developed nations to help developing countries adjust to the ban without harming their living standards.[39]

Confronting the Evidence

By the late 1980s many environmentalists and scientists believed human activities were affecting Earth's climate and that policy makers needed to act. In 1988 the United Nations established the Intergovernmental Panel on Climate Change (IPCC) to advise national governments about climate science and potential impacts from global warming. But critics, including large

Some critics have claimed that as a result of these conflicts of interest and other problems, carbon markets, in effect, are generating "rights to pollute."

"We require project developers to make positive contributions to local communities in two out of three categories — economic, social and environmental — and our screening process gives them numbers they can use to rate what they're delivering in each area," says Caitlin Sparks, U.S. marketing director for Gold Standard. "We monitor those promises through the full life of the project. U.N.-accredited auditors validate and verify all of the documents, and the information is re-verified after the project starts."

For instance, all CDM projects are supposed to promote "sustainable development," but it's usually left up to the host country to define what that means. However, Gold Standard makes its own judgment.

"They are doing the sorts of things that should be applied wholesale to CDM," says Wara. "They dig in and do better verification, which costs more and makes the process more time-consuming, but that needs to happen. We need more scrutiny of these projects."

Gold Standard projects have three key features: They must focus on renewable energy or energy efficiency to help promote a transition to a clean-energy economy; developers must prove that the carbon reductions will be "additional" to business as usual (this test is optional when projects go through CDM review but is required by Gold Standard); and they must show that their projects will make measurable economic contributions to sustainable development in host communities.

"A free market for credits will tend to focus on quantities of tons," says Sparks. "The Gold Standard is meant to focus on quality" of emission reductions.

Gold Standard projects in India and South Africa reflect the program's diversity and focus on quality:

- The Shri Chamundi biomass co-generation power plant in Karnataka, India, will generate 16 megawatts of electricity from biomass fuels such as eucalyptus branches, coconut fronds, rice husks and cashew shells. It will also use waste heat to produce steam for manufacturing, replacing boilers that run on heavy fuel oil. The plant will create more than 800 jobs, including collecting and preparing biomass, converting previously useless crop residues into fuel. It also will reduce open burning of crop wastes in fields, which pollutes the atmosphere and local water supplies.
- In Cape Town, South Africa, the Kuyasa housing service upgrade project installed ceiling insulation, solar hot water heaters and energy-efficient lighting in a low-income housing development and will install similar improvements in future developments. Making homes more energy-efficient will reduce CO_2 emissions, local air pollution and the danger of household fires.[1]

[1] Information about these projects comes from validation reports in the Gold Standard Registry, http://goldstandard.apx.com; and "Reducing the Carbon Footprint of the UN: High-Level Event on Climate Change," U.N. Headquarters, Sept. 24, 2007, www.un.org/climatechange/2007highlevel/climatefriendly.shtml.

corporations and President George H. W. Bush, argued that the scientific evidence was uncertain and that reducing GHG emissions would seriously harm economic growth.

Other nations, led by Western European countries with strong Green parties, wanted a binding agreement to limit greenhouse emissions. The Framework Convention on Climate Change (FCCC), signed at the 1992 Earth Summit in Rio de Janeiro, Brazil, amounted to a compromise: It called only for voluntary reductions in greenhouse gases to 1990 levels but laid out a path for further action. Some countries — including the Netherlands, Sweden, Finland, Norway and Denmark — passed domestic carbon taxes to reduce their emissions. But total GHG emissions from industrialized nations kept rising, making it clear that mandatory targets and timetables would be needed.

In 1997 FCCC members adopted the Kyoto Protocol, which required signatories to make specific reductions (averaging 5.2 percent below 1990 levels) by 2012. U.S. President Bill Clinton supported the goal, but his administration was worried about costs. A U.S. carbon tax was not an option: The administration had suffered an embarrassing defeat in 1993 when it proposed a BTU tax (a levy on the energy content of fuels), only to be blocked by fellow Democrats in Congress. Instead, U.S. negotiators at Kyoto pushed to include emissions trading and credits for funding offset projects in developing countries and former Eastern Bloc nations.

Although the final agreement included these policies and the Clinton administration signed the treaty, the Senate voted 95-0 for a resolution against ratifying it unless developing countries also had to make binding reduction pledges. President George W. Bush, who had promised during his campaign to limit carbon dioxide emissions, repudiated the Kyoto agreement shortly after taking office, arguing that mandatory GHG reductions (even through market-based mechanisms) would harm the U.S. economy.

Nonetheless, President Bush embraced the idea of emissions trading to address domestic air pollution issues and sought to build on a successful program initiated a decade earlier under the first Bush administration. In 1990 Congress had amended the Clean Air Act to create an emissions trading program for sulfur dioxide (SO_2) and nitrogen oxide (NO_x), two pollutants from fossil fuel-fired power plants. These emissions formed acids in the atmosphere that fell back to Earth in rain and snow, damaging forests, soils and buildings. The so-called acid rain trading program, which began in 1995, capped emissions of SO_2 (with looser limits for NO_x) and set up a trading market for emission allowances.

The program was widely viewed as a success. EPA reported in 2004 that a decade of emissions trading had reduced the power sector's SO_2 and NO_x emissions 34 and 38 percent, respectively, below 1990 levels.[40] Economists estimated trading had saved $1 billion or more per year over command-and-control approaches.[41] Touting these results, President Bush proposed emissions trading initiatives to cut U.S. SO_2 and NO_x emissions even further and suggested using a trading scheme to control mercury emissions. But congressional critics argued that these measures did not cut far or fast enough and that emissions trading was the wrong way to reduce toxic pollutants like mercury.[42]

As the Bush administration continued to oppose cutting GHG emissions, other U.S. leaders grew increasingly worried about climate change. Sens. John McCain, R-Ariz., and Joseph Lieberman, D-Conn., offered carbon cap-and-trade legislation in 2003 and 2005 and reintroduced the bill in 2007. Seeing the political handwriting on the wall, large U.S. corporations began to endorse carbon controls.

"We know enough to act on climate change," said the U.S. Climate Action Partnership, an alliance of major corporations including Alcoa, Dupont and General Motors. The group called on Congress to pass mandatory GHG limits and create a cap-and-trade system to attain them.[43]

CURRENT SITUATION

A New Player?

As Americans increasingly worry about climate change, many observers expect the United States to limit its greenhouse gas emissions and create a domestic carbon trading system after the 2008 elections. Multiple cap-and-trade bills were introduced in both houses of Congress in 2007 and 2008, including several with bipartisan support.[44] And the two major-party presidential candidates, Sens. McCain and Barack Obama, D-Ill., both pledged to set up a cap-and-trade system and to pursue deep cuts in U.S. GHG emissions.

> "Marginal women farmers in Burkina Faso or Ethiopia are not well placed to negotiate with carbon brokers in the City of London."
>
> — *U.N. Human Development Report 2007/2008*

Since the United States is one of the world's largest GHG emitters, U.S. entry into carbon trading would dramatically expand global carbon markets. New Carbon Finance, a market research firm in London, estimated in October that the total value of world carbon trading would reach $550 billion by 2012 and just over $2 trillion by 2020, even without U.S. participation. If the United States introduces a federal cap-and-trade system, however, those figures would increase to $680 billion by 2012 and more than $3 trillion by 2020.[45] By way of comparison, $3 trillion is roughly the size of the combined world markets for oil, coal, natural gas and electricity today.[46]

Two legislative proposals — one debated by the Senate in mid-2008 and a House Energy and Commerce committee proposal released on Oct. 7 — offer some indication of what national cap-and-trade legislation might look like. Both bills would cap U.S. greenhouse gas emissions and set up a trading system to reduce them. The House bill would require a 6 percent cut below 2005 levels by 2020, and the Senate bill calls for a 19 percent cut. By 2050, however, the House measure would reduce emissions by 80 percent below 2005 levels, compared to 71 percent under the Senate bill.

Along with public concern and growing scientific evidence that human activities are warming the planet, another factor pushing U.S. policy makers to act is a 2007 Supreme Court ruling which held — contrary to the Bush administration's position — that carbon dioxide was a pollutant under the Clean Air Act and that the EPA had authority to regulate it.[47] "CO_2 controls are clearly coming. The only remaining questions are when and who is going to do the controlling," said Rep. Rick Boucher, D-Va., chair of the House Energy and Commerce Committee's Subcommittee on Energy and Air Quality, in late 2008. A coauthor of the committee's cap-and-trade proposal, Boucher said he thought Congress rather than the EPA should lead on regulating carbon and that he planned to hold hearings on cap-and-trade legislation early in 2009.[48]

If Congress does pass such legislation, its effectiveness will depend on which sectors it covers, how quickly it cuts emissions and whether it compensates businesses and consumers for higher costs. Carbon marketers will watch closely to see how strictly the U.S. limits the use of offset credits from foreign sources such as CDM projects.

Some states are launching regional cap-and-trade schemes to show the approach can work and to build support for national action. In September, 10 Northeastern states, stretching from Maryland to Maine, launched the Regional Greenhouse Gas Initiative (RGGI) — the first mandatory U.S. carbon cap-and-trade system. RGGI is designed to reduce GHG emissions from electric power plants 10 percent below current levels by 2018. Unlike systems that have given polluters emission allowances for free, RGGI auctioned off its first batch of allowances and will invest the proceeds — $38.5 million, at a final price of $3.07 per ton of CO_2 — in energy efficiency and renewable energy programs.

State officials called the first RGGI auction a success. "Demand was high, and fears of low-ball bidding did not come to pass," said Democratic New York Gov. David Paterson. "Instead, RGGI has used market forces to set a price on carbon."[49]

River waters crash into a Buddhist temple during high tide on the outskirts of Bangkok, Thailand. Climatologists say higher global temperatures are causing polar ice caps to melt, raising sea and river levels in low-lying coastal areas. Carbon trading schemes are the world's current answer to the question of how to control global warming.

AP Photo/Somnuk Attipanyo

At nearly the same time, seven Western states and four Canadian provinces agreed on the basics of a broader regional cap-and-trade program that would cover emissions from electricity generation, industry, transportation and residential and commercial energy use. The initiative would cut members' GHG emissions to 15 percent below 2005 levels by 2020. Trading is scheduled to start in 2012, with a second phase beginning in 2015.[50]

"The Western Climate Initiative is increasingly the system that many observers see as a possible precursor to a U.S. federal system because of its size and design features. They've received input from some key experts who were involved in setting up the EU system," says Hasselknippe of the Point Carbon research firm. However, if Congress enacts national GHG controls, that system would almost certainly replace regional cap-and-trade programs.

Beyond Kyoto

Global negotiators are working on a follow-on agreement to the Kyoto Protocol, which only limits signatories' emissions through 2012, although some countries have made longer-term commitments. For example, in 2007 EU countries pledged to cut their total GHG emissions 20 percent by 2020 and to increase this target to 30 percent if other nations sign a post-Kyoto treaty.

Thousands of planes will be required to cut their carbon emissions now that the European Union has decided that airliners should be included in EU carbon emission caps under Phase 3 of the Kyoto Protocol climate change treaty, beginning in 2012. Airlines are resisting, saying that their industry has been hit hard by high oil prices and that the EU does not have legal authority to regulate emissions from flights that originate in other countries. Above, planes in Glasgow, Scotland.

At a contentious international conference in 2007 in Bali, Indonesia, negotiators agreed on basic principles for crafting a post-Kyoto agreement. The plan calls for finalizing a new treaty in 2009 (to take effect in 2013) that includes deep cuts in developed countries' greenhouse emissions and unspecified "mitigation actions" by developing countries. It also pledges to develop policies that reward tropical countries for protecting their forests and creates a fund using a surcharge on CDM projects to help poor countries adapt to climate change impacts.[51]

Many developed countries wanted emissions cuts of 25 to 40 percent in rich countries by 2020, but the United States refused to approve an agenda with specific targets. U.S. representatives were booed during the talks, and at one point Papua New Guinea's representative was cheered when he told them, "If you're not going to lead, get out of the way." Ultimately, however, the U.S. supported the principles — the first time that the Bush administration had agreed to negotiate climate targets with other nations.[52]

It is not yet clear what shape a post-Kyoto agreement may take. It could set binding national emissions targets, like the Kyoto treaty, or build on pledges by individual countries or groups of countries. Some nations have already made significant commitments outside the Kyoto framework. The European Parliament, for example, is already setting emissions caps and planning to auction some carbon allowances in the third phase of EU ETS, to start in 2013.[53]

Some developing countries have also pledged to reduce their contribution to climate change. China's current five-year plan, which runs through 2010, calls for reducing the energy intensity of gross domestic product (the amount of energy used to produce each unit of income) 20 percent below 2005 levels by 2010. Beijing is also working to generate 10 percent of national energy demand with renewable sources by 2010 and 15 percent by 2020; by contrast, the U.S. currently gets about 7 percent of its energy from renewables. And Costa Rica has pledged to become carbon-neutral, as have New Zealand, Monaco, Norway and Iceland.[54]

Beyond these steps, however, experts warn that unless large developing countries like China, India, Indonesia and Brazil accept binding carbon caps soon, it will be impossible to avoid disastrous climate change. "If China and India keep doing what they're doing, their emissions will be tremendous," says Kollmuss of the Stockholm Environment Institute. "At the same time, these countries need to develop, so we need to find a just and equitable climate solution that will get them to buy in."

The U.N. Development Programme seconded this view in its 2007/2008 *Human Development Report*, which urged large developing countries to accept emissions targets proportional to what they could accomplish. "Any multilateral agreement without quantitative commitments from developing countries will lack credibility," the report asserted. However, it also argued that it would be impossible to negotiate such an agreement unless wealthy countries provided money and technology to help poorer nations adopt low-carbon strategies.[55]

Some advocates in developing countries worry that they will be asked to take on GHG reduction commitments when many rich nations have not cut their emissions significantly (or, in the case of the United States, at all).

"The message from Bali is that the fight against climate change will be brutal and selfish," says Sunita Narain, director of the Centre for Science and Environment in New Delhi. She agrees that India is "devastatingly vulnerable" to climate change impacts like floods and heat waves. By signing an action plan in Bali without hard reduction targets or timetables, she argues,

Should the European Union cap aviation carbon emissions?

YES
Joao Vieira
Policy Officer, European Federation for Transport and Environment

From *T&E Bulletin*, July 22, 2008

After years of us and others highlighting the environmental damage caused by aviation, the [European Union] has finally done something to try and counteract its impact. It has shown courage, in particular, in standing up to threats from the USA and against a background of abysmal inaction from the International Civil Aviation Organisation, the body charged with regulating emissions from aircraft under the Kyoto Protocol. . . .

So why are we at *T&E* so reluctant to be happy about this? There are two reasons. The terms on which aviation has entered the ETS [Emissions Trading Scheme] will mean very limited reductions in emissions from aircraft [which] might create the illusion that other measures that would do much more to reduce emissions . . . are no longer needed. And . . . the ETS might now be seen as a "silver bullet" solution for emissions from transport. . . .

Airlines will be allowed to buy permits from other sectors without restrictions, so their emissions will continue to grow. Instead of changing to greener technologies and operations, the aviation sector is likely to limit its climate efforts to buying permits in the carbon market. In addition, this directive only addresses CO_2 [carbon dioxide] emissions, ignoring the fact that NO_x [nitrogen oxides] is emitted from aircraft . . . and aviation-induced clouds also have climatic impact. It will mean aviation remains the least-efficient and most climate-intensive mode of transport.

The limitations of a cap-and-trade system's ability to effectively reduce emissions from transport should be a lesson for EU decision-makers, some of whom seem tempted by the idea of emissions trading for road transport.

The ETS is . . . for large, fixed-emission facilities. Transport . . . has numerous operators of mobile emissions sources, which do not face international competition [since] transport is a geographically bound activity.

T&E has said all along that including aviation in the ETS can only be a first step. If the transport sector is to reduce its emissions, other measures to address the climatic impacts of all modes of transport will be needed.

Without the courage to apply fuel taxation, fair and efficient infrastructure charging and strict emission standards, applying emissions trading to transport will simply allow transport to keep growing its emissions. . . . That is unfair to [other] industries, and irresponsible to future generations.

NO
Giovanni Bisignani
Director General and CEO, International Air Transport Association (IATA)

From remarks at the Farnborough [England] International Air Show, July 18, 2008

Today, airlines are in crisis. Oil is above $140. Jet fuel is over $180. In five years fuel went from 14 percent of operating costs to over 34 percent. If oil averages $135 for the rest of the year, the industry bill will be $190 billion. And next year it could be over $250 billion. . . .

IATA's environment leadership is delivering results. We worked with our members to implement best practices in fuel management. In 2007 this saved 6.7 million tonnes of CO_2 and $1.3 billion in cost.

We also worked with governments and air navigation service providers. Optimising 395 routes and procedures in 81 airports saved 3.8 million tonnes of CO_2 and $831 million in costs.

We could save up to 73 million tonnes of CO_2 with better air traffic management, but, while painting themselves green to win votes, governments are slow to deliver results. . . .

IATA supports emissions trading, but it must be global, fair and effective. Europe's approach could not be more wrong.

First, it's not an effective incentive. Developed when oil was $55 per barrel, it was meant to be an economic stick to force airlines to become more fuel-efficient. Europe's politicians had not foreseen the giant club of $140 oil.

It has beaten the life out of 25 airlines already this year, and we expect many more to follow into bankruptcy protection if they can afford it or straight into liquidation if they cannot. To survive, airlines are doing everything possible to reduce fuel burn. The [Emissions Trading Scheme] will add costs but will not improve the results. . . .

Second, the timing is wrong. Why make long-range policy decisions in the moment of a crisis when the future is completely uncertain — even five years out. And why make fuel more expensive when it is at its highest level ever — an 87 percent increase in the last year? Clearly, green politics has got in the way of good policy. . . .

How can Europe expect to charge an Australian airline for emissions over the Middle East on a flight from Asia to Europe? This will be challenged at [the International Civil Aviation Organisation] and in the International Court of Justice. And a responsible industry could easily be caught in a trade war of a layering of punitive economic measures.

Instead of cleaning up the environment, Europe is creating an international legal mess.

AP Photo/Ed Wray

Growers burned down a dense forest in Sumber, Kalimantan, Indonesia, to make way for a palm oil plantation. Deforestation accounts for about 20 percent of human-generated greenhouse gas emissions worldwide. Environmentalists point out that forest preservation is one of the most cost-effective ways to address climate change.

"The world powers have reneged on all of us. Now developing countries will be even more reluctant to engage. Hardliners will say, 'We told you so.' "

In September U.N. Secretary-General Ban Ki-moon announced a cooperative program to test ways of managing tropical forests to keep them healthy and store large amounts of carbon. Norway donated $35 million for the first phase, which will involve at least nine countries in Africa, Asia and Latin America. The program seeks to pave the way for including forest conservation in a post-Kyoto treaty.

"This initiative will not only demonstrate how forests can have an important role as part of a post-2012 climate regime," said Ban, "it will also help build much needed confidence that the world community is ready to support the implementation of an inclusive, ambitious and comprehensive climate regime, once it is ratified."[56]

OUTLOOK

Cost of Inaction

As world leaders struggle to address this fall's global financial meltdown, some policy makers say now is the wrong time to impose further limits on greenhouse gas emissions. Putting a price on carbon, they worry, will raise energy costs when economies are already sputtering.

In October, for example, some East European countries tried unsuccessfully to delay the auctioning of EU ETS emission allowances, and conservative U.S. legislators questioned whether the economy could handle the added impact of cap-and-trade legislation.[57] If the world goes through a prolonged recession, energy prices are likely to fall, which would ease the financial crunch somewhat but would also reduce some of the imperative to shift away from fossil fuels.

Indeed, controlling carbon emissions won't be cheap. The total cost of controlling global warming could cost 1-2 percent of world gross domestic product — or roughly $350 to $700 billion — per year over the next few decades, according to several prominent economists, including Nicholas Stern of Great Britain and Jeffery Sachs of the United States.[58]

But advocates say it's more urgent than ever to act on climate change. Since renewable fuels like wind, solar and geothermal energy are free or low-cost, investing in them now will not only reduce GHG emissions but also make nations less dependent on oil and gas. And, they argue, green technologies can generate thousands of new, high-paying jobs.

Supporting this view, a 2008 study by David Roland-Holst, an economist at the University of California, calculated that energy efficiency policies in California from 1976 through 2006 had saved households some $56 billion and created about 1.5 million jobs.[59]

"The longer we wait to cap our emissions, the farther we fall behind in the remaking of a $6 trillion economy," says Environmental Defense Fund President Krupp.

Moreover, the cost of inaction is likely to be much higher than those of cutting emissions. Climate change will have major impacts worldwide, especially in poor countries that have few resources to protect people or move them out of harm's way. Global policy experts warn that recent progress against poverty in developing countries could be wiped out by climate change impacts like crop failures, water shortages and catastrophic flooding in river deltas that could leave millions hungry and homeless.

"If we are to avoid the catastrophic reversals in human development that will follow in the wake of climate change, we need to more than halve emissions of greenhouse gases," wrote Kevin Watkins, lead author of the U.N.'s *Human Development Report*, during the Bali climate conference. "That will not happen without a global accord that decarbonises growth and extends access to affordable energy in the developing world: a shake-up in energy policy backed by a programme similar to the post-Second World War Marshall Plan."[60] Under that initiative, the United States spent about $13 billion from 1947 through 1951 to rebuild war-torn Western Europe. The price tag for a program on the same scale, measured in 2007 dollars, would be roughly $740 billion.[61]

Rising concerns about costs make it increasingly likely that carbon trading will be a central part of the climate change solution, since it offers the opportunity to make cuts where they are most affordable. But cap-and-trade programs alone will not be enough. Government also must fund energy research and development; tighten energy efficiency standards and create markets for new technologies by setting national renewable energy targets. The overall goal, says IPCC Chair Pachauri, is to create a cleaner, less resource-intensive development path.

Pachauri often recalls Mahatma Gandhi's quip when asked whether India's people should have the same standard of living as the British. "It took Britain half the resources of the planet to achieve this prosperity," Gandhi replied. "How many planets will a country like India require?"[62]

NOTES

1. Mamuni Das, "Germany To Buy Carbon Credits From TTD Solar Kitchen," *The Hindu Business Line. com*, Aug. 24, 2005, www.thehindubusinessline .com/2005/08/24/stories/2005082402960100.htm; "Solar Amenities Way Above Sea Level," *The Statesman*, Oct. 15, 2006, www.thestatesman.net/ page.arcview.php?clid=30&id=161337&usrsess=1; Madhur Singh, "India's Temples Go Green," *Time*, July 7, 2008, www.time.com/time/world/article/ 0,8599,1820844,00.html.

2. Singh, *ibid.*

3. http://cdm.unfccc.int/UserManagement/File Storage/ 4WZXEVUUTRCJDV4AC6SY7VSL0KBFC5.

4. David Adam, "World Carbon Dioxide Levels Highest for 650,000 Years, Says U.S. Report," *The Guardian*, May 13, 2008, www.guardian.co.uk/ environment/2008/may/13/carbonemissions.climate change.

5. For background, see Colin Woodard, "Curbing Climate Change," *CQ Global Researcher*, February 2007, pp. 27-52.

6. For background, see Mary H. Cooper, "Global Warming Treaty," *CQ Researcher*, Jan. 26, 2001, pp. 41-64.

7. Garrett Hardin, "The Tragedy of the Commons," *Science*, Dec. 13, 1968, pp. 1243-1248.

8. "Carbon 2008" Point Carbon, March 11, 2008, p. 3.

9. Fiona Harvey, "World Carbon Trading Value Doubles," *Financial Times*, May 7, 2008, http://us.ft.com/ ftgateway/superpage.ft?news_id=fto05072008 2214562909.

10. "Regional Initiatives," Pew Center on Global Climate Change, www.pewclimate.org/what_s_ being_done/in_the_states/regional_initiatives.cfm.

11. Sen. Barack Obama (D-Ill.) endorsed cutting U.S. emissions 80 percent below 1990 levels by 2050, while Sen. John McCain (R-Ariz.) called for reducing at least 60 percent below 1990 levels on the same timetable. "Science Debate 2008," www.sciencedebate2008.com.

12. "Emission Impossible: Access to JI/CDM Credits in Phase II of the EU Emissions Trading Scheme," World Wildlife Fund-UK, June 2007, p. 10, http:// assets.panda.org/downloads/emission_impossible__ final_.pdf.

13. A. Denny Ellerman and Paul Joskow, "The European Union's Emissions Trading System in Perspective," Pew Climate Center, May 2008, figure 1, p. 13, www.pewclimate.org/docUploads/EU-ETS-In-Perspective-Report.pdf.

14. "Europe's Dirty Secret: Why the EU Emissions Trading Scheme Isn't Working," *Open Europe*, 2007, p. 16, www.openeurope.org.uk/research/etsp2.pdf.

15. "What's Really Going On in the European Carbon Market," Environmental Defense Fund, June 27, 2007, http://blogs.edf.org/climate411/2007/06/27/ eu_carbon_market/.

16. Ellerman and Joskow, *op. cit.*, pp. 12-15.

17. James Kanter, "Europe Forcing Airlines to Buy Emissions Permits," *The New York Times*, Oct. 25, 2008, p. B2.

18. "Emission Impossible . . . ," *op. cit.*, pp. 3-4.

19. Michael W. Wara and David G. Victor, "A Realistic Policy on International Carbon Offsets," *Working Paper #74*, Program on Energy and Sustainable Development, Stanford University, April 2008, p. 5, http://pesd.stanford.edu/publications/a_realistic_policy_on_international_carbon_offsets/.

20. Yvo de Boer, "Prepared Remarks for Public Debate on the Kyoto Mechanisms," New York, Oct. 9, 2008.

21. Leila Abboud, "An Exhausting War On Emissions," *The Wall Street Journal*, Sept. 30, 2008, p. A15.

22. Fred Krupp and Miriam Horn, *Earth: The Sequel: The Race to Reinvent Energy and Stop Global Warming* (2008), p. 247.

23. "A Conversation with Nobel Prize Winner Rajendra Pachauri," *Yale Environment 360*, June 3, 2008, http://e360.yale.edu/content/print.msp?id=2006.

24. Barbara Haya, "Failed Mechanism: How the CDM is Subsidizing Hydro Developers and Harming the Kyoto Protocol," *International Rivers*, November 2007, http://internationalrivers.org/files/Failed_Mechanism_3.pdf.

25. Oliver Balch, "Forests: A Carbon Trader's Gold Mine?" ClimateChangeCorp.com, May 7, 2008, www.climatechangecorp.com/content.asp?ContentID=5305; for project details and review documents, see "Project 1051: Mitigation of Methane Emissions in the Charcoal Production of Plantar, Brazil," United Nations Framework Convention on Climate Change, http://cdm.unfccc.int/Projects/DB/DNV-CUK1175235824.92/view.

26. Michael S. Northcott, *A Moral Climate: The Ethics of Global Warming* (2007), p. 136.

27. William F. Laurance, "A New Initiative to Use Carbon Trading for Tropical Forest Conservation," *Biotropica*, vol. 39, no. 1 (2007), pp. 20-24, www.globalcanopy.org/themedia/NewCarbonTrading.pdf.

28. Keya Acharya, "Rainforest Coalition Proposes Rewards for 'Avoided Deforestation,'" *Environmental News Network*, Aug. 15, 2007, www.enn.com/ecosystems/article/21854.

29. "Forests in the Fight Against Climate Change," www.forestsnow.org.

30. De Boer, *op. cit.*

31. "CDM Experiences and Lessons" (presentation), slide 5, U.N. Development Programme, April 1, 2008, http://unfccc.meta-fusion.com/kongresse/AWG_08/downl/0401_1500_p2/Krause%20UNDP%20JI_CDM1.pdf.

32. "Fighting Climate Change: Human Solidarity in a Developed World, *Human Development Report 2007/2008* (2008), United Nations Development Programme, p. 155.

33. " 'Global Green Deal' — Environmentally-Focused Investment Historic Opportunity for 21st Century Prosperity and Job Generation," United Nations Environment Programme, press release, Oct. 22, 2008.

34. Richard N. L. Andrews, *Managing the Environment, Managing Ourselves: A History of American Environmental Policy* (1999), pp. 127-128.

35. J. H. Dales, *Pollution, Property and Prices* (1968), p. 801.

36. The final conference declaration is online at www.unep.org/Documents.Multilingual/Default.asp?DocumentID=97&ArticleID=1503.

37. See Thomas H. Tietenberg, *Environmental and Natural Resource Economics*, 5th ed. (2000), pp. 454-455.

38. Randall A. Bluffstone, "Environmental Taxes in Developing and Transition Economies," *Public Finance and Management*, vol. 3, no. 1 (2003), pp. 152-55.

39. Richard Elliot Benedick, *Ozone Diplomacy: New Directions in Safeguarding the Planet* (1998), pp. 314-320.

40. "Acid Rain Trading Program, 2004 Progress Report," U.S. Environmental Protection Agency, October 2005, pp. 2, 10, www.epa.gov/airmarkt/progress/docs/2004report.pdf.

41. Robert N. Stavins, "Lessons Learned from SO2 Allowance Trading," *Choices*, 2005, p. 53, www.choicesmagazine.org/2005-1/environment/2005-1-11.htm; Nathaniel O. Keohane and Sheila M. Olmstead, *Markets and the Environment* (2007), p. 184.

42. For background see Jennifer Weeks, "Coal's Comeback," *CQ Researcher*, Oct. 5, 2007, pp. 817-840. The Bush administration then issued regulations through EPA to promote emissions trading, but in 2007 the D.C. Circuit Court held that the EPA did not have authority under the Clean Air Act to develop such broad trading programs.

43. "A Call for Action," Jan. 22, 2007, U.S. Climate Action Partnership, p. 2, www.us-cap.org/Climate Report.pdf.

44. For a summary of bills pending in September 2008, see "Comparison of Legislative Climate Change Targets," World Resources Institute, Sept. 9, 2008, www.wri.org/publication/usclimatetargets.

45. "Carbon Market Round-Up Q3 2008," *New Carbon Finance*, Oct. 10, 2008; www.newcarbonfinance.com/download.php?n=2008-10-10_PR_Carbon_Markets_Q3_20082.pdf&f=fileName&t=NCF_downloads.

46. Simon Kennedy, " 'Carbon Trading' Enriches the World's Energy Desks," *Marketwatch*, May 16, 2007.

47. *Massachusetts v. Environmental Protection Agency*, 549 U.S. 497 (2007).

48. Rep. Rick Boucher, remarks at the Society of Environmental Journalists annual conference, Roanoke, Va., Oct. 17, 2008.

49. "Governor Paterson Hails Nation's First Global Warming Cap and Trade Auction A Success," Sept. 29, 2008, www.ny.gov/governor/press/press_0929083.html.

50. For details see www.westernclimateinitiative.org/.

51. Robert N. Stavins and Joseph Aldy, "Bali Climate Change Conference: Key Takeaways," Harvard Project on International Climate Agreements, Dec. 18, 2007, http://belfercenter.ksg.harvard.edu/publication/17781/bali_climate_change_conference.html.

52. Daniel Howden and Geoffrey Lean, "Bali Conference: World Unity Forces U.S. to Back Climate Deal," *The Independent*, Dec. 16, 2007, www.independent.co.uk/environment/climate-change/bali-conference-world-unity-forces-us-to-back-climate-deal-765583.html; Gary LaMoshi, "Bumpy Ride Ahead for Bali Road Map," *Asia Times*, Dec. 18, 2007, www.atimes.com/atimes/Southeast_Asia/IL18Ae01.html.

53. Ian Traynor and David Gow, "EU Promises 20% Reduction in Carbon Emissions by 2020," *The Guardian*, Feb. 21, 2007, www.guardian.co.uk/environment/2007/feb/21/climatechange.climatechangeenvironment; Pete Harrison and Gerard Wynn, "EU Lawmakers Watch Credit Crisis in Climate Fight," Reuters, Oct. 7, 2008.

54. Stefan Lovgren, "Costa Rica Aims to Be 1st Carbon-Neutral Country," *National Geographic News*, March 7, 2008, http://news.nationalgeographic.com/news/2008/03/080307-costa-rica.html.

55. "Fighting Climate Change, . . ." *op. cit.*, pp. 27-28.

56. " 'Redd'-Letter Day for Forests: United Nations, Norway United to Combat Climate Change from Deforestation, Spearheading New Programme," U.N. press release, Sept. 24, 2008.

57. Pete Harrison and Gerard Wynn, "EU Lawmakers Watch Credit Crisis in Climate Fight," Reuters, Oct. 7, 2008, www.reuters.com/article/rbssIndustryMaterials UtilitiesNews/idUSL711408420081007?sp=true; Dina Cappiello, "Economic Woes Chill Effort to Stop Global Warming," The Associated Press, Oct. 12, 2008, http://ap.google.com/article/ALeqM5jFaQmoL WbpKq8HH1AAQ5GoGZjz0gD93OTVC00; James Kanter, "Europe's Leadership in Carbon Control at Risk in Credit Crisis," *The New York Times*, Oct. 21, 2008, p. B10.

58. Juliette Jowit and Patrick Wintour, "Cost of Tackling Global Climate Change Has Doubled, Warns Stern," *The Guardian*, June 26, 2008, www.guardian.co.uk/environment/2008/jun/26/climatechange.scienceofclimatechange; Jeffrey D. Sachs, *Common Wealth: Economics for a Crowded Planet* (2008), pp. 308-311.

59. David Roland-Holst, "Energy Efficiency, Innovation, and Job Creation in California," Center for Energy, Resources and Economic Sustainability, University of California, Berkeley, October 2008.

60. Kevin Watkins, "Bali's Double Standards," *The Guardian*, Dec. 14, 2007, www.guardian.co.uk/commentisfree/2007/dec/14/comment.bali.

61. Niall Ferguson, "Dollar Diplomacy: How Much Did the Marshall Plan Really Matter?" *The New Yorker*, Aug. 27, 2007, p. 81.

62. "A Conversation with Nobel Prize Winner Rajendra Pachauri," *op. cit.*

BIBLIOGRAPHY

Books

Krupp, Fred, and Miriam Horn, *Earth: The Sequel,* **Norton, 2008.**
The president and senior staff writer, respectively, at the U.S.-based Environmental Defense Fund describe innovators who are leading a clean-energy revolution and argue that the United States should adopt a carbon cap-and-trade system to boost investments in innovative energy technologies.

Northcott, Michael S., *A Moral Climate: The Ethics of Global Warming, Orbis,* **2007.**
An Episcopal priest and divinity professor at the University of Edinburgh views climate change as an ethical issue and criticizes carbon trading as biased toward rich countries and large greenhouse gas emitters.

Tietenberg, Thomas H., *Emissions Trading: Principles and Practice,* **2nd edition,** *Resources for the Future,* **2006.**
An environmental economist shows how emissions trading became popular as an alternative to command-and-control regulation and assesses successes, failures and lessons learned in 25 years of application.

Zedillo, Ernesto, ed., *Global Warming: Looking Beyond Kyoto, Brookings,* **2008.**
Authors from around the globe examine how to structure a post-Kyoto climate change agreement that can reduce emissions quickly enough to avert disastrous warming.

Articles

"C is for Unclean," *Down to Earth,* **Dec. 15, 2007.**
A critique of the Clean Development Mechanism (CDM) by India's Centre for Science and Environment argues that the program has been taken over by carbon entrepreneurs and turned into a financial tool instead of fighting climate change.

"First Africa Carbon Forum Fosters Clean Climate Projects," *Environment News Service,* **Sept. 4, 2008.**
Only a fraction of CDM projects are in Africa, but African leaders and international development officials want to increase the continent's share.

Arrandale, Tom, "Carbon Goes to Market," *Governing,* **September 2008, p. 26.**
As Congress debates cap-and-trade policies, nearly half the states are working on their own carbon trading schemes.

Scott, Mark, "Giant Steps for Carbon Trading in Europe," *Business Week,* **Jan. 23, 2008.**
The EU Emissions Trading Scheme is setting stringent, new targets, which will make carbon credits more valuable.

Szabo, Michael, "Problems Plague Canada's Emissions Trading Plans," *Reuters,* **May 8, 2008.**
Canada wants to start carbon trading, but some of its provinces have already adopted their own schemes, and emissions from the Canadian oil industry are rising.

Turner, Chris, "The Carbon Cleansers," *Canadian Geographic Magazine,* **October 2008, p. 3.**
Norway's carbon tax on the oil and gas industry, adopted in 1992, has spurred research into cleaner energy technologies, as well as carbon capture and storage.

Reports and Studies

"Carbon 2008," *Point Carbon,* **March 11, 2008, www .pointcarbon.com/polopoly_fs/1.912721!Carbon_ 2008_dfgrt.pdf.**
An international market research firm focusing on carbon markets provides an overview of global carbon trading and major carbon policy trends.

"Fighting Climate Change: Human Solidarity in a Developed World," *Human Development Report 2007/2008,* **2008,** *United Nations Development Programme,* **http://hdr.undp.org/en/media/ hdr_20072008_en_complete.pdf.**
Climate change is a major threat to human development and is already undercutting global efforts to reduce poverty in some parts of the world. This report calls for urgent action on a post-Kyoto agreement and policies to help poor countries adapt to unavoidable climate change impacts.

Ellerman, A. Denny, and Paul Joskow, "The European Union's Emissions Trading System in Perspective," *Pew Center on Global Climate Change,* **May 2008,**

www.pewclimate.org/docUploads/EU-ETS-In-Perspective-Report.pdf.
Two economists from the Massachusetts Institute of Technology conclude that the EU ETS is still a work in progress but has successfully set a European price for carbon emissions and offers important lessons for U.S. leaders as they debate cap-and-trade policies.

Wara, Michael W., and David G. Victor, "A Realistic Policy on International Carbon Offsets," *Working Paper #74, Program on Energy and Sustainable Development, Stanford University,* **April 2008, http://iis-db.stanford.edu/pubs/22157/WP74_final_final .pdf.**
Two Stanford University law professors recommend major reforms to the Kyoto Protocol's Clean Development Mechanism, which they say awards credits for projects that don't really reduce emissions, and argue the United States should not rely on offsets to lower the cost of reducing carbon emissions.

For More Information

Centre for Science and Environment, 41 Tughlakabad Institutional Area, New Delhi, India; (+91)-11-29955124; www.cseindia.org. An independent public interest organization that works to increase awareness of science, technology, environment and development issues.

China Sustainable Energy Program, The Energy Foundation, CITIC Building, Room 2403, No. 19, Jianguomenwai Dajie, Beijing, 100004, P.R. China; (+86)-10-8526-2422; www.efchina.org. A joint initiative funded by U.S. foundations to support China's policy efforts to promote energy efficiency and renewable energy.

The Gold Standard, 22 Baumleingasse, CH-4051, Basel, Switzerland; (+41)-0-61-283-0916; www.cdmgoldstandard .org. A nonprofit that screens carbon offset projects and certifies initiatives that provide measurable economic, environmental and social benefits.

Institute for Sustainable Futures, University of Technology, L11, 235 Jones St., Broadway, Sydney, Australia; (+61)-2-9514-4590; www.isf.uts.edu.au. Research institute that works with Australian businesses and communities to promote sustainable environmental and design policies.

Intergovernmental Panel on Climate Change, 7bis Ave. de la Paix, C.P. 2300, CH-1211 Geneva 2, Switzerland; (+41)-22-730-8208; www.ipcc.ch. A U.N.-sponsored organization created to advise national governments on climate change science.

Regional Greenhouse Gas Initiative, 90 Church St., 4th Floor, New York, NY 10007; (212) 417-7327; www.rggi .org. A joint venture launched in 2008 by 10 Northeastern states to reduce greenhouse gas emissions from the electric power sector through carbon emissions trading.

U.N. Development Programme, One United Nations Plaza, New York, NY 10017; (212) 906-5000; www.undp.org. Works to cut poverty and use aid effectively.

World Wildlife Fund — UK, Panda House, Weyside Park, Godalming, Surrey GU7 1XR, United Kingdom; (+01)-483-426444; www.wwf.org.uk. The British arm of an international conservation organization.

Race for the Arctic

Who Owns the Region's Undiscovered Oil and Gas?

Brian Beary

A young Nenets woman harnesses her reindeer in Siberia, Russia. Indigenous groups worry that the race for Arctic riches will affect their traditional way of life and deprive them of their fair share of the resources.

From *CQ Global Researcher*, August, 2008.

Along with several other nations, Russia claims a vast swath of the oil-rich Arctic. But last summer the Russians got fed up with the glacial pace of international efforts to settle the claims. In a swashbuckling move that outraged other Arctic players, Russia sent a pair of submersible vessels more than two miles under the Arctic ice cap to plant a titanium Russian flag in the seabed.

"This isn't the 15th century," fumed Canadian Foreign Minister Peter MacKay. "You can't go around the world and just plant flags and say, 'We're claiming this territory.'"[1]

But while MacKay scoffed at Moscow's antics, Canada, albeit more discreetly, also has been asserting its sovereignty in the Arctic — as are Norway, Denmark and the United States — prompted by high energy prices and the melting ice cap.

In recent decades the Arctic's climate has changed more dramatically than other parts of the world. Alaska, for instance, has warmed by 4.9 degrees Fahrenheit since 1950, compared to a 1.8-degree increase since 1908 in the rest of the United States.[2] Average Arctic air temperatures were 10.4 degrees higher in November 2007 than during the same period in the 1980s and '90s. More Arctic sea ice melted in 2007 than in any other year on record, with summer ice levels 20 percent lower than the previous record, set in 2005.[3]

"Many scientists who track Arctic change recognized that an abrupt decline in sea ice was possible, but nearly all were surprised that a dramatic sea-ice decline could occur so fast," according to James E. Overland, an oceanographer at the National Oceanic and Atmospheric Administration's (NOAA) Pacific Marine Environmental Laboratory in Seattle.[4]

Huge Area at Stake in Race for Arctic Resources

Eight nations have territory within the Arctic Circle, a vast region that encompasses the Arctic Ocean, the North Pole, 24 time zones, 5 million people, 30 ethnic groups and three transcontinental shipping routes. A recent U.S. Geological Survey report estimated the area could contain 22 percent of the world's undiscovered oil and gas deposits. Of the eight Arctic countries, five with borders on the mostly ice-covered Arctic Ocean — Russia, Canada, the United States, Norway and Denmark (which owns Greenland) — are scrambling to extend their offshore boundaries beyond the traditional 200-mile limit in order to claim potential offshore resources.

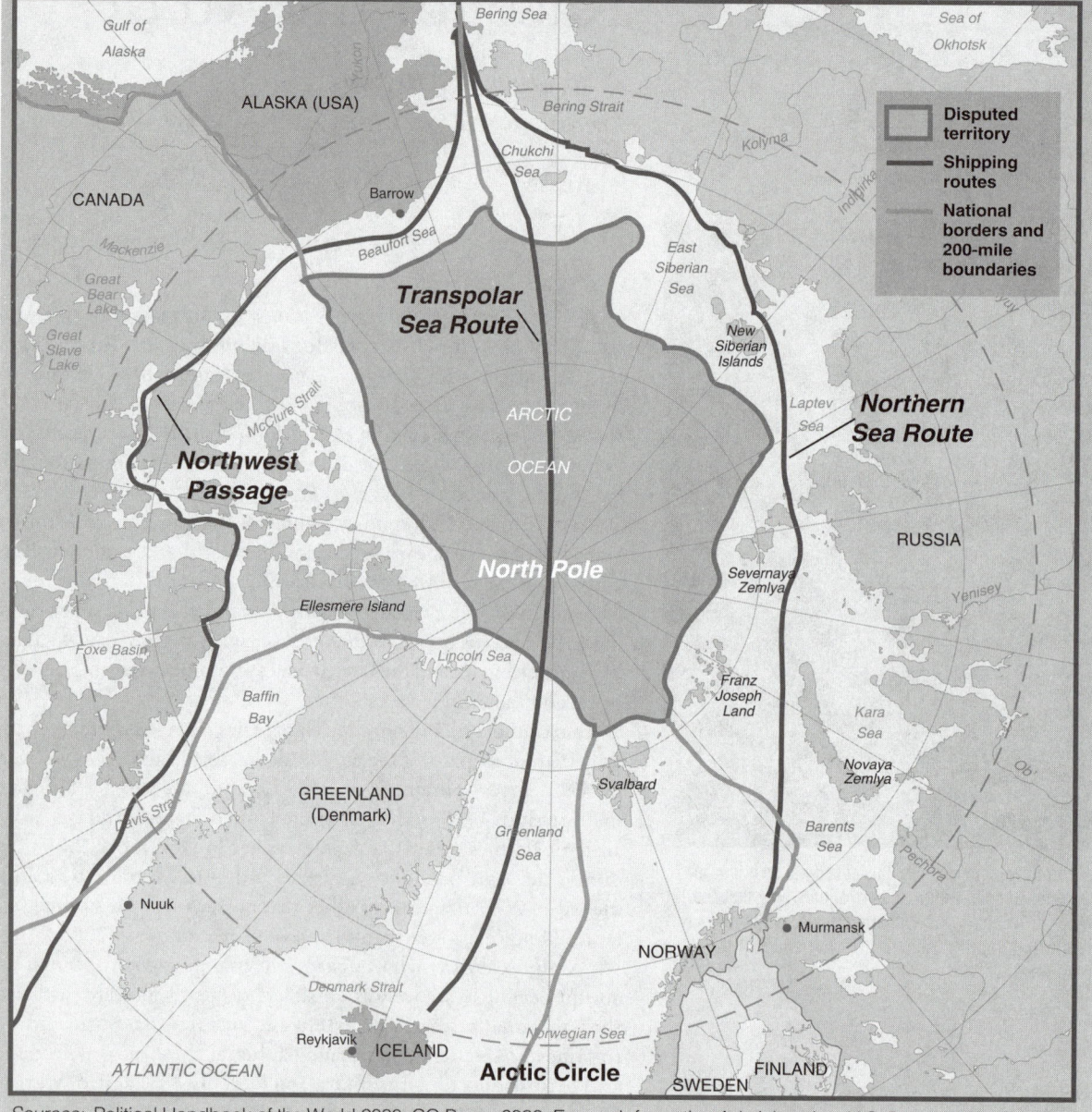

Sources: Political Handbook of the World 2008, CQ Press, 2008; Energy Information Administration, U.S. Department of Energy

Unlike Antarctica, which is a continent covered by mile-high glaciers, the Arctic is mostly an ocean covered with sea ice that has declined in minimum thickness from about 12 feet in the 1980s to eight feet today.*

But melting ice has been a boon in Greenland, a huge, glacier-covered Danish island located almost entirely within the Arctic Circle, making extraction of the rich resources beneath the ice simpler. "Climate change has a positive impact on Greenland," says Foreign Affairs Minister Aleqa Hammond. "But we are aware of severe impacts both globally and locally."

As the ice melts, Hammond says global warming's "winners and losers" are becoming obvious, such as the polar bear. Last May, the U.S. Department of Interior listed the iconic Arctic predator as a threatened species because it relies on sea ice as both a home and a feeding area.[5] For indigenous Arctic peoples, global warming has its advantages and disadvantages. On the one hand, the shrinking ice cap makes access to oil, gas and minerals easier, and warmer weather allows more agriculture. But the loss of sea ice also disrupts the habitats of seals and other marine mammals, threatening the livelihood of indigenous hunters.

In the end, however, environmentalists say the Earth itself could be the biggest loser, as a vicious cycle plays itself out: Melting ice triggers more oil and gas drilling, causing more global warming when the carbon-based fuels are burned.[6]

The most sought-after Arctic area is the huge Lomonosov Ridge — an underwater mountain range as big as California, Indiana and Texas combined that straddles the North Pole. When Russia planted its flag in the middle of the Lomonosov, it angered the Danes and Canadians, who also claim the area. In total, Russia claims sovereignty over half of the Arctic Ocean.[7] Norway and the United States — the other two countries with Arctic Ocean coastlines — claim more southerly Arctic waters.**

Under the United Nations Convention on the Law of the Sea (UNCLOS), countries can claim an area 350 nautical miles or more from their shores if they can prove the adjacent seabed is an extension of their continental shelves.[8] But the United States cannot file such a claim because the Senate has refused to ratify UNCLOS. Were such a claim filed and accepted, the United States would gain almost as much territory as it did when it purchased Alaska from Russia in 1867 for $7.2 million.

Many senators regret the Senate's refusal, including Sen. Lisa Murkowski, R-Alaska. "The Arctic is one of the last spaces on Earth whose borders are not set," she says. "The U.S. needs to be a player, not an outsider. We have an opportunity that is unparalleled around the world."

Meanwhile, the Arctic's indigenous communities fear being sidelined once again in the rush to develop the region's resources (*See sidebar, p. 130.*) "This is Inuit

Arctic Region at a Glance			
Country	Population (in millions, 2006, unless otherwise indicated)	Area (in square miles)	Net petroleum exports/imports (-), 2007 (thousand barrels per day)
Canada	32.8**	3,855,081	1,026
Russia	142.4	6,592,800	7,018
Norway	4.7	149,282	2,321
Greenland (Danish)	0.06*	840,000	-4
United States	304.6**	3,732,396	-12,210
Iceland	0.3	39,768	-19
Finland	5.2	130,119	-224
Sweden	9.1	173,731	-357

* 2005 estimate

** 2007 estimate

Sources: Political Handbook of the World 2008, CQ Press, 2008; Energy Information Administration, U.S. Department of Energy

---

* The Danes are involved because Greenland, which is located mostly within the Arctic Circle, is an independent Danish province.

** Arctic sea ice is melting much faster than Antarctic ice because the South Pole is protected somewhat by a hole in the region's ozone layer, Overland notes, which has caused winds to increase, keeping the warmer temperatures out.

territory," says Aqqaluk Lynge, president of the Inuit Circumpolar Council (ICC) in Greenland, which represents the Arctic's 150,000 Inuit, once known as Eskimos. "While we are very loyal to our respective governments, they must assist us in helping build Inuit unity and help the Inuit use the resources in a sustainable manner."

With oil prices now topping $127 a barrel, gasoline at nearly $4 a gallon and global oil consumption rising, a rush to find new supplies in the Arctic has begun.[9] Unlike in Antarctica, where mining is banned until 2041, no international moratorium on Arctic drilling exists. Arctic states already extract "black gold" in large quantities and are stepping up their operations. (*See table, p. 125.*)

Some 90 billion barrels of undiscovered oil and 1,670 trillion cubic feet of natural gas could lie onshore and offshore within the Arctic Circle region, according to a July report from the U.S. Geological Survey (USGS). That represents 30 percent of the world's undiscovered gas reserves and 13 percent of the oil reserves.[10] The United States produces 1.85 billion barrels of oil each year and 19.3 trillion cubic feet of natural gas.[11]

Russia is already the biggest player in the Arctic, with 75 percent of the known Arctic oil and 90 percent of the gas — and validation of its territorial claims would only enhance its energy-kingpin status.[12] The Norwegians, who operate offshore fields in the North Sea, are moving operations north as old wells dry up. Petroleum, which represented 31 percent of Norway's revenues in 2007 and 48 percent of its exports, is key to Norway's wealth.[13] Greenland has quintupled the number of exploitation licenses it grants and expanded the area earmarked for oil and gas exploration from 2,657 sq. miles to nearly 39,000 sq. miles.[14] Meanwhile, both the United States and Canada are opening up their sections of the Beaufort Sea to drilling. (*See map, p. 124.*)

The European Union (EU) — which recently predicted the scramble for resources will intensify in the Arctic — will probably end up in the Arctic "loser" category, because it has no territory in the region. Although Denmark is a member, its Arctic province Greenland left the EU in 1985, and Norway stood on the threshold of EU membership twice, but referenda in 1972 and 1994 narrowly failed.[15]

Despite the attention being paid to the Lomonosov Ridge, USGS geologist Don Gautier, says it "is not an interesting place from the petroleum point of view" because the vast majority of Arctic oil and gas lies elsewhere. "Offshore Alaska is the most obvious place to look for oil, while the area with the most gas is the West Siberian Basin in Russia." Although the Lomonosov contains sedimentary rock — a critical component for petroleum reserves to be present — there is no evidence of a previous tectonic event that would have sealed reserves under the seabed, Gautier explains.

And, even if oil and gas are found, countries will drill closer to their coastlines first, Gautier says, because they have undisputed sovereignty over these areas and because it's easier to operate there than in the Lomonosov, which is hundreds of miles offshore.

The shrinking sea ice also is beginning to affect global shipping. In summer 2007 the legendary Northwest Passage through northern Canada, which connects the Atlantic and Pacific oceans, was ice-free for the first time in recorded history, raising the promise of new, shorter trans-Arctic shipping routes. By 2030 the Arctic may be entirely ice-free during the summer months, NOAA's Overland predicts.

Savings on shipping costs could be enormous if the Arctic routes were to become usable for longer periods. A ship sailing from New York to Tokyo, for instance, could shave 2,600 miles off its journey by taking the Northwest Passage instead of a conventional route through the Panama Canal. Vessels traveling from London to Tokyo could reduce their journey by some 5,000 miles by taking the Northern Sea Route — also called the Northeast Passage — through Russian waters instead of the Suez Canal. (*See map, p. 133.*)[16]

And even partly ice-covered passages are navigable now with new "double acting" ships, which sail through ice-free waters using their V-shaped bow, and then turn around when they hit icy waters and navigate with their U-shaped stern, eliminating the need for an accompanying icebreaker.

Initially, with expanded offshore energy exploitation and warmer waters attracting more warm-water fish, most of the increased trans-Arctic sea travel would probably be petroleum-laden tankers or commercial fishing vessels. The jury is still out, however, on whether trans-Arctic shipping of consumer goods will be commercially viable anytime soon — because savings in distance would be offset by other expenses, such as building more ice-resistant ships.

In any case, Russia — which already has 18 icebreakers that escort cargo ships along the Northern Sea

Route — seems best positioned to exploit new opportunities.[17] A rise in commercial traffic along North America's Northwest Passage seems less likely, because the route is more difficult to navigate, and the United States and Canada disagree about its legal status. The United States says the passage is an international strait open to all; Canada says it is Canadian waters.

As the race for Arctic treasure intensifies, here are some of the key questions political leaders are grappling with:

Is an Arctic treaty needed?

"This is an absolute necessity," says Rob Huebert, a politics professor and Arctic expert at the University of Calgary. "We have no multilateral system of governance for the Arctic. The U.S. is not a party to UNCLOS, and the treaty does not deal with certain things — for example the rights of indigenous peoples."

Huebert insists a new treaty should be concluded between all eight states with territory within the Arctic Circle — Canada, Denmark, Russia, the United States, Norway, Iceland, Sweden and Finland — rather than just the five whose coastlines border the Arctic Ocean (Canada, Denmark, Russia, the United States and Norway), who were invited to a ministerial meeting in May in Greenland to discuss territorial issues. A treaty should also contain a conflict-resolution mechanism and provisions on navigation, fishing and tourism, he says.

"Right now, everyone is going it alone," he continues. "We need a champion like Malta was in the 1960s for UNCLOS. It would be nice to see Canada assume this role." (*See p. 137.*)

Craig Stewart, director of the World Wildlife Fund's (WWF) Ottawa Bureau, adds, "We need a framework convention on resource extraction that sets environmental and oil and gas recovery standards. This should enshrine the 'integrated management planning concept' under which the impact of all activities — fishing, shipping, oil drilling — are assessed, all stakeholders are involved and resource extraction is banned in certain areas."

He says Canada's 1996 Oceans Act would be a good model for such a convention.

Britain's Diana Wallis, vice president of the European Parliament, says an international Arctic treaty would be "appropriate," especially now. "The timing is good, with 2007-2008 being International Polar Year."

So far, she says, at least "people are honoring the legal frameworks" of the UNCLOS territorial-claims

National Snow and Ice Data Center

Satellite images of the top of the Earth show how the polar ice cap has shrunk dramatically over the past 27 years. Scientists say more Arctic ice melted in 2007 than in any other year on record, with summer ice levels 20 percent lower than the previous record — set in 2005.

procedure. "If it works, OK. But in the long term we should think about drafting an Arctic Charter and strengthening the political dimension of the Arctic Council."

Set up in 1996, the Norway-based council includes representatives from all eight Arctic states plus indigenous community organizations. Yet so far, it has not been much of a player: A U.S. secretary of State has never

© B&C Alexander/Arcticphoto.com (both)

Moving the "Gold"

The huge oil facility at Prudhoe Bay, on Alaska's Beaufort Sea coast, sits next to the largest oil field in the United States (top). With gasoline prices at nearly $4 a gallon and global oil consumption rising, Arctic countries are racing to develop the region's "black gold" — both onshore and offshore. Canada is building a 750-mile natural gas pipeline to transport natural gas from its Northwest Territory fields to southern markets. And in Norway, drilling rigs are being moved northward toward the Arctic as its North Sea wells dry up (bottom).

attended one of the council's biannual ministerial-level meetings.[18] And when asked to outline the council's vision for development of the Arctic, a spokesman said he was "not in position to speak to political issues on behalf of its eight member states."

Environmental groups are favorably disposed to such a treaty and to beefing up the council's role. "The council has not developed policies yet — it just releases studies, although this is useful, too," says Chris Krenz, Arctic

Project Manager in Juneau, Alaska, for the Oceana environmental group. "UNCLOS may be useful for deciding territorial rights, but there needs to be something else just for the Arctic."

But Norway's ambassador to the United States, Wegger Strommen, says an Arctic treaty is superfluous. "UNCLOS has worked well," he says. "If disputes arise from overlapping claims, it is best to resolve them through bilateral negotiations. Once we have the technical data, I am confident they will be resolved."

Norway's Foreign Minister Jonas Gahr Store agrees. "We do not exclude future new regulation in particular fields," he said, "but only if real needs have been identified with precision. The actual challenges related to the legal regime in the Arctic may have more to do with a lack of implementation of existing rules than a lack of rules."[19] As evidence, a Norwegian embassy official responsible for fisheries policy cites agreements Norway concluded with other countries in 2005 setting fishing quotas for blue whiting and herring.[20]

The Norwegian view was endorsed in May by Canada, Denmark, the United States and Russia when ministers met in Ilulissat, Greenland, to discuss this issue. A post-meeting joint declaration said UNCLOS provides a "solid foundation for responsible management by the five coastal states and other users of this ocean." It concluded: "We therefore see no need to develop a new, comprehensive international legal regime to govern the Arctic Ocean."[21]

Given such opposition from the key governments, an Arctic treaty looks politically unfeasible.

Oran Young, a professor of environmental science and international governance at the University of California, Santa Barbara, dismissed the idea of an Arctic treaty as "utopian — both politically and legally. Legally binding agreements are hard to negotiate, often lacking in substance, and commonly slow to enter into force. They are clumsy instruments that are apt to cause trouble in highly dynamic settings."[22]

And although Young supported enhancing the Arctic Council's role somewhat, he also recommended "keeping its decision-making authority and organizational capacity to a minimum."[23]

Gunnar Sander, Arctic adviser at the Copenhagen-based European Environment Agency (EEA), a network of EU environmental agencies, suggests something slightly more modest than an Arctic treaty: a regional protocol for the Arctic Ocean within the UNCLOS framework. Twelve regional-seas conventions already have been adopted under the UNCLOS framework, including a 1992 treaty for protecting the North-East Atlantic.[24] Yet, with the five key Arctic governments clearly favoring bilateral and sector-specific pacts, even this modest suggestion looks to be a long shot.

Should Arctic oil and gas reserves be exploited?

While environmentalists are more enthusiastic than governments about an Arctic treaty, the situation is reversed on the question of oil and gas drilling: Governments are much more enthusiastic than environmentalists on the issue.

International mineral and oil companies "are flocking to Greenland," says Foreign Affairs Minister Hammond. "I would, too, if I were in their position." Greenland, with a population 56,000, would get a massive windfall if major oil or gas deposits are found, notes Hammond, who is also minister for finance.

Claudia A. McMurray, the U.S. State Department's assistant secretary for oceans, environment and science, supports exploration if it is done "in a sustainable manner." Guidelines are needed on how to conduct operations and contingency plans for spills, she says, but "the U.S already has rules for this."

Environmentalists are more fearful. "The rush to exploit Arctic resources can only perpetuate the vicious cycle of human-induced climate change," said Greenpeace International spokesman Mike Townsley.[25] Extracting oil and gas will only lead to more fossil fuels being burned, which will trigger further global warming and more melting of the ice caps, he explained.

But Danish Ambassador to the United States Friis Arne Petersen says, "We cannot give up on oil and gas. We want to drill offshore for oil in western Greenland and gas in eastern Greenland."

Oceana's Krenz worries about the impact exploration will have on the surrounding environment, noting that Alaskan beaches still have not recovered from the 1989 *Exxon Valdez* oil spill.[26] "If you dig a hole, you can still see oil seeping its toxic compounds into the ocean," he says. "This has been very detrimental to pink salmon. Herring stocks have never really recovered either."

Oil spills are especially lethal for seabirds and seals, because the oil covers their feathers and fur, making it harder for them to escape from predators, causing seals to drown by sticking to their flippers and causing hypothermia in seal pups and birds. "Placing wells, pipelines and vessels in the remote Arctic creates a substantial risk of a catastrophic oil spill, and there is no proven method to clean up an oil spill in the icy conditions often found in the Arctic," Oceana warns.[27] And the noise caused by drilling could drive whales and other marine life away from feeding areas, it added.

For these reasons, the World Wildlife Fund is calling for a moratorium on Arctic development. "The U.S. Minerals Management Service (MMS) estimates that there is a 20 to 52 percent risk of an oil spill in the Chukchi or Beaufort seas," says WWF's Stewart. "The British-based energy company BP did a test in 2000 that concluded you could not clean up a spill if there was 30 percent ice coverage. It is highly irresponsible to proceed without a recovery system."

The European Environmental Agency's Sander says drilling in the High Arctic would be "very risky." The large quantities of ice, 24-hour darkness in winter and extremely low temperatures make conditions for operating a facility treacherous, he says.

EU parliament member Wallis is more circumspect: "In a sense, it is fair for countries to exploit the resources. But you must proceed with caution, getting the best science, not taking risks with the environment and respecting what the local populations want."

According to a recent Arctic Council report, "knowledge about effects on the environment and human health of oil and gas activities is limited."[28] To date there have been no large oil spills in the Arctic Ocean from oil and gas activities (the *Exxon Valdez* ran aground in the Pacific), it noted, and seismic exploration has left "no long-lasting effects on fish stocks or marine ecosystems."[29] Most animals revert to normal behavior when the noise ceases, the report said, except for bowhead whales in the Beaufort Sea, which had been observed changing swimming direction in response to noise sources up to 20 miles away.

In addition, the report continued, the local communities experienced increased employment during the construction phase, but many workers were brought in from the outside because the locals did not have the necessary

Arctic's Indigenous People Fight for Their Resources

Big nations are rushing to exploit offshore gas, oil.

Exploitation of the Arctic's resources is ancient history to its indigenous peoples, says Aqqaluk Lynge, president of the Inuit Circumpolar Council (ICC), which represents 150,000 Inuit. When Arctic-area ministers met recently in breathtakingly picturesque Ilulissat, Greenland, to discuss sharing the region's natural resources, he reminded them the debate stretches back to the 1600s, "when the first foreign whaling ship came to hunt our big whales and decimate our stocks, from which they have never recovered."[1]

Today Arctic governments have their sights set on offshore oil and gas and new shipping and fishing opportunities. And indigenous communities want to know whether they will be winners or losers in the new race for Arctic resources.

"All this is nothing new for us," says Gun-Britt Retter, a member of the indigenous Sami community's parliament in Norway.* "We used to have to pay taxes to four different kings — Sweden, Norway, Denmark and Russia. Today we have governments making nice speeches about indigenous peoples having the right to their culture. But they do not give us the basis for that culture — our land. We have no right to veto drilling operations and no right to revenues from oil and gas extraction on our land."

Indeed, throughout modern times indigenous Arctic peoples have fought to preserve their language, culture and way of life as neighboring colonial powers encroached on their turf. In 1953, for instance, Canada pushed the Inuit in Nunavik, Quebec, into the High Arctic in an effort to assert Canada's sovereignty over the region. The same year Eskimos were forced out of their homes in northwestern Greenland to make room for a Danish-backed U.S. Air Force base in Thule.

_____

* The Sami were formerly known as Laplanders.

Nenets reindeer herders meet with gas company officials in Yamal, Siberia, to discuss how oil development is affecting their community.

Native peoples have scored some successes, however. In 1971, under the Alaska Native Claims Settlement Act, the U.S. government gave the Inuit $962.5 million and 44 million acres of land in Alaska after complaints that oil developers were robbing locals' land and destroying the environment.[2] In 1999 Canada created the Inuit-dominated Territory of Nunavut by splitting the Northwest Territories in two. Greenland, which is 90 percent Inuit, gained home rule from Denmark in 1979, after nearly three centuries of domination. A referendum this November would give the Inuit in Greenland further autonomy and divide up future oil and gas revenue between the Greenlandic and Danish governments.

But Edward Itta, the mayor of Alaska's North Slope Borough, is critical of how the U.S. government is conducting its current policy review of the Arctic.

"We have not been formally involved in the review," says Itta, an Inuit. "We have lived here for 10,000 years, yet the bureaucrats in Washington think they know it all."

training. And when oil and gas activity ceases, old sites need to be safely removed and the surrounding environment cleaned up — something the industry does not always bother to do.[30]

Perhaps for these reasons, the Inuit conference's Lynge says tough questions must be answered before energy exploitation gets the green light. "How many new jobs will be created?" he asks. "How many of them

Besides fighting for a seat at the table, indigenous peoples are trying to forge a strong and unified stance among themselves. Inuit from Russia, Alaska, Greenland and Canada will meet in Nunavik in November to devise a common position, which is vital to resisting the Arctic powers' "divide-and-conquer approach," says Lynge.[3]

In addition to the Inuit, the 70,000-strong Sami — residing in Norway, Sweden, Finland and Russia — are the second-largest Arctic indigenous group. Other smaller groups include the Aleut, who live on the Pacific Aleutian islands between Russia and Alaska, the Athabaskans and Gwich'in from Alaska and Canada plus 41 indigenous groups who live in Arctic Russia.

The rights of indigenous peoples vary widely. For example, the Sami have their own parliaments in Norway, Sweden and Finland, but not in Russia. "Our people face their biggest challenge in Russia," says Retter. "The government there draws up maps for pipelines and mining development, ignoring the people who live there. Reindeer herding is a huge part of our culture, but because of this new infrastructure, the reindeer, which move homes between summer and winter, become blocked."

Now global warming is forcing indigenous communities to adapt quickly. According to Kenneth Hoegh, Greenland's agriculture adviser in Qaqortog, climate change has been a mixed blessing in southwest Greenland. The reduction in drift ice has hurt Inuit hunters because the ice calms the sea, enabling the hunters to shoot seals.

"If this continues, they will need to find other livelihoods — maybe fishing, eco-tourism or ethnic tourism," he says.

On the other hand, warmer seas have attracted more cod, which fetch good prices. Fishermen have had to invest in new gear and boats, however, since they previously fished mainly for shrimp, which are eaten by the cod. Global warming also has given a boost to farming, allowing more grazing and hay, silage and vegetable cultivation.

Meanwhile, industrial pollution from faraway regions threatens indigenous peoples' health. Inuit mothers' breast milk has become dangerous because the polar bears, seals, walruses, fish and whales they eat are contaminated by

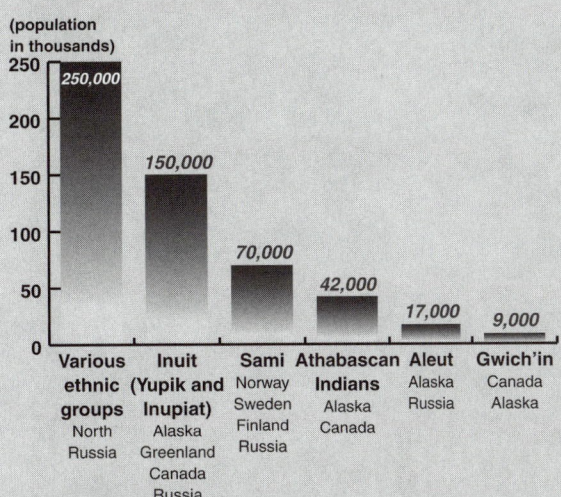

Indigenous People of the Arctic

(population in thousands)

Various ethnic groups	Inuit (Yupik and Inupiat)	Sami	Athabascan Indians	Aleut	Gwich'in
250,000	150,000	70,000	42,000	17,000	9,000
North Russia	Alaska Greenland Canada Russia	Norway Sweden Finland Russia	Alaska Canada	Alaska Russia	Canada Alaska

Sources: Inuit: www.inuitcircumpolar.com; Sami: www.galdu.org; Aleut: www.apiai.com; Athabaskan: www.arcticathabaskan council.com; Gwich'in: www.gwichin.org; Russian indigenous: www.raipon.org.

heavy metals, PCBs and other industrial compounds found in seawater and stored in the animals' fat.[4]

While much is known already about the environmental challenges, more research is needed for policymakers to make the right decisions, according to Mayor Itta. "Our ocean is getting more acidic," he says. "We need more baseline data to understand the impact on the entire food chain — from the krill to the bowhead whale."

[1] Aqqaluk Lynge, president, Inuit Circumpolar Council (ICC) Greenland, address to the Ministerial Summit of Arctic Oceans, "Issues relating to the local inhabitants and indigenous communities," May 28, 2008, Ilulissat, Greenland, www.inuit.org/index.asp?lang=eng&num=3 (Inuit version)

[2] *Encyclopaedia Britannica Online*, www.britannica.com.

[3] Lynge, *op. cit.*

[4] Colin Woodard, "Oceans in Crisis," *CQ Global Researcher*, October 2007, pp. 237-264.

will go to Greenlanders? Who will be getting the high-paid jobs?"

In Alaska, some say the issue is complicated by the polar bears, which the U.S. government recently listed as threatened. "If the Department of Interior decides that exploration will further threaten the polar bears' habitat, it will be difficult to grant development leases," says the State Department's McMurray.

Life is treacherous these days for Arctic polar bears — like this one at Cape Churchill, Canada — as Arctic ice melts away due to global warming. The U.S. Department of Interior in May listed the iconic predator as a threatened species because it relies on sea ice as both a home and a feeding area. The listing could block or delay development of Alaskan oil reserves.

"This finding, given the inflexibility of the 1973 Endangered Species Act, makes it easier to legally challenge oil and gas lease sales in the Beaufort and Chukchi seas," says Professor Jonathan Adler, an environmental law expert at Case Western Reserve University in Cleveland. "I think the matter will be resolved in the courts."

Will the melting ice caps revolutionize international shipping routes?

The receding ice caps are likely to affect Arctic shipping, but how quickly things will change and what routes will be affected is unknown.

Three basic routes cross the Arctic Ocean: the Northwest Passage in North America, the Northern Sea Route through Russia's northern waters and the Transpolar Route over the North Pole. (*See map, p. 133.*)

"The greatest potential saving is probably over the Northern Sea Route" because it's the most ice-free, according to Mead Treadwell, chairman of the U.S. Arctic Research Commission.

A 2006 study funded by the Alaska-based Institute of the North concluded that shipping containers from the Aleutian Islands in western Alaska to Iceland using the Northern Sea Route would cost $354 to $526 per container compared to the current cost of $1,500 per container from Japan to Europe using the southern route.[31] Other costs also must be factored in, such as having to build and operate new terminals, the study stresses. Until now, the northern route has not been used for shipping goods between continents because its icy waters make it treacherous to navigate.

The Transpolar Route also has potential, says Ragnar Baldursson, an official at Iceland's Department of Natural Resources and Environmental Affairs, because it avoids treacherous coastal areas, such as the Northwest Passage, where ice is often swept towards the straits. "The Transpolar route is easier for political reasons, too, because no one disputes ships' right to sail over the North Pole, which is not the case for the Northwest Passage," he says. In an ongoing dispute, the United States claims the Northwest Passage is an international strait through which all ships can pass, while Canada argues it is Canadian waters and that Canada can impose environmental regulations and demand to be notified of passing ships.

Diplomatic squabbles aside, Canadian shipping executive Thomas Paterson says greater commercial use of the Northwest Passage is not viable. "It would need to be completely ice-free to be economical, but this will not happen," says Paterson, vice president of Montreal-based Fednav Ltd. "Ships coming up Greenland's coast [to reach the passage] will encounter icebergs broken off from Greenland's glaciers and will have to slow down to avoid them, so the journey could end up taking more time despite the shorter distance."

In addition, icebreaking ships are more expensive to build — $100 million compared to $40 million for a standard ship, he points out. Businesses shipping goods across continents will not take on these extra risks and costs, he says, although oil companies shipping Arctic oil in and around the Northwest Passage may be willing to pay.

The greatest potential for improved Arctic shipping lies with regional, not trans-continental, shipping, says Lawson W. Brigham, director of the Arctic Research Commission's Alaska Office and a former U.S. Coast Guardsman who commanded ice-breakers in the Arctic and Antarctic. There is already a thriving seasonal trade in shipping minerals, he notes, including zinc from Alaska's Red Dog mine and nickel and copper from Siberia.

"This trade has nothing to do with climate change," says Brigham, who earned a Ph.D. in polar ocean-ography from England's Cambridge University. With seven nuclear-powered icebreakers to escort ships, Russia has used the Northern Sea Route for 60 years to transport fuel, food, minerals and machinery during the summer months, according to a Russian official.

The University of Calgary's Huebert predicts that most of the new shipping will support the oil and gas industry rather than regular cargo, a view shared by Brigham. "The distances may be shorter, but there will still be ice," Brigham says. "The Northwest Passage was open for less than a month in 2007, and even then there may have been small ice floes that the satellite images did not pick up. If you go too fast, you risk damaging things."

In 1994 Brigham captained the U.S icebreaker *Polar Sea*, which, in a joint expedition with its Canadian counterpart the *Louis S. St. Laurent*, became the first surface ships to cross the central Arctic Ocean. They approached the polar sea via the Bering Strait and came out at Svalbard. "It was a slow crossing, about 40 days," he

Arctic Melting Opens Up Shorter Shipping Routes

The melting of the Arctic ice cap could create more efficient shipping routes from Europe to the Far East. For example, the distance from Hamburg, Germany, to Yokohama, Japan, via traditional shipping routes — around the Cape of Good Hope or through the Panama or Suez canals — could be as long as 14,500 nautical miles. By contrast, the distance is half that amount via the Northern Sea Route (see below), and even less for the Transpolar Route and Northwest Passage.

Nautical Miles from Hamburg, Germany, to Yokohama, Japan

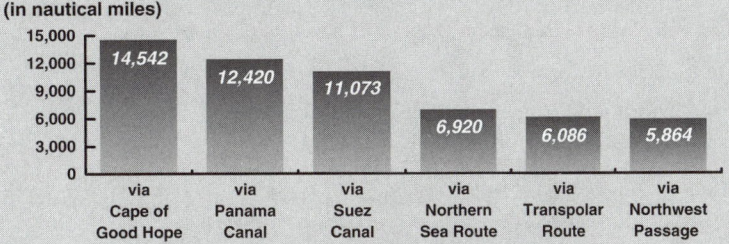

(in nautical miles)

Route	Nautical Miles
via Cape of Good Hope	14,542
via Panama Canal	12,420
via Suez Canal	11,073
via Northern Sea Route	6,920
via Transpolar Route	6,086
via Northwest Passage	5,864

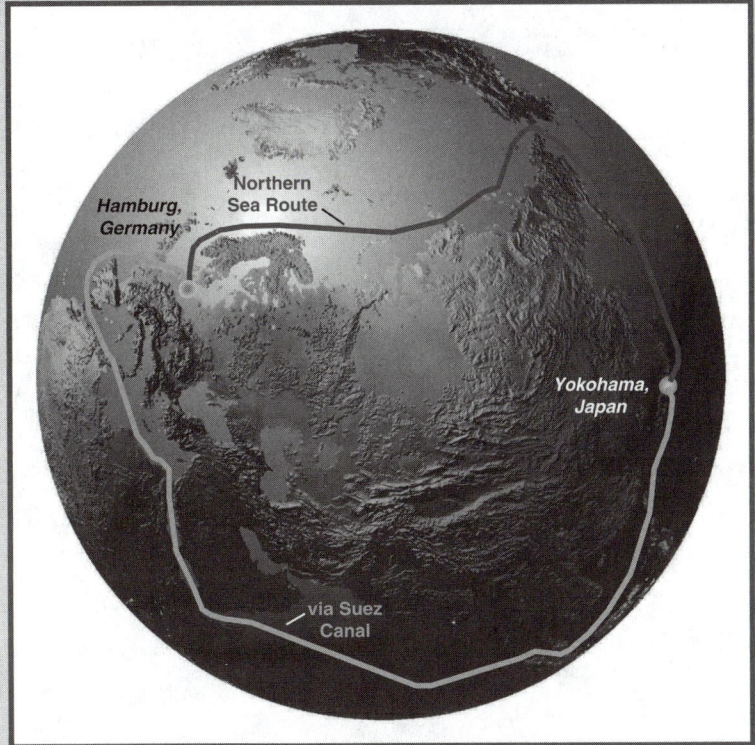

Source: Ray Chartier Jr., "Arctic Sea Ice Recent Trends and Causes; Impact on Arctic Operations," U.S. Naval Ice Center

CHRONOLOGY

35,000-10,000 B.C. *First settlers arrive in the Arctic.*

11,000 B.C. Ice cap thaws, and land bridge linking Asia and North America floods.

900-1910s *Explorers and colonial powers arrive in the Arctic.*

986 A.D. Erik the Red establishes a small Norse colony in Greenland.

1609 Dutch jurist Hugo Grotius publishes *Mare Liberum*, establishing free-seas principle.

1845 An expedition led by Britain's Sir John Franklin in search of Canada's Northwest Passage disappears, never to be heard from again.

1867 Russia sells Alaska to the United States for $7.2 million.

1909 U.S. explorer Robert Peary claims to be first to reach North Pole.

1920s-1960s *Governments begin exploiting the Arctic's natural resources and questioning Grotius' free-seas principle.*

1920 Oil exploration begins in Canada's Northwest Territories.

1922 Oil exploration begins on Alaska's North Slope.

1945 President Harry S. Truman claims all resources on the U.S. continental shelf.

1958 U.S. government issues first lease for oil exploration on the North Slope.

1967 Malta's ambassador to the U.N. gives a groundbreaking speech calling for an international treaty on the sea.

1968 First surface expedition, led by American Ralph Plaisted, reaches the North Pole, using snowmobiles.

1970s-1990s *Global governments regulate the seas. Economic development of the Arctic continues to grow.*

1973 U.N. conference convenes to write a global oceans treaty.

1977 Trans-Alaska pipeline begins pumping oil 800 miles from northern Alaska to the ice-free southern seaport of Valdez. . . . Inuit establish the Inuit Circumpolar Council to represent their interests. . . . Soviet nuclear-powered icebreaker *Arktika* is first ship to reach the Pole.

1981 First exploratory well is drilled on Alaska's outer continental shelf.

1982 U.N. adopts the Convention on the Law of the Sea (UNCLOS) and opens it for ratification. Eventually 156 nations, but not the United States, will ratify it.

1984 Snohvit gas field is discovered in Norway's Barents Sea.

1987 Soviet leader Mikhail Gorbachev proposes transforming the Arctic into a "zone of peace."

1994 UNCLOS enters into force.

2000s *Melting ice caused by global warming triggers a new rush for Arctic land and natural resources.*

2001 Russia becomes the first Arctic nation to claim sovereignty over the North Pole, using a process set up under UNCLOS.

2007 The Northwest Passage is ice-free for the first time on record. . . . Russia plants its flag on the North Pole seabed, galvanizing other Arctic nations into asserting their own sovereignty. . . . U.S. Senate Foreign Relations Committee approves UNCLOS, bringing it a step closer to ratification.

2008 U.S. authorizes oil and gas exploration in the Chukchi Sea. . . . U.S. lists the polar bear as a threatened species due to loss of its sea-ice habitat. . . . Russia, Canada, Denmark, the United States and Norway agree to use UNCLOS to resolve Arctic territorial claims. . . . U.S. and Canada begin collaborating on Arctic seabed mapping to pursue continental shelf claims.

says. "Certain commodities — toys, fresh fruit, clothing, cars — are very time-sensitive and you may not be able to afford to arrive a few days late." Brigham says "there are strong differences of opinion about the use of trans-Arctic navigation on a routine basis" and that solid economic analyses of its viability have yet to be performed.

Ice itself isn't the only obstacle to trans-Arctic shipping, notes Winn Dayton, a director of transportation policy at the U.S. State Department's Bureau of Economic and Business Affairs. Special ice-resistant hulls are expensive, and Arctic ports lack road and rail connections, Dayton says. Extracting materials in such remote areas is costly and dangerous, since it is far from Coast Guard crews who could launch search-and-rescue operations, he adds.[32]

"Conditions are extremely tough up there, with the storms and rough seas," says Petter Meier, fisheries counselor at the Norwegian Embassy in Washington. "In ice-covered waters, the ice can actually screw a ship right down into the sea."

Arctic tourism — which is experiencing something of a boom, with hundreds of cruises crisscrossing Arctic waters last summer — is a potential growth sector. Yet lack of infrastructure in the remote regions of Canada and Greenland limits the potential, according to Capt. Ted Thompson, senior vice president of the Cruise Lines International Association.

"Tourists will have nothing to do if you dump them at the ports there," he says. "Even if the Northwest Passage is open for a week and a half this year, it will not be long enough to make it through all the way. We will see expeditionary cruises but not big-scale tourist cruises."[33]

Bill Sheffield, director of the Port of Anchorage and a former Alaska governor, notes that only "120 ships crossed the Northwest Passage last year, whereas 5,000 passed through the Panama Canal. I do not think the Northwest Passage will be commercially viable in my age. But if it does happen, Anchorage will be very important because it is a deepwater port."[34]

BACKGROUND

Exploration and Migration

The first human settlers arrived in the Arctic — from the Greek word arktos, meaning "bear" — some 30,000 years

ago.[35] At the time a land bridge across the Bering Strait linked the North American and Eurasian continents, but around 11,000 B.C. the climate warmed and melting ice flooded the land bridge.[36] The warmer temperatures enabled forests to grow and led to better hunting and fishing possibilities.

By the Middle Ages (900-1400 A.D.) Europeans looking for fur and foodstuffs made trading and raiding forays into the northern parts of what is now Norway, Sweden, Finland and Russia. During the modern era, Russia emerged as the dominant Arctic power, expanding its borders, subjugating indigenous peoples, exploiting the region's fishing, forestry, mineral and energy resources and establishing a strong military presence. They colonized Alaska after Tsar Peter the Great ordered the exploration of Russia's Pacific coast; a Russian expedition landed in Alaska in 1741.[37] The United States purchased Alaska from a financially strapped Russia in 1867 for $7.2 million, although Alaska did not become a U.S. state until 1959.[38]

Greenland was settled more than 4,000 years ago by North American Inuit. In 986 A.D. the Vikings settled the huge island during a warm spike, led by Erik the Red, but they left when it got colder in the early 15th century. In 1721, a Danish-Norwegian priest, Hans Egede, settled in Godthab (today's capital, Nuuk), marking the beginning of Danish sovereignty over the island.[39] Norway occupied and tried to claim part of Greenland in 1931, but the International Court of Justice ruled in 1933 that the whole island belonged to Denmark.

During World War II, Nazi Germany's occupation of Denmark blocked Danish contact with Greenland. The United States, recognizing its geopolitical importance, started to trade more with Greenland and in 1946 even offered $100 million for the island, which the Danes rejected.[40] In 1951 the United States opened an Air Force base at Thule in northwest Greenland.[41] Meanwhile, Greenlanders began to seek more autonomy, winning home rule in 1979.

Between the 16th and 20th centuries, explorers mapped out the Arctic sea routes. Dutchman Willem Barents discovered the island of Novaya Zemlya off the north Russian coast in 1594 and the Svalbard archipelago north of Norway in 1596. An Austro-Hungarian expedition led by Karl Weyprecht discovered the Franz Josef Land archipelago north of Novaya Zemlya in 1873. In 1845

Territorial Disputes Roil the Arctic

Many nations eyeing gas and oil reserves.

On a tiny, uninhabited island in the remotest reaches of the Arctic, Danish naval officers stake their nation's claim to the island once a year by planting bottles of Old Danish bitter in the snow. Troops from Canada also claim the barren patch of land, but with Canadian Club whiskey, drinking the bitters to remove all traces of a Nordic colony. The Danes return the favor when they come back, downing the Canadian whiskey and replacing it with more Danish spirits.

This good-humored sparring continued for years until recently, when the dispute between Canada and Denmark over Hans Island — about 300 acres wedged between Canada's Ellesmere Island and Greenland — suddenly was no longer a joke.

At an Arctic foreign ministers meeting in Ilulissat, Greenland, in May, Greenlandic Prime Minister Hans Enoksen declared, "We traditionally have already named the island The Kidney-Shaped Island. . . . should anyone have any claims prior, they would have named it already before we did." Canada's natural resources minister, Gary Lunn, retorted tersely, "I'm not going to comment on that," adding, "we're here to affirm Canada's sovereignty by our strong presence in the North."[1]

While the row may seem as silly as a "Monty Python" sketch, no one is giving a square inch — keenly aware of the precedent it might set for other territorial claims and, ultimately, control of the Arctic's vast resources.

Southwest of Hans Island, the United States and Canada have been entangled in a similar standoff since 1969 over the status of the Northwest Passage, the stretch of water in northern Canada that connects the Atlantic and Pacific oceans. The United States insists the fabled passage is an international strait open to all vessels.[2] Canada insists it is part of Canada's territorial waters.

"If Canada is right," says Professor Rob Huebert, an Arctic sovereignty expert at the University of Calgary, "Canadian authorities will decide who can or cannot pass and what safety and environmental rules they must follow."

Until now, the dispute has been largely academic, because the passage historically has been frozen and unnavigable for most of the year. But global warming made the passage ice-free last summer for the first time in observational record and has catapulted the dispute into the political realm.

"There is no room to move. We have agreed to disagree," says Claudia McMurray, the State Department's assistant secretary for oceans, environment and science. "It is not a major issue right now, but it will be if the ice melts forever and the passage becomes a shipping lane." Neither

Britain's Sir John Franklin led the most famous and tragic expedition, searching vainly for a navigable path through Canada's Northwest Passage. Franklin and his men were never seen again, but expeditions launched to find him greatly expanded knowledge of the area's geography. Remains of the expedition, including bones of crew members, were later discovered, indicating they perished from a combination of bad weather, disease and starvation.[42] In 1906 Norwegian explorer Roald Amundsen became the first to successfully traverse the passage.

The race to reach the North Pole began in the late 1800s, with American explorer Robert E. Peary declaring he had won in 1909 — although his claim is widely disputed today. The first surface expedition definitely to reach the Pole was led by American Ralph Plaisted in 1968, using snowmobiles. The Soviet nuclear-powered icebreaker *Arktika* in 1977 became the first surface vessel to reach the Pole.[43]

Global Treaties

Historically, the seas were regulated by the "cannon-shot-rule," which held that countries controlled the seas up to three miles from their coast — or the range of a 17th-century cannon. In 1609, Dutch philosopher and jurist Hugo Grotius' influential treatise, Mare Liberum, established the right to freely navigate the seas for trade purposes.[44]

In the mid-20th century, however, countries began pushing to expand their maritime territory to exploit offshore natural resources. In 1945 President Harry S Truman extended U.S. jurisdiction over all oil, gas and

side has brought a case to the International Court of Justice (ICJ) yet, but this could well happen given the increasing inflexibility Arctic nations are showing in territorial disputes.

A 1949 ICJ ruling on the use of the Corfu Channel in the Mediterranean Sea found that the channel was an international strait only if the passage was used for international navigation. So far the Canadians have argued that is not the case for the Northwest Passage, because so few ships use it. But that may soon change.

Canada and the United States also are at odds over how to draw their border in the Beaufort Sea. The Canadians say it should be a continuation of the land border between Alaska and Canada, while the United States says it should be a line equidistant from both countries' coastlines. At stake are rights to the rich, underwater oil and gas deposits.

Some 10,000 miles to the east, Russia and Norway are contesting the sovereignty of a 60,000-square-mile area in the Barents Sea, with no resolution in sight. Oslo and Moscow have agreed to allow their military, commercial and fishing vessels to use the waters, but the oil or gas reserves remain untouched.

Meanwhile, Iceland contests Norway's sovereignty — gained under a 1920 treaty — over the Svalbard archipelago. "It is not obvious that Norway owns Svalbard, yet it has taken unilateral control of fishing rights there," complains an Icelandic diplomat, who asked that his name not be used. In another Arctic dispute, Norway, Denmark and Iceland have overlapping claims on a section under the Norwegian Sea called the Banana Hole.[3]

But the granddaddy of Arctic territorial disputes is now before the U.N. Continental Shelf Commission. Russia, Canada and Denmark each have their eyes set on the enormous, underwater Lomonosov Ridge, which straddles the North Pole. The ridge is as big as California, Indiana and Texas combined and is thought to contain rich mineral and possibly oil and gas deposits, although the U.S. Geological Survey recently concluded that most Arctic oil and gas are located elsewhere.[4]

For now, diplomacy remains the favored channel for resolving the disputes, but as the Arctic's geopolitical significance grows, that could change. As Denmark's ambassador to the United States, Friis Arne Petersen, notes, "In the 1930s and 1940s when Denmark and Norway contested a part of Greenland in the northeast, we went to the ICJ to get our sovereignty confirmed. If we cannot agree on Hans Island, we could go to the ICJ again."

[1] Randy Boswell, "Hans Island ours first: Greenland; Premier rejects Canada's claim to disputed Arctic territory," Canwest News Service, May 29, 2008, www.canada.com/ottawacitizen/news/story.html?id=582509c7-fe1a-46f9-887d335a1b100e72.

[2] "Documents on the law of the sea — historical perspective," United Nations Web site, www.un.org/Depts/los/convention_agreements/convention_historical_perspective.htm#Historical%20Perspective.

[3] "Continental Shelf Submission of Norway in respect of areas in the Arctic Ocean, the Barents Sea and the Norwegian Sea," Government of Norway, 2006, www.un.org/Depts/los/clcs_new/submissions_files/submission_nor.htm.

[4] "Circum-Arctic Resource Appraisal," U.S. Geological Survey, July 2008, http://energy.usgs.gov/arctic.

minerals on the "continental shelf" — a term not clearly defined at the time.[45] In 1970, in an effort to prevent its waters from becoming polluted, Canada asserted its right to regulate navigation for 100 nautical miles from its shores.[46] Iceland then extended its maritime boundary to 200 miles, provoking three bloodless "cod wars" with Britain, which dispatched warships to protect its trawlers against the Icelandic coast guard.[47]

Such tensions underscored the need for a global treaty to regulate the seas. In 1967, a passionate address to the General Assembly by Malta's ambassador to the United Nations, Arvid Pardo, helped launch a 15-year negotiation process that led to the signing of UNCLOS in 1982.[48] Another groundbreaking moment came five years later, when Soviet leader Mikhail Gorbachev declared

the Arctic should be transformed into "a zone of peace." At the time, the Soviet and U.S. navies were conducting Cold War maneuvers in the region as a display of their military preparedness.[49]

UNCLOS gave coastal countries the right to exploit all marine resources in their "exclusive economic zone," or the area up to nautical 200 miles from shore. The provision especially benefited coastal states without a big continental shelf, guaranteeing them a minimum of 200 miles of control. States could extend that limit even farther if their continental shelf extended beyond 200 miles.[50]

In 2001 Russia became the first Arctic coastal state to request such an extension, claiming four separate areas of the Arctic Ocean. The U.N. Continental Shelf Commission has asked for more data.[51] In 2006 Norway, whose

A family of indigenous Sami — formerly called Laplanders — prepares a meal during the reindeer migration in northern Norway.

sovereignty over the Svalbard archipelago in the Barents Sea has proved extremely useful in the claims process, submitted a claim for parts of the Norwegian Sea, Barents Sea and Arctic Ocean.[52]

Under a 1995 UNCLOS agreement, global commercial fishing is also being regulated, with countries obliged to set total allowable catches for certain species.[53]

In 1982 President Ronald Reagan objected to UNCLOS provisions on deep seabed mining in international waters, arguing they went against U.S. economic and security interests. The provisions empowered a new international body to license such activities, including the right to collect and distribute royalties.[54] While President Bill Clinton secured an agreement in 1994 aimed at allaying such concerns, the Senate continued to balk at ratification, fearing it undermined U.S. sovereignty.

Last October, the Senate Committee on Foreign Relations approved UNCLOS, but it still must pass the full Senate by a two-thirds majority. Sen. Richard G. Lugar, R-Ind., who supports passage, noted that "unlike some treaties, such as the Kyoto Agreement and the Comprehensive Test Ban Treaty — where U.S. non-participation renders the treaties virtually ineffective — the Law of the Sea will continue to form the basis of maritime law regardless of whether the U.S. is a party."[55] Lugar was referring to the fact that the United States applies the Law of the Sea in practice, even though it hasn't ratified the treaty.

Another UNCLOS backer in the Senate, Foreign Relations Committee Chairman Joseph R. Biden, D-Del., argues the treaty gives the United States the opportunity to extend its control up to 600 miles off the Alaska coast. "The oil and gas industry is unanimous in support of the convention," said Biden.[56]

Environmental Threats

The reduction in sea ice has devastated marine mammals, causing mass walrus deaths along the Chukotka coast in northeastern Russia, notes Oceana's Krenz. Fish populations have been affected too. Shrimp and crab, which prefer the cold, have become rarer while stocks of cod, salmon, mackerel and pollock have increased.[57] For unknown reasons, fish stocks are moving from the coastal areas to the open sea, causing problems for the seabirds that feed on them, which don't venture that far from shore; sea parrots, for instance, are declining significantly.[58]

Meanwhile, Greenland's stunning Ilulissat glacier, a UNESCO World Heritage Site, moves toward the sea at seven feet per hour as it melts — three times its pace in 2002.[59] When the glacial ice reaches the sea and breaks off into the ocean it raises sea levels, threatening coastal populations. (Melting sea ice, on the other hand, does not raise sea levels because the ice is already floating on the sea.)

The Arctic's permafrost — or frozen soil — is melting as well, buckling highways, bursting pipelines and weakening the foundations of buildings. In Vorkuta, Russia, for example, resident Lyubov I. Denisova complained that "everything is falling apart. The ceiling has warped, the walls cracked, the window frames splintered."[60] Melting permafrost also releases methane into the atmosphere, further accelerating global warming.

The Arctic environment also has been polluted by industrial emissions transported by air and sea, often from installations thousands of miles away, such as coal-fired power plants. "The Arctic is a sink for a lot of contaminants like mercury, pesticides and PCBs," says Sander at the European Environment Agency. "Arctic species have no capacity to resist these chemicals. They get stored in fat deposits and enter the food chain." A new study from the University of Northern British Columbia found that mercury levels in the Arctic remain stubbornly high, with coal-fired power plants the main culprit.[61]

© B&C Alexander/Arcticphoto.com (all)

Arctic Life Is Changing

Traditional Arctic culture and ways of life are disappearing as temperatures rise and oil and gas exploration intensifies. Inuit hunters in Northwest Greenland today rarely build igloos like this one built during a long 1986 hunting trip because the warmer atmospheric temperatures make construction difficult (top). Reindeer herders like this Tundra Nenets man in Western Siberia say oil and gas pipelines make it difficult to move the herds (bottom). An Inuit man in Igloolik, Nunavut, Canada (right), wears a traditional caribou-skin outfit.

Opportunity Knocks

Commercial oil activity in the Arctic began in 1920 in Canada's Northwest Territories, with ventures in Russia and Alaska following soon after.[62] The U.S. government issued its first oil exploration lease on Alaska's North Slope in 1958, bringing in big producers like ConocoPhillips.[63] Given the difficulty of Arctic Ocean shipping, a land-based pipeline was constructed in the 1970s to transport oil from northern Alaska to the ice-free port of Valdez in the south.

Oil companies began drilling off the Alaskan, Canadian, Norwegian and Russian coasts in the 1980s. Interest in Greenland has intensified in recent years, especially after a 2007 U.S. Geological Survey assessment of reserves ranked an area of northeastern Greenland as 19th among the world's 500 biggest oil and gas regions.[64]

Offshore oil and gas drilling in the Arctic was initially concentrated along shorelines due to the harsh climate, but companies are gradually venturing northward. In August 2007 the Snohvit natural gas field went online in the Barents Sea, 90 miles from the Norwegian coast.[65]

Snohvit operates some 300 meters below sea level, sending extracted gas via pipeline to a processing plant on Melkoya Island, which liquefies it for export to Europe and the United States.[66] Petroleum has made Norway one of the globe's richest nations, with total revenues from Snohvit alone expected to top $39 billion, or $8,200 per citizen, over its estimated 25-year lifecycle.[67]

Russia, with help from two foreign energy firms, Norway's huge StatoilHydro and France's Total, has begun developing the Shtokman gas field in the Barents Sea, 373 miles offshore, although it is not expected to produce for several years.

Russian Foreign Minister Sergey Lavrov has noted how "global warming not only creates additional problems for us but opens up new possibilities as well."[68] As for environmental concerns about resource extraction, Lavrov said he had helped set up a public-private partnership, Emercom, to monitor and respond quickly to risks arising from "oil and gas production, nuclear energy, the transportation and processing of hydrocarbons and other raw materials."[69]

Meanwhile, the development of the double acting ship has made it easier for ships to navigate the Arctic's icy waters. Pat Broe, a Denver businessman, has spent $50 million modernizing a derelict Hudson Bay port that he bought for $7 million from Canada in 1997 and hopes will figure prominently in a coming boom in Arctic shipping. Broe has estimated that the port in Churchill, Manitoba, could make $100 million a year serving as a terminal for ships from Murmansk, a major Russian port.[70] Churchill could also service the increasingly popular Arctic tourist cruises, some carrying more than 1,000 passengers.

The development of huge factory fishing ships that can stay at sea for months has led to severe depletions of fish stocks.[71] Governments responded by setting catch quotas and limiting fishing rights of foreign vessels within their 200-mile boundaries. Norway and Russia now have agreements allowing some non-Arctic nations like Poland, Spain, France, Germany and the U.K. to fish in the Barents Sea.[72] Norway, which exports $6 billion worth of fish a year, also has been clamping down on Russian vessels that poach in Norwegian waters.[73] Meanwhile, the shrinking sea ice is encouraging vessels to move further north.

"It is happening in the Barents Sea — not yet in Canadian and U.S. waters, but the potential is there," says Oceana's Krenz.

Arctic coastal states traditionally have maintained a strong military presence in the region. In the past year, however, Canada has beefed up its military profile. The government announced in October 2007 that "as part of asserting sovereignty in the Arctic . . . new Arctic patrol ships [costing $3.1 billion] and expanded aerial surveillance will guard Canada's Far North and the Northwest Passage."[74]

Canadian forces also have stepped up patrols in the world's most northerly settlement — the community of Alert on Ellesmere Island — to "look for evidence of incursions into the area by Inuit from Greenland to hunt polar bears."[75] It also launched a space satellite, *Polar Epsilon*, to provide land and sea surveillance for Canadian forces beginning this summer.[76]

CURRENT SITUATION

Ilulissat Fallout

The joint declaration adopted at the May 27-29 Ilulissat ministerial meeting asserts the primacy of UNCLOS for resolving territorial claims.[77] Danish Foreign Minister Per Stig Moller proclaimed "hopefully we have eradicated all the myths about a 'race for the North Pole.' The legal framework is in place, and the five states have now declared that they will abide by it."[78]

But Huebert at the University of Calgary insists "not everyone is getting along like they pretend. In reality, there is a race to the North Pole."

To begin with, the meeting ruffled feathers by its exclusivity. "This is a very strange way of discussing what is a pan-Arctic issue or indeed an international issue," protested EU Parliament Vice President Wallis. "Why have not Finland, Sweden and Iceland been invited, countries which are also full Arctic Council member states?"[79]

Indeed, an Icelandic diplomat says his government was "not amused" at being left out. "We agree that territorial claims can be resolved by bilateral agreements, but in Ilulissat they also talked about shipping, Inuit rights and security. We should have been invited."

The State Department's McMurray, who attended the meeting, says the most concrete thing to emerge was a green light for Norway to draft a proposal to improve search and rescue services. "This will cover airplane and shipping accidents," she says. "Greenland presently has no capability to cope with the numbers of tourists going there, most of whom are Americans."

New Energy Leases

More than 400 oil and gas fields have been discovered north of the Arctic Circle, and that figure is set to rise.[80] In February 2008 the U.S. government's Minerals Management Service approved the extraction of oil and gas from a portion of the Chukchi Sea off Alaska's northern coast. It plans to open four other sections of the Chukchi and Beaufort seas between now and 2012.[81] The World Wildlife Fund says the leases should not have been awarded, because the impact of exploration on polar bears and indigenous communities has not been determined.[82]

Sen. John Kerry, D-Mass., agrees and has introduced a bill to ban exploration until the assessment is made.[83] But President Bush is calling for more offshore oil drilling to help bring down high oil prices. "Congress should permit exploration in currently restricted areas of northern Alaska, which could produce roughly the equivalent of two decades of imported oil from Saudi Arabia," Bush recently said.[84]

Although Bush was talking about drilling inland, the USGS's recent conclusion that Arctic Alaska is the region's most oil-rich area will undoubtedly increase pressure to drill — especially offshore, where most of the Arctic's undiscovered oil and gas is thought to be found. The Arctic's 90 billion barrels of undiscovered oil compares to U.S. reserves of 22 billion barrels and annual production of 1.6 billion barrels.[85]

This June Canada awarded a $1.2 billion lease to Britain's BP to develop oil and gas in the Beaufort Sea.[86] The World Wildlife Fund's Stewart criticizes the move and notes that the Canadian government has no consistent energy-exploration policy because the responsible departments disagree over whether drilling should go ahead. One indication of that internal disarray: Despite numerous efforts, the Canadian Embassy in Washington was unable to provide a single Canadian official willing to discuss the topic for this article, because, according to an embassy official, no single agency is in charge of Arctic policy.

Meanwhile, Russia is stepping up its activity. In the Shtokman gas operation in the Barents Sea, it is using the expertise of foreign companies — StatoilHydro of Norway and Total of France — to produce the gas, but they must sell it all to Russia's state-owned energy giant Gazprom.[87] A new oil terminal at Varandey, 14 miles offshore in the Barents Sea, became operational in June 2008. It will load oil onto ships for transport to Europe and America.

"The infrastructure we have been able to establish helps develop new fields in Timan-Pechora oil and gas province," noted Vagit Alekperov, president of Russia's Lukoil, which spearheaded the project.[88]

In other developments, Greenland awarded numerous exploration licenses this year to U.S., Canadian, British, Danish and Swedish companies, and in July StatoilHydro began mapping the seabed of northeast Greenland.[89] Iceland plans to grant licenses within the next year to develop undersea resources on the Jan Mayen Ridge, off its northeastern coast.

Revamping Policies

The EU is paying more attention to the Arctic than ever before, with the Parliament planning to pass a resolution in September providing direction to the European Commission on its Arctic policy paper, due out in the autumn. EU Parliament Vice President Wallis feels the EU, with no Arctic territory, could play the role of an honest broker in future talks.

The Bush administration also is due to unveil its new Arctic policy soon, but none too soon for Alaska's Sen. Murkowski. "We have not accepted the responsibility of being an Arctic nation yet. I want a policy that does not simply say, 'We value the Arctic' or 'The Arctic is a lovely place,' but provides specifics, such as how many icebreakers we will acquire." The United States currently has only three: One is laid up in Seattle for repairs, another was designed mainly for scientific expeditions and a third, a more heavy-duty design, is in use.[90] Consequently, the United States contracts with foreign icebreakers to meet its needs. Meanwhile, Russia has 18, Finland and Sweden each have seven and Canada has six. Apart from helping other ships navigate icy seas, icebreakers can be used to support search and rescue and oil-spill clean-up operations as well as to gather seabed data to evaluate extended continental shelf claims.

The Arctic Council is scheduled to publish an assessment of the long-term potential for Arctic shipping. Inuit leader Lynge believes a moratorium on increased commercial shipping should be imposed until a stricter regime can ensure that only "Arctic-proof" ships enter Arctic waters.

Canada and Russia Dominate Arctic Production

The Arctic contains 22 percent of the world's undiscovered oil and gas deposits (top). Russia produces more oil and gas per day than any other Arctic country and has more gas reserves than all the other Arctic nations combined. Canada holds the most known oil reserves. Finland, Sweden, Iceland and Greenland produce almost no oil or gas and have no known reserves, although a recent study estimated that Greenland, which is owned by Denmark, is likely to have large, undiscovered deposits.

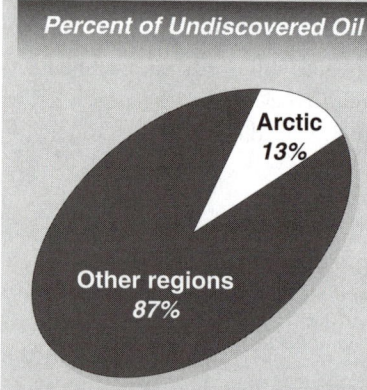

Percent of Undiscovered Oil

Arctic 13%

Other regions 87%

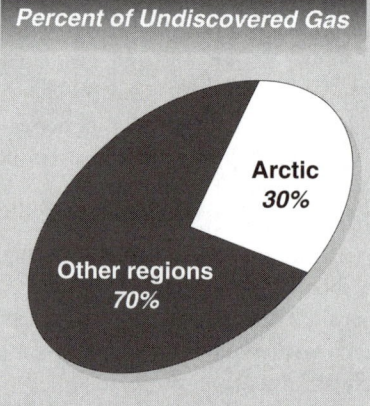

Percent of Undiscovered Gas

Arctic 30%

Other regions 70%

Arctic Energy Production and Known Reserves

Country	Daily oil production, 2007 (thousand barrels)	Proved oil reserves, 2007 (billion barrels)	Annual natural gas production, 2006 (billion cubic feet)	Proved natural gas reserves, 2006 (billion cubic feet)
Canada	3,355.79	179.21	6,548	56,577
Russia	9,875.77	60.00	23,167	1,680,000
Norway	2,565.27	7.85	3,196	84,260
U.S.	8,487.40	21.76	18,531	204,385
Greenland	0	0	0	0
Iceland	0	0	0	0
Finland	8.95	0	0	0
Sweden	2.35	0	0	0

Source: Energy Information Administration, U.S. Department of Energy; U.S. Geological Survey 2008

"Think of a continent as a big rock sitting in a bathtub, and imagine that a chunk of it rises out of the water," wrote *Wired* reporter Geoffrey Gagnon. "The question for scientists is, where does the rock end and the acrylic tub begin? It sounds simple enough, but imagine now that your tub is also made of rock and that smaller rocks are piled up all over the place."[91]

In Nunavut, Canada, researchers 375 miles north of Grise Fjord are trying to determine whether their shelf extends as far as the Eurasian side of the North Pole, where Russian geologists are also gathering data.[92]

"The need to assert our sovereignty and take action to protect our territorial integrity in the Arctic has never been more important," Canadian Natural Resources Minister Gary Lunn has said.[93]

Equally assertive, Danish Ambassador Petersen says, "We already have a lot of geological data. We believe Russia's claim to the Lomonosov Ridge to be unfounded." The Danes have until 2014 to make their claim, Canada until 2013 and Norway and Russia until 2009.

The United States has just begun gathering data for a claim. The Coast Guard's largest icebreaker, *Healy*, is conducting a joint collaboration in the Arctic Ocean this summer with Canada's *Louis S. St. Laurent*.[94] "We are far behind other countries," Assistant Secretary McMurray admits. But the United States cannot submit a claim unless and until the Senate ratifies UNCLOS. Most senators support ratification, but the Democratic leadership has not put it to a vote yet, fearing it will not pass by the necessary two-thirds majority.

Meanwhile, Arctic governments continue mapping the Arctic seabed in pursuit of continental shelf claims. But there probably won't be global scientific consensus on where those geological borders lie because finding the shelf can be tricky.

The United States is at another disadvantage because it does not own any islands near the North Pole. Calculating

Offshore Drilling Poses Special Challenges

Access and cleanup are more difficult in the Arctic.

Exploring for oil and gas under the sea usually begins with geological mapping and a search for two key factors: sedimentary rock at least 1.8 miles thick and evidence of an ancient "tectonic event." The thick rock is a precondition for oil and gas to be present, geologists say. And a shift in one or more of the Earth's tectonic plates typically would have sealed the oil into a confined space.[1]

In the early days, oil explorers simply drilled holes to find oil. Today images of the seabed are created by seismic surveys, in which explosions are triggered that send shockwaves into the Earth, which then are reflected back in radio waves that provide a picture of the ocean floor. Next, well data is gathered by boring into the ground to obtain core samples.

Before a well can be drilled, an area must be at least temporarily ice-free. If oil is discovered, facilities and pipelines must be constructed. Rigs may be installed either above the sea surface or on the seabed. Surface rigs can be either fixed or floating units, with the latter providing necessary flexibility to cope with icy Arctic conditions. The Snohvit gas rig in Norway's Barents Sea, which is ice-free, stands entirely on the seabed, with no surface installations. Snohvit is "over-trawlable" and does not interfere with trawl nets and other fishing equipment. Pipes along the sea floor transport the gas from the wells to the shore 90 miles away for processing.

Drillers avoid areas where the sea is permanently ice-covered, because access to oil and gas is more complicated and spillages more difficult to clean up. Extreme cold and the need to work during the winter months, in 24-hour darkness, also deter Arctic petroleum exploration.

Once extracted, oil is transported by pipeline or tanker to a refinery or storage depot; gas is converted into liquefied natural gas (LNG) and shipped. Once a well is exhausted, the rig must be removed in an environmentally safe manner. Depending on the country, exploration may need to be accompanied by environmental-impact assessments and public consultations with neighboring communities.

Spillages can be caused by oil-well explosions, collisions of oil-laden ships or leaking pipelines. Clean-ups pose particular challenges because ice makes it hard to reach the spills and more difficult to detect spills that are trapped under the ice. On the other hand, if contained by the ice, the oil can be easier to clean up because it is less emulsified than when mixed with the water.

Sometimes a spill is cleaned up by setting it on fire. But the resulting thick, black smoke plume releases toxic chemicals into the atmosphere and may not be feasible if there is a community nearby. An experimental, controlled spill and so-called *in situ* burning are planned for the Barents Sea in May 2009, organized by Norway in collaboration with Statoil, Chevron and ConocoPhillips.

---

[1] Arctic Monitoring and Assessment Programme, "Arctic Oil and Gas 2007," Oslo, Norway, 2007, www.amap.no/oga; Don Gautier, geologist at United States Geological Survey; Amy Merten, co-director, Coastal Response Research Center, National Oceanic and Atmospheric Administration.

---

the continental shelf limit can begin at any of a country's islands.

It will be several years before the U.N. commission assessing the claims passes judgment. And that probably will not be the final word on the matter. In its submission to the commission, Norway said the final boundaries will have to be determined through bilateral agreements with its Arctic neighbors.[95]

McMurray agrees: "It is not going to be the U.N. that sorts out overlapping claims. The countries will have to agree among themselves." Petersen says "if we fail to agree bilaterally we can still go to the International Court of Justice."

Lynge believes indigenous communities are the key to avoiding an ugly dispute. "They must look for partnership with us — otherwise they will simply fight among themselves for decades. The Inuit can be the glue that stops this from disintegrating into a territorial fight." Indigenous community representatives are quick to point out that they have shared the Arctic's resources for thousands of years without resorting to conflict with one another.

The polar bears' threatened-species designation could throw a monkey wrench into the oil developers' plans, because U.S. law bars government agencies from taking any action that could further endanger a listed species. Conservation

© B&C Alexander/Arcticphoto.com

Arctic Wildlife Abounds

A variety of mammals are able to survive the Arctic's harsh climate, including walruses in Spitsbergen, Norway (top), reindeer in northern Norway being herded by a Sami woman (right) and bull musk-oxen in Canada's Northwest Territories (bottom).

groups can argue before the courts that drilling poses a threat — both directly from spillages and indirectly through more fossil fuels being consumed, triggering more global warming and more loss of sea ice.[96]

In June conservationists scored another success when President Bush signed a congressional resolution aimed at preventing a mad dash to exploit Arctic fish stocks. The resolution's sponsor, Republican Sen. Ted Stevens of Alaska said, "with less summer ice in the Arctic, our northern waters will be open for exploitation from pirate fishing fleets. But the passage of the resolution will help protect our marine resources."[97]

The measure calls on the United States to consult with other Arctic nations for an agreement on managing fish stocks.[98] Oceana has called the move "the first significant step the U.S. government has taken to protect the Arctic Ocean," adding, "hopefully this starts a trend towards conservation and away from the 'too much, too fast and too soon' pace we've seen so far."[99]

OUTLOOK

Strategic Importance

Most scientists believe the Arctic will continue to warm faster than the rest of the planet. "It seems nearly impossible for summer Arctic sea ice to return to the climatological extent that existed prior to 1980," according to NOAA's Overland, who predicts that within 12 years the Arctic may be entirely ice-free in summer.[100]

Meanwhile, offshore oil and gas development will expand, especially within Arctic nations' exclusive economic zones, where reserves are easier to access and where most oil and gas is thought to be located. There will be more onshore development as well. A 750-mile natural gas pipeline connecting gas fields in Canada's Northwest Territories with markets to the south is being planned, although its development has slowed recently due to land-ownership disputes with indigenous communities.[101] A rival pipeline starting in Prudhoe Bay in neighboring Alaska is also being touted.[102]

Russia is expanding operations in western Siberia — where most of the Arctic's gas is thought to lie — and in the Timan-Pechora Basin. But concerns about global warming could stall drilling operations, especially in Canada and the United States, where environmental groups are likely to mount strong legal challenges.

Rich oil profits should flow into the region, although foreign energy firms could do well, too, since four of the five Arctic coastal states have no restrictions on foreign ownership of oil companies.[103] Cash-strapped governments may demand a bigger slice of the pie. Currently, their revenue share ranges from 46-65 percent in Greenland to 90-100 percent in Russia.[104] The people of Greenland will vote in November on a revenue-sharing agreement signed in June with Denmark. Exploration could creep higher into the Arctic if the sea ice continues to recede and the seas become more accessible — but only if companies are convinced there is enough oil and gas to make it worth their while.

Shipping may be the more viable option for transporting fuels, given how costly and complicated it is to construct pipelines and how vulnerable they are to being ruptured by melting permafrost.[105] Thus, Arctic shipping routes will become busier, and the necessary support infrastructure must be developed. An immediate boom in transcontinental shipping of other non-fuel cargo looks less likely, because ice-related delays or the cost of extra fuel needed to cut through ice-covered seas will cancel out the cost-savings from the shorter travel distances. Oceana's Krenz says an increase in shipping also could further hasten the melting of the ice cap, because ships' carbon emissions darken the ice, increasing its absorption of heat.

Exporting freshwater — either from icebergs or, more likely, from existing lakes, of which Canada has many — is

A fur-clad Inuit hunter in northwest Greenland scans the sea ice for polar bears. His world is rapidly changing as global warming melts the ice and introduces increased tourism, energy development and transcontinental shipping.

another potential profit source, says the Arctic Research Commission's Brigham. "No one is doing it yet, but with freshwater increasingly scarce and expensive, it may become commercially interesting to ship it to countries with shortages."[106]

"The amount of ice that comes into the ocean [from melting glaciers] could provide the water supply for any of the largest cities in the world for an entire year," according to Robert Corell, director of the Global Change Program at the H. John Heinz III Center for Science, Economics and the Environment, in Washington, D.C.[107]

The European Environment Agency's Sander predicts Arctic waters will become a center for genetic resources, a growing industry involving the harnessing of plant or animal substances for use in medicines. And, as job opportunities grow in the oil and gas, agriculture, fishing, shipping and tourism industries, so, too, could immigration, which may heighten tensions between indigenous communities and newcomers.

The burgeoning economic activity may motivate countries to step up their military presence, as Canada and Russia are doing. Russian Gen. Vladimir Shamanov has announced plans to deploy more naval vessels, adding, "We are also planning to increase the operational radius of the Northern Fleet's submarines."

A prominent military hawk, Shamanov insists Russia has the capability to defend its claim to half of the Arctic Ocean.[108]

Should the U.S. Senate ratify the U.N. Convention on the Law of the Sea?

YES
Sen. Lisa Murkowski, R-Alaska
Member, Senate Foreign Relations and Energy and Natural Resources Committees

Written for *CQ Global Researcher*, August 2008

Recent actions by Russia, Canada and other northern-tier nations to strengthen or establish claims in the Arctic Ocean underscore why it's so critical for the U.S. Senate to ratify the U.N. Convention on the Law of the Sea (UNCLOS). Otherwise, we may be watching from the sidelines as other nations divvy up the significant energy resources contained in the Arctic seabed.

It is believed that the Arctic may hold 22 percent of the world's undiscovered oil and gas — a number that could rise considerably as additional survey work is completed in the region. An expedition by the Coast Guard cutter *Healy* last winter showed that the United States could lay claim to an area the size of California as part of our extended continental shelf.

The problem? The United States has no legal claim to most of this area — and the oil or gas it contains — unless we become a party to the UNCLOS. If we don't claim it, others certainly will.

Russia already has claimed almost half of the Arctic, including parts of what we believe to be Alaska's extended continental shelf, while Canada is looking to establish military bases in the north.

For those who think Russia's claims, or those of other nations, will not be recognized, think again. On April 21 of this year, Australia's claim to 2.5 million square kilometers of extended continental shelf — an area three times the size of Texas — was recognized. It is only a matter of time before other claims are accepted as well.

It would be naïve to believe we could reach multiple bilateral agreements with nations once their claims in the Arctic, and to its oil and natural gas, are internationally recognized. What is their incentive? What would the United States need to give up in return?

When we talk about sovereignty, those who say the United States already enjoys the benefits of the Law of the Sea Treaty ignore that we do so only by the grace of other nations. They ignore that our military commanders believe UNCLOS is vital to ensuring the passage of U.S. naval vessels through international waters. They ignore that if we cede the Arctic to Russia and other Arctic nations, we could very well be importing oil that should belong to us in the first place.

In a time of rising energy costs and demands, that does not seem like a sound policy for the United States to follow.

NO
Lawrence A. Kogan
President and CEO, Institute for Trade, Standards and Sustainable Development

Written for *CQ Global Researcher*, August 2008

Since 2007, a growing body of evidence has revealed that UNCLOS, if ratified by the United States, would ensure much more than what the U.S. Navy recognizes as America's absolute right to freedom of navigation.

Granted, UNCLOS codifies this customary international-law principle. But UNCLOS parties, especially European governments, also increasingly embrace recent U.N. concepts of environment-centric sustainable development, which ultimately are based on environmental and health regulation that reflect hypothetically possible rather than empirically probable harms. These nostrums already have been used to reshape international environmental law, which will now be implemented and enforced through the treaty's dynamic environmental provisions, putting new conditions on the exercise of that right to freedom of navigation.

Indeed, there are 45-plus environmental articles, annexes, appendices, protocols and regulations within UNCLOS that can expand and evolve over time to reflect the most current international environmental law. Ironically, these same provisions have captured the imagination of creative, transatlantic policy makers, who, aided by sensationalist media, have triggered public anxieties about the potential environmental and health hazards posed by observable (but likely cyclical) global warming and melting ice.

UNCLOS ratification raises several important questions. For instance, what connection, if any, exists between UNCLOS, global warming, carbon dioxide emissions and other types of air and water "pollution" generated both within U.S. jurisdiction and beyond? What legislative, regulatory and judicial obligations would UNCLOS place on the U.S. government to prevent such pollution from materializing in the first place? What economic, technological and legal burdens would U.S. businesses and individual Americans consequently face as U.S. laws are made more stringent and costly due to UNCLOS ratification? Why is UNCLOS ratification necessary to drill for oil and gas in Alaska's inland and offshore sites, since most of the untapped reserves are reportedly within 200 miles of the coast — where the United States can drill without U.N. permission? And finally, why do administration officials, congressional representatives and environmental activists oppose holding open, public and transparent Senate and House hearings to investigate the potential impact of UNCLOS' "green" provisions on the U.S. economy, national security and sovereignty?

If UNCLOS isn't the green Trojan Horse that opponents say it is, why not prove it?

On the governance side, the European Union will seek ways to assert itself, despite owning no Arctic territory. A recent EU policy paper noted "an increasing need to address the growing debate over territorial claims" and new trade routes, which challenge Europe's trade and resource interests in the region and "may put pressure on its relations with key partners."[109]

The Arctic Council may also have a chance to play a more prominent role. "The council could focus on policy development in specific areas like combating mercury pollution," says Sander. Icelandic official Baldursson says the council "could be used as a venue for information exchange and preliminary negotiations." Danish Ambassador Petersen says the council should address not just environmental but also economic activities.

In the inevitable pursuit of the Arctic's resources, Gun-Britt Retter, a member of the Sami indigenous people's parliament in Norway, fears governments will pay scant regard to the environmental impact of it all. "We have lived off the land for 10,000 years without extracting all the resources. We think long-term, not about filling our budgets. Governments only think four years ahead until the next election."

NOTES

1. See James Graff, "Fight for the Top of the World," *Time*, Oct. 1, 2007, pp. 28-36, www.time.com/time/world/article/0,8599,1663445,00.html.

2. Presentation by Thomas Armstrong, Senior Advisor for Global Change Programs, U.S. Geological Survey, at the Danish Embassy to the U.S., May 7, 2008.

3. James Overland, *et al.*, "The Arctic and Antarctic: Two Faces of Climate Change," *EOS*, American Geophysical Union, May 6, 2008, www.noaanews.noaa.gov/stories2008/images/5-6-08_Overland.pdf.

4. *Ibid.*

5. Documentation concerning the U.S. Interior Department's May 14, 2008, decision to list the polar bear as a threatened species is at www.doi.gov/issues/polar_bears.html.

6. See Scott. G. Borgerson, "Arctic Meltdown," *Foreign Affairs*, March/April 2008, www.foreign

affairs.org/20080301faessay87206/scott-g-borgerson/arctic-meltdown.html.

7. Adrian Blomfield, "Russia plans military build-up in the Arctic," *The Daily Telegraph*, June 12, 2008, www.telegraph.co.uk/news/worldnews/europe/russia/2111507/Russia-plans-Arctic-military-build-up.html. For a detailed map of the various territorial claims filed by the five Arctic states, go to http://news.bbc.co.uk/go/em/fr/-/2/hi/staging_site/in_depth/the_green_ room/7543837.stm.

8. See "Decision regarding the date of commencement of the ten-year period for making submissions to the Commission on the Limits of the Continental Shelf set out in article 4 of Annex II to the United Nations Convention on the Law of the Sea," May 14-18, 2001, www.un.org/Depts/los/convention_agreements/convention_historical_perspective.htm.

9. Market price on July 24, 2008.

10. "Circum-Arctic Resource Appraisal," U.S. Geological Survey, July 2008, http://energy.usgs.gov/arctic.

11. United States Energy Information Administration, http://tonto.eia.doe.gov/dnav/ng/hist/n9070us2A.htm.

12. "Arctic Oil and Gas 2007," Arctic Monitoring and Assessment Programme (AMAP), 2007,www.amap.no/oga, p. ix.

13. For more information, see "Facts 2008 — The Norwegian Petroleum Sector," Norwegian Petroleum Directorate, www.npd.no/English/Produkter+og+tjenester/Publikasjoner/Faktaheftet/Faktaheftet+2008/fakta2008.htm.

14. "Swedish oil company joins hunt for oil and gas in Greenland," press release, Greenland Home Rule Web site, May 23, 2008, http://uk.nanoq.gl/Emner/News/News_from_Parliament/2008/05/2008_may_Swedish_oil_company.aspx.

15. "Climate change and international security," paper from the High Representative and the European Commission to the European Council, March 14, 2008, p. 5, www.consilium.europa.eu/ueDocs/cms_Data/docs/pressData/en/reports/99387.pdf.

16. Graff, *op. cit.*

17. The 18 figure is provided by U.S. Coast Guard, Department of Homeland Security. Presentation by Niels Bjorn Mortensen, Head of Marine, BIMCO (Baltic and International Maritime Council), at a conference on Arctic Transportation, U.S. Maritime Administration, June 5, 2008.

18. Interview with Friis Arne Petersen, Danish Ambassador to the United States.

19. Remarks at a seminar, "Arctic Governance in a global world: is it time for an Arctic Charter?" European Parliament, Alliance of Liberals and Democrats for Europe, May 7, 2008. For seminar presentations, see www.alde.eu/index.php?id=42&L=0&L=ht&tx_ ttnews[tt_news]=9348&cHash=76d92ab815.

20. Norwegian Ministry of Fisheries and Coastal Affairs, press release, Dec. 16, 2005, www.regjeringen.no/ se/dep/fkd/Preassaguovdda/Preassadieahusat/2005/ Broad-agreement-on-fisheries-between-Norway- and-the-EU.html?id=419750.

21. "The Ilulissat Declaration," Governments of Denmark, United States, Canada, Russia and Norway, May 28, 2008, www.um.dk/NR/rdonlyres/ BE00B850-D278-4489-A6BE-6AE230415546/ 0/ArcticOceanConference.pdf.

22. "Arctic Governance in a global world: is it time for an Arctic Charter?" *op. cit.*

23. *Ibid.*

24. *Ibid.*

25. Quoted in Graff, *op. cit.*

26. NOAA Fisheries, National Marine Service Regional Alaska Office, www.fakr.noaa.gov/oil/default .htm.

27. See Web page of Oceana, www.protectthearctic .org.

28. AMAP, *op. cit.*, p. xii.

29. *Ibid.*, p. 25.

30. *Ibid.*, p. vii.

31. "Arctic shuttle container link from Alaska US to Europe," Aker Arctic Technology Inc, March 2006, p. 28, www.institutenorth.org/servlet/ content/studies.html.

32. *Ibid.*

33. *Ibid.*

34. *Ibid.*

35. Jeff Hechts, "Ancient site hints at first North American settlers," *New Scientist*, January 2004, www.newscientist.com/article.ns?id=dn4526.

36. *Britannica Online Encyclopaedia*, www.britannica .com.

37. "Alaska's Heritage," Alaska History and Cultural Studies, www.akhistorycourse.org/articles/article .php?artID=155.

38. *Ibid.*

39. Rasmus Ole Ramussen, "Factsheet: Denmark — Greenland," Royal Danish Ministry of Foreign Affairs, January 2004.

40. John J. Miller, "Let's Buy Greenland!" *National Review Online*, May 7, 2007, www.nationalreview .com/nr_comment/nr_comment050701b.shtml.

41. See U.S. Air Force Web site, www.thule.af.mil.

42. See Derek Hayes, *Historical Atlas of the Arctic* (2003).

43. *Britannica Online, op. cit.*, p. 79.

44. See "Documents on the law of the sea: historical perspective," U.N. Web site, www.un.org/ Depts/los/convention_agreements/convention_ historical_perspective.htm#Historical percent 20Perspective.

45. *Ibid.*

46. *Ibid.*

47. For background, see Colin Woodard, "Oceans in Crisis," *CQ Global Researcher*, October 2007, pp. 237-264.

48. Speech of Malta's Ambassador to the U.N., Arvid Prado, Nov. 1, 1967, www.un.org/Depts/los/ convention_agreements/texts/pardo_ga1967 .pdf. Also see "Documents on Law of the Sea," *op. cit.*

49. Philip Taubman, "Soviet Proposes Arctic Peace Zone," *The New York Times*, Oct. 2, 1987, http:// query.nytimes.com/gst/fullpage.html?res=9B0DE 0DC173CF931A35753C1A961948260.

50. "Documents on Law of the Sea," *op. cit.*

51. "Russia's 2001 submission to the Commission on the Limits of the Continental Shelf," www.un.org/

Depts/los/clcs_new/submissions_files/submission_rus.htm.

52. "Continental Shelf Submission of Norway in respect of areas in the Arctic Ocean, the Barents Sea and the Norwegian Sea, 2006," Government of Norway, www.un.org/Depts/los/clcs_new/submissions_files/submission_nor.htm.

53. "Documents on Law of the Sea — historical perspective," *op. cit.*

54. See www.oceanlaw.org/downloads/references/reagan/PresidentalStmt-Jan82.pdf.

55. Senate Committee on Foreign Relations, hearing on Convention on the Law of the Sea, Oct. 4, 2008. For full testimonies go to http://foreign.senate.gov/hearings/2007/hrg071004a.html.

56. Biden statement, Oct. 31, 2007. See http://biden.senate.gov/press/press_releases/release/?id=15d1b23d-4d04-4e3b-8727-932dd1352bd2.

57. Woodard, *op. cit.*

58. Petter Meier, Fisheries Counselor, Embassy of Norway to the United States, Washington, D.C.

59. See Colin Woodard, "In Greenland, an Interfaith Rally for Climate Change," *The Christian Science Monitor*, Sept. 12, 2007, Ilulissat, Greenland, www.csmonitor.com/2007/0912/p06s01-woeu.html.

60. Steven Lee Myers, Andrew C. Revkin, Simon Romero and Clifford Krauss, "Old Ways of Life are Fading as the Arctic Thaws," *The New York Times*, Oct. 20, 2005, www.nytimes.com/2005/10/20/science/earth/20arctic.ready.html.

61. Bob Weber, "Toxic chemical levels in Arctic food animals dropping: study," The Canadian Press, July 14, 2008, http://cnews.canoe.ca/CNEWS/Canada/2008/07/14/6155656-cp.html.

62. AMAP, *op. cit.*

63. *Ibid.*

64. "New Oil and Gas Assessment of Northeastern Greenland," U.S. Geological Survey, press release, Aug. 28, 2007, www.usgs.gov/newsroom/article.asp?ID=1750.

65. Graff, *op. cit.*

66. For more information on the Snohvit operation, see www.statoil.com/STATOILCOM/snohvit/svg02699.nsf?OpenDatabase&lang=en.

67. Revenue estimates from Statoil Web site, www.statoil.com/STATOILCOM/snohvit/svg02699.nsf?OpenDatabase&lang=en.

68. Remarks, Russian Minister of Foreign Affairs Sergey Lavrov at Conference of Five Arctic Coastal States, Ilulissat, Greenland, May 28, 2008, www.mid.ru/brp_4.nsf/0/A7DABB275A1E95CFC325745800497B84.

69. *Ibid.*

70. Clifford Krauss, Steven Lee Myers, Andrew C. Revkin and Simon Romero, "As Polar Ice Turns to Water, Dreams of Treasure Abound," *The New York Times*, Oct. 20, 2005, www.nytimes.com/2005/10/10/science/10arctic.html?pagewanted=1&_r=1.

71. Woodard, *CQ Global Researcher*, *op. cit.*

72. Meier, *op. cit.*

73. *Ibid.*

74. See "Ottawa buying up to 8 Arctic patrol ships," CBC News, www.cbc.ca/canada/story/2007/07/09/arctic-cda.html. Also see "Strong Leadership. A Better Canada — Speech from the Throne," Government of Canada, Oct. 16, 2007, www.sft-ddt.gc.ca/eng/media.asp?id=1364.

75. "Canadian Forces Patrol to Confirm Arctic Sovereignty," National Defence and the Canadian Forces, March 22, 2007, www.dnd.ca/site/Newsroom/view_news_e.asp?id=2224.

76. "Polar Epsilon to assert Canada's arctic sovereignty," National Defence and the Canadian Forces, press release, Jan. 10, 2008, www.forces.gc.ca/site/newsroom/view_news_e.asp?id=2547.

77. "The Ilulissat Declaration," *op. cit.*

78. "Conference in Ilulissat, Greenland: Landmark political declaration on the future of the Arctic," Ministry of Foreign Affairs of Denmark, edited June 6, 2008, www.missionfnnewyork.um.dk/en/menu/statements/CONFERENCEINILULISSATGREENLAND.htm.

79. Diana Wallis, European Parliament Vice President, statement on Arctic Five meeting in Greenland,

May 28, 2008, http://dianawallismep.org.uk/news/000590/diana_wallis_responds_to_meeting_of_arctic_five.html.

80. "Circum-Arctic Resource Appraisal," *op. cit.*

81. For map of planned oil and gas exploration areas in Chukchi and Beaufort seas, U.S. Minerals Management Services Scoping Report, Environmental Impact Assessment, March 2008, p. 17, www.mms.gov/alaska/cproject/ArcticMultiSale/scoping_rpt.pdf.

82. "Native and Conservation Groups Voice Opposition to Lease Sale 193 in the Chukchi Sea," World Wildlife Fund, press release, Feb. 2, 2008, www.worldwildlife.org/who/media/press/2008/WWFPresitem5921.html.

83. Sen. John Kerry, press release, Jan. 30, 2008, http://kerry.senate.gov/cfm/record.cfm?id=291475.

84. "President Bush Discusses Outer Continental Shelf Exploration," White House, July 14, 2008, www.whitehouse.gov/news/releases/2008/07/20080714-4.html.

85. Circum-Arctic Resource Appraisal, *op. cit.*

86. David Ebner, "BP signals start of Arctic oil rush," *The Globe and Mail* (Canada) June 7, 2008, www.uofaweb.ualberta.ca/govrel/news.cfm?story=79420.

87. Guy Chazan, "Oil Sees End of Sweet Deals," *The Wall Street Journal*, July 14, 2008, http://online.wsj.com/public/search/page/3_0466.html?KEYWORDS=Shtokman&mod=DNH_S.

88. "LUKoil starts oil exports through Varandey terminal," *New Europe*, June 16, 2008, www.neurope.eu/articles/87870.php.

89. "Swedish oil company joins hunt for oil and gas in Greenland," Greenland Home Rule Web site, May 23, 2008, http://uk.nanoq.gl/Emner/News/News_from_Parliament/2008/05/2008_may_Swedish_oil_company.aspx. Also see "Geological investigations offshore North East Greenland in the summer of 2008," Greenland Home Rule Web site, May 2, 2008, http://uk.nanoq.gl/Emner/News/News_from_Parliament/2008/05/2008_apr_geological_investigation_offshore.aspx.

90. Testimony by Admiral Thad Allen, U.S. Coast Guard Commandant, hearing, House Subcommittee on Coast Guard and Maritime Transportation, July 16, 2008, http://transportation.house.gov/News/PRArticle.aspx?NewsID=681.

91. Geoffrey Gagnon, "The Last Great Landgrab," *Wired*, February 2008, www.wired.com/science/planetearth/magazine/16-02/mf_continentalshelf.

92. Randy Boswell, "Scientist warns over Arctic quest," Canwest News Service, June 2, 2008, www.canada.com/vancouversun/news/story.html?id=5131cf5a-d7fc-47f1-b487-39c4d0c972bc.

93. "Minister Lunn Visits Canadian Scientists in Far North: Research Supports Canada's Claim to Arctic Sovereignty," Natural Resources Canada, press release, April 17, 2008, www.nrcan-rncan.gc.ca/media/newcom/2008/200824-eng.php.

94. Kathy Eagen, public affairs officer, U.S. State Department, June 13, 2008.

95. Government of Norway, 2006, *op. cit.*

96. See Kenneth P. Green, "Is the Polar Bear Endangered, or Just Conveniently Charismatic?" American Enterprise Institute, May 2008, www.aei.org/publications/filter.all,pubID.27918/pub_detail.asp.

97. Sen. Ted Stevens, press release, June 4, 2008, www.stevens.senate.gov/public/index.cfm?FuseAction=NewsRoom.PressReleases&ContentRecord_id=5538fa34-d757-3e73-f6cd-ec6c3628762c&Region_id=&Issue_id=.

98. S.J. Res. 17, "A joint resolution directing the United States to initiate international discussions and take necessary steps with other nations to negotiate an agreement for managing migratory and transboundary fish stocks in the Arctic Ocean," P.L. 110-243.

99. Oceana, press release, June 3, 2008, www.oceana.org/north-america/media-center/press-releases/press_release/0/788/.

100. Overland, *et al.*, *op. cit.*

101. See www.mackenziegasproject.com/theProject/index.html.

102. Ed Struzik, "Pipeline or Pipe Dream?" Canwest News Service, July 18, 2008, www.canada.com/topics/news/national/story.html?id=45752856-72d2-4cbd-b988-d374b73a03e9.

103. Rachel Halpern, " 'Above-Ground' issues and Arctic Oil and Gas Development," International Trade Administration, U.S. Department of Commerce, presentation at National Defense University and Forces Transformation and Resources Seminar, May 14, 2008, pp. 136-145, www.ita.doc.gov/td/energy/arctic%20paper.pdf.

104. *Ibid.*

105. For background, see Trans-Alaska Pipeline Web site, at www.alyeska-pipe.com/Pipelinefacts/Permafrost.html.

106. See Lawson W. Brigham, "Thinking about the Arctic's Future: Scenarios for 2040," *The Futurist*, Sept-Oct 2007, www.wfs.org/Sept-Oct07 percent20files/FuturecontSO07.htm.

107. Woodard, *The Christian Science Monitor, op. cit.*

108. Blomfield, *op. cit.*

109. "Climate change and international security," paper from the High Representative and the European Commission to the European Council, March 14, 2008, p. 8, www.consilium.europa.eu/ueDocs/cms_Data/docs/pressData/en/reports/99387.pdf.

BIBLIOGRAPHY

Books

Brandt, Anthony, ed., *North Pole, A Narrative History, National Geographic Society,* 2005.
Drawing on extensive Society archives, an adventure expert chronicles the race to the North Pole using memoirs, letters, ships' logs and diaries of the great Arctic explorers.

Hayes, Derek, *Historical Atlas of the Arctic, University of Washington Press,* 2003.
An award-winning author and book designer uses nearly 200 historical maps to illustrate all the significant Arctic explorations from the 16th century well into the 20th.

Vaughan, Richard, *The Arctic: A History, Phoenix Mill,* 1994.
A former history professor describes man's struggle to survive in the Arctic from the Stone Age until modern times, including an examination of the impact of exploration on the lives of indigenous peoples.

Articles

Borgerson, Scott G., "Arctic Meltdown," *Foreign Affairs*, March/April 2008, www.foreignaffairs.org/20080301faessay87206/scott-g-borgerson/arctic-meltdown.html.
A fellow at the Council on Foreign Relations discusses how the melting Arctic ice cap is opening up access to natural resources and shipping shortcuts.

Brigham, Lawson W., "Thinking about the Arctic's Future: Scenarios for 2040," *The Futurist Magazine*, September-October 2007, www.wfs.org/Sept-Oct07%20files/FuturecontSO07.htm.
The deputy director of the U.S. Arctic Research Commission — a Ph.D. in polar oceanography and former icebreaker commander — describes how the Arctic might look in 30 years if global warming continues.

Gagnon, Geoffrey, "The Last Great Landgrab," *Wired*, February 2008, www.wired.com/science/planetearth/magazine/16-02/mf_continentalshelf.
A science writer charts the ongoing efforts by Arctic nations to map the sea floor in an effort to bolster claims to expand their continental shelves.

Graff, James, "Fight for the Top of the World," *Time*, Oct. 1, 2007, www.time.com/time/world/article/0,8599,1663445,00.html.
Arctic nations are racing to assert their sovereignty over large swaths of unclaimed Arctic territory, including the North Pole.

Green, Kenneth P., "Is the Polar Bear Endangered, or Just Conveniently Charismatic?" *American Enterprise Institute*, May 2008, www.aei.org/publications/filter.all,pubID.27918/pub_detail.asp.
A scholar at a conservative think tank examines whether scientific evidence justifies the designation of the polar bear as an endangered species — a step the U.S. government has taken since the article was published.

Myers, Steven Lee, Andrew C. Revkin, Simon Romero and Clifford Krauss, "Old Ways of Life are Fading as the Arctic Thaws," *The New York Times*, Oct. 20, 2005, www.nytimes.com/2005/10/20/science/earth/20arctic.ready.html.
This installment of a series examining the impact of climate change on Arctic communities focuses on how melting permafrost threatens buildings, highways and pipelines.

Overland, James, et al., "The Arctic and Antarctic: Two Faces of Climate Change," *EOS, National Oceanic and Atmospheric Administration,* May 6, 2008, www.noaanews .noaa.gov/stories2008/images/5-6-08_Overland.pdf.
Scientists explain how the polar ice caps are reacting in different ways to climate change.

Reports and Studies

"Arctic Climate Impact Assessment, Impacts of a Warming Arctic," *Cambridge University Press,* 2004.
A joint collaboration among more than 300 scientists — commissioned by the Arctic Council and the International Arctic Science Committee — evaluates the global impact of climate change.

"Arctic Oil and Gas 2007," *Arctic Monitoring and Assessment Programme,* 2008, www.amap.no/oga.

A report mandated by the Arctic Council describes past, present and future oil and gas exploration projects around the Arctic.

"Circum-Arctic Resource Appraisal: Estimates of Undiscovered Oil and Gas North of the Arctic Circle," *U.S. Geological Survey,* July 2008, http://energy.usgs .gov/arctic.
The first publicly available resource assessment of the area north of the Arctic Circle estimates it contains 22 percent of the world's undiscovered oil and gas.

"Climate change and international security," *Policy Paper, EU High Representative and European Commission,* March 14, 2008, www.consilium.europa.eu/ueDocs/ cms_Data/docs/pressData/en/reports/99387.pdf.
The European Union examines international security issues relating to resource-exploitation opportunities in the Arctic.

For More Information

Arctic Council, Polarmiljøsenteret, NO-9296 Tromsø, Norway; +47-77-75-01-40; www.arctic-council.org. High-level forum for cooperation between Arctic states and their indigenous communities.

Embassy of Denmark to the United States, 3200 Whitehaven St., N.W., Washington, DC 20008; (202) 234-4300; www.ambwashington.um.dk. Denmark owns the self-governing Arctic territory of Greenland, making the Danes a major player in the race for Arctic resources.

Embassy of Russia to the United States, 2650 Wisconsin Ave., N.W., Washington, DC 20007; (202) 598-5700; www.russianembassy.org. The largest Arctic nation, which has claimed sovereignty over the North Pole.

International Maritime Organization, 4, Albert Embankment, London, SE1 7SR, United Kingdom; +44 (0)20-7735-7611; www.imo.org. U.N. agency responsible for improving maritime safety and preventing pollution from ships.

Inuit Circumpolar Council, Dronning Ingridsvej 1, P.O. Box 204, 3900 Nuuk, Greenland; +11 299-3-23632; www.inuit .org. Greenlandic branch of the organization that represents 150,000 Inuits in Russia, Canada, Alaska and Greenland.

National Snow and Ice Data Center, 449 UCB University of Colorado, Boulder, CO 80309-0449; (303) 492-6199; www.nsidc.org. Studies snow, ice, glacier, frozen ground and climate interactions around the world; provides regular updates on extent of Arctic sea ice.

Norwegian Petroleum Directorate, P.O. Box 600, 4003 Stavanger, Norway; +47 51-87-60-00; www.npd.no. Norwegian government agency responsible for managing the country's abundant petroleum resources.

Oceana, 1350 Connecticut Ave., 5th floor, N.W., Washington, DC 20036; (202) 833-3900; www.oceana .org. Environmental advocacy group with offices in the United States, Chile, Spain and Belgium; dedicated to protecting and restoring the world's oceans.

U.S. Arctic Research Commission, Alaska Office, 420 L St., Suite 315, Anchorage, AK 99501; (907) 271-4577; www .arctic.gov. Government agency set up in 1984 to promote research and provide policy guidance on Arctic matters.

WWF Canada, 245 Eglinton Ave. East, Suite 410, Toronto, ON M4P 3J1, Canada; (416) 489-8800; www .wwf.ca. A leading Canadian conservation organization and a member of the World Wildlife Fund's global network.

7

Future of Recycling

Is a Zero-Waste Society Achievable?

Jennifer Weeks

New York City sanitation workers collect paper for recycling ahead of roving scrap scavengers. Almost half of the 250 million tons of household trash generated by Americans annually is diverted to other uses. About a third is recovered for recycling or composting, and 13 percent is burned to generate electricity.

AP Photo/Seth Wenig

From *CQ Researcher*, December 14, 2007.

Back in the early days of recycling, critics argued that recycling not only cost more than dumping waste in a landfill but also used more energy than it saved.

Tell that to the enterprising thieves cruising the streets of New York City nowadays. With scrap material prices rising, New York has an unusual recycling problem: Thieves are stealing metal, bundled paper and other recyclables from curbside bins and selling them on underground markets. The improbable "green" crime wave prompted Mayor Michael Bloomberg to sign a bill in October raising the penalty for using a vehicle to steal curbside materials from $100 to $2,000.[1]

Few New Yorkers would have predicted that old glass and plastic could become so valuable back in 2002, when the city stopped recycling them to save money during a budget crisis. But as costs rose to send these items to landfills, and neighborhoods opposed building new incinerators, the city made a new commitment to recycling.

"With landfill and incineration disposal costs rising steeply and their current reliability in question, it is important that [New York City] move beyond its traditional reliance on dump-and-burn solutions," Comptroller William Thompson, Jr. warned in an October 2004 report.[2]

New York City's waste problem is especially challenging because the city closed its vast Fresh Kills landfill on Staten Island (the world's largest) in 2001 after local politicians sued to shut it down, and trucking waste to out-of-state landfills is costly.

Americans have debated the benefits and costs of recycling for several decades.[3] Although U.S. recycling rates have climbed

One-Third of Solid Waste Is Paper

Paper accounted for 34 percent of the 251 million tons of U.S. municipal solid waste in 2006. Yard trimmings and food scraps together were 25 percent of the total.

U.S. Municipal Solid Waste, by Material, 2006

- Other 3.3%
- Paper 33.9%
- Glass 5.3%
- Metals 7.6%
- Food scraps 12.4%
- Yard trimmings 12.9%
- Plastics 11.7%
- Wood 5.5%
- Rubber, leather and textiles 7.3%

* Figures do not total 100 due to rounding.

Source: "Municipal Solid Waste Generation, Recycling, and Disposal in the United States: Facts and Figures for 2006," Environmental Protection Agency

steadily since the 1970s, advocates say that the nation can do more. At the same time, technologies for producing energy from trash offer new options for managing solid waste.

Americans generate about 250 million tons of municipal solid waste (MSW), or household trash, annually. This amount has nearly tripled since 1960, but the rate of growth has slowed in recent years. In 1960 nearly all MSW was dumped into landfills, but in 2006 almost half was diverted to other uses. More than 32 percent was recovered for recycling or composting (breaking down organic materials such as food and paper into a soil-like mixture that can be used as fertilizer). Another 13 percent was incinerated in waste-to-energy (WTE) plants — facilities equipped with advanced pollution controls that burn garbage under controlled conditions to generate electricity.[4] (*See chart, p. 159.*)

State and local governments, which are responsible for solid waste disposal, typically support recycling as a way to reduce littering and disposal costs. Environmentalists endorse recycling because it conserves natural resources and reduces environmental impacts from logging and mining. And because manufacturing products from scrap instead of virgin materials often requires less energy, recycling saves fuel and reduces greenhouse gas (GHG) emissions that contribute to global climate change.[5] (*See graph, p. 155.*) Recycling also combats global climate change directly by reducing generation of methane, a powerful greenhouse gas produced when organic waste decays in landfills.

"People understand recycling — it's the most widely practiced environmental activity in the U.S.," says Allen Hershkowitz, a senior scientist with the Natural Resources Defense Council (NRDC). "Recycling is ecologically superior to using virgin materials. When you make aluminum from recycled cans instead of bauxite ore, you save 95 percent of the energy." Relying on virgin resources also threatens biodiversity, Hershkowitz contends. "Earth is losing an acre of tropical forest every second, and the paper industry is the top world cause of deforestation," he says.

Municipal recycling is part of a larger scrap-recycling industry that also processes materials from industrial and other sources, such as automobiles, appliances and construction and demolition wastes. This sector generates an estimated $65 billion in revenues annually and employs some 50,000 people. In 2006 U.S. scrap recyclers exported $15.7 billion worth of materials to 143 countries.[6]

"With the developing world taking off economically, demand for resources is picking up, and this trend is not going to subside. There just aren't enough raw materials out there at decent prices for manufacturers to get what they want," says Jeffrey Morris, a principal with Sound Resource Management Group, a consulting firm in Washington state. "Energy is scarce, too, and it takes energy to process materials into products. Disposal isn't a good use of these resources, which is why China is buying them as fast as it can."

Skeptics say that materials in municipal waste have low value and are expensive to reuse or recycle. Daniel K. Benjamin, an economics professor at Clemson University in South Carolina, argues that mandatory recycling programs "force people to squander valuable resources in a quixotic quest to save what they would sensibly discard." In Benjamin's view, society is better off letting low-income scavengers cull valuable materials from trash. "[R]ecycling household discards is the business of the poor, but only until they have improved their lot enough to pass it on to those who would follow in their footsteps," he writes.[7]

Nearly 60 percent of U.S. household discards are organic materials that can be readily composted or recycled (food scraps, yard trimmings, paper and paperboard). Other products pose harder challenges. Only two of the six major types of commercial plastic resins have well-developed recycling markets. (*See sidebar, p. 166.*) And unlike glass, plastic typically cannot be processed directly back into its original form, so recycling often means "downcycling" it into a lesser-quality product — for example, shredding plastic beverage bottles to make fiber for fleece garments.

Another concern is e-waste — used electronic goods like televisions, computers and cell phones, which contain many toxic materials. The United Nations Environment Programme estimates that 20-50 million metric tons of e-waste are generated worldwide every year.[8] E-waste currently accounts for about 2 percent of U.S. municipal solid waste, but it is the fastest-growing segment of the municipal waste stream. According to the Environmental Protection Agency (EPA), only 15 to 20 percent of the roughly 2 million tons of U.S. electronics discarded in 2005 were recycled, with most of the remainder going to landfills.[9]

The short life cycle of electronic products is contributing to the prevalence of e-waste. "Invariably, after you

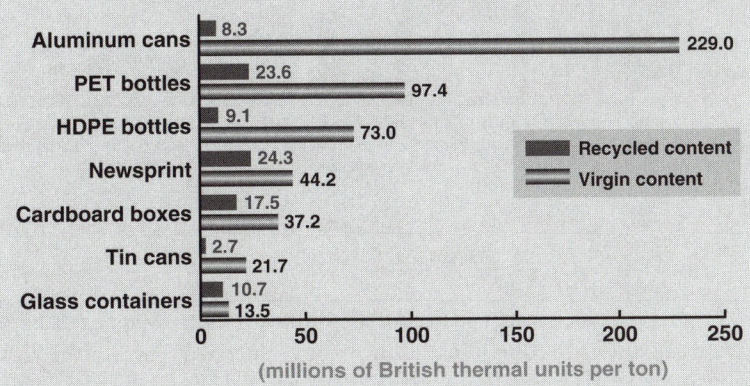

Recycled Content Saves Energy

Products made with recycled material often require far less energy than making the same products with virgin content. Aluminum cans, for example, require about 8 million BTUs if made with recycled material vs. 229 million BTUs using virgin materials.

Energy Usage of Products Made with Virgin vs. Recycled Content

Product	Recycled content	Virgin content
Aluminum cans	8.3	229.0
PET bottles	23.6	97.4
HDPE bottles	9.1	73.0
Newsprint	24.3	44.2
Cardboard boxes	17.5	37.2
Tin cans	2.7	21.7
Glass containers	10.7	13.5

(millions of British thermal units per ton)

Source: Sound Resource Management

buy the newest electronic widget, you dump the old one," observes Canadian writer Giles Slade.[10] Government standards can also make products obsolete. Notably, U.S. television broadcasters are scheduled to shift from analog to digital technology in early 2009, a step that could prompt consumers to scrap millions of older televisions.[11]

Waste managers and environmentalists worry that e-waste will be crushed in landfills and release contaminants, polluting ground water and threatening human health. Cathode ray tubes in televisions and computer monitors contain several pounds of lead, which can cause brain and nerve damage. Computers also contain heavy metals such as copper, zinc, cadmium, beryllium and arsenic that are hazardous in small quantities. Liquid-crystal displays in laptops, flat-panel televisions and other digital equipment contain mercury, another strong neurotoxin.[12] Electronics recycling is a fast-growing industry because the metallic components are valuable, but many operations — especially in developing countries — provide little or no protection for workers or the environment.

Almost All Car Batteries Are Recycled

Virtually all of the nation's old automotive batteries are recycled, as required by most state laws. Recycling rates for household products such as paper and aluminum cans are significantly lower.

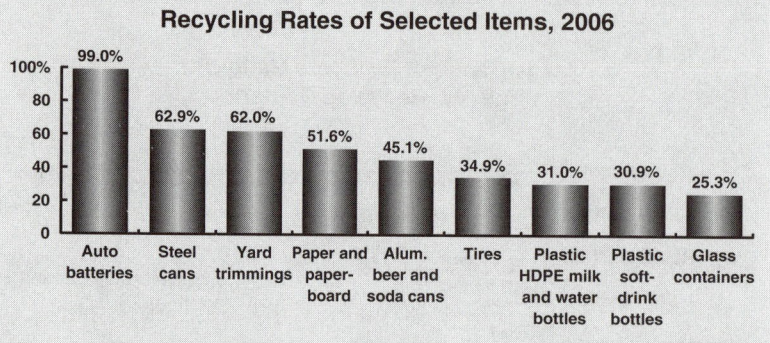

Recycling Rates of Selected Items, 2006

Source: "Municipal Solid Waste Generation, Recycling, and Disposal in the United States: Facts and Figures for 2006," Environmental Protection Agency

High fossil fuel prices in recent years have raised interest in alternative fuels, including energy generated from waste.[13] WTE plants are one way to turn garbage into power; in addition, many large landfills capture their methane emissions, clean the gas to remove impurities and burn it to generate electricity. As of 2006 the U.S. had 3,134 megawatts of generating capacity from landfill gas and WTE plants, the equivalent of five or six medium-sized coal-fired power plants.[14]

More landfill methane projects are on the drawing boards, but no new WTE plants have been built in the United States for a decade, although several plants are expanding. Today's WTE plants have advanced pollution controls and produce much lower emissions than older waste incinerators. WTE advocates say that electricity from waste combustion should receive the same legal benefits and subsidies as other renewable fuels, but many environmental advocates oppose classifying WTE as "green" power. (*See "At Issue," p. 171.*)

As regulators, businesses and advocacy groups look for ways to manage America's trash, here are some of the issues they are debating:

Is there a waste disposal crisis in the United States?

Since the first Earth Day celebration in 1970, many recycling advocates have warned that the nation faces disaster if Americans keep recycling only a fraction of the solid wastes they produce. In the past, some observers worried the United States could run out of landfill space. Today most recycling supporters acknowledge it is possible to bury all of our trash, but they say landfills pose lasting environmental risks and that some wastes are too toxic to bury or burn. And some regions lack disposal space or systems for managing trash.

In 2006 there were 1,754 municipal landfills operating in the United States.[15] The number has declined sharply in the past several decades, but their average size has increased as site owners seek to achieve economies of scale. According to recent industry estimates, the United States has 20-50 years of landfill disposal capacity, although some states have as little as five years' worth.[16] A 2004 survey by *BioCycle* magazine identified 30 states that were adding landfill capacity.[17]

Some observers argue that the world has plenty of room for its trash. In his 2001 bestseller *The Skeptical Environmentalist*, Danish political scientist Bjorn Lomborg projected that all of the garbage generated in the United States in the 21st century would fit into a landfill measuring 18 miles on each side and 10 stories high. "Garbage is something we can deal with. It is a management problem," Lomborg asserted.[18]

But many environmental and community groups say that even state-of-the-art landfills are not an acceptable way to manage trash. As waste breaks down in landfills it produces landfill gas, a mix of methane, carbon dioxide and small amounts of other substances that can cause odors or health risks.[19] Landfills also produce leachate, a liquid runoff that can be toxic, when water leaks in and picks up contaminants from garbage.

Current standards require landfill operators to install liners to contain leachate, and to capture and treat gas at large landfills. But neither system is foolproof. "Most professionals acknowledge that no one knows how long modern liners will actually function," says Sego Jackson, principal solid waste management planner for Snohomish County in northwest Washington state. EPA's guidelines for estimating landfill air emissions assume that on average, collection systems will capture about 75 percent of the landfill gas.[20]

"We still do have a solid-waste management crisis. The issue isn't landfill capacity, it's the long-term impact of landfills on public health," says Brenda Platt, co-director of the Institute for Local Self-Reliance, a non-profit community development group in Washington, D.C. "We know all landfill liners will eventually leak, so we're just postponing the impact of our consumption."

Waste managers want to improve technologies for managing trash but say that the system is working. "Solid waste management is a local issue, so it's hard to generalize that the U.S. is facing a crisis," says Brent Dieleman, manager of the technical division for the Solid Waste Association of North America (SWANA), which includes industry and government agencies. "There are local crises because of landfill space shortages and high disposal prices. But when people raise this issue, often they're really saying that we generate more garbage than we did in the past, and that's not true."

In the 1970s and '80s, U.S. MSW generation rates rose by 30 percent or more each decade. The rate leveled off considerably in the 1990s as the concept of source reduction (preventing waste from ever entering the waste stream) started to influence business practices. For example, many manufacturers found ways to use less material in packaging as a cost-cutting measure. Beverage companies reduced the weight of two-liter plastic bottles by 25 percent between 1977 and 2000, and made steel beverage cans 40 percent lighter between 1970 and 2000.[21] And producers increased the lives of some products, such as tires, so fewer were thrown away over time.

These trends gradually moderated the rate at which Americans produced trash. Total municipal waste generation increased by about 16 percent between 1990 and 2000, and from 2000 through 2006 trash output increased by only 5.4 percent. The national per-capita generation rate actually fell slightly, from 4.64 pounds per day in 2000 to 4.60 pounds in 2006 (total garbage quantities rose because population increased).[22] "We're not producing substantially more waste now than we have in the past, so for the most part we can handle it effectively," says Dieleman.

But for public officials in areas with high waste disposal costs the issue is urgent. The nationwide average "tipping fee" for disposing of trash at a landfill rose from $8.20 per ton in 1985 to $34.29 in 2004, and prices are much higher where space is scarce. Northeast state tipping fees averaged $70.53 per ton in 2004; in contrast, fees in Southern and Western states were roughly $25 per ton.[23]

And siting new landfills can be challenging. "We have room, but landfilling is not what citizens want to do with open space. When you ask consumers about landfills, no one wants to live near them or drive by them," says Kate Krebs, executive director of the National Recycling Coalition.

In one recent instance, when proposals for six large landfills in eastern North Carolina became public in 2006, the state legislature passed a one-year moratorium on new landfills by votes of 50-0 in the Senate and 99-11 in the House. Later, North Carolina placed a surcharge on all trash sent to landfills and tightened environmental

Most Trash Is Discarded

Fifty-five percent of all municipal solid waste was discarded in 2006. Only about one-third was recycled. One-eighth was combusted with energy recovery.

Management of Municipal Solid Waste, 2006

Recycling **32.5%**

Discarded **55%**

12.5%

Combustion with Energy Recovery

Source: "Municipal Solid Waste Generation, Recycling, and Disposal in the United States: Facts and Figures for 2006," Environmental Protection Agency

standards for new facilities.[24] States are forbidden from discriminating against out-of-state waste shipments under a 1978 U.S. Supreme Court ruling, which held that such policies violated the Constitution's Commerce Clause, but some have used strategies such as surcharges and special waste-management districts to regulate imported waste.[25]

Many areas with growing populations are having trouble keeping up with rising waste generation. California has an aggressive solid waste program that already recycles, reuses and composts 54 percent of household garbage, but the state's population is projected to rise from 36 million today to 60 million by 2050. "We're looking at that and we're thinking, 'Wow, that's going to be a lot of trash,'" acknowledged Jon Myers, public affairs director for the California Integrated Waste Management Board.[26]

Growth and development in many Western states are worsening a longstanding problem: illegal waste dumping on public lands. The Interior Department's Bureau of Land Management reported more than 6,000 illegal dump sites strewn with household waste, car parts, appliances and other trash between 2000 and 2006. Cleaning up those dumps could cost several thousand dollars apiece if they contain hazardous materials or require laboratory testing.[27] Illegal dumping is especially common in areas that do not have enough trained personnel and facilities for managing solid waste.

Even everyday consumer items such as automobile tires can create hazards if they are not managed safely. Between 1983 and 1985 two separate fires at a tire pile in Everett, Wash., burned more than 1 million tires, leaving five acres of ash that contained carcinogenic residues and required a multi-million-dollar cleanup.[28] "A lot has been done to address tire piles, but they still exist in Snohomish County and around Washington today. They're very expensive to clean up, and the public still doesn't have many good options for dealing with unwanted tires," says Jackson.

Do product bans reduce waste?

Plastic bags, once a convenience that shoppers took for granted, have become a prime environmental target. About 100 billion bags are sold to retailers worldwide every year, and only 1-3 percent are recycled. Plastic bags and films make up about 4.5 percent of the waste in landfills, where they can take centuries to break down.[29] They blow around easily outdoors, where they tangle in tree branches, block drains and choke animals and birds that accidentally ingest them. Ubiquitous as litter, plastic bags are known derisively as "the national flower" in South Africa, "white pollution" in China and "witches' knickers" in Ireland.

Plastic bags are made of several types of polyethylene (#2 and #4 resins). Only about 1 percent of bags used in the U.S. each year are recycled. Most curbside recycling programs do not collect them because they clog sorting machinery. In response to growing concerns about litter and environmental impacts, at least 18 countries have adopted or considered taxes, consumer-education campaigns, usage-reduction targets or outright bans on plastic bags in the past five years.[30]

San Francisco banned plastic shopping bags at large grocery and drug stores in 2007, and other cities have debated similar measures, including Annapolis, Boston and Austin. In November 2007 a bill was introduced in New Jersey to ban the bags at large retail stores statewide.[31]

Proponents argue that banning hard-to-recycle and environmentally harmful products will force users to find more benign substitutes. "[M]erely emphasizing greater recycling of plastic bags is an inadequate response; rather, we must fundamentally alter policy to significantly reduce our use and consumption of plastic bags," argues Ramey Ko, a member of the Bag the Bags Coalition in Austin, Texas. As Ko acknowledges, even in environmentally conscious Austin many people choose plastic bags over alternatives such as paper bags or reusable tote bags.[32]

Bag manufacturers say the best way to deal with plastic bag litter is to boost support for recycling. The industry is working with grocery stores to increase at-store collection and train employees not to double-bag purchases in plastic. Producers also note that technology improvements have made bags much lighter: grocery sacks were 2.3 mils (thousandths of an inch thick) in 1976, but are 0.7 mils thick today. Because plastic bags are so light, they require less fuel to transport than paper grocery bags. They also consume about four times less energy to produce and require only about 10 percent as much energy to recycle.[33]

"From a litter standpoint, plastic bags are very aggravating, so it's understandable that people are focusing on them," says the NRC's Krebs. "But there's very strong end-use demand for them from companies that use them as feedstock for plastic decking, and the industry is working hard to get users to recycle them."

Other plastic goods have attracted similar treatment. Roughly 100 cities, mostly in California, have banned takeout food containers made of polystyrene foam (known as Styrofoam, a trademarked brand) over the past 20 years, seeking to promote biodegradeable alternatives such as paper cups.[34] Polystyrene can be recycled but has a low scrap value because it is lightweight and bulky, so collecting and transporting enough material for recycling is expensive, and food containers must be cleaned before processing. Like other disposable plastic products, it is a major component of litter and breaks down very slowly.

As with plastic bags, producers say that polystyrene containers cause less environmental harm than alternatives, such as plastic-coated paper cups.

Many food retailers also object to container bans. "It places the burden on restaurants when we should be focusing attention on the people who are throwing away the containers," said Lara Diaz Dunbar of the California Restaurant Association in March 2007, when legislation banning non-recyclable food containers by 2012 was introduced in the state legislature.[35]

Instead of banning hard-to-recycle products altogether, many states and communities forbid landfilling them. Numerous states bar wastes including yard trimmings, tires, used motor oil, various types of batteries, appliances and oil-based paint from landfills.[36] These rules force sources to recycle the materials or find other uses for them and help to reduce waste generation over time. "Disposal bans that put responsibility for recycling on producers create a direct incentive not to make that item," says Snohomish County's Jackson.

For example, in 2006 Massachusetts banned sending construction and demolition wastes such as asphalt, brick, wood and metal to landfills in order to extend state landfill capacity. "The state targeted aggregates [crushed stone, sand and gravel], metal and wood because recycling markets could accept at least 75 percent of the calculated waste stream with no problem," says Amy Bauman, founder of greenGoat, a Boston consulting firm that works with the building industry to reduce and recycle wastes. "Otherwise a ban might lead to illegal dumping, which doesn't help anyone."

In Bauman's view, the ban has benefited Massachusetts builders by giving them a new incentive to reduce waste and take advantage of markets for recyclables. "The industry was already recycling aggregates and metal, so wood was the only controversial issue," she says. "The ban reinforces the growing popularity of green building."

Dieleman of SWANA emphasizes that disposal bans only work as part of a broader waste reduction and recycling strategy. "Before you ban landfilling wastes, you need to establish alternative ways to regulate, collect and

Nation Recycles 82 Million Tons Annually

The amount of solid waste in the United States has nearly tripled in the past half-century, to 251 million tons. During the same period, the amount of waste recycled — including composting — increased more than 15-fold, to 82 million tons.

Management of Municipal Solid Waste, 1960-2006

Source: "Municipal Solid Waste Generation, Recycling, and Disposal in the United States: Facts and Figures for 2006," Environmental Protection Agency

Remnants of a 'Throwaway Society'

Pharmaceutical products await incineration at the Covanta Energy Corp. in Indianapolis (top). Last year the facility burned some 6.5 million pounds of pills from pharmacies and drug manufacturers around the country. Electronic equipment to be recycled is warehoused at The Computer Service Center in Blaine, Minn. (bottom). A half-dozen states, including Minnesota, ban computer monitors, televisions and other e-waste in landfills because of their toxic content.

process them that will achieve the overall goal," he points out. "Otherwise, you're imposing an unfunded mandate on waste managers."

Some cities are working with producers instead. In July 2007 Los Angeles partnered with plastic bag manufacturers, grocers and environmental groups to launch a pilot plastic bag recycling program in the wake of a new state law requiring grocery and retail stores to offer in-store bag collection. City agencies are publicizing the program in designated "high-trash areas" and offering collection bins, pickup services, promotional materials and media support to stores that participate.[37]

Taxes and fees can also promote sustainable choices. Ireland cut plastic shopping bag use by 90 percent after it placed a 15 Euro-cent tax on the bags in 2002. In 2007 the tax was raised to 22 cents per bag after its initial impact began to erode.[38] And a "green bag" movement in which stores offer inexpensive, reusable polypropylene tote bags as an alternative to paper or plastic, is spreading from Europe and Australia to the United States. "Hardly anyone pays for a shopping bag in those countries," says Jackson. "They've all got their own."

Should producers be responsible for disposing of used products?

Few Americans think of their homes as hazardous waste storage sites, but according to EPA the cans of old house paint sitting in millions of basements nationwide are household hazardous waste. Modern paints may contain a variety of toxic solvents and pigments, and some older house paints contain lead (added to make the finish last longer) or mercury (used to prevent mildew).

The EPA regulates hazardous waste disposal under the Resource Conservation and Recovery Act (RCRA), but households and small businesses that generate minimal quantities of waste are essentially exempt from RCRA requirements. Instead, municipal waste programs are responsible for safe disposal of household hazardous wastes. Communities may collect paint and other hazardous materials year-round, accept them on special collection days or refer residents to drop-off centers elsewhere. People who live far from collection centers have few options. Some agencies suggest mixing old paint with kitty litter or sawdust to thicken it, pouring half-inch layers of paint into a cardboard box lined with plastic (letting each layer harden before adding more), and then throwing away the box.[39]

In contrast, residents of British Columbia, Canada, can call a hotline for directions to more than 100 depots across the province that accept leftover house paint.[40] The centers are run by Product Care, an industry-funded nonprofit association that also collects flammable liquids, pesticides and gasoline.[41] Under provincial regulations, companies that make, sell and distribute these products must provide environmentally safe ways for users to dispose of leftovers — a philosophy known as extended producer responsibility.

Producer responsibility requirements are common in Canada and the European Union, but the concept has been applied less often in the United States. Examples include deposit/return systems for beverage bottles and voluntary producer initiatives to recycle items that are landfilled in large quantities, such as carpet, or that contain hazardous materials, such as home thermostats equipped with mercury switches. Most states have laws requiring car-battery retailers to take back used batteries for recycling. Many service stations and chains like Jiffy Lube and Auto Zone also take back and recycle used motor oil, antifreeze and tires.

Concerns about the growing volume of electronic goods entering the municipal waste stream are spurring a grassroots push for producer responsibility laws focused on e-waste. "We think corporations should be required to take back their e-waste, and should be barred from exporting it," says Silicon Valley Toxics Coalition campaign Director Lauren Ornelas. "They also should have to reduce and eventually eliminate the toxic chemicals that they use now."

Today most e-waste recycling takes place in developing countries, where labor costs are lower and environmental standards are less stringent than those in the United States. Press reports indicate that a large share of global e-waste is exported illegally in violation of the Basel Convention, a pact that bans international shipment of hazardous wastes without consent from receiving states.[42] The convention has been ratified by 170 countries, including most European nations, but not the United States.

The Silicon Valley coalition and the nonprofit Basel Action Network estimated in 2002 that 50-80 percent of the roughly 13 million computers recycled in the United States that year were exported to Asia.[43] In 2005 significant amounts of e-waste were also beginning to flow to Africa, and a case study in Nigeria found that most secondhand electronics were either refurbished or thrown directly into unregulated dumps.[44]

Many Asian e-waste processors do little more than smash up electronics to recycle them and harvest valuable materials. Environmental samples collected by Greenpeace in 2005 at e-waste recycling facilities in Guiyu, China, and New Delhi, India, contained high levels of toxic metals including lead, cadmium, copper, antimony and mercury, as well as PCBs and PBDEs — persistent, toxic manmade chemicals that are widely used in plastic and electronic products as insulators and flame retardants.[45] Exposure to PCBs can damage victims' skin and liver as well as their hormonal and immune systems and increase cancer risks.[46] PBDEs have caused harmful thyroid and liver effects in animal studies, and EPA has classified one type as a possible human carcinogen.[47]

A 2007 study by researchers from Hong Kong found elevated levels of dioxins and furans (persistent toxic chemicals that are by-products of many industrial processes), in surface soils and waste combustion residues in Guiyu. "[T]he crude processing of e-waste has become one of the main contributors of [these chemicals] to the global environment," the authors concluded.[48]

Since 2003 California, Connecticut, Maine, Maryland, Minnesota, North Carolina, Oregon, Texas and Washington have passed laws that require certain electronic products to be recycled and set up systems to pay for it. Arkansas, Massachusetts, New Hampshire, and Rhode Island have banned landfilling or incinerating e-waste.[49] Most state recycling laws require manufacturers to pay for collecting and recycling their products. California uses an alternate system under which retailers collect a $6-$10 advance recycling fee from buyers at the time of purchase. The fees go into a fund to cover recycling costs without involving producers.

Under pressure from advocacy groups and consumers, some companies have started providing takeback services. Dell Computer offers free recycling for its own products at any time and for other brands when customers buy a Dell replacement. Other companies, including Hewlett-Packard, Apple and Toshiba will take back certain products, often with a service charge. Among television manufacturers, only Sony will recycle its products for free.[50]

Some waste managers observe that no toxic leaks from landfilled e-waste have been documented and say that risks from e-waste have been exaggerated. "Of course, we should eliminate the use of toxic materials whenever possible, and we should also learn how to best collect and process electronic materials for recycling. However, we should not ban e-waste disposal unless we

San Francisco Pioneers in Recycling Food Scraps

City to collect 75 percent of all waste by 2010.

About 60 percent of U.S. municipal solid waste is food scraps, soiled paper, yard trimmings and other compostable materials. Homeowners and municipal landscapers typically bag yard waste separately from other garbage, so it is easy to collect. Some 62 percent of U.S. yard waste was composted in 2006. But few jurisdictions collect food scraps, which are usually mixed into household garbage and require special handling to manage odors and avoid attracting rats and other pests.

San Francisco is the first large U.S. city to collect and compost food scraps as a waste-diversion strategy. Food and other compostable materials like soiled paper and waxed cardboard make up about 20 percent of San Francisco's solid waste (the city is highly urbanized and has few yards, so it produces little yard waste). Sunset Scavenger and Golden Gate Disposal, the city's two waste-hauling companies, have collected food waste from restaurants and other commercial customers since 1996 and from residences since 2000. Thanks partly to this program San Francisco was diverting 63 percent of its waste by 2005 and is aiming for a 75 percent diversion rate by 2010.[1]

Some 40 percent of San Francisco's population does not speak English, so the food-diversion process is designed to be simple and user-friendly. Curbside collection of household waste uses a color-coded system called the "Fantastic Three": organic wastes go into green wheeled collection carts, other recyclables like glass and plastic into blue carts and trash into black carts. Businesses, which also use a color-coded collection system, receive a 25 percent discount on their trash pickup costs for separating food waste. Hauling companies provide multilingual training and posters to help employees learn the system.

As of 2007, San Francisco haulers were collecting over 300 tons of organic wastes every day from some 2,100 businesses and 75,000 homes.[2] Trucks take the materials from a downtown processing center to two composting facilities about an hour away. There the waste is ground, mixed and stored for several months until natural decomposition processes turn it into compost. The resulting blends, including a mix called Four Course Compost that is approved for use on organic soils, are sent to local vineyards, small farms and landscaping suppliers. San Francisco also holds a yearly free compost giveaway for residents.

Rather than viewing the food collection program as a burden, restaurants praise it. "It's increased the morale in the kitchens," said Jonathan Cook, operations supervisor at the Metreon, a San Francisco entertainment complex with eight restaurants. "People feel they're not throwing things out, they're doing something good for the environment while they're working." Separating food scraps saves Metreon restaurants $1,600 per month in waste hauling fees.[3]

Growers also praise the end product, which costs no more than traditional compost. Linda Hale, vineyard supervisor for the Madrone Vineyard Management Group

have sound data that support such a ban. Public-sector budgets can't afford new recycling mandates," argues Chaz Miller, state programs director for the Environmental Industry Associations, a trade group for the solid waste management industry.[51]

Other experts point out that although producer responsibility requirements in Europe have helped to reduce waste and increase recycling, it is not clear that they are the most effective way to achieve these goals, or that they are spurring manufacturers to make their goods more eco-friendly.[52] "The main arguments for takeback in Europe were to reduce costs for local governments and to encourage producers to redesign products," says Margaret Walls, an economist with the think tank Resources for the Future. "But no programs actually work that way because they're all collective — companies hire contractors to manage takeback. No producer takes back its own merchandise from consumers, so signals to redesign products are very muted."

Takeback programs also are expensive and can be complicated to administer, Walls notes. "Systems that require consumers to pay a deposit fee up front when they buy an item and refund it to them when they're done with it [often retaining part of the deposit to pay for recycling] are more cost-effective, and the rebate offers an incentive to bring things back," she says.

in Sonoma County, calls Four Course Compost "really rich, and just fabulous stuff." The diversity of ingredients collected from restaurants gives the compost a rich nutrient content, says David Di Loreto, owner of Di Loreto Cellars in Camron Park, Calif.: "They have developed a consistent, high quality, well-composted product, which all of our field trials and use have shown very beneficial and environmentally clean and friendly."[4]

Other cities are starting to follow San Francisco's lead. Seattle has banned paper and cardboard from non-recyclable garbage and allows residents to mix food scraps with yard waste, which is collected for composting. Starting in 2009 the city will require food-scrap recycling.[5] Meanwhile, nearly 200 businesses in Portland, Ore., and another 33 companies at Portland's airport are participating in a city program that collects commercial food waste and soiled paper for composting.[6]

"Food and green wastes are the new recycling frontier," says Kate Krebs, executive director of the National Recycling Coalition. "The biggest opportunities we have within the municipal stream are all compostable materials like food, yard trimmings, wood scraps, paper and cardboard. This trend is going to spread east because it makes so much sense to turn food waste into nutrients in a non-chemical way."

Food scraps go into a compost container at The Slanted Door restaurant in San Francisco, which began collecting and composting residential and commercial food wastes in 1996.

[1] Jeremy Bates, "City Surges Toward 75 Percent Waste Diversion," *San Francisco Observer Online*, May 17, 2005.

[2] Norcal Waste Systems, "New Annex Becomes Green Central in S.F.," March 22, 2007.

[3] Elizabeth Davies, "Four-Course Compost Completes the Food Chain," *Independent* (London), Nov. 5, 2004.

[4] Tina Caputo, "Restaurant Scraps Find New Life in Northern California Vineyards," *Wines & Vines*, February 2004.

[5] J. Michael Kennedy, "Seattle's Recycling Success Is Being Measured in Scraps," *The New York Times*, Oct. 10, 2007.

[6] Portland Composts!, www.portlandonline.com/osd.

Deposit-refund systems have worked well for beverage containers in the United States: 65-95 percent of these items are recycled in the 11 "bottle bill" states, compared to 30 percent on average in other states.[53] Some states also use deposit-refund systems to promote recycling of lead-acid car batteries.

BACKGROUND

'The Throwaway Society'

Humans have recycled since ancient times, especially prior to the Industrial Revolution, when labor was cheaper than most finished goods. Through the late 19th century, many American families sewed quilts out of worn clothing, fed table scraps to their animals and made soap from wood ashes and animal fat.

As industry expanded during the 1800s, factories needed increasing quantities of rags (used to make paper), ropes, rubber, scrap metal and other inputs. Scrap recycling expanded from an activity practiced mainly at home and in small craft shops into a commercial industry. By the 1890s large U.S. cities such as New York and Philadelphia had hundreds of scrap and junk dealers, some of whom shipped goods throughout the United States and across the Atlantic to Europe. Thousands of immigrants earned

The Top 10 Items to Recycle

These items make up significant shares of the municipal solid waste stream and are readily recyclable in most areas of the United States:

1. **Aluminum**
2. **PET plastic bottles**
3. **Newspaper**
4. **Corrugated cardboard**
5. **Steel cans**
6. **HDPE plastic bottles**
7. **Glass containers**
8. **Magazines**
9. **Mixed paper**
10. **Computers**

Source: National Recycling Coalition; for a map showing places to recycle, visit www.nrc-recycle.org/localresources.aspx

their first American wages collecting, processing and peddling scrap materials.[54]

At the same time, public health experts recognized that garbage could spread disease, and local governments came to see trash disposal as a civic responsibility. New York City, with its notoriously crowded and dirty tenements, was the locus for many waste-management innovations. It built the first U.S. trash incinerator on Governor's Island in New York Harbor in 1885, created the first public garbage-collection system in 1895 and set up the first U.S. trash sorting plant for recycling in 1899. Other cities followed suit: A survey conducted by MIT in 1902 found that more than 120 American cities provided regular residential waste collection.[55]

Through World War I, as immigration swelled the U.S. population and incomes rose, Americans generated growing quantities of trash. New York City residents threw out four pounds per person per day between 1900 and 1920, mostly ashes from coal and wood heating.[56] But

consumers also were buying more single-use disposable products such as razors, facial tissue and sanitary napkins, which producers touted as more modern and hygienic than traditional homemade versions. Using these items eroded the thrift ethic, making it more socially acceptable to throw things away.[57]

The Great Depression forced many Americans back into recycling household items and composting food scraps out of economic necessity. When the United States entered World War II, government officials touted recycling as a civic duty. Millions of families collected used metal, rags, paper, string and household fats (a source of glycerin for explosives) for scrap drives to support war production. President Franklin D. Roosevelt exhorted radio listeners in 1942 to join a used-rubber collection drive that brought in 400 tons of material, including girdles, pet toys and rubber bands.[58]

The pendulum swung back toward consumption in the postwar boom years as consumers spent their rising wages on new homes, cars and appliances. To encourage repeat purchases, manufacturers updated products regularly. Some deliberately shortened the design lives of popular items like radios, a practice known as planned obsolescence or "death-dating."[59] In 1955 *Life* magazine dubbed the United States "The Throwaway Society."

Although people were buying more packaged goods, they also were using less coal and wood for heating and burning more oil, which did not leave ashes behind. As a result Americans generated only 2.68 pounds of solid waste per person per day in 1960 — the same amount or less than in the 1930s and '40s.[60] Most of the refuse was dumped into "sanitary landfills" that compacted alternating layers of garbage and dirt in trenches, a technique pioneered by the U.S. Army Corps of Engineers during World War II and widely adopted by American cities. But as consumers scooped up televisions, hula hoops and other "must-have" items, the municipal waste stream expanded and junkyards — increasingly filled with manufactured products and packaging — spread across the nation.

Confronting Waste

Converging worries about municipal and hazardous wastes pushed the federal government into the waste management arena in the 1960s. In 1965 Congress passed the Highway

CHRONOLOGY

1945-1960 *Postwar boom makes disposable products more widely available, increasing waste generation. Marketing promotes culture of mass consumption.*

1948 Fresh Kills landfill, which will become the world's largest city dump, opens in Staten Island, N.Y.

1954 Industrial designer Brooks Stevens calls "planned obsolescence" the goal of marketing.

1955 *Life* magazine labels America a "throw-away society."

1960s-1970s *Emerging environmental movement warns about hazardous wastes and argues that Americans generate too much trash.*

1960 Americans recycle about 6 percent of the more than 82 million tons of municipal solid waste they generate.

1965 Solid Waste Disposal Act provides funds for research, demonstrations.

1970 The first Earth Day raises awareness of the growing waste problem and recycling. . . . Congress establishes Environmental Protection Agency. . . . Resource Recovery Act shifts focus of federal waste-management activities from disposal to recycling, resource recovery and converting waste to energy. . . . College student Gary Anderson designs the "chasing arrows" recycling symbol.

1971 Oregon enacts first U.S. "bottle bill" on beer and soft-drink containers.

1976 Resource Conservation and Recovery Act (RCRA) creates first federal permit program for hazardous-waste disposal and sets standards for "sanitary landfills" and waste incinerators.

1980s *Perceived waste-disposal crisis spurs public and government support for recycling.*

1984 Amended RCRA sets environmental-protection standards for landfills and requires all facilities not meeting these standards to close by 1993.

1987 *Mobro 4000* garbage barge receives widespread media coverage as it sails from Long Island to the Caribbean looking for a disposal site, sparking public fears the U.S. is running out of landfill space.

1988 Society of the Plastics Industry develops coding system sorting plastics into six categories. . . . Hypodermic needles and medical waste wash up on East Coast beaches.

1990s-2000s *Ups and downs in scrap markets trigger debate over the economic value of recycling. Increasing energy prices and concerns about climate change prompt companies to explore ways of turning waste into energy.*

1990 U.S. waste generation rises to 205 million tons, of which 14 percent is recycled, 14 percent is burned for energy and 2 percent is composted. . . . Pressure from consumers and environmentalists leads McDonald's restaurants to stop selling food in Styrofoam "clamshell" packages. . . . Congress amends Clean Air Act to tighten emission standards for solid-waste incinerators.

1994 EPA launches outreach program to reduce landfill methane emissions, promote landfill gas energy projects.

1996 San Francisco launches pilot program to collect and compost food waste. . . . U.S. achieves 25 percent recycling rate.

2002 Mayor Michael Bloomberg, R-N.Y., suspends glass and plastic recycling in response to major budget deficits.

2004 Suspension of recycling fails to generate major savings, and New York City resumes recycling, sets a goal of diverting 70 percent of municipal waste from landfills by 2015.

2005 Nation produces 245 million tons of municipal solid waste; 23 percent is recycled, 8 percent is composted and 13 percent is burned for energy.

2006 Dell Computer institutes free recycling for all of its hardware without requiring a replacement purchase.

2007 San Francisco bans plastic shopping bags at large grocery and drug stores. . . . Five states pass e-waste recycling laws. . . . Eighteen nations ban or regulate plastic bags.

Recycling Focuses on Two Types of Plastic
Market for other types is less developed.

Plastics have become essential in packaging as well as products from clothing to furniture. In 1988 the Society of the Plastics Industry introduced seven codes identifying the basic types of plastic resin. These numbers, which were intended to make recycling easier, appear inside the small "chasing arrows" triangle imprinted on the bottoms of plastic jars and bottles.

But this imprint does not guarantee that plastic items will be recycled. Recyclers focus mainly on #1 and #2 narrow-neck containers, such as beverage bottles, because there are more commercialized applications for these resins. (Wide-mouth containers such as yogurt tubs and baby wipe boxes are often rejected, even if they are made from #2 plastic, because they have a different melting point from bottles, so the containers cannot be processed together.) Fewer jurisdictions collect plastics #3 through #7 because markets for these materials are less developed.

Resin	Products made with virgin material	Products made with recycled content
#1 Polyethylene Terephthalate (PET/PETE)	Plastic beverage and grocery bottles; food jars; film wrap; microwaveable food trays; textiles; carpet	Fiber for carpet, clothing, and comforter fill; food and beverage containers; film; strapping
#2 High Density Polyethylene (HDPE)	Milk, water, juice, shampoo, and detergent bottles; grocery bags; shipping containers; extruded pipe; plastic wood composites; wire covering	Bottles for non-food items such as shampoo and cleaning supplies; plastic lumber; pipe; floor tiles; buckets, crates, recycling bins, and other containers
#3 Polyvinyl Chloride (PVC)	Many types of rigid and flexible packaging; shrink wrap; pipe; siding; window frames; fencing; medical tubing; carpet backing	Pipe; decking; fencing; paneling; gutters; flooring; garden hose; packaging
#4 Low Density Polyethylene (LDPE)	Bags for dry cleaning, newspapers, produce, and household trash; shrink wrap; coatings for beverage containers; toys, squeezable bottles; moldings, adhesives, and sealants	Floor tiles; paneling; furniture; compost bins and trash cans
#5 Polypropylene (PP)	Yogurt, margarine, and deli food tubs; medicine bottles; appliances, carpeting, and other durable consumer products	Automobile parts; garden equipment
#6 Polystyrene (PS)	Takeout food containers and disposable utensils; Styrofoam "peanuts" and other types of foam packaging; building insulation; medical products; toys	Thermal insulation; foam packaging; plastic moldings
#7 Other (resins other than #1-6 or a multi-layer combination of several of these resins)	Large reusable water bottles; packaging materials bottles; plastic lumber	Bottles; plastic lumber

Source: American Chemistry Council, Plastics Division

Beautification Act, championed by Lady Bird Johnson, which regulated junkyards and billboards along major highways. Congress also adopted the Solid Waste Disposal Act, which authorized federal research and demonstration projects of waste-disposal practices and provided aid to states to create waste management plans. Five years later the Resource Recovery Act expanded the focus to recovering energy and materials from solid waste and required the newly formed Environmental Protection Agency to report annually on ways of promoting recycling and reducing solid-waste generation.

States and towns also took up the issue. In 1971, over opposition from the beverage industry, Oregon passed the nation's first "bottle bill" requiring refundable deposits on beer and soft-drink containers. Next-door-neighbor Washington state quickly jumped on the recycling bandwagon, opening the first U.S. buy-back center for newspapers, beer bottles and aluminum cans in 1972. By the mid-1970s several communities, including Madison, Wis., and University City, Mo., had established curbside recycling collection.[61]

With the 1976 Resource Conservation and Recovery Act (RCRA), Congress created a national waste management policy framework. Many of the law's provisions focused on hazardous wastes, but Subtitle D urged states to develop comprehensive programs for managing non-hazardous wastes, including MSW and other materials such as batteries, construction debris and medical waste. The law established criteria for municipal landfills and incinerators and banned open dumping of solid waste.

Many states and communities embraced recycling as a way to reduce litter and disposal costs, particularly on the East and West coasts where landfill tipping fees were relatively high. These efforts received a boost in 1987, when the *Mobro 4000* garbage barge sailed up and down the East Coast seeking a place to dump a load of trash from Long Island. When operators in other states rejected the barge — which did not have a disposal permit — out of fear that it was carrying hazardous waste, news stories wrongly reported that the United States was running out of space for its trash. After six months the barge owner was finally allowed to send the garbage to a Brooklyn incinerator.

By 1988 some 1,050 communities offered curbside pickup for recycling, a figure that would double to 2,711 in 1990 and double again to 5,404 in 1992.[62] Nine states had followed Oregon's lead and passed bottle bills. In 1989 California adopted a goal of diverting 50 percent of its solid waste from landfills and waste-to-energy plants by the year 2000.[63]

Like other commodities, recycled materials were subject to price swings influenced by market conditions, government policies and investor actions. Rapidly expanding community recycling programs produced a flood of materials in the early 1990s, driving U.S. prices down from an average of $50-$60 per ton in the late 1980s to around $33 per ton in 1993. Then in 1994 and '95, prices abruptly spiked as high as $200 per ton before falling back to around $50 by 1996.

These wild swings roiled the recycling industry: Many companies that had invested when prices were high quickly went bankrupt. Some critics blamed state and federal mandates requiring use of recycled paper for the spike. However, other assessments concluded the episode was an unusual confluence of events in a developing industry and that such dramatic swings were less likely to recur as global recycling capacity expanded and producers signed more long-term contracts.[64]

Domestic Debate

Gyrating markets for recycled materials prompted critics to argue that environmentalists had oversold recycling and that it produced more costs than benefits. A 1996 *New York Times Magazine* cover story proclaimed, "Recycling is Garbage," calling it a waste of time and resources that

---

Did You Know?

- Recycling 82 million tons of solid waste saved the energy equivalent of 10 billion gallons of gasoline in 2006.

- Recycling a ton of mixed paper saves the energy equivalent of 185 gallons of gasoline.

- Recycling a ton of aluminum cans saves the energy equivalent of 1,655 gallons of gasoline.

- Approximately 31.4 million tons of materials were combusted for energy recovery in 2006.

- There were 8,660 curbside recycling programs in U.S. communities in 2006.

Source: "Municipal Solid Waste Generation, Recycling, and Disposal in the United States: Facts and Figures for 2006," Environmental Protection Agency

---

disrupted markets.[65] Others supported recycling to a point but disagreed that the United States could achieve a "zero-waste" society as some advocates urged.

"We already recycle the items that make the most environmental and economic sense," argued former EPA Assistant Administrator J. Winston Porter in 1997. During his tenure at EPA a decade earlier, the agency had established a national goal of diverting 25 percent of municipal waste for recycling. "As we force ourselves to go after less valuable wastes in more difficult locations — say, hotdog wrappers at ballparks or leftover napkins at the airport — the costs will skyrocket. Recovered items will be trucked greater distances, or more resources will be used to clean and process dirty recyclables."[66]

Recycling skeptics also pointed out that new controls were reducing the environmental impacts of landfills and

AP Photo/Eric Risberg

AP Photo/Kalamazoo Gazette/Mark Bugnaski

From Vineyards to Greenhouses

High-grade compost made from restaurant and household food scraps is delivered to the Saintsbury winery in Napa, Calif. (top). Pipes collect methane gas from a solid-waste landfill in Watervliet, Mich. (bottom). Some of the gas is burned in furnaces to heat neighboring greenhouses. Environmentalists say recycling combats global climate change directly by reducing the generation of methane, a powerful greenhouse gas produced when organic waste decays in landfills.

waste-to-energy plants. Many small landfills and dumps had closed since 1991, when EPA began requiring municipal landfills to install liners, leachate-collection systems and groundwater monitoring. Integrated waste-management companies — a growing force in all facets of the industry, from trash collection to recycling and disposal — had opened new, larger landfills in their place.[67] In 1995 EPA required advanced pollution controls at municipal incinerators and waste-to-energy plants.[68] A

year later the agency directed large landfills to collect landfill gas emissions and burn them, either directly at the site or in engines or boilers to generate energy.[69]

Recycling supporters contended that the new requirements still produced serious air and water pollution and that properly designed collection programs were cost-competitive with incinerators and landfills. They also charged that critics understated energy and environmental benefits from recycling.[70] By 2000 the United States was diverting more than 29 percent of municipal solid waste for recycling and composting, and rapid economic growth in Asia was creating new markets for both new and used paper, plastics and metals. Thanks in large part to rising Asian demand, average prices for recycled materials rose steadily from the late 1990s through 2007.[71] In 2006 the United States shipped $6.7 billion worth of scrap materials to China, some 42 percent of its total scrap exports worldwide.[72]

Even with demand growing, diversion rates for various materials remained uneven. By 2005 the United States was recovering 50 percent (by weight) of paper products in municipal solid waste and 35-72 percent of major metals, but less than 6 percent of plastics. The situation was similar for organic wastes, which accounted for one-fourth of waste generation, about half from yard trimmings (of which almost 62 percent were composted) and half from food wastes (less than 3 percent composted).[73]

Some areas with advanced recycling programs began to tackle new and neglected classes of waste. Starting in 1996 San Francisco developed a system for collecting and composting residential and commercial food wastes. (*See sidebar, p. 162.*) And as environmentalists and regulators grew increasingly alarmed about electronic waste, states began to ban e-waste from landfills and debate whether producers or consumers should pay to recycle it.

CURRENT SITUATION
Federal Action?

Growing concern about e-waste disposal and climate change may stimulate national action to boost recycling rates. Although states and communities manage most recycling programs, advocates say the federal government should do more to help create markets and educate the public about recycling's benefits.

Several studies by the Government Accountability Office (GAO) have called for more federal support for recycling. In 2005 the agency recommended that EPA should take the lead in developing national legislation to encourage and finance e-waste recycling. But EPA responded that the problem was "fundamentally a business and economic issue, rather than an environmental issue," and that it would be inappropriate for the agency to choose how to fund e-waste recycling when manufacturers did not agree on the best approach.[74]

Another GAO study in 2006 pointed out that EPA worked with businesses and government agencies to promote recycling but did not have data or performance measures. Nor, GAO reported, was the Commerce Department carrying out its responsibility under the Resource Conservation and Recovery Act to help develop new markets for recycled materials in the United States. Based on a survey of recycling program managers and other experts, the report identified three major federal actions that could increase recycling rates:

- more public education;
- passage of a national bottle bill; and
- support for producer takeback programs focusing on toxic or hard-to-recycle products. [75]

Facing a patchwork of state e-waste laws, the Electronic Industries Association (EIA) called in 2007 for Congress to pass national legislation regulating computer and television recycling. EIA's proposal would set up two systems: TV recycling would initially be paid for by fees assessed on buyers of new TVs, until a large number of "legacy" TV sets (televisions sold in the past by companies no longer in business) had been recovered, while computer makers would collect and recycle information-technology equipment at no cost to consumers.[76]

"This is an issue crying out for a national solution," said EIA interim president and CEO Matt Flanigan. "Congress can do right by the environment, consumers and the electronics industry by adopting a national recycling plan."[77] Several members of Congress have formed a working group on e-waste, and Rep. Mike Thompson, D-Calif., has introduced legislation (H.R. 233) that would assess fees of up to $10 on computer purchases to fund recycling grants.

Liaison/Stephen Ferry

The Fresh Kills landfill — the world's largest — on Staten Island, was closed in 2001 adding to New York City's trash-disposal problems. While in operation, the 3,000-acre dump took in 14,000 tons of trash and released 2,650 tons of methane gas per day.

Congress may also consider a bill (H.R. 4238) introduced by Rep. Edward M. Markey, D-Mass., to place a five-cent national deposit on bottled water, iced tea, sport drink and carbonated beverage containers. Other legislators have advocated national bottle bills in the past, but Markey, who chairs the House Select Committee on Energy Independence and Global Warming, described his bill as a way to save energy and reduce greenhouse gas (GHG) emissions. "If all of the 58 billion aluminum cans that are thrown away every year in the United States were recycled, it would cut the emissions of heat-trapping carbon pollution by nearly 6 million tons — the equivalent of the pollution from more than 1 million cars," Markey said.

Some bottle-bill states, including California, and Oregon, have broadened their coverage to include popular products like bottled water. But it can be hard to expand state laws, according to Jeffrey Morris at the Sound Resource Management Group, because beverage manufacturers and grocers lobby hard against such measures. "National legislation would make a big difference, especially on plastic bottles and items that people consume away from home, so they don't go into curbside bins," says Morris. Many retailers dislike handling returned bottles because they take up space, but the process can be structured in other ways. For example, California accepts bottles and cans at more than 2,100 state-certified bottle and can redemption centers.

Getty Images/Chien-min Chung

Environmental activist Wen Bo, here at a recycling center in Beijing, heads up China operations for the U.S.-based group Pacific Environment. China buys about 42 percent of all U.S. scrap, but environmentalists say many Asian recyclers use unsafe practices. Environmental samples collected by Greenpeace in 2005 at e-waste recycling facilities in Guiyu, China, contained high levels of toxic metals and chemicals.

Beyond these waste categories, some advocates say U.S. energy and climate-change policy should reward recycling for reducing overall energy use. One option, says the National Recycling Coalition's Krebs, would be awarding tradable credits to companies and agencies for increasing the quantity of materials they collect and recycle. "Recycling helps to sequester carbon, and we hope that Congress will include it in a multi-pronged assault on global warming," says Krebs.

Slimmer Packages

Under pressure to reduce their environmental footprints, many consumer product manufacturers are reducing waste by redesigning packages to make them even lighter and use less material. In doing so, they also are cutting production, shipping and disposal costs. Some companies are using recycled materials or designing readily recycled packages.

As part of a broad push to make its operations greener, mega-retailer Wal-Mart has set a long-term goal of producing zero waste from its stores by reducing waste generation and recycling more materials. As a first step, the company is working to reduce solid-waste generation at its U.S. stores 25 percent below 2005 levels by October 2008.

Wal-Mart has sent scorecards to its network of more than 60,000 suppliers to rate the environmental soundness of their packaging materials and will start factoring the results into its purchasing decisions in 2008. "Our aim is to reach a day when there are no dumpsters behind our stores and [Sam's] Clubs, and no landfills containing Wal-Mart throwaways," the company said.[78]

This strategy is good business, says NRDC senior scientist Hershkowitz. "Wal-Mart doesn't want to incur the ecological liabilities and costs of disposing of so much packaging, so that's why they're saying that all the packages they sell have to be recyclable or contain reduced amount of waste," he says. Other companies are also "greening" their packages by reducing material content or using more recycled and recyclable inputs, including Procter & Gamble (toothpaste packages), Coca-Cola (Dasani water bottles), Estée Lauder (makeup tubes), Kraft (beverage bottles), and Johnson & Johnson (Aveeno moisturizer bottles and tubes).[79]

Technical advances are making it possible to incorporate more recycled materials in packaging. Seventh Generation, a Vermont-based company that makes environmentally safe household products, has developed HDPE (#2 plastic) bottles with 50 percent recycled content, rigid containers that are 80-90 percent recycled and trash bags made from 65-100 percent recycled content.

The economics of recycling are challenging, says Reed Doyle, Seventh Generation's director of advanced innovation. "Recycling is expensive in the U.S. because we have stringent environmental regulations, so the profit margins for recyclers are low," says Doyle. "But sustainable packaging is a huge movement. The whole consumer products industry is doing this because it has to do it to stay in business."

Many recycling advocates agree that China's voracious demand for scrap materials is a mixed blessing for recycling

Is generating energy from waste good for the environment?

YES   Ted Michaels
President, Integrated Waste
Services Association (IWSA)

Written for *CQ Researcher*, December 2007

How can communities best manage post-recyclable garbage? How can a newly carbon-conscious America reduce greenhouse gas emissions? Which homegrown energy source can help promote energy independence and reduce fossil fuel consumption? Waste-to-energy is the answer to these questions, and many others just like them.

Americans generate more than 300 million tons of garbage each year. About one-third of it gets recycled, about 8 percent goes to waste-to-energy plants and more than 160 million tons is landfilled. Modern waste-to-energy plants generate clean, renewable energy through the combustion of household trash that would otherwise be landfilled. All waste-to-energy facilities comply with extremely stringent federal and state requirements. After a thorough examination of waste-to-energy facilities, the U.S. Environmental Protection Agency concluded that waste-to-energy facilities produce electricity "with less environmental impact than almost any other source of electricity."

Use of waste-to-energy has been shown to be an important component of successful solid-waste management programs. IWSA and its members vigorously encourage and support community programs to reduce, reuse and recycle waste. The EPA and many states, as well as the European Union, have established a solid-waste management hierarchy, showing that, after the 3Rs (Reduce, Reuse, Recycle) direct recovery of energy from waste through waste-to-energy is preferable to landfill disposal. Far from competing with recycling, waste-to-energy is compatible with recycling. In fact, recycling rates of communities that utilize waste-to-energy plants are nearly 20 percent greater than the national average.

Not surprisingly, European nations that enjoy the highest recycling rates emphasize the use of waste-to-energy to process what cannot be recycled. For example, Germany and Denmark, with recycling rates of more than 60 percent, employ waste-to-energy for the remainder of their combustible waste.

Waste-to-energy plants are also valuable contributors in the fight against global warming. EPA studies show that American waste-to-energy plants prevent the release of nearly 30 million tons of carbon dioxide equivalents per year. The U.S. Conference of Mayors and the Global Roundtable on Climate Change have both recognized waste-to-energy as a tool to fight global warming.

Increased use of waste-to-energy will promote energy independence and reduce greenhouse gas emissions through the generation of clean, renewable energy. It's an important component of America's energy and solid-waste policies.

NO   Brenda Platt
Co-Director, Institute
for Local Self-Reliance

Written for *CQ Researcher*, December 2007

The incinerator industry falsely promotes waste incineration as safe and clean, and as a source of renewable energy. Yet, incineration is not "waste to energy," it is a waste of energy. Here are four key reasons to say no to incineration and in its stead favor waste prevention, reuse, recycling and composting:

Incinerators Waste Energy and Resources — Recycling saves three to five times the amount of energy as burning the same materials. For example, when a ton of office paper is burned for its heating value, it generates about 8,200 mega joules. But when this same ton is recycled, it saves about 35,200 mega joules. For every ton of material burned, many more tons of raw materials must be processed to make new products to take its place. More trees cut down to make paper. More ore mined for metal production. More petroleum processed into plastics. Incineration encourages a one-way flow of materials on a finite planet. It makes the task of conserving resources and reducing waste more difficult, not easier.

Incinerators Pollute — All incinerators release pollutants, including acid gases, particulate matter, carbon monoxide, nitrogen oxides, metals, dioxins and furans and at least 190 volatile organic compounds. Many are persistent, bioaccumulative and toxic. A U.N. report indicated that waste incinerators contribute 69 percent of the dioxin in the global environment. The better the air-pollution control, the more toxic the ash. An alarming new trend is the increase in efforts to use and disperse incinerator ash in commercial products. Moreover, waste prevention and recycling can reduce greenhouse gases and pollution much more effectively than burning trash to displace coal.

Incinerators Are Costly — Facilities cost hundreds of millions of dollars to build and operate — far higher than recycling and composting. (Recycling also sustains 10 times more jobs than incineration on a per-ton basis.) Indeed, many existing incinerators have become white elephants for their communities. Some jurisdictions have raised property taxes to subsidize their incinerators. In New Jersey, counties that built incinerators accumulated $1.35 billion in debt. Voters had to approve a multimillion-dollar state bailout.

Burning Encourage Wasting and Limit Recycling — Incinerators rely on minimum guaranteed waste flows, often called "put-or-pay" contracts. As a result, facility operators regularly burn readily recyclable materials rather than pay extra fees for tonnage shortfalls. Incinerators perpetuate the throwaway society and impede sustainable production and consumption.

Ocean Conservancy

Plastic bags — known as "the national flower" in South Africa and "white pollution" in China — are a global problem. About 100 billion bags are sold to retailers worldwide every year. Plastic bags and films make up about 4.5 percent of the waste in landfills, where they can take centuries to break down. At least 18 countries have adopted or considered taxes, consumer-education campaigns, usage-reduction targets or outright bans on plastic bags in the past five years.

in the United States. "China's growth has helped grow the paper-recycling infrastructure in the United States, Japan and the European Union," says Doyle. "The better and smarter we get at collecting this stuff, the more of their supply we'll be able to produce."

Better still, say some, would be to process scrap at home. "I doubt that overseas recyclers follow the same environmental standards that we use here, so I'm skeptical that there's an overall environmental benefit in sending material abroad," says Boston consultant Bauman. "And if we had a manufacturing base big enough to accept all of that post-consumer scrap, it would ultimately drive down production costs and make these manufacturers healthier. But you can't ignore the reality of overseas opportunities."

OUTLOOK

Zero-Waste Visions

Although U.S. solid-waste generation continues to inch upward, some 30 U.S. cities and counties, plus dozens of others worldwide, share Wal-Mart's long-range goal of achieving zero waste.[80] They view waste as a resource that can be used in more productive ways than landfilling or incinerating it.

"It's a planning strategy, like a zero-defect policy for manufacturers," says Platt at the Institute for Self Reliance. "The goal isn't literally to eliminate every shred of waste, but it does say that we won't set an artificial cap on recycling by saying that our goal is 25 or 35 percent and then stopping there. We want to get to an efficient society in which all materials, products and packaging can be recovered and recycled at the end of their lives."

Snohomish County's Jackson echoes this perspective. "Unless you look toward zero waste, you're completely off the path to true sustainability," he says. "You may not get to zero, but you should be able to get very close, and the small residual should not contain harmful elements."

Architect William McDonough and chemist Michael Braungart sketched a paradigm for a zero-waste society in their 2002 best-seller *Cradle to Cradle*, which called for shifting from "cradle-to-grave" industrial production — make something, use it, throw it away — to a waste-free society in which objects are designed to be reused. "Products can be composed either of materials that biodegrade and become food for biological cycles, or of technical materials that stay in closed-loop technical cycles, in which they continually circulate as valuable nutrients for industry," the authors wrote.[81]

Some waste professionals see this vision as utopian. Dieleman of the Solid Waste Association of North America says that managing 65 percent of America's municipal waste through source reduction, recycling, composting and energy recovery projects is an ambitious but realistic goal. "Zero-waste ambitions and aggressive recycling targets aren't bad, but at this point we can't recycle 100% of our waste, and we aren't likely to be able to do that any time," he says.

Zero-waste goals can make sense in certain settings, says the National Recycling Coalition's Krebs. "We're seeing the idea come up quite a bit in the private sector, and we applaud that. It also makes sense in venues like sporting arenas and national parks, where you can control who comes in, who leaves and how concessionaires run their businesses. In those contexts you can set up systems to capture wastes and hit a high target," Krebs says. "It's trickier when you get out into communities with homes, schools, playgrounds and other elements that aren't as tightly controlled."

Current debates about nuisance items like plastic shopping bags and disposable water bottles suggest that Americans are becoming more concerned about trash and waste. Another trend that echoes the idea of using fewer goods is the growth of so-called product-service systems, in which customers buy a product or service instead of an object. For example, Zipcar is a car-sharing company whose members pay for occasional use of cars from a company fleet.[82] Interface, a Georgia-based carpet manufacturer, offers a carpet leasing program under which it will supply, install, and replace flooring for a monthly fee (recycling used carpet).[83] Some products, such as photocopying machines, are more commonly leased than purchased.

According to theorists like McDonough and Braungart, product-service systems combined with extended producer-responsibility requirements will create a system in which manufacturers want to design their goods for eventual disassembly and recycling. Under such a system consumers would not have to feel guilty about upgrading to new models, because they would return durable goods to manufacturers, who in turn would have access to a constant stream of high-quality materials for new production.

"We're moving forward now from a very primitive perspective on recycling and materials management into a more modern era," says Jackson in Snohomish County. "It's inevitable from a climate change, resource and energy perspective. The transition will be bumpy for a while, but it's going to happen."

NOTES

1. Thomas J. Lueck, "Hot Items On the Streets: Recyclables," *The New York Times*, Oct. 15, 2007, p. B1.

2. "No Room To Move: New York City's Impending Solid Waste Crisis," Office of the Comptroller, City of New York, October 2004.

3. For background see Mary H. Cooper, "The Economics of Recycling," *CQ Researcher*, March 27, 1998, pp. 265-288.

4. U.S. Environmental Protection Agency, "Municipal Solid Waste Generation, Recycling, and Disposal in the United States: Facts and Figures for 2006,"

November 2007, p. 2, www.epa.gov/epaoswer/non-hw/muncpl/pubs/msw06.pdf.

5. For background see Marcia Clemmitt, "Climate Change," *CQ Researcher*, Jan. 27, 2006, pp. 73-96; and Colin Woodard, "Curbing Climate Change," *CQ Global Researcher*, February 2007, pp. 25-48.

6. Institute of Scrap Recycling Industries, "Scrap Recycling Industry Facts," www.isri.org.

7. Daniel K. Benjamin, "Eight Great Myths of Recycling," PERC Policy Series No. PS-28, Property and Environment Research Center, September 2003, pp. 19-22, 25.

8. United Nations Environment Programme, "E-waste, The Hidden Side of IT Equipment's Manufacturing and Use," *Environment Alert Bulletin*, January 2005, p. 1.

9. U.S. Environmental Protection Agency, "Management of Electronic Waste in the United States," April 2007, www.epa.gov/epaoswer/hazwaste/recycle/ecycling/docs/fact4-30-07.pdf.

10. Giles Slade, *Made To Break: Technology and Obsolescence in America* (2006), p. 268.

11. Analog televisions can be equipped with converter boxes that will enable them to receive digital signals, but many consumers may take the occasion to upgrade to digital televisions. For information on the digital TV transition, see www.dtv.gov/index.html.

12. Elizabeth Grossman, *High-Tech Trash: Digital Devices, Hidden Toxics, and Human Health* (2006), pp. 17-20.

13. For background see Jennifer Weeks, "Domestic Energy Development," *CQ Researcher*, Sept. 30, 2005, pp. 809-832, and Mary H. Cooper, "Alternative Fuels," *CQ Researcher*, Feb. 25, 2005, pp. 173-196.

14. U.S. Energy Information Administration, "Renewable Energy Consumption and Electricity: Preliminary 2006 Statistics," August 2007, p. 14.

15. U.S. Environmental Protection Agency, *op. cit.*, p. 8.

16. National Solid Wastes Management Association, "MSW (Subtitle D) Landfills," Nov. 8, 2006, http://wastec.isproductions.net/webmodules/webarticles/anmviewer.asp?a=1127; American Chemistry Council, Chlorine Chemistry Division, "Landfilling FAQs," www.americanchemistry.com/s_plastics/sec_content.asp?CID=1182&DID=4393.

17. Phil Simmons, *et al.*, "The State of Garbage in America," *BioCycle*, April 2006, p. 40.

18. Bjorn Lomborg, *The Skeptical Environmentalist: Measuring the Real State of the World* (2002), pp. 206-209. Lomborg assumed that U.S. waste generation would continue to rise at the 1990-2000 rate and that the nation's population would more than double by 2100.

19. U.S. Agency for Toxic Substances and Disease Registry, "Landfill Gas Primer" (November 2001), chapter 2, p. 4, www.atsdr.cdc.gov/HAC/landfill/html/toc.html.

20. U.S. Environmental Protection Agency, "AP 42, Fifth Edition: Compilation of Air Pollutant Emission Factors," vol. 1, November 1998, pp. 2.4-6, www.epa.gov/ttn/chief/ap42/ch02/final/c02s04.pdf.

21. Testimony of Katharine Hornbarger, Grocery Manufacturers Association, before the Connecticut Bottle Bill Task Force, Oct. 24, 1970, www.gmabrands.com/news/docs/Testimony.cfm?DocID=649.

22. EPA, November 2007, *op. cit.*, p. 1.

23. National Solid Wastes Management Association, *op. cit.*

24. "No Trash Can Range," *Winston-Salem Journal*, Aug. 7, 2007, p. A8.

25. The case is *City of Philadelphia v. New Jersey*, 437 U.S. 617 (1978). For information on state regulation of imported waste, see Institute for Local Self-Reliance, "Trashing Transport: Strategies To Ban Imported Garbage," Feb. 8, 1991, www.ilsr.org/recycling/FTAO_17-TrashingTransport.pdf, and Michael J. Podolsky and Menahem Spiegel, "When Does Interstate Transportation of Municipal Solid Waste Make Sense and When does It Not?" *Public Administration Review*, vol. 59, no. 3, May-June 1999.

26. David Lazarus, "Talking Trash Disposal," SFGate.com, July 13, 2007.

27. U.S. Department of the Interior, Bureau of Land Management, Colorado, "Help Stop Illegal Dumping On Your Public Lands," press release, Aug. 15, 2006; Benjamin Spillman, "Illegal Dumps Alter Western Landscape," *USA Today*, Oct. 9, 2006, p. 3A.

28. Rachel Tuinstra, "Development Envisioned At Landfill As $15 Million Cleanup Nears End," *Seattle Times*, March 5, 2003.

29. Progressive Bag Alliance, "Plastic Bag Backgrounder," www.progressivebagalliance.com/background.html.

30. For current reports, see http://reusablebags.typepad.com/newsroom/reusablebagscom/index.html.

31. Terrence Dopp, "NJ To Ban Plastic Shopping Bags?" Bloomberg News, Nov. 20, 2007.

32. Ramey Ko, "Why a Ban?" www.bagthebags.com/ban.html.

33. "Paper Bags Are Better Than Plastic, Right?" Reusablebags.com, www.reusablebags.com/facts.php?id=7.

34. Jim Herron Zamora, "Styrofoam Food Packaging Banned in Oakland," *San Francisco Chronicle*, June 28, 2006.

35. "Restaurant Owners Fire Back At Anti-Styrofoam, Plastic Bill," NBC11.com, March 1, 2007.

36. Phil Simmons, *et al.*, "The State of Garbage in America," *BioCycle*, April 2006, p. 36.

37. City of Los Angeles plastic bag recycling program, www.plastics.lacity.org.

38. "Ireland To Raise 'Green Tax' On Plastic Bags," Reuters UK, Feb. 21, 2007.

39. For example, see Ohio Environmental Protection Agency, "Storage and Disposal of Paint Facts," www.epa.state.oh.us/pic/facts/hhwpaint.html, and New York Department of Environmental Conservation, "Paint Disposal," www.dec.ny.gov/docs/materials_minerals_pdf/paint.pdf.

40. Recycling Council of British Columbia, "Frequently Asked Questions," www.rcbc.bc.ca/resources/frequently_asked_questions.htm.

41. Product Care, "Product Stewardship Solutions," www.productcare.org.

42. "China's Massive High-Tech Waste Woes," *Business Week*, Aug. 9, 2007; Christopher Bodeen, "China Not Fighting Off E-waste Nightmare," *The Miami Herald*, Nov. 19, 2007, www.miamiherald.com. For information on the Basel Convention, see www.basel.int/index.html.

43. Basel Action Network and Silicon Valley Toxics Coalition, "Exporting Harm: The High-Tech Trashing of Asia," Feb. 25, 2002.

44. Basel Action Network, "The Digital Dump: Exporting Re-use and Abuse to Africa," Oct. 24, 2005, pp. 10-25.

45. Greenpeace International, "Recycling of Electronic Wastes In China and India: Workplace and Environmental Contamination," August 2005, pp. 3-6.

46. U.S. Centers for Disease Control and Prevention, "Spotlight On Dioxins, Furans, and Dioxin-Like Polychlorinated Biphenyls," July 2005, www.cdc .gov/exposurereport/pdf/factsheet_dioxinsfurans .pdf; U.S. Food and Drug Administration, "Questions and Answers About Dioxins," updated July 2006, www.cfsan.fda.gov/~lrd/dioxinqa.html#g2.

47. U.S. Agency for Toxic Substances and Disease Registry, "ToxFAQs for Polybrominated Diphenyl Ethers (PBDEs)," www.atsdr.cdc.gov/tfacts68-pbde .html#bookmark05.

48. Anna O. W. Leung, *et al.*, "Spatial Distribution of Polybrominated Diphenyl Ethers and Polychlorinated Dibenzo-p-dioxins and Dibenzofurans in Soil and Combusted Residue at Guiyu, an Electronic Waste Recycling Site in Southeast China," *Environmental Science & Technology*, vol. 41, no. 8, April 15, 2007, pp. 2730-2737.

49. Electronics Takeback Coalition, "State Legislation on E-Waste," www.e-takeback.org/ docs%20open/Toolkit_ Legislators/state%20legislation/state_leg_main.htm.

50. For updated information, see Electronics Takeback Coalition, "Corporate Responsibility," www .computertakeback.com/corporate_accountability/ company_takeback.cfm.

51. Chaz Miller, "Toxic Trash," *Waste Age*, Oct. 1, 2005, www.wasteage.com.

52. Carola Hanisch, "Is Extended Producer Responsibility Effective?", *Environmental Science & Technology*, vol. 34, no. 7, April 1, 2000, pp. 170-75; Noah Sachs, "Planning the Funeral at the Birth: Extended Producer Responsibility in the European Union and the United States," *Harvard Environmental Law Review*, vol. 30 (2006), pp. 51-98.

53. Container Recycling Institute, *The 10¢ Incentive To Recycle*, July 2006, p. 1.

54. Carl A. Zimring, *Cash for Your Trash: Scrap Recycling in America* (2005), pp. 14-34.

55. U.S. Environmental Protection Agency, "Milestones in Garbage: A Historical Timeline of Municipal Solid Waste Management," www.epa.gov/msw/timeline_alt.htm#2.

56. Helen Spiegelman and Bill Sheehan, "The Next Frontier for MSW," *BioCycle*, February 2006, p. 30; Kirk Johnson, "Throwaway Societies of Yesteryear," *The New York Times*, Nov. 22, 2002, p. B1.

57. Slade, *op. cit.*, pp. 13-24.

58. Doris Kearns Goodwin, *No Ordinary Time: Franklin and Eleanor Roosevelt: The Home Front in World War II* (1994), pp. 357-58.

59. Slade, *op. cit.*, pp. 164-72.

60. U.S. Environmental Protection Agency, "Municipal Solid Waste in the United States: 2005 Facts and Figures," October 2006, p. 142.

61. U.S. Environmental Protection Agency, "Milestones in Garbage," *op. cit.*; Greater Madison Convention and Visitors Bureau, www.visitmadison.com/ visitorinfo/index.php?category_id=94&subcategory_ id=239&printable=1.

62. California Integrated Waste Management Board, "Curbside Recycling: The Next Generation," updated Oct. 26, 2007, Table 1, www.ciwmb.ca .gov/lglibrary/innovations/Curbside/Program.htm.

63. California Integrated Waste Management Board, "History of California Solid Waste Law, 1985-1989," www.ciwmb.ca.gov/Statutes/Legislation/ CalHist/1985to1989.htm.

64. Jeffrey Morris, "There Must Be 50 Ways to Pick A Number," *Resource Recycling*, May 1998; Frank Ackerman and Kevin Gallagher, "Mixed Signals: Market Incentives, Recycling and the Price Spike of 1995," Global Development and Environment Institute, Tufts University, Working Paper 01-02 (January 2001), p. 16.

65. John Tierney, "Recycling is Garbage," *The New York Times Magazine*, June 30, 1996.

66. J. Winston Porter, "Too Much Recycling Can Be a Waste of Resources," *Atlanta Journal-Constitution*, March 9, 1997.

67. Zimring, *op. cit.*, pp. 155-56.

68. U.S. Department of Energy, "Public Policy Affecting the Waste to Energy Industry," *Renewable Energy Annual 1996*, http://www.eia.doe.gov/cneaf/solar .renewables/renewable.energy.annual/chap08.html.

69. U.S. Environmental Protection Agency, "Fact Sheet: Final Air Regulations for Municipal Solid Waste Landfills," March 1, 1996.

70. Institute for Local Self-Reliance, "The Five Most Dangerous Myths About Recycling," September 1996, www.ilsr.org/recycling/wrrs/fivemyths.html; Allen Hershkowitz, *Recycling: Too Good To Throw Away* (Natural Resources Defense Council, February 1997).

71. Brian Taylor, "Pushing Demand," *Recycling Today*, July 2002; Dan Sandoval, "Throwing Its Weight Around," *Recycling Today*, October 2003; Amy Bauman, "Finding the Afterlife," GoStructural.com, June 1, 2005.

72. Daniel Gross, "The Tao of Junk," *Slate*, Sept. 8, 2007.

73. U.S. Environmental Protection Agency, Municipal Solid Waste in the United States: 2005 Facts and Figures (October 2006), p. 7.

74. U.S. Government Accountability Office, "Electronic Waste: Strengthening the Role of the Federal Government in Encouraging Recycling and Reuse," November 2005 (EPA response on pp. 54-56).

75. U.S. Government Accountability Office, "Recycling: Additional Efforts Could Increase Municipal Recycling," December 2006.

76. Electronic Industries Association, "As E-cycling Laws Proliferate, EIA Urges a Federal Approach," www.eia.org/print/print.phtml?article=351.

77. EIA, *op. cit.*

78. Wal-Mart, "Sustainablity Progress to Date 2007-2008," p. 45, http://walmartstores.com.

79. Pan Demetrakakes, "How To Sustain 'Green' Packaging," *Food & Drug Packaging*, June 2007; Claudia H. Deutsch, "Incredible Shrinking Packages," *The New York Times*, May 12, 2007, p. C1.

80. Zero Waste International Alliance, www.nrc.gov/materials/sp-nucmaterials.html.

81. William McDonough and Michael Braungart, *Cradle to Cradle: Remaking the Way We Make Things* (2002), p. 104.

82. www.zipcar.com.

83. www.interfaceeurope.com/internet/web.nsf/webpages/554_EN.html.

BIBLIOGRAPHY

Books

Recycle: The Essential Guide, Black Dog Publishing, 2006.
This comprehensive guide includes descriptions of how glass, plastic, paper and other materials are processed and case studies of successful recycling initiatives around the world. Also includes contact information for government recycling organizations, non-governmental organizations active on waste issues and retailers offering "green" goods.

McDonough, William, and Michael Braungart, *Cradle to Cradle: Remaking the Way We Make Things*, North Point Press, 2002.
Architect McDonough and chemist Braungart envision an "eco-effective" world where products are designed so that when they reach the end of their useful lives, they serve as ingredients for other high-quality products instead of being thrown away. To illustrate its theme, the book is printed on synthetic paper made of plastic resins and inorganic fillers that can be infinitely recycled.

Royte, Elizabeth, *Garbage Land: On the Secret Trail of Trash*, Little, Brown, 2005.
Journalist Royte follows each element in her household waste stream — from food scraps to sewage — to its ultimate recycling or disposal site and reveals how little most Americans know about what happens to their trash.

Strasser, Susan, *Waste and Want: A Social History of Trash*, Henry Holt, 1999.
A history professor at the University of Delaware recounts how Americans have used and managed their trash since the early 19th century and traces the cultural shift from reuse to consumption and convenience.

Articles

"New Recycling Era for NYC," *BioCycle*, October 2004.
A report on New York City's decision to resume recycling glass and plastic after a two-year suspension is accompanied by views from recycling and waste-management experts on lessons from New York's experience.

Burger, Michael, and Christopher Stewart, "Garbage After Fresh Kills," *Gotham Gazette*, Jan. 28, 2002, www.gothamgazette.com/iotw/garbage.
The authors look at New York City's waste management dilemma after the closure of the Fresh Kills landfill.

Fishman, Charles, "Message in a Bottle," *Fast Company*, **July 2007.**
The $15 billion U.S. bottled-water industry demonstrates the power of marketing and how the energy and waste involved in bottling water affects America's consumer culture.

Mariansky, Gal, "Plastics — Solution, Or Pollution," *California Engineer*, **spring 2006.**
An overview of current techniques for recycling plastics includes options for making new types of resin that are more easily recyclable.

Nowak, Rachel, " 'Total Recycling' Aims To Make Landfill History," *New Scientist*, **Oct. 20, 2007.**
Mechanical biological treatment plants, which decontaminate and separate the wastes in household garbage and compost the organic portion, could greatly reduce the amount of municipal garbage sent to landfills.

Selin, Henrik, and Stacy D. VanDeveer, "Raising Global Standards: Hazardous Substances and E-waste Management in the European Union," *Environment*, **December 2006.**
The article examines the impact — on EU members and on manufacturers worldwide who want to sell into the EU market — of EU directives to restrict the use of hazardous substances in electronic equipment and increase recycling of e-waste.

Swartz, Nikki, "The San Francisco Feat," *Waste Age*, **April 2002.**
Swartz provides an overview of San Francisco's ambitious organic-waste composting program.

Reports and Studies

Benjamin, Daniel K., "Eight Great Myths About Recycling, Property and Environment Research Center," *PERC Policy Series No. PS-28*, **September 2003.**
A professor of economics at Clemson University critiques what he terms "errors and misinformation" in standard arguments advocating recycling.

Fishbein, Bette K., "Waste in the Wireless World: The Challenge of Cell Phones," *INFORM*, **2002.**
Fishbein examines the growing world cell phone market, environmental impacts of cell phone components and options to promote cell phone recycling.

U.S. Department of Commerce, **"Technology Administration, Recycling Technology Products: An Overview of E-waste Policy Issues," July 2006.**
Comments at a government-sponsored roundtable provide an overview of stakeholder positions and concerns about possible national e-waste recycling legislation.

For More Information

American Chemistry Council, Plastics Division, 1300 Wilson Blvd., Arlington, VA 22209; (703) 741-5000; www .americanchemistry.com/s_plastics/index.asp. Trade organization representing leading manufacturers of plastic resins and offering information on plastic products and recycling.

Institute for Local Self-Reliance, 927 15th St., N.W., 4th floor, Washington, DC 20005; (202) 898-1610; www.ilsr .org. Promotes strategies and policies that help create ecologically and economically sound communities.

National Recycling Coalition, 805 15th St., N.W., Suite 435, Washington, DC 20005; (202) 789-1430; www .nrc-recycle.org. Nonprofit advocacy group promoting waste reduction and recycling.

Natural Resources Defense Council, 40 W. 20th St., New York, NY 10011; (212) 727-2700; www.nrdc.org. National environmental advocacy group supporting recycling efforts to reduce waste and conserve energy and natural resources.

Product Stewardship Institute, 137 Newbury St., 7th floor, Boston, MA 02116; (617) 236-4855; www.product stewardship.us. Works to reduce the health and environmental impacts of consumer products by promoting partnerships between government agencies, manufacturers, retailers and environmental groups.

Silicon Valley Toxics Coalition, 760 N. First St., San Jose, CA 95112; (408) 287-6707; http://svtc.etoxics.org. Strives to make computer and electronic equipment more eco-friendly.

Solid Waste Association of North America, 100 Wayne Ave., Suite 700, Silver Spring, MD 20910; (800) 467-9262; www.swana.org. Provides information on all aspects of waste management.

U.S. Environmental Protection Agency, Office of Solid Waste and Emergency Response, 1200 Pennsylvania Ave., N.W., Washington, DC 20460; (202) 272-0167; www.epa .gov. Develops guidelines and provides technical support to state and local governments for managing solid and hazardous waste and underground storage tanks.

Buying Green

8

Buying Green

Does It Really Help the Environment?

Jennifer Weeks

Actor Brad Pitt is spearheading the construction of 150 "affordable and sustainable" homes in hurricane-battered New Orleans. Activists say the key to protecting the environment is "buying green" — choosing products designed to reduce pollution and waste. Consumer spending accounts for about two-thirds of the $14 trillion U.S. gross domestic product, making eco-consumerism a potentially powerful influence on policy and the economy.

From *CQ Researcher*, February 29, 2008.

During Lent, many Christians commemorate the time that Jesus spent fasting and praying in the desert, according to the Bible, before taking up his ministry. Most churchgoers mark Lent by giving up alcohol, red meat or other luxuries. But this year two prominent British bishops called on the faithful to sacrifice something else: carbon emissions. Through steps such as insulating hot-water heaters, sealing drafts in their houses and changing to energy-efficient light bulbs, the church leaders urged observers to reduce their carbon footprints — the greenhouse gases (GHGs) emitted from human activities that contribute to global climate change. "We all have a pivotal role to play in tackling the stark reality of climate change," said Richard Chartres, Bishop of London. "Together we have a responsibility to God, to future generations and to our own well-being on this earth to take action."[1]

Although they may not cast the issue in religious terms, Americans are increasingly willing to take personal action to protect the environment. And while conservation has long been associated with sacrifices, such as driving smaller cars and turning down the heat, today some advocates argue that a comfortable lifestyle can be eco-friendly. The key, they say, is "buying green" — choosing products designed to reduce pollution, waste and other harmful impacts.

Activists have long recognized that consumer spending, which accounts for about two-thirds of the $14 trillion U.S. gross domestic product, can be a powerful influence on national policy. Consumer campaigns often stigmatize a product to highlight suppliers' unacceptable behavior. For example, civil rights activists in the 1950s and '60s boycotted segregated buses in Montgomery, Ala., and held sit-ins at lunch counters that refused to serve African-Americans.

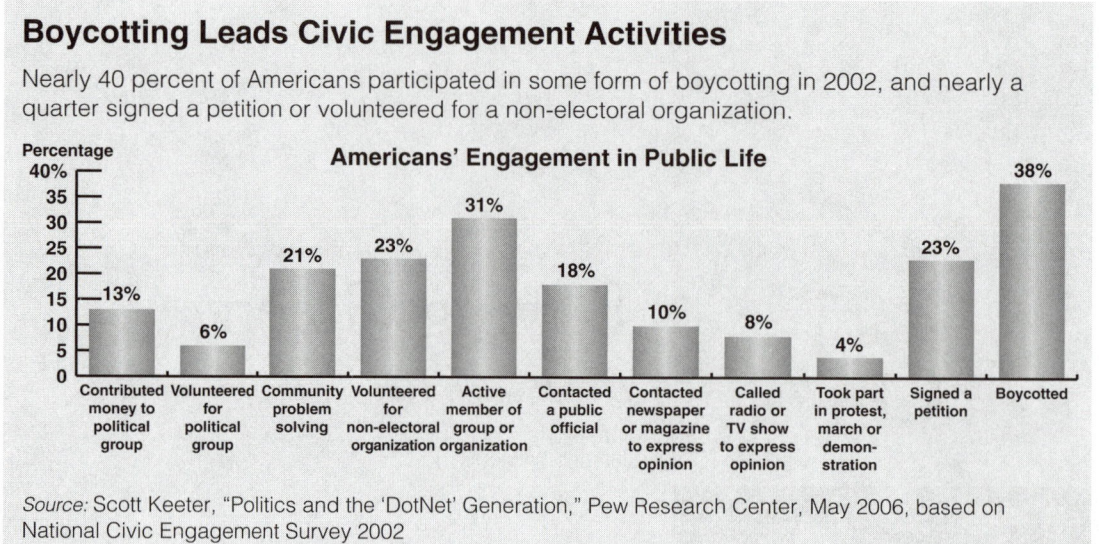

Boycotting Leads Civic Engagement Activities

Nearly 40 percent of Americans participated in some form of boycotting in 2002, and nearly a quarter signed a petition or volunteered for a non-electoral organization.

Americans' Engagement in Public Life

Source: Scott Keeter, "Politics and the 'DotNet' Generation," Pew Research Center, May 2006, based on National Civic Engagement Survey 2002

Both strategies drew national attention to segregation in the South and built support for new civil rights laws.

Consumers can also reward positive behavior with their dollars. In the 1970s, the garment workers' union urged Americans to "Look for the union label" that identified clothing made in the United States instead of choosing products from low-wage foreign sources. Today eco-conscious shoppers are buying organically grown food, fuel-efficient cars and shares in socially responsible investment funds that target companies with strong environmental records.

According to the annual Green Brands Survey, U.S. consumers will spend about $500 billion on environmentally friendly products and services in 2008, double last year's amount.[2] A typical American family spends roughly $50,000 each year on food, clothing, shelter, transportation, health care, entertainment and other items.[3] (*See graph, p. 181.*) And consumers frequently use buying power to communicate their opinions: Boycotting or "buycotting" (deliberately choosing) products for political or ethical reasons are among the most common ways in which Americans express political views.[4] (*See graph, above.*)

"The consumer movement has quietly become part of the fabric of American society," says Caroline Heldman, an assistant professor of politics at Occidental College in Los Angeles and author of a forthcoming book on consumer activism. "Environmental concerns are the most important motives that drive people to engage in

consumer activism, and with concern about global warming so high, the public is primed to act if environmental groups can find tangible things for people to do."

However, not all green products deliver on their promises. Since it first issued guidelines for environmental marketing in 1990, the Federal Trade Commission (FTC) has acted against 37 companies for misleading consumers with green claims.[5] A recent survey by TerraChoice, an environmental marketing firm, suggests that "greenwashing" — making misleading environmental claims about a company or product — is becoming more pervasive as companies bring new green products to market. In a review of 1,108 consumer products that made environmental claims, TerraChoice found that all but one provided some form of false or misleading information. (*See sidebar, p. 189.*)

"Green labeling today is where auto-safety information was in the 1950s. Standards and certification programs are still emerging," says TerraChoice Vice President Scot Case. "This is unexplored territory, so marketers may be stretching the truth unintentionally. We think that the sudden interest in green just caught a lot of people off guard, and marketers were busy slapping buzzwords on packaging. But FTC's guidelines are clearly 15 to 20 years out of date."

Many issues are spurring interest in green products. In 2007 the Intergovernmental Panel on Climate Change, an international scientific association created to advise national governments, called global warming unequivocal and concluded with at least 90 percent certainty that human activities since 1750 had warmed the planet.[6] Repeated warnings about climate change are prompting many companies and individuals to shrink their carbon footprints. New products like renewable energy certificates and carbon offsets, which allow buyers to pay for green actions that happen elsewhere, make this task easier. (*See glossary, p. 183.*) But critics say that these commodities are feel-good gestures and do not always promote new, clean technologies.

Recent cases of contaminated food and toxic ingredients in common household products like pet food and toothpaste also are spurring consumers to seek out green alternatives.[7] Green consumption is a logical response to environmental threats, but Andrew Szasz, a sociologist at the University of California, Santa Cruz, believes that it could actually threaten environmental progress if consumers see it as a substitute for political action.

"A lot of people get environmentally conscious enough to get worried. Then they go buy everything green that they can afford and move on to something else," says Szasz, who calls the trend an example of "inverted quarantine" — citizens protecting themselves from danger by building barriers instead of organizing to reduce the threat. "Pressure from social movements to take toxic substances out of our water and air will create more progress than individual consumer actions," he argues.

Eco-consumption mirrors a similar trend in the business sector. Many U.S. companies are working to green their operations, both to appeal to the fast-growing market and because leaders are finding that environmental strategies can help cut costs and make their operations more efficient.[8] Many large corporations that have clashed with environmentalists in the past, such as DuPont, Monsanto and Waste Management, Inc., now highlight their commitments to environmental stewardship and sustainability.[9]

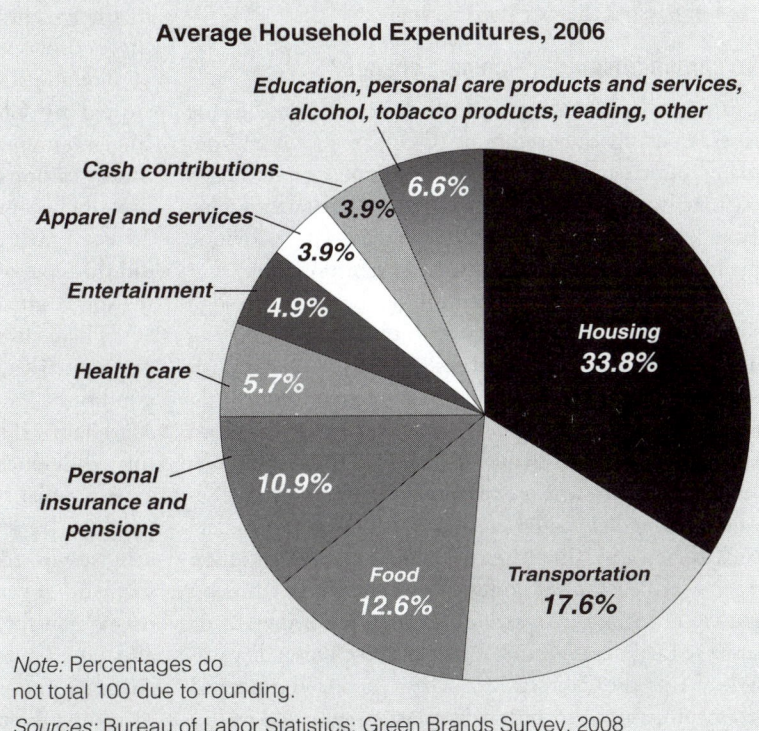

Average Household Spends Nearly $50,000

The average household spent $48,398 in 2006, including more than one-third on housing and 18 percent on transportation. According to a recent survey, U.S. consumers will spend about $500 billion on environmentally friendly products and services in 2008, double last year's amount.

Average Household Expenditures, 2006

- Education, personal care products and services, alcohol, tobacco products, reading, other — 6.6%
- Cash contributions — 3.9%
- Apparel and services — 3.9%
- Entertainment — 4.9%
- Health care — 5.7%
- Personal insurance and pensions — 10.9%
- Food — 12.6%
- Transportation — 17.6%
- Housing — 33.8%

Note: Percentages do not total 100 due to rounding.

Sources: Bureau of Labor Statistics; Green Brands Survey, 2008

In a notable sign of corporate greening, the U.S. Climate Action Partnership (a coalition including Alcoa, General Electric, Shell and Xerox) called in early 2007 for prompt mandatory limits to slow and reverse the growth of GHG emissions. Many large companies have opposed mandatory GHG limits in the past, arguing that putting a price on carbon emissions would drive up energy costs.[10] However, U.S.-CAP members contended that addressing climate change "will create more economic opportunities than risks for the U.S. economy."[11]

Corporate greening appears to be widespread but hard to measure because there is no authoritative definition of a green business. A recent report by Greener World Media found that green businesses are making progress toward some milestones, such as disclosing their carbon emissions and investing in new clean technologies. It also judged, however, that corporate America is treading water or falling behind on other targets, such as using more renewable energy and emitting fewer GHGs per unit of economic activity. "Green business has shifted from a movement to a market. But there is much, much more to do," the authors asserted.[12]

As environmentalists, business executives and consumers ponder what buying green can accomplish, here are some issues they are considering:

Do carbon offsets slow climate change?

Curbing climate change is difficult because greenhouse gases, especially carbon dioxide (CO_2), are produced from many routine activities like powering appliances and driving cars. Every year the average American generates roughly 10 to 20 metric tons of CO_2 through day-to-day activities, mainly through home energy use and transportation.[13]

Consumers can shrink their carbon footprints through steps such as adding insulation to their houses, buying more energy-efficient appliances and using public transit for some trips instead of cars. But if people want to do more, or have carbon-intensive lifestyles because they own large homes or travel frequently, they can buy carbon offsets from brokers, who use the money to fund projects elsewhere that reduce GHG emissions. Pollution offsets date back to the mid-1970s, when the Environmental Protection Agency (EPA) allowed industries to build new emission sources in regions with serious air pollution if they made larger reductions at existing sources nearby. This policy was written into the Clean Air Act in 1977 and later expanded to let companies earn and trade emission-reduction credits if they cut emissions below thresholds required by law.

"Offsets have an important role to play as we try to shrink our carbon footprint," says Mike Burnett, executive director of the Climate Trust, an Oregon nonprofit created to implement a 1997 state law that requires new power plants to offset some CO_2 emissions. The trust invests money from power plants, as well as businesses and individuals, in energy efficiency, renewable energy and other low-carbon projects to offset clients' emissions. "Oregon has pledged to reduce its GHG emissions 75 percent below 1990 levels by 2050. Investing in high-quality offsets can help us address climate change at the lowest overall cost, which will leave more money for other priorities," says Burnett.

The Climate Trust uses strict criteria to screen potential investments. Emission reductions must be rigorously quantified, and sponsors have to show that offset projects would not happen without funding from the trust — a concept called "additionality" to indicate that resulting GHG reductions must be additional to business as usual. For example, although installing underground systems at landfills to capture methane (a potent greenhouse gas produced when waste decomposes) is a popular type of offset, the trust would not invest in a methane-capture project if regulations already required the landfill operator to control methane emissions.

Not all providers are as strict. A 2006 study commissioned by Clean Air-Cool Planet (CACP), a New England nonprofit group, found that the market for voluntary carbon offsets was largely unregulated and had no broadly accepted standards for defining or measuring offsets. Prices to offset a ton of carbon varied widely, as did the types of offsets available and the amount of information companies provided to customers.[14]

"There clearly are good offsets and not-so-good ones on the market, so the problem for buyers is finding the good ones," says CACP Chief Executive Officer Adam Markham. "If they don't buy good ones, they're not making a difference, and they're wasting their money."

A popular strategy that has raised questions is paying to plant trees. Growing plants absorb CO_2 from the atmosphere to make plant tissue, and trees also offer many other benefits, such as stabilizing soils and providing habitat for animals and birds. Movie stars Brad Pitt and Jake Gyllenhaal, along with Home Depot, Delta Airlines and other corporations, have funded tree-planting projects from suburban Atlanta to Bhutan.

But trees don't always help the environment. Planting non-native species can soak up local water supplies and replace other valuable ecosystems such as prairie grassland. Moreover, calculating how much carbon various types of forests take up is an inexact science. And since trees eventually release carbon when they die and decompose (or are logged or burned down), they cycle carbon quickly and only remove it from the atmosphere for a matter of decades. In contrast, today's oil, coal and natural gas supplies represent much more permanent carbon reserves that formed when carbon-based plant materials were compressed in ancient, underground fossil beds. Burning these fossil fuels permanently releases carbon stores that have been sequestered for thousands of years and will not be recreated in the foreseeable future.[15]

"Forest offsets tend to be more risky because we know less about how much carbon they displace than we do

A 21st-Century Carbon Glossary

The pollutant plays a key role in today's environmental efforts.

Carbon footprint — The sum of all greenhouse gas (GHG) emissions caused during a specified time period by a person's activities, a company's operations or the production, use and disposal of a product.

Carbon neutral — Operating in a way that does not produce any net addition of GHGs to the atmosphere. For both businesses and individuals, becoming carbon neutral typically involves two steps: reducing GHG emissions that they generate directly, through steps such as conserving energy; and buying carbon offsets that equal whatever direct GHG emissions they cannot eliminate.

Carbon offset — An activity that reduces GHG emissions, such as planting trees to take up atmospheric carbon dioxide or producing energy from carbon-free fuels like wind and solar energy. Buying carbon offsets is a way of contracting out GHG emission reductions, typically because the offset project can reduce emissions more cheaply than the buyer can.

Carbon trading — Buying and selling GHG emission allowances (government permits to release a specific quantity of pollution) or emission-reduction credits, which may be issued by government under mandatory regulations or created by companies and individuals through voluntary trading schemes.

Greenhouse gases (GHGs) — Heat-trapping gases that absorb solar energy in the atmosphere and warm earth's surface. Six major GHGs are controlled under the Kyoto Protocol, but since carbon dioxide (CO_2) is the most abundant and causes the most warming, companies and governments convert their total emissions into CO_2 equivalents.

Renewable energy certificates (RECs) — Certificates that represent the environmental attributes of electricity produced from renewable sources and can be sold separately from the electricity itself. Investors can buy RECs to support green energy whether or not they are located close to the source. Some companies may market themselves as "powered by green energy," even though they use electricity from coal- or gas-fired power plants, because they buy RECs to equal their total electric power usage (thus helping to put that amount of carbon-free energy into the electric power grid).

---

for energy projects, and they're less likely to be permanent," says Markham. Instead, he prefers energy projects because it's easier to quantify the emissions that they displace and demonstrate additionality. "Wind power and methane-capture projects tend to be pretty high-quality investments," Markham says.

But nothing is guaranteed. After the for-profit broker TerraPass provided offsets to help green the 2007 Academy Awards ceremony, an investigation by *Business Week* magazine found that six projects that generated TerraPass offsets would have taken place in any case. One, a methane-capture system installed by Waste Management, Inc. at an Arkansas landfill, was initiated in response to pressure from state regulators. TerraPass's investment was "just icing on the cake" for another project, a county official in North Carolina told *Business Week*.[16]

"There are a lot of new entrants into the market, so some offerings probably aren't as robust as others, and it's causing some confusion," says Burnett. "If this sector doesn't become more standardized within the next five years, government will have to step in. We don't

necessarily need a single federal scheme, but it would be very useful to have a federally sanctioned panel of experts who could review offset products."

Beyond the characteristics of specific projects, some critics argue that carbon offsets don't reduce climate change because they let people keep doing high-carbon activities, which the offsets counterbalance at best. Worse, offsets may serve as cover for carbon-intensive activities. For example, a recent report from the Transnational Institute in Amsterdam, the Netherlands, points out that British Airways offers passengers an option to buy carbon offsets for their flights but is also pushing to expand British airports and short-haul flights, which will increase the company's total GHG emissions.[17]

"Offsets may be tarnished by revelations of practices that aren't credible. That would be a problem, because these tools can be quite useful if they're applied effectively," says Thomas Tietenberg, a professor of economics at Colby College in Waterville, Maine. "The consumer offset market is facing an important moment in terms of its credibility. It needs to get some agreement about what the standards are."

Should government require green purchases?

Government officials often want to boost demand for green products, even if they cost somewhat more, because these goods reduce pollution, conserve energy or keep waste out of landfills. One option is to mandate the use of green goods and services. But critics argue that government interference distorts markets and that setting environmental performance standards may deliver inferior products.

Renewable energy is perhaps the most widely mandated green commodity. As of January 2008, 26 states and the District of Columbia had adopted renewable portfolio standards (RPSs) requiring electricity suppliers to generate certain fractions of their power from renewable fuels like wind, solar energy and biomass.[18] Advocates would like to see a national renewable-energy requirement, but so far Congress has failed to enact one.

Most recently, in 2007 the House passed an energy bill that included a 15 percent RPS requirement by 2020, with utilities allowed to meet up to 4 percent of their targets through energy conservation. Supporters argued that the measure would reduce air pollutants and greenhouse gas emissions from fossil fuel combustion and spur the growth of a domestic renewable-energy industry. But the provision was dropped after critics charged that it would raise electricity prices and penalize regions with fewer renewable resources. (*See "At Issue," p. 195.*)

"The market should be allowed to work things out. We don't support having the government impose a mandate that says, "Thou shalt do this," says Keith McCoy, vice president for energy and resources policy at the National Association of Manufacturers. "Utilities and regulators in RPS states are looking at the right fuel mixes for their regions, but we need to take into account what's possible in different parts of the country."

RPS advocates want a national standard to push states that have been less aggressive in developing renewable energy. A national RPS "is absolutely achievable," said Rep. Tom Udall, D-N.M., a sponsor of the measure, during House debate. "[B]ut the full potential for renewable electricity will be left unrealized without the adoption of a federal program to enhance the efforts of these states."[19]

Governments can also ensure that products are at least somewhat green by establishing content or performance requirements. Measures such as building codes and energy-efficiency standards for appliances are one way to remedy a common problem: Many buyers don't know much about products, so it's hard to choose the best even if they want to. "If you're walking around a house looking at it, you have no idea what kind of insulation is in the walls or how efficient the heating system is, but building codes set some basic thresholds for performance," says Colby College economist Tietenberg.

Forcing manufacturers to comply with new standards may spur technical advances, but it can also challenge businesses to meet the new goals. When new energy-efficiency standards for top-loading washing machines went into effect in 2007, *Consumer Reports* gave low performance ratings to the first models that it tested. The Competitive Enterprise Institute (CEI), a think tank that opposes excessive regulation, accused the Energy Department of ruining a once-dependable home appliance. "Send your underwear to the undersecretary," CEI urged dissatisfied consumers.[20]

"If these technologies really are that good, we shouldn't need laws to force them down people's throats," says CEI General Counsel Sam Kazman. "We don't think that promoting energy efficiency is an appropriate role for government, but if that's the goal, the way to do it is with an energy tax, which would reduce energy use and create incentives to develop energy-saving technologies. One big attraction of regulations is that the public doesn't see them as tax increases — people perceive them as relatively cost-free."

Today, however, those energy-efficient washers look better. "What a difference a year makes," *Consumer Reports* commented in February 2008. The best high-efficiency top-loading washers were performing better, testers found, and *CR* pointed out that high-efficiency models could end up costing the same or less than standard machines over their lifetime when energy savings were factored in.[21]

Posing the issue as a choice between a free market or regulations is misleading, says Bill Prindle, deputy director of the American Council for an Energy-Efficient Economy (ACEEE). "The real issue is what the rules should be for market players. When you set boundaries and targets, manufacturers come up with very ingenious solutions that give customers great value," Prindle contends. He also notes that manufacturers and conservation advocates have negotiated some two dozen energy-efficiency standards since 2005 that subsequently were enacted into law. "These are largely consensus-based agreements. They wouldn't have passed otherwise," Prindle argues.

Another way to promote green technologies is through voluntary labeling programs that identify environmentally preferable products. The Energy Star program, administered by EPA and the Department of Energy, was launched in 1992 in response to a Clean Air Act provision directing EPA to find non-regulatory strategies for reducing air pollution. Energy Star defines superior energy efficiency standards for more than 50 types of residential, commercial and industrial equipment, including consumer electronics, heating and cooling systems and lighting.[22] EPA estimates that over 2 billion products with Energy Star labels were sold in 2006, saving 170 billion kilowatt-hours of electricity, or enough to power more than 15 million average American households for a year.[23]

Another program, Leadership in Energy and Environmental Design (LEED), was developed by the U.S. Green Building Council to identify highly energy-efficient buildings with extremely healthy indoor environments.[24] More than 800 buildings in the U.S. and worldwide have received LEED certification by scoring points on a fixed scale for features like energy and water conservation and indoor air quality. Many large corporations and universities have built LEED buildings to demonstrate environmental commitments.

Labeling programs complement requirements to use green products, says Tietenberg. "Mandates make sense as a floor, but you don't want to stop there. Labels like LEED provide something that performs above the minimum," he says. "They let buyers know that they are

Some Buyers Are Greener Than Others

A 2006 study by the Natural Marketing Institute classified adult U.S. consumers into five categories based on their attitudes toward ethical consumption.

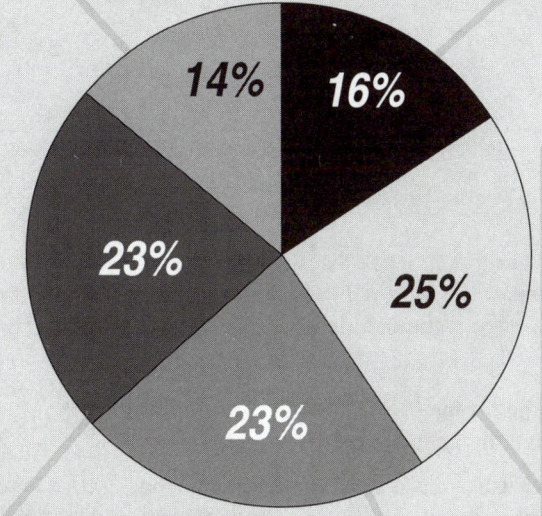

Unconcerneds — Do not consider social or environmental values in buying decisions.

LOHAS (Lifestyles of health and sustainability) — Make purchases based on belief systems and values, including environmental protection and social responsibility.

Naturalites — Are interested in natural and healthy products, but their choices are driven more strongly by personal and family health concerns than by broader environmental views.

Conventionals — May recycle or give money to environmental groups, but do not shop based on a cohesive set of values; sometimes buy green products, especially items that offer economic savings.

Drifters — May believe in protecting the environment, but often think that measuring the impact of their consumer choices is too hard or don't know how to do it.

Note: Percentages add to more than 100 due to rounding.

Source: LOHAS Forum, "Understanding the LOHAS Consumer: The Rise of Ethical Consumerism," www.lohas.com

getting a certain value for their investment and communicate that fact to other people."

CEI's Kazman argues that green labeling programs can also be problematic. "Consumers don't get the full story if labels omit repair issues and the risk that very new technologies will have problems," he says. "And

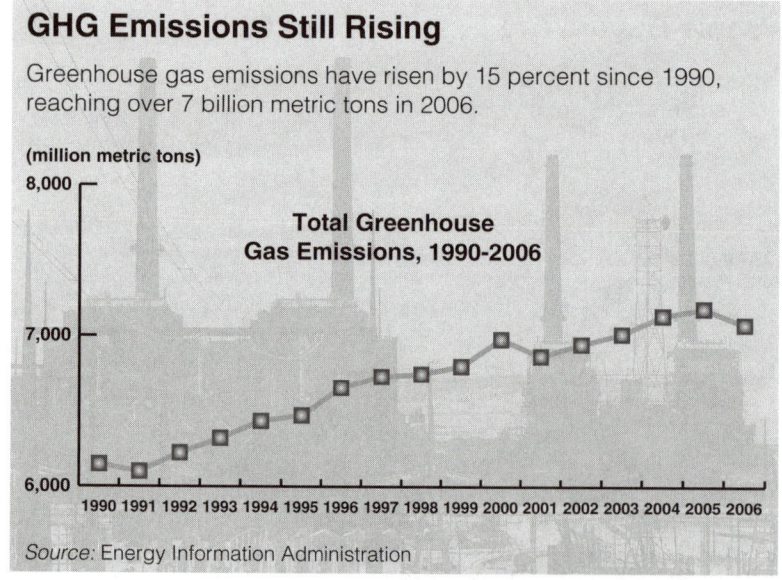

GHG Emissions Still Rising

Greenhouse gas emissions have risen by 15 percent since 1990, reaching over 7 billion metric tons in 2006.

(million metric tons)

Total Greenhouse Gas Emissions, 1990-2006

Source: Energy Information Administration

to sustain it," said entrepreneur and satellite radio host Josh Dorfman, the self-styled "Lazy Environmentalist," in a 2007 interview. "As a nation, we don't really want to deal with [global warming]. We have neither the political leadership nor the political will, which is why I think that for now the environmental solutions presented have to be both effective and painless."[25]

This is a new perspective for the environmental movement, which has long argued that rampant economic growth and high consumption are root causes of environmental harm. Not all environmentalists agree that so-called checkbook environmentalism can save the planet. For one thing, critics argue, the green product boom has had little impact so far on U.S. greenhouse gas emissions. Since 1990 the emissions intensity of the U.S. economy (the amount of GHG emissions produced for every dollar of economic activity) has declined, but total GHG emissions have increased nearly every year due to overall economic growth. (*See graph, above.*)

"True, as companies and countries get richer they can afford more efficient machinery that makes better use of fossil fuel, like the hybrid Honda Civic I drive," writes bestselling author Bill McKibben. "But if your appliances have gotten more efficient, there are also far more of them: The furnace is better than it used to be, but the average size of the house it heats has doubled since 1950. The 60-inch TV? The always-on cable modem? No need for you to do the math — the electric company does it for you, every month."[26]

Complicating the issue, many green living guides fail to distinguish between actions that have a major impact, like insulating your house, and those with smaller effects such as buying a natural-fiber shower curtain or dog leash. "People tend not to sort through which choices are important and which are insignificant. They view most actions as equally important," says Warren Leon, coauthor of *The Consumer's Guide to Effective Environmental Choices* and director of the Massachusetts Renewable Energy Trust.[27] (*See sidebar, p. 191.*) "I worry about products that are sold as green, often by promoters who

once items earn stars, there's a risk that the next step will be to mandate them. But we'd rather have government give advice and make recommendations than impose mandates."

Is buying green better for the environment than buying less?

Most observers agree that today's green consumption boom signals the mainstreaming of environmental values. In the 1980s eco-friendly products like soy milk and recycled paper were of uneven quality and were viewed as niche goods for a small subset of dedicated customers. Today megastores like Wal-Mart and Target offer green cleaning supplies, organic food and energy-efficient light bulbs.

"We've seen green waves before, but today there's better understanding of environmental issues, higher quality products and more consumer understanding," says Case at TerraChoice Environmental Marketing. "This issue has penetrated the heads of the average consumer and business executive."

With more consumers buying more earth-friendly products, some advocates say that environmental protection no longer has to mean scaling back affluent lifestyles. Instead, they assert, we can shop our way to sustainability. "We all need to be presented with better product choices that enable us to maintain the way of life to which we're accustomed without overtaxing the planet's ability

sincerely believe in them, but that either don't work well or don't have a serious impact. Mediocre or trivial green products will turn consumers off in the long run," he warns.

"Greenwashing" further undercuts the impact of buying green by marketing products with vague claims like "All Natural," "Earth Smart" and other labels that are too general to document whether goods will help the environment or not. Some consumers analyze these slogans critically, but many are likely to take them at face value. According to a 2006 study by the Natural Marketing Institute, LOHAS (Lifestyles of Health and Sustainability) buyers, who make purchases based on belief systems and values, including environmental protection and social responsibility, account for only about 16 percent of U.S. consumers. (*See graph, p. 185.*)

Although LOHAS consumers are a relatively small segment of the market, green business experts say that they have significant influence. "LOHAS consumers push the envelope. They're always testing the boundaries, and they make decisions for the sake of the mission," says Ted Ning, who directs an annual business gathering in Colorado called the LOHAS Forum. "Once their items become mainstream, they move on to the next issue. For example, instead of just buying organic food or locally grown food, now they're choosing food based on its carbon footprint."

LOHAS buyers also size up companies critically, says Ning. "They expect a lot of in-depth information to show whether products are authentic. Blogs and Web sites give people lots of ways to communicate, so if companies don't make that data available, there's an assumption that they have something to hide. And LOHAS consumers are evangelists, so they're proud to share their information. If you get on their wrong side, they'll bad-mouth you to death."

Businesses are keenly interested in LOHAS consumers, who represent an estimated $209 billion market for goods including organic food, personal and home care products, clean energy technologies, alternative transportation and ecotourism.[28] But it's not clear that this group's preferences can steer the entire U.S. economy toward sustainability.

"Consumers are most interested in high-quality, affordable products. That's still a larger driver than other environmental considerations, although green aspects

AFP/Getty Images/Jaime Reina

Growing numbers of eco-conscious shoppers are buying organically grown food today. Demand for organic and natural groceries has made Whole Foods the nation's largest natural food market chain.

often are tie-breakers," says TerraChoice's Case. Recent polls show that while Americans are increasingly willing to make lifestyle changes to protect the environment, they prefer easy actions like recycling over more demanding steps like reducing their carbon footprints.[29]

"Green labeling and marketing are market-based instruments that can be adopted quickly as our environmental knowledge grows, but in the long term they'll be seen as transitional steps," says Case. "Ultimately, we'll address these issues with other mechanisms like cap-and-trade systems and taxes."

BACKGROUND

Conservation Focus

Before the United States was a century old, early conservationists began to warn about threats to precious lands and resources. In his 1854 classic *Walden*, Henry David Thoreau decried loggers and railroads that encroached on his forest retreat. In 1876 naturalist John Muir wrote that California's forests, which he called "God's first temples," were "being burned and cut down and wasted like a field of unprotected grain, and once destroyed can never be wholly restored even by centuries of persistent and painstaking cultivation."[30]

Congress began putting lands under federal protection with the creation of Yellowstone National Park in 1872. It also established scientific agencies to manage

CHRONOLOGY

1960-1980 *Environmentalists use lobbying, litigation and citizen action to curb pollution.... Congress imposes new regulations on businesses.*

1967 Congress enacts Clean Air Act.

1969 Congress passes National Environmental Policy Act, requiring environmental-impact studies for federal projects with potentially significant effects on the environment.

1970 Millions of Americans celebrate Earth Day on April 22....Congress establishes Environmental Protection Agency and expands Clean Air Act.

1973 Endangered Species Act enacted.

1974 Safe Drinking Water Act enacted.

1978 Homeowners in New York's Love Canal neighborhood force federal government to pay for evacuating them from houses built atop toxic-waste dump.

1979 Three Mile Island nuclear power plant in Pennsylvania partially melts down, stalling the growth of nuclear energy.

1980 Superfund law assigns liability and fund cleanup at hazardous-waste sites....Ronald Reagan is elected president on platform calling for reducing government's role.

1980-2000 *Global climate change emerges as major environmental issue.*

1987 Twenty-four nations initially sign Montreal Protocol, pledging to phase out chemicals that deplete Earth's ozone layer; dozens more sign in subsequent years.

1989 *Exxon Valdez* runs aground in Alaska, contaminating more than 5,000 kilometers of pristine coast with oil and killing thousands of animals and birds.

1990 Congress creates market-based allowance trading system to reduce emissions that cause acid rain....Federal Trade Commission (FTC) brings first enforcement case against deceptive green marketing, challenging claims for "pesticide free" produce sold by Vons supermarkets.

1992 Delegates to the Earth Summit in Rio de Janeiro, Brazil, adopt first international pledge to cut greenhouse gas (GHG) emissions....FTC issues marketing guides for green products and services.

1997 International conference approves Kyoto Protocol requiring GHG reductions but lets wealthy nations meet some of their obligations with offset projects in developing countries; U.S. signs but fails to ratify pact.

1998 U.S. Green Building Council launches Leadership in Energy and Environmental Design (LEED) program for rating energy-efficient, healthy buildings.

2000 British Petroleum re-brands itself BP and pledges to go "Beyond Petroleum" by investing in clean energy.

2000 Department of Agriculture issues final rule for certifying organic food.

2001-2007 *As environmental concern grows, more companies offer eco-friendly products. Skeptics warn of "greenwashing."*

2001 President George W. Bush rejects mandatory controls on GHG emissions....Following the Sept. 11 terrorist attacks, Bush urges Americans to shop to help fend off economic recession.

2005 General Electric launches "Ecomagination" advertising campaign to demonstrate its environmental commitment....Kyoto Protocol enters into force, including credits for carbon offset projects in developing countries....European Union members begin trading carbon credits.

2006 Democrats recapture control of Congress, increasing support for policies to boost renewable energy and curb greenhouse gas emissions.

2007 FTC initiates review of green marketing guidelines and environmental products, including carbon offsets....Toyota Prius hybrids surpass top-selling sport-utility vehicles.

The Six Sins of 'Greenwashing'

Misleading environmental claims are common.

A perfectly green product may not exist, but some certainly are much greener than others, according to a recent study by Pennsylvania-based TerraChoice Environmental Marketing.[1] It examined 1,018 consumer products that made a total of 1,753 environmental claims and found that every product but one offered false or misleading information. The firm identified six broad categories of misleading environmental claims, or "greenwashing":

- **The hidden trade-off:** Marketing a product as eco-friendly based on a single green attribute like recycled content, without addressing other issues such as where its materials come from or how much energy is required to produce it.
- **No proof:** Making environmental claims without providing information backing them up at the point of purchase or on the manufacturer's Web site.
- **Vagueness:** Touting products based on claims that are too vague to have any real meaning, such as "Non-Toxic," "All Natural" or "Earth-Friendly."
- **Irrelevance:** Offering a claim that is true but not important or helpful to consumers. For example, some products are labeled "CFC-Free," but ozone-destroying chlorofluorocarbons (CFCs) have been outlawed in the U.S. for several decades.
- **Lesser of two evils:** Selling a product with an environmental label even though it belongs to a class of goods that is generally bad for consumers' health or the environment, such as organic cigarettes.
- **Fibbing:** Providing false information or claiming a certification, such as USDA Organic, that the product has not actually earned.

Greenwashing matters for several reasons, the study contends. First, consumers will waste money and may conclude that environmentally friendly products do not work. Second, greenwashing takes business away from legitimate green products. This makes it harder for honest manufacturers to compete and slows the rate at which high-quality products penetrate the market.

Indeed, greenwashing was a factor in the demise of an early wave of green consumerism in the 1980s, says TerraChoice Vice President Scot Case, but more scrutiny this time may deter cheaters. "We'll know if things are improving when we repeat the study in a few months," says Case. "We're hopeful that attention from the media and the Federal Trade Commission [FTC] will help."

Consumers who want to ensure that they are getting green products have several options. First, they can look for seals of approval from organizations such as EcoLogo and Green Seal, both of which certify green products based on multiple criteria.[2] These eco-labeling programs are standardized under a set of principles developed by the International Organization for Standards.

Consumers also can check product labels and manufacturers' Web sites for information that supports green marketing claims. "Companies should be very careful not to claim that things are green, only that they are greener," says Case. "They shouldn't suggest that just because they've addressed one issue, it's a green product." The FTC has published guidance to help consumers sort through green advertising claims.[3]

Although greenwashing may be pervasive today, TerraChoice argues that green marketing can be a positive force. "[G]reen marketers and consumers are learning about the pitfalls of greenwashing together," the report states. "This is a shared problem and opportunity. When green marketing overcomes these challenges, consumers will be better able to trust green claims, and genuinely environmentally preferable products will penetrate their markets more rapidly and deeply. This will be great for consumers, great for business and great for the planet."[4]

---

[1] TerraChoice Environmental Marketing, "The 'Six Sins of Greenwashing," November 2007, www.terrachoice.com.

[2] For more information see www.ecologo.org and www.greenseal .org.

[3] U.S. Federal Trade Commission, "Sorting Out 'Green' Advertising Claims," www.ftc.gov/bcp/edu/pubs/consumer/general/gen02.pdf.

[4] TerraChoice, *op. cit.*, p. 8.

natural resources, including the U.S. Fisheries Commission (later the Fish & Wildlife Service) in 1871 and the U.S. Geological Survey and Division of Forestry (later the Forest Service) in 1879.

But politicians mainly sought to develop and use resources, not to protect them in their natural states. To settle the West, Congress passed laws like the 1872 Mining Law, which allowed prospectors to buy mining rights on public lands for $5 per acre, and the 1878 Timber and Stone Act, which made land that was "unfit for farming" available for $2.50 per acre for timber and stone resources. These statutes often allowed speculators and large corporations to exploit public resources at far less than fair market value.[31]

Environmental advocates formed many important conservation groups before 1900, including the Appalachian Mountain Club, American Forests and the Sierra Club. Their members, mainly affluent outdoorsmen, focused on preserving land for hunting, fishing and expeditions. One notable exception, the Massachusetts Audubon Society, was founded in 1896 by two Boston society women who opposed killing exotic birds to provide feathers for fashionable ladies' hats. Within a year the group persuaded the state legislature to ban commerce in wild bird feathers. Its work later spurred Congress to pass national legislation and support a treaty protecting migratory birds.[32]

Although early groups won some notable victories, most conservation work was mandated by the federal government. Congress and Presidents Theodore Roosevelt (1901-1909) and William Howard Taft (1909-1913) set aside many important tracts of land as parks and monuments. Congress created the National Park Service in 1916 to manage these new preserves. But national policy also spurred harmful development, such as federally funded irrigation projects to help settlers farm in dry Western states. With government agencies urging them on, farmers plowed up the Great Plains, destroying their natural grass cover and helping to create the Dust Bowl when drought struck in the 1930s.

During the long tenure of President Franklin D. Roosevelt, (1933-1945), several important conservation programs were launched even as Western dam building accelerated. The Civilian Conservation Corps (CCC), also known as "Roosevelt's Tree Army," hired more than 3 million unemployed Americans to build fire towers,

plant trees and improve parks across the nation. More than 8 million people worked for the Works Progress Administration on projects including roads, bridges and park lodges.

These were top-down programs, writes anthropologist Michael Johnson: "The federal government defined the problems, defined the solutions and then 'fixed' the problems by employing lots of people . . . the average citizen had an almost blind trust in the federal definition of problems and solutions." Moreover, while the CCC and other initiatives treated symptoms such as soil erosion, they failed to address human actions like plowing and over-grazing that caused the problems.[33]

Environmental Awakening

As the economy grew rapidly after World War II, human impacts on the environment became obvious. Pollutants from power plants, factories and passenger cars mixed in the atmosphere to create toxic smog. Offshore oil-drilling platforms appeared along California's scenic coastline. And Rachel Carson's 1962 book *Silent Spring* warned that widespread use of pesticides threatened ecosystems and human health.

Alarmed environmentalists began fighting back. In 1955 they rallied against a hydropower dam that would have flooded part of Dinosaur National Monument in Utah. A decade later, a coalition led by the Sierra Club helped to block a dam that would have inundated the Grand Canyon. Conservationists won a big victory in 1965 when a federal court allowed them to sue against a proposed electric power plant on Storm King Mountain in New York's Hudson Valley.[34] Courts previously had decided such siting issues on narrow technical grounds but in this case held that groups not directly involved in development projects could intervene to protect scenic resources. Litigation quickly became an important tool for environmental advocates.

Congress passed several key environmental laws in the 1960s, including the Wilderness Act (1964), which created a process for protecting land permanently from development, and the National Environmental Policy Act (1969), which subjected major federal actions such as building dams to environmental-impact studies. But new disasters spurred calls for further action. In 1969 an offshore oil well near Santa Barbara, Calif., ruptured and spilled oil along 30 miles of coastline. Five months later

Guidelines for Eco-minded Consumers

Here's how to have the most impact.

For many consumers, the biggest challenge of buying green is not finding earth-friendly goods but figuring out which choices have the biggest environmental impact. Green buying choices can be complicated, and green products often cost more than conventional alternatives.

Moreover, as journalist Samuel Fromartz observes in his history of the organic food business, few shoppers buy everything from premium suppliers like Whole Foods. Instead, regardless of income level, they buy organic in categories that matter to them, such as milk for their children, and choose other items of lower concern from conventional or discount stores.[1]

To help eco-minded consumers focus on purchases with the biggest environmental impact, *The Consumer's Guide to Effective Environmental Choices* identifies the biggest environmental problems related to household consumption: air and water pollution, global warming and habitat alteration. Then, by quantifying environmental impacts and linking these impacts to consumer products and services, authors Michael Brower and Warren Leon identify three household activity areas that account for most of these impacts: food, household operations and transportation.

To address these issues, Brower and Leon urge consumers to take steps such as driving fuel-efficient, low-polluting cars, eating less meat and making their homes energy-efficient.[2]

"A green purchase can have at least three results," says Leon. "First, it can favor a lower-impact product over conventional options. Second, it may allow you to consume fewer resources over the lifetime of the product. That's why energy choices are important — not only does energy use have significant environmental impacts, but you will use less energy every time you turn that appliance on."

As another example, consider a gardener who spends several hundred dollars on outdoor furniture. If she chooses items made from sustainably harvested wood, she may preserve several trees in a threatened forest. But if she uses the same money to buy a backyard composting bin, she can divert hundreds of pounds of food waste from landfills

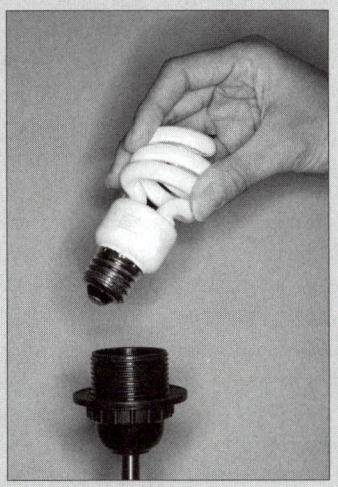

Installing compact fluorescent light bulbs is one of several tips for responsible consumption recommended by the Center for a New American Dream.

Getty Images/Steve Wisbauer

(which produce greenhouse gases as wastes break down and can leak and contaminate groundwater) during the years that she uses the bin.

Third, Leon argues, some green purchases can favor new environmentally friendly technologies or industries with big growth potential. "By joining the early adapters who reinforce demand for a new product, you can help create a perception that it's a success," he says. However, it is important to note that some products will never become market phenomena because they have small niche markets. Only a small fraction of the Americans who drink wine will buy organic wine, but nearly everyone has to clean a bathroom at some point, so green cleaning supplies have a bigger prospective market.

The nonprofit Center for a New American Dream, which advocates for responsible consumption, offers a similar list of personal steps to "Turn the Tide":

- Drive less.
- Eat less feedlot beef.
- Eat eco-friendly seafood.
- Remove your address from bulk mailing lists.
- Install compact fluorescent light bulbs.
- Use less energy for home heating and cooling.
- Eliminate lawn pesticides.
- Reduce home water usage.
- Inspire your friends.

"None of Turn the Tide's nine actions involve drastic changes in your life, yet each packs an environmental punch," says the center. "In fact, every thousand participants prevent the emission of 4 million pounds of climate-warming carbon dioxide every year."[3]

---

[1] Samuel Fromartz, *Organic, Inc.: Natural Foods and How They Grew* (2006), pp. 248-53.

[2] Michael Brower and Warren Leon, *The Consumer's Guide to Effective Environmental Choices* (1999), pp. 43-85.

[3] Center for a New American Dream, "Turn the Tide," www.newdream .org/cnad/user/turn_the_tide.php.

Ohio's Cuyahoga River caught fire when flammable chemicals on its surface ignited.

On April 22, 1970, the first Earth Day, more than 20 million Americans attended rallies and teach-ins designed to force environmental issues onto the national agenda. Activists followed up with lobbying and lawsuits. In response Congress passed a flurry of new laws, including an expanded Clean Air Act (1970), the Endangered Species Act (1973), the Safe Drinking Water Act (1974), the Resources Conservation and Recovery Act (1976) and the Clean Water Act (1977).

"Citizens across the country became aware of what was happening to their physical surroundings," writes journalist Philip Shabecoff. "Equally important, they also acquired a faith — not always requited — that in the American democracy change was possible, that they could act as individuals and communities to obtain relief from the environmental dangers with which they were threatened."[35] Slogans like "Reduce, reuse, recycle" and "Think globally, act locally" underlined the importance of personal action.

While national groups pressured Congress and the new EPA, grassroots activists attacked local problems. In 1978 residents of the Love Canal neighborhood in upstate New York, led by housewife Lois Gibbs, forced the federal government to pay for moving them out of homes that had been built on top of an industrial-waste site. Groups with names like the Abalone Alliance sprang up to oppose new nuclear power plants, blocking some and delaying others.

Businesses and free-market advocates pushed back. President Ronald Reagan was elected in 1980 on a platform that called for reforming regulation and ensuring that benefits from environmental controls justified their costs.[36] During the campaign Reagan argued that air pollution had been "substantially controlled" in the United States and that laws like the Clean Air Act were forcing factories to shut down.[37] When he installed anti-regulation appointees like Interior Secretary James G. Watt and EPA Administrator Anne Gorsuch, many environmentalists worried that their recent victories would be reversed.

Working With Markets

As the Reagan administration learned, most Americans did not support a broad rollback of environmental laws. Public backlash against proposals such as selling off millions of acres of public lands drove Watt and Gorsuch from office. But environmentalists still faced a Republican administration and Senate majority that opposed new controls.

In response some groups began working with the private sector and developing market-based policies. Proponents of this environmental "third wave" contended that if regulations were more cost-effective and flexible, industries could be persuaded to cut pollution instead of having to be forced.

Their most visible success was promoting tradable permits to cut pollution. EPA had started experimenting in the 1970s with programs that allowed companies to earn and trade credits for reducing air pollutants such as carbon monoxide and particulates. Business leaders preferred this approach because instead of mandating specific control technologies, it let them decide how and where to make reductions. For example, instead of installing pollution controls a company might make its operations more efficient or switch to cleaner methods or products.

When Congress amended the Clean Air Act in 1990, some environmentalists supported a cap-and-trade system to reduce sulfur dioxide (SO_2) and nitrogen oxide emissions that caused acid rain. This approach set an overall cap on emissions and issued a fixed number of tradable emission permits to sources. Factories emitting less pollution than their allotments could sell extra permits to other sources — giving polluters an economic incentive to clean up, advocates asserted.[38]

The SO_2 trading program went into effect in 1995 and expanded in 2000. Many supporters praised it for cutting SO_2 releases sharply at a lower cost than industry had predicted.[39] However, acid rain remained a problem in areas located downwind from major pollution sources, such as the Adirondack Mountains, and emissions trading did not prove to be a panacea for other U.S. air pollution problems.[40]

During the 1990s some economic experts began to argue that going green made sound business sense. By reducing pollution, the theory held, companies would make their operations more efficient, which meant that they would use less energy and waste fewer raw materials. "Innovation to comply with environmental regulation often improves product performance or quality," business professors Michael Porter and Claas van der Linde asserted in 1995.[41]

As one step, some companies forged relationships with large environmental groups.[42] McDonald's worked with Environmental Defense to design a paperboard alternative to its polystyrene "clamshell" hamburger package, and the Rainforest Alliance helped Chiquita Brands develop social and environmental standards for its banana farms in Latin America.[43] However, critics argued that by accepting corporate donations and putting business executives on their boards of directors, environmentalists risked becoming too sympathetic to private interests.[44]

Some smaller groups stuck to more aggressive tactics. San Francisco's Rainforest Action Network carried out scrappy direct-action campaigns that persuaded Burger King to stop using beef raised on former rainforest lands and Home Depot to sell only sustainably produced wood. The Earth Island Institute used negative publicity and a consumer boycott to make tuna companies adopt fishing practices that avoided killing dolphins in tuna nets. And major groups continue to vilify companies like oil giant Exxon Mobil, whose opposition to action on global warming and support for oil drilling in the Arctic National Wildlife Refuge made it a prime environmental target.[45]

The 1997 Kyoto Protocol applied offsets to climate change in a provision called the Clean Development Mechanism (CDM), under which developed countries could meet part of their commitments by paying for projects that reduced GHG emissions in developing countries. This process was designed to reduce costs by letting industrialized nations cut GHG emissions in locations where environmental upgrades were cheaper. (GHGs dissipate widely throughout the atmosphere, so eliminating a ton of CO_2 emissions has the same impact on climate change wherever it occurs.)

Shopping for Change

National environmental policy became more contentious after George W. Bush was elected president in 2000 with strong support from energy- and resource-intensive industries. Many administration appointees pushed to loosen environmental regulations, and President Bush reversed a campaign pledge to limit greenhouse gas emissions that caused global warming, arguing that doing so would hurt the economy.[46]

Stymied at the federal level, environmentalists looked for other ways to leverage public support for green policies. Many advocacy groups deepened ties with businesses to influence corporate policies and earn political support from the private sector. They also urged members to target their buying power toward green goals. "People got tired of the gloom and doom approach. They wanted to hear about solutions," explained Bud Ris, executive director of the Union of Concerned Scientists from 1984 through 2003.[47]

Even as scientific consensus increased that human actions were causing global climate change, President George W. Bush opposed calls for mandatory controls on U.S. GHG emissions. Instead, in 2002 Bush pledged to reduce U.S. GHG emissions per dollar of economic activity by 18 percent by 2012. "This will set America on a path to slow the growth of our greenhouse gas emissions and, as science justifies, to stop and then reverse the growth of emissions," Bush said. However, many analysts noted, even if the American economy became 18 percent less carbon-intensive, its total GHG emissions would increase during that time as a result of normal economic growth.

Many corporations joined voluntary initiatives, however, like EPA's Climate Leaders program or the privately funded Pew Center on Global Climate Policy, both to show stockholders that they were paying attention to the environment and to discuss what kind of climate change policies would be most workable for businesses.[48] These partnerships required companies to measure their GHG emissions and develop strategies for reducing them. Companies also began exploring options like renewable energy certificates (RECs) and carbon offsets to reduce their carbon footprints.

Some companies turned growing concerns about pollution and climate change to their advantage with products that were both high-quality and green. Toyota's gas-electric hybrid Prius hatchback, which promised drivers 60 miles per gallon in city driving, debuted with limited sales in U.S. markets in 2000. By 2005 the Prius had become a symbol of green chic, and Toyota was selling 100,000 per year. And after the U.S. Department of Agriculture finalized standards for certifying organic food in 2000, Whole Foods rode growing demand for organic and natural groceries to become the largest natural food market chain in the nation.

CURRENT SITUATION

Keeping Standards High

As consumer interest in green products rises, regulators and environmentalists are taking a critical look at definitions and marketplace practices. Strong standards are needed, observers say, to prevent a new wave of greenwashing and help consumers avoid wasting money.

"The nature of marketing is to puff up products. That's why we have labeling laws, and there are struggles over who regulates what," says University of California sociologist Szasz. "The first struggle is over how regulated a product like organic food will be and who will do it. Then once the rules are written, debate over practices like greenwashing takes place within those boundaries."

In late 2007 the Federal Trade Commission (FTC) announced plans to review its green marketing guidelines and new green products such as carbon offsets.[49] FTC's guidelines offer advice for manufacturers on a variety of green products, but the commission may issue specific guidance on carbon offsets and RECs.

"We want to learn more about what these products are, how they work and how much activity is going on in the marketplace. We're also exploring how marketers are substantiating their claims and what consumers need to know about these products that we can provide," says FTC attorney Hampton Newsome.

The FTC is not an environmental agency, so it will not set specifications for individual products. Rather, it considers questions such as whether labels provide enough clear information for consumers to make judgments. For example, according to agency guidelines, a bottle labeled "50% more recycled content" would be ambiguous because the comparison could refer to a competing brand or to a prior version of the product. A label reading "50% more recycled content than our previous package" would be clearer.[50]

"Marketers have to substantiate express or implied marketing claims with competent and reliable evidence," says Newsome. "How consumers understand the claim is key, because that determines their purchasing decisions, not what the seller intended." Under the Federal Trade Commission Act, which outlaws unfair and deceptive trade practices, companies that make false or misleading claims could face penalties including injunctions or forfeiture of profits.

Many organizations are working to help standardize carbon offsets and define high-quality versions. There are a number of issues to consider, says Colby College's Tietenberg. "Quantification is important. The fact that something reduces greenhouse gases is useful, but you need to quantify how much it reduces them," he says. "You need to ensure that the initial reductions prevail through the life of the offset — for example, if you plant trees and the forest burns down, you don't get the offset. And you need a tracking system to keep people from selling the same offsets to multiple buyers."

Advocates also want to make green certification programs more rigorous. Some have criticized the LEED rating system for green buildings, saying that its checklists are simplistic and give too much weight to small steps, like installing bicycle racks, and not enough to bigger ones, such as renovating a historic building instead of razing it.[51] But the green building movement remains strong: By 2010, trade publications estimate that about 10 percent of commercial construction starts will be green projects (not all of which may seek LEED ratings).[52]

Watchdogs also see room for improvement in the Energy Star program. In 2007 EPA's inspector general reported that the agency was not doing enough to confirm that Energy Star products (which are tested by manufacturers, not EPA) performed at the promised level, or to prevent unqualified products from being labeled as Energy Star models.[53] The Government Accountability Office also criticized relying on manufacturers to test products and urged EPA and the Energy Department to look more closely at issues such as how many products are purchased because of Energy Star ratings.[54]

More Mandates?

Congressional supporters of a national renewable electricity portfolio standard have pledged to bring RPS legislation up again this year. Countering the argument that this policy would penalize some states, a study by the American Council for an Energy-Efficient Economy (ACEEE) projects that electricity prices would be lower across the U.S. in 2020 and 2025 under a standard like that passed by the House in 2007 (combining renewable electricity and conservation) than without an RPS. A more aggressive standard that met 15 percent of electricity demand with renewable fuels and 15 percent through conservation would push prices even lower, ACEEE found.[55]

Does the United States need a national renewable electricity portfolio standard?

YES
Gov. Bill Ritter, Jr., D-Colo.

From testimony before House Select Committee
on Energy Independence and Global Warming, Sept. 20, 2007

It has been our experience that [a renewable electricity portfolio standard] creates new jobs, spurs economic development and increases the tax base all while saving consumers and businesses money and protecting our environment. In 2004, following three years of failed legislative efforts, the people of Colorado placed the nation's first citizen-initiated renewable portfolio standard (RPS), Amendment 37, on the ballot. While the effort was opposed by virtually all Colorado utilities, including the state's largest utility — Xcel Energy — the effort passed by a wide margin. The Colorado RPS established a goal of 10 percent renewable resources by 2015 for Xcel Energy (along with the other Colorado Public Utilities Commission-regulated utility, Aquila).

In 2004, 10 percent was an ambitious goal: a little over 1 percent of Xcel's electricity was generated from renewable sources at that time. Today, it is the country's leading provider of wind energy. Xcel will meet the 10-percent-by-2015 goal at the end of 2007 — nearly eight years ahead of schedule.

Xcel has done what all successful businesses do — it adapted. While Xcel originally viewed the RPS as a burden, it soon recognized it as an opportunity, and the utility is now a great example of the successes that will come from our New Energy Economy. . . .

Renewable energy development of the future is not limited to wind. In Colorado, we are fortunate to have a broad mix of renewable resources, including wind on our Eastern Plains, solar in the San Luis Valley and southwest part of the state and geothermal all along our Western Slope. . . .

The committee has asked how a national renewable electricity standard will impact technologies in Colorado. Developments in wind technology have led the industry to be cost competitive with fossil fuel generation, but we need similar developments in both solar electric as well as concentrated solar technology. With the appropriate leadership from the federal government, these resources have the opportunity to join wind as a primary source of renewable power. . . .

As we saw with the RPS in Colorado — we encouraged the market through the RPS, and the market has responded. Investment, research and development are following the establishment of the RPS. A federal RPS provides more markets for renewable energy, prosperity for Americans in the heartland and a more responsible energy future for our nation.

NO
Chris M. Hobson
*Senior Vice President, Research
and Environmental Affairs,
Southern Company*

From testimony before House Select Committee
on Energy Independence and Global Warming, Sept. 20, 2007

Southern Company opposes a national renewable-energy mandate. We believe that mandates are an inefficient and potentially counterproductive means of increasing the production of cost-effective, reliable electric power from renewable sources. We prefer to seek cost-effective additions to our generation portfolio based on technological maturity, technical performance, reliability and economic cost. . . .

Our estimates show that a 15 percent federal renewable-energy mandate would far exceed the available renewable resources in the Southeastern region. To replace 15 percent of the nation's retail energy by 2020 would require approximately 80,000 wind turbines of 2 megawatt capacity each, or 2,200 square miles of land — an area larger than Delaware — for solar photovoltaic arrays, or 87,000 square miles of switch grass fields — an area the size of Minnesota. To replace 15 percent of just Southern Company's retail energy by 2020 would require approximately 6,900 wind turbines of 2 megawatt capacity each, or 200 square miles of land for solar photovoltaics, or 6,000 square miles of switchgrass fields — an area the size of Connecticut. . . .

Because the renewable resources that would be required to comply with a 15 percent mandate are not available in the Southeast, Southern Company would be required to comply largely by making alternative compliance payments to the federal government. . . . Because of the limited availability of renewable resources in our region and the fact that most of what is available will likely be more expensive than the 3 cents/kilowatt-hour price cap, the majority of the $19 billion cost to our customers will simply be payments to the federal government. Thus a nationwide [renewable portfolio standard] mandate could cost electricity consumers in the Southeast billions of dollars in higher electricity prices, with no guarantee that additional renewable generation will actually be developed. . . .

Not every technology will be well-suited to every region of the country. We do believe that the use of renewable energy to produce electricity can be increased, and we intend to play a key role in the research and development needed to reach such an objective. This is best reached by the enhancement of current strategies to provide incentives for the R&D as well as the use of renewable energy as compared to the adoption of a federal mandate for a single standard across the country.

Getty Images/Mario Tama

Many grocery stores have begun selling reusable shopping bags as an alternative to environmentally unfriendly plastic bags.

"Including energy efficiency brings down wholesale prices," explains ACEEE Deputy Director Prindle. Efficiency and renewables also complement each other, he says, because conservation projects can be put in place more quickly while new renewable energy projects are sited and built.

But opponents are likely to fight any new RPS proposals in 2008. Energy producers in the Southeast maintain that a national RPS will penalize their region, and the White House threatened to veto the 2007 energy bill over its RPS requirement. "A federal RPS that is unfair in its application, is overly prescriptive in its definition by excluding many low-carbon technologies and does not allow states to opt out would hurt consumers and undercut state decisions," National Economic Council Chair Allan Hubbard wrote to congressional leaders in late 2007.[56]

First Congress may have to revisit another controversial green mandate — the Renewable Fuels Standard (RFS), enacted in 2005 and expanded in 2007, which promotes bio-based transportation fuels like ethanol and biodiesel.[57] The original RFS, which was adopted to reduce U.S. dependence on imported oil and cut pollution from transportation, required refiners to use 5.4 billion gallons of renewable fuels (mostly blended with conventional gasoline) in 2008, rising to 7.5 billion gallons by 2012. The new law mandates 9 billion gallons in 2008, increasing to 36 billion gallons by 2022.

Most biofuel sold in the United States is ethanol made from corn, although researchers are starting to make ethanol from cellulosic sources (crop wastes and woody plants), which have a higher energy content and require fewer resources to produce. For the moment, however, much support for the RFS comes from farm-state lawmakers and agribusinesses invested in corn ethanol.

Many observers believe that the RFS is poorly designed and is producing unintended consequences. Two recent studies suggest that the push to expand biofuel crops may trigger such widespread land clearing that it increases climate change (by destroying forests that take up carbon) instead of reducing it.[58] And by driving up demand for corn, which also is used in animal feed and processed foods, critics say the mandate is increasing food prices.[59]

"The RFS has a narrow focus on a particular technology, and it doesn't strike a balance between demand and supply," says Prindle. "Also, it will take a lot of new capacity to meet the targets, including inputs like water and electricity as well as grain. You have to develop a massive new infrastructure across the middle of the country [where most corn is grown]." Colby College's Tietenberg seconds this perspective. "Mandates should be performance-based instead of requiring a specific input," he says. "You want to make sure the standard is clear but that there are flexible options for meeting it."

Green Is Red-Hot

Amid these debates, green marketing is spreading across much of the nation's economy. Today green labeling is most commonly found on office products, building materials, cleaning products and electronics. "In the 20 years between the last green bubble and this one, the only people who expressed strong interest in green products were large institutional purchasers like government agencies, colleges and hospitals, so green labeling had a very business-centric focus," explains TerraChoice's Case.

But now the message is penetrating into new sectors. Transportation, for example, accounts for about 27 percent of U.S. GHG emissions and is a major contributor to regional air pollution. A decade ago gas-guzzling sport utility vehicles (SUVs) and light trucks dominated the U.S. auto market, but in 2007 sales of gas-electric hybrid Toyota Prius hatchbacks surpassed the Ford Explorer, long the top-selling SUV.[60]

Now, with gas prices high and new fuel-efficiency standards signed into law, U.S. automakers are terminating some SUV lines, converting others to smaller "crossovers" and putting more money into alternative vehicles. In 2007 General Motors unveiled a concept model of the Chevrolet Volt, a plug-in electric car that uses a small gasoline engine as a generator to charge its batteries. GM is still designing the Volt but hopes to have it on the market by late 2010.[61] Other companies, including Toyota and Ford, are developing plug-in hybrids that can be recharged at standard 120-volt outlets.

Home and personal care products are also becoming increasingly green, in response to consumer alarm over recent reports describing toxic, hazardous and untested ingredients in common consumer goods. For example, laboratory testing carried out for the Campaign for Safe Cosmetics in 2007 found detectable levels of lead, a neurotoxic chemical, in many brand-name lipsticks.[62] Another recent study found increased levels of phthalates (chemical softeners that have been linked to reproductive problems and are banned from personal care products in the European Union) in infants who were treated with baby lotions, powders and shampoos.[63] Toys, food and beverage containers, upholstery, and other goods have also been found to contain compounds known or suspected to be hazardous to human health.

But this area is a major greenwashing zone, with marketers often relying on slogans that have no standard meaning. "While splashy terms and phrases such as 'earth-friendly,' 'organic,' 'nontoxic,' and 'no harmful fragrances' can occasionally be helpful, the ugly truth is in the ingredients list," the environmental magazine *Grist* advises in its green living guide.[64]

OUTLOOK

Focus on Carbon

Whichever party wins the White House in 2008, it appears likely that the United States will adopt binding GHG limits sometime after a new president takes office in 2009. All of the front-runners for president, including Democrats Hillary Rodham Clinton and Barack Obama and Republican John McCain, support cap-and-trade legislation that would sharply reduce U.S. emissions by 2050 — a timetable that many scientists believe is needed to avert catastrophic global warming.[65]

Many companies can read the writing on the wall and are working to turn the issue to their advantage. "The business community sees tremendous opportunity in green products. It's a chance for companies to push technology and come up with innovative solutions," says the National Association of Manufacturers' McCoy. "We're on the cusp of some fascinating discoveries that could help solve our energy needs. We need to consider what research and development incentives government can offer to facilitate that, with manufacturers and the business community involved." Even Exxon Mobil, long one of the strongest foes of binding GHG limits, has started to discuss what national controls should look like.[66]

With mandatory GHG limits in place, will green consumerism still have a role to play? Many observers see buying green as an important piece of the larger solution. "The reality is that we consume products every day. This is not going to change any time soon," says Dorfman, the "Lazy Environmentalist." "So we have to find more environmentally conscious ways to consume if we want to maintain our quality of lives and not see them degraded by climate change. . . . However, the solutions have to fit our lifestyles or the great majority of us won't even consider them."[67]

But green consumption and business/environment partnerships are not substitutes for political action, says Colby College's Tietenberg. "You need policies to level the playing field. If some firms are out there doing more and it costs more, they may have trouble competing and lose market share," he argues. "But if government sets rules that create a level playing field, business will take the ball and run with it. Many businesses are asking for national standards now."

Consumers who want to make a serious impact with their purchases need to learn which steps make the most difference. "People have a limited understanding of their carbon footprints," says Climate Trust Director Burnett. "They don't necessarily know what kind of fuel generates their electricity, or how significant airplane flights are." And comparing products' full life-cycle impacts can get complicated. For example, today many consumers are debating whether it is preferable to buy organically grown food that is shipped over long distances to market (generating GHG emissions in the process) or locally grown food that has been raised using less earth-friendly methods.[68]

"Wisdom is a curse — once you learn about these issues, you can't overlook them," says LOHAS Forum Director Ning. "But as we confront more problems like environmental toxins that stem from manufacturing processes, people are becoming more aware of design impacts. They're trying to understand more about how products work, and producers are trying to learn more about sustainability. Now that these ideas are becoming part of school curriculums, and people are talking about them more, our consciousness is only going to grow."

NOTES

1. Tearfund, "Senior Bishops Call For Carbon Fast This Lent," Feb. 5, 2008, www.tearfund.org.

2. Penn, Schoen, & Berland Associates, "Consumers Will Double Spending on Green," Sept. 27, 2007.

3. U.S. Bureau of Labor Statistics, Consumer Expenditure Survey, 2000-2006, www.bls.gov/cex/2006/standard/multiyr.pdf.

4. Karlo Barrios Marcelo and Mark Hugo Lopez, "How Young People Expressed Their Political Views in 2006," Center for Information & Research on Civic Learning & Engagement, University of Maryland, November 2007; Scott Keeger, "Politics and the 'DotNet' Generation," Pew Research Center, May 30, 2006; Lori J. Vogelgesang and Alexander W. Astin, "Post-College Civic Engagement Among Graduates," Higher Education Research Institute, University of California, Los Angeles, April 2005.

5. U.S. Federal Trade Commission, "The FTC's Environmental Cases," www.ftc.gov/bcp/conline/edcams/eande/contentframe_environment_cases.html.

6. Intergovernmental Panel on Climate Change, *Climate Change 2007: The Physical Science Basis, Summary for Policymakers* (2007), pp. 3, 5. For background, see Marcia Clemmitt, "Climate Change," *CQ Researcher*, Jan. 27, 2006, pp. 73-96, and Colin Woodard, "Curbing Climate Change," *CQ Global Researcher*, February 2007, pp. 27-50.

7. For background see Peter Katel, "Consumer Safety," *CQ Researcher*, Oct. 12, 2007, pp. 841-864, and Jennifer Weeks, "Factory Farms," *CQ Researcher*, Jan. 12, 2007, pp. 25-48.

8. For background see Tom Price, "The New Environmentalism," *CQ Researcher*, Dec. 1, 2006, pp. 985-1008, and Tom Price, "Corporate Social Responsibility," *CQ Researcher*, Aug. 3, 2007, pp. 649-672.

9. For details on these companies' pledges, see www.dupont.com/Sustainability/en_US/; www.monsanto.com/who_we_are/our_pledge.asp; and www.thinkgreen.com.

10. For background see Marcia Clemmitt, "Climate Change," *CQ Researcher*, Jan. 27, 2006, pp. 73-96.

11. U.S. Climate Action Partnership, *A Call for Action* (2007), p. 3, www.us-cap.org/USCAPCallForAction.pdf.

12. Joel Makower, *et al.*, *State of Green Business 2008* (2008), p. 3, www.stateofgreenbusiness.com/.

13. CarbonCounter.org, www.carboncounter.org/offset-your-emissions/personal-calculator.aspx; Union of Concerned Scientists, "What's Your Carbon Footprint?" www.ucsusa.org/publications/greentips/whats-your-carb.html.

14. *A Consumer's Guide to Retail Carbon Offset Providers* (2006), www.cleanair-coolplanet.org/ConsumersGuidetoCarbonOffsets.pdf.

15. Ted Williams, "As Ugly As a Tree," *Audubon*, September/October 2007.

16. Ben Elgin, "Another Inconvenient Truth," *Business Week*, March 26, 2007.

17. Kevin Smith, *The Carbon-Neutral Myth: Offset Indulgences for Your Climate Sins* (2007), pp. 10-11, www.carbontradewatch.org.

18. Federal Energy Regulatory Commission, "Electric Market Overview: Renewables," updated Jan. 15, 2008, www.ferc.gov/market-oversight/mkt-electric/overview/elec-ovr-rps.pdf.

19. *Congressional Record*, Aug. 4, 2007, p. H9847.

20. "Send Your Underwear to the Undersecretary," Competitive Enterprise Institute news release, May 16, 2007.

21. "Washers and Dryers: Performance For Less," *Consumer Reports*, February 2008.

22. For details see www.energystar.gov.

23. U.S. Environmental Protection Agency, "Energy Star and Other Climate Protection Partnerships 2006

Annual Report," September 2007, p. 15, www .energystar.gov/ia/news/downloads/annual_report_2006 .pdf. According to the Department of Energy, the average U.S. household uses about 11,000 kilowatt-hours of electricity annually; see www.eere.energy .gov/consumer/tips/appliances.htm.

24. For details see www.usgbc.org.

25. Jenny Shank, "An Interview With 'Lazy Environmentalist' Josh Dorfman," July 2, 2007, www .newwest.net/topic/article/an_interview_with_lazy_ environmentalist_josh_dorfman/C39/L39/.

26. Bill McKibben, "Reversal of Fortune," *Mother Jones*, March/April 2007.

27. Michael Brower and Warren Leon, *The Consumer's Guide To Effective Environmental Choices* (1999).

28. LOHAS Forum, "About LOHAS," www.lohas.com/ about.htm.

29. Patrick O'Driscoll and Elizabeth Weise, "Green Living Takes Root But Habits Die Hard," *USA Today*, April 19, 2007; Anjali Athavaley, "A Serious Problem (But Not My Problem)," *Wall Street Journal Classroom Edition*, February 2008.

30. John Muir, "God's First Temples: How Shall We Preserve Our Forests?" reprinted in John Muir, *Nature Writings* (1997), p. 629.

31. For background see Tom Arrandale, "Public Land Policy," *CQ Researcher*, June 17, 1994, pp. 529-552.

32. Massachusetts Foundation for the Humanities, "Mass Moments," www.massmoments.org/moment .cfm?mid=262.

33. Michael D. Johnson, "A Sociocultural Perspective on the Development of U.S. Natural Resource Partnerships in the 20th Century," USDA Forest Service Proceedings (2000), p. 206.

34. *Scenic Hudson Preservation Conference v. Federal Power Commission*, 354 F. 2d 608 (1965).

35. Philip Shabecoff, *Earth Rising: American Environmentalism in the 21st Century* (2000), p. 7.

36. Republican Party Platform of 1980, adopted July 15, 1980, online at The American Presidency Project, www.presidency.ucsb.edu/showplatforms .php?platindex=R1980.

37. Joanne Omang, "Reagan Criticizes Clean Air Laws and EPA as Obstacles to Growth," *The Washington Post*, Oct. 9, 1980.

38. See "Acid Rain: New Approach to Old Problem," *CQ Researcher*, March 3, 1991.

39. Environmental Defense, *From Obstacle to Opportunity: How Acid Rain Emissions Trading Is Delivering Cleaner Air* (September 2000); Robert N. Stavins, "Experience with Market-Based Environmental Policy Instruments," Discussion Paper 01-58, Resources for the Future, November 2001, pp. 27-29.

40. See Charles T. Driscoll, *et al.*, *Acid Rain Revisited: Advances in Scientific Understanding Since the Passage of the 1970 and 1990 Clean Air Act Amendments* (2001); Mary H. Cooper, "Air Pollution Conflict," *CQ Researcher*, Nov. 14, 2003, pp. 965-988; and Jennifer Weeks, "Coal's Comeback," *CQ Researcher*, Oct. 5, 2007, pp. 817-840.

41. Michael E. Porter and Claas van der Linde, "Toward a New Concept of the Environmental-Competitiveness Issue," *Journal of Economic Perspectives*, vol. 9, no. 4, fall 1995, p. 99.

42. For background see Tom Price, "The New Environmentalism," *CQ Researcher*, Dec. 1, 2006, pp. 985-1008.

43. Daniel C. Esty and Andrew S. Winston, *Green to Gold: How Smart Companies Use Environmental Strategy to Innovate, Create Value, and Build Competitive Advantage* (2006), pp. 70-71.

44. Mark Dowie, *Losing Ground: American Environmentalism at the Close of the Twentieth Century* (1995), pp. 114-124.

45. For details see "Exxpose Exxon," www. exxpose-exxon.com.

46. See Mary H. Cooper, "Energy Policy," *CQ Researcher*, May 25, 2001, pp. 441-464, and Mary H. Cooper, "Bush and the Environment," *CQ Researcher*, Oct. 25, 2002, pp. 865-896.

47. Steve Nadis, "Non-Government Organizations (NGOs) Mini-Reviews," New England BioLabs, www.neb.com.

48. For more information, see www.epa.gov/stateply/ index.html and www.pewclimate.org/companies_ leading_the_way_belc.

49. For more information see www.ftc.gov/bcp/workshops/carbonoffsets/index.shtml.

50. U.S. Federal Trade Commission, "Complying With the Environmental Marketing Guides," www.ftc.gov/bcp/conline/pubc/buspubs/greenguides.pdf.

51. Auden Schendler and Randy Udall, "LEED Is Broken; Let's Fix It," *Grist*, October 26, 2005; Stephen Del Percio, "What's Wrong With LEED?" *Green Building*, spring 2007.

52. McGraw Hill, *Green Building Smart Market Report 2006*, cited in "Green Building by the Numbers," U.S. Green Building Council, February 2008.

53. U.S. Environmental Protection Agency, Office of the Inspector General, "Energy Star Program Can Strengthen Controls Protecting the Integrity of the Label," Aug. 1, 2007, www.epa.gov/oig/reports/2007/20070801-2007-P-00028.pdf.

54. U.S. Government Accountability Office, "Energy Efficiency: Opportunities Exist for Federal Agencies to Better Inform Household Consumers," GAO-07-1162 (September 2007).

55. American Council for an Energy-Efficient Economy, "Assessment of the Renewable Electricity Standard and Expanded Clean Energy Scenarios," Dec. 5, 2007, http://aceee.org/pubs/e079.htm.

56. The full letter is posted online at http://gristmill.grist.org/images/user/8/White_House_letter_on_CAFE.pdf.

57. For background see Peter Katel, "Oil Jitters," *CQ Researcher*, Jan. 4, 2008, pp. 1-24, and Adriel Bettelheim, "Biofuels Boom," *CQ Researcher*, Sept. 29, 2006, pp. 793-816.

58. Joseph Fargione, *et al.*, "Land Clearing and the Biofuel Carbon Debt," *Sciencexpress Report*, Feb. 7, 2008; Timothy Searchinger, *et al.*, "Use of U.S. Croplands for Biofuels Increases Greenhouse Gases Through Emissions from Land Use Change," *Sciencexpress Report*, Feb. 7, 2008.

59. Randy Schnepf, "Agriculture-Based Renewable Energy Production," Congressional Research Service, Oct. 16, 2007, pp. 16-20; Colin A. Carter and Henry I. Miller, "Hidden Costs of Corn-Based Ethanol," *The Christian Science Monitor*, May 21, 2007; "Food Prices: Cheap No More," *The Economist*, Dec. 6, 2007.

60. Bernard Simon, "Prius Overtakes Explorer in the U.S.," *Financial Times*, Jan. 11, 2008.

61. "Chevy Volt FAQs," www.gm-volt.com/chevy-volt-faqs.

62. Campaign for Safe Cosmetics, "A Poison Kiss: The Problem of Lead in Lipstick," October 2007, www.safecosmetics.org.

63. Sheela Sathyanarayana, *et al.*, "Baby Care Products: Possible Sources of Infant Phthalate Exposure," *Pediatrics*, February 2008.

64. Brangien Davis and Katharine Wroth, eds., *Wake Up and Smell the Planet: The Non-Pompous, Non-Preachy Grist Guide to Greening Your Day* (2007), p. 20.

65. "Compare the Candidates," *Grist*, www.grist.org/candidate_chart_08.html.

66. Jeffrey Ball, "Exxon Mobil Softens Its Climate-Change Stance," *The Wall Street Journal*, Jan. 11, 2007.

67. Jenny Shank, *op. cit.*

68. For example, see Mindy Pennybacker, "Local or Organic? I'll Take Both," *The Green Guide*, September/October 2006, www.thegreenguide.com/doc/116/local, and John Cloud, "Eating Better Than Organic," *Time*, March 2, 2007.

BIBLIOGRAPHY

Books

Brower, Michael, and Warren Leon, *The Consumer's Guide to Effective Environmental Choices*, Three Rivers Press, 1999.
Although somewhat dated, this guide prioritizes consumer actions according to the scale of their environmental impacts based on extensive data and analysis. Brower and Leon, both senior environmental experts, draw on research by the Union of Concerned Scientists, a national environmental advocacy group.

Esty, Daniel C., and Andrew S. Winston, *Green To Gold: How Smart Companies Use Environmental Strategy to Innovate, Create Value, and Build Competitive Advantage*, Yale University Press, 2006.

Two Yale experts on business and the environment show how green strategies can help companies manage environmental challenges and gain an edge over competitors.

Szasz, Andrew, *Shopping Our Way to Safety: How We Changed from Protecting the Environment to Protecting Ourselves,* **University of Minnesota Press, 2007.**
Szasz, a sociologist, warns that the current green consumption boom could have negative impacts if it turns people away from broader political action.

Articles

"Climate Business/Business Climate," *Harvard Business Review,* **October 2007.**
A special report on the business challenges posed by climate change offers views from a dozen corporate and academic experts.

Davenport, Coral, "A Clean Break in Energy Policy," *CQ Weekly,* **Oct. 8, 2007.**
A national renewable electricity portfolio standard would trigger widespread changes in the ways that utilities produce power and state regulators oversee them.

Elgin, Ben, "Little Green Lies," *Business Week,* **Oct. 29, 2007.**
Auden Schendler, environmental director for Aspen Skiing Co., argues that many corporate greening actions are misleading and empty feel-good gestures.

Farenthold, David A., "Value of U.S. House's Carbon Offsets is Murky," *The Washington Post,* **Jan. 28, 2008.**
Critics say Congress wasted money by buying carbon offsets that funded activities already occurring.

Finz, Stacy, "Food Markets Getting Greener, More Sensual," *San Francisco Chronicle,* **Jan. 27, 2008.**
Consumers want healthier food raised using eco-friendly methods, and the grocery industry is responding.

Koerner, Brendan I., "Rise of the Green Machine," *Wired,* **April 2005.**
Koerner explains how Toyota made it cool to own a hybrid car.

Lynas, Mark, "Can Shopping Save the Planet?" *The Guardian* **(United Kingdom), Sept. 17, 2007.**

Numerous corporations are entering the green product market, but observers argue that at heart green marketing is all about sales, not sustainability.

Schultz, Abby, "How To 'Go Green' on a Budget," *MSN Money,* **June 29, 2007.**
Many green products are more expensive than conventional options, but consumers can make a difference if they choose their purchases carefully.

Underwood, Anne, "The Chemicals Within," *Newsweek,* **Feb. 4, 2008.**
Many common household products contain chemicals that could be harmful to humans. Concerns about health effects are driving many shoppers to seek alternatives.

Williams, Alex, "Don't Let the Green Grass Fool You," *The New York Times,* **Feb. 10, 2008.**
Many suburban Americans would like to shrink their carbon footprints, but skeptics argue that a lifestyle centered on big houses and multiple cars is inherently unsustainable.

Reports and Studies

A Consumer's Guide to Retail Carbon Offset Providers, **Clean Air-Cool Planet, 2006, www.cleanair-coolplanet .org/ConsumersGuidetoCarbonOffsets.pdf.**
An advocacy group that helps businesses, universities and cities and towns reduce greenhouse gas emissions describes key factors that contribute to the quality of carbon offsets and identifies some of the most credible offset providers.

Makower, Joel, *et al.,* *State of Green Business 2008,* **January 2008, www.stateofgreenbusiness.com.**
A report on the spread of green business practices finds that companies are gradually becoming more eco-friendly, but economic growth is offsetting many of the gains, and that the trend is very hard to quantify.

TerraChoice Environmental Marketing, **"The Six Sins of Greenwashing," November 2007, www.terrachoice .com/Home/Six%20Sins%20of%20Greenwashing.**
A study of environmental claims in North American consumer markets finds that virtually all purportedly eco-friendly products mislead consumers to some degree. More accurate green marketing, it asserts, will benefit consumers, businesses and the environment.

For More Information

American Council for an Energy-Efficient Economy, 1001 Connecticut Ave., N.W., Suite 801, Washington, DC 20036; (202) 429-8873; www.aceee.org. Supports energy-efficiency measures to promote economic prosperity and environmental protection.

Clean Air-Cool Planet, 100 Market St., Suite 204, Portsmouth, NH 03801; (603) 422-6464; www.cleanair-coolplanet.org. A nonprofit organization that partners with businesses, colleges and communities throughout the Northeast to reduce carbon emissions and educate the public and opinion leaders about global warming impacts and solutions.

Climate Trust, 65 SW Yamhill St., Suite 400, Portland, OR 97204; (503) 238-1915; www.climatetrust.org. Created to implement an Oregon law that requires new power plants to offset some of their carbon emissions, the Climate Trust produces greenhouse gas offset projects for energy companies, regulators, businesses, and individuals.

Competitive Enterprise Institute, 1001 Connecticut Ave., N.W., Suite 1250, Washington, DC 20036; (202) 331-1010; www.cei.org. A public policy research center dedicated to advancing the principles of free enterprise and limited government.

Consumers Union, 101 Truman Ave., Yonkers, NY 10703; (914) 378-2000; www.consumersunion.org. A nonprofit expert group that promotes a fair and safe market for all consumers; activities include testing and rating products and publishing *Consumer Reports* magazine, as well as Greener-Choices.org, a Web site focusing on green products.

Federal Trade Commission, 600 Pennsylvania Ave., N.W., Washington, DC 20580; (202) 326-2222; www.ftc.gov. Protects consumers' interests, promotes competition and advises businesses on eco-labeling; it is currently reviewing its green marketing guidelines.

LOHAS Forum, 360 Interlocken Blvd., Broomfield, CO 80021; (303) 822-2263; www.lohas.com. An annual business conference focused on the marketplace for goods and services related to health, the environment, social justice, personal development and sustainable living.

National Association of Manufacturers, 1331 Pennsylvania Ave., N.W., Washington, DC 20004; (202) 637-3000; www.nam.org. Promotes legislation and regulations conducive to economic growth and highlights manufacturers' contributions to innovation and productivity.

TerraChoice Environmental Marketing Inc., 1706 Friedensburg Road, Reading, PA 19606; (800) 478-0399; www.terrachoice.com. Conducts market research and advises on strategy, communication and policy issues.

Regulating Toxic Chemicals

Do We Know Enough About Chemical Risks?

Jennifer Weeks

Concern about exposure to the chemical bisphenol A (BPA), widely used in hundreds of products, is prompting consumers and retailers to switch to BPA-free products. The National Toxicology Program warned recently that BPA poses some concern for "effects on the brain, behavior and prostate gland in fetuses, infants and children." Wal-Mart, Target, and other large companies have stopped selling products containing BPA.

From *CQ Researcher*, January 23, 2009.

I n October 2007, the Eastman Chemical Co. of Kingsport, Tenn., introduced Tritan, a new plastic boasting "faster molding cycles compared to many other types of transparent polymers," plus enhanced durability and high gloss.[1]

But Tritan had another feature that made the plastics market take special notice: The new resin did not contain bisphenol A (BPA), a chemical widely found in rigid plastic products like food containers and baby bottles.

BPA has been used in consumer products for decades, although researchers have known since the 1930s that in mammals the chemical mimics estrogen, the natural hormone that regulates female sexual development and reproductive cycles. Endocrine disruption, as the effect is known, has been linked to developmental, reproductive and other problems in wildlife and laboratory animals, and some researchers believe it has a similar impact in humans.[2]

Until the late 1990s scientists thought BPA was only harmful at high doses, but then some studies showed that quantities as low as a few parts per billion could have toxic effects. They also demonstrated that BPA could leach from bottles and can linings into infant formula and food.[3] Then in 2008 the federally funded National Toxicology Program warned that current exposure levels to BPA posed some concern for "effects on the brain, behavior and prostate gland in fetuses, infants and children."[4] In contrast, the Food and Drug Administration (FDA), which regulates exposure to BPA from food packaging, maintained it was safe.

Consumers and retailers opted to be safe rather than sorry, especially after Canada banned BPA from baby bottles in April. Wal-Mart,

Getty Images/Scott Olson

A sign warns that dangerous industrial chemicals were dumped in a lake near Gary, Ind. In 1979 the Environmental Protection Agency banned production of polychlorinated biphenyls (PCBs), which cause cancer and birth defects in laboratory animals, and set timetables for phasing out their use in various industries.

Target, REI, Costco and other large companies pulled products containing BPA from their shelves or found substitutes. Many of these stores now sell hard plastic water bottles made with Tritan copolyester, prominently marked as BPA-free.

"They're selling fantastically," says Carolyn Beem, public affairs manager for L.L. Bean, the Maine outdoor retailer. "We're not experts in science, but we are experts in listening and responding to our customers. With all of the reports out there, it seemed like a good time to start again." In March 2008 Eastman expanded Tritan production to keep up with demand.[5]

In addition to BPA, environmentalists and consumer advocates warn that many other materials in commercial products may be harmful to human health, including:

- polyvinyl chloride (PVC) plastic, used in items such as shower curtains and water pipes;
- phthalates, a group of chemicals used to make plastics soft and pliable; and
- polybrominated diphenyl-ethers (PBDEs), chemicals added to foams and fabrics as flame retardants.

In addition, some consumer goods contain materials widely known to be toxic, such as lead in popular brands of lipstick.[6]

"Consumers assume when they buy a product that someone has vetted it to make sure it's safe, but that doesn't always happen," says Sarah Janssen, a physician and environmental health expert at the Natural Resources Defense Council (NRDC), an advocacy group. "They're at a disadvantage because most of the important information isn't even on the label."

Humans are exposed to many potentially harmful substances in their daily lives, from air and water pollutants to household contaminants like mold and dust. Over time some of these exposures may cause cancer or other serious problems, such as birth defects or organ damage. Some of these illnesses result from lifestyle choices: for example, smoking, inactivity and obesity are major causes of cancer in the United States.[7] But workers and consumers also can be exposed unknowingly to risky materials that are legally used in commercial products.

Human exposure to toxic chemicals is controlled by several different agencies, depending on how the chemical is used and where people come in contact with it. The Environmental Protection Agency (EPA) regulates industrial chemicals and pesticides, while the FDA controls food additives, drugs and cosmetics and the Consumer Product Safety Commission (CPSC) oversees thousands of other consumer goods, from personal care products to toys. Workplace exposure to chemicals is regulated by the Occupational Safety and Health Administration (OSHA). Some materials must be tested for toxicity before marketing, but in other cases manufacturers merely have to notify regulators that they are going to start producing them.

Many experts think federal policy should be more consistent. "The agencies have very different approaches because they are covered by laws that find wildly varying levels of risk acceptable," says David Michaels, a professor of environmental and occupational health at George

Washington University and a former assistant secretary of Energy. "We should be thinking about ways to harmonize standards across these agencies, because their actions affect each other. They allow different levels of exposure for many of the same chemicals."

Chemical manufacturers say the Toxic Substances Control Act (TSCA) — the core law that regulates industrial chemicals — is working. "TSCA has protected human health and the environment," says Michael Walls, managing director for regulatory and technical affairs at the American Chemistry Council (ACC), a chemical industry trade group. "There are areas where we can reform it, and we're encouraged that proposals have been offered to amend the law, not to replace it." The chemical industry is working with EPA to make more data available on hazards from widely used chemicals and assess how chemical exposures affect children's health.

Many critics worry that it is too easy for new materials to enter commerce before their effects have been well studied. They are especially concerned about the growing field of nano-technology, which uses microscopic particles to enhance products ranging from sunscreen to medications. Reducing materials to the nano scale makes it easier to apply them precisely: for example, chemotherapy drugs can be targeted directly at tumors. But materials acquire new properties at this scale, and scientists are still analyzing the toxicity of many nanomaterials.

"Nanotechnology is taking our understanding of what makes something harmful and how we deal with that, and turning it upside down," said Andrew Maynard, chief science advisor to the Project on Emerging Nanotechnologies, in April 2008 congressional testimony. "New, engineered nanomaterials are prized for their unconventional properties. But these same properties may also lead to new ways of causing harm to people and the environment."[8]

Concerns Linger Over Exposure to Bisphenol A

Scientists say they have "negligible concern" to "some concern" about the health effects of exposure to bisphenol A, a chemical commonly used in the production of plastics.

The National Toxicology Program uses the following five-level scale of concern for adverse effects from exposure to BPA:

- Serious concern
- Concern
- Developmental toxicity for fetuses, infants and children (effects on the brain, behavior and prostate gland) — Some concern
- Developmental toxicity for fetuses, infants and children (effects on the mammary gland and early puberty in females, and reproductive toxicity in workers) — Minimal concern
- Reproductive toxicity in adult men and women and malformations in newborns — Negligible concern

How to Reduce Your Exposure to Bisphenol A:

Don't microwave polycarbonate plastic food containers. Bisphenol A may break down from repeated use at high temperatures.

Avoid plastic containers with the number 7 on the bottom. (www.recyclenow.org/r_plastics.html)

Don't wash polycarbonate plastic containers in the dishwasher with harsh detergents.

Reduce your use of canned foods.

When possible, opt for glass, porcelain or stainless steel containers, especially for hot foods or liquids.

Use infant formula bottles and toys that are bisphenol A-free.

Source: National Toxicology Program

In 2007 the European Union (EU) launched a new system for regulating chemicals that differs markedly from the U.S. approach. Under the REACH (Registration, Evaluation, Authorization and Restriction of Chemicals) policy, companies that produce or import chemicals in large volumes have to register their products with the EU and provide data on their properties and uses. Chemicals must be shown to be safe before they can enter commerce. U.S. companies doing business in Europe have to comply with the directive.[9] (*See sidebar, p. 218.*)

REACH is based on the so-called precautionary principle, which can be traced back through history but was articulated as a basis for environmental regulation at an international conference in 1998: "When an activity raises threats of harm to the environment or human health, precautionary measures should be taken even if some cause-and-effect relationships are not fully established scientifically."[10]

In contrast, many U.S. laws require regulators to produce scientific evidence that a substance is harmful before it can be removed from the market. Environmental and health advocates want the United States to adopt a more precautionary approach to regulation. But critics say the precautionary principle is too vague to be a viable basis for regulation and fails to balance risks and benefits. (*See "At Issue," p. 220.*)

For example, EPA banned use of the insecticide DDT in the U.S. in 1972 because it harmed the environment, but in 2006 the World Health Organization endorsed DDT for controlling mosquito-borne malaria in developing countries.[11] Some environmental groups want DDT banned worldwide, along with other persistent organic pollutants, but other advocates — including health experts — say it should remain in use until safer alternatives are developed.[12]

As Congress, regulators, businesses and advocates debate how to protect consumers from harmful exposures, here are some issues they are considering:

Do we know enough about chemical risks?

Chemicals are central to the economy and to many products that Americans associate with modern living. They underpin a $637 billion industry in the United States and generated over $135 billion in export revenues as of 2006.[13] Innovations in chemistry have contributed to technical advances such as composite materials for vehicles, stronger adhesives, faster microprocessors for computers and recyclable plastics.

Core responsibility for regulating the massive chemical industry falls to the EPA, which is authorized under the Toxic Substances Control Act of 1976 (TSCA) to collect information about industrial chemicals from manufacturers and to limit or ban those that pose unreasonable risks.[14] Today EPA has some 82,000 chemicals in its TSCA inventory, of which about 62,000 were already in use when the law was passed. On average, more than 700 new chemicals are introduced each year.[15]

Although TSCA gives EPA the power to review chemicals already in commerce, the testing burden falls mainly on the agency rather than on manufacturers. As a result, EPA has required testing for fewer than 200 of the 62,000 chemicals that were in commerce in the 1970s. TSCA also requires the agency to show substantial evidence that a substance already in use poses an unreasonable risk in order to limit its use. EPA has banned only five chemicals or classes of chemicals under TSCA, and one of these efforts was overruled by a federal court in 1991.[16]

For new chemicals, manufacturers have to notify EPA before they start production and provide information on production volumes, expected uses and any test data that they have. However, most companies do not voluntarily test their products. Instead of testing new chemicals directly, EPA uses scientific models to compare their properties to similar existing chemicals and identify potential hazards. According to the Government Accountability Office (GAO), these reviews have led to actions that reduced risks from over 3,600 new chemicals.[17]

Critics say that the U.S. needs a broader and more proactive policy for regulating chemicals. "Our approach is barbaric and out of date. We used to be the leader decades ago, but now we're behind," says Lois Gibbs, founder and director of the Center for Health, Environment & Justice. In the late 1970s Gibbs organized homeowners in Niagara Falls, N.Y., after learning that their neighborhood had been built on top of a leaking toxic waste dump called Love Canal; after two years, the federal government relocated the families.

"The U.S. is much more science-bound than other countries. There's a presumption that we understand all of the harmful interactions from exposure to toxics, but we don't," Gibbs argues. "Industry doesn't want anything changed until there's proof beyond the shadow of a doubt that it will cause harm, but we're just not that smart."

Manufacturers say that the U.S. regulatory system is fundamentally sound. "TSCA gives EPA broad authority to collect information, order testing, prohibit new uses of a substance and label or ban substances," says Walls at the American Chemistry Council. "We can enhance it to promote more systematic review and give the public more information about what chemicals are being produced." Under a program called the High Production Volume (HPV) Challenge, launched in 1998, chemical companies are voluntarily testing about 2,800 chemicals that are produced or imported in quantities of at least 1 million pounds per year and providing the information to EPA. About 1,400 data sets have been completed to date.

But GAO, while calling the HPV Challenge "laudable," has concluded that TSCA makes it too expensive and time-consuming for EPA to review chemical hazards.[18] In order to force companies to do testing EPA has to issue a regulation, a process that can take several years. "Given the difficulties involved in requiring testing, EPA officials do not believe that TSCA provides an effective means for testing a large number of existing chemicals," GAO reported in 2006. As a solution, it recommended empowering EPA to require companies to do chemical testing and provide the data to regulators.

Both EPA and FDA also need better testing methods in order to regulate toxic substances effectively. Scientists agree that current approaches, which rely heavily on animal testing, are too slow and expensive to cover hundreds of new chemicals each year and are not well-suited to predict harm from very low doses. "We need to bring our methodologies into the 21st century by making them less animal-intensive and getting higher throughputs," or testing many substances quickly, says John Bucher, associate director of the federally funded National Toxicology Program (NTP), which studies the impact of chemicals on human health.

Current test methods typically give rats or mice large doses of chemicals, look for end points like cancer or organ damage and then extrapolate those responses from animals to humans — a complex and often controversial process. A 2007 report by the National Research Council called for a new approach focused on "toxicity pathways" — changes that occur in networks of cells due to chemical exposure and which eventually may lead to adverse health

Getty Images/China Photos

Scientists agree that animal testing is generally too slow and expensive to cover hundreds of new chemicals each year and is not well-suited to predict harm from very low doses. The National Research Council has called for testing chemicals in cell cultures, a shift it predicted would greatly reduce the need for animal testing.

effects. For example, exposure might initially cause hormone levels to change or tissues to become inflamed. The study recommended developing rapid systems for testing chemicals in cell cultures to identify toxicity pathways — a shift that it predicted would greatly reduce the need for animal testing and focus more attention on human biology and exposures.[19]

The NTP shares this vision, says Bucher. "These would be short-term assays [tests] with very simple readouts that could be run 24/7 just by punching buttons and would give a signature of biological interactions that a particular chemical would have," he says. "We hope that certain structures will be related to particular chemical classes and that that will let us make judgments about which chemicals should go through more sophisticated studies or should not be authorized for significant human exposures."

Are we commercializing nanotechnologies too quickly?

Many nanoscale materials (particles as small as 1/100,000th of the width of a human hair) have unique chemical, physical or biological characteristics that are different from larger particles of the same materials. Because they have distinctive properties such as high electrical conductivity, nanomaterials have special uses and are showing up in hundreds of consumer products, from kitchenware with anti-bacterial silver coatings to paints impregnated with silica particles that repel graffiti.

Consumer advocates worry that some of these applications could pose health risks, and that government agencies do not know enough about nanomaterials to regulate them effectively. An EPA fact sheet states the challenge bluntly: "At this early stage of the development of nanotechnology, there are few detailed studies on the effects of nanoscale materials in the body or the environment . . . it is not yet possible to make broad conclusions about which nanoscale substances may pose risks."[20]

Twenty-six federal agencies, including EPA, FDA and the CPSC, participate in the National Nanotechnology Initiative, a federal program that supports research on promising applications of nanotechnology and on environmental health and safety (EHS) issues. From fiscal 2005 through 2008, these agencies spent an estimated $180 million on research to address EHS questions.[21]

But keeping up with this fast-growing field is challenging for regulators. "I do not pretend to understand nanotechnology, and our agency does not pretend to have a grasp on this complicated subject either," CPSC Commissioner Thomas H. Moore told a Senate subcommittee in March 2007. "For fiscal year 2007, we were only able to devote $20,000 in funds to do a literature review on nanotechnology. Other agencies are asking for, and getting, millions of dollars for research in this area."[22]

Four months later an FDA task force report on regulating nanomaterials pointed out that because of their unique properties, the agency might need new testing equipment and methods to predict how they will react in body tissues.[23] Other agencies studying nanotechnologies confirm they often behave in surprising ways. "It is a daily occurrence in our labs that one of our standard assays doesn't work because of the unusual properties of these nanomaterials," said Scott E. McNeil, director of the National Cancer Institute's Nanotechnology Characterization Laboratory, at a conference last March.[24]

Some watchdog groups want to stop the marketing of nanoproducts until they are proven safe. Last May a coalition of health, environmental, and consumer groups petitioned EPA to control products containing nano-silver, which is highly effective at killing bacteria, fungi and other microorganisms. Because of this property, nano-silver has been added to garments (to kill odor), food storage containers, soaps, air purifiers and dozens of other products.

The petitioners argued that nano-silver in the environment could kill plants, benign microbes, fish and other aquatic species and might also threaten human health. They called on EPA to regulate the material as a pesticide and require comprehensive safety testing before any products containing it could be marketed.[25]

At a minimum, critics say, manufacturers should be required to label products containing nanoparticles so that consumers can choose whether or not to buy them. A study by Consumers Union found that four out of five sunscreens that claimed to be nano-free actually contained nanoparticles of titanium dioxide and/or zinc oxide, two compounds that help protect against ultraviolet radiation.[26]

"Size matters. Materials at the nanoscale should be considered new particles and have to go through new safety assessments," says Michael Hansen, senior staff scientist at Consumers Union. "Right now, it's assumed that if a material has been tested for bulk applications, it's safe. But when you reduce things to such small sizes, their behavior and surface area can change drastically. You can't assume that something safe at the macro scale is safe at the nano scale."

Some experts say that health concerns may be exaggerated. "When we started looking at them, we found that the properties of nanomaterials in products, such as particle size, often were different from what manufacturers said they were. People didn't always know what they were studying," says the NTP's Bucher. "We completely characterized the materials we were working with and then administered them to animals in ways that might mimic human exposures. Our studies suggest that some risks are lower than reports in the literature have suggested."

For example, according to Bucher, many reports predicted that titanium dioxide in sunscreen would penetrate skin readily, but the NTP concluded that won't happen unless the skin is cut or scraped. However, he cautions, this does not prove that all nanomaterials are harmless. "Every product is going to be different," he says.

Even if many nanomaterials are harmless, weak and underfunded regulatory agencies may have trouble distinguishing benign products from risky ones. Marla Felcher, an expert on marketing and consumer issues at Harvard University's Kennedy School of Government, says the Consumer Product Safety Commission is unprepared for the challenge. "CPSC is playing catch-up," she says. "More than half of the nanotechnology goods on the market come under its jurisdiction, and the funding it has to work with is a drop in the bucket."

But Felcher says the CPSC needs more than additional staffing and funding to ensure that nanomaterials in consumer products are safe. It also needs new authority to make manufacturers identify products that contain these substances and to impose mandatory safety standards for products based on new technologies, she says. (Today the agency relies on industry to develop and comply with voluntary safety standards).[27]

Hansen is hopeful the EPA will regulate nano-silver as a pesticide, but he says the FDA has so far refused to agree that nanomaterials are categorically different from their conventional counterparts. "The biggest exposures come from items that you put on or in your body and that contain free [non-bound] nanoparticles, like food ingredients and personal care products," says Hansen. "Scientific studies are saying that these materials need to be regulated."

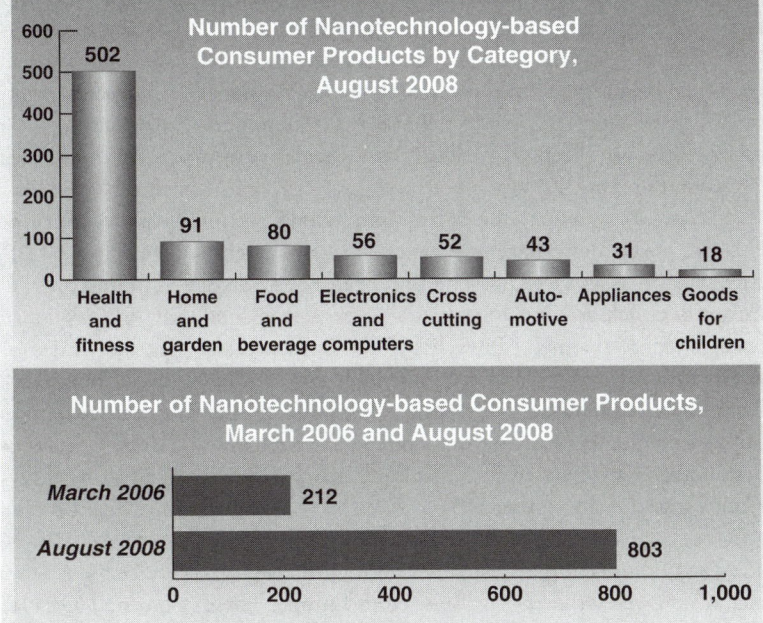

Use of Nanotechnology Is Increasing

More than 800 consumer products containing nanomaterials were in the marketplace as of August 2008 — nearly quadruple the amount from just two years earlier. Some 60 percent of the products were related to health and fitness.

Number of Nanotechnology-based Consumer Products by Category, August 2008

Category	Number
Health and fitness	502
Home and garden	91
Food and beverage	80
Electronics and computers	56
Cross cutting	52
Automotive	43
Appliances	31
Goods for children	18

Number of Nanotechnology-based Consumer Products, March 2006 and August 2008

	Number
March 2006	212
August 2008	803

Source: The Project on Emerging Nanotechnologies, Woodrow Wilson International Center for Scholars

Would stricter regulations hurt manufacturers and consumers?

Regulating chemicals in consumer products more stringently would affect chemical companies and manufacturers that use those chemicals to make retail goods. Chemical toxicity testing is expensive, and many business leaders say that substitutes for widely used materials like BPA will be more expensive and could produce inferior products. Health, environmental and consumer groups respond that safer products don't always cost much more, and in any case are worth a cost premium.

Even if a chemical poses risks, only some uses may require substitutes. "Health and safety concerns about a chemical like BPA are dictated as much by how it's used as by its chemistry. I'm more concerned about using it in baby bottles than in auto parts or compact discs," says

Terry Collins, a professor of chemistry and director of the Institute for Green Science at Carnegie Mellon University.

Industry representatives say the risks of BPA have been widely studied and that removing it from food containers, as many critics urge, will be difficult. "BPA has been part of epoxy resin can linings for more than 50 years, and that's why we have canned goods with long shelf lives," says Steven Hentges, executive director of the American Chemistry Council's Polycarbonate/ BPA Global Group. These linings prevent metallic flavors from migrating into food and keep acidic foods like tomatoes from corroding the cans.

"Substitutes have to be safer than what's being replaced, and no alternatives have been as thoroughly tested as BPA" says Hentges. The European Food Safety Authority concluded last July that BPA was safe in food packages. Canada banned BPA in baby bottles as a precautionary measure and declared it a toxic substance, but has not removed the material from food packaging for adults. Canadian regulators are funding studies to see whether further steps are needed to limit how much BPA is released into the environment.[28]

But other options exist. Many Americans buy juices, soups, sauces and chopped tomatoes in brick-shaped cartons, which were originally introduced in Europe. These containers, which are about 75 percent paper, 20 percent polyethylene plastic and 5 percent aluminum, typically cost more than canned goods, but foods packaged this way retain more color and flavor than canned foods because the food and the container are sterilized separately. The boxes can be recycled with milk and juice cartons.[29]

"There also are ways to can food so that it doesn't contain such high levels of BPA," says Janssen at the Natural Resources Defense Council. "Japan set voluntary standards for reducing BPA use in canned food, and now a lot of Japanese canned goods have a polyethylene layer inside that seals the epoxy resin lining so that BPA doesn't migrate into food. Industry should be thinking about more sustainable techniques instead of fighting to maintain the status quo."

Chemical companies and consumer advocates are also debating risks associated with phthalates, especially in children's toys. In 1998 a coalition of environmental and consumer groups petitioned the CPSC to ban toys that contained phthalates and were designed for children under age 6, citing studies suggesting that these materials could be toxic and the fact that young children commonly chewed on soft plastic toys. An expert panel convened by the commission found some risk from the phthalate DINP and asked toy makers to remove phthalates from toys voluntarily. According to the American Chemistry Council most companies removed phthalates from teethers, rattlers and pacifiers.[30]

The European Union also studied phthalates and imposed a temporary ban on six forms of the chemicals in toys and teething items in 1999. In 2005 it made the ban permanent, requiring manufacturers to eliminate three phthalates (DEHP, DBP and BBP) from all toys and to remove three others (DINP, DIDP and DNOP) from toys and child-care items that could be mouthed by children.[31]

EU regulators acted in response to studies that suggested, but did not prove, that exposure to phthalates could have toxic effects or cause abnormal reproductive development, especially in boys. A 2005 study in the United States reached a similar conclusion, but a U.S. government review panel found that animal studies that showed a connection were not necessarily applicable to people.[32] However, California, Washington and Vermont passed state-level bans. In 2008 Congress permanently banned DEHP, DBP and BBP from toys and set an interim ban on the other three types pending a safety review by the CPSC.[33]

Many businesses opposed the measure. "[M]anufacturers would be forced to use more expensive alternatives that may subject them to additional safety and legal liability concerns, and consumers would be exposed to products containing alternatives that have not been approved for use in children's products by any federal agency," the U.S. Chamber of Commerce wrote to Senate members early in 2008.[34]

Chemical industry representatives maintain that scientific evidence shows phthalates to be safe. "The pro-regulatory side considers phthalates guilty until proven innocent. They want to act even though the data is not conclusive," says Allen Blakey, vice president of the Vinyl Institute, a trade group for companies that manufacture vinyl and vinyl products (many of which contain phthalates to make them soft and flexible).

But toy manufacturers seem to be adapting to phthalate restrictions. Observers predicted the U.S. ban could drive some of China's small and uncompetitive toy manufacturers out of business, but other Chinese companies already make toys with phthalates for U.S. markets and without them for sale in the EU.[35] BASF, a major German chemical company, still produces DEHP in the United States but developed a new plasticized version called Hexamoll DINCH, which it markets to toy makers as a product "whose health safety is beyond all question" and "an ideal solution to adapting their products to the requirements of the new EU regulation."[36]

BACKGROUND

Reactive Regulation

Through the 19th century, as the United States grew from a nation of small-scale farmers into an industrial powerhouse, few standards protected people from hazardous materials. And even when government began to regulate dangerous products and substances in the early 20th century, controls were almost always put in place belatedly after scandals or disasters.

Muckraking journalist Upton Sinclair spurred passage of early consumer-protection laws with his 1906 novel *The Jungle*, which described filthy conditions in Chicago's meatpacking industry. Simultaneously, a series of articles in *Collier's* magazine spotlighted false claims and unsafe ingredients in so-called patent (non-prescription) medicines. Many of these concoctions were sold as cure-alls for numerous diseases but contained addictive substances like cocaine, heroin or alcohol. "[F]raud, exploited by the skillfulest [sic] of advertising bunco men, is the basis of the trade," author Samuel Hopkins Adams charged.[37]

In response Congress passed the Meatpacking Act and the first Food and Drug Act, which authorized government regulators to inspect meat processing plants and to seize products that were mislabeled or contained harmful or spoiled ingredients. However, manufacturers were not required to list all of the ingredients in foods or medicines or submit any information to the government before marketing them.

In 1933 the Food and Drug Administration proposed a complete revision of the Food and Drug Act, but Congress failed to act until 107 people in 15 states died in 1937 after taking elixir of sulfanilamide for strep infections.

A chemist had created a liquid form of sulfanilamide, a new and effective prescription medicine, by dissolving the powdered medication in diethylene glycol, a chemical normally used as antifreeze, which he failed to realize was poisonous.[38] This tragedy spurred passage of the Federal Food, Drug, and Cosmetic Act, which required new drugs to be tested for safety before marketing.

As Congress debated safety standards, the fast-growing chemical industry was inventing myriad new materials. Important chemical products developed in the 1920s and '30s included polychlorinated biphenyls (PCBs), used as coolants and lubricants; synthetic estrogens (female hormones); and organic pesticides like the mosquito-killer DDT. Nineteenth-century inventors had already discovered many basic types of plastic, and by World War II these materials were widely used in applications including cellophane, vinyl, nylon and Teflon coatings.

During this period the labor movement gained strength as workers formed unions and won the right to collective bargaining. One of their priorities was making workplaces safer. Government agencies started to regulate safety, initially focusing on industries like mining and manufacturing, where workers were frequently injured by machinery, fires and explosions. Toxic exposure was also emerging as a serious hazard. For example, by the 1930s manufacturers knew that workers who inhaled silica dust or asbestos had high rates of lung disease, and medical researchers were starting to connect asbestos inhalation with cancer.

Under President Franklin D. Roosevelt (1933-1945), the Labor Department worked with industry and unions to improve workplace safety, mainly through voluntary safety codes and better training programs. During the economic boom of the 1950s occupational safety became a more established professional field, but it focused on traumatic injuries such as falls or machine accidents rather than exposure to dangerous materials. In one industrial hygienist's words, it was hard to draw attention to safety issues "unless people saw the blood drip."[39]

New Guardians

As corporations shifted from wartime manufacturing to civilian products, new materials streamed into commercial use, including vaccines, food additives, pesticides and herbicides and an avalanche of consumer goods. Most Americans welcomed these products, but research soon showed that some were unsafe.

By the late 1950s government regulators had banned more than a dozen food additives because they caused cancer, organ damage or other toxic effects in animals. [40] In 1958 Congress adopted the Delaney Clause, which barred all food additives that had been shown to cause cancer in laboratory animals. Six years later Surgeon General Luther Terry released a report stating that smoking caused cancer, and Congress passed a law requiring cigarette packs to carry health warning labels.[41] However, the tobacco industry — which had created its own scientific arm, the Tobacco Industry Research Committee, to refute incriminating studies — argued that smoking was a personal choice, and successfully lobbied against any limits on cigarette advertising or marketing.

By this time other toxic exposures were in the news. Rachel Carson's 1962 bestseller *Silent Spring* warned that persistent organic pesticides like DDT were accumulating in the environment, harming fish and birds and contaminating food supplies. In the same year it was disclosed that thousands of babies in Asia, Africa and Europe had been born with deformed or missing limbs after their mothers took thalidomide, a new sedative that the FDA was then close to approving for sale in the United States.

In 1965 consumer activist Ralph Nader amplified pressure on the government to regulate dangerous products with his book *Unsafe at Any Speed*, which attacked U.S. automakers for refusing to include safety devices like seat belts and filling cars with confusing and distracting features.[42] The book and subsequent congressional hearings generated new safety requirements and oversight agencies for passenger cars.

The Nixon administration created other agencies to regulate industry more tightly and protect consumers, including the Environmental Protection Agency (EPA) in 1970, the Occupational Safety and Health Administration (OSHA) in 1971 and the Consumer Product Safety Commission (CPSC) in 1972. Along with the FDA, each of the new agencies had some responsibility for protecting workers and the public from toxic threats, although the scope of their powers varied.

During the 1970s federal regulators passed some important protective measures. EPA banned DDT use in 1972 because of its harmful environmental impacts. In 1979 the agency banned production of PCBs, which had been shown to cause cancer and birth defects in laboratory animals, and set timetables for phasing out their use in various industries. In 1977 the CPSC banned lead paint and its use on toys and furniture. OSHA set occupational exposure standards for many hazardous substances and developed requirements (finalized in the early 1980s) for businesses to identify and label hazardous chemicals in the workplace and tell employees how to use them safely.

Business Pushes Back

Many controls adopted in the 1970s made the environment cleaner and improved public health. But industry and conservative politicians argued that government regulators were becoming high-handed and that excessive regulations slowed economic growth. President Ronald Reagan (1981-1989) made reducing government's power a centerpiece of his administration, cutting budgets at EPA, OSHA and CPSC and appointing officials who were hostile to regulation.

Reagan also required the White House Office of Management and Budget to review proposed new rules — a policy that his successors continued — and signed an executive order directing agencies not to issue new ones unless their potential benefits to society were greater than their costs.[43] Many policy experts agreed that cost-benefit analysis was a useful tool for setting priorities, but others worried that health and environmental benefits were hard to quantify and would be undervalued.

Critics charged the Reagan administration with leading a "retreat from safety." "The agencies no longer respond to the needs of unorganized victims of technological hazards. Instead, they service the business executives and stockholders who are responsible for the hazards," wrote Joan Claybrook, president of the Nader-founded activist group Public Citizen and former head of the National Highway Traffic Safety Administration, in 1984.[44]

In this climate some of the most significant new steps were so-called right-to-know policies, which did not limit the use of risky materials but gave people more information about potential exposures. After methyl isocyanate, a deadly industrial gas, leaked from a chemical plant in Bhopal, India, in 1984 (killing some 4,000 people) and a plant in West Virginia the next year (with no deaths), Congress passed the Emergency Planning and Community Right to Know Act in 1986. The law required companies to tell EPA and state officials what hazardous chemicals were used in significant quantities at their plants and to notify emergency responders about any chemical releases.

CHRONOLOGY

1900-1960 *Government begins regulating consumer goods to protect buyers; fast-growing chemical industry produces thousands of materials that are quickly put to use.*

1906 Congress authorizes federal inspections of meatpacking plants and outlaws adulterated or mislabeled foods and drugs.

1929 Chemical companies start making polychlorinated biphenyls (PCBs).

1930 Food and Drug Administration (FDA) is established . . . . Studies show asbestos can cause cancer.

1938 After tainted medicine kills 105 people, Congress passes Food, Drug and Cosmetic Act, requiring food additives and drugs to be proven safe. . . . British scientists produce diethylstilbestrol (DES), a synthetic estrogen, which is approved to treat gynecological ailments.

1939 Swiss chemist Paul Müller discovers that the synthetic chemical DDT is an effective insect killer. Müller later wins Nobel Prize after DDT-B is widely used to protect troops from typhus and malaria during World War II.

1954 Cigarette manufacturers create Tobacco Industry Research Council in response to scientific findings of health threats from smoking.

1958 Delaney Clause to Food, Drug and Cosmetic Act bans food additives that cause cancer in animals.

1960-1980 *New agencies protect consumers and workers from hazardous substances. Studies find popular chemicals can harm health.*

1962 Rachel Carson's bestseller *Silent Spring* warns of environmental and health threats from DDT.

1964 Surgeon general declares smoking hazardous to health; warning labels are required on cigarettes.

1970 Environmental Protection Agency (EPA) is created.

1971 Occupational Safety and Health Administration (OSHA) is established. . . . DES is linked to vaginal cancer.

1972 Consumer Product Safety Commission (CPSC) is established. . . . EPA bans DDT.

1976 Toxic Substances Control Act (TSCA) authorizes EPA to regulate chemicals but exempts 62,000 substances.

1977 CPSC bans nearly all uses of lead paint, including on toys.

1980-2000 *Anti-regulatory forces challenge new, protective standards.*

1980 Supreme Court's "benzene decision" says OSHA must show significant risks before limiting a chemical's use.

1983 OSHA requires employers to show workers how to use toxic chemicals.

1986 California mandates warning labels for products with chemicals that cause cancer or birth defects.

1990 Congress requires leaded gasoline to be phased out by 1996.

1996 Food Quality Protection Act tightens standard for pesticide residues in food and requires special protection for infants and children.

1997 Study finds bisphenol A (BPA) alters reproductive development in mice.

2000-Present *Support grows for natural and organic products.*

2000 National Nanotechnology Initiative is launched.

2003 Congress approves $3.7 billion over four years for nanotech research, but only a small amount is earmarked for studying health impacts.

2007 European Union's REACH chemical regulation enters into force.

2008 Congress strengthens CPSC and bans lead and six phthalates from children's toys. . . . Canada bans BPA from baby bottles. . . . FDA committee concludes BPA is not harmful in food packaging, but the agency's review panel faults the study's methods.

Americans' Bodies Contain Over 100 Chemicals

Some Cause Cancer and Other Health Problems.

Studies indicate that all human beings alive today carry traces of many industrial chemicals in their bodies. Some of these substances enter during fetal development or infanthood, carried by maternal blood and breast milk. In addition, we inhale airborne pollutants, ingest pesticide residues and chemical additives with our food and drinking water and absorb others through our skin. Exposure can happen in the workplace, outdoors or inside homes and schools.

Some so-called "chemical body burdens" in humans are harmless, but others can cause cancer, birth defects, developmental problems and other serious health impacts. Many are still being studied. The presence of a chemical in the body does not necessarily mean it will cause harm, but scientists say chemical exposure is pervasive in modern society, and they underscore the importance of testing widely used chemicals for toxic effects.

"I find it remarkable that in this day and age one of the primary ways by which the toxic effects of chemicals are discovered is still the 'body in the morgue' method," writes epidemiologist and former Assistant Secretary of Energy David Michaels. "An industrial worker dies from some very unusual condition, and we ask why. Well, some of us ask."

For example, Michaels notes, chemical companies that make diacetyl (the main ingredient in artificial butter flavor) did not know that breathing the compound could cause lung damage until workers in popcorn factories became ill. Manufacturers had been required to test diacetyl as a food ingredient, but not as an airborne contaminant in the workplace.[1]

According to a 2005 report from the Centers for Disease Control and Prevention (CDC), well over 100 chemicals are present in Americans at detectable levels, including heavy metals like cadmium and mercury, phthalates and many pesticides. Levels of some chemicals have fallen in recent years, notably lead (which has been banned from gasoline and house paint) and substances found in second-hand cigarette smoke.[2]

Others are more worrisome. For example, the CDC found that almost 6 percent of women of childbearing age had blood levels of mercury that were borderline dangerous. Mercury is a potent neurotoxin that can cause birth defects, nervous system damage and other harmful effects. It is emitted into the air from sources including coal-burning power plants and incinerators, then falls back to the surface and concentrates in the food chain. Humans are exposed mainly by eating fish that contain high amounts of mercury.

Another major step in 1986 was the passage in California of Proposition 65, a ballot initiative that directed the state to publish an annual list of chemicals used in California that were known to cause cancer, birth defects or other reproductive harms. Businesses had to warn people before exposing them to significant risks from listed chemicals — for example, by putting warning labels on processed food or signs in workplaces where listed substances were used.[45]

The Clinton administration (1993-2001) was more receptive to new health and safety regulations than its predecessors. FDA Commissioner David Kessler declared cigarettes to be "drug delivery devices," an acknowledgment that nicotine was addictive, and called for limiting marketing and sales to young people. In 1996 Clinton signed the Food Quality Protection Act, which tightened standards for pesticide residues in foods and required EPA to consider children's higher sensitivity to these chemicals when it set tolerance levels.

In 1998 the administration called for chemical companies to perform voluntary toxicity testing on chemicals in use that had not been tested — and threatened to require it if industry did not comply. Subsequently the EPA, the chemical industry and the advocacy group Environmental Defense announced the High Production Volume (HPV) Challenge, which aimed to complete toxicity testing by 2004 on about 2,800 industrial chemicals made or imported into the U.S. in large quantities.

Along with cancer and birth defects, Americans started to hear in the 1990s about so-called endocrine disruptors — chemicals that interfered with hormones responsible for regulating biological processes throughout the body, such as brain growth and sexual development. Scientists were finding evidence that endocrine disruptors were causing reproductive abnormalities, population declines and other negative impacts in

Another 2005 study commissioned by two advocacy organizations, Commonweal and the Environmental Working Group, tested umbilical cord blood from 10 babies born in U.S. hospitals during the previous year. Researchers found an average of 200 industrial chemicals and pollutants in the samples, including mercury, environmental pollutants known as dioxins and pesticides. This study showed that pollutants cross the placenta from mother to fetus as infants grow in utero, exposing the gestating infants to a complex mixture of chemicals during critical months of development.[3]

Living far from industrial sources does not necessarily make people safer from exposures. Indigenous peoples in the Arctic have some of the highest body concentrations of mercury, PCBs and other pollutants of any region on the planet, thanks to global wind patterns and ocean currents that carry pollutants to the poles. Inuit, Aleut, and other native people in Greenland, Alaska and Canada eat large quantities of locally caught meat and fish, which contain high concentrations of chemicals.[4]

Recent studies show that concentrations of some toxins in Arctic food animals are stabilizing, thanks to international agreements limiting use of some of the most hazardous chemicals.[5] However, toxic chemicals remain a major threat to Arctic indigenous peoples' traditional way of life — an ironic fate for people who neither produce nor use most of these products.

An Inuit woman in Iqaluit, Nunavut, Canada, dries a caribou skin. Toxic chemicals remain a major threat to traditional ways of life in the Arctic.

---

[1] David Michaels, *Doubt Is Their Product: How Industry's Assault on Science Threatens Your Health* (Oxford University Press, 2008), p. 247.

[2] "Third National Report on Human Exposure to Environmental Chemicals," 2005, www.cdc.gov/exposurereport/report.htm, and "Spotlight on Mercury," both Centers for Disease Control and Prevention, www.cdc.gov/ExposureReport/pdf/factsheet_mercury.pdf.

[3] "Body Burden — The Pollution in Newborns," *Environmental Working Group*, July 14, 2005, http://archive.ewg.org/reports/bodyburden2/contentindex.php.

[4] Marla Cone, *Silent Snow: The Slow Poisoning of the Arctic* (2006).

[5] "Toxic Chemical Levels Finally Dropping in Arctic Food Animals, New Study Shows," The Canadian Press news agency, July 14, 2008.

---

wildlife. Some studies linked pesticides that mimicked estrogen, the female sex hormone, with increased risk of breast cancer.

Other researchers were alarmed by falling human sperm counts. "Every man sitting in this room today is half the man his grandfather was," University of Florida zoologist Louis Guillette told a Senate committee in 1993. "Are our children going to be half the men we are?" Three years later, the best-selling book *Our Stolen Future* argued that endocrine disruptors posed pervasive health risks but that federal controls on toxic chemicals were overly focused on detecting and controlling cancer risks. "The assumptions about toxicity and disease that have framed our thinking for the past three decades are inappropriate and act as obstacles to understanding a different kind of damage," the authors contended.[46]

New Worries

Under President George W. Bush (2001-2009), momentum once again swung from strong regulation to voluntary compliance strategies in which companies agreed to police themselves. With pro-business officials in charge at many regulatory agencies and limited budgets, the pace of federal regulation dropped sharply. Rulemaking fell by more than 50 percent at FDA and 57 percent at EPA between 2001 and 2008 compared with those agencies' records during the Clinton administration. OSHA withdrew more than a dozen regulations that had been proposed under Clinton and delayed taking action on silica dust after identifying it as a workplace health threat.[47]

Conservative advocates generally supported the shift to deregulation, arguing that excessive health and safety regulations were burdens on the economy and often were not the most effective way to protect public health or the environment. "Regulations unquestionably force the issue, but usually at a

The Polluted Arctic

Atmospheric and ocean currents carry persistent organic pollutants around the world far from their sources and concentrate them in some regions, notably the Arctic, where they are a threat to indigenous peoples and wildlife. Even relatively "clean" air from non-industrial areas contains low levels of pesticides and other chemicals.

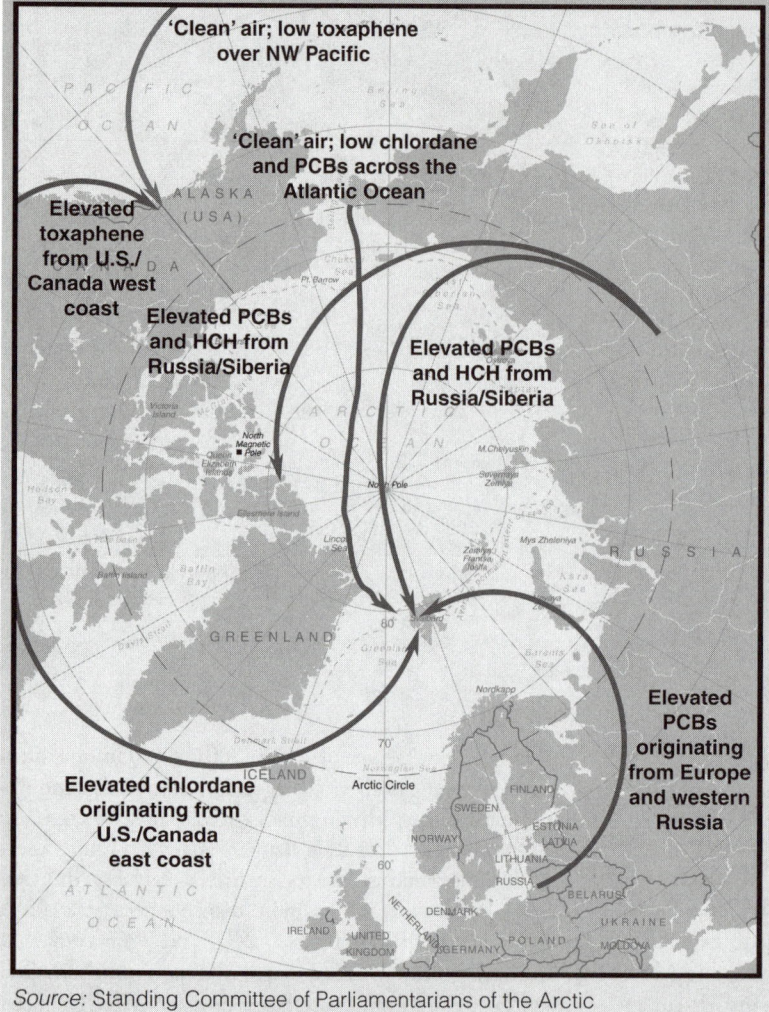

Source: Standing Committee of Parliamentarians of the Arctic

At the same time, however, consumers and even some large industries were asking federal agencies for more regulation. From 2007 through mid-2008 a string of product scares made headlines, including U.S.-grown spinach carrying hazardous bacteria, imported pet food and seafood adulterated with chemicals, and recalls of toys found to contain lead paint.[49] Many of these products, including the tainted pet food and toys, came from China, while contaminated fish was shipped from China and other countries in Asia and from Latin America. In May 2008 FDA Commissioner Andrew von Eschenbach asked Congress for $275 million in immediate funding to improve oversight of drugs, medical products and imported food.[50]

Two months later Congress passed the Consumer Product Safety Act of 2008, which overhauled the CPSC and increased its staffing, required toys and other children's products to be tested for safety before they entered the market and banned lead and several types of phthalates from children's products. "This reform is much needed, long overdue and necessary to ensure that CPSC can successfully ensure the safety of consumer products," said Rachel Weintraub, director of product safety and senior counsel at the Consumer Federation of America.

CURRENT SITUATION

FDA and BPA

very high cost to the economy and to property rights," wrote American Enterprise Institute analyst Steven Hayward in 2008. "This kind of bureaucratic environmentalism has about played itself out, and is decreasingly relevant to the local environmental problems that remain to be tackled."[48]

As debate continues over potential health risks from BPA, the FDA is at the center of controversy. Last August the agency released a draft assessment concluding that BPA in food packaging did not pose a health risk. But an advisory panel that reviewed the draft report found a number of flaws, such as omitting studies suggesting BPA could have harmful effects, using too few infant formula samples and not considering cumulative exposures. The reviewers concluded that "the Margins of Safety defined by the FDA as 'adequate' are, in fact, inadequate."[51] (A margin of safety is the gap between the lowest dose of BPA expected to cause harm and the actual exposure that scientists expect to occur.)

The FDA is reviewing these arguments and has pledged to provide a response by this February. "FDA agrees that, due to the uncertainties raised in some studies relating to the Potential effects of low-dose exposure to bisphenol A, additional research would be valuable," says agency spokesperson Michael Herndon. "[The agency] is already moving forward with planned research to address the potential low-dose effects of bisphenol A, and we will carefully evaluate the findings of these studies."

Critics argue the FDA has deliberately downplayed low-dose exposures to avoid having to issue new regulations. "We're replaying what happened with lead regulation," says Carnegie Mellon chemistry Professor Terry Collins. "Trade associations fought against banning lead from house paint and gasoline for 70 years by beating up doctors who said lead was bad for children and funding studies that only looked at high doses. EPA chose for years not to look at risks from ultra-low doses, and FDA is doing the same thing now. It's very confusing to the public, and these impacts are showing up across the population."

The National Toxicology Program's Bucher agrees that the FDA needs new methods to evaluate BPA. "The academic studies that found effects at low doses assessed exposures to very fine degrees," he says. "FDA's guidelines for industry studies don't require such detail, and they're just not adequate to pick up subtle changes that can occur from low-dose exposures, such as behavior differences between male and female mouse pups."

The NTP is still trying to answer important questions about BPA, says Bucher: "We know what doses animals receive in studies, but we don't know much about where it goes and how much of it reaches different tissues, or how quickly it's eliminated from the body. It's not eliminated as quickly in young animals as in older ones, and we think that's true in humans as well." He expects that the NTP will soon initiate a study to see whether prenatal exposure to BPA can lead to cancer. "Earlier studies started dosing in young adults, but clearly the most sensitive periods are earlier than that," Bucher adds.

Activist Congress

Although research is ongoing, some members of Congress have already called for new limits on chemicals in consumer products, starting with a ban on BPA in food and beverage containers. Several legislators cited a November 2008 study by the *Milwaukee Journal Sentinel* that found plastic products labeled as "microwave safe" leached potentially harmful doses of BPA when they were heated. "Parents always err on the side of caution when it comes to their kids' health. We think the law should do the same," said Sen. Charles E. Schumer, D-NY.[52] He introduced legislation in 2008 that would have banned BPA from products designed for children ages 7 and under, while Rep. Edward J. Markey, D-Mass., introduced a House bill that would have eliminated BPA from all food and beverage packaging.[53]

At least 13 states are also considering BPA bans. However, one such proposal failed in California in August 2008. Food processors, chemical manufacturers and packaging companies opposed the bill, which would have banned use of BPA in products for children ages 3 and under. "California's legislators made the right decision for consumers," said the American Chemistry Council's Hentges.

Another 2008 congressional bill that is likely to be reintroduced, the Kid-Safe Chemicals Act, would require more sweeping reforms to the Toxic Substances Control Act and the chemical-testing process.[54] The measure seeks to "eliminate the exposure of all children, workers, consumers and sensitive subgroups to harmful chemicals distributed in commerce by calendar year 2020." The measure would:

- require industry to demonstrate that chemicals in use are safe;
- authorize EPA to require additional testing for health effects at low doses and for nanomaterials;
- expand analysis by the Centers for Disease Control and Prevention (CDC) of chemical residues in humans; and
- provide new funds to promote safer alternatives.

"It is critical that we modernize our nation's chemical safety laws," said Rep. Henry A. Waxman, D-Calif., a sponsor of the House bill and the new chair of the Energy

European Regulators Take 'Precautionary' Approach

Chemical companies must show products are safe.

Chemicals are big business in Europe as well as in the United States, but the European Union (EU) has taken a sharply different approach to regulating chemical risks. In 2007 the EU's new REACH policy (Registration, Evaluation, Authorization, and Restriction of Chemicals) went into effect. In the United States, regulators must show that chemicals pose risks to human health or the environment before they can limit their production or use. But REACH takes essentially the opposite approach: Companies must show that chemicals will not harm human health or the environment before they can be marketed.

During an 11-year phase-in period, businesses that produce or import any chemical into the EU in quantities greater than one metric ton per year will have to register it with the new European Chemicals Agency and submit information about its physical and chemical properties, how it will be made, how to use it safely and how it affects human health and the environment. More detailed information is required for chemicals that are produced in larger volumes. EU officials estimate that about 30,000 chemicals now in use will be subject to REACH.[1]

Manufacturers of chemicals deemed to pose especially high risks — such as those that cause cancer, birth defects or endocrine disruption or that persist and are toxic in the environment — will have to apply to the European Commission for authorization. They will have to show that it is not technically or economically feasible to use safer substitutes, and that the risks from using the chemical can be controlled. REACH allows regulators to ban or restrict the use of chemicals that pose unacceptable risks to human health or the environment and limits the amount of health-related data that manufacturers can shield as proprietary information.

Many U.S. health and environmental advocates say REACH is a better model for regulating hazardous substances than the Toxic Substances Control Act (TSCA), and that the U.S. should emulate Europe by moving in a more precautionary direction. "TSCA is really ineffective and needs to be updated," says Sarah Janssen, a scientist at the Natural Resources Defense Council. "It limits EPA's ability to request toxicity information from manufacturers; there are thousands of chemicals on the market now without

and Commerce Committee. "The Kid-Safe Chemicals Act will deliver what its name implies — a non-toxic environment for our children."

Another chemical issue on Congress's agenda is reauthorization of the National Nanotechnology Initiative (NNI), which coordinates nanotechnology research by federal agencies. The House passed a reauthorization bill with little controversy in 2008, but nanotechnology may face a bumpier ride in the Senate. In December 2008 the National Research Council released a review of NNI's research plan for studying potential health and environmental risks of nanotechnologies. While the study did not address whether current uses of nanomaterials posed risks to the public, it found that NNI did not have an adequate strategy for answering that question.

NNI's plan "does not describe a clear strategy for nanorisk research. It lacks input from a diverse stakeholder group,

and it lacks essential elements, such as a vision and a clear set of objectives, a comprehensive assessment of the state of the science, a plan or road map that describes how research progress will be measured, and the estimated resources required to conduct such research," the NRC review stated.[55]

Making Exceptions

Banning products does not always end debate over them. Bans on phthalates in children's products under the 2008 Consumer Product Safety Improvement Act were scheduled to start on Feb. 10, 2009, but lawyers representing toy wholesalers and retailers wrote to the CPSC in late 2008 that the ban would impose "significant financial hardship" on their clients — especially if they were left with useless products after the deadline passed.

In response CPSC General Counsel Cheryl Falvey held that the law did not contain a "clear statement of

toxicity information; and there's no requirement for companies to notify EPA if they increase production or start using chemicals in new ways. REACH isn't perfect, but it's definitely a lot better than what we have, which is basically a free-for-all."

U.S. chemical companies and the Bush administration lobbied hard against REACH, arguing that it was too complex and expensive, posed a barrier to foreign exporters outside of Europe and could cause American workers to lose their jobs. C. Boyden Gray, the U.S. ambassador to the EU, said REACH would "be hell for American multinationals. . . . Our position is if we don't stop it, it will multiply like kudzu."[2] Now, however, U.S. manufacturers are reformulating their products for sale in Europe and preparing to register them.

Michael Walls, managing director at the American Chemistry Council, the main U.S. chemical industry trade group, acknowledges that REACH breaks some valuable ground. "It's raised the issue of how we assure safe use, and it's promoted dialogue about how certain chemicals are used in sectors like electronics, automobiles and aerospace," he says. But, Walls argues, REACH does not pay enough attention to how chemicals are used, which is one determinant of how risky they are. "There are some opportunities to consider specific uses, but chemicals are identified for regulation specifically based on hazardous characteristics, and we don't think that's the way to prioritize," he says.

No regulatory decisions have been made under REACH yet. A preregistration phase for existing chemicals ended last November, and regulators now are considering which substances should require authorization before they can be used. By December 2010 companies must submit data on high-volume chemicals (those produced in quantities over 1,000 metric tons per year) and highly toxic chemicals produced in smaller quantities. "REACH is still untested and unproven, and we have concerns about whether some of its provisions are workable," says Walls.

But some activists already would like to make REACH even more stringent. For example, Janssen argues the system does not pay enough attention to endocrine-disrupting chemicals. "Some chemicals aren't produced in very big volumes, but they have serious impacts at very low volumes," she says. "Hormones work in the parts-per-billion to parts-per-trillion range in your body — very small doses have really big impacts." And REACH does not explicitly cover nanomaterials, although manufacturers who want to use an existing chemical substance at the nano level will have to supply additional information on the nanoform's specific properties and describe measures to minimize risks from them.[3]

---

[1] "Chemical Regulation: Comparison of U.S. and Recently Enacted European Union Approaches to Protect Against the Risks of Toxic Chemicals," U.S. Government Accountability Office, August 2007.

[2] Mark Schapiro, *Exposed: The Toxic Chemistry of Everyday Products and What's at Stake for American Power* (2007), p. 253.

[3] "REACH and Nanomaterials," European Commission, http://ec.europa.eu/enterprise/reach/reach/more_info/nanomaterials/index_en.htm.

---

unambiguous intent" to apply the ban to existing toys, so manufacturers could keep selling items in their inventories that contained the proscribed materials.[56] Two advocacy groups, the Natural Resources Defense Council and Public Citizen, filed suit against the agency, arguing that all items containing the phthalates in question should be removed from shelves by the February 2009 deadline. "The CPSC decision will generate and prolong exposure to known hormone-disrupting chemicals. . . . There is no way for [consumers] to know whether products on store shelves after the ban date contain phthalates or not," the groups argued.[57]

Many toy vendors and manufacturers also say the law's Feb. 10 deadline for applying tough, new lead levels could cost them heavily. By that date toys may contain no more than 600 parts per million by weight of lead, a trace amount that will ratchet further down over time. Falvey ruled in November that unlike the phthalate ban, the new lead ban (which was worded differently in the law) did apply to existing toys. But some toy company owners said that testing their entire inventories for lead would be extremely expensive, and that retailers might send entire shipments back if there were worries about whether some items met the standard.[58] According to the CDC, only certified laboratories can test toys accurately for lead.[59]

Another proposed ban, on polyvinyl chloride (PVC) plastics, passed through the California Assembly and two Senate committees last year but then stalled in the Senate Appropriations Committee. PVC is used for many applications, including water pipes, medical tubing and numerous types of packaging. But critics like the Center for Health, Environment, and Justice (CHEJ) call PVC "poison plastic" because it can release chemicals such as phthalates and dioxins (a family of persistent, toxic, chlorinated hydrocarbon

Does the precautionary principle make us safer?

YES
Wendy E. Wagner
Professor of Law, University of Texas

Written for *CQ Researcher*, January 2009

The regulation of chemicals in the United States epitomizes what can go wrong when a legal system adopts a non-precautionary approach. Under the Toxic Substances Control Act (TSCA), manufacturers are not required to do any pre- or post-market testing on their chemicals unless mandated by the Environmental Protection Agency. At the same time, there are few to no rewards under the act for producing safer or better-tested chemicals, at least with regard to latent hazards.

In fact, chemical manufacturers that do voluntarily test their chemicals may put themselves at a competitive disadvantage: They not only produce evidence that can be used against them by regulators and plaintiffs' attorneys but also dedicate resources to testing that are unlikely to be recouped in sales — either because the testing reveals unwelcome risks or because the positive results cannot be validated readily by consumers or investors.

The TSCA's non-precautionary approach is partly to blame for the resulting ignorance about the long-term safety of most chemicals and for the lack of incentives to develop safer, "greener" chemicals. Over the 30-year-plus history of the legislation, EPA has required testing for fewer than 200 chemicals. Most of the remaining 75,000 chemicals produced during that period are essentially unrestricted and unreviewed with regard to their health and environmental impacts. While such a counterproductive regulatory scheme would seem at first blush a perfect candidate for public-spirited reform, the highest-stakes participants in toxics policy are the chemical manufacturers, who not surprisingly have become well-organized and steadfast in their opposition to reform.

Fortunately, the European Union's REACH directive will produce valuable toxicity information on chemicals, whether U.S. manufacturers want it or not. Through its mandatory testing requirements, REACH (registration, evaluation, authorization and restriction of chemicals) may also generate incentives for safer chemical substitutes.

In the United States, the precautionary features of REACH could be supplemented by creating additional rewards for producing safer chemicals. For example, EPA could preside over petitions filed by manufacturers seeking regulatory certification of a chemical's superiority relative to its competitors. Pitting manufacturers against one another through such adjudication will help draw out information on the toxicity of chemicals and reward greener chemical companies, while at the same time undermining the unified resistance of chemical manufacturers to modifications in TSCA's non-precautionary approach.

NO
Gary Marchant
Professor of Law, Arizona State University

Written for *CQ Researcher*, January 2009

The precautionary principle (PP) attempts to address a serious problem: How should we deal with uncertain risks? Bisphenol A, Teflon, thimerosal in vaccines, melamine in baby formula and phthalates in fire retardants are just some of the uncertain risks on the front pages of newspapers today. Which ones should we restrict now, and which should we just study more before taking action?

Unfortunately, the PP fails to provide a coherent or useful answer to this critical question. The problem, as H. L. Mencken once noted: "[t]here is always an easy solution to every human problem — neat, plausible, and wrong."

Since originating in Europe approximately 40 years ago, the PP is now binding law in Europe, Canada, Australia and several Asian nations, has been incorporated in over 60 international treaties and has been adopted by several U.S. cities. Yet, the PP is problematic, especially when enacted as a binding legal rule. First, there is no standard or official definition of "the" precautionary principle, and dozens of unofficial versions exist. Which version applies will make a huge difference in many decisions.

Second, available interpretations of the PP offer no clear guidance on key questions, such as what manufacturers must do to satisfy the PP and how costs are factored in. Without answering these fundamental questions, the PP opens the door to arbitrary decisions motivated by political bias, protectionism and other inappropriate motives, rather than objective scientific evidence of risk.

Thus, relying on the PP, Norway banned Kellogg's Corn Flakes because the added vitamins could theoretically harm some ultrasusceptible person. France banned Red Bull energy drinks because the caffeine might harm pregnant women (but did not ban coffee or wine) and Denmark banned cranberry fruit drinks because vitamin C might harm some people.

More tragically, Zambia cited the PP to deny U.S. food aid to its starving population because of the possible presence of genetically modified corn (which Americans routinely eat with no apparent consequences). The European Union even used the PP to justify governmental subsidization of the coal industry, even though coal is not generally perceived as the most environmentally friendly energy source. With the PP, however, no further explanation is needed.

Finally, the PP fails to consider that many new technologies, such as biotechnology and nanotechnology, offer the promise of enormous benefits, including health and environmental gains. By failing to consider these effects, the PP fails its own test for seeking to prohibit dangerous innovations.

chemicals) during its life cycle, and its production exposes workers to other hazardous materials.

Debate over the California bill showed the difficulty of making up-or-down decisions about substances that have many uses but also pose risks. As the bill moved through various committees, legislators exempted a number of products from the ban, including medical devices, packaging for medications and containers for petroleum products. "It's easy for attackers to dismiss PVC, but not so easy for the marketplace," says the Vinyl Institute's Blakey.

Many large manufacturers and retailers have adopted policies to phase out PVC in products or packaging, including Mattel, Nike, Sony, Target, Wal-Mart, K-Mart and Sears. But Blakey calls these steps responses to political pressure and argues that PVC products are safe. Retailers, he says, "are misinformed and pressured. They don't have a lot of staff to verify critiques, and they want the issue to go away."

Activists don't deny that they're pushing companies to drop PVC, but they say safer alternatives are available. "There are some substances that don't have substitutes, so we have to use them carefully. But there are all kinds of substitutes for PVC," says CHEJ President Lois Gibbs. The center published a guide in 2008 that lists dozens of sources for toys, clothing, mattresses and other goods made without PVC. (However, as the guide notes, the center does not endorse any of the listed substitute products, manufacturers, or retailers.)[60]

The Obama Administration

Many environmentalists are optimistic about what the newly inaugurated President Barack Obama will do about toxic chemicals. Obama has embraced green issues during his campaign and since his election. Although the economic meltdown undoubtedly will force Obama to pare down his campaign wish list, his transition team has been examining new environmental policies that could be adopted quickly, including some Clinton-era initiatives that could be resurrected.

During his inaugural speech on Jan. 20, Obama said he would "restore science to its rightful place" and has vowed to listen more closely to scientific advisers and environmental experts, whose advice the Bush administration often ignored or overruled. "I think we are in store for something new," said William Reilly, who led the Environmental Protection Agency under President George

H. W. Bush. "His pledge to follow the science will be reassuring to a lot of people, including those who fear the regulators are going to run amok."[61]

Within hours after Obama's inauguration, his Chief of Staff Rahm Emmanuel ordered a halt on all work on unfinished Bush administration regulations until they can be reviewed by the new team. Bush issued 100 new rules after Obama was elected in November, including one that President Obama strenuously opposes, which would make it much harder for the government to regulate toxic substances and hazardous chemicals in the workplace.[62]

Earlier, Obama and four other senators had proposed a measure to block the new rule and wrote a letter urging the department to scrap it, saying it would "create serious obstacles to protecting workers from health hazards on the job."[63]

The administration probably will also reconsider a Jan. 15 EPA health advisory urging Americans not to drink water with more than 0.4 parts per billion (ppb) of perfluorooctanoic acid (PFOA) — a toxic chemical linked to cancer, liver damage and birth defects that is used to make Teflon and other non-stick coatings.[64]

Some scientists have urged limits as low as 0.02 parts per billion of PFOA, and, in fact, his pick to lead the EPA, New Jersey Environmental Protection Commissioner Lisa Jackson, recommended a level of 0.04 parts per billion in her state — 10 times stricter than the new federal limit.

Richard Wiles, executive director of the Environmental Working Group — a nonprofit organization that has pushed for stricter regulation of PFOA — said the EPA's new advisory was "essentially legalizing unsafe exposure levels. Nobody should have to drink a cancer-causing Teflon chemical in their water."[65]

OUTLOOK

Green Chemistry

The task of regulating the chemical industry's constant stream of new products for health and safety risks can seem hopelessly daunting. But some experts see a way: green chemistry, which seeks to design chemicals and chemical processes with reduced environmental impacts.[66]

Since the mid-1990s, green chemistry has developed into an active research field. The EPA provides grants, awards and fellowships for green chemistry achievements, and the American Chemical Society's Green Chemistry Institute works to advance green principles across all fields of chemical research. About a dozen U.S. universities offer green chemistry programs, and major corporations like GE and BASF are investing billions of dollars in green applications, such as alternative energy systems.

Winners of the EPA's green chemistry awards for 2008 included Battelle, which developed bio-based resins and toners for office copiers and printers. Made from soy and corn feedstocks instead of petroleum products, the inks are easier to remove from paper than conventional toner, which reduces the amount of energy needed to recycle waste paper. Another winner, Nalco, designed technology to monitor the water that circulates through many building cooling systems. The Nalco system adds chemicals to keep cooling water clean only when needed, saving water and energy and reducing the quantity of chemicals in discharged cooling water.[67]

Although the field is growing rapidly, Carnegie Mellon Professor Collins says government leadership is needed. "Federal investment in green chemistry is almost nonexistent, and we desperately need it," he says. "We need to prioritize hazards and figure out how to design against them." Collins recently invented an environmentally friendly catalyst that can break down harmful pollutants into less-toxic substances.[68]

The Green Chemistry Research and Development Act, which was passed by the House in 2007 and introduced in the Senate, would provide $188 million over three years for agencies to support research, development, education and training in green chemistry.

"Modern science keeps giving us new warnings about many of the chemicals we use every day, from home cleaning products to the food we put on our family's table," said Sen. John Kerry, D-Mass., a cosponsor of the Senate bill. "It's time for Washington to respond by helping to build a whole, new chemistry industry that's on a mission to make America greener."

Reducing serious risks is key, says Collins. "Green chemistry could exist without focusing on hazardous products, and it would probably do all kinds of nice little things. But to be authentic, it has to deal with hazards."

NOTES

1. "All About Eastman Tritan Copolyester," www.eastman.com/company/news_center/News_archive/2007.

2. "Endocrine Disruptors," National Institute of Environmental Health Sciences, February 2007.

3. "Timeline: BPA from Invention to Phase-Out," Environmental Working Group, April 22, 2008, www.ewg.org/node/26291/print.

4. "Bisphenol A (BPA)," National Toxicology Program, September 2008, www.niehs.nih.gov/health/docs/bpa-factsheet.pdf.

5. "Eastman Expanding Tritan Copolyester Capacity," Reuters, March 13, 2008. For background, see Jennifer Weeks, "Buying Green," *CQ Researcher*, Feb. 29, 2008, pp. 193-216.

6. "A Poison Kiss: The Problem of Lead in Lipstick," Campaign for Safe Cosmetics, October 2007, www.safecosmetics.org/docUp-loads/A%20Poison%20Kiss.pdf.

7. For background, see Marcia Clemmitt, "Preventing Cancer," *CQ Researcher*, Jan. 9, 2009, pp. 25-48.

8. Testimony of Andrew D. Maynard before Committee on Science and Technology, U.S. House of Representatives, April 16, 2008, p. 5.

9. For background, see Brian Beary, "The New Europe," *CQ Global Researcher*, August 2007, pp. 181-210, and Kenneth Jost, "Future of the European Union," *CQ Researcher*, Oct. 28, 2005, pp. 909-932.

10. "Wingspread Statement on the Precautionary Principle," www.sehn.org/ppfaqs.html.

11. "WHO gives indoor use of DDT a clean bill of health for controlling malaria," World Health Organization, Sept. 15, 2006.

12. "Alternatives to DDT on International Radar," United Nations Environment Programme, November 2008.

13. "The Business of Chemistry," American Chemistry Council, August 2007.

14. Exceptions include pesticides, which EPA regulates under a separate law, and food additives, drugs, and cosmetics, which are controlled by the Food and Drug Administration.

15. "Chemical Regulation: Actions Are Needed to Improve the Effectiveness of EPA's Chemical Review Program," U.S. Government Accountability Office, Aug. 2, 2006, p. 1.

16. The five chemicals are PCBs, chlorofluorocarbons, dioxin, asbestos, and hexavalent chromium for use as a water treatment chemical. EPA's decision banning asbestos was reversed in *Corrosion Proof Fittings v. EPA*, 947 F. 2d 1201 (1991).

17. GAO, *op. cit.*, p. 3.

18. "Toxic Substances Control Act: Legislative Changes Could Make the Act More Effective," Sept. 26, 1994; "Chemical Regulation: Options Exist to Improve EPA's Ability to Assess Health Risks and Manage Its Chemical Review Program," June 1, 2005; and "Chemical Regulation: Actions Are Needed to Improve the Effectiveness of EPA's Chemical Review Program," Aug. 2, 2006, all U.S. Government Accountability Office.

19. "Toxicity Testing in the 21st Century: A Vision and a Strategy," National Research Council (2007), pp. 48-52.

20. "Fact Sheet for Nanotechnology Under the Toxic Substances Control Act," U.S. Environmental Protection Agency, www.epa.gov/oppt/nano/nano-facts.htm.

21. E. Clayton Teague, Director, National Nanotechnology Coordination Office, testimony before House Subcommittee on Research and Science Education, Oct. 31, 2007, pp. 1-4.

22. Thomas H. Moore, Commissioner, Consumer Product Safety Commission, testimony before Senate Commerce Subcommittee on Consumer Affairs, Insurance, and Automotive Safety, March 21, 2007, p. 7.

23. "Nanotechnology: A Report of the U.S. Food and Drug Administration Nanotechnology Task Force," July 25, 2007, pp. 12-15.

24. David J. Hanson, "FDA Confronts Nanotechnology," *Chemical & Engineering News*, March 17, 2008.

25. Online at www.nanoaction.org/nanoaction/doc/CTA_nano-silver%20petition__final_5_1_08.pdf.

26. "No-Nano Sunscreens?" *Consumer Reports*, December 2008.

27. E. Marla Felcher, "The Consumer Product Safety Commission and Nanotechnology," *PEN 14*, Project on Emerging Nanotechnologies, August 2008.

28. "Baby Bottle Chemical Levels Safe, EU Agency Says," Reuters, July 23, 2008; "Health Canada Responds to Concerns Raised About Bisphenol A in Canned Food," Health Canada, May 29, 2008; "Canada Declares BPA a Health Hazard," *USA Today*, Oct. 18, 2008.

29. Kate Murphy, "Business: Thinking Outside the Can," *The New York Times*, March 14, 2004; "Frequently Asked Questions," Hain Celestial Canada, www.hain-celestial.ca/index.php/faq/.

30. For a chronology see "Phthalates and Children's Toys," American Chemistry Council, Phthalate Information Center, www.phthalates.org/yourhealth/childrens_toys.asp.

31. "New EU Phthalates Directive Finalised," *Intertek Labtest*, July 2005.

32. Jocelyn Kaiser, "Panel Finds No Proof That Phthalates Harm Infant Reproductive Systems," *Science*, Oct. 21, 2005.

33. "Congress Passes Consumer Product Safety Improvement Act," *Beveridge & Diamond*, July 31, 2008.

34. Letter online at www.uschamber.com/issues/letters/2008/080304_phthalate_ban.htm.

35. Bohan Loh and Judith Wang, "U.S. Ban To Shake up China Toy Sector," *ICIS News*, July 31, 2008; Mark Schapiro, *Exposed: The Toxic Chemistry of Everyday Products and What's at Stake for American Power* (2007), pp. 56-57.

36. "A Plasticizer for Sensitive Applications," *Science Around Us*, BASF, June 2007.

37. Samuel Hopkins Adams, "The Great American Fraud: Articles on the Nostrum Evil and Quacks," Reprinted from *Collier's Weekly* (Collier, 1905), p. 3.

38. "Taste of Raspberries, Taste of Death: The 1937 Elixir Sulfanilamide Incident," *FDA Consumer Magazine*, U.S. Food and Drug Administration, June 1981.

39. Gregg LaBar, "Seven Decades of Safety: Good Times Take Their Toll," *EHS Today*, Oct. 1, 2008.

40. "Food Additives," Center for Science in the Public Interest, www.cspinet.org/reports/chemcuisine.htm#Food%20additive.

41. "The Reports of the Surgeon General," National Library of Medicine, http://profiles.nlm.nih.gov/NN/Views/Exhibit/narrative/smoking.html.

42. Ralph Nader, *Unsafe at Any Speed: The Designed-In Dangers of the American Automobile* (1965).

43. Philip Shabecoff, "Reagan Order on Cost-Benefit Analysis Stirs Economic and Political Debate," *The New York Times*, Nov. 7, 1981.

44. Joan Claybrook *et al.*, *Retreat From Safety: Reagan's Attack on America's Health* (1984), p. xi.

45. "Proposition 65 in Plain Language," California Office of Environmental Health Hazard Assessment, www.oehha.org/prop65/background/p65plain.html.

46. Theo Colborn, Dianne Dumanoski and John Peterson Myers, *Our Stolen Future: Are We Threatening Our Fertility, Intelligence, and Survival?* (1996).

47. Stephen Labaton, "OSHA Leaves Worker Safety in Hands of Industry," *The New York Times*, April 25, 2007.

48. Steven Hayward, "Happy Earth Day," *Human Events Online*, April 22, 2008.

49. For background see Jennifer Weeks, "Fish Farming," *CQ Researcher*, July 27, 2007, pp. 625-648, and Peter Katel, "Consumer Safety," *CQ Researcher*, Oct. 12, 2007, pp. 841-864.

50. Gardiner Harris, "F.D.A. Chief Writes Congress for Money," *New York*, May 14, 2008.

51. "Scientific Peer-Review of the Draft Assessment of Bisphenol A for Use in Food Contact Applications," U.S. Food and Drug Administration Science Board Subcommittee on Bisphenol A, Oct. 31, 2008, p. 4.

52. Meg Kissinger, "Lawmakers to Seek Ban on BPA," *Milwaukee Journal Sentinel*, Nov. 17, 2008.

53. S. 2928, introduced April 29, 2008, and H.R. 6228, introduced June 10, 2008.

54. S. 3040 and H.R. 6100, both introduced May 20, 2008.

55. National Research Council, *Review of Federal Strategy for Nanotechnology-Related Environmental, Health, and Safety Research* (2008), prepublication version, p. 6.

56. The letter and CPSC advisory opinion are online at www.cpsc.gov/LIBRARY/FOIA/advisory/320.pdf.

57. The complaint is online at http://docs.nrdc.org/health/files/hea_08120401a.pdf.

58. Melanie Trottman, "Vendors Urge Relaxed Lead-Safety Rule," *The Wall Street Journal*, Nov. 18, 2008.

59. "Toys and Childhood Lead Exposure," Centers for Disease Control and Prevention, www.cdc.gov/nceh/lead/faq/toys.htm.

60. "Pass Up the Poison Plastic," Center for Health, Environment and Justice, November 2008, www.besafenet.com/pvc/documents/PVC-Guide-1.pdf.

61. Michael Hawthorne, "Change gets green light; His plans for environmental legislation may have big impact," *Chicago Tribune*, Nov. 19, 2008, p. C4.

62. Robert Pear, "Bush Aides Rush to Enact a Rule Obama Opposes," *The New York Times*, Nov. 29, 2008, www.nytimes.com/2008/11/30/washington/30labor.html?ref=us.

63. Quoted in *ibid*.

64. See Michael Hawthorne, "U.S. warns of Teflon chemical in water," *Chicago Tribune*, Jan. 16, 2009, p. C18.

65. *Ibid.*

66. "Introduction to the Concept of Green Chemistry," U.S. Environmental Protection Agency, www.epa.gov/greenchemistry/pubs/about_gc.html.

67. "Award Winners," U.S. Environmental Protection Agency, www.epa.gov/greenchemistry/pubs/pgcc/past.html.

68. "Green Catalysts Provide Promise for Cleaning Toxins and Pollutants," *Science Daily*, Aug. 20, 2008.

BIBLIOGRAPHY

Books

Hilts, Philip J., *Protecting America's Health: The FDA, Business, and One Hundred Years of Regulation*, Knopf, 2003.
A health and science reporter traces the history of the Food and Drug Administration and business resistance to regulation.

Michaels, David, *Doubt Is Their Product: How Industry's Assault on Science Threatens Your Health,* **Oxford University Press, 2008.**

An epidemiologist and former assistant secretary of Energy criticizes what he calls the "product defense industry" for promoting doubt and uncertainty about whether unsafe products should be regulated.

Schapiro, Mark, *Exposed: The Toxic Chemistry of Everyday Products and What's at Stake for American Power, Chelsea Green,* **2007.**

An investigative journalist argues that Europe is replacing the United States as a commercial leader by setting high standards that require manufacturers to develop safer products.

Shabecoff, Philip, and Alice Shabecoff, *Poisoned Profits: The Toxic Assault on Our Children, Random House,* **2008.**

Two journalists link rising levels of childhood illness and death to toxic exposures in children's homes, schools and neighborhoods.

Articles

Cone, Marla, "A Greener Future," *Los Angeles Times,* **Sept. 14 and 19, 2008.**

Once an obscure subfield, green chemistry is slowly changing the chemical industry, but more funding and training are needed before it becomes the mainstream approach.

Henig, Robin Marantz, "Our Silver-Coated Future," *On Earth,* **fall 2007.**

Nano-silver, the most widely used nanomaterial, illustrates the need for safety testing and new regulations for nanotechnologies.

Hogue, Cheryl, "The Future of U.S. Chemical Regulation," *Chemical & Engineering News,* **Jan. 8, 2007.**

American Chemistry Council Managing Director Michael Walls and University of Massachusetts-Lowell Professor Joel Ticknor debate whether U.S. law regulating commercial chemicals is stringent enough.

Pereira, Joseph, "Protests Spur Stores to Seek Substitute for Vinyl in Toys," *The Wall Street Journal,* **Feb. 12, 2008.**

Under pressure from consumers and advocacy groups, toy makers are exploring substitute materials without vinyl or phthalates.

Rosenberg, Tina, "What the World Needs Now is DDT," *The New York Times Magazine,* **April 11, 2004.**

DDT is a cheap way to kill mosquitoes that carry malaria, but the pesticide's toxic reputation and the challenging logistics of effective spraying campaigns have made it hard for the countries that most need help to use it.

Spivak, Cary, Susanne Rust and Meg Kissinger, "Are Your Products Safe? You Can't Tell," *Milwaukee Journal Sentinel,* **Nov. 25, 2007.**

Shampoo, carpets, skin lotions, clothing and many other consumer products contain endocrine-disrupting chemicals that cause cancer and other health problems in laboratory animals. Critics call U.S. government efforts to regulate these substances "an abject failure."

Reports and Studies

"Chemical Regulation: Comparison of U.S. and Recently Enacted European Union Approaches to Protect Against the Risks of Toxic Chemicals," *U.S. Government Accountability Office,* **Aug. 17, 2007.**

The report compares U.S. chemical regulation under the Toxic Substances Control Act (TSCA) and the European Union's REACH directive.

"Third National Report on Human Exposure to Environmental Chemicals," *Centers for Disease Control and Prevention,* **2005, www.cdc.gov/exposurereport/report.htm.**

This ongoing assessment of human exposure to environmental chemicals, based on human specimens such as blood and urine, finds that levels of some substances such as blood lead and secondhand cigarette smoke have fallen, but that many other chemicals are widely present throughout the U.S. population, including known hazardous substances.

"Toxicity Testing in the 21st Century: A Vision and a Strategy," *National Research Council,* **2008.**

The council charts a course for making chemical toxicity testing faster, more affordable and more accurate while reducing reliance on animal studies.

Felcher, E. Marla, "The Consumer Product Safety Commission and Nanotechnology," *Project on Emerging Nanotechnologies,* **August 2008, www.nanotechproject.org/process/assets/filed/7033/pen14.pdf.**

An expert on business and consumer protection argues that the commission is ill-prepared to regulate nanomaterials in consumer products.

For More Information

American Chemistry Council, 1300 Wilson Blvd., Arlington, VA 22209; (703) 741-5000; www.american-chemistry.com. The main trade organization for the U.S. chemical industry.

Center for Health, Environment and Justice, P.O. Box 6806, Falls Church, VA 22040; (703) 237-2249; www.chej.org. A grassroots advocacy group that works to protect communities from exposure to dangerous environmental chemicals.

Consumer Product Safety Commission, 4330 East West Highway, Bethesda, MD 20814; (301) 504-7921; www.cpsc.gov. The federal agency charged with protecting the public from unreasonable risks from products.

Consumers Union, 101 Truman Ave., Yonkers, NY 10703; (914) 378-2000; www.consumersunion.org. A nonprofit group that tests products.

National Nanotechnology Coordination Office, 4201 Wilson Blvd., Stafford II Room 405, Arlington, VA 22230; (703) 292-8626; www.nano.gov. Provides information about federal research and development of nanotechnologies.

National Toxicology Program, 111 T.W. Alexander Dr., Research Triangle Park, NC 27709; (919) 541-3665; http://ntp.niehs.nih.gov. A Department of Health and Human Services agency that studies the impact of chemicals on human health.

Project on Emerging Nanotechnologies, One Woodrow Wilson Plaza, 1300 Pennsylvania Ave., N.W., Washington, DC 20004; (202) 691-4282; www.nanotechproject.org. Provides independent, objective analysis of nanotechnology.

Project on Scientific Knowledge and Public Policy, 2100 M St., N.W., Suite 203, Washington, DC 20052; (202) 994-0774; www.defendingscience.org. Examines how science is used and misused in government decision-making.

10

Coal's Comeback

Can Coal Become a Clean Energy Source?

Jennifer Weeks

AP Photo/The Daily Tribune News/Dayton P. Strickland

Georgia Power's huge Bowen power plant in Euharlee burns 1,100 tons of coal per hour and is the third-largest emitter of carbon dioxide — the main greenhouse gas that causes global warming — among all coal plants nationwide. Energy firms like Georgia Power are investing heavily in environmental controls to offset pollutants from coal combustion, especially in the face of looming government regulation.

From *CQ Researcher*, October 5, 2007.

By any measure, Georgia Power's 2,500-acre Bowen generating facility is big. Two 1,000-foot smokestacks at the site northwest of Atlanta vent emissions from four coal-fired boilers high into the atmosphere. Bowen generated 22.6 million megawatt-hours of electricity in 2006, enough to power more than 2.3 million households.[1] When all of its units are firing, the plant burns three trainloads of coal daily — about 1,100 tons per hour.

Bowen has generated more electricity than any other fossil-fuel plant nationwide at least 10 times since it began operating in the early 1970s. "Bowen provides more than a quarter of the power we generate in the state of Georgia. It's very important to our company," says Lolita Jackson, a Georgia Power spokeswoman. "We're spending more than $900 million to put in state-of-the-art environmental controls, and we're going to run it for a long time."

Bowen needs controls because it also produces huge amounts of air pollution. In 2006 it generated more carbon dioxide (CO_2), the main greenhouse gas (GHG) that causes climate change, than all but two other coal-burning power plants nationwide. Bowen was the top emitter of sulfur dioxide (SO_2), which causes acid rain and particulate pollution, and 14th for nitrogen oxides (NO_x), which contribute to acid rain and smog. It is also a major source of mercury, a toxic heavy metal that causes neurological damage.[2] (*See sidebar, p. 229.*)

Americans depend on coal for more than half of their electricity, and that share could grow. As of May 2007, 151 new coal-fired power plants were under construction or planned to meet steadily rising demand.[3] The Department of Energy projects that U.S. electricity sales will

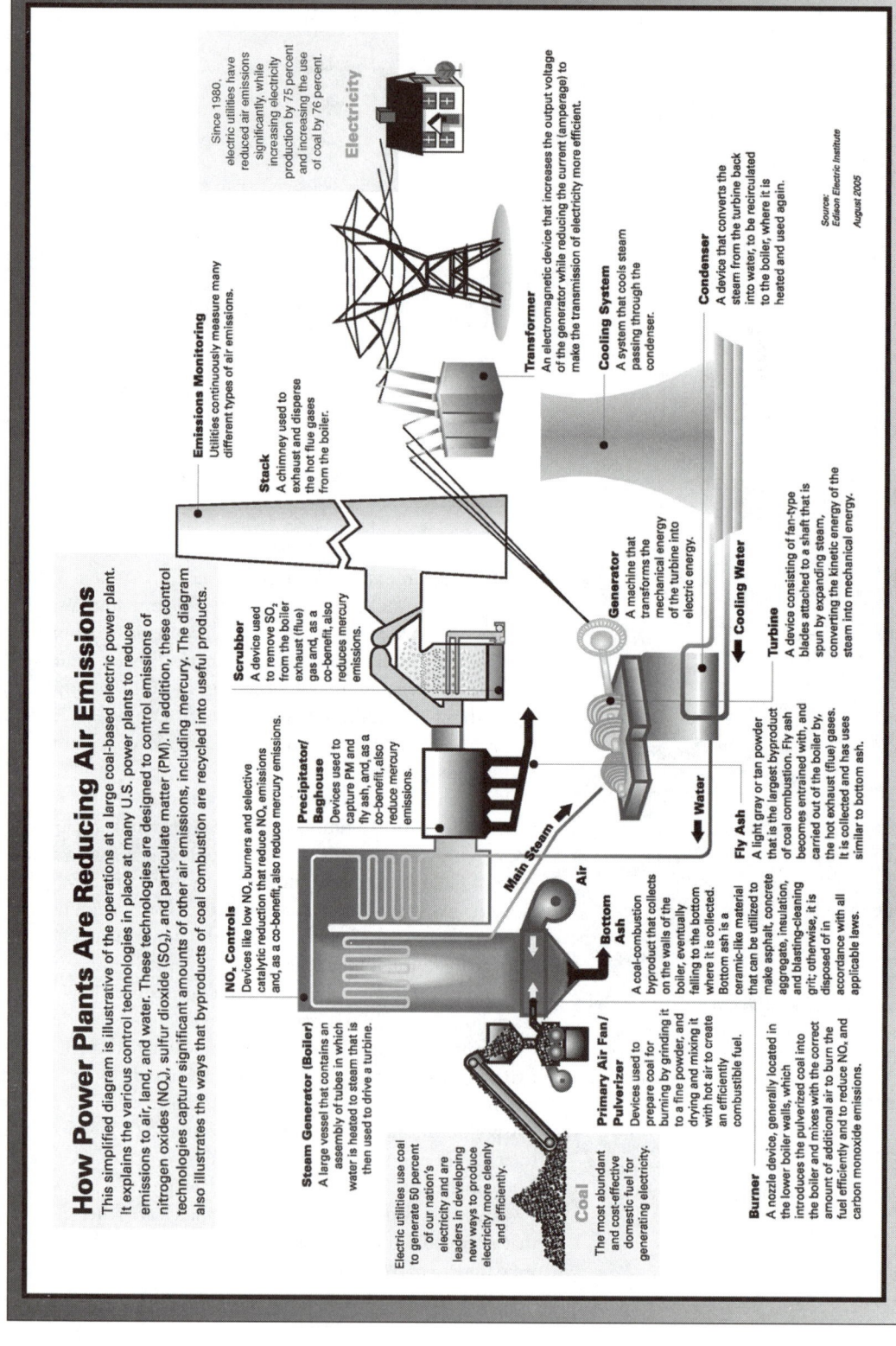

Pollutants Caused by Coal Combustion

Pollutant	Effects	Control technologies
Sulfur dioxide (SO_2) Formed when sulfur is exposed to oxygen at high temperatures.	• Causes breathing difficulty and aggravates heart disease. • Dissolves in cloud droplets to form acid rain, which damages plants, acidifies lakes and kills aquatic organisms. • Reacts in atmosphere to form fine-particle pollution. • Sulfate particles create haze, reducing visibility.	• Flue gas-desulfurization units (scrubbers) remove SO_2 from gas exiting power plant boilers. • Switching to low-sulfur coal reduces production of SO_2 during combustion.
Nitrogen oxides (NO_X) Formed when fuel is burned at high temperatures.	• Forms acid rain, fine particles and haze, with impacts similar to SO_2. • Reacts with other pollutants to form ozone, a toxic air pollutant that causes lung damage, and smog.	• Low-NO_X burners and other combustion technologies change the combustion process to reduce NO_X formation. • Post-combustion processes inject chemicals into flue gas to remove NO_X before it is emitted.
Fine particles Formed when SO_2 and NO_X react with other chemicals in the atmosphere.	• Aggravate respiratory problems like asthma and bronchitis, and heart ailments such as irregular heartbeats. Exposure causes premature deaths in people with heart and lung diseases. • Particles create haze, reducing visibility.	• Electrostatic precipitators and filters remove particles from flue gas.
Mercury Released when coal is burned.	• Accumulates in the environment and is passed up the food chain. • Causes growth and reproductive problems in fish, animals and birds, and neurological damage and birth defects in humans.	• SO_2 and NO_X controls reduce some mercury emissions. • Municipal waste and medical waste incinerators inject activated carbon into flue gas to remove more mercury; this process is being studied for use at power plants.
Carbon dioxide (CO_2) Produced when any fuel containing carbon is burned.	• Promotes global climate change by trapping heat in the atmosphere.	• CO_2 can be chemically separated from flue gas after combustion in a conventional coal plant or from gasified coal before combustion in an IGCC (integrated gasification combined cycle) plant.

increase by 41 percent between 2005 and 2030, with coal's share growing from 50 percent of generation to 57 percent if current environmental policies remain unchanged.[4]

But coal's health and environmental impacts could darken that forecast. The deaths of nine miners in August at Utah's Crandall Canyon mine were a reminder that coal mining is one of the most dangerous occupations in the United States. From 1900 through 2006 more than 104,000 coal mine workers died on the job.[5] Above-ground methods such as strip mining and mountaintop removal can wreak heavy environmental damage, although some mined lands have been reclaimed for other uses.

Burning coal has broader impacts. Studies have shown that air pollutants from coal-burning power plants and other large combustion sources cause thousands of deaths and illnesses every year.[6] They also contribute to acid rain, smog, and haze and contaminate oceans and streams with mercury.

Environmentalists want the United States to use more low-emission options like wind, solar power and biofuels.[7]

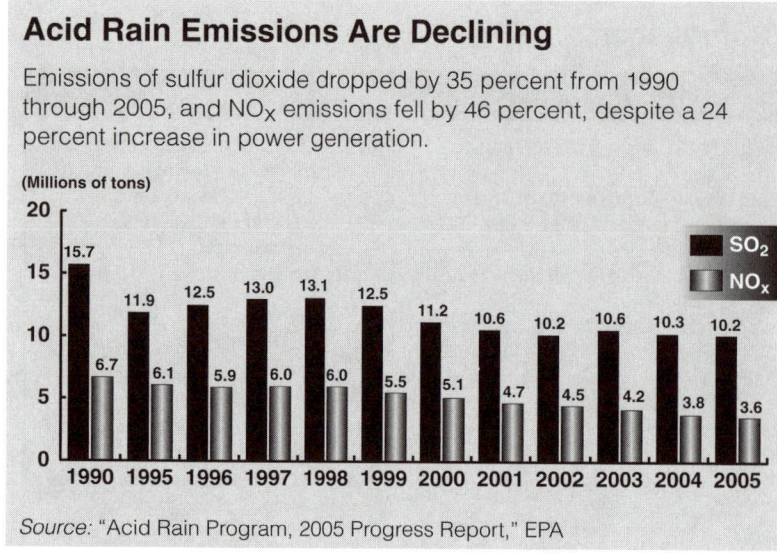

Acid Rain Emissions Are Declining

Emissions of sulfur dioxide dropped by 35 percent from 1990 through 2005, and NO_x emissions fell by 46 percent, despite a 24 percent increase in power generation.

(Millions of tons)

Source: "Acid Rain Program, 2005 Progress Report," EPA

As of 2005, amendments to the Clean Air Act that were adopted in 1990 had cut SO_2 emissions by about 35 percent from 1990 levels and NO_x emissions by 46 percent, at costs well below original government and industry projections. (*See graph, at left.*) "Air quality has continuously improved in the United States for particulate matter, ozone and acid rain," says John Kinsman, director of air quality programs for the Edison Electric Institute, which represents shareholder-owned electric power companies. "It will continue to improve in the future, and electric power SO_2 and NO_x emission reductions are a major reason."

"Coal power plants are the largest manmade source of CO_2 in our atmosphere," says Jennifer Coken, a campaign director for Western Resource Advocates (WRA), a Colorado-based environmental advocacy group. "Smokestack emissions reduce visibility at national parks. Water is a critical resource in the West, and coal plants divert huge amounts of water for cooling."

Other advocates see nuclear power as a clean alternative to coal, since nuclear reactors do not emit conventional air pollutants or CO_2 when they generate electricity. But critics say nuclear power is too dangerous and generates too much long-lived, difficult-to-dispose-of radioactive waste to be an acceptable energy mainstay.[8]

The Bush administration's national energy policy, issued in 2001, called for spending $2 billion over 10 years to develop plants that burn coal more efficiently and produce less pollution. "We've got 250 years of coal, at least, in America. If we're interested in becoming less dependent on foreign sources of energy, we ought to be using energy here at home in a wise way," President George W. Bush told a Cleveland audience on July 10. "But coal can be dirty and, therefore, we're spending a lot of your money on developing clean coal technologies."

According to a recent National Research Council study, Bush's 250-year supply estimate is impossible to confirm because it is based on 30-year-old data and methods. However, the United States probably does have enough coal to last for more than a century at current consumption rates.[9]

But in many parts of the nation SO_2 and NO_x still contribute to high levels of secondary pollutants (contaminants that form through reactions in the atmosphere) such as ozone and fine particulates. "Air quality is much better than it was 20 years ago, but cleaner air is not clean air," says Janice Nolen, assistant vice president of the American Lung Association. "There is documented evidence of dreadful health effects from these pollutants at levels that all too frequently exist in the United States. Pollution from coal power plants is still a problem."

Coal-fired electricity plants in the United States are a mix of old and new, including some that went into operation before World War II. Most plants have taken steps to reduce SO_2 and NO_x emissions. Some, like Bowen, are adding controls now to meet the latest SO_2 and NO_x targets, set by the Environmental Protection Agency (EPA) in 2005.

The EPA also issued a rule in 2005 designed to reduce mercury emissions from power plants for the first time, but critics argue that it is too slow and too weak. Meanwhile, CO_2 emissions from power plants are not controlled yet at the federal level. Bush contends that doing so would drive up energy prices, but some states are adopting their own greenhouse gas controls, and support is growing in Congress for national limits.

New clean-air standards, such as limits on CO_2 emissions, could force power plant owners to spend hundreds of millions of dollars to install additional control systems. Electric utilities would have to raise prices, reducing coal's competitive advantage over cleaner but more expensive fuels like natural gas, nuclear power and renewable sources like solar and wind. New environmental controls thus could prevent currently planned coal plants from being built, as many environmentalists hope.

Some companies already have backed away from planned new plants. In April 2006 the TXU Corp. announced plans to build 11 new coal-fired generating units in Texas, an expansion equivalent to more than 3.5 percent of the entire U.S. coal-burning fleet. The company asserted the plants would make the air cleaner because they would replace older, dirtier units without modern pollution controls. Critics replied that building coal plants instead of cleaner power sources would be disastrous for public health and the environment. They also accused TXU of pushing for quick permits so that it could build the plants before any future limits on greenhouse gas emissions took effect.[10]

"Here we are in the 21st century, and the governor and TXU are trying to meet our state's energy needs with a 19th-century fuel source," said Neil Carman, clean air program director of the Sierra Club's Lone Star chapter.[11]

With more than 30 Texas cities and towns opposing the new plants and TXU's stock price dropping, shareholders grew nervous. In February 2007 the corporation's board voted to accept a $45 billion leveraged-buyout offer from two private equity firms. As part of the deal investors agreed to cancel eight of the new coal plants, support mandatory national controls on carbon emissions and invest $400 million in energy efficiency and conservation measures, plus other environmental commitments.[12]

"All of the issues at play in Texas are applicable to other companies," says Dan Bakal, electric power program director at Ceres, a network of investor, environmental and public interest groups that promotes corporate social responsibility.[13] "As electricity providers plan future investments they need to analyze business risks associated with climate change, explore technologies for managing carbon emissions and plan for cost increases, including policies that put a price on carbon."

As lawmakers, state officials and energy companies try to balance coal's energy value against its negative effects on health and the environment, here are some of the issues they are debating:

Should new coal plants be required to capture carbon emissions?

As evidence mounts that greenhouse gas (GHG) emissions are causing significant climate change, Congress is debating proposals for mandatory national GHG limits.[14] Coal-burning power plants emit more CO_2 per unit of electricity produced than any other fuel. But an evolving technology called carbon capture and storage (CCS) holds the promise of making coal-based electricity nearly carbon-free.[15]

CCS systems chemically separate CO_2 from power plant flue gas and compress it into a fluid for underground injection. A 2007 study by a panel of scientists and engineers at MIT called CCS "the critical enabling technology that would reduce CO_2 emissions significantly while also allowing coal to meet the world's pressing energy needs." The authors recommended more than doubling current U.S. spending to address the two-part challenge of demonstrating advanced coal-generation technologies using carbon capture and finding potential underground storage sites.[16]

Adding CCS to power plants is technically challenging and raises plant costs. The chemical conversion processes involved in capturing carbon emissions use some of the steam output that normally would turn turbines to generate electricity, so the plant makes less electric power from a given amount of coal. Plants with CCS thus need bigger boilers and steam turbines to produce as much power as conventional plants. Companies designing plants with CCS need roughly 20 percent more space for these larger components and for equipment to capture, recover and compress CO_2.

The MIT study concluded that plant owners were unlikely to retrofit existing coal-fired plants with CCS given the costs and technical challenges. However, it said CCS could work with many types of new coal plants, including high-efficiency versions of today's pulverized-coal plants (so called because they burn coal that has been ground to a fine powder).

Environmentalists favor a newer integrated gasification combined cycle (IGCC) plant, which converts coal to gas, cleans most pollutants from the gas before combustion and then burns the gas. Only two IGCC power plants (without CCS) are operating today in the United States, but about one-fifth of the coal plants on the drawing boards are IGCC plants. IGCC generates electricity at a higher cost today than pulverized-coal plants but uses less water and produces fewer air pollutants.

Carbon storage is also an evolving field. Energy companies routinely inject CO_2 and other gases underground to increase pressure and maximize yields from oil and gas deposits, but only three projects worldwide, in Norway,

Burning Coal Produces Most Pollutants

Burning coal at U.S. power plants creates, on average, more pollutants per megawatt-hour (MWh) of electric-power generation than any other fuel.

Pollutants From Fossil Fuel-Burning Power Plants

	Natural Gas	Oil	Coal
Sulfur dioxide (SO_2)	0.1 lbs/MWh	12 lbs/MWh	13 lbs/MWh
Nitrogen oxides (NO_x)	1.7 lbs/MWh	4 lbs/MWh	6 lbs/MWh
Carbon dioxide (CO_2)	1,135 lbs/MWh	1,672 lbs/MWh	2,249 lbs/MWh

Source: EPA

Canada and Algeria, are injecting up to 1 million metric tons per year. Offsetting a significant fraction of human-generated CO_2 emissions could require capturing and storing a billion tons or more yearly. The MIT study called for about a dozen major demonstrations in different geological settings around the world, plus government support for three to five commercial-sized coal-burning plants with carbon capture.

"We need large-scale demonstration projects, which will take 8 to 10 years," says MIT chemical engineering professor and study coauthor Howard Herzog. "At that point CCS should be ready to go mainstream if the government has provided economic incentives for capturing and storing carbon, either by putting a price on carbon emissions or limiting power plant emission rates."

Many observers expect that within the next several years Congress will set national limits on CO_2 emissions. Lawmakers will either tax them at a certain fee per ton or cap total emissions and require power plants to buy allowances to cover any CO_2 they release above their individual quotas (a so-called cap-and-trade system because plants with extra allowances can sell them to others that need them). The MIT study estimated that pricing CO_2 emissions at $30 per ton through one of these methods would make it economically competitive to build new coal plants with CCS instead of today's designs. Owners would pay more for CCS technology up front but would not have to pay taxes on emissions or buy allowances to cover them.

But if the government sets a lower price on CO_2, fewer energy companies are likely to invest in power plants with expensive CCS technology. "We need a serious carbon policy for coal plants with CCS to be built

on a large scale. A small carbon tax won't lead to many new plants being built quickly," says Herzog.

Some environmental advocates say that no more coal plants should be built until CCS is ready. "There should be a moratorium on building any more coal-fired power plants until we have the technology to capture and sequester the CO_2," prominent climate scientist James Hansen, director of NASA's Goddard Institute for Space Studies, told a National Press Club audience in February. "It will become clear over the next 10 years that coal-fired power plants that do not capture and sequester CO_2 are going to have to be bulldozed."[17]

Some politicians agree with Hansen. Sen. Christopher J. Dodd, D-Conn., and former Sen. John Edwards, D-N.C., both seeking the Democratic presidential nomination in 2008, say they would ban new coal plants without CCS.[18] Others support emission performance targets that coal plants could only meet by capturing CO_2. Earlier this year California barred electric utilities from signing new contracts with sources that produce more than 1,000 pounds of CO_2 per megawatt-hour, including out-of-state plants.[19] Sen. John Kerry, D-Mass., has introduced legislation requiring all new coal-fired plants to emit no more than 285 pounds of CO_2 per megawatt-hour.[20]

Energy companies say that moratorium proposals are unrealistic with electricity demand rising. "[G]iven the growth of power demand in the U.S., we're getting to the point where many regions of the country are starting to look at shortages over the next couple of years, and we're going to have to start building some baseload coal plants, using the best available technologies," DTE Energy Chair Anthony Earley said in July.[21]*

According to the MIT study, adding CCS to IGCC plants is cheaper than adding it to pulverized coal plants with current technology. But the authors concluded that it

---

* Baseload plants run almost constantly except when they are shut down for maintenance, and are used by power companies to meet the bulk of customer demand. Smaller "peaking" plants are brought into service at times when demand is highest, such as the hottest days of summer. Coal plants are best suited to provide baseload power because they are slow to fire up and cool down.

was too early to anoint one preferred CCS option because research to improve coal generation is under way around the world. They were also skeptical of a concept, advocated by some officials and environmentalists, that future plants should be made "capture ready" through steps such as designing them with extra space for CCS equipment.

"CCS isn't like a cable-ready TV that you can plug right in," says MIT's Herzog. "There's not a lot you can do up front to make that switch-over to carbon capture at an operating plant any easier. We're better off spending money to build plants with capture systems today, and those will need government support. That's where large-scale demonstrations come in, to set the stage."

Others want to move faster. The Natural Resources Defense Council (NRDC), an environmental advocacy group, argues that technologies for CCS at IGCC plants are available today. In NRDC's view, the most urgent need is for policies that will make coal plant owners start using these systems — for example, a national emission-performance standard like California's that limits how much CO_2 plants can release per unit of electricity generation.

"Decisions being made today in corporate board rooms, government ministries and congressional hearing rooms are determining how the next coal-fired power plants will be designed and operated," NRDC analysts David Hawkins and George Peridas wrote earlier this year. "If all 3,000 of the next wave of coal plants [forecast worldwide] are built with no CO_2 controls, their lifetime emissions will impose an enormous pollution lien on our children and grandchildren."[22]

Is mercury emissions trading safe?

Mercury is a natural element found in trace amounts in rocks and ores, including coal. But a little bit goes a long way: According to the EPA, the maximum daily amount of mercury that a 140-pound adult can be exposed to without health effects is 6.3 millionths of one gram.[23] In larger doses mercury interferes with the brain and central nervous system. The expression "mad as a hatter" is based on the experiences of 19th-century English hatmakers, who developed muscle tremors, distorted speech and hallucinations after they used mercury solutions to cure furs.

Mercury enters the environment from natural sources, like volcanic eruptions, and human activities such as burning coal. It travels through the atmosphere, then falls to Earth, where bacteria in soils and wetlands convert it to a toxic form called methylmercury that accumulates in living tissues. As of 2006, 48 states had issued warnings against eating certain species of fish caught in local rivers, lakes or coastal waters because of mercury contamination.[24]

Coal-fired power plants produced nearly 48 tons of mercury in 1999, about 42 percent of U.S. mercury emissions. The Bush administration, energy companies and health and environmental groups agree that mercury emissions from coal plants should be reduced but disagree sharply on how to do it.

The Clean Air Act classifies mercury as a hazardous air pollutant. More than a decade ago, the EPA agreed in a legal settlement to set mercury emissions standards for power plants by 2004, using "Maximum Available Control Technology" as required by the act. The agency convened a working group in 2001 to help develop standards, but halted work in 2003. "There was total silence for nine months, and then EPA took a very different approach," says panel member Praveen Amar, science and policy director at Northeast States for Coordinated Air Use Management (NESCAUM), a Boston nonprofit that analyzes air-quality issues for state governments.

EPA's Clean Air Mercury Rule (CAMR), which became final in 2005, uses allowance trading to reduce mercury emissions. Like the SO_2 trading program that Congress created in 1990, CAMR caps total allowable mercury releases and gives each state an emissions "budget" to allocate among power plants. Plants that reduce emissions below their allotted levels can sell extra allowances to higher emitters. EPA estimates that the rule will reduce mercury emissions from coal plants by 70 percent from current levels, to 15 tons per year when fully implemented in 2025.[25]

Energy companies support trading because, instead of making them install specific control technologies at every plant, it lets them choose whether to reduce emissions or buy allowances, and if they reduce, how to do it. "A national cap-and-trade program is the most cost-effective means to achieve substantial mercury emission reductions," says Michael Rossler, manager of environmental programs at the Edison Electric Institute. "It's also an efficient and flexible approach for states, which ultimately translates into a low-cost option for electric consumers."

Critics say that the rule will take too long to reduce mercury emissions and could create dangerous mercury concentrations near sources that buy allowances instead of cutting emissions. The rule "leaves hundreds of plants using antiquated control technology for two or more decades and significantly increases the risk of toxic hotspots downwind of such plants," Sens. Patrick J. Leahy, D-Vt., and Olympia J. Snowe, R-Maine, wrote to colleagues in August 2005. Forty-seven senators voted for a resolution offered by Leahy and Snowe opposing the rule.[26]

EPA officials say agency modeling shows that mercury emissions trading will not produce hotspots. "We found that on average, CAMR would reduce power plant mercury emissions by about 70 percent across the United States when it's fully implemented," says Robert Wayland, director of the energy strategies group at EPA's Office of Air Quality Planning and Standards. "Some studies have shown higher-than-average mercury deposition in selected spots, but we concluded that overall reductions on this scale would prevent hotspots from occurring."

But recent studies in the Northeast paint a different picture. A report published in 2007 by scientists affiliated with the Hubbard Brook Research Foundation in New Hampshire identified five actual and nine potential biological mercury hotspots in the Northeast (areas where mercury levels in many samples of key fish, birds or mammals, such as yellow perch and common loons, exceed human and ecological health thresholds).[27] A companion study reported high mercury concentrations in fish and fish-eating wildlife across the region. The authors estimated that cuts required under the mercury rule would probably not be deep enough to protect human and environmental health.[28]

The EPA asserts that much of the mercury contaminating U.S. waters comes from non-U.S. sources, but these analyses concluded that nearby coal-fired power plants produced about 40 percent of regional mercury deposition. The authors suggested that EPA's computer models might be underestimating mercury pollution from nearby sources, and that mercury emissions trading might perpetuate or worsen hotspots.[29]

"I don't think atmospheric modeling of mercury is a very mature science. We're learning more all the time, but it's an area that's growing rapidly," says Syracuse University environmental engineering Professor Charles Driscoll, a coauthor of the Hubbard Brook studies. "There are problems with a lot of the information in national emission inventories, and many numbers for various forms of mercury are estimated rather than measured."

The EPA has discussed modeling methods with the Hubbard Brook scientists, says Driscoll, but the agency needs to work with states and regions to monitor

mercury deposition and environmental concentrations. "That's what has made the SO_2 trading system work — they have detailed measurements of ecosystem levels and air-quality measurements, so they can track effects. But there's much less data on mercury," says Driscoll. "If that kind of program was in effect, you would know how a trading program was working and whether it was reducing mercury levels in the environment."

EPA does not contest the Hubbard Brook findings, although the agency says its models do a better job of predicting complex chemical reactions that mercury undergoes in the atmosphere. "They did their analysis in a different way, but studies like [the Hubbard Brook reports] will continue to influence the science and provide information that we need to develop a comprehensive mercury-monitoring network," says EPA's Wayland.

Sixteen states have filed a lawsuit challenging the mercury rule. Many of these states, along with others not involved in the lawsuit, have adopted or are developing more stringent technology-based mercury limits than the EPA rule.

EPA and energy companies also say that activated-carbon injection, the most advanced technology for removing mercury emissions from plant flue gas, needs more study to make it work on large plants that burn various types of coal. But some experts, including NESCAUM's Amar, disagree.

"The technology is here. It's widely used on municipal waste incinerators, which used to be big mercury sources," says Amar. "Many states have decided that technology controls are more straightforward than trading and are cost-effective. Mercury controls are not just about averages, and small cost savings to industry from trading may not be worth introducing more uncertainty about hotspots."

Should mountaintop removal mining be banned?

As Congress and regulators work to reduce air pollution from coal combustion, fuel providers are looking for low-sulfur coal to mine. One source is the central Appalachian basin, which reaches from southern West Virginia into southwestern Virginia, eastern Kentucky and small areas in Tennessee. But grassroots organizations argue that mining these coal seams is destroying ecologically valuable lands and traumatizing local communities.

Surface miners use a range of methods to remove overlying rock and soil, known as overburden, and expose coal seams. In Western states where coal seams lie just a few feet below the prairie, overburden can be plowed away with gigantic bulldozers and earth-movers. But Appalachia's high, narrow hills and deep valleys require a different approach.

Mountaintop removal, a technique that has come into increasing use over the past 30 years, clears away topsoil and vegetation, then uses millions of pounds of explosives to blast away rock, sometimes reducing site elevation by hundreds of feet. Since slopes are too steep to pile overburden beside the mine, the material is dumped into adjoining valleys.

"Coal in these areas is found in very narrow seams, and the surrounding rock geology is less stable than in areas with larger seams, so the only safe way to mine it is to go straight at it from the top," says National Mining Association Senior Vice President Carol Raulston. "It creates flat terrain on what was the top of the mountain, but the mountain is still there."

A 2005 EPA review estimated that mountaintop mining and valley fills (MTM/VF) would affect more than 800,000 acres (1,250 square miles) of Appalachian forests between 1992 and 2012. Some 1,200 miles of headwater streams — the small creeks and streams that feed most major rivers — were buried by MTM/VF between 1992 and 2002.[30]

Southern Appalachia has unusually diverse plant and animal populations, and many scientists believe that MTM/VF threatens this ecologically rich area. EPA's environmental review called Appalachia's ecoregions "unique in the world," with many native plants, animals and fish, as well as rich forests that "have been profoundly altered over the past few centuries and are becoming increasingly threatened."[31]

Local groups say mountaintop mining is stressful and dangerous for people living nearby. The process worsens local flooding, says Judy Bonds, outreach director for Coal River Mountain Watch (CRMW), a West Virginia citizens' group. "When mountains are denuded and local streams fill up with sediment, there's more runoff from steep slopes that causes flooding for miles downstream," says Bonds. "I know people who sleep in their street clothes at night because they've been through flooding and worry about having to run again in the middle of the night."

Flat land is all that remains after miners blasted away the top of a mountain in the Appalachians. As regulators seek to reduce pollution from coal combustion, energy providers are increasingly turning to mountaintop-removal mining for low-sulfur coal.

Mountaintop mining also "breaks windows and cracks house foundations," she says. "You can smell and taste the explosive dust in your mouth afterward. It's all over your property and in your lungs. Mine runoff and selenium discharges contaminate our fishing streams and drinking water, so people have to go out and pay for public water access instead.* We can't even swim in our own streams any more."[32]

Regulators at the federal Office of Surface Mining, Reclamation and Enforcement (OSM) and state agencies say surface mining is much more stringently regulated today than it was before Congress passed the Surface Mining Control and Reclamation Act (SMCRA) in 1977 to curb abuses in strip mining, in which operators scrape away soil and rock to expose large coal seams lying near the surface. "Although there are still impacts from mining, the practice is now carefully planned and permitted with extensive scientific, regulatory and public input," West Virginia Secretary of Environmental Protection Stephanie Timmermeyer told the House Natural Resources Committee in July.[33]

Community groups disagree. "OSM has used, and has allowed the states to use, [SMCRA] as a perverse tool to justify the very harm that Congress sought to prevent,"

---

* Selenium, a naturally occurring mineral that is toxic in moderate doses, has leached from mountaintop removal sites and contaminated a number of West Virginia rivers and streams.

CHRONOLOGY

1920s-1960 *Mechanization makes coal mines bigger and more efficient. Miners win basic workplace safeguards.*

1920s Mechanical loading equipment replaces hand loading.

1930 Molded protective helmets for miners are introduced.

1937 Coal shuttle car is invented; electric hauling equipment for coal and refuse starts replacing mules at mines.

1943 President Franklin D. Roosevelt nationalizes U.S. coal mines to maintain production during a wartime strike.

1945-1960 Coal use for heating and powering trains and ships declines. Oil replaces coal as largest primary U.S. energy source.

1960s-1990s *Rising demand for electricity spurs surge in coal production. Concerns about environmental impacts of mining and burning coal spur new regulations.*

1970 Clean Air Act sets national air-quality standards for pollutants including sulfur dioxide, nitrogen oxides and fine particulates.

1972 Congress adopts Clean Water Act, which bars dumping wastes into U.S. waters without a permit. . . . Flooding kills 125 people and leaves 4,000 homeless after a coal slurry impoundment dam bursts in Logan County, W. Va., on Feb. 4, releasing 132 million gallons of mine wastewater.

1973-74 Arab oil embargo increases demand for coal, raising prices. . . . Surface mining, especially in Western states, generates growing share of U.S. coal output.

1977 Surface Mining Control and Reclamation Act (SMCRA) regulates strip mines and requires operators to restore sites after mining. . . . Congress adds New Source Review (NSR) program to Clean Air Act, grandfathering existing plants unless they expand their capacity.

1979 Accident at Three Mile Island nuclear plant near Harrisburg, Pa., stalls expansion of nuclear power.

1992 Congress amends Clean Air Act, creating a cap-and-trade system to reduce emissions that contribute to acid rain.

1993 Price ceilings on natural gas are eliminated, increasing production but letting prices rise and fall with supply and demand.

1997 United States signs Kyoto Protocol on greenhouse gas emissions, but Senate opposition deters Clinton administration from submitting it for ratification.

1999 Justice Department files 51 lawsuits against electric power producers in 10 states for NSR violations.

2000s *Rising energy prices and supply crises spur new demand for coal. The Bush administration supports increased production, but critics say the U.S. needs to use less coal, not more.*

2000 Oil and gas prices rise as domestic output falls, energy demand increases in developing countries and production drops because of conflicts in major exporting countries.

2001 President George W. Bush reverses a campaign pledge to regulate CO_2 emissions. . . . Administration's energy plan calls for funding clean-coal technology research, offering new emission-trading legislation and reviewing the NSR program and pending enforcement cases to see whether they are preventing companies from building or expanding power plants.

2002 EPA releases new rules allowing companies to modify plants without seeking NSR permits as long as emissions will not exceed caps on specific pollutants.

2005 Energy Policy Act of 2005 provides $1.8 billion for research on clean-coal technologies and $3 billion to promote pollution-control upgrades at existing plants and construction of new, advanced coal plants.

2007 TXU Energy Corp. cancels eight of 11 planned coal plants and accepts a leveraged-buyout offer after controversy over the plants drives the company's stock price down. . . . Nine miners die at Crandall Canyon mine in Huntington, Utah.

Beyond Picks and Shovels

Today's miners use computers and GPS.

Humans have been extracting coal from the Earth since the Middle Ages. For centuries, miners hacked coal from underground deposits with picks and hammers and hauled it out in carts, often using children to pull loads through narrow tunnels.[1] Today, however, coal mining in the United States and other industrialized nations has entered the computer age.

"There's a misunderstanding that coal mining is an antiquated business that relies on manual labor," says Mike Mosser, manager of the Mining Industries of the Future program at the Energy Department's National Energy Technology Laboratory. "Mining coal in 2007 is a technologically sophisticated, highly engineered discipline for extracting energy. It's capital-intensive, and it generates a lot of jobs."

Cutting, cleaning and transporting coal are all highly mechanized processes today. Operators use wireless communications, sensors and computerized controls to guide machinery. The traditional approach to underground mining is called the "room and pillar" method: Miners remove coal in sections, leaving large pillars of coal intact to support the rock and soil above. In the 1950s and '60s, hand-drilling and blasting was replaced by "continuous mining" machines, which carve coal from the rock face with spinning toothed cylinders and feed it onto conveyor belts for transport to the surface.

A newer technique, longwall mining, instituted in the 1980s, uses specialized machines to cut swaths from blocks of coal up to 15,000 feet long, working back and forth across the coal face under movable roof supports. "It's just like mowing grass," says Mosser. "Longwall mining has kept U.S. coal companies competitive in world markets." As of 2003, more than half of U.S. underground coal production came from longwall mining.[2]

Surface-mining methods also have changed radically with mechanization. In the 19th century, surface miners hitched horses to plows and steel scrapers to uncover coal seams near the surface. Now huge trucks, bulldozers and excavators move vast quantities of material. The "buckets," or scoops, on large dragline excavators can be large enough to hold several automobiles. Some operators use global positioning systems (GPS) to guide machinery as it exposes coal seams.

Technical advances have also made mining safer. For centuries miners stabilized tunnel roofs with timber supports, which often collapsed, especially when each miner was responsible for securing his own work area in the years before regulation. Roof bolting, introduced in the 1950s and required by law in 1969, replaced timbers with high-strength bolts drilled upward to tie overlying rock layers together. Newer mining machines with sensors and video monitors can be controlled remotely hundreds of feet away from the rock face. And researchers are working to design robots that can map mines and detect dangerous gases.[3]

But some technical advances create new safety issues. For example, moving-vehicle accidents are a leading cause of deaths and injuries at coal mines. Some 300 workers are injured every year by falling as they climb in and out of gigantic mining trucks, and drivers often collide with people or smaller vehicles nearby or accidentally back their enormous vehicles off the road. Federal regulators are studying ways to reduce these accidents by equipping mining vehicles with sensors and cameras.[4]

Accidents such as the collapses at West Virginia's Sago mine in 2006 and the Crandall Canyon mine in Utah this year have also highlighted the need for better communications technology underground. "When you have an accident or flood, if you're communicating by wire you lose contact with your people," says Mosser. "Wireless communications are a research priority for underground mining. It's better than it was 50 years ago, but we need to get it to a higher level."

---

[1] Barbara Freese, *Coal: A Human History* (2003), pp. 46-47, 77-78.

[2] U.S. Energy Information Administration, "Coal Production in the United States: An Historical Overview," October 2006, p. 5.

[3] Eric Weiner, "Could Robots Replace Humans in Mines?" National Public Radio, Aug. 7, 2007.

[4] National Institute for Occupational Safety and Health, "Safety Enhancements for Off-Road Haulage Trucks." http://0-www.cdc.gov/niosh/nas/mining/researchproject62.htm.

Joe Lovett, director of the Appalachian Center for the Economy and the Environment, told the same hearing. "The members of Congress who voted to pass the Act in 1977 could not have imagined the cumulative destruction that would be visited on our region by the complete failure of the regulators to enforce the act."[34]

Mountaintop removal critics have won a series of favorable rulings from the U.S. District Court for the

Southern District of West Virginia, although some have been reversed on appeal. Most recently, Judge Robert Chambers ruled in March that the U.S. Army Corps of Engineers failed to comply with the National Environmental Policy Act and the Clean Water Act in issuing four mountaintop removal permits without fully considering the ecological importance of streams that would be buried.[35]

In June, Chambers ruled against another mountaintop removal practice: damming streams below valley fills to create sediment-control ponds, where solids washing down from the mine waste settle out before the stream flows on downhill. The Corps of Engineers classifies these ponds as waste-treatment systems and exempts them from Clean Water Act water-quality standards. But Chambers held that the act applied starting at the lower edge of valley fills, so the Corps could not let mining companies turn streams into waste-filtering systems.[36]

"The decisions prove our point that these steep slopes and narrow valleys are valuable," says Bonds. "You can't strip mine coal in Appalachia without destroying the water supply because of our topography. People think this is a throwaway region, but these streams are the sources of important water supplies for East Coast cities."

Coal industry representatives argue that they need settling ponds to treat pollution and meet Clean Water Act requirements. "This judge's decision says the Clean Water Act is illegal. It says SMCRA is illegal. It's surreal," said West Virginia Coal Association Vice President Jason Bostic.[37] Coal companies are appealing the ruling, with support from the National Mining Association. "There's a history of troubling decisions from this court that have ultimately been reversed on appeal," says Raulston.

According to the association, mountaintop removal accounted for about 16 percent of national coal production and one-third of annual production from Appalachia in the past several years. Not all of the coal seams could be accessed by other means. "Just because you can doesn't mean you should. We have a lot of asbestos left, but we don't mine that any more," says Bonds, who hopes to end mountaintop mining within the next five years.

But it won't be easy to replace sources that are providing about one-sixth of the nation's coal supply, Bonds acknowledges, especially if electricity demand keeps rising. "It's going to take public outcry, litigation and a national energy shift," she says.

BACKGROUND
Powering America

Americans have put coal to many uses since colonial times, from heating homes to operating steam engines and manufacturing glass, iron and steel. In 1882 inventor Thomas Edison opened a new chapter when he started operations at Pearl Street Station in lower Manhattan, the nation's first commercial electric generating station (powered by coal-fired boilers). As this new form of energy gained acceptance, coal surpassed wood as the dominant U.S. energy source for the next 70 years.

Coal was less bulky than wood, had a higher energy content and created steady, long-lasting fires. By the turn of the 20th century, millions of Americans depended on coal for heat and cooking and to run factories. Leading industrialists like Andrew Carnegie and Henry Clay Frick amassed fortunes by linking railroad and steel companies into huge conglomerates powered by coal.

Rising demand for coal intensified struggles within the industry over low wages and dangerous conditions. Many coal companies violently suppressed miners' efforts to form unions. In a notorious 1914 instance, National Guard troops machine-gunned and burned a camp of striking miners at Ludlow, Colo., killing 21 people, including 11 children. The Ludlow Massacre capped a 14-month strike in which some 66 miners died. It focused scathing criticism on magnate John D. Rockefeller, owner of the largest coal company in Colorado, and helped draw public attention to the hardships of coal mining.[38]

Conditions for miners finally started to improve in the 1930s with New Deal reforms. The 1933 National Industrial Recovery Act and the 1935 National Labor Relations Act guaranteed most private-sector workers the right to unionize, while the 1938 Fair Labor Standards Act established a minimum wage, maximum work week and standards for overtime and restricted the use of child labor. Previously, youths had long been employed in mines or as "breaker boys," who bent over chutes for 10 or more hours a day sorting waste and rock from fast-moving streams of coal.

Coal helped power Allied forces to victory in World War II, but after the war oil became America's fuel of choice. New oilfields in the Middle East and Latin America pumped out such abundant supplies that oil became cheaper than coal. Liquid fuels were easier to handle and transport, and oil burned more cleanly than coal, although it still produced significant pollution.

Repeated strikes in the U.S. coal industry also drove manufacturers to seek more reliable substitutes. During a strike in 1943, President Franklin D. Roosevelt placed U.S. coal mines under federal control and used a "fireside chat" radio address to urge striking miners back to work.[39] A Venezuelan oil producer jokingly suggested building a statue of John L. Lewis, the combative president of the United Mine Workers of America, in Caracas' central square to honor his indirect role in boosting Venezuelan oil exports.[40]

Throughout the 1950s many users switched from coal to petroleum for heat and for powering ships and trains. Coal remained a crucial source of electricity, however, as demand for electric power swelled. Newly prosperous consumers spent their new postwar wealth on televisions, appliances and other goods, and industry and agriculture became increasingly automated. U.S. electricity generation more than quintupled between 1949 and 1970, with nearly half produced from coal-fired power plants.[41]

Focus on Pollution

By 1970 many Americans worried that rapid economic growth was damaging the environment. Air pollution was a major concern. Since the late 1940s a number of "killer smog" events and temperature inversions (situations in which a mass of cold air settled on a region, preventing air pollutants from rising and dispersing) had killed thousands of people in urban areas, including London and New York City.[42] Deadly ingredients in these smogs included SO_2 and toxic metals, emitted from power plants and factories that burned coal and heavy fuel oil.[43]

Congress passed clean air laws in 1955 and 1963, but they mainly helped states to address local air pollution, a strategy that was dwarfed by the national scope of the problem. A few months after the first Earth Day in April 1970, Congress adopted a major set of amendments to the Clean Air Act that directed the EPA to develop National Ambient Air Quality Standards for six so-called "criteria" pollutants, including SO_2, NO_x, ozone and particulate matter. To meet the standards, states were required to develop implementation plans that covered

AP Photo/Debbie Caldwell

Coal miner Allen Turner's children greet him every morning after his shift in Caswood, Ky. The August deaths of nine miners at Utah's Crandall Canyon mine were a grim reminder that coal mining is among the nation's most dangerous occupations. From 1900 through 2006 more than 104,000 American mine workers died on the job.

major pollution sources such as factories, refineries, power plants and motor vehicles.

Congress amended the Clean Air Act again in 1977, setting New Source Performance Standards to ensure that new air pollution sources installed advanced emission controls. Existing power plants were exempted, or "grandfathered," on the grounds that it would be extremely expensive to retrofit them to these standards, and many older plants were expected to cease operating within a few years in any case. If the plants made major modifications that increased their capacity, however, they were required to go through the same New Source Review (NSR) permitting process as newly built facilities.

The amended laws spurred research into pollution controls for power plants. Many new plants installed devices such as flue gas-desulfurization units ("scrubbers"), which removed SO_2 from the gas exiting coal boilers, and low-NO_X burners designed to reduce nitrogen oxide formation during combustion. Some electric utilities turned to low-sulfur coal or cleaner fuels. Nuclear power's share of U.S. electric generation rose from less than 2 percent in 1970 to more than 10 percent in 1980 as reactors ordered in the 1960s and '70s came online, and electric generation from natural gas rose sharply in the early 1970s.

Coal received a boost when Arab countries embargoed oil exports to the United States in 1973, driving oil prices up sharply. Mining expanded, and most oil-burning power plants were converted to coal or natural gas. The Carter administration initiated research on liquefying and gasifying coal to replace imported oil, but these projects proved to be extremely expensive and were tabled a few years later when oil prices declined.

Congress also moved to address the environmental impacts of coal mining by enacting the Surface Mining Control and Reclamation Act (SMCRA) in 1977. Strip mining had been widely practiced since the 1930s, scarring land and damaging rivers and streams with eroded dirt and mine waste. Minerals in coal produced acidic runoff when they came in contact with water, creating toxic drainage that polluted surrounding areas long after mines were shut down.

Critics sought to ban strip mining altogether, but SMCRA regulated the practice instead. The law barred strip mining in areas where it was deemed to be too damaging to the environment and required coal producers to pay per-ton fees into a fund to support reclamation projects on abandoned mine lands.

While mining impacts were debated mainly at the local level, controversy raged nationally through the 1980s over whether SO_2 and NO_x emissions from coal-burning power plants were causing acid rain. In 1990 Congress amended the Clean Air Act yet again to create a cap-and-trade system for SO_2. The law cut total allowable SO_2 emissions to 10 million tons below 1980 levels and assigned emission allowances to large sources, which they could either use to cover their emissions or sell to other generators who needed more allowances. The amendments also set less-stringent controls on NO_x that limited plant emission rates but did not cap total emissions.

SO_2 emissions trading accelerated an ongoing shift away from traditional Eastern coal fields in northern Appalachia, which produced mainly bituminous coal, toward subbituminous coal that produced less heat but also contained less sulfur. The largest such deposits were in Wyoming,

Montana and North Dakota. To service the new demand for subbituminous, railroads deployed massive long-haul coal trains with more than 100 cars each, and Western energy companies developed large-scale surface mines that could be worked with gigantic bulldozers, excavators and draglines weighing thousands of tons.

President Bill Clinton's administration (1993-2001) brought further pressure to bear on the coal industry. Responding to a 1995 petition from Eastern states, EPA issued the Ozone Transport Rule requiring upwind sources to curb NO_x emissions that were contributing to high ozone levels along the East Coast. In 1997 the agency set new standards limiting pollution from fine particulates with diameters of 2.5 micrometers or less (about 3 percent of the width of a human hair). Since sulfates and NO_x contributed to fine-particle formation, the step was a new constraint on coal power plants.

President Clinton also endorsed the 1997 Kyoto Protocol, which required industrialized nations to make specific cuts in greenhouse gas emissions by 2012 in order to limit global climate change. Since coal power plants were one of the largest U.S. sources of CO_2, energy and mining companies strongly opposed the pact. "It's really a double whammy when you combine this with the clean air regulations," said Taylor Pensoneau, vice president of the Illinois Coal Association.[44] Legislators were also concerned about the economic impacts of restricting CO_2 emissions: The U.S. Senate voted 95-0 against ratifying any climate change agreements unless developing countries also were required to limit emissions, and mandatory cuts could be shown not to threaten U.S. economic growth.

The administration further challenged coal-burning utilities when it filed suit against seven utilities in the Midwest and South and issued a separate administrative order against the Tennessee Valley Authority for violating the Clean Air Act by making major modifications to plants without going through the new source review (NSR) process. The Justice Department charged owners of 32 coal plants with illegally emitting tens of millions of tons of SO_2, NO_x and particulates over many years.[45]

Reversal of Fortune

In 1998 oil and natural gas prices, which had been quite steady for a decade or more, began to rise sharply due to factors that included rapid economic growth in China and India, tightening U.S. supplies and instability in many producing countries.[46] President George W. Bush's election in 2000, which was strongly supported by energy companies, dramatically altered prospects for the coal industry. The Bush administration saw coal as crucial to productivity and a healthy economy and moved quickly to alter policies that it viewed as harmful to coal use.

Less than two months after taking office, President Bush reversed a campaign pledge to limit CO_2 emissions, arguing that doing so would raise electricity prices and that CO_2 was not a pollutant under the Clean Air Act.[47] The Bush energy plan, released in May 2001, called for increased research on clean coal technologies and for a new market-based program to further reduce emissions of SO_2, NO_x and mercury. It also recommended reviewing NSR regulations and pending lawsuits to give plant owners more certainty about environmental controls.[48] Four days after the plan was released, the Ohio-based Cinergy Corp. backed out of an NSR settlement that would have reduced its emissions by 500,000 tons per year.[49]

The administration also eased restrictions on coal mining. Under the Clean Water Act, "dredged or fill materials" — which generally are used for a beneficial purpose, such as development — can be added to U.S. waterways under general permits rather than detailed individual permits. In 2002 EPA and the Army Corps of Engineers issued a rule that allowed mine waste to be treated as "fill," making it easier for mountain-removal mining operations to dump waste into adjoining valleys and streams.[50] Another rule proposed in 2004 relaxed a regulation barring coal mining on land within 100 yards of streams that would be harmed by the activity.[51]

Environmental advocates strongly opposed the Bush administration's actions, arguing "Clear Skies" emissions-trading legislation proposed by the White House in 2003 did not reduce its targeted pollutants (SO_2, NO_x, and mercury) far enough or fast enough. After several years of stalemate on Capitol Hill, the EPA in 2005 proposed the Clean Air Interstate Rule (CAIR), which sets new limits on SO_2 and NO_x emissions in 28 Eastern states, and the Clean Air Mercury Rule, which creates a national trading system to reduce mercury emissions from coal-fired power plants.

"CAIR will result in the largest pollution reductions and health benefits of any air rule in more than a decade," said Acting EPA Administrator Stephen Johnson, who stressed that the administration still aimed to pass national clean air legislation. Environmentalists called the measure a step forward but sharply opposed trading mercury emission allowances. Although President Bush's proposals built on the emissions-trading ideas that his father had helped to enact as president in the 1990 Clean Air Act amendments, the second Bush administration was unable to strike similar compromises.

CURRENT SITUATION

Environmental Challenges

Although dozens of new coal-burning power plants are planned or under construction, the latest coal boom is meeting resistance from critics who want to shift the U.S. economy toward cleaner fuels. Even if electricity from coal is cheaper than other sources, they argue, the savings are far outweighed by its environmental and health impacts.

Greenhouse gas emissions are becoming coal's biggest environmental liability, as scientific and public support grows for action to slow global warming. In February 2007 the Intergovernmental Panel on Climate Change (IPCC), an organization created to advise national governments, released its fourth multi-year assessment of the scientific evidence for climate change. Weighing all natural and human influences on climate, the panel concluded in its strongest language to date that Earth was unquestionably warming and that most warming observed since the 1950s was "very likely" (more than a 90 percent chance) due to human activities.[52]

Polls indicate Americans are concerned about global climate change and ready to pay for solutions. In surveys conducted by researchers at MIT, public willingness to pay for solutions to climate change through higher electricity bills rose by 50 percent (from an average of $10 to $15 per month) between 2003 and 2006.[53] The findings indicate the public is increasingly open to policies such as carbon taxes that would raise the price of electricity.

With climate-change science growing clearer and state and public concern rising, many corporate leaders now believe the U.S. will adopt national limits on GHG emissions in the next decade. Some are asking Congress to act now so that they can make informed decisions about future investments. In January the U.S. Climate Action Partnership, a coalition including Alcoa, DuPont, General Electric and Caterpillar, called for binding limits to slow and reverse the

Coal Use Exploding in China and India

Environmental impacts more severe than in U.S.

Three nations account for 60 percent of world coal use: China (which burned 2.3 billion tons of coal in 2005), the United States (1.2 billion tons) and India (500 million tons).[1] Energy demand is growing rapidly in China and India, and both nations get most of their electricity from coal. The U.S. Department of Energy projects that world coal consumption will rise by 74 percent from 2004 through 2030, and that China and India will account for nearly three-fourths of the increase.[2]

Environmental and health impacts from coal use in developing countries are much more severe than those seen in the United States. Air pollution levels in China far exceed both the country's own national standards and recommended air-quality guidelines from the World Health Organization, partly because the nation burns huge quantities of coal in inefficient power plants and factories.

China is the world's biggest source of SO_2, which produces industrial smog and acid rain. Many rural Chinese families also use coal for indoor heating and cooking, creating indoor air pollution that causes thousands of premature deaths every year. "The coal that has powered China's economic growth . . . is also choking its people," writes Elizabeth Economy, director for Asia studies at the influential Council on Foreign Relations, a nonpartisan think tank.[3]

On average, China opens a new coal-burning power plant every week. China displaced the United States in 2007 as the top global CO_2 emitter, making Beijing's heavy reliance on coal a global concern.[4] Some advocates argue the United States should help China adopt advanced clean-coal technologies, but others say outsiders have little leverage over fragmented and poorly coordinated Chinese energy policies. China has begun to research and design advanced, clean coal power plants that can capture carbon emissions, but its near-term focus is on building a string of coal-to-liquid fuel plants to displace some of its oil imports with synthetic fuels.

Significant economic aid could help persuade China and other developing countries to clean up their energy policies. Many experts also say that the U.S. needs to lead. "Without a strong U.S. commitment [on greenhouse gas reductions],

growth of GHG emissions. Addressing climate change, the group said, "will create more economic opportunities than risks for the U.S. economy."[54]

The prospect of GHG limits complicates planning for energy companies, which make decisions about new power plants on multidecade timetables.

"The industry probably took longer than it should have to accept the science," says Mayo Shattuck, president and CEO of Constellation Energy, a *Fortune* 200 company that generates electricity from nuclear power, coal, oil, gas and renewable fuels. "But now companies are trying to formulate policies so that we can deal with climate change in a manageable way. We need to find incentives for new technologies and migrate away from traditional coal."

Many factors influence utility decisions to use particular fuels, including cost, availability and government policies. Providing a steady supply of energy is a prime concern, especially with demand rising. "Our capital is limited, and reliability is a huge issue," says Shattuck. "People expect that the lights will always go on, so we don't want to make many investment mistakes."

Even if utilities try to innovate, regulators may favor a tried-and-true path. For example, Wisconsin-based We Energies proposed to build a coal gasification plant in 2003, but the state public service commission held that the technology was too expensive and technically risky and rejected the unit. Now Wisconsin companies are building conventional coal plants.[55]

The Bush administration has resisted proposals for mandatory GHG reductions, arguing that would drive up energy prices and harm the U.S. economy. Recently, Bush has supported international proposals for negotiating an international agreement that, unlike the Kyoto Protocol, will require action from developing as well as industrialized countries to address global warming. However, the Bush administration's biggest step toward this goal has been to call for a meeting of heads of state in 2008 to agree on a long-term reduction goal.[56]

National Legislation

Since Democrats won majorities in both houses of Congress in 2006, momentum has grown for national legislation to promote clean energy sources and limit GHG emissions.

the international community has no credibility in pressuring the Chinese," Economy observes.[5]

India's population is almost as large as China's, and its economy is also growing quickly, although per-capita energy use in India is currently only about one-third of that in China. India is exploring many energy options and would like to use more of its domestic coal supplies, but much Indian coal has a high ash content, which makes it more polluting and reduces its heat content. As a result, Indian plants must burn more coal to produce a given amount of heat. According to the Brookings Institution, a centrist think tank, India will exhaust its proven coal reserves within 80 years if it keeps burning coal at current rates.[6]

In 2005 the United States and India began discussing ways to mine coal more efficiently and use it more cleanly. And both India and China are participating in FutureGen, a 10-year effort announced by President George W. Bush in 2003 to build a clean coal-burning plant that can produce electricity and hydrogen fuel while capturing and storing carbon emissions.

Meanwhile, because its fastest growth in energy use is projected to take place in the decade after 2020, India may have greater opportunities to introduce clean-coal technologies than China, where dozens of conventional coal plants are already being built.

Cooling towers dwarf the surroundings at a power plant near Zhangjiakou, in China's Hebei province.

[2] U.S. Energy Information Administration, "International Energy Outlook 2007," May 2007, pp. 49, 53.

[3] Elizabeth C. Economy, "The Great Leap Backward?" *Foreign Affairs*, September/October 2007.

[4] John Vidal and David Adam, "China Overtakes U.S. as World's Biggest CO₂ Emitter," *The* [Manchester] *Guardian*, June 19, 2007.

[5] Elizabeth Economy, "China vs. Earth," *The Nation*, May 7, 2007.

[6] Tanvi Madan, India, Brookings Foreign Policy Studies Series, November 2006, pp. 81-83.

[1] U.S. Energy Information Administration, "International Coal Consumption," www.eia.doe.gov/emeu/international/coalconsumption .html.

But both issues affect virtually every sector of the U.S. economy, so agreement will not be quick or easy.[57]

Both houses of Congress have passed energy bills that would speed up work on carbon capture and storage (CCS) by requiring the Energy Department to carry out at least seven large-scale carbon-sequestration demonstrations (storing at least 1 million tons of CO_2 per year) in a variety of geologic formations, as recommended in the MIT coal study. Each bill would increase federal CCS funding by about $1.5 billion over the next five years.[58]

The energy measures, however, are part of broader bills that contain many controversial provisions, such as a national renewable-energy mandate and higher vehicle fuel-economy standards. House and Senate leaders plan to resolve the bills in conference this fall, but the schedule is undetermined. If the CCS provisions are not enacted into law, current Energy Department work to demonstrate CCS could remain at a level the MIT study called "completely inadequate," warning that slow progress on CCS technology and regulations could keep the United States from enacting carbon controls in a timely way.[59]

"A lot of moving parts have to fit together to make carbon capture and storage work," says MIT study coauthor Howard Herzog. "We should be getting the technology figured out, so it can be ready to go when the market conditions are right."

During its debate on the House carbon capture and storage bill, the Senate rejected two amendments that would have revived federal support for producing coal-to-liquids (CTL) fuels, a step that advocates said would reduce U.S. dependence on imported oil. (*See "At Issue," p. 244.*) Coal-state legislators may try to revive federal support for CTL during conference on the energy bill, but with climate change looming in the background, many legislators are wary of measures that would increase U.S. reliance on coal.

Democratic leaders in Congress plan to move legislation in both houses during this session to reduce U.S. GHG emissions by roughly 70 percent by 2050, a level that many scientists say is needed to avoid catastrophic levels of global climate change. Such action would raise the cost of generating electricity from coal and spur a

AT ISSUE

Should the U.S. government subsidize liquid fuels from coal?

YES
John N. Ward
Vice President, Headwaters Inc.

Testimony before House Subcommittee on
Energy and Environment, Sept. 5, 2007

With coal-to-liquids technology, the United States can take control of its energy destiny. Any product made from oil can be made from coal. At today's oil prices, coal-to-liquids is economical and has the power to enhance energy security, create jobs here at home, lessen the U.S. trade deficit and provide environmentally superior fuels that work in today's vehicles. By building even a few coal-to-liquids plants, the U.S. would increase and diversify its domestic production and refining base — adding spare capacity to provide a shock absorber for price volatility. . . .

From a production perspective, coal-to-liquids refineries are very similar to petroleum refineries. They make the same range of products, including gasoline, diesel fuel, jet fuel and chemical feedstocks. These fuels can be distributed in today's pipelines without modification. They can be blended with petroleum-derived fuels if desired. They can be used directly in today's cars, trucks, trains and airplanes without modifications to the engines. . . .

The production of coal-to-liquids fuels is also environmentally responsible. Because coal-liquefaction processes remove contaminants from coal prior to combustion, emissions from coal-to-liquids plants are much lower than traditional pulverized-coal power plants. . . .

[C]oal liquefaction plants generate carbon dioxide in highly concentrated form, allowing carbon capture and storage. Coal-to-liquids plants with carbon-dioxide capture and storage can produce fuels with life-cycle greenhouse-gas-emission profiles that are as good as or better than that of petroleum-derived products. . . .

Although larger-scale coal-to-liquids projects appear to be economically viable in today's oil-price environment, there are still significant hurdles to get the first projects built. There are no coal-to-liquids plants operating in the U.S. that would serve as commercially proven models. Until that happens, financial institutions will be reluctant to fund multibillion-dollar projects without significant technology and market-performance guarantees. . . .

As long as oil prices remain high or climb higher, market forces will lead to the development of a coal-to-liquids infrastructure in the United States. But that development will come slowly and in measured steps. If, for energy-security reasons, the United States would like to speed development of a capability for making transportation fuels from our most abundant domestic energy resource, then incentives for the first coal-to-liquids project are appropriate.

NO
David Hawkins
*Director, Climate Center,
Natural Resources Defense Council*

Testimony before House Subcommittee on
Energy and Environment, Sept. 5, 2007

Coal is a carbon-intensive fuel, containing double the amount of carbon per unit of energy compared to natural gas and about 50 percent more than petroleum. When coal is converted to liquid fuels, two streams of CO_2 are produced: one at the liquid-coal production plant and the second from the exhausts of the vehicles that burn the fuel. . . . [E]ven if the CO_2 from the synfuel production plant is captured, there is no prospect that liquid fuel made with coal as the sole feedstock can achieve the significant reductions in fossil carbon content that we need to protect the climate. . . .

EPA's analysis finds that without carbon capture life-cycle greenhouse-gas emissions from coal-to-liquid fuels would be more than twice as high as from conventional diesel fuel (118 percent higher). Assuming carbon capture and storage, EPA finds that life-cycle greenhouse-gas emissions from coal-to-liquid fuels would be 3.7 percent higher than from conventional diesel fuel. . . .

In the West, as in the East, surface-mining activities cause severe environmental damage as huge machines strip, rip apart and scrape aside vegetation, soils [and] wildlife habitat and drastically reshape existing land forms and the affected area's ecology to reach the subsurface coal. Strip mining results in industrialization of once quiet open space along with displacement of wildlife, increased soil erosion, loss of recreational opportunities, degradation of wilderness values and destruction of scenic beauty. . . .

According to the Department of Energy's Idaho National Lab, approximately 12-14 barrels of water are used for every barrel of liquid coal. Therefore the water requirement necessary to meet the needs of an 80,000 BPD [barrels per day] liquid-coal plant could require sourcing about 40 million gallons of water per day (14 billion gallons per year). The 40 million gallons of water per day needed for an 80,000 BPD liquid coal facility is enough water to meet the domestic needs of more than 200,000 people. . . . There are already serious water-supply problems in Western states such as Montana and Wyoming, where most of our cheap coal supplies are located. . . .

The impacts that a large liquid-coal program could have on global warming pollution, conventional air pollution and damage from expanded coal production are substantial — so substantial that using coal to make liquid fuel would likely create far worse problems than it attempts to solve.

move away from traditional coal plants and toward more efficient designs with CCS as well as lower-carbon fuels.

Some energy companies are rushing to build new coal plants before climate legislation passes, but prominent Democrats have warned that they will not "grandfather" operating plants from complying with GHG reductions. "Any company planning to spend billions of dollars on new coal-fired power plants, and any investor in such a company, should think carefully about how to spend their funds so as to be part of the solution to climate change, not a part of the problem," Senate committee chairs Jeff Bingaman, D-N.M. (Energy and Natural Resources) and Barbara Boxer, D-Calif. (Environment and Public Works) wrote in a January op-ed.[60]

Congress is addressing other coal issues this fall as well. Responding to the August Crandall Canyon mining disaster, several Senate committees are holding hearings on mine safety and the adequacy of federal oversight. Legislators in both houses have already introduced bills to speed up technical improvements in mine communications and increase fines for accidents.[61] And 92 House members have cosponsored the Clean Water Protection Act, introduced by Rep. Frank Pallone Jr., D-N.J., which would end dumping of mountaintop mining waste into streams.

Muffled Boom?

Concerns about pollution could deflate the nascent U.S. coal boom. Some two-dozen coal plants have been cancelled since early 2006, including the TXU cancellations in Texas and projects in Florida, Montana, North Carolina and Oregon.[62] Senate Majority Leader Harry Reid of Nevada is publicly opposing three proposed plants in his home state. "I will use every means at my disposal to prevent the construction of new coal-fired plants in Nevada that do not capture and permanently store greenhouse gas emissions," Reid wrote in July.[63]

Many facilities are still moving forward, including planned or proposed coal gasification plants in a dozen states. But investors are cooling on the coal industry. In July Citigroup's equity research division downgraded coal stocks across the board, based on low expected earnings and a hostile political outlook. "[P]rophesies of a new wave of coal-fired generation have vaporized, while clean-coal technologies such as IGCC [integrated gasification combined cycle] with carbon capture and coal-to-liquids remain a decade away, or more," wrote Citigroup analyst John Hill.[64] Prices of a dozen large coal companies were down 11 to 38 percent from their 52-week highs in early September.[65]

"A lot of countervailing trends have emerged in the past year," says Ceres electric power program director Bakal. "There's new awareness of climate change and discussion of regulating carbon emissions. Also, the cost of building any kind of new generating plant is rising because the costs of commodities and labor are rising. And there's increasing recognition that energy-efficiency measures are a cheaper and quicker way to address rising electricity demand than building new plants, so states are providing new incentives for energy-efficiency programs."

OUTLOOK
Energy Choices

Coal's role in the nation's energy portfolio in the coming decades will be shaped by market signals from government officials. If Congress moves quickly to set greenhouse gas reduction targets and boosts support for clean-coal technologies like gasification and carbon capture, energy company investments will follow. Without policy and economic incentives, corporations will have less reason to take the low-carbon path.

"We need a strong partnership with the federal government to develop new technologies for managing coal emissions, including carbon," says National Mining Association Vice President Raulston. "That's going to be very expensive, and the industry needs help to bring these systems to the deployment stage."

Conventional pollutants like SO_2 and NO_x are still serious concerns. The American Lung Association's most recent report card on U.S. air quality found that fine-particulate air pollution rose in the Eastern United States from 2003-2005, after consistent decreases from 1999 through 2003, mainly because of increased generation by coal-burning power plants. Building more coal-burning plants will increase pollution levels in some areas, the study warned, even if all new plants use the best available pollution-control technology — which is not guaranteed under current law.[66]

"We need tighter limits on coal-fired plants," says the lung association's Nolen. "Delaying and weakening regulations will mean more unnecessary deaths and more harm to public health."

Meanwhile, major investments in energy efficiency could buy time to expand less-polluting energy sources. Saving a kilowatt-hour of electricity through energy-efficiency measures is often quicker and cheaper than generating it at a power plant and can help avert the need to build new plants. Statewide conservation initiatives launched in California after its energy supply crisis in 2000-2001 have reduced per-capita electricity use to record lows. In 2005 the average Californian used 7,032 kilowatt-hours, two to four times lower than consumers in many other states.[67]

"Demand management and efficiency should be priorities, because we can do something about that now," says Constellation Energy's Shattuck. "There's no more cheap power — people have to use less energy, and they have to understand the technologies and their own usage patterns so they can reduce their energy use. We can't build ourselves out of this situation."

Critics want to phase conventional coal plants (without carbon capture and sequestration) out of U.S. energy policy, given the environmental and health impacts of mining and transporting as well as burning it. "The trend is going to be toward energy efficiency and renewables, and toward carbon capture. We can't afford to keep automatically building coal plants, from a human-health standpoint or an economic standpoint," says Coken of Western Resource Advocates.

Ironically, however, the MIT coal study concluded that if carbon capture and storage is adopted successfully, the world will use more coal, not less, in coming decades.[68] Given how heavily other nations rely on coal, especially India and China, the United States has a long-term interest in making coal energy cleaner and safer, even if our own fuel mix shifts toward lower-carbon sources. Rep. Edward Markey, D-Mass., chairman of the House Select Energy Committee on Energy and Global Warming, warns, "If we do not solve this challenge, our fight to protect the planet from global warming will be lost before it even gets started."[69]

NOTES

1. According to the Department of Energy, average residential energy use in 2005 was 938 kilowatt hours per month, or 11,256 kilowatt hours (11.25 megawatt

hours) per year. U.S. Department of Energy, Energy Information Administration, "Frequently Asked Questions — Energy," http://tonto.eia.doe .gov/ask/electricity_faqs.asp#electricity_use_home.

2. Environmental Integrity Project, "Dirty Kilowatts: America's Most Polluting Power Plants" (July 2007). Bowen's mercury emissions ranked 14th among power plants nationwide in 2005, the most recent year for which data was available.

3. U.S. Department of Energy, National Energy Technology Laboratory, "Tracking New Coal-Fired Power Plants," May 1, 2007, www.netl.doe.gov/ coal/refshelf/ncp.pdf.

4. U.S. Energy Information Administration, "Annual Energy Outlook 2007," pp. 82-84.

5. U.S. Department of Labor, Mine Safety and Health Administration, "Coal Fatalities for 1900 through 2006," www.msha.gov/stats/centurystats/coalstats.asp. For background see Pamela M. Prah, "Coal Mining Safety," *CQ Researcher*, March 17, 2006, pp. 241-264.

6. For example, see Douglas W. Dockery, *et al.*, "An Association Between Air Pollution and Mortality in Six U.S. Cities," *The New England Journal of Medicine*, vol. 329, no. 24 (1993), pp. 1753-1759; C. Arden Pope, *et al.*, "Lung Cancer, Cardiopulmonary Mortality, and Long-Term Exposure to Fine Particulate Air Pollution," *JAMA (Journal of the American Medical Association)*, vol. 287, no. 9 (2002), pp. 1132-1141; and Abt Associates, Inc., "Power Plant Emissions: Particulate Matter-Related Health Damages and the Benefits of Alternative Emission Reduction Scenarios," June 2004, www.catf.us/ publications/reports/Power_Plant_Emissions.pdf.

7. For background see Adriel Bettelheim, "Biofuels Boom," *CQ Researcher*, Sept. 29, 2006, pp. 793-816; Barbara Mantel, "Energy Efficiency," *CQ Researcher*, May 19, 2006, pp. 433-456; and Mary H. Cooper, "Alternative Fuels," *CQ Researcher*, Feb. 25, 2005, pp. 173-196.

8. For background see Jennifer Weeks, "Nuclear Energy," *CQ Researcher*, March 10, 2006, pp. 217-240.

9. National Research Council, "Coal: Research and Development To Support National Energy Policy," prepublication copy, 2007, p. 3.

10. Matthew L. Wald, "Committed To Coal, and In A Hurry, Too," *The New York Times*, Nov. 7, 2006.

11. Sierra Club, "TXU Announces New Coal Fired Power Plants," April 21, 2006.

12. Andrew Ross Sorkin, "A $45 Billion Buyout Deal With Many Shades of Green," *The New York Times*, Feb. 26, 2007; *Independent Assessment of Proposed Leveraged Buyout of TXU: The Impact on Consumers* (Washington, DC: GF Energy LLC), June 2007, pp. 59-61.

13. For background see Tom Price, "Corporate Social Responsibility," *CQ Researcher*, Aug. 3, 2007, pp. 649-672.

14. For background see Marcia Clemmitt, "Climate Change," *CQ Researcher*, Jan. 27, 2006, pp. 73-96.

15. Carbon dioxide (CO_2) is a molecule containing one carbon atom and two oxygen atoms. By weight, CO_2 is about 27 percent carbon. Since carbon is the substance that traps heat in the atmosphere and causes global climate change, regulators often talk interchangeably about controlling either CO_2 emissions or carbon emissions. In either case the objective is to prevent the carbon component from being released.

16. Stephen Ansolabehere, *et al.*, *The Future of Coal: Options For a Carbon-Constrained World* (2007).

17. Amanda Griscom Little, "Let's Call the Coal Thing Off," Grist, March 9, 2007; James Hansen, "Why We Can't Wait," *The Nation*, May 7, 2007.

18. Chris Dodd For President, "The Dodd Energy Plan," http://chrisdodd.com/energy_independence/plan; John Edwards For President, "Edwards Calls For Cleaner Use of Coal as Part of Fight Against Global Warming," http://johnedwards.com/news/headlines/20070326-cleaner-coal/.

19. Margot Roosevelt, "State Acts To Limit Use of Coal Power," *Los Angeles Times*, May 24, 2007.

20. S. 1227, the Clean Coal Act of 2007, introduced April 26, 2007.

21. "Climate Policy, Energy Efficiency Take Center Stage at State Regulators' Summer Conference," *Electric Utility Week*, July 23, 2007.

22. David Hawkins and George Peridas, "No Time Like the Present: NRDC's Response to MIT's 'Future of Coal' Report," March 2007, pp. 6-9, www.nrdc.org/globalWarming/coal/mit.pdf.

23. Based on EPA's reference dose for mercury of 0.1 micrograms per kilogram of body weight per day.

24. U.S. Environmental Protection Agency, Office of Water, "2005/2006 National Listing of Fish Advisories," July 2007, www.epa.gov/waterscience/fish/advisories/2006/tech.pdf.

25. Rick Srivastava. Nick Hutson, and Frank Princiotta, U.S. Environmental Protection Agency, Office of Research and Development, "Reduction of Mercury Emissions From Coal-Fired Electric Utility Boilers," July 12, 2005, www.netl.doe.gov/publications/proceedings/05/Mercury/pdf/Srivastava-071205-am.pdf.

26. Senate Joint Res. 20, defeated 47-51 with two members not voting, Sept. 13, 2005.

27. David C. Evers, *et al.*, "Biological Mercury Hotspots in the Northeastern United States and Southeastern Canada," *BioScience*, Vol. 57, No. 1, January 2007, pp. 29-43.

28. Charles T. Driscoll, *et al.*, "Mercury Contamination in Forest and Freshwater Ecosystems in the Northeastern United States," *BioScience*, Vol. 57, No. 1, January 2007, pp. 17-28.

29. "Mercury Matters: Linking Mercury Science With Public Policy in the Northeastern United States," Hubbard Brook Research Foundation, January 2007, p. 6.

30. U.S Environmental Protection Agency, Region 3, "Mountaintop Mining/Valley Fills In Appalachia: Final Programmatic Environmental Impact Statement," October 2005, p. 4. "Mountaintop mining" as defined in the report includes mountaintop removal and other surface-mining methods on mountain slopes.

31. EPA, "Mountaintop Mining/Valley Fills in Appalachia: Draft Programmatic Environmental Impact Statement," p. III. A-6.

32. Ken Ward Jr., "Mines Might Get More Time on Selenium," *Charleston Gazette*, March 4, 2007.

33. Testimony before House Committee on Natural Resources, July 25, 2007, p. 2.

34. Testimony before House Committee on Natural Resources, July 25, 2007, p. 6.

35. *Ohio Valley Environmental Coalition, et al., v. United States Army Corps of Engineers, et al.,* Civil Action No. 3:05-0784, March 23, 2007.

36. Ken Ward Jr., "Mine Ponds Ruled Illegal," *Charleston Gazette,* June 14, 2007; Beth Gorczyca Ryan, "Federal Pond Ruling Troubles Coal," *The State Journal,* June 21, 2007.

37. Ryan, *op. cit.*

38. For background see University of Denver Department of Anthropology, Colorado Coal Field War Project, "A History of the Colorado Coal Field War," www.du.edu/anthro/ludlow/cfhist.html.

39. See University of California, Santa Barbara, The American Presidency Project, Fireside Chat #46, May 2, 1943, www.presidency.ucsb.edu/ws/index.php?pid=16393.

40. Daniel Yergin, *The Prize: The Epic Quest For Oil, Money and Power* (1991), p. 543.

41. U.S. Energy Information Administration, "Annual Energy Review 2006" (2007), p. 226.

42. U.S. Environmental Protection Agency, Region 10, "Air Pollution Events in History," Sept. 15, 2003, http://yosemite.epa.gov/r10/homepage.nsf.

43. Coal emissions were mainly a problem in the Eastern United States, while Los Angeles' notorious air-pollution problems stemmed from other sources such as vehicle exhaust and hydrocarbons from oil refineries. South Coast Air Quality Management District, "The Southland's War on Smog: Fifty Years of Progress Toward Clean Air," May 1997, www.aqmd.gov/news1/Archives/History/marchcov.html.

44. William Flannery, "Global Warming Treaty: What It Would Mean for St. Louis," *St. Louis Post-Dispatch,* Dec. 12, 1997.

45. "U.S. Sues Electric Utilities in Unprecedented Action to Enforce the Clean Air Act," EPA press release, Nov. 3, 1999.

46. For background see Jennifer Weeks, "Domestic Energy Development," *CQ Researcher,* Sept. 30, 2005, pp. 809-832.

47. Robert Schlesinger, "Bush Bars New Control on Emission," *The Boston Globe,* March 14, 2001.

48. National Energy Policy Development Group, "Reliable, Affordable, and Environmentally Sound Energy for America's Future" (May 2001), pp. 3-3, 5-13 to 5-15, www.whitehouse.gov/energy/2001/National-Energy-Policy.pdf.

49. Clear the Air, "Timeline: Power Plant Cleanup and New Source Review," www.cleartheair.org/proactive/newsroom/release.vtml?id=21840#12.

50. Jeff Nesmith, "Bush Pushes Mountaintop Removal Mining," *Atlanta Journal-Constitution,* April 14, 2002.

51. "Interior Department Set to Relax Rules Regarding Mining Near Streams," *U.S. Coal Review,* Jan. 12, 2004.

52. Intergovernmental Panel on Climate Change, *Climate Change 2007: The Scientific Basis, Summary for Policymakers* (2007), p. 8.

53. Ansolabehere, *et al., op. cit.,* p. 90.

54. United States Climate Action Partnership, *A Call for Action* (2007), p. 3.

55. Thomas Content and Lee Bergquist, "Our Insatiable Appetite For Coal," *Milwaukee Journal Sentinel,* Feb. 10, 2007.

56. "President Bush Participates in Major Economies Meeting On Energy Security and Climate Change," White House press release, Sept. 28, 2007.

57. For background see Coral Davenport, "Facing the 50-Year Carbon Challenge," *CQ Weekly,* Sept. 3, 2007.

58. H.R. 6 as amended by the Senate, passed on June 21, Title III; H.R. 3221, passed by the House Aug. 4, Title IV, Subtitle F.

59. Ansolabehere, *et al., op. cit.,* p. xii.

60. Jeff Bingaman, and Barbara Boxer, "Utilities That Rush New Coal Plants Now Won't Get Bigger Emission Breaks Later," *Dallas Morning News,* Jan. 19, 2007.

61. Libby George, "Utah Mine Disaster Has Congress Considering Stricter Mandates for Safety," *CQ Today,* Sept. 4, 2007.

62 Rebecca Smith, "Coal's Doubters Block New Wave of Power Plants," *The Wall Street Journal,* July 25, 2007; Steven Mufson, "Coal Rush Reverses, Power Firms Follow," *The Washington Post,* Sept. 4, 2007.

63. Bernie Woodall, "Reid Tells Four Companies No Coal Power in Nevada," Reuters, July 26, 2007.

64. "Coal: Missing the Window," Citigroup, July 18, 2007, available online at http://switchboard.nrdc

.org/blogs/ngreene/media/Citibank%20071807
.pdf.

65. Andrew T. Gillies, "Getting Burned," Forbes.com,
Sept. 5, 2007.

66. American Lung Association, *State of the Air: 2007*
(2007), pp. 9-12, 56-57.

67. California Energy Commission, "U.S. Per Capita
Electricity Use by State In 2005," www.energy.ca
.gov/electricity/us_per_capita_electricity_2005.

68. Ansolabehere, *et al.*, *op. cit.*, pp. 14-15.

69. Rep. Edward Markey, "What Role Coal?" *Grist*, June 21,
2007, http://gristmill.grist.org/story/2007/6/20/
16282/1355.

BIBLIOGRAPHY

Books

Freese, Barbara, *Coal: A Human History*, Perseus,
2003.
A former state environmental regulator recounts how
coal helped to make the Industrial Revolution possible
and chronicles its human impacts worldwide.

Goodell, Jeff, *Big Coal: The Dirty Secret Behind
America's Energy Future*, Houghton Mifflin, 2006.
Journalist Goodell argues the nation is addicted to coal
energy and is in denial about its health, safety and environmental consequences.

National Research Council, *Coal: Research and
Development To Support National Energy Policy*,
National Academies Press, 2007.
A congressionally requested study identifies areas where
research is needed to support use of coal to meet U.S. energy
goals, including new estimates of national coal reserves, steps
to make coal mining safer and new techniques for mitigating
the environmental impacts of mining.

Reece, Erik, *Lost Mountain: A Year in the Vanishing
Wilderness*, Penguin, 2006.
Reece describes the leveling of a Kentucky peak during a
year of mountaintop-removal mining.

Articles

Fairley, Peter, "China's Coal Future," *Technology Review*,
January 2007.

To reduce its dependence on imported oil, China is making huge investments in all kinds of coal technology, from
traditional pulverized-coal power plants to coal-to-liquids
refineries. So far, however, Beijing is paying more attention to increasing energy supply than to reducing the
accompanying pollution.

Gribben, Roland, "Coal Cleans Up Its Act and Makes a
Comeback," *Daily Telegraph* [London], March 22, 2007.
Electricity producers in Britain are investing in technologies
to reduce greenhouse gas emissions from coal-fired power
plants. England is also looking to carbon emissions trading
to meet stringent greenhouse gas reduction targets.

McPhee, John, "Coal Train," *The New Yorker*, Oct. 3
and 10, 2005.
Hauling coal across the United States generates more
than one-fifth of railroad industry revenues. McPhee
rides with coal train operators and describes the vast scale
of surface mining operations in Wyoming's Powder River
Basin, the nation's largest source of low-sulfur coal.

Stier, Ken, "Eco-Friendly CEO?" *The Chief Executive*,
April 2005.
James Rogers, now head of Duke Energy, says that carbon
limits are inevitable and that his industry needs to prepare
for them.

Ward, Ken Jr., *et al.*, "Mining the Mountains," *The
Charleston Gazette Online*, www.wvgazette.com/static/
series/mining.
A collection of award-winning investigative reports, follow-up articles and opinion pieces document the impact
of mountaintop-removal mining in West Virginia.

Whitman, David, "Burning Atlanta," *Washington
Monthly*, September 2005.
Two decades of debate over sulfur dioxide and nitrogen
oxide emissions at Georgia Power's Plant Bowen illustrate
the pros and cons of different approaches to regulating air
pollution.

Reports and Studies

American Lung Association, "State of the Air: 2007."
The association's annual report card on U.S. air quality
finds that almost half of the U.S. population lives in counties with unhealthful levels of ozone or particulate pollution. The report recommends steps to make air cleaner,
including tighter limits on power plant emissions.

Ansolabehere, Stephen, *et al.,* "The Future of Coal," Massachusetts Institute of Technology, 2007.
A panel of MIT energy and public policy experts examines the role of coal as an energy source in a world where limits on carbon emissions are likely to be adopted to slow global climate change. The study finds that continued reliance on coal as a primary fuel will require technologies to be developed and commercialized to capture and store carbon emissions from coal combustion.

Hubbard Brook Research Foundation, "Mercury Matters: Linking Mercury Science with Public Policy in the Northeastern United States," January 2007.
Based on two articles in the peer-reviewed journal *BioScience,* this report presents new findings on environmental mercury concentrations in the Northeastern United States and eastern Canada. The authors conclude that local and regional sources, including coal-burning power plants, are important contributors to Northeast mercury hotspots, and that mercury emissions trading may not alleviate the problem if it allows emissions at these sources to continue unabated.

U.S. Energy Information Administration, "Annual Energy Outlook 2007," www.eia.doe.gov/oiaf/aeo/index .html.
The agency's latest annual report analyzes U.S. energy supply, demand and prices with projects through 2030, with chapters on coal and other fuels.

For More Information

American Lung Association, 61 Broadway, 6th Floor, New York, NY 10006; (212) 315-8700; www.lungusa.org. Funds research and carries out advocacy and public education on issues associated with fighting lung diseases, including environmental health.

Clean Air Markets Program, U.S. Environmental Protection Agency, 1200 Pennsylvania Ave., N.W., Mail Code 6204J, Washington, DC 20460; (202) 343-9150; www.epa.gov/airmarkets. Administers market-based programs to reduce emissions.

Coal River Mountain Watch, P.O. Box 651, Whitesville, WV 25209; (304) 854-2182; www.crmw.net. Works to halt mountaintop mining in West Virginia.

Coal-to-Liquids Coalition, (202) 463-9789; www.future coalfuels.org. A coalition of labor, mining, and industry groups promoting liquefied-coal fuels.

Edison Electric Institute, 701 Pennsylvania Avenue, N.W., Washington, DC 20004; (202) 508-5000; www.eei.org. Represents shareholder-owned electric companies.

Energy Information Administration, U.S. Department of Energy, 1000 Independence Ave., S.W., Washington, DC 20585; (202) 586-8800; www.eia.doe.gov. Central source for U.S. government data and forecasts on energy.

Hubbard Brook Research Foundation, 16 Buck Road, Hanover, NH 03755; (603) 653-0390; www.hubbardbrook foundation.org. Supports long-term research at the Hubbard Brook experimental forest in central New Hampshire.

National Mining Association, 1010 Constitution Ave., N.W., Suite 500 East, Washington, DC 20001; (202) 463-2600; www.nma.org. Represents the mining industry.

Office of Surface Mining Reclamation and Enforcement, U.S. Department of the Interior, 1951 Constitution Ave., N.W., Washington, DC 20240; (202) 208-2719; www .osmre.gov. Regulates mountaintop removal.

Western Resource Advocates, 2260 Baseline Road, Suite 200, Boulder, CO, 80302; (303) 444-1188; www.westernre-sourceadvocates.org. Nonprofit law and policy group that advocates for environmental protection in interior Western states.

Ecotourism

*Does It Help or Hurt
Fragile Lands and Cultures?*

Rachel S. Cox

Marine iguanas show little fear of visitors to the Galapagos Islands, where the Ecuadorian government tightly controls tourism. Ecotourism supporters say such "sustainable" travel brings environmental and economic benefits to isolated communities, but critics warn that even well-managed ecotourism can destroy the very attractions it promotes.

Terra Incognita Ecotours/Gerard "Ged" Caddick

From *CQ Researcher*,
October 20, 2006.

11

A week-long cruise to the fabled Galapagos Islands last summer took members of the Sturc family of Washington, D.C., back into history. As they clambered out of their rubber landing raft, boobies and penguins, iguanas and sea lions greeted them as nonchalantly as their forebears had greeted British naturalist Charles Darwin when he arrived in 1835 to collect evidence that led to his theory of natural selection.

"It was beautiful in a very stark way," Susan Sturc recalls. "We were impressed at how clean everything was. There was no trash anywhere." But, she adds, the islands 600 miles off the coast of Ecuador were "not as untouched as I had thought they would be. I was surprised at how much development there was. I thought it would be pristine."

The Sturcs' experience typifies the paradox of ecotourism, a relatively new and increasingly popular form of tourism that The International Ecotourism Society defines as "responsible travel to natural areas that conserves the environment and improves the well-being of local people."

To its supporters, ecotourism offers a model with the potential to remake the travel industry, bringing environmental and economic benefits to destination communities while providing tourists with more meaningful experiences than conventional tourism offers. But critics warn that the environmental and social changes that accompany even well-managed ecotourism threaten to destroy the very attractions it promotes.

Over the last 25 years, travelers have enjoyed expanding opportunities to visit locations once considered impossibly remote. Even

Hotels Going 'Green' Around the World

Many tourism companies are trying to reduce their impact on the environment — and save money — by cutting consumption of water, energy and other resources and improving the disposal of waste.

Hotel "Greening" Success Stories

Hilton International

The chain saved 60 percent on gas costs and 30 percent on both electricity and water in recent years, cutting waste by 25 percent. Vienna Hilton and Vienna Plaza reduced laundry loads by 164,000 kilograms per year, minimizing water and chemical use.

Singapore Marriott and Tang Plaza Scandic

Efforts to save some 40,000 cubic meters of water per year have reduced water use by 20 percent per guest. The chain pioneered a 97 percent "recyclable" hotel room and is building or retrofitting 1,500 rooms annually.

Sheraton Rittenhouse Square, Philadelphia

Boasts a 93 percent recycled granite floor, organic cotton bedding, night tables made from discarded wooden shipping pallets, naturally dyed recycled carpeting and nontoxic wallpaper, carpeting, drapes and cleaning products. The extra 2 percent 'green' investment was recouped in the first six months.

Inter-Continental Hotels and Resorts

Each facility must implement a checklist of 134 environmental actions and meet specific energy, waste and water-management targets. Between 1988 and 1995, the chain reduced overall energy costs by 27 percent. In 1995, it saved $3.7 million, reducing sulfur dioxide emissions by 10,670 kilograms, and saved 610,866 cubic meters of water — an average water reduction of nearly 7 percent per hotel, despite higher occupancies.

Forte Brighouse, West Yorkshire, United Kingdom

Energy-efficient lamps reduced energy use by 45 percent, cut maintenance by 85 percent and lowered carbon emissions by 135 tons. The move paid for itself in less than a year.

Hyatt International

Energy-efficiency measures in the United States cut energy use by 15 percent and now save the chain an estimated $15 million annually.

Holiday Inn Crowne Plaza, Schiphol Airport, Netherlands

By offering guests the option of not changing their linens and towels each day, the hotel reduced laundry volume, water and detergent — as well as costs — by 20 percent.

Source: Lisa Mastny, "Traveling Light, New Paths for International Tourism."

than the tourism industry as a whole, according to the World Tourism Organization.[1]

Tourism activist Deborah McLaren, the founder of Indigenous Rights International, says many tourists are no longer interested in the fantasy tourism culture of "sand, sun, sea and sex" offered by packaged tours to beach resorts and cruise ships.[2] Many travelers now prefer what the industry calls "experiential" tourism — encounters with nature, heritage and culture. Many also want a sense of adventure and discovery or philanthropic activities, such as restoring historic buildings or teaching.[3]

While ecotourism has brought new income to isolated parts of the world, it has come at a price, critics say. When archeologist Richard Leventhal, director of the Museum of Archaeology and Anthropology at the University of Pennsylvania, began his field work in 1972 in Cancun, Mexico, grass huts bordered the island's white-sand beaches. Today, Cancun's 20,000 hotel rooms attract more than 2.6 million visitors a year, and a sprawling shanty town houses the 300,000 workers drawn to the new industry.[4]

"Ecotourism has brought a lot of attention to a lot of places that wouldn't have gotten it otherwise," Leventhal observes. "That's generally good, because the economies are so fragile." But "tourism is one of the most fickle stimuli that exist. A hurricane comes, and the tourists are gone."

"Ecotourism is not the cost-free business option that its supporters suggest," argues Rosaleen Duffy, a senior lecturer at the Centre for International Politics at Manchester University in England. "Because ecotourism often takes place in relatively remote areas and small communities, the effects of

Antarctica is now visited by more than 10,000 travelers per year. Tourism in general is considered by many to be the world's largest industry, and one of the fastest growing. Indeed, eco/nature tourism is growing three times faster

establishing a small-scale hotel or food outlet can have the same impact as building a Hilton in a large town or city."[5]

As a Maya scholar, Leventhal has worked closely with communities throughout Central America, especially in Belize — considered a leading ecotourism success story similar to nearby Costa Rica. "What I always ask," he says, "is, 'Does it really benefit local people?' "

Development economists call the problem "leakage." Studies have shown that up to half of the tourism revenue entering the developing world reverts to the developed world in profits earned by foreign-owned businesses, promotional spending abroad or payments for imported labor and goods.[6]

And, as "ecotourism" has become a popular gimmick in travel marketing, another sort of leakage has emerged. "Ten years ago, I could tell you what ecotourism was," Leventhal says. "Today, everyone's trying to claim it, because it's a hook people really like."

Ron Mader, a Mexico-based travel writer and founder of the ecotourism Web site Planeta.com, agrees. "Look at national travel Web sites," he says. "Even Cancun has a page on ecotourism," with a picture of a contented drinker lounging at a pool bar, suggesting that just getting a sunburn is "practicing ecotourism."

Partly to clarify such public misperceptions, some ecotourism advocates support creation of a certification system reflecting a destination's environmental and cultural sensitivity. Conservation groups like the Rainforest Alliance and Conservation International see the plan as a way to encourage responsible ecotourism and sound environmental practices.

"'Eco-travel' can come in many shades of green," senior editor Rene Ebersole writes in *Audubon* magazine. "Without a global certification label — something as recognizable as, say, the [U.S. Department of Agriculture] 'Organic' sticker on produce —- it's hard to be sure" which trips qualify as genuine ecotourism.[7]

Critics contend, however, that ecotourism certification will further diminish the involvement of indigenous people and exacerbate many of the problems ecotourism already creates for its communities. "It really pits people against each other," says McLaren.

Conservation International and other major non-governmental conservation organizations (NGOs) say ecotourism can give indigenous people a stake in

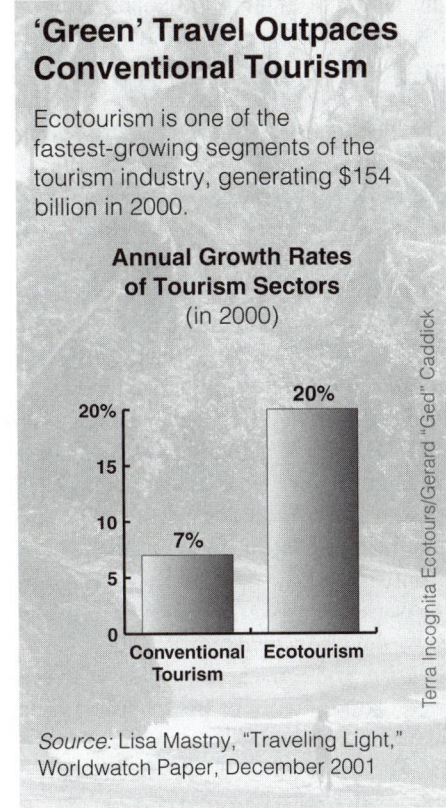

'Green' Travel Outpaces Conventional Tourism

Ecotourism is one of the fastest-growing segments of the tourism industry, generating $154 billion in 2000.

Annual Growth Rates of Tourism Sectors
(in 2000)

- Conventional Tourism: 7%
- Ecotourism: 20%

Terra Incognita Ecotours/Gerard "Ged" Caddick

Source: Lisa Mastny, "Traveling Light," Worldwatch Paper, December 2001

protecting their environment, with income from tourism compensating for the loss of traditional lifeways, such as hunting and slash-and-burn agriculture.

"Carefully planned and implemented tourism can . . . offer a powerful incentive to conserve and protect biodiversity," says Conservation International. "People who earn their living from ecotourism are more likely to protect their natural resources and support conservation efforts."[8]

But Luis Vivanco, an anthropology professor at the University of Vermont who has studied the effects of ecotourism in Costa Rica, is skeptical. "For elites and people with the ability to make money, it's a great opportunity," he says. But in real life, "ecotourism is redefining people's lives and landscapes. It's impossible not to wonder if they could be destroying what they love."

As conservationists, tourism operators, development banks and anthropologists evaluate ecotourism, here are some of the key questions in the debate:

Does ecotourism threaten fragile ecosystems?

Traveling in Nepal in the early 1980s, Steve Powers, a tour operator in Long Beach, N.Y., witnessed the effects of uncontrolled tourism. "Nepal was a prime example of how not to do tourism in the Third World," he says. "The government policy was to let everybody in with no controls. Tourists just trashed the trekking sites, and backpackers living on $2 a day really weren't benefiting the community."

Even the native porters contributed to the problem. He remembers seeing them conscientiously collect all the trash at a campsite, then dump it in a river.

By 2003, more than 25,000 trekkers were visiting the Khumbu Valley near Mt. Everest. Much of the area that Sir Edmund Hillary described as being superbly forested in 1951 had become "an eroding desert."[9]

The main culprit in the area's massive deforestation was the tourists, and the demand they created not only for fuel to warm themselves and their porters but also to build the "teahouses" where they stayed.

"Do tourists who come here consider what their need for hot water costs in terms of wood?" asked Gian Pietro Verza, field manager at an Italian environmental research station near a Sherpa village. "One trekker can consume an average of five times more wood per day than an entire Sherpa family uses — and the porters and guides they bring with them need firewood, too."[10]

Other ecotourism skeptics tell the story of Brazil's first "eco-resort," Praia do Forte, a 247-room hotel whose developer bought thousands of acres of rain forest on a spectacular beach, then leveled much of the forest to build his hotel.[11]

In Africa, uncontrolled "nature" tourism has been linked to a decline in cheetah survival rates. As tourists clamor to watch the cats up close, according to Costas Christ, Sr., director of ecotourism at Conservation International, they frighten the cheetahs and their young away from hard-won kills, the food is scavenged by hyenas and the cubs go hungry.[12]

The Third World Network, a Malaysia-based coalition that supports development in developing countries, recently reported that tourism was destroying the "World's Eighth Wonder" — the Banaue rice terraces, a UNESCO World Heritage site in the northern Philippines. The group said timber cutting in the Banaue watershed to provide wood for handicrafts for tourists was reducing water flow to the terraces and encouraging giant earthworms to bore deeper into their banks.

In addition, a recent study by the Tebtebba Foundation, a Philippines-based indigenous peoples' advocacy and research center, found the terraces also were being damaged by the water demands of hotels, lodges and restaurants, as well as the conversion of rice paddies into lots for lodges and shops. At the same time, the study said, rice farmers are giving up their traditional livelihoods to take jobs in tourism.[13]

Similarly, the development in the Galapagos Islands that surprised ecotourist Susan Sturc reflected social changes brought about by increased tourism. The Ecuadorian government tightly controls Galapagos tourism, limiting the number of cruise ships, requiring visitors' groups to be accompanied by guides and prohibiting the carrying of food onto the islands.[14]

Nonetheless, the influx of tourists has attracted many Ecuadorians from the mainland who seek better economic opportunities. Between 1974 and 1997 the population of the Galapagos grew by almost 150 percent, and today there are about 27,000 year-round residents. In 2004, a study about the future of the Galapagos warned "tourism is the main economic driver, yet the migration it induces threatens the future of tourism."[15]

These and many other environmental impacts are being addressed by governments and NGOs. Tour operator Powers helped to establish Nepal's Kathmandu Environmental Education Project, now being run by Nepalis. It educates both tourists and locals by conducting eco-trekking workshops, encouraging trekking companies to be environmentally responsible and even paying porters for the trash they bring home. "It's better now," he says, but finding funds for such educational efforts is a perennial problem.

Powers believes organizations like the American Society of Travel Agents (ASTA) can help educate businesses, especially since its code of conduct includes respecting destination cultures and environments. But in-country operators — the local hotels and guides with whom travel agents arrange tours — also should be held accountable, he says.

But defining and measuring practices that promote environmental sustainability is a very new field, says David Weaver, a professor of tourism management and an ecotourism expert at the University of South Carolina in Columbia. "We're working to pin down the variables and criteria you would need to measure to determine whether an operation is sustainable," he says, but "we still have a long way to go. There aren't a lot of mature programs, and a lot of it is learn as you go."

For instance, a recent study of Magellanic penguins nesting at Punta Tombo, in Argentina, found that the birds adjusted relatively quickly to tourists. To study stress in the birds, researchers measured their number of head turns when humans approached and the level of stress-related hormones they secreted.

Greg Wetstone, U.S. director for the International Fund for Animal Welfare, calls the findings encouraging. "We still have a lot to learn, but this study reinforces the sense that responsible ecotourism can be a low-impact way to create economic pressure for protecting threatened wildlife." The study's authors cautioned, however, that "long-term consequences are much harder to document, especially in long-lived animals."[16]

Ecotourism consultant Megan Epler Wood, the first executive director of the Ecotourism Society (now The International Ecotourism Society), sees the problem of managing environmental effects more in terms of money than methodology. "With the participation of large conservation agencies, it has been shown that as long as an ecotourism project is appropriately planned, zoning the infrastructure well away from protected areas, people can visit without harming," she says.

But even in the United States, Epler Wood notes, the National Park Service has trouble implementing new methodologies because of funding gaps, a situation that is even more dire in developing countries.[17] "You may have one or two staff overseeing hundreds or thousands of acres," she says. "The idea of them controlling and managing so much requires a budgetary level that many can't approach."

Even the best-managed ecotourism facility can pave the way for less-benevolent permanent development, say other observers. In the remote Canadian province of Newfoundland, for instance, the tourism infrastructure gradually improved as the fishing industry gave out. "There has always been the hook and bullet crowd," says Larry Morris, president of the Quebec-Labrador Foundation/Atlantic Center for the Environment. "Now it's 'non-consumptive use.'"

Declining survival rates of African cheetahs have been linked to heavy tourism in game preserves. According to Conservation International, clamoring tourists frighten adult cheetahs and their young away from their kills, allowing hyenas to scavenge the food and forcing cubs to go hungry.

Getty Images/Win McNamee

The sophistication of the outfitters has increased dramatically, Morris notes, and the province is capitalizing on concerns about global warming by promoting itself as a reliable destination for snow lovers. Now some of the visitors are purchasing permanent homes — a trend the industry labels "amenity migration." The province just got its first gated community, in Deer Lake, and its "wilderness cottages" — next to a new golf course — are attracting buyers from the United Kingdom.

The University of South Carolina's Weaver suggests that environmental damage caused by ecotourism can be diminished if it is practiced in areas that are already heavily altered. In downtown Austin, Texas, for instance, crowds gather every night at the Congress Street Bridge between March and November to watch up to 1.5 million Mexican free-tailed bats — North America's largest urban bat colony — emerge from their nests in deep crevices.

"You can have very high-quality ecotourism in highly disturbed areas," he says. "People go to see whooping cranes in the stubble of farmers' fields in Saskatchewan."

Others view peregrine falcons roosting in Pittsburgh skyscrapers, and even in the much-maligned New Jersey Meadowlands — just five miles from Manhattan — a bird-watching and fishing guidebook now promotes ecotourism.[18]

"The perception that [ecotourism] is a threat comes mostly from indigenous groups," says anthropologist Vivanco. "When you don't have control over tourism in your community, things leave." About five years ago, he points out, "bioprospecting" — in which pharmaceutical companies send people into the rain forest to see if they can find useful plants — became identified as ecotourism.

"Indigenous groups felt that things were being taken from them," he says, and it made them "very politicized," even though the evidence of biological theft was mostly anecdotal. "There is the notion that this is yet another effort to bring us into the modern world, to get control of our land — the latest version of the white man telling us what we should do with our land."

Some indigenous peoples involved with ecotourism projects are simply calling it quits. In Santa Maria, Costa Rica, where for several years Vivanco took his students on field trips, the community-based tourism project that sent paying guests to stay in local homes began to arouse resentment because not all families got guests. Recently, the villagers decided to end the program. "People are saying, 'We've had enough. It's causing division in the community,'" Vivanco says. "Their own conflicts play out in tourism."

Does ecotourism offer a realistic alternative to more traditional commercial development?

In the early 1990s, archeologist Leventhal worked with a group of Mayan Indians studying the future of their communities in southern Belize. At the time Belize — following Costa Rica's lead — was in the process of transforming itself into a major ecotourism destination. The group went on a tour of Mexico's popular Yucatan Peninsula.

"They were fascinated by being waited on by other Maya," Leventhal recalls. But not all the encounters were positive. When they'd walk into the big hotels, the Mayan security guards would immediately stop them.

"They really understood the impact of tourism," Leventhal says. "Yes, it brought money in, but they got very worried about certain aspects of it. They got involved with the idea that these were their cousins. Living in a subsistence economy in their own villages, they basically controlled the show. They didn't need to borrow money. When you borrow money, you have to pay it back." In the end they rejected ecotourism.

A 1999 study commissioned by the environmental group Greenpeace and conducted by American resource economist Christopher LaFranchi, however, suggests that while ecotourism may not be perfect, it is far more advantageous for indigenous peoples than "industrial" options such as logging and plantation-style agriculture. The study compared such traditional development tactics with small-scale development options, including ecotourism in the forest lands of the Marovo lagoon area in the Solomon Islands. It found negative long-term repercussions despite "rapid and considerable cash returns available from abruptly selling the forest for logging" and potential governmental revenues derived from taxing the timber industry.

"The rapid exploitation of tropical forests, although very profitable for international timber companies, has produced only limited long-term economic gain for the nations of the Pacific, and at great environmental and social cost," the study said.[19]

In comparing the costs and benefits of exploiting the reef and forest resources of the area, the study found that "the economic benefits of the small-scale options considerably exceed those of the industrial options. Moreover, they leave landowners in more direct control of their resources, distribute benefits more equitably and do not expose them to the high risks of fluctuations in international commodity markets."[20]

The present value of industrial options — mainly logging and palm oil — to landowners was estimated at $8.2 million, while small-scale options were valued at $29 million.

Tourism Professor Weaver calls this advantage the "one shot" angle. With traditional development, he says, "You get a lot of money in a limited time, but then it's done. With ecotourism, it's never exhausted."

Within the world of international aid agencies and development banks, says ecotourism consultant Epler Wood, ecotourism is "increasingly gaining credibility as a development tool because of its clear economic statistics and because there aren't that many other tools." Proposed development projects must now be sustainable, she says. "The economic growth potential is on a par with textiles. The reception is growing, and all the statistics have been clearly presented."

Often, she points out, the poorest countries stand to gain the most from ecotourism. Many studies show that traditional development strategies "have created a gap between rich and poor and between urban and rural," she explains. "Rural people have been left out of grand development schemes. But as long as they are an ecotourism attraction, rural people can get a nice growth trend."

Ecotourism has other advantages over traditional development schemes, she adds. Start-up takes a much lower investment and, thanks to the Internet, projects can be marketed directly to consumers, allowing the benefits to be delivered directly to the producer.

"It's very viable," says Benjamin Powell, a managing partner of Agora Partnerships, an American NGO that promotes Nicaraguan entrepreneurship. "Certain countries have completely branded themselves as ecotourism destinations to great effect. If it is done right, people are often willing to pay, and it often does trickle down to the locals."

Traditionally, institutional and cultural barriers have prevented native people from owning local businesses. Besides lacking a cultural tradition of entrepreneurship, Powell explains, "Most aspiring entrepreneurs in poor countries are caught in a development blind spot: They're too big for microfinance, yet too small for traditional lending."

'Green' Certification on the Rise

Tourism companies increasingly are participating in voluntary certification programs that provide a seal of approval to businesses that demonstrate environmentally or socially sound practices.

Selected Tourism-Certification Efforts Worldwide

Green Globe 21 — Has awarded logos to some 500 companies and destinations in more than 100 countries. Rewards efforts to incorporate social responsibility and sustainable resource management into business programs. But may confuse tourists by rewarding not only businesses that have achieved certification but also those that have simply committed to undertake the process.

ECOTEL® — Has certified 23 hotels in Latin America, seven in the United States and Mexico, five in Japan and one in India. Assigns hotels zero to five globes based on environmental commitment, waste management, energy efficiency, water conservation, environmental education and community involvement. Hotels must be reinspected every two years, and unannounced inspections can occur at any time. A project of the industry consulting group HVS International.

European Blue Flag Campaign — Includes more than 2,750 sites in 21 European countries; being adopted in South Africa and the Caribbean. Awards a yearly ecolabel to beaches and marinas for their high environmental standards and sanitary and safe facilities. Credited with improving the quality and desirability of European coastal sites. Run by the international nonprofit Foundation for Environmental Education.

Certification for Sustainable Tourism, Costa Rica — Has certified some 54 hotels since 1997. Gives hotels a ranking of one to five based on environmental and social criteria. Credited with raising environmental awareness among tourism businesses and tourists. But the rating is skewed toward large hotels that may be too big to really be sustainable.

SmartVoyager, Galapagos, Ecuador — Since 1999, has certified five of more than 80 ships that operate in the area. Gives a special seal to tour operators and boats that voluntarily comply with specified benchmarks for boat and dinghy maintenance and operation, dock operations and management of wastewater and fuels. A joint project of the Rainforest Alliance and a local conservation group.

Green Leaf, Thailand — Had certified 59 hotels as of October 2000. Awards hotels between one and five "green leaves" based on audits of their environmental policies and other measures. Aims to improve efficiency and raise awareness within the domestic hotel industry.

Source: Lisa Mastny, "Traveling Light, New Paths for International Tourism."

Powell promotes the advantages to small investors of small investments in local businesses. "From an investment perspective, you have more leverage if you invest in a local operation because you can put some corporate-responsibility standards in place," he says. "There's no correlation with the stock market at all. It's a very specific market, very local. It's not affected by anything macro. But still, it is very risky."

Should ecotourism businesses and programs be certified?

As ecotourism has become highly marketable, numerous schemes have sprung up that offer a "green" imprimatur for businesses. Some certification proposals require high standards while others set the bar lower; some are operated for profit, others are run by nonprofit organizations; some can be purchased, others are awarded.

"We're seeing nearly 100 different programs," says Katie Maschman, a spokeswoman for The International Ecotourism Society. Some programs are worldwide, national or regional in scope and others relate to specific resources, such as Blue Flag certification for healthy beaches. Other examples include the worldwide program Green Globe 21 and the World Wildlife Fund's PAN Parks network in Europe. The American Hotel & Lodging Association lets its most energy-efficient members display a Good Earthkeeping logo. The association estimates 43 million domestic travelers each year are "environmentally minded."

In recent years, the Rainforest Alliance and the ecotourism society have spearheaded an effort to regularize certification, supported by the Inter-American Development Bank, foundations and other development groups. Now they are studying how to develop and judge standards and certify eco-ventures that practice sustainable tourism, inspired by successful certification programs in other industries — such as the Forest Stewardship Council's approval of sustainably harvested lumber and the fair trade movement's certification of "green" coffee beans and bananas.

Advocates argue that a more coherent certification system is the only way to protect the market advantages of genuine ecotourism and encourage development of sustainable practices in the broader marketplace.

But critics say certification programs now being discussed raise more questions than they answer. For one thing, deciding who qualifies is not a simple matter. At an ecolodge in Australia, for example, visitors can buy packets of seeds to feed the colorful, parrot-like lorikeets, which will then flock around and alight on tourists' arms and heads.

"It's a paradox that this park lodge has advanced accreditation," says tourism professor Weaver. "They do a lot of fantastic things," but the bird feeding is a "demonstrable ecological problem." It keeps a lot of weak birds alive, which spreads diseases, he explains, and when the birds, gorged on seeds, return to the wild and defecate, weeds and other invasive species are introduced.

Nonetheless, a good ecolabel or certification "would give the public some confidence in what they're buying," Weaver says.

The difficulties lie in deciding how such a system would be monitored, he says, and what penalties should be levied for violations. To Planeta.com founder Mader, certification based on sustainability does not address questions many travelers are concerned about. "Most of the travelers I talk to would love certification if it would tell them where there's a clean bathroom," he says. Mader sees a far greater need for certification in safety- and service-related areas such as scuba diving, rock climbing or massage therapy.

Certification efforts so far have been "prioritized far too ahead of the curve, before we have reliable information, let alone communication," Mader argues. "In countries that are developing rural travel, there are usually six to 12 state or federal entities involved — none of whom ever want to talk to one another. The tourism section and the environmental, labor, agriculture and forestry sections each want to protect its place in the pipeline. Communication that could improve the marketability of the ecotourism product is all too rare. They're not sharing information, and none is very transparent or public."

McLaren, of Indigenous Rights International, questions the parallel being drawn between products like lumber and ecotourism. "It's really hard, because tourism is a service instead of a product. You can follow the trail from farm to market with a potato, but it's much more difficult to certify all these different parts" of tourism.

McLaren says the certification process so far looks to some observers like "another grab at money and control" that has left the local communities out of the process.

"We need to talk to the businesses," says Mader, echoing her concern. "There's a lot of discussion at the consultancy level, but at the operator level we're just not speaking their language."

Martha Honey, executive director of The International Ecotourism Society and a leader of the certification effort, says that while many certification programs came into being without consultation with indigenous people, those involved in current efforts are "extremely concerned about and sensitive to" the issue. Last September, she notes, the first meeting in an effort to bring indigenous peoples to the table was held in Quito, Ecuador, and future meetings are scheduled in Fiji and Norway. She cites as a possible model the Respecting Our Culture program in Australia, run by indigenous peoples through a program called Aboriginal Tourism Australia.

Critics of certification also worry that it will be too costly. "The field is not ready for certification," says Epler Wood. "There's no identifiable market for it, and without a market driver you get a lot of investment in systems that are not selling with the public."

"Ecotourism is a small, micro-business phenomenon," she continues. "The profit margins barely justify staying in business." While certification could have a viable role in developing a bigger market, she says, until the companies are more stable and profitable, they cannot afford it.

Honey agrees that cost is an issue. "Certification cannot be so expensive that it sets the bar too high for small-scale operators," she says, but she feels the problem is surmountable. One solution would be scaled fees, with larger operators paying more. Another might be government subsidies drawn from revenues such as airport taxes or "negative taxes" on less eco-friendly businesses, such as the cruise industry.

Honey explains that existing certification programs failed to develop a large market because most of them had virtually no marketing budget. And, she says, what marketing they did was misdirected. The key to greater success, she believes, is to market the label not to travelers — the ultimate consumers — but to the tourist industry's equivalent of dealers or middle men — tour operators who stand to save money by not having to investigate individual accommodations and attractions for themselves.

Honey also argues that a reliable certification program also would be extremely useful to guidebook publishers, national parks — which must evaluate the reliability of concessionaires — and development agencies like the U.N. Development Programme, the U.S.

Terra Incognita Ecotours/Gerard "Ged" Caddick

The Karawari Lodge in Papua New Guinea's East Sepik Province sits on the edge of a lowland rain forest in one of the country's most remote regions. Visitors can explore the area's varied flora and fauna and visit villages on the Karawari River.

Agency for International Development and the World Bank.

But Xavier Font, a lecturer in tourism management at Leeds Metropolitan University in England, says "certification is most suited to those countries with well-established infrastructures and the finances to support industry to reduce its negative impacts. It is not the best tool for livelihood-based economies or sectors, be it tourism, forestry, agriculture or any other at the center of attention of certification today."[21]

Brian Mullis, president of Sustainable Travel International, a nonprofit organization that is developing the first certification program in North America, disagrees. "Having spent a good part of the last four years looking at the problem," Mullis says, "I don't think it is premature. At the end of the day, the only way sustainable travel can really be defined is to have verification that companies are doing what they say they're doing.

"More and more consumers are supporting businesses that define themselves as green," he continues. "But if they're not doing what they say they're doing, it doesn't really matter what they say."

BACKGROUND

Tourism Is Born

Travel for pleasure came on the world scene with the emergence of wealth and leisure. Affluent Greeks and Romans vacationed at thermal baths and visited exotic locales around Europe and the Mediterranean. The first guidebook for travelers is credited to the French monk Aimeri de Picaud, who in 1130 wrote a tour guide for pilgrims traveling to Spain. In the 18th and 19th centuries, European and British aristocrats as well as wealthy Americans took the "grand tour" of continental Europe's natural and cultural attractions, including the Swiss Alps, and health spas became popular destinations.[22]

Until the Industrial Revolution, travel had more to do with its etymological root — the French word for "work," travailler — than with pleasure. The development of railroads, steamships and, later, the automobile and airplane, made travel easier and faster. The Englishman Thomas Cook set up a travel agency in 1841 and organized tourist excursions by train to temperance rallies in the English Midlands. By the mid-1850s he was offering railway tours of the Continent.

In the United States, the American Express Co. introduced Travelers Cheques and money orders, further easing the logistics of tourism. By the end of the 19th century, the tourism industry had fully emerged, complete with guidebooks, packaged tours, booking agents, hotels and railways with organized timetables.[23]

Earlier, the dawning of the Romantic era in around 1800 had fired a new passion for the exotic among Europeans and an upwelling of scientific curiosity that fueled journeys of exploration and discovery. Beginning in 1799, Alexander von Humboldt, a wealthy German, spent five years exploring in the uncharted reaches of Central and South America, gathering data and specimens. Three decades later, a young British aristocrat keen on biology, Charles Darwin, sailed to the Galapagos Islands and developed the foundations of his revolutionary theory of evolution.[24]

Armchair adventurers avidly sought reports of explorers supported by the British Royal Geographic Society, founded in 1830. Among them were the legendary missionary/explorer David Livingstone in Africa and the man who went to find him, journalist Henry Stanley, in the mid-19th century; Antarctic explorers Robert Scott, the British naval officer who perished on his journey to the South Pole, and Ernest Shackleton in the early 20th century; and Sir Edmund Hillary, the New Zealander who in 1953, with his Nepalese guide Tensing Norgay, first climbed Mt. Everest.

By the late 19th century, the beauty of unspoiled nature was attracting more and more ordinary visitors. In the United States, Congress set aside more than 2 million acres in 1872 to create Yellowstone National Park, the world's first national park. Reserving public lands for "public use, resort and recreation," became a guiding principle of the National Park Service, established in 1916.

Private tourism promoters also played a large role in the creation and expansion of the National Park System, with the Northern Pacific Railroad urging the creation of Yellowstone as a draw for its passengers. The railroads later played similar roles in promoting the creation of Sequoia and Yosemite (1890), Mount Rainier (1899) and Glacier (1910) national parks.[25]

Beginning in Australia in 1879, other countries also set aside protected areas for parks, including Mexico (1898), Argentina (1903) and Sweden (1909). The Sierra Club began its Outings program in 1901 with an expedition for 100 hikers, accompanied by Chinese chefs, pack mules and wagons, to the backcountry wilderness of the Sierra Nevada Mountains. The trips not only provided healthful diversion for the members but also encouraged them to "become active workers for the preservation of the forests and other natural features" of the area.

The political implications behind the early trips would continue to motivate nonprofit organizations to sponsor travel outings in the years ahead.

In the 1950s, big-game hunters began flocking to luxury safari lodges in Kenya, South Africa and, later, Tanzania. The creation of national parks and wildlife

CHRONOLOGY

1860s-1960s *Interest in nature travel grows after first being limited largely to the wealthy.*

1916 U.S. National Park Service is founded.

1920s "Bush walker" movement in Australia increases the popularity of wilderness excursions.

1953 Sir Edmund Hillary and Tenzing Norgay are the first to climb Mount Everest.

1970s *Tourism spreads into remote and fragile regions after wide-bodied jets make travel cheaper.*

1970 First cruise ship visits Antarctica.... First Earth Day on April 22 signals birth of environmental movement.

1980s *Environmental and cultural impact of tourism sparks concern.*

1980 Manila Declaration on World Tourism declares that "tourism does more harm than good" to people and societies in the Third World. ... Ecumenical Coalition on Third World Tourism takes shape to fight such negative impacts as poverty, pollution and prostitution.

1989 Hague Declaration on Tourism calls on states "to strike a harmonious balance between economic and ecological considerations."

1990s *Ecotourism is promoted as a "win-win" for economic development and the environment. Tourism increases 66 percent in 10 years on the Galapagos Islands.*

1990 The Ecotourism Society (later renamed The International Ecotourism Society) is founded.

1992 First World Congress on Tourism and the Environment is held in Belize.

1995 *Conde Nast Traveler* magazine publishes its first annual "Green List" of top ecotourism destinations.

1996 World Tourism Organization, World Travel & Tourism Council and Earth Council draft Agenda 21

for the travel and tourism industry, outlining key steps governments and industry need to take for sustainability.

1997 Governments and private groups from 77 countries and territories pledge in the Manila Declaration on the Social Impact of Tourism to better involve local communities in tourism planning and to address social abuses.

1999 World Bank and World Tourism Organization agree to cooperate in encouraging sustainable tourism development.

2000s *"Sustainable travel" is embraced by governments and the travel industry. The number of tourists visiting Antarctica tops 10,000 a year.*

2000 Mohonk Agreement sets out terms for international ecotourism certification. ... One-in-five international tourists travels from an industrial country to a developing one, compared to one-in-13 in the mid-1970s.

2002 U.N. celebrates International Year of Ecotourism; more than 1,000 participants at World Ecotourism Summit approve Quebec Declaration on Ecotourism — stressing the need to address tourism's economic, social and environmental impacts.

2003 The once heavily forested base of Mt. Everest has become an "eroding desert" due to 10,000 trekkers a year burning trees for fuel.

2004 A study about the Galapagos Islands warns that tourism-induced human migration "threatens the future of tourism."

2005 Between 1950 and 2004, the number of tourist arrivals worldwide grows by more than 3,000 percent — from 25 million arrivals to some 760 million in 2004.

2006 International tourist travel jumps 4.5 percent worldwide in the first three months. The fastest-growing destinations are Africa and the Middle East, each rising about 11 percent.

Taking the Guilt Out of Ecotravel

Travel — even by the most dedicated ecotourists — invariably takes a toll on the environment. But now environmentally sensitive travelers are finding ways to compensate.

When the World Economic Forum sponsored a meeting of its Young Global Leaders Summit this year in Vancouver, British Columbia, the forum offered attendees the opportunity to "offset" the negative environmental effect of the emissions generated by their plane flights by contributing to the rehabilitation of a small hydropower plant in Indonesia.

Concerns about the negative impact of their own airplane emissions also prompted conservationists and community-development activists who gathered in Hungary in April 2006, to offset their emissions by planting trees on a Hungarian hillside.

Airplanes contribute 3 to 5 percent of global carbon dioxide emissions — 230 million tons in the United States alone in 2003 — and air transport is one of the world's fastest-growing sources of emissions of carbon dioxide and other so-called greenhouse gases, according to the Worldwatch Institute.[1]

The only sure-fire way to eliminate negative environmental impacts is to stay home — an option some travel writers actually are promoting.[2] But short of that, say those promoting ecotourism, travelers can "give back" to Mother Nature by donating "carbon offsets."

At the Web site for ClimateCare.org, a British organization started in 1998, travelers can learn how many tons of carbon dioxide their trip will produce and donate money to underwrite renewable-energy projects, energy-efficiency improvements and reforestation efforts in developing countries to produce a comparable reduction in carbon emissions.

A round trip between New York and Chicago, for example, produces the equivalent of 0.27 tons of CO_2, which the organization translates into a $3 donation per traveler to renewable-energy projects.

A 2004 German program, atmosfair (www.atmosfair .de/index.php?id=08L=3) converts carbon emissions into euros, then contributes donated sums to climate-protection projects in India and Brazil. Its installation of solar power instead of diesel- and wood-fired equipment in 10 industrial kitchens in India, for example, will save roughly 570 tons of CO_2 — the equivalent of 2,000 round-trip flights between New York and Chicago.

The Portland, Ore.-based Better World Club claims it's "the first travel company in the world to offer a carbon-offset program." Its TravelCool! Program offers offsets in $11 increments, which it equates to roughly one ton of CO_2, or a tenth of the emissions produced annually by the typical automobile. The funds collected have helped replace old oil-burning boilers in Portland public schools.

The Web site nativeenergy.com, based in Charlotte, Vt., will calculate all the carbon dioxide emissions from an entire vacation, including hotel stays. The Native American group supports American Indian and farmer-owned wind, solar and methane projects. Contributions to offset automobile and other travel emissions can be made in the form of regular monthly contributions.

---

[1] Lisa Mastny, "Traveling Light: New Paths for International Tourism," Worldwatch Paper 159, December 2001, p. 29; and Esther Addley, "Boom in green holidays as ethical travel takes off, *The Guardian*, July 17, 2006; and P. W. McRandle, "Low-impact vacations (Green Guidance)," *World Watch*, July-August 2006.

[2] See Ian Jack and James Hamilton-Paterson, "Where Travel Writing Went Next," *Granta*, Summer 2006.

---

sanctuaries by Kenya's British colonial government, however, forced the nomadic Maasai people from their ancestral lands. The resulting resentments led to poaching and vandalism, problems that to this day complicate conservation efforts.

Rise of Ecotourism

The powerful combination of the labor movement and 20th-century industrialization brought tourism within reach of a vast, new universe — the burgeoning population of middle-class wage earners seeking diversion for their annual vacations.

In 1936, the International Labor Organization called for a week's paid vacation every year. A 1970 ILO convention expanded the standard to three weeks with pay.

But it was the rise of the aviation industry after World War II that sparked mass, intercontinental tourism. In 1948 Pan American World Airways introduced tourist class, and the world suddenly grew smaller. In 1957 jet engines made commercial travel faster still.

The introduction of wide-bodied jets in the 1970s made international travel between developed and developing nations practical for holiday travelers. By 1975, international tourist arrivals had surpassed 200 million annually — and double that number by 1990.[26]

In the mid-1970s, 8 percent of all tourists were from developed countries traveling on holidays to developing countries. By the mid-1980s the number had jumped to 17 percent.

Developing countries and international aid institutions initially welcomed the burgeoning source of foreign exchange sparked by the spurt in tourism. The World Bank's first tourism-related loan was made in 1967 for a hotel in Kenya that was partly owned by a subsidiary of Pan American Airways. In the 1970s the bank loaned about $450 million directly to governments for 24 tourism projects in 18 developing countries, and other international aid and lending institutions followed suit.

But the bank's support of conventional tourism and large hotel projects provoked criticism that it encouraged indebtedness while failing to address the problems of poverty in Third World countries. Concern about the environmental effects of resort development, along with a string of financial failures, caused the bank to close down its Tourism Projects Department in 1979.

As the emergence of the environmental movement in the 1960s and '70s pushed international aid agencies to re-examine their commitments, other forces were also pushing the development of a less intrusive, more eco-friendly form of travel.

Despite setbacks among local operators and growing discontent among indigenous peoples, by the turn of the millennium the notion that tourism could be both more lucrative and less resource-intensive than heavy industry or plantation-style monoculture was gaining currency in the international community. In 1998 it was reported to be the only economic sector in which developing countries consistently ran a trade surplus. It represented roughly 10 percent of developing-world exports and accounted for more than 40 percent of the gross domestic product in some countries.[27]

In 2002, more than 1,000 participants from 132 countries gathered in Quebec, Canada, to attend the World Ecotourism Summit, organized by the U.N. Environment Programme and the World Tourism Organization. In adopting the Quebec Declaration on

Watched by local experts, an ecotourist gives a blowgun a try in Peru's Amazon rain forest. Tour groups now flock to the Amazon for trips up the river and forays into the forest in search of the region's animals and colorful birds.

Ecotourism, they embraced "the principles of sustainable tourism, concerning the economic, social and environmental impacts of tourism" — which would come to be seen as the "triple bottom line" in development circles.

The declaration also pointed out that ecotourism differed from the broader concept of "sustainable tourism" by four key characteristics:

- contribution to the conservation of natural and cultural heritage;
- inclusion of local and indigenous communities;
- interpretation of natural and cultural heritage; and
- affinity for independent and small-group travelers.[28]

The summit also boosted ecotourism certification efforts by endorsing "the use of certification as a tool for measuring sound ecotourism and sustainable tourism" while also stressing that certification systems "should reflect regional and local criteria."[29]

Giving native peoples a stake in conservation outcomes was a prime force behind the development of ecotourism, says Harold Goodwin, director of the International Centre for Responsible Tourism at the University of Greenwich in England. To win the support of indigenous peoples, international conservation organizations began creating environmentally responsible tourist accommodations near private conservation areas

G.A.P Adventures

Terra Incognita Ecotours/Gerard "Ged" Caddick

G.A.P Adventures

Mixing People and Nature

Penguins in Antarctica show no fear of humans (top); tourists in Baja, Calif., watch a blue whale (middle); and a visitor gets acquainted with giant turtles in the Galapagos Islands (bottom).

"You have to give the local community economic benefits so they don't poach," Goodwin says.

Ecotourism also opened up new marketing possibilities, Goodwin says. Costa Rica, for example, unable to compete in the world tourism market on the quality of its beaches, began promoting its rich, unspoiled biodiversity as an attraction — with great success. Belize followed suit.

Ecotourism also introduced a new type of competition, he says, because "there are only so many places to go and things to do," and only so much elasticity in pricing. Introducing the values of environmentalism, conservation and education, he says, "avoids competing on price. You can compete on interpretation."

But many of the first small, local ecotourism endeavors that sprang up in the 1990s failed because there was a disconnect between the international market and the local entrepreneurs, Goodwin says. Those that succeeded, however, transformed their surroundings.

"In the early 1990s, everybody was talking about ecotourism," says anthropologist Vivanco, who did his field research at that time near the private Monte Verde Cloud Forest Preserve, considered the jewel in the crown of Costa Rica's extensive park system. "Over 10 years ago, there were about 45,000 to 50,000 tourists a year in an area of about 3,500 to 4,000 inhabitants," he says. But as the number of visitors increased and new facilities went up, hundreds of Costa Rican workers moved to the area, creating a negative environmental impact on the fringe of the preserve — a problem that has afflicted ecotourism sites as remote as the Galapagos Islands.

"Nowadays, there are at least 140,000, and as many as 200,000 visitors, "and it's grown up in a completely unmanaged way at the edge of the park," he says.

"The population explosion has an impact on their whole way of life," Vivanco continues. "Class differences emerged that didn't exist before. Locally, many people were saying, 'It's a bit out of hand, we need to get greater control.' "

CURRENT SITUATION
Global Presence

Growing awareness of the environmental costs of travel, such as its contribution to global warming, increasingly

that would provide some income to native peoples. Foundations were established to return earnings to the community in the form of water projects and other physical improvements, educational opportunities, even clinics and health services. Besides being altruistic, the program had practical outcomes as well.

Making Sure Your Travel Is Really 'Green'

The term ecotourism is used so loosely by marketers these days that tourists may be getting "ecotourism lite," not a truly "green" experience, says Katie Maschman, a spokeswoman for The International Ecotourism Society.

"It's great to see ecotourism principles incorporated from a mass-tourism perspective," Maschman says, "but there is a lot of green-washing going on. A hotel simply advertising that they only change the sheets every three days does not, by any means, suggest they've given it real attention."

Research is vital to planning a trip that minimizes negative environmental and cultural impacts, experts say. And while a variety of Web sites and guidebooks focus on "green" travel, nothing substitutes for direct questioning of tour and facility operators and of other travelers.[1]

"The best thing to do is to ask to speak to former clients," says Steve Powers, of Hidden Treasure Tours, in Long Beach, N.Y. Like many other tour packagers, Powers tries to support small, grassroots programs. But it can be difficult to determine whether operators at a far-off destination are actually doing what they say.

A tourist also can ask travel companies for their policies, which may already be codified and thus easily communicated. "If you want to book a tour," says Ron Mader, founder of the ecotourism Web site Planeta.com, "ask [tour operators] if they support conservation or local development projects. Many agencies and operators are very proud of their environmental conservation and community-development work."[2]

Helpful Web sites featuring ecotourism destinations are operated by nonprofit organizations, travel marketers and for-profit online travel clubs and information exchanges, including www.sustainabletravelinternational.org, ecoclub.com, responsibletravel.com, eco-indextourism.org, eco-tourism.org, ecotour.org, tourismconcern.org, travelersconservationtrust.org, and visit21.net.

Travel-award programs are another good source of ideas, such as the Tourism for Tomorrow awards of the World Travel & Tourism Council at www.tourismfortomorrow.com; the annual ecolodge award of the International Ecotourism Club, available at ecoclub.com; and the First Choice Responsible Tourism Awards from responsibletravel.com.

In addition to consulting those and similar sites, adding terms such as "green travel" or "ecotourism" to a country- or destination-based Internet search can bring results.

Here are the questions experts say travelers should ask their tour firm or the operator of the destination:

- Do you have an ethical ecotourism policy?
- What steps have you taken to reduce waste and water use?
- Do you practice recycling?
- How do you minimize damage to wildlife and marine environments?
- What community members do you employ and do they have opportunities for advancement? What local products do you purchase, and do you use local produce whenever possible? What community projects are you involved in?
- Do you donate to community organizations and/or conservation programs?
- What energy-saving activities do you practice?
- Are your buildings built with locally available materials?
- Do you use environmentally friendly products?

---

[1] P. W. McRandle, "Low-impact Vacations (Green Guidance)," *World Watch*, July-August 2006; and Esther Addley, "Boom in Green Holidays as Ethical Travel Takes Off," *The Guardian*, July 17, 2006.

[2] Quoted in Clay Hubbs, "Responsible Travel and Ecotourism," *Transitions Abroad*, May/June 2001, www.transitionsabroad.com/publications/magazine.

affects travel decisions. More than three-quarters of U.S. travelers "feel it is important their visits not damage the environment," according to a study by the Travel Industry Association of America and *National Geographic Traveler* magazine. The study estimated that 17 million U.S. travelers consider environmental factors when deciding which travel companies to patronize.[30]

A survey by the International Hotels Environmental Initiative found that more than two-thirds of U.S. and Australian travelers and 90 percent of British tourists consider active protection of the environment — including support of local communities — to be part of a hotel's responsibility.[31] Another industry study found that 70 percent of U.S., British and Australian travelers

AFP/Getty Images/Romeo Gacad

Tourism is threatening the Philippines' ancient Banaue rice terraces, created 2,000 years ago by Ifugao tribesmen. The naturally irrigated paddies are endangered by deforestation to supply wood for tourist handicrafts and by the water demands of hotels and restaurants.

would pay up to $150 more for a two-week stay in a hotel with a "responsible environmental attitude."[32]

Overall, the travel industry employs 200 million people, generates $3.6 trillion in economic activity and accounts for one in every 12 jobs worldwide.[33] Between 1950 and 2004, the number of tourist arrivals worldwide grew by more than 3,000 percent — from 25 million arrivals in 1950 to some 760 million in 2004.[34]

Moreover, travelers' destinations have shifted, with visits to the developing world increasing dramatically while travel to Europe and the Americas has dropped. By 2000, one-in-five international tourists from industrial countries traveled to a developing nation, compared to one-in-13 in the mid-1970s.[35] The fastest-growing areas for international travel in the first quarter of 2006 were Africa and the Middle East, with estimated increases of 11 percent each.[36]

For example, Wildland Adventures conducts tours to Central America, the Andes, Africa, Turkey, Egypt, Australia, New Zealand and Alaska. The Seattle-based tour operator created the nonprofit Traveler's Conservation Trust, which contributes a portion of the firm's earnings to community-improvement projects and conservation organizations in the countries they visit.

In the Ecuadorian Amazon rain forest, Yachana, an eco-lodge constructed in 1995 by the Foundation for Integrated Education and Development, attracts nearly 2,000 visitors a year — but limits the number to 40 at a time — who reach the lodge by canoe. Visitors spend time with indigenous families, participate in traditional rituals and visit the foundation's model farm and tree nursery. The lodge has generated more than $3.5 million for the foundation's programs in conservation, poverty reduction, health care and community development.

International Development

"Nearly every country with national parks and protected areas is marketing some type of ecotourism," according to the Center on Ecotourism and Sustainable Development. "Lending and aid agencies are funneling hundreds of millions of dollars into projects that include ecotourism; major environmental organizations are sponsoring ecotourism projects and departments; and millions of travelers are going on ecotours."

"It's absolutely excellent," says ecotourism consultant Epler Wood. "I used to tell people I was a consultant on ecotourism, and they'd give me a blank stare. Now they are, like, 'Wow, you are so lucky.' It's been one of our greatest goals to make it an accepted, mainstream profession."

Moreover, many of the basic tenets of ecotourism are being embraced by the international development world as goals for economic development generally. In choosing which development projects to fund, the new "triple bottom line" adds environmental and social/cultural effects to the longstanding criterion of profitability — at least on paper.

At a tourism policy forum at George Washington University in October 2004 — the first of its kind — Inter-American Development Bank (IDB) President Enrique Iglesias and World Bank Vice President James Adams joined delegates from donor agencies, developing countries and academia in endorsing tourism's potential as a sustainable-development strategy. They also agreed, however, that the complex nature of the industry presents special challenges.

The IDB, after being involved with tourism projects for 30 years, has changed its focus from big infrastructure projects to more community-based projects, Iglesias said. Adams reported the World Bank had undertaken approximately 100 projects, including tourism in 56 countries — 3 percent of the bank's total investment.[37]

Will improved certification make ecotourism more marketable?

YES   Martha Honey
Executive Director,
The International Ecotourism Society

Written for *CQ Researcher*, October 2006

Reputable "green" certification programs that measure environmental and social impacts will promote ecotourism — but it will take time to educate consumers. It took some 30 years to build the U.S. market for certified organic foods, and now consumer demand for organics is booming. In tourism, AAA and 5 Star quality-certification programs for hotels and restaurants have been around for nearly a century and are part of the "fabric" of the tourism industry.

U.S. consumers want to travel responsibly. But they are not yet actively asking for "green" certification, in part because there is no national program.

Around the world, my colleague Amos Bién notes there are some 60 to 80 "green" tourism-certification programs, but most are less than 10 years old. Costa Rica's Certification for Sustainable Tourism (CST) program, launched in 1998, awards one to five green leaves to hotels and tour operators. Lapa Rios Eco-lodge is one of only two hotels there to have earned five leaves. Owner Karen Lewis sees a link between certification, improved sustainability and increased marketability. "Certification is the best internal audit out there, for any owner and/or management team," she says.

Adriane Janer, of EcoBrazil, who has been involved in creating Brazil's new Sustainable Tourism Program, says "certification has been very successful in improving quality and reliability of products and services." In Guatemala, the Green Deal program principally certifies small businesses at a minimal cost of $300. In Costa Rica, certification is free, and the CST cannot keep up with all the hotels wanting to be audited.

In tourism, as in retailing, we're beginning to see the successful use of "retailers" — tour operators — who are choosing to use certified hotels and other "green" supplies. The Dutch tour operators association, which represents over 850 travel companies, requires all members to use hotels and other businesses that have a credible sustainability policy. In Costa Rica, seven leading tour operators are giving preference to CST-certified hotels, and at least two are hoping within three years to be using only certified hotels.

Indeed, without certification, the danger of 'greenwashing' — businesses that use "eco" language in their marketing but don't fit any of the criteria of ecotourism — greatly increases. Certification provides a necessary tool to separate the wheat from the chafe, the genuine ecotourism businesses from the scams and the shams.

As Glenn Jampol, owner of the Finca Rosa Blanca Inn, the other Costa Rican hotel to have earned five green leaves, puts it, "I envision a day when guests will routinely check for Rosa Blanca's green leaf rating as well as our star rating."

NO   Ron Mader
Founder, Planeta.com

Written for *CQ Researcher*, October 2006

Indigenous peoples, tour operators and others claim that many certification programs for ecotourism and sustainable travel do not deserve support. I agree.

Certification has a number of serious problems, starting with the lack of consumer demand. Moreover, most stakeholders have been left out of the process, including indigenous people, community representatives and owners of travel businesses. When invited to participate, many of these leaders opt out, reminding organizers they have other priorities.

Stakeholders around the world confided during the International Year of Ecotourism that certification does not enhance business. In fact, some leading tour operators believe certification and accreditation schemes are a scam that creates a cottage industry for consultants.

In short, ecotourism certification is not a "market-driven" option.

Said one tour operator during the Ethical Marketing of Ecotourism Conference: "First, get consumers to care, then worry about rating and certification. Doing it any other way is not only putting the cart before the horse, it is putting the wheel before the cart, the spoke before the wheels."

Much more effective are industry awards. They are conducted in the public eye and cost a fraction of formal certification programs. Likewise, an investment in Google ads pays better dividends than certification.

In 2006 Planeta.com invited tourism professionals — particularly those at the forefront of ecotourism — to participate in a candid review of tourism promotion. Respondents gave government marketing campaigns around the world a low mark. Comments indicate that in-country and outbound travel operators do not know the PR agencies that represent the country.

These are alarming results for those interested in ecotourism and responsible travel as they indicate that rather than promoting what's available, the promotion departments are seen as an obstacle, particularly for small- and medium-sized in-country businesses.

If our collective goal is to improve the marketing of ecotourism, the solution is simply to improve the dialogue among operators and national tourism campaigns. The reality is that by far the most "eco" and "community-focused" services are the ones that receive the least promotion.

While little or no consumer demand may exist for certified "eco" vacations, we should not accept the status quo. The emphasis needs to be placed on evaluating the industry and offering training and promotion for local providers who strive toward sustainability and ecotourism.

Terra Incognita Ecotours/Gerard "Ged" Caddick

Visitors can come within a few yards of wild mountain gorillas in Volcanoes National Park, on the Rwanda side of the Virunga Volcanoes. "I just about burst open with happiness every time I get within one or two feet of them," said naturalist Dian Fossey, who studied the gorillas for years.

USAID Administrator Andrew Natsios similarly stressed the need for community involvement to ensure tourism is sustainable. "Properly planned tourism requires good natural-resource management and good local governance to protect and enhance the resources on which it depends," he said.[38]

Until recently, says Epler Wood, ecotourism funds typically were funneled through conservation-oriented NGOs, which often lacked the business experience needed to make new enterprises succeed. Another handicap was the paucity of small-scale loans. In 1995, she recalls, the International Finance Corp., profit-making arm of the World Bank, was investing no less than $500 million per project. Now, she says, they're down to about $1 million — still high for community-based ecotourism undertakings. And they're looking for partners with expertise in business development, not conservation.

"We're at the very beginning phase in a new era of enterprise development," Epler Wood says. "It's still a new paradigm. Economic growth still gets the big players and the big money, while the environmental and humanitarian development goals tend to be evaluative afterthoughts, instead of being integral to the projects."

But, she says, the big players are taking an interest. "The donor architecture is still not quite built to accommodate the potential of ecotourism as a sustainable-development tool. It's a very big, slow-moving world, but you do see change happening within it."

Variations on a Theme

As ecotourism joins the tourism mainstream, it is spinning off numerous new tourism genres. In Europe, especially, so-called pro-poor tourism, responsible tourism and ethical tourism aim to extend the benefits of tourism to developing countries while improving its effects on destination communities and the environment.

Evidence is mounting that travelers are embracing the concept's values. In England this past summer, ethical holidays reportedly were the fastest-growing travel sector. According to a recent survey, by 2010 the number of British visitors going on "ethical" holidays outside England will have grown to 2.5 million trips a year, or 5 percent of the market. The Web site ResponsibleTravel.com has seen bookings double in the last year.[39]

Other variations of ecotourism are viewed less favorably by ecotourism advocates. Adventure travel to exotic and often physically challenging destinations — "ecotourism with a kick," ecotourism society executive director Honey calls it — has been a particularly fast-growing style of nature tourism.

Adventure travel proponents argue that adventurers, like ecotravelers, have an interest in protecting the resources they enjoy, but critics blame them for a wide range of damaging intrusions — helicopter trips causing noise and air pollution while taking skiers to pristine mountain tops; growing numbers of tourists struggling to ascend Mt. Everest (and risking their lives and the lives of others in the process); polar bear watchers who ride bus-like vehicles on monster-truck tires along the south shore of Hudson Bay in Manitoba in the fall, dangerously stressing the bears when they should be building up fat reserves for the long winter season.[40]

"Whereas nature, wildlife and adventure tourism are defined solely by the recreational activities of the tourist," Honey explains, "ecotourism is defined as well by its benefits to both conservation and people in the host country."

'Green' Chic

An essay in *The New York Times* fall travel magazine, "Easy Being Green," portrays ecotourism as the latest fashion trend. "In luxury resorts, eco is the flavor du jour," proclaims author Heidi S. Mitchell.[41]

"There has been a real movement toward high-end ecotourism," Honey said. A 2004 survey found that 38 percent would be willing to pay a premium to patronize travel companies that use sustainable environmental practices.[42]

But as green travel goes upscale, environmentalists worry that the original goals of environmental conservation paired with community betterment will be lost under a misleading "greenwash."

"Ecotourism has been watered down from the beginning," says Planeta.com founder Mader. "The NGOs have watered it down. They're even participating in Antarctic travel."

But others, like Honey, see the upscale trend as a sign that environmental sustainability — a key aspect of ecotourism — is having a real effect on the travel industry as a whole. In a less glamorous example, the Rainforest Alliance, with support from the Inter-American Development Bank, is working with small- and medium-sized travel businesses in Latin America to improve sustainable practices, whether or not the businesses meet all the requirements of classic ecotourism.

In Costa Rica, Guatemala, Belize and Ecuador, more than 200 tourism operations in or near sensitive or protected areas are receiving training in the "best practices" of sustainable tourism, including waste management and water and electricity conservation, as well as such social factors as paying adequate salaries and including local and indigenous people in decision-making.

Businesses that adopt best practices become eligible for certification by existing national programs and gain access to marketing networks and trade-show appearances organized by the Rainforest Alliance. The program has had two benefits, says Alliance marketing specialist Christina Suhr: "It has let people know what we do, and they have gained confidence in us."

OUTLOOK

Setting Limits

The latest worry for travelers who care about the Earth's environment is global warming, especially since air transport is one of the world's fastest-growing sources of emissions of carbon dioxide and other greenhouse gases. If global warming continues unabated, many of the attractions most favored by eco-travelers will be among the most vulnerable. A report for the United Kingdom's World Wide Fund for Nature warned of soaring temperatures, forest fires and other consequences that could drive wildlife from safari parks in Africa, damage Brazil's rain forest ecosystems and flood beaches and coastal destinations worldwide.[43]

Some observers say the costs of global travel in environmental damage, cultural homogenization and economic displacement are so serious that would-be travelers should just stay home.

"The more we flock to view the disappearing glaciers, the faster they will vanish," mused novelist James Hamilton-Paterson.[44]

Similarly, travel writer Anneli Rufus observes ruefully, "Colonialism isn't dead. Colonialism is alive and well every time you travel from the First World to the Third and come home bearing photographs of sharks and storms and slums . . . and then you tell your friends and co-workers, 'Oh man, it was so great, you gotta go.' "

But the quandary Rufus faces as she considers ending her travel writing is common to affluent travelers visiting poor countries: "Am I saving some tribe from extinction by not looking for it, much less telling you about it? Or am I starving some shopkeeper by not buying his sandals? Both. Neither. I am out of that [travel writing] game now."[45]

But indigenous-rights activist McLaren feels that the interpersonal connections and first-person impressions derived from independent travel are more important than ever. "In an age where the media dominates and shapes our views of the world," she writes, "it is imperative to utilize tourism as a means to effectively communicate with one another. In fact, there is no better way to understand the global crisis that we face together than through people-to-people communication."[46]

McLaren finds hope in the growing number of successful projects that blend tourism, environmentalism and sustainability, like Elephant Valley eco-resort in India. "There are lots of good examples, though not everybody calls them ecotourism," McLaren says. "A lot of workable projects tend to be more regional, more of public-private partnerships. Elephant Valley, she says, is "a beautiful, low-impact place. Money is really being used to conserve the area, employ local people, produce food, teach about sustainability and work with schools in the region."

In Tasmania, ecotourism has been proposed as an alternative to logging in Australia's largest temperate rain forest, the Tarkine.[47]

In the Patagonia region of southern Chile, environmentalists are seeking to block plans to build a series of hydro-electric dams that would flood thousands of acres of rugged, pristine lands that, they say, could better serve as ecotourism attractions and ranchland.[48]

And in Puerto Rico, environmentalists and other groups are fighting the proposed development of resorts and residential complexes in one of the territory's "last remaining pristine coastal areas," seeking to preserve it "for wildlife, the citizens of Puerto Rico and ecotourism." According to the Waterkeeper Alliance, an organization leading the fight, the developments threaten local water supplies and also mean that "tourists who flock to Puerto Rico to enjoy its cultural and natural resources . . . will have one less reason to visit the island."[49]

NOTES

1. The International Ecotourism Society, Fact Sheet, June 2004, p. 2.

2. Deborah McLaren, "Rethinking Tourism," Planeta Forum, updated June 16, 2006, www.planeta.com/planeta/97/1197rtpro.html; Martha Honey, *Ecotourism and Sustainable Development: Who Owns Paradise?* (1999), p. 9.

3. A 2003 study by the Travel Industry Association of America and *National Geographic Traveler* found that 55.1 million U.S. travelers could be classified as "geo-tourists" interested in nature, culture and heritage tourism; see The International Ecotourism Society, *op. cit.*

4. Jacob Park, "The Paradox of Paradise," *Environment*, October 1999. For a detailed discussion of the environmental costs of resort development, see Polly Patullo, *Last Resorts: the Cost of Tourism in the Caribbean* (1996).

5. Rosaleen Duffy, *A Trip Too Far: Ecotourism, Politics & Exploitation* (2002), pp. x-xii.

6. Lisa Mastny, "Traveling Light," *Worldwatch Paper 159*, Worldwatch Institute, 2001, p. 10.

7. Rene Ebersole, "Take the High Road," *Audubon Travel Issue*, July-August 2006, p. 39.

8. Conservation International Web site; www.conservation.org/xp/CIWEB/programs/ecotourism/.

9. Finn-Olaf Jones, "Tourism Stripping Everest's Forests Bare," *National Geographic Traveler*, Aug. 29, 2003.

10. *Ibid.*

11. Simon Davis, "So Can Tourism Ever Really Be Ethical?" *The* [London] *Evening Standard*, July 19, 2006, p. 51.

12. Costas Christ Sr., "A Road Less Traveled," Conservation International Web site; www.conservation.org/xp/frontlines/partners/focus32-1.xml.

13. Maurice Malanes, "Tourism Killing World's Eighth Wonder," Third World Network, www.twnside.org.sg/title/mm-cn.htm.

14. An exception to the low-impact policy was recently permitted, allowing small kayaking groups to camp in preapproved sites on some islands.

15. Juliet Eilperin, "Despite Efforts, Some Tours Do Leave Footprints," *The Washington Post*, April 2, 2006, p. A1.

16. Juliet Eilperin, "Science Notebook," *The Washington Post*, Jan. 30, 2006, p. A5.

17. For background, see Thomas Arrandale, "National Parks Under Pressure," *CQ Researcher*, Oct. 6, 2006, pp. 817-840.

18. Janet Frankston, "State to push unlikely site for eco-tourists: the Meadowlands," The Associated Press, Aug. 8, 2006.

19. Christopher LaFranchi and Greenpeace Pacific, "Islands Adrift: Comparing Industrial and Small-Scale Economic Options for Marovo Lagoon Region of the Solomon Islands," Greenpeace, 1999, p. 4; www.greenpeace.org/international.

20. *Ibid.*

21. Xavier Font, "Critical Review of Certification and Accreditation in Sustainable Tourism Governance," www.Planeta.com.

22. Unless otherwise noted, background drawn from Honey, *op. cit.*, pp. 7-8.

23. Mastny, *op. cit.*, p. 10.

24. For background, see Marcia Clemmitt, "Intelligent Design," *CQ Researcher*, July 29, 2005, pp. 637-660.

25. Rachel S. Cox, "Protecting the National Parks," *CQ Researcher*, June 16, 2000, p. 521-544.

26. Mastny, *op. cit.*, p. 13.

27. *Ibid.*

28. See "Ecotourism: a UN Declaration," *The Irish Times*, Aug. 5, 2006.

29. Martha Honey, "Protecting Eden: Setting Green Standards for the Tourism Industry," *Environment*, July-August, 2003.

30. *Ibid.* For background, see Marcia Clemmitt, "Climate Change," *CQ Researcher*, Jan. 27, 2006, pp. 73-96.

31. Zoe Chafe, "Consumer Demand and Operator Support for Socially and Environmentally Responsible Tourism," CESD/TIES Working Paper No. 104, Center on Ecotourism and Sustainable Development and The International Ecotourism Society, revised April 2005, p. 4.

32. *Ibid.*, p. 6.

33. Mintel report cited in The International Ecotourism Society, Ecotourism Fact Sheet, "Eco and Ethical Tourism-UK," October 2003.

34. Mastny, *op. cit.*, and "Ecotourism Fact Sheet," The International Ecotourism Society and World Tourism Organization, *World Tourism Barometer*, January 2005, p. 2.

35. Martha Honey, *Ecotourism and Sustainable Development: Who Owns Paradise?* (1999), p. 8.

36. World Tourism Organization, news release, *op. cit.*

37. Cited in www.dantei.org/wto.forum/background-papers.html

38. Theodoro Koumelis, "WTO Policy Forum: Tourism is top priority in fight against poverty," Oct. 22, 2004, TravelDailyNews.com.

39. Simon Davis, "So Can Tourism Ever Really Be Ethical?" *The* [London] *Evening Standard*, July 19, 2006, p. A51.

40. Mark Clayton, "When Ecotourism Kills," *The Christian Science Monitor*, Nov. 4, 2004, p. 13.

41. Heidi S. Mitchell, "Easy Being Green," *The New York Times Style Magazine*, fall travel 2006, Sept. 24, 2006, p. 14.

42. Christopher Solomon, "Where the High Life Comes Naturally," *The New York Times*, May 1, 2005, Sect. 5, Travel, p. 3.

43. Mastny, *op. cit.*, p. 29. The report is by David Viner and Maureen Agnew, "Climate Change and Its Impact on Tourism," 1999.

44. James Hamilton-Paterson, "The End of Travel," *Granta*, summer 2006, pp. 221-234.

45. Anneli Rufus, "There's No Such Thing as Eco-Tourism," AlterNet; posted Aug. 14, 2006; www.alternet.org/story/40174/.

46. McLaren, *op. cit.*

47. Leisa Tyler, "Next Time You're In . . . Tasmania," *Time International*, Dec. 27, 2004, p. 120.

48. Larry Rohter, "For Power or Beauty? Debating the Course of Chile's Rivers," *The New York Times*, Aug. 6, 2006, p. 3.

49. Waterkeeper Alliance Web site, "Marriott and Four Seasons: Do Not Disturb PR"; www.waterkeeper.org/mainarticledetails.aspx?articleid=262.

BIBLIOGRAPHY

Books

Buckley, Ralf, ed., *Environmental Impacts of Ecotourism*, CABI Publishing, 2004.
This collection of articles analyzes the cost of various types of ecotourism and what is being done to mitigate negative impacts of the industry.

Duffy, Rosaleen, *A Trip Too Far: Ecotourism, Politics and Exploitation*, Earthscan, 2002.
Based on her field work in Belize, a senior lecturer at the Centre for International Politics at the University of Manchester in England critiques positive assumptions about ecotourism by examining its place in the complex web of "green capitalism."

Honey, Martha, *Ecotourism and Sustainable Development: Who Owns Paradise? Island Press*, 1999.
Using a clear, engaging writing style, Honey outlines the history and development of ecotourism, including a country-by-country study of the industry.

Weaver, David B., ed., *The Encyclopedia of Ecotourism*, CABI Publishing, 2001.
Papers by leading experts cover a range of ecotourism issues — from defining the term and its impact on host destinations to the practicalities of business planning and management.

Articles

Boynton, Graham, "The Search for Authenticity," *The Nation*, Oct. 6, 1997.
Paradoxes and compromises emerge when tourists search for "the real thing" in the developing world.

Duffy, Rosaleen, ed., "The Politics of Ecotourism and the Developing World," *Journal of Ecotourism*, Vol. 5, Nos. 1 and 2, September 2006.
An ecotourism scholar explores the range of issues raised by the politics of ecotourism in the developing world — from abstract theories to specific cases.

Ebersole, Rene, "Take the High Road," *Audubon Travel Issue*, July-August 2006, p. 39.
Without a globally recognizable certification label, travelers cannot be sure which trips and hotels qualify as genuinely ecologically friendly.

Honey, Martha, "Protecting Eden: Setting Green Standards for the Tourism Industry," *Environment*, July-August, 2003.
The writer provides an excellent overview of the background and rationale for creating a regularized certification program for ecotourism.

Jones, Finn-Olaf, "Tourism Stripping Everest's Forests Bare," *National Geographic Traveler*, Aug. 29, 2003.
As of 2003, more than 25,000 trekkers were visiting the Khumbu Valley near Mt. Everest, turning into "an eroding desert" much of the area described by Sir Edmund Hillary in 1951 as being superbly forested.

Nicholson-Lord, David, "The Politics of Travel: Is Tourism Just Colonialism in Another Guise?" *The Nation*, Oct. 6, 1997.
The writer offers a negative take on the cultural, political and economic conundrums posed by ecotourism.

Vivanco, Luis A., "The Prospects and Dilemmas of Indigenous Tourism Standards and Certification," in R. Black and A. Crabtree, eds., *Quality Assurance and Certification in Ecotourism*, CAB International, 2007, pp. 218-240.
An anthropologist examines ecotourism certification from the point of view of native peoples.

Reports and Studies

Chafe, Zoe, "Consumer Demand and Operator Support for Socially and Environmentally Responsible Tourism," *CESD/TIES Working Paper No. 104, Center on Ecotourism and Sustainable Development/ The International Ecotourism Society*, revised April 2005.
Statistics and trends are presented from a range of studies focusing on the U.S., Europe, Costa Rica and Australia.

Christ, Costas, Oliver Hillel, Seleni Matus and Jamie Sweeting, "Tourism and Biodiversity: Mapping Tourism's Global Footprint," *Conservation International*, 2003, p. 7.
The authors document the overlap between biodiversity "hotspots" and tourist destinations, making a case for carefully managed, sustainable tourism.

LaFranchi, Christopher, and Greenpeace Pacific, "Islands Adrift? Comparing Industrial and Small-scale Economic Options for Marovo Lagoon Region of the Solomon Islands," *Greenpeace*, March 1999; www.greenpeace.org/international/press/reports/ islands-adrift-comparing-indu.
An analysis of the subsistence-based economy of a small but biologically rich region illuminates the complex issues that arise when ecotourism is chosen over more conventional, extractive development routes.

Mastny, Lisa, "Traveling Light: New Paths for International Tourism," *Worldwatch Paper 159, Worldwatch Institute*, 2001.
A well-documented study examines the environmental implications of global travel in light of the massive economic forces it entails and considers the challenges and opportunities of achieving sustainable travel.

For More Information

Center on Ecotourism and Sustainable Development, 1333 H St., N.W., Suite 300, East Tower, Washington, DC 20005; (202) 347-9203; www.ecotourismcesd.org. Designs, monitors, evaluates and seeks to improve ecotourism practices and principles.

Conservation International, 1919 M St., N.W., Suite 600, Washington, DC 20036; (202) 912-1000; www.conservation .org. Seeks to protect endangered plants and animals around the world.

EplerWood International, www.eplerwood.com. Consultancy that offers insights into the challenges and opportunities of ecotourism from specific projects to broader economic and organizational issues.

The International Ecotourism Society, 1333 H St., N.W., Suite 300, East Tower, Washington, DC 20005; (202) 347-9203; www.ecotourism.org. Works to foster responsible travel to natural areas that conserves the environment and improves the well-being of local people.

Planeta.com, www.planeta.com. An ecotourism Web site featuring news, blog articles and links to other relevant Internet sites.

Transitions Abroad, P.O. Box 745, Bennington, VT 05201; (802) 442-4827; www.transitionsabroad.com. Web site offering information on working, studying, traveling and living abroad.

World Tourism Organization, Calle Capitan Haya, 42, 28020 Madrid, Spain; (34) 91 567 9301; www.unwto.org. United Nations agency that promotes economic development through responsible, sustainable tourism.

Rebuilding New Orleans

Should Flood-Prone Areas Be Redeveloped?

Peter Katel

12

The working-class Lower Ninth Ward was among the hardest-hit New Orleans neighborhoods. A rebuilding plan proposed by the Bring New Orleans Back Commission in early January would give residents a role in deciding whether heavily flooded neighborhoods would be resettled. An earlier plan by the Urban Land Institute sparked controversy among African-Americans when it proposed abandoning unsafe areas, including parts of the Lower Ninth.

From *CQ Researcher*, February 3, 2006.

Hurricane Katrina's floodwaters surged through tens of thousands of houses in New Orleans, including Dennis and Linda Scott's tidy, two-story brick home on Farwood Drive. The first floor has since been gutted, the ruined furnishings and appliances discarded.

Five months after floodwaters breached the city's levees and drainage canals, every other house for miles around is in the same deplorable shape.[1]

Like the Scotts, most of the residents who evacuated the sprawling New Orleans East area cannot decide whether to return, uncertain if their solidly middle class, mostly African-American neighborhoods will ever come back to life.

The disaster that began when Katrina's Category 3 winds hit New Orleans on Aug. 29, 2005, grinds on.[2] Yet the Scotts and their neighbors feel lucky to be alive.

"I'm one of the fortunate ones," says Scott, 47, who fled to Houston with his wife before the storm hit.

Linda's teaching job was swept away when the floods closed down the schools, so she's staying in Texas while Dennis works on the house and goes to his job as a communications specialist at Louis Armstrong International Airport. Their next-door neighbors, an elderly couple who stayed home, were drowned. Some three-quarters of Louisiana's 1,070 Katrina deaths occurred in New Orleans, where about 70 percent of the victims were age 60 and older.[3]

But "the east" is not alone. Similar devastation also afflicts some older neighborhoods, where lush gardens and sprawling villas reflect the city's French and Spanish heritage.[4]

Flooding Affected Most of Greater New Orleans

Flood water up to 20 feet deep covered more than three-quarters of New Orleans when storm surges pushed by Hurricane Katrina breached levees in 34 places. The Lower Ninth Ward and the New Orleans East district were among the hardest-hit areas.

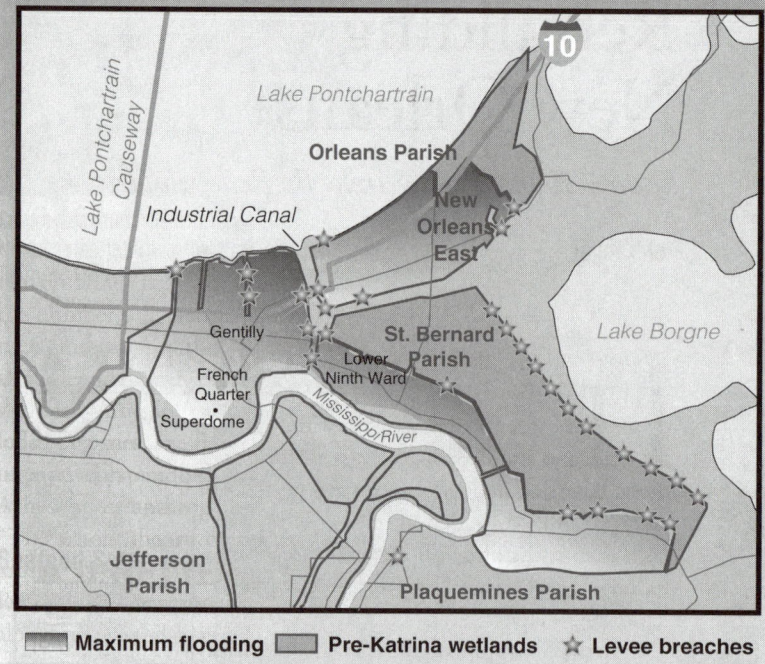

Maximum flooding   **Pre-Katrina wetlands**   ☆ **Levee breaches** (not all shown)

Source: Federal Emergency Management Agency

Losses in destroyed and damaged property, added to losses resulting from the shrinkage of the city's economy, amount roughly to $35 billion, estimates Stan Fulcher, research director of the Louisiana Recovery Authority in Baton Rouge.

Most residents are still gone, largely because most jobs — except those that involve either tearing down houses or fixing them up — have disappeared. Plans are only starting to be made to rebuild the city, and no one knows how much reconstruction money will be available.

Does Scott have a future in New Orleans? "I'm on hold," he replies.

That response comes up a lot among the city's residents and evacuees, often accompanied by a sense that the rest of the country has moved on — or views the French-founded, majority-African-American city as somehow foreign or not worth rebuilding.

"This is America you're talking about," lawyer Walter I. Willard says in frustration.

So American, in fact, that jazz was born there — amid a culture formed by the peculiarities of the city's slavery and segregation traditions.[9] "The West Africans [slaves] were allowed to play their music in Congo Square on Sundays. That happened nowhere else in the United States," famed New Orleans-born trumpeter Wynton Marsalis says.[10]

Slavery's legacy of racial and class divide has been part of the Katrina story from the beginning. New Orleans is two-thirds African-American, and the thousands of impoverished residents who were without cars to flee the approaching hurricane were overwhelmingly black.[11] "As all of us saw on television," President Bush acknowledged, "there's . . . some deep, persistent poverty in this region. That poverty has roots in a history of racial discrimination, which cut off generations from the opportunity of America."[12]

The continuing devastation mocks President Bush's stirring promise two weeks after the storm to mount "one of the largest reconstruction efforts the world has ever seen."[5]

Indeed, when the Senate Homeland Security and Governmental Affairs Committee toured the city four months later, members were "stunned" to see that "so much hasn't been done," said Chairwoman Susan Collins, R-Maine.[6]

Floodwaters up to 20 feet deep covered about 80 percent of the city and didn't recede until late September.[7] Fully half the city's homes — 108,731 dwellings — suffered flooding at least four feet deep, according to the Bring New Orleans Back Commission (BNOBC) formed by Mayor Ray Nagin. In some neighborhoods, Hurricane Rita, which struck later in September, brought additional flooding.[8]

Bush also conceded that the federal response to Katrina amounted to less than what its victims were entitled to — a point reinforced in early 2006, when Sen. Collins' committee released a strikingly accurate prediction of Katrina's likely effects, prepared for the White House two days *before* Katrina hit.[13]

But in a sense, New Orleans was crumbling from within even before the floods washed over the city. "The city had a lot of economic and social problems before — economics, race, poverty, crime, drugs," says musician and Xavier University Prof. Michael White. "Our failure to deal with harsh realities has sometimes been the problem."

In 2004, for example, the city's homicide rate hit 59 per 100,000 — the nation's highest.[14]

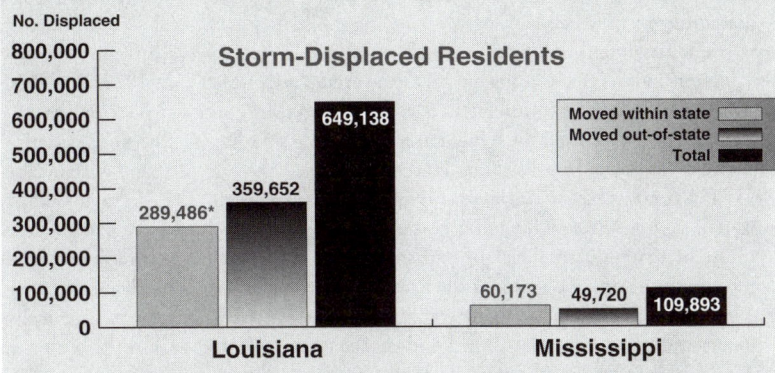

More Than 400,000 Residents Left Home States

Six times more Louisiana residents are still displaced from their homes than Mississippians. Of the more than 750,000 residents from both states displaced by Katrina, more than half are still living outside their home states.

Storm-Displaced Residents

No. Displaced

Louisiana: 289,486* (Moved within state), 359,652 (Moved out-of-state), 649,138 (Total)

Mississippi: 60,173 (Moved within state), 49,720 (Moved out-of-state), 109,893 (Total)

Legend: Moved within state / Moved out-of-state / Total

* Based on the number of FEMA aid applicants who have not returned to their pre-Katrina addresses.

Source: Louisiana Recovery Authority

In that post-Katrina climate — fed by bitter memories of institutional racism — the African-American community is concerned that developers are planning to reduce the black portion of the city's population. U.S. Housing and Urban Development Secretary Alphonso Jackson, who is African-American, intensified those fears when he said, "New Orleans is not going to be as black as it was for a long time, if ever again."[15]

The concern remained an issue into early 2006, when Mayor Nagin, also African-American, declared on Jan. 16 that the city "should be a chocolate New Orleans . . . a majority-African-American city. It's the way God wants it to be."[16] The following day, after furious reactions from both the white and black communities, Nagin apologized.[17]

Nagin's provocative language aside, fears of a demographic shift seem well-founded. In late January, sociologist John R. Logan of Brown University said he had conducted a study that showed about 80 percent of New Orleans' black residents were unlikely to come back, in part because their neighborhoods wouldn't be rebuilt.[18]

The BNOBC sparked the most recent chapter of the race and redevelopment debate. The commission's rebuilding plan, unveiled in early January, would give residents of the most heavily flooded neighborhoods four months to help figure out if their districts could be resettled. Homeowners in neighborhoods that can't be revived could sell their houses to a government-financed corporation for 100 percent of the pre-Katrina values, minus insurance payouts and mortgage obligations. The overall plan would cost more than $18 billion.[19] Federal, state and city approval is needed.[20]

Nowhere did the commission say that the poorest and most heavily damaged African-American neighborhoods should be abandoned. But the Washington-based Urban Land Institute (ULI), flatly recommended against extensive rebuilding in the most flood-prone areas, by implication including much of the working-class, largely African-American Lower Ninth Ward.[21]

Under the Jim Crow segregation system that lasted into the 1960s, residents point out, the Lower Ninth was the only place where African-Americans could buy property. "These people struggled to buy a little bit of land they could call home," says contractor Algy Irvin, 60, standing in the wrecked living room of his mother's house on Egania Street.

Can New Orleans' Musical Culture Be Saved?

Sunpie and the Louisiana Sunspots have the crowd at the House of Blues rocking as the group pounds out "Iko-Iko," a New Orleans standard with Creole lyrics and an irresistible beat.

The first night of Carnival is under way in the French Quarter, and the club is filling up for a long evening of music, with three more acts to follow. In the less touristy Marigny neighborhood, jazz pianist Ellis Marsalis is starting a slightly more sedate set at popular Snug Harbor.

Four months after Katrina hit, New Orleans is making music again. "So far, it's gone better than I would have thought, given the total lack of tourism," says Barry Smith, proprietor of the Louisiana Music Factory, where CDs and vinyl records of New Orleans artists account for some three-quarters of the stock of jazz, blues and gospel artists — both world-renowned and known only to locals. "I've definitely experienced a big increase in the number of local customers coming to the store, and a lot of the people who came here to work — from construction workers to Red Cross volunteers."

Few if any places in the United States come even close to New Orleans as an incubator of musical style and talent. As far back as 1819, a visitor wrote about the African music being played at Congo Square. And by the early 20th century, a musical tradition had formed in which Louis Armstrong — arguably the century's most influential musician — came of age.[1]

"All American music in the 20th century was profoundly shaped and influenced by New Orleans music," Tom Piazza writes in *Why New Orleans Matters*.[2]

The career of famed musician/producer Allen Toussaint illustrates the city's musical power. Toussaint wrote such 1960s hits as "Mother in Law" and produced and arranged the 1973 hit "Right Place, Wrong Time" for fellow New Orleans resident "Dr. John," as well as the disco standard "Lady Marmelade."

"He helped invent things we take as everyday in music — certain beats, certain arrangements," his partner in a record label said recently.[3]

Toussaint fled New Orleans after Katrina and has spoken optimistically of the city's future prospects.[4] But away from the club scene and music stores, the future looks less bright.

That's because the city's music springs from the very streets that Katrina emptied — the fabled "social aid and pleasure clubs," fraternal organizations that sponsor the Mardi Gras "Indian tribes," as well as the brass-band funeral processions that nourished jazz. All these influential institutions are maintained by people who mostly live paycheck to paycheck, says Michael White, a clarinetist and music scholar who holds an endowed chair in arts and humanities at New Orleans' Xavier University.[5]

Irvin recalls earning $35 a week mopping hospital floors and paying $18 a week for his own $1,200 lot on nearby Tupelo Street — now also a ruin. "You can see why people don't want a fat-cat developer coming in, making millions," he says, giving voice to a common suspicion that declaring the neighborhood unsafe is merely a cheap means of clearing out its present inhabitants to make way for lucrative development. But Irvin adds, "If people are compensated, that's another story."

Post-Katrina television coverage also gave the impression that New Orleans' African-American population was uniformly poor. In fact, the city had a substantial black middle class. "I had no clue that people couldn't get out of here," says Anne LaBranche, an African-American from New Orleans East, who returned to the city in January after staying with friends in Birmingham, Ala. "I do not know a person who doesn't own a car."

The LaBranches are moving into a house owned by her father-in-law. Her physician husband Emile, whose family practice was destroyed by Katrina along with all the patients' records, has been looking for work. But other medical offices say they aren't hiring until they know how many people are coming back.

Across town, Cory Matthews, 30, a medical-technology salesman, also wonders whether he still has a place in the city. He is rebuilding the flood-damaged Uptown house he shares with his girlfriend, but as he puts up new Sheetrock and rewires, he worries that his physician customer base has shrunk. "I'm hoping we're making the right move," he says.

Certainly, nobody is expecting redevelopment to bring speedy population growth. An estimated 135,000 people remain in New Orleans — less than a third of the 462,000 pre-Katrina population. Nagin's commission projects

The New Orleans establishment recognizes the problem. "Financial losses for social aid and pleasure clubs, Mardi Gras Indian tribes and [brass band] second-line companies are conservatively estimated at over $3 million," the Bring New Orleans Back Commission reports.[6]

"These were poor people, but people who spent a lot of money on these events," says White, a New Orleans native who comes from a long line of musicians. "The thing of money is serious. If people don't have jobs, they're not going to be able to participate."

White himself suffered another kind of loss — his vast collection of vintage instruments and memorabilia that included a trumpet mouthpiece from jazz saint Sidney Bechet; 4,000 rare CDs and even rarer vinyl recordings; photographs of New Orleans musical legends and notes and tapes of interviews with musicians who have since died. All were stored at his house — and it's all gone.

Is resurrecting an entire popular culture any more possible than restoring White's collection? "It's not like there's a central entity that can be rebuilt," says Piazza. "What steps can be taken to repatriate as many members of the African-American community and other communities — people who don't have the same kinds of resources as others to come back and rebuild, or who lived in areas where logistical challenges to rebuilding are all but insurmountable? That is the most difficult question about cultural renewal."

Legendary jazz pianist Ellis Marsalis is a popular performer in Old New Orleans, which was largely spared by the flooding.

Courtesy www.ellismarsalis.com

---

[1] For background, see Geoffrey C. Ward and Ken Burns, *Jazz: A History of America's Music* (2000), pp. 7-16; 40-46.

[2] Tom Piazza, *Why New Orleans Matters* (2005), p. 37.

[3] Quoted in Deborah Sontag, "Heat, and Piano, Back in New Orleans," *The New York Times*, Sept. 20, 2005, p. E1; for additional background see, "Inductees: Allen Toussaint," Rock+Roll Hall of Fame and Museum, undated, http://rockhall.com/hof/inductee.asp?id=200.

[4] *Ibid.*

[5] Ward and Burns, *op. cit.*, pp. 7-16.

[6] "Report of the Cultural Committee, Mayor's Bring New Orleans Back Commission," Jan. 17, 2006, pp. 8-9, www.bringneworleansback.org.

247,000 residents by September 2008, while a more optimistic consultant projects 252,000 by early 2007.[22] The totals, however, don't specify whether the residents will be laboring at construction sites or behind desks.

Jay LaPeyre, president of the Business Council of New Orleans and the River Region, says laborers are desperately needed "for every type of manual labor — from skilled electricians and plumbers to low-skilled apprentices and trainees to service jobs at Burger King."

That kind of talk makes white-collar New Orleanians nervous. Tulane University, one of the city's major high-end employers, laid off 230 of its 2,500 professors.[23] Nearly all 7,500 public school employees were laid off as well, though some were rehired by the handful of charter schools that have sprung up.[24]

"It's become a blue-collar market," says Daniel Perez, who lost his night-manager job at the swanky Royal Sonesta Hotel after business dropped off. Perez applied in vain for dozens of professional or managerial jobs. He had almost decided to leave New Orleans before finally landing a position as a sales manager for *USA Today*.

For now, at least, even the service-industry job market is thinning, though the profusion of help-wanted signs in the functioning parts of the city convey a different impression. A planned Feb. 17 reopening of Harrah's Casino, for example, will take place with only half the pre-Katrina payroll of 2,500, says Carla Major, vice president for human resources.

On his Jan. 11 visit, President Bush touted New Orleans as still "a great place to visit." But his motorcade had skirted most of the devastation, going nowhere near, for instance, the Scotts' deserted neighborhood.[25]

"We can't move forward until we have positive information on what's happening," Scott says. "There are no

Katrina Costs Dwarf Previous Disasters

Hurricane Katrina cost the Federal Emergency Management Agency $25 billion in the Gulf Coast — nearly three times more than the 2001 terrorist attacks on the World Trade Center and eight times more than Hurricane Rita, which followed on the heels of Katrina. The money pays for such services as temporary housing, unemployment assistance, crisis counseling and legal aid.

Disaster	FEMA Cost Estimate* ($ in billions)
Hurricane Katrina (2005)	$24.6
World Trade Center (2001)	$8.8
Hurricane Rita (2005)	$3.4
Hurricane Ivan (2004)	$2.6
Hurricane Wilma (2005)	$2.5
Hurricane Georges (1998)	$2.3
Hurricane Andrew (1992)	$1.8
Hurricane Hugo (1989)	$1.3
Loma Prieta Earthquake (1989)	$0.87
Hurricane Alberto (2000)	$0.6

* Flood-insurance reimbursements not included

Source: FEMA, December 2005

banks, no schools, no electricity. We just want to be home."

As officials plan the city's future, here are some of the questions being debated:

Should some neighborhoods not be rebuilt?

The buzzword summing up the single toughest question about New Orleans' future is "footprint." That's urban-planner jargon for a city's shape and the amount of space it occupies. In New Orleans, the term has become code for the idea that flood-prone districts are best turned back into open-space "sponges" to absorb nature's future onslaughts.

But would that help? New Orleans and the entire Gulf Coast are sinking. New Orleans was built on sandy soil to begin with, but oil and gas extraction and upriver levee construction — which reduces the delta area's natural landfill process, called silting — have exacerbated the problem. And sea levels are rising due to global warming.[26] As a result, writes Virginia R. Burkett of the U.S. Geological Survey's National Wetlands Research Center in Louisiana, by 2100 parts of New Orleans "could lie [about 23 feet] below water level during a Category 3 hurricane."[27]

Even so, the extensive levee system was designed to defend the entire metropolitan area from floods. So the Katrina disaster didn't grow out of the development of flood-prone lands that never should have been urbanized, say opponents of shrinking the footprint. Instead, they argue, the catastrophe grew out of human failure in engineering, construction or maintenance — or in all three.

"If we can build levees in Iraq, we can build levees on the Gulf Coast," says Sen. Mary Landrieu, D-La. "And if we can build hospitals in Baghdad and Fallujah, we can most certainly rebuild our hospitals in this metropolitan area."[28]

But congressional power brokers aren't in the mood to redevelop flood-prone areas. "We are committed to helping the people of Louisiana rebuild," said House Appropriations Committee member Rep. Ray LaHood, R-Ill. But, "we are not going to rebuild homes that are going to be destroyed in two years by another flood. We are not just going to throw money at it."[29]

Some who call the flood a man-made failure don't oppose redesigning the city in a more environmentally sensible way — even if it means abandoning their own neighborhoods. "It's not what I want, but I could live with it," says LaBranche, who with her husband owns a home, an office building and rental properties in New Orleans East. "I don't want to go through this again."

But who should decide? "The idea that everybody gets to have what they want" is not practical, says business leader LaPeyre. He wants the government to use its power of eminent domain — the right to condemn private property and compensate the owner — to prevent redevelopment of areas unsuitable for residential and business use.[30]

Private companies, such as utility and insurance companies — will also influence decisions about where development will occur. "The market will do better than most people claim," he says. "If you're not going to have good services, most people will say, 'I don't want to live there.' "

Others argue that a neighborhood's residents should have a big voice. The Bring New Orleans Back Commission proposed letting residents of heavily damaged neighborhoods work with urban and financial planners to determine if their districts could be revived. The "neighborhood planning teams" would have until May to decide. The procedure grew out of opposition to the Urban Land Institute's recommendation against rebuilding in flood-prone areas.

"In an arbitrary and capricious manner to say that these areas — which were populated by black people because they were directed there — should now be turned into green space deepens the wound," says Councilwoman Cynthia Willard-Lewis, who represents several of the city's eastern neighborhoods. Many of the houses can be repaired and the communities brought back, she says, adding that she suspects the plan "was not based on what was safe but on whom they wanted to return."

William Hudnut, a former mayor of Indianapolis who holds the Urban Land Institute's public policy chair, says city leaders do not have the courage to tell residents what they don't want to hear. "The footprint has to be smaller and development more compact," he says. "An honest, tough-minded approach to rebuilding is part of what leadership is all about. It may be that some people would lose their political base or lose their jobs. But if a thing is worth doing, it's worth doing well and worth standing up for."

Ari Kelman, an environmental historian at the University of California at Davis, concedes that some neighborhoods should be abandoned. At the same time,

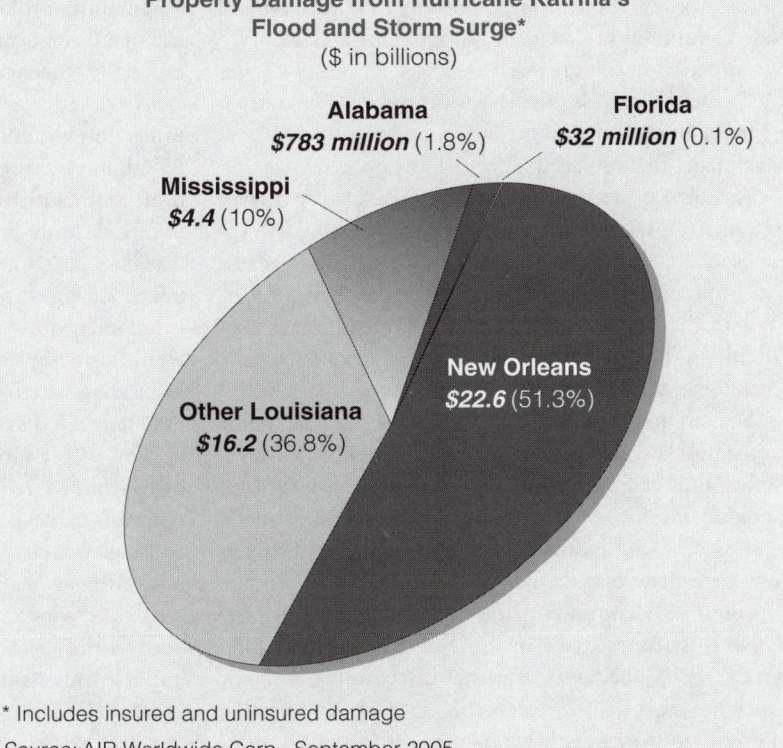

Katrina Saved Worst for New Orleans

Nearly 90 percent of Katrina's flood and storm damage occurred in Louisiana — more than half of it in New Orleans. The other three states affected by Katrina suffered only 12 percent of the damages.

Property Damage from Hurricane Katrina's Flood and Storm Surge*
($ in billions)

Alabama *$783 million* (1.8%)
Florida *$32 million* (0.1%)
Mississippi *$4.4* (10%)
New Orleans *$22.6* (51.3%)
Other Louisiana *$16.2* (36.8%)

* Includes insured and uninsured damage

Source: AIR Worldwide Corp., September 2005

he says, low-income African-American residents have well-founded fears that any planning and decision system will be stacked against them.

"People who don't have money also don't have power," says Kelman, author of a 2003 book on the interplay between human design and nature in New Orleans. "When politics get cooking in New Orleans, it's likely that the poor are going to get screwed."

Should the levee system be upgraded to guard against a Category 5 storm?

The levee system surrounding New Orleans was designed to withstand a Category 3 hurricane. Katrina had weakened to Category 3 by the time it made landfall, but the wall of water it sent ashore — the hurricane's "surge" — was born when the storm was still offshore and raging at Category 4 and 5 strength.[31]

So far, official attention has focused on possible errors in design, construction or maintenance of the levees. But many are also asking whether the system should be upgraded to protect against a Category 5 hurricane — the most powerful. Among Louisianans in general and New Orleanians in particular, support for a Category 5 system seems nearly universal.

"I would like to see the levees brought to Category 5 for my safety and that of my family and properties," says LaBranche, the displaced New Orleans homeowner.

But some government experts say a Category 5 levee system is a pipe dream. They point out Category 5 is open-ended, taking in all hurricanes whose winds exceed 155 mph and create storm surges greater than 18 feet. "What's the top end for a Cat 5 hurricane?" asked Dan Hitchings, director of Hurricane Katrina recovery for the Corps of Engineers. "There isn't one."[32]

That argument carries little weight in Louisiana. Some Louisiana lawmakers say that if the below-sea-level Netherlands can protect itself from floods, New Orleans shouldn't settle for less. "They built once-in-1,000-years flood protection," Sen. Landrieu told a rally of some 75 displaced New Orleanians outside the White House last December. "We don't even have once-in-100-years [protection]."

No hurricanes strike in the North Sea, which surrounds the Netherlands. But the tiny country, some of which lies more than 20 feet below sea level, is vulnerable to powerful storms with winds that can reach 60 mph. Following a 1953 storm that killed more than 1,800 people, the country redesigned its protective system in ways that many New Orleanians say should serve as a model.[33]

The Netherlands system was designed to withstand a once-in-10,000-years storm. New Orleans' levees were designed for a once-in-200-300-years storm, says the Corps of Engineers.[34]

In addition, say Louisiana officials, a Category 5 system would probably cost about $32 billion.[35]

"It will probably be a pretty staggering price tag," acknowledges Craig E. Colten, a geography professor at Louisiana State University in Baton Rouge and author of a recent book on New Orleans' flood-protection history. But the long-term value of property protection would make an upgraded system a wise investment, he added,

citing the prosperous Netherlands, an international shipping center.

But Rep. Richard Baker, R-La., cautions that debating a Category 5 upgrade now could distract from the immediate and urgent tasks facing New Orleans. "Construction toward a Category 5 standard would be a decade-long project," he says. "The statistical probabilities of a Category 5 hitting New Orleans are fairly small, especially since we just got hit. I think we have time."

No one denies the need for fixing the existing flood-protection system. The Bush administration has proposed $1.6 billion to restore the system to a Category 3 level of protection, and another $1.5 billion for further improvements.[36] Thus far, however, it has stayed out of the Category 5 argument. At a White House briefing on the new flood-protection plan, Donald E. Powell, the administration's coordinator of post-hurricane recovery projects, would only say that after the proposed improvements, "The levee system will be better, much better, and stronger than it ever has been in the history of New Orleans."[37]

The White House plan also includes a study, backed by Mayor Nagin, of whether a substantial upgrade to the system is needed. A preliminary report is due in May.

However, city officials argue that a system capable of protecting against a Category 5 storm is well within the range of engineering possibilities and would be good for both the city's and the country's economy. "We need to build toward Category 5 to provide . . . assurance to [potential] investors," says Gary P. LaGrange, director of the Port of New Orleans, and to protect the port, an essential part of the nation's trade system.

Should the nation pay for New Orleans to be rebuilt?

So far, Congress has committed $98.9 billion for post-hurricane recovery and rebuilding programs throughout the Gulf Coast, the Senate Budget Committee calculated. The funding came in two emergency appropriations in September totaling $62.3 billion, followed by several smaller spending authorizations. In December, expanding on a request by Bush, Congress redirected $23.4 billion in funds previously appropriated.[38]

It's uncertain, however, how much will go to New Orleans.

In any event, money appropriated so far includes $6.2 billion in Community Development Block Grants intended for Louisiana, and $22 billion for reimbursements to Gulf Coast homeowners from the federal flood-insurance program. But even with the emergency injections of cash, the flood-insurance program is "bankrupt," Senate Banking Committee Chairman Richard Shelby, R-Ala., said on Jan. 25. The acting director of the Federal Emergency Management Agency (FEMA) insurance division said the agency has paid out $13.5 billion in claims arising from the 2005 hurricane season — nearly as much as the agency has paid out in its 37-year existence. And 30 percent of the 239,000 claims have yet to be resolved.[39]

Federal hurricane-recovery coordinator Powell has been advocating directing much of the block grant money to the estimated 20,000 New Orleans homeowners who didn't have flood insurance because their neighborhoods weren't designated as flood plains.[40]

Given the huge costs involved and all the unknowns, lawmakers from other parts of the country are not exactly champing at the bit to pay for rebuilding New Orleans. The city's tenuous hydrological situation and the likelihood that it will be flooded again by other hurricanes lead some Americans to question whether the rest of the country should have to pay to rebuild the city in such a precarious location.

"There is a lot of — I suppose you can call it 'Katrina fatigue' — that people are dealing with out in the heartland," Rep. Henry Bonilla, R-Texas, told Louisiana Gov. Kathleen Babineaux Blanco, a Democrat, at a House Select Katrina Response Investigation Committee hearing last Dec. 14.

The situation has rekindled a long-simmering debate about whether Americans in the heartland should pay to constantly bail out people — usually those living on the coasts — who choose to live in areas prone to floods, hurricanes, landslides and earthquakes. "Is it fair to make people living in Pennsylvania or Ohio pay billions for massive engineering projects so that some of the people of New Orleans can go back to the way things were and avoid the hard choices that nature presents them?" asks economist Adrian Moore of the libertarian Reason Foundation of Los Angeles.[41]

Some lawmakers agree, although only a few have spoken out. "It looks like a lot of that place could be bulldozed," House Speaker Dennis Hastert, R-Ill. said shortly after the hurricane, raising hackles. He later explained he only meant that danger zones shouldn't be resettled.[42]

Getty Images/Robyn Beck

Skip LaGrange takes a break from cleaning out his flooded home in the Mid-City section of New Orleans, on Oct. 5, 2005. An estimated 135,000 people are now living in New Orleans — less than a third of the 462,000 pre-Katrina population.

New Orleanians respond that other disaster-prone areas, including hurricane-exposed Florida coastal cities, get rebuilt with few questions asked about viability. "People build on mountainsides in California that fall in the ocean," notes Perez, the newspaper sales manager. "We're not the only vulnerable area in the country."

In addition, points out Republican Louisiana Sen. David Vitter, 25 percent of the nation's energy and most of the Midwest's grain exports are shipped through the port of New Orleans. "If people don't think there's a national stake in rebuilding New Orleans, that's fine. But they should get used to much higher gasoline prices," he said. "And people can forget about getting crops to foreign markets. You need a major city as the hub of all that activity."

But if federal funds are forthcoming to rebuild the city, they should have some serious accountability strings attached, given the city's long history of corruption and dysfunction, some argue. "A lot of . . . our constituents now are telling us that they [don't] want us to support funding for the Gulf region at this point without strong plans of accountability," Bonilla said.

Recognizing those sentiments — as well as the reality that the country is at war and its debt and deficits are

CHRONOLOGY

1700s-1800s *From the time of its founding, New Orleans' vulnerability to nature is seen as the price of its incomparably strategic location.*

1718 New Orleans is founded on a natural levee along a bend in the Mississippi River.

1892 Adolph Plessy of New Orleans is arrested after testing segregation laws by riding in a "white" train car. U.S. Supreme Court later upholds his conviction in landmark *Plessy v. Ferguson* decision.

1900-1947 *A catastrophic flood reminds the city of its dangerous location.*

1927 Massive Mississippi floods see many African-Americans forced into levee-reinforcement work; two rural parishes are deliberately flooded to save New Orleans.

1929 The U.S. Army Corps of Engineers begins building a spillway on the Mississippi to channel floodwater away from New Orleans.

1930s *Expansion of city drainage systems allows urban expansion, but new neighborhoods are strictly segregated.*

Sept. 17-19, 1947 A Category 4 hurricane overwhelms levees, causing flooding over nine square miles of the city.

1950s-1970s *The city expands into drained wetlands, increasing its vulnerability to floods.*

1950 Land drained for suburban expansion reaches 49,000 acres.

Sept. 7, 1965 Hurricane Betsy slams the city with Category 3 winds, pushing a 10-foot storm surge through some levees.

Oct. 27, 1965 President Lyndon B. Johnson signs the Flood Control Act, which includes funding for a hurricane-protection system in New Orleans.

Aug. 17, 1969 Category 5 Hurricane Camille devastates Mississippi and Alabama, but reinforced protective systems keep most of New Orleans safe.

May 3, 1978 Heavy rainstorm flooding damages more than 70,000 homes.

1980s-1990s *Attempts by the city to guard against rainstorm floods prove inadequate, as fears of vulnerability to hurricanes begin to grow.*

April 1982 Rainstorm-caused floods damage 1,400 homes and other buildings.

1983 City expands pumping and drainage systems.

May 8-10, 1995 Flooding damages thousands of homes, causes six deaths.

2000-Present *Fears of hurricane vulnerability grow, as journalists and government officials warn about the weakness of the city's defenses.*

June 23-June 26, 2002 *Times-Picayune* warns of New Orleans' hurricane vulnerability.

Sept. 26, 2002 Hurricane Isidore hits Louisiana after weakening to a tropical storm, but still causes major flooding.

July 2004 FEMA officials conduct a drill featuring Category 3 "Hurricane Pam" hitting New Orleans and predict serious flooding, massive evacuation.

Aug. 29, 2005 Hurricane Katrina makes landfall east of New Orleans.

Sept. 15, 2005 President Bush visits New Orleans and pledges a massive disaster-recovery effort.

Jan. 11, 2006 Bring New Orleans Back Commission releases an "Action Plan" for re-creating the city.

Jan 17, 2006 Senators of both parties visit New Orleans and criticize slow progress on recovery.

Jan. 26, 2006 President Bush explains why he refused to support the creation of a public corporation to buy flood-damaged homes.

June 1, 2006 Hurricane season begins; repairs and improvements to levee system due for completion.

rising — Louisiana politicians have proposed two major plans that they say would lower the federal spending burden for rebuilding New Orleans and the rest of the state.

But the White House has already refused to back one of these plans. Its author, Rep. Baker, proposed establishing a public corporation to buy or finance repairs on storm-damaged property. Homeowners who sold their houses to the corporation would get 60 percent of the pre-Katrina value of their holdings. The corporation would then resell the homes, if possible, and turn the proceeds back to the Treasury. Nagin's BNOBC adopted the idea, which some of its members called crucial to reviving the city.

"We were concerned about creating additional federal bureaucracies, which might make it harder to get money to the people," Bush said, explaining his rejection of Baker's idea.[43]

On Feb. 1, according to Baker's office, three former Republican governors of Louisiana — Murphy J. "Mike" Foster, Charles E. "Buddy" Roemer III, and David Treen — urged Bush to change his mind concerning Baker's bill, which they called the only practical method of disposing of thousands of ruined residential and business properties.

The congressman has been vowing to press ahead with his proposal, sponsored in the Senate by Sen. Landrieu. Bush's negative response would "constrict the opportunities for rapid redevelopment, and that's tough," said Reed Kroloff, architecture dean at Tulane University and a BNOBC member.[44]

But developer Joseph Canizaro, who helped put together the commission's plan, said block grant money and other unspecified funds could be found for a property buyback.[45]

The other plan to lower direct federal spending is a longstanding proposal to boost the state's share of money that the federal government earns from petroleum leases on the Outer Continental Shelf in the Gulf of Mexico off Louisiana's coast. One-quarter of U.S. crude oil production comes from Louisiana's offshore waters.[46]

The cost of repairing the state's hurricane-protection system "can be paid for simply by giving Louisiana our fair share of oil and gas revenues from the Outer Continental Shelf," Gov. Blanco told Bonilla at the House Select Committee hearing.

Coastal states like Louisiana receive 27 percent of the revenues from oil and gas leases from waters within their three-mile jurisdictions (federal waters extend another 197 miles). By contrast, states with oil and gas production on public lands receive 50 percent of the federal revenues, leading coastal states to feel they are entitled to a larger share of offshore revenues.[47]

Sen. Landrieu last year pushed a bill to grant coastal states 50 percent of the take from oil and gas leases in the areas off their shores. The bill died at year's end, but she is planning to revive it this year (*see p. 292*).

Rather than creating a new revenue source, however, the proposal would merely divert money to the state before the funds reach federal coffers, which bothered Bonilla. "It is wise when states and local governments come before us to show what they are doing to help themselves in terms of raising whatever revenue dollars you can," Bonilla told Blanco. "People would want to know . . . what is Louisiana doing in terms of everything you possibly can do to help yourself and not just look at the federal government and say, 'We need you to help us pay for these things.' "

But, he added, Americans would not "turn their back on those who want to help themselves."

BACKGROUND

Island City

New Orleans has been battling with nature ever since explorer Jean-Baptiste Le Moyne de Bienville founded the city in 1718. Its original name, in fact, reflected the city's relationship to the four bodies of water surrounding it — the Mississippi River, Lake Pontchartrain, Lake Borgne and the Gulf of Mexico. He called it L'Isle de la Nouvelle Orléans — the Island of New Orleans.[48]

"His enthusiasm for the river's commercial benefits blinded him to many of the challenges of building a city in the delta," environmental historian Kelman writes. These included: epidemics; "terrible to nonexistent" drainage; dampness; and "the threat of catastrophic flooding."

Still, Bienville's insight into the river's economic importance was on the money. The Mississippi was unrivalled as a highway deep into the North American continent, and remains so today. Some 500 million tons of goods — including about 60 percent of U.S. grain exports — are

Experts Blame Levees, Not Storm

The newspaper headlines blamed "Killer Storm Katrina" for devastating New Orleans. But engineers largely blame the levees designed and built by the U.S. Army Corps of Engineers.

A team of experts who examined the protective system found no fewer than 34 storm-induced levee breaches, indicating that the engineering failures were far wider than initial reports indicated.[1]

"The performance of many of the levees and floodwalls could have been significantly improved, and some of the failures likely prevented, with relatively inexpensive modification," the team concluded. The simple addition of concrete "splash slabs," for instance, might have prevented soil levee tops from eroding.

In fact, even a task force assembled by the Corps of Engineers itself concluded "integral parts of the . . . hurricane-protection system failed."[2]

With the June 1 start of the 2006 hurricane season approaching, the Corps is trying to patch the immediate problems. Engineers and lawmakers, meanwhile, are evaluating the system's performance. So far, a lethal combination of design, construction and maintenance errors appears to underlie the disaster.

Blame extends from state-appointed "levee boards" responsible for inspection and maintenance to the Corps of Engineers, Sen. George Voinovich, R-Ohio, told the Senate Homeland Security and Governmental Affairs Committee on Dec. 14. And Congress deserved blame too, he said: "We have been penny-wise and pound-foolish" on funding upkeep and completion of the New Orleans levee system.

The Lake Pontchartrain and Vicinity Hurricane Protection Project includes 125 miles of levees, floodwalls and other structures. The system was supposed to bar storm surges from Lake Pontchartrain and channel any flooding out of the city via a series of canals.[3]

Though Congress approved the project in 1965, it was unfinished when Katrina struck. In the city itself, construction was 90 percent complete, but the lack of completion has not been blamed for the system's failure.[4] Rather, the devastation was intensified by the environmental changes in southern Louisiana since the system was first designed, the *Times-Picayune* reported as early as 2002.[5]

As the oil and gas industry expanded, the Corps of Engineers built or approved the necessary navigation channels in southern Louisiana and the Gulf of Mexico. And the industry expansion swallowed one-third to one-half of the wetlands — which have been disappearing at a rate of at least 25 square miles a year. Experts now know wetlands play a critical role during hurricanes, slowing storms as they make landfall.[6]

shipped downriver to the southern Louisiana port complex, which includes New Orleans.[49]

The first of New Orleans' protective barriers — called levees from the French verb "to lift" — were natural. In fact, New Orleans exists in the first place because the Mississippi's waters helped create a high section of riverbank along the section of the river that forms a crescent embracing old New Orleans — known today as the French Quarter. The sloping, natural levee was only 12 feet above sea level.

Settlers soon began adding to nature's work. Throughout the 18th and early 19th centuries — during the first period of French rule, the Spanish colonial period that followed in 1768-1801 and the French restoration in 1801-1803 — levees were built far upstream, and raised continually after flooding.

The levee work continued after the United States bought the city and vast swaths of the new nation's interior in 1803 for $15 million, or about 3 cents an acre. Nine years after the so-called Louisiana Purchase, Louisiana became a state.

From the beginning, many people realized that building ever-higher levees up and down the river prevented its energy from being dissipated naturally in periodic floods. By the time the Mississippi reached New Orleans, it would be dangerously high and flowing at maximum force.

"We are every year confining this immense river closer and closer to its own bed — forgetting that it is fed by over 1,500 streams — and regardless of a danger becoming every year more and more impending," State Engineer P. O. Herbert warned in 1846. He argued for flood outlets along the river, but landowners resisted, not wanting their plantations flooded.[50]

In 1849, the river broke through several upstream levees, one of them 17 miles above New Orleans. The resultant flooding in the lowest section of New Orleans forced 12,000 mostly poor residents to abandon their dwellings or try to coexist with the water.

Afterward, the city raised the levees higher still. But A. D. Wooldridge, the state engineer who succeeded

So when Katrina made landfall across the region's depleted wetlands, the poorly designed and built levees and floodwalls couldn't withstand the full force of the storm surge.

A section of floodwall along the London Avenue Canal was so weakened that it likely would have been breached by the floodwaters — if the barrier on the opposite side of the canal hadn't failed first, an engineer told the Senate Environment and Public Works Committee on Nov. 17. "Multiple, concurrent failure mechanisms" were present, said Larry Roth, deputy executive director of the American Society of Civil Engineers. "The wall was badly out of alignment and tilting landward; as a result of the tilt, there were gaps between the wall and the supporting soil."

Additional pressure on the flood barriers came from the Mississippi River Gulf Outlet (MRGO), a 76-mile long canal built to give ships a shortcut from the Gulf to the Port of New Orleans. Instead, it gave Katrina a straight shot into the city — a "hurricane alley" — said Sen. David Vitter, R-La., who has called, along with others, for the canal's closure. The Corps says it will not conduct its annual dredging of the waterway, and hurricane experts say it may become less dangerous as it becomes shallower.[7]

Meanwhile, engineers have suggested that some residential areas be abandoned — to provide a flood-absorbing floodplain — and building codes amended to require that houses be elevated.

But the levee system also must be dealt with, Roth said. "If we are to rebuild the city," he said, "we must also rebuild its protections."[8]

[1] The team was assembled by the National Science Foundation (NSF), the American Society of Civil Engineers (ASCE) and the University of California at Berkeley. See R. B. Seed, *et al.*, "Preliminary Report on the Performance of the New Orleans Levee Systems in Hurricane Katrina on Aug. 29, 2005," Nov. 2, 2005, Figure 1.4, p. 1-10, www.ce.berkeley.edu/~inkabi/KRTF/CCRM/levee-rpt.pdf.

[2] "Performance Evaluation Plan and Interim Status, Report 1 of a Series: Performance Evaluation of the New Orleans and Southeast Louisiana Hurricane Protection System," Interagency Performance Evaluation Task Force, Jan. 10, 2006, Appendix A, p. 2, https://ipet.wes.army.mil.

[3] *Ibid*, pp. 1.2-1.3; Seed, *et al.*, *op. cit.*, p. A-2.

[4] "Performance Evaluation Plan," *op. cit.*, Appendix A, p. 2.

[5] John McQuaid and Mark Schleifstein, "Evolving Danger; experts know we face a greater threat from hurricanes than previously suspected," *The Times-Picayune* (New Orleans), June 23, 2002, p. A1.

[6] John McQuaid and Mark Schleifstein, "Shifting Tides," *The Times-Picayune* (New Orleans), June 26, 2002, p. A1.

[7] John Schwartz, "New Orleans Wonders What to Do With Open Wounds, Its Canals," *The New York Times*, Dec. 231, 2005, p. A26; Seed, *et al.*, *op. cit.*, p. 3.1; Matthew Brown, "Corps suspends plans to dredge MRGO," *The Times-Picayune* (New Orleans), Breaking News Weblog, Nov. 21, 2005, www.nola.com/t-p/.

[8] For background, see Larry Roth statement to Senate Committee on Environment and Public Works, Nov. 17, 2005, http://epw.senate.gov/hearing_statements.cfm?id=249000.

Herbert, declared in 1850 that reliance on levees "will be destructive to those who come after us." By then, some rose 15 feet.

Dynamiting the Levee

The engineers' warnings came to pass in early 1927. A series of rainstorms, coupled with unusually heavy spring runoff, swelled the huge river and overwhelmed the levees. Floodwater inundated 28,545 square miles of the Mississippi Valley as far north as Illinois, killing 423 people. By mid-April, more than 50,000 people had fled their homes.[51]

In New Orleans, powerful pumps kept floodwaters at bay — until a bolt of lightning disabled the power plant that kept the pumps humming.

A group of city leaders, who had formed the Citizens Flood Relief Committee, began campaigning to stop the flooding of the city by blowing a hole in the levee some 12 miles downstream.

Residents of the two thinly populated wetland parishes downstream, St. Bernard and Plaquemines, largely made their living fishing and trapping muskrats for their fur. The New Orleans political class persuaded Louisiana Gov. Oramel Simpson that those rural activities were worth sacrificing to protect New Orleans. Simpson gave the "river parish" residents three days to clear out. Muskrat trapping took years to recover.

For the poor African-Americans living along the river's southern reaches, the 1927 flood left bitter memories of racial oppression and death. Especially in Mississippi, thousands of black men were conscripted into labor gangs that shored up the levee, often working at gunpoint. Some drowned as they worked, and a community leader who refused a summons because he'd been working all night was shot on the spot.

The race-hatred exacerbated by the flood triggered a vast expansion of the "great migration" of African-Americans from South to North.[52] For the black community, 1927 established a connection between natural disaster, racism

Getty Images/Robyn Beck

Engineers inspect a Katrina-damaged section of the London Avenue Canal on Sept. 21, 2005, three days before Hurricane Rita hit and reopened some levees that had been partially repaired. The city's flood-control system may not be completely repaired by June 1, the start of the 2006 hurricane season.

and black exodus — a chain of events that many would later see repeating itself with Katrina.

New Expansion

The 1927 disaster led to improved federal flood-control systems and also launched a continuing debate over whether all Americans should have to pay to protect people living in disaster-prone places.[53]

In New Orleans, the 1927 flood also undermined the total dependence on levees for protection. Two years later, the Corps of Engineers began building a spillway at Bonnet Carré that could release river water into Lake Pontchartrain if the Mississippi rose to 20 feet in New Orleans. The spillway was completed in 1936.

By then, New Orleans residents had other reasons to feel safer. Electric and gasoline-powered motors had relieved major drainage problems. In a city sitting below sea level in a swampy area, difficulties in disposing of human and other waste had long endangered health and lowered the quality of life. Mosquito-borne yellow fever alone killed about 41,000 people between 1817 and 1905.

Draining surrounding swampland also allowed the opening up of new lands for settlement. From the 1930s to the post-World War II years, acreage to the north, east and west of the original city were transformed from wetlands into tract-housing territory. The suburbanization expanded into Jefferson Parish, just outside of the city.

Within New Orleans itself, the amount of land that had been drained for settlement expanded from 12,349 acres in 1895 to more than 90,000 by 1983.

On a dry day, the newly drained territory appeared suitable for housing. But after Katrina, the local paper, the *Times-Picayune*, published an 1878 map showing that nearly every part of the city that flooded in 2005 had been uninhabited in the years before the land was drained. Early residents understood exactly where not to live, the paper concluded.[54]

Hurricanes and Floods

Since the city's founding, the protective levee system had aimed mainly at holding back Mississippi flooding. But beginning in the mid-20th century, a series of powerful hurricanes changed the perception of where danger lay.

In 1947, a 112-mile-an-hour hurricane (they didn't have names yet) brought two-foot floods in a nine-square-mile area. Hurricanes Flossy (1956) and Hilda (1964) caused some damage but were dwarfed by the 160-mile-an-hour winds of Hurricane Betsy in 1965. Floodwaters reached eight feet in parts of the city; 75 people died, and 7,000 homes suffered damage.

In response, Congress passed the Flood Control Act of 1965, which funded expansion of the levee and canal system in and around New Orleans to protect against what today would be classified as a Category 3 hurricane.[55]

In 1969, just as construction of the expanded system began, Hurricane Camille slammed the Gulf Coast. Mississippi was hit hardest, but a section of the New Orleans levee complex also failed, flooding part of the city.

In succeeding years, even rainstorms became problematic. Nine inches of rain during a 1978 storm caused flooding of up to 3.5 feet in low-lying sections, damaging 71,500 homes. A series of heavy rainstorms between 1979 and 1995 also caused widespread damage, and in 1998, Hurricane Georges, a Category 2 storm that barely touched New Orleans, brought a water surge to within a foot of topping the levees.[56]

Waiting for the Big One

The steady growth in the number and intensity of hurricanes during the 1990s fed unease in New Orleans and prompted the Times-Picayune to publish — at the beginning of the 2002 hurricane season — a series of articles unflinchingly examining the risks New Orleans faced. "Officials at the local, state and national level are convinced the risk is genuine and are devising plans for alleviating the aftermath of a disaster that could leave the city uninhabitable for six months or more," the authors presciently wrote.[57]

In January 2005, Ivor van Heerden, deputy director of the Louisiana State University (LSU) Hurricane Center, told a conference on "coastal challenges" that a Category 3 or above storm striking New Orleans or any other coastal Louisiana city would be a "disaster of cataclysmic proportion."[58]

By then, the city's new-and-improved flood-protection system consisted of about 125 miles of levees, floodwalls and flood-proofed bridges and other barriers. In Orleans Parish, the renovation work was 90 percent complete.[59]

On Aug. 28, as Hurricane Katrina was rolling through the Gulf and heading for New Orleans, the National Weather Service called it "a most powerful hurricane with unprecedented strength." After landfall, "Most of the area will be uninhabitable for weeks, perhaps longer."[60]

Mayor Nagin, a newcomer to politics, had ordered the city evacuated. But buses for the tens of thousands of elderly and poor residents who didn't own cars were never dispatched.

Even before Katrina touched down near New Orleans on the morning of Aug. 29, a storm surge breached the levees along the Inner Harbor Navigation Canal (the "Industrial Canal"). At about the same time, an 18-foot surge from Lake Borgne pushed through a wall along the Mississippi River Gulf Outlet east of St. Bernard Parish and the Lower Ninth Ward. The resulting flooding soon reached the Lower Ninth.[61]

Over the next few hours, additional surges over the Industrial Canal sent even more floodwater into the Lower Ninth. Then, with Katrina moving westward near Lake Pontchartrain, another section of levee along the Industrial Canal gave way, followed by a breach of the 17th Street Canal floodwall, flooding the western end of the parish.[62]

In the days following the storm, New Orleans became an international symbol of government dysfunction. Tens of thousands of residents unable to evacuate clung to rooftops or flocked to the New Orleans Superdome, which was unequipped to receive them. By Sept. 12, FEMA Director Michael Brown had resigned under pressure — only days after being congratulated by President Bush. Belatedly, federal officials organized bus convoys and flights out of the city.[63]

Then, on Sept. 24, Hurricane Rita, a Category 3 storm, hit the Gulf Coast. New Orleans didn't lie directly in the storm's path, but the hurricane reopened some partly repaired levee breaches. As a result, the Lower Ninth Ward and the Gentilly neighborhood flooded again. Elsewhere in Louisiana and East Texas, the damage was far worse, with tens of thousands left homeless.[64]

By early December, only 10 percent of the city's businesses were up and running, and 135,000 residents, at most, had stayed or returned. They had a name for the only fully functioning part of the city — a strip of high ground that includes the French Quarter and other sections of old New Orleans: Like explorer Bienville, they called it "the island."[65]

CURRENT SITUATION

Redevelopment Plans

On Jan. 11, the Bring New Orleans Back Commission released its "Action Plan" for rebuilding the city, but action doesn't seem to be on the near horizon.

The plan recommended the formation of 13 neighborhood-planning committees, with work on recommendations to start on Feb. 20, finish by May 20 and be submitted to the city for approval by June 20. Reconstruction would begin by Aug. 20.[66]

Within days of the plan's release, however, a FEMA official said updated floodplain maps of the city wouldn't be available until the summer, depriving crucial information to homeowners considering rebuilding.

"If I were putting my lifetime savings in the single, biggest investment I'll ever make, I'd want to make sure I had minimized every possible risk," said Tulane's Kroloff, chairman of the commission's urban-design subcommittee.[67]

The delay in obtaining the updated flood-zone information would slow the reconstruction timetable, Kroloff said, but wouldn't prevent the neighborhood committees from canvassing past and present residents. "There are some people who are going to return no matter what, and some who aren't," he said.[68]

Other obstacles could further slow the plan's execution. Congress may not approve Rep. Baker's proposal to create a public corporation to buy and sell distressed properties, although BNOB Commissioner Canizaro hopes funds can be rounded up from FEMA and elsewhere.[69] The Louisiana legislature would have to create the nonprofit entity, provisionally entitled the Crescent City Recovery Corp., and New Orleans voters would have to OK changes to the city charter to authorize it.[70]

That vote could come as soon as April. But it remains to be seen how receptive voters will be to measures recommended by Nagin and the commission, especially in light of the criticism that greeted the plan when it was unveiled. Some property owners attacked the proposal as a land grab.

"If you come to take our property, you'd better come ready," homeowner Rodney Craft of the Lower Ninth Ward told the commissioners.[71]

"I hear the politicians talk, and nothing is being said — nothing," says Gail Miller, a retired New Orleans police officer who has returned to her home in New Orleans East, living upstairs but cooking in a motor home she and her husband park in the driveway. "The political situation worries me — the levees don't worry me a bit."

Another widespread worry is education. Since the state took over 102 of the city's 117 schools by designating them as a "recovery district," only about 8,000 of 60,000 pre-Katrina students are attending the handful of public and parochial schools that are operating.[72]

"One of the barriers to families returning is that the state took over the schools and is not opening them," says Councilwoman Willard-Lewis.

Many residents say, however, that reopening the schools as they were wouldn't be much help. The Urban Land Institute reported that before Katrina the public school system had an "educational quotient" ranking of 1 out of 100 — the nation's lowest.[73]

"Everybody knew that public education was broken before the storm," says Heather Thompson, a New Orleans native and Harvard Business School student. A graduate of the public schools' only secondary-level crown jewel, Benjamin Franklin High School, Thompson helped organize a consulting project by four dozen of her fellow business students to recommend recovery ideas for schools and other elements of civic life.[74]

Meanwhile, the shortage of school space seems likely to continue. "I want to get the very best leaders and the very best teachers for every child in Orleans Parish," said State Education Superintendent Cecil Picard, adding that he expects 15,000 public-school students when classes reopen in August.[75]

Port Bounces Back

Giant cranes are swinging containers off and on ships, warehouses are filled with bundles of rubber and coils of steel, and trucks headed inland are filling up with coffee beans. The Port of New Orleans is back up and running, though only months ago a quick comeback seemed improbable.

"On Aug. 30, somebody told me it would be six months before we got the first ship back," port Director LaGrange says. "I said our goal was to be at 70 percent of pre-Katrina activity by March 1 — the six-month anniversary [of Katrina]. We're pushing 65 percent now."

Immediately after Katrina struck, while Americans watched thousands of human tragedies unfolding in real time on television, shippers and merchants focused on the southern Louisiana port complex — the country's fourth-largest.[76] "The longer the ports remained closed, the greater the risk that we'd all be paying higher prices for coffee, cocoa, lumber, steel, zinc, aluminum and any number of other things," said Mark M. Zandi, chief executive of the Economy.com research firm.[77]

In a seeming paradox, Katrina largely spared the riverfront port area. Like the old French Quarter, most of the port sits atop the natural levee on which Bienville founded the city. However, a major container terminal and a new cold-storage warehouse in eastern New Orleans were both destroyed.

Louisiana politicians frequently cite the port's importance to the economy as an argument for rebuilding New Orleans to its pre-Katrina scale. When she heard that the port might be able to function at full strength with a city

Should New Orleans be completely rebuilt on its old footprint?

YES
Sen. Mary Landrieu, D-La.
Member, Senate
Appropriations Committee

Written for the *CQ Researcher*, January 2006

More than five months ago, Hurricane Katrina and the subsequent breaks in numerous flood-control levees decimated one of our nation's greatest cities, my hometown, New Orleans.

Some have since questioned whether or not we should rebuild New Orleans, saying that we should abandon a city that has contributed so much to our great nation.

New Orleans is the capitol of our nation's energy coast. It was put there for a reason. We did not go there to sunbathe. We went there to set up the Mississippi River, to tame that river, to create channels for this country to grow and prosper. New Orleans was established so the cities and communities along the Mississippi River would have a port to trade with the world.

The indispensible Higgins boats that saved us during World War II were built in New Orleans. Forty-three thousand people built those boats and headed them out to Normandy. We're going to rebuild our shipping industry. We're going to rebuild our maritime industry, we will maintain our great port and we will continue to provide the energy that keeps our lights on across the nation.

Just because parts of New Orleans are below sea level is no reason to allow this great city to die. The Netherlands is a nation that is 21 feet below sea level at its economic heart, yet they still operate Europe's largest port — just as we operate America's largest port system.

The Dutch have proved that you can live below sea level and still keep your feet dry. They believe in an integrated system of water management. After a flood destroyed their nation in 1953, the Dutch said "Never again," and today they have created the world's most advanced storm-protection and flood-control system. If a nation half the size of Louisiana can do it, then surely the United States of America can.

We can and should rebuild every neighborhood — but maybe not exactly the way we did it the first time. This time we can build better, smarter, stronger neighborhoods.

One fact is certain: Every, single American citizen who calls New Orleans home has a right to come back and rebuild their neighborhoods, and the federal government should generously support that right.

New Orleans helped build America, and now America must help rebuild New Orleans, because America needs that great city — right where it is.

NO
William Hudnut
Joseph C. Canizaro Chair
in Public Policy, Urban Land Institute

Written for the *CQ Researcher*, January 2006

There are those who understandably feel that New Orleans should be rebuilt in its entirety, and that blocks and neighborhoods throughout the pre-Katrina city should be rebuilt house by house as resources permit.

The emotional tug of going back to one's "roots" is strong. One cannot blame the City Council and others for demanding that all areas of the city, especially East New Orleans and the Lower Ninth, as well as Lakeview and Gentilly, be rebuilt simultaneously. But we need to ask: Is such a plan realistic? Does it make sense?

The city will not have the resources to take care of a widely dispersed population, and not all the evacuees will be returning. Critics of a smaller city dismiss such plans and ideas as "arrogant," "elitist" and "racist," because the low-lying areas are where mostly black and low-income residents lived before Katrina. But the questions persist.

I can think of two compelling reasons to envision a smaller New Orleans in the future. It will have a smaller population, and it will be safer.

As is often said, "Demography is destiny." If New Orleans once had 465,000 people, that was once and no more. The city was losing population before Katrina and has shrunk to a little over 100,000 today, with prospects of that number climbing to perhaps 250,000 by the time Katrina's third anniversary rolls around.

Is it prudent to think that this smaller number of people should occupy all the territory that almost twice that number did before August 2005, especially when the city will not have the financial resources, police, fire and EMS services and the like to care for such a scattered population? Two keys to a successful, vibrant city are diversity and density, which a sprawled-out land base does not provide.

Katrina has given New Orleans a chance to reinvent itself as a more compact, connected city on a smaller footprint. The city's recovering economy built on restored building blocks — culture, food, music, art, entertainment, tourism, bioscience and medical research, the port, energy production — will attract people back into mixed-use, mixed-income, racially balanced, pedestrian-friendly neighborhoods carefully planned by citizens, with parks, open space, new wetlands and light-rail transit added to the mix. All of that can be accomplished on less space than the city occupied heretofore.

Who was it that said, "Small is beautiful?"

somewhat smaller than pre-Katrina New Orleans, Sen. Landrieu, responded: "Where are the workers going to come from? You can't have a port without New Orleans."

LaGrange takes a more nuanced view. "You've got to have the work force here," he says, and they will need "the support services that a city provides — transit, schools, places to worship, grocery stores, gasoline stations. But if the city, for some reason, is smaller, I don't think that would be a tremendous effect on the output of the port."

Politics and Legislation

New Orleans' future lies in many hands, but federal law-makers may be the most important, because they control the biggest money source.

"We are at your mercy," Gov. Blanco told Senate Homeland Security Committee members as they toured the disaster zone on Jan. 17. "We are begging you to stay with us."[78]

Landrieu plans to revive her proposal to channel 50 percent of offshore petroleum-lease revenues to the state. The money would be earmarked for post-Katrina reconstruction, says her spokesman, Adam Sharp.

Besides the Landrieu and Baker proposals, Louisiana politicians will continue to push for $2.1 billion in supplemental Medicaid funds to help pay for health care for Katrina victims — many suddenly homeless and unemployed — who had to enter the federally subsidized medical insurance program for low-income people. Congress adjourned at year's end without passing the Medicaid bill, but Landrieu says she'll also continue to push for that.

The fact that none of these proposals passed while Katrina's devastation was fresh would seem to show that the state's politicians "have some work to do" to get Congress' attention, said one of Baker's aides. Blanco, meanwhile, is preparing to call a special 12-day legislative session, beginning on Feb. 6. She wants state lawmakers to make the "levee boards" that supervise maintenance more accountable. The boards were widely criticized — even ridiculed — for laxity, following Katrina.[79]

Getting the schools going again remains a priority, and Blanco must hammer together by May a plan to reorganize the city's school system, now largely under state control. The state Board of Elementary and Secondary Education would have to rule on the plan. The BNOBC in January proposed a leaner administrative office — one superintendent and four or five assistants — and expanded authority for principals, who would be able to hire and fire their own staffs. Differences between "have" and "have-not" schools would be eliminated under the plan, and early-education programs would be initiated.[80]

Meanwhile, the often-criticized Blanco tangled with the City Council over what she called its resistance to installing FEMA-supplied trailers for needy families. The council was responding, in part, to complaints from some residents who objected to trailer villages in their neighborhoods.

"Disagreements over housing must end — and must end now," she told the council on Jan. 5. Council members denied that they had obstructed trailer installation. After a subsequent meeting between the governor and council members, sites for a total of 40,000 trailers were identified.[81]

Even the demolition of unsafe houses stirred controversy. When it appeared the city was about to bulldoze some Lower Ninth Ward houses deemed unsafe, residents and some council members sought a court order to stop it. U.S. District Judge Martin L. C. Feldman then OK'd a deal between the Nagin administration and Lower Ninth Ward residents requiring at least seven-days' notice before demolition.[82]

The court-approved settlement apparently resolved the demolition issues, but political conflicts between Nagin and the council remain. The beleaguered mayor is among the candidates up for re-election on April 22.

OUTLOOK
Pessimism and Paralysis

Optimism is in short supply in New Orleans, notwithstanding the brave talk of Louisiana politicians. The failure of the flood-protection system, the tragedy and chaos of the early days of the disaster and the devastated conditions that remain in much of the city five months after Katrina have not provided grounds for much hope.

President Bush, in his State of the Union address on Jan. 31, devoted 162 of the speech's 5,432 words to New Orleans, proposing no specific, new remedies. "As we meet . . . immediate needs, we must also address deeper challenges that existed before the storm arrived," Bush said, citing a need for better schools and economic opportunity.

Among Louisiana politicians, even the president's fellow Republicans felt left out. "I was very disappointed at how small a part those national challenges — and I think are national challenges — were given in the speech," Sen. Vitter told the *Times-Picayune*.

"There's no sense of urgency from the city government, the state government or the federal government," says Dennis Scott, looking out on his devastated New Orleans East neighborhood.

Indeed, as of late January, the U.S. Army Corps of Engineers had completed only 16 percent of the levee repairs scheduled for completion by June 1, when the 2006 hurricane season begins.[83]

An outsider draws essentially the same conclusion as Scott. "The lack of unity in the political establishment is the paralyzing factor," says the Urban Land Institute's Hudnut. "There's almost a political stand-off between the governor's office, the mayor's office, the City Council and the Bring New Orleans Back Commission; but this is also partially a Washington issue. I don't see a lot of leadership coming from the White House team."

Republican Hudnut is one of many politicians and ordinary citizens to question the high cost of the war in Iraq with the needs of New Orleans. The war's direct cash cost alone through November 2005 was calculated at $251 billion, according to a study released in January by two former Clinton administration officials.[84] Thompson, the Harvard Business School student working on redevelopment plans, observes that the government ought to be able to "make money appear" for New Orleans in the same way as deficit financing is arranged for the war.

If talking openly about race relations holds promise for making them better, the New Orleans disaster might have served some purpose. Some black New Orleanians wonder aloud, though, if the color of the majority of the city's residents hasn't also slowed down the pace of recovery. Anne LaBranche, the doctor's wife from New Orleans East, can't think of any other reason.

"This was a man-made problem," she says, referring to the failure of the flood-protection system. And yet, previous hurricane damage in Florida and other Gulf Coast states has been paid for without debate on whether people should be living in such potentially risky areas, she says. "President Bush says he resents it when people say 'racism,' so tell me what it is," she says quietly. "Why the different treatment?"

If New Orleans has one advantage concerning race, it may be that the city's geography tends to throw people of different colors together more than in other locales. Another point in the city's favor is New Orleanians' loyalty to their city. It remains to be seen whether that's enough to overcome the economic, political and environmental obstacles.

Piano technician David Doremus has lived in New Orleans most of the past 30 years. He and his wife live in the unflooded Algiers neighborhood on the Mississippi's west bank, and they are committed to remaining in town with their daughters.

While he's unsure about how much piano tuning and rebuilding work he'll have in the near future, he can't imagine anywhere else that offers the pace of life, the social graces and the fishing that he enjoys in New Orleans — as well as the musical variety. "I work for a recording studio, and one of the first sessions I worked on after the storm was with Allen Toussaint and Elvis Costello," he says.

So Doremus is ready to commute 40 miles to work at a friend's piano business in Covington, La., for a year, if he has to, or even work at Home Depot. "My family back in Virginia thinks I'm nuts," he adds. "And my wife's family in Pittsburgh thinks she's nuts."

If the Doremuses are crazy, New Orleans needs all the nuts it can muster.

NOTES

1. Gary Rivlin, "Anger Meets New Orleans Renewal Plan," *The New York Times*, Jan. 12, 2006, p. A18.

2. When Hurricane Katrina made landfall at Buras, La., 35 miles east of New Orleans at about 6 a.m., it was originally rated at Category 4, the classification for storms with wind speeds of 131-155 mph. The National Hurricane Center later revised that classification down to Category 3, with winds of 111-130 mph. Some 24 hours before reaching Louisiana, Katrina varied between categories 4 and 5. For further detail, see Peter Whoriskey and Joby Warrick, "Report Revises Katrina's Force," *The Washington Post*, Dec. 22, 2005, p. A3; Richard D. Knabb, *et al.*, "Tropical Cyclone Report: Hurricane Katrina, 22-30 August, 2005," National Hurricane Center, Dec. 20, 2005, p. 3, www.nhc.noaa.gov/pdf/TCR-AL122005_Katrina.pdf; and

National Aeronautics and Space Administration, "Hurricane Season 2005: Katrina," www.nasa.gov/vision/earth/lookingatearth/h2005_katrina.html.

3. Nicholas Riccardi, "Most of Louisiana's Identified Storm Victims Over 60," *Los Angeles Times*, Nov. 5, 2005, p. A11; Nicholas Riccardi, Doug Smith and David Zucchino, "Katrina Killed Along Class Lines," *Los Angeles Times*, Dec. 18, 2005, p. A1.

4. While Katrina had weakened to Category 3 upon reaching Louisiana, the surges it created began when the storm was at categories 4 and 5 strength. For further detail, see "Tropical Cyclone Report," *op. cit.*, p. 9.

5. "President Discusses Hurricane Relief in Address to the Nation," White House, Sept. 15, 2005, www.whitehouse.gov/news/releases/2005/09/print/20050915-8.html.

6. Bill Walsh, "Senators say recovery moving at snail's pace," *The Times-Picayune* (New Orleans), Jan. 18, 2006, p. A1.

7. Ralph Vartabedian, "New Orleans Should be Dry by End of Week," *Los Angeles Times*, Sept. 19, 2005, p. A8; "Performance Evaluation Plan and Interim Status, Report 1 of a Series: Performance Evaluation of the New Orleans and Southeast Louisiana Hurricane Protection System," Interagency Performance Evaluation Task Force, Jan. 10, 2006, p. 1, https://ipet.wes.army.mil.

8. "Action Plan for New Orleans: The New American City," Bring New Orleans Back Commission, Urban Planning Committee, Jan. 11, 2006, Introduction, www.bringneworleansback.org.

9. "It was not unusual for slaves to gather on street corners at night, for example, where they challenged whites to attempt to pass. . . ," historian Joseph G. Tregle is quoted in Eugene D. Genovese, *Roll, Jordan, Roll: The World the Slaves Made* (1972), pp. 412-413.

10. Quoted in Reed Johnson, "New Orleans: Before and After," *Los Angeles Times*, Sept. 5, 2005, p. E1. For more background on Congo Square, see Craig E. Colten, *An Unnatural Metropolis: Wresting New Orleans From Nature* (2005), p. 72; and Gerald Early, "Slavery," on Web site for "Jazz," PBS documentary, www.pbs.org/jazz/time/time_slavery.htm.

11. "A Strategy for Rebuilding New Orleans, Louisiana," Urban Land Institute, Nov. 12-18, 2005, p. 17, www.uli.org/Content/NavigationMenu/ProgramsServices/AdvisoryServices/KatrinaPanel/ULI_Draft_New_Orleans%20Report.pdf.

12. "President Discusses Hurricane Relief," *op. cit.*

13. Joby Warrick, "White House Got Early Warning on Katrina," *The Washington Post*, Jan. 24, 2005, p. A2.

14. Steve Ritea and Tara Young, "Cycle of Death: Violence Thrives on Lack of Jobs, Wealth of Drugs," *The Times-Picayune* (New Orleans), p. A1; Adam Nossiter, "New Orleans Crime Swept Away, With Most of the People," *The New York Times*, Nov. 10, 2005, p. A1. Dan Baum, "Deluged, When Katrina hit, where were the police?" *The New Yorker*, Jan. 9, 2006, p. 59.

15. Quoted in, Joel Havemann, "New Orleans' Racial Future Hotly Argued," *Los Angeles Times*, Oct. 1, 2005, p. A14.

16. Brett Martel, The Associated Press, "Storms Payback From God, Nagin Says," *The Washington Post*, Jan. 17, 2006, p. A4.

17. Manuel Rog-Franzia, "New Orleans Mayor Apologizes for Remarks About God's Wrath," *The Washington Post*, Jan. 18, 2006, p. A2.

18. James Dao, "Study Says 80% of New Orleans Blacks May Not Return," *The New York Times*, Jan. 27, 2006, p. A16.

19. *Ibid.*; see also "Action Plan," (pages unnumbered); Frank Donze and Gordon Russell, "Rebuilding proposal gets mixed reception," *The Times-Picayune* (New Orleans), Jan. 12, 2006, p. A1.

20. Donze and Russell, *ibid.*; Rivlin, *op. cit.*

21. "A Strategy for Rebuilding," *op. cit.*; Frank Donze, "Don't write us off, residents warn," *The Times-Picayune* (New Orleans), Nov. 29, 2005, p. A1.

22. "Action Plan," Introduction, *op. cit.*; Gordon Russell, "Comeback in Progress," *The Times-Picayune* (New Orleans), Jan. 1, 2006, p. A1.

23. "Battered by Katrina, Tulane University forced into layoffs, cutbacks," The Associated Press, Dec. 9, 2005.

24. Susan Saulny, "Students Return to Big Changes in New Orleans," *The New York Times*, Jan. 4, 2006,

p. 13; Steven Ritea, "School board considers limited role," *The Times-Picayune* (New Orleans), Dec. 7, 2005, p. A1.

25. Elizabeth Bumiller, "In New Orleans, Bush Speaks With Optimism But Sees Little of Ruin," *The New York Times*, Jan. 13, 2006, p. A12.

26. For background, see Marcia Clemmitt, "Climate Change," *CQ Researcher*, Jan. 27, 2006, pp. 73-96.

27. Virginia R. Burkett, "Potential Impacts of Climate Change and Variability on Transportation in the Gulf Coast/Mississippi Delta Region," Center for Climate Change and Environmental Forecasting, Oct. 1-2, 2002, p. 7, http://climate.volpe.dot.gov/workshop1002/burkett.pdf. Burkett is chief of the Forest Ecology Branch of the U.S. Geological Survey's National Wetlands Research Center, in Lafayette, La.

28. In 2006, the Bush administration does not plan to seek new funds for reconstruction in Iraq. See, Ellen Knickmeyer, "U.S. Has End in Sight on Iraq Rebuilding," *The Washington Post*, Jan. 2, 2006, p. A1.

29. Michael Oneal, "GOP Cools to Katrina Aid," *Chicago Tribune*, Nov. 12, 2005, p. A7.

30. For background, see Kenneth Jost, "Property Rights," *CQ Researcher*, March 4, 2005, pp. 197-220.

31. R. B. Seed, *et al.*, "Preliminary Report on the Performance of the New Orleans Levee Systems on August. 29, 2005," University of California at Berkeley, American Society of Civil Engineers, Nov. 2, 2005, pp. 1.2-1.4.

32. Schwartz, *op. cit.*

33. For details, see John McQuaid, "The Dutch Swore It Would Never Happen Again," "Dutch Defense, Dutch Masters," "Bigger, Better, Bolder," *The Times-Picayune* (New Orleans), Nov. 13-14, 2005, p. A1.

34. "Performance Evaluation Plan," *op. cit.*, appendix A-2. John Schwartz, "Category 5: Levees are Piece of $32 Billion Pie," *The New York Times*, Nov. 29, 2005, p. A1.

35. *Ibid.*

36. Richard W. Stevenson and James Dao, "White House to Double Spending on New Orleans Flood Protection," *The New York Times*, Dec. 16, 2005, p. A1.

37. *Ibid.*

38. President Bush said on Jan. 26 the congressional appropriations amounted to $85 billion. For background and detail, see Joseph J. Schatz, "End-of-Session Gift for the Gulf Coast," *CQ Weekly*, Dec. 26, 2005, p. 3401; "Cost of Katrina Nearing $100 Billion, Senate Budget Says," *CQ Budget Tracker News*, Jan. 18, 2006; "Senate Budget Committee Releases Current Tally of Hurricane-Related Spending," Budget Committee, Jan. 18, 2006, http://budget.senate.gov/republican. "Press Conference of the President," [transcript] Jan. 26, 2006, www.whitehouse.gov/news/releases/2006/01/20060126.htm.

39. Quoted in Jacob Freedman, "Additional Flood Funds Needed to Cover Extensive Gulf Coast Damage," *CQ Today*, Jan. 25, 2006; Statement of David I. Maurstad, Acting Director/Federal Insurance Administrator, Mitigation Division, Federal Emergency Management Agency, Committee on Senate Banking Housing and Urban Affairs, Jan. 25, 2006, http://banking.senate.gov/_files/ACF43B7.pdf.

40. Frank Donze, Gordon Russell and Lauri Maggi, "Buyouts torpedoed, not sunk," *The Times-Picayune* (New Orleans), Jan. 26, 2006, p. A1.

41. Adrian Moore, "Rebuild New Orleans Smarter, Not Harder," Reason Foundation, Jan. 11, 2006, www.reason.org/commentaries/moore_20060111.shtml.

42. David Greising, *et al.*, "How Do They Rebuild a City?" *Chicago Tribune*, Sept. 4, 2005, p. A1.

43. "Press Conference of the President," *op. cit.*

44. Donze, Russell and Maggi, *op. cit.*

45. *Ibid.*

46. Robert L. Bamberger and Lawrence Kumins, "Oil and Gas: Supply Issues After Katrina," Congressional Research Service, updated Sept. 6, 2005, p. 1, www.fas.org/sgp/crs/misc/RS22233.pdf. For background on offshore leases, see Jennifer Weeks, "Domestic Energy Development," *CQ Researcher*, Sept. 30, 2005, pp. 809-832.

47. Marc Humphries, "Outer Continental Shelf: Debate Over Oil and Gas Leasing and Revenue Sharing," Congressional Research Service, Updated Oct. 27, 2005, pp. 1-4. http://fpc.state.gov/documents/organization/56096.pdf.

48. Unless otherwise indicated, all material in this section comes from Colten, *op. cit.*; and Ari Kelman, *A River and Its City: The Nature of Landscape in New Orleans* (2003).

49 Caroline E. Mayer and Amy Joyce, "Troubles Travel Upstream," *The Washington Post*, Sept. 5, 2005, p. A23.

50. Colten, *op. cit.*, pp. 25-26.

51. For background, see C. Perkins, "Mississippi River Flood Relief and Control," *Editorial Research Reports*, 1927, Vol. 2; and M. Packman, "Disaster Insurance," *Editorial Research Reports 1956*, Vol. I.

52. John M. Barry, *Rising Tide: The Great Mississippi Flood of 1927 and How it Changed America* (1998), pp. 311-317; p. 332.

53. For background, see "Economic Effects of the Mississippi Flood," *Editorial Research Reports, 1928*, Vol. I.

54. Gordon Russell, "An 1878 Map Reveals that Maybe Our Ancestors Were Right to Build on Higher Ground," *The Times-Picayune* (New Orleans), Nov. 3, 2005, p. A1.

55. "Performance Evaluation Plan," *op. cit.*, Appendix A, p. 1; Willie Drye, " 'Category Five': How a Hurricane Yardstick Came To Be," *National Geographic News*, Dec. 20, 2005, http://news.nationalgeographic.com/news/2005/12/1220_051220_saffirsimpson.html.

56. John McQuaid and Mark Schleifstein, "The Big One," *The Times-Picayune* (New Orleans), June 24, 2002, p. A1.

57. *Ibid.*

58. Ivor van Heerden, "Using Technology to Illustrate the Realities of Hurricane Vulnerability," Jan. 25, 2005, www.laseagrant.org/forum/01-25-2005.htm.

59. "Performance Evaluation Plan," *op. cit.*, Appendix A, pp. 2-3.

60. "Urgent Warning Proved Prescient," *The New York Times*, Sept. 7, 2005, p. A21.

61. "How New Orleans Flooded," in "The Storm That Drowned a City," NOVA, WGBH-TV, October 2005, www.pbs.org/wgbh/nova/orleans/how-nf.html.

62. *Ibid.*

63. See Pamela Prah, "Disaster Preparedness," *CQ Researcher*, Nov. 18, 2005, pp. 981-1004.

64. "Rita's Aftermath," *Los Angeles Times*, Sept. 28, 2005, p. A1; Shaila Dewan and Jere Longman, "Hurricane Slams Into Gulf Coast; Flooding Spreads," *The New York Times*, Sept. 25, 2005, p. A1.

65. Anne Rochell Konigsmark, "Amid ruins, 'island' of normalcy in the Big Easy," *USA Today*, Dec. 19, 2005, p. A1; Gordon Russell, "Comeback in Progress," *The Times-Picayune* (New Orleans), Jan. 1, 2006, p. A1.

66. "Action Plan," *op. cit.*, Sec. 4, (pages unnumbered).

67. Gordon Russell and James Varney, "New flood maps will likely steer rebuilding," *The Times-Picayune* (New Orleans), Jan. 15, 2006, p. A1.

68. *Ibid.*

69. *Ibid.*

70. *Ibid.*

71. Russell and Donze, *op. cit.*, Jan. 12, 2006.

72. Ritea and Saulny, *op. cit.*

73. "A Strategy for Rebuilding New Orleans," *op. cit.*, p. 19.

74. For background, see, George Anders, "How a Principal in New Orleans Saved Her School," *The Wall Street Journal*, Jan. 13, 2006, p. A1.

75. Steve Ritea, "La. won't run N.O. schools by itself," *The Times-Picayune* (New Orleans), Jan. 3, 2006, p. B1.

76. Vanessa Cieslak, "Ports in Louisiana: New Orleans, South Louisiana, and Baton Rouge," Congressional Research Service, Oct. 14, 2005, p. 1, http://fpc.state.gov/documents/organization/57872.pdf.

77. Keith L. Alexander and Neil Irwin, "Port Comes Back Early, Surprisingly," *The Washington Post*, Sept. 14, 2005, p. D1.

78. Bill Walsh, "Senators say recovery moving at a snail's pace," *The Times-Picayune* (New Orleans), Jan. 18, 2006, p. A1.

79. Ed Anderson, "Special session set to begin Feb. 6," *The Times-Picayune* (New Orleans), Jan. 12, 2006, p. A2.

80. Steve Ritea, "Nagin's schools panel issues reforms," *The Times-Picayune* (New Orleans), Jan. 18, 2006, p. A1; "Rebuilding and Transforming: A Plan for

World-Class Public Education in New Orleans," Bring New Orleans Back Commission, Jan. 17, 2006, pp. 10, 48.

81. Ed Anderson, "N.O. needs 7,000 more trailer sites, Blanco says," *The Times-Picayune* (New Orleans), Jan. 9, p. A1.

82. Adam Nossiter, "New Orleans Agrees to Give Notice on Home Demolitions," *The New York Times*, Jan. 18, 2006, p. A10.

83. Spencer S. Hsu, "Bush's Post-Katrina Pledges," *The Washington Post*, Jan. 28, 2006, p. A12.

84. Linda Bilmes and Joseph Stiglitz, "The Economic Costs of the Iraq War: An Appraisal Three Years After the Beginning of the Conflict," http://ksghome.harvard.edu/~lbilmes/paper/iraqnew.pdf. Former Deputy Assistant Commerce Secretary Bilmes is now at the Kennedy School of Government at Harvard; Stiglitz, a Nobel laureate economist, teaches at Columbia University.

BIBLIOGRAPHY

Books

Colten, Craig E., *An Unnatural Metropolis: Wresting New Orleans from Nature, Louisiana State University Press,* **2005.**
A Louisiana State University, Baton Rouge, geographer chronicles the city's ongoing efforts to tame its watery environment.

Dyson, Michael Eric, *Come Hell or High Water: Hurricane Katrina and the Color of Disaster, Basic Civitas Books,* **2006.**
A professor of humanities at the University of Pennsylvania — and a prolific author and commentator on issues of race and culture — dissects what he views as structural racism, government incompetence and class warfare against the poor in the Katrina disaster.

Kelman, Ari, *A River and its City: The Nature of Landscape in New Orleans, University of California Press,* **2003.**
Using New Orleans' long and complicated relationship with the Mississippi River as a framework, an environmental historian at the University of California, Davis, examines why New Orleans developed as it did.

Piazza, Tom, *Why New Orleans Matters, HarperCollins,* **2005.**
A jazz historian, novelist and New Orleans resident who evacuated the city during Katrina argues that American culture will be poorer if the working people who keep the city's traditions alive are permanently uprooted from the city.

Ward, Geoffrey C., and Ken Burns, *Jazz: A History of America's Music, Alfred A. Knopf,* **2000.**
An author of popular history (Ward) and a renowned documentary filmmaker provide — with contributions by jazz scholars — a one-volume history of America's major cultural creation, with much attention to New Orleans' role.

Articles

Baum, Dan, "Deluged: When Katrina hit, where were the police?" *The New Yorker,* **Jan. 9, 2006, p. 50.**
A writer recounts how police and city government coped — or failed to — in the post-hurricane disaster.

Cooper, Christopher, "Old-Line Families Escape Worst of Flood and Plot the Future," *The Wall Street Journal,* **Sept. 8. 2005, p. A1.**
A profile of one of New Orleans' aristocrats brings the city's social inequalities to light in dispassionate fashion.

McQuaid, John, and Mark Schleifstein, "In Harm's Way," "Evolving Danger," "Left Behind," "The Big One," "Exposure's Cost," "Building Better," "Model Solutions," "Tempting Fate," "Shifting Tides," [series] *The Times-Picayune,* **June 23-June 26, 2002.**
Three years before Katrina, two reporters spell out the city's growing vulnerability to a massive hurricane, virtually telling the Katrina story.

Sontag, Deborah, "Delrey Street," *The New York Times,* **Oct. 12, 2005, p. A1; Oct. 24, 2005, p. A1; Nov. 12, 2005, p. A9; Nov. 14, 2005, p. A1; Dec. 2, 2005, p. A20; Jan. 9, 2006, p. A1.**
In a series of detailed profiles, a *New York Times* reporter examines how the lives of families from New Orleans' Lower Ninth Ward have been upended by Katrina.

Tizon, Alex Tomas, and Doug Smith, "Evacuees of Hurricane Katrina Resettle Along a Racial Divide," *Los Angeles Times,* **Dec. 12, 2005, p. A1.**
Two reporters analyzed change-of-address data to draw early conclusions on the racial effects of the disaster.

Reports and Studies

"Action Plan for New Orleans: The New American City," *Bring New Orleans Back Commission, Urban Planning Committee,* Jan. 11, 2006, www.bringneworleansback.org. Civic leaders and officials provided the first detailed plan for redevelopment of New Orleans.

"An Unnatural Disaster: The Aftermath of Hurricane Katrina," *Scholars for Progressive Reform,* Sept. 2005, www.progressivereform.org/Unnatural_Disaster_512.pdf. A liberal organization analyzes the disaster as a failure of unrestrained energy development and inadequate government regulation.

Katz, Bruce, *et al.,* "Katrina Index: Tracking Variables of Post-Katrina Reconstruction," updated Dec. 6, 2005, *The Brookings Institution,* www.brookings.edu/metro/pubs/200512_katrinaindex.htm. To be updated periodically, this report compiles and organizes statistics in order to show economic and social trends as New Orleans recovers.

Seed, R. B., *et al.,* "Preliminary Report on the Performance of the New Orleans Levee Systems in Hurricane Katrina on August 29, 2005," *University of California at Berkeley, American Society of Civil Engineers, National Science Foundation,* Nov. 2, 2005, www.berkeley.edu/news/media/releases/2005/11/leveereport_prelim.pdf. Engineering experts provide an early look at the failures of the levee system that led to disaster.

For More Information

Bring New Orleans Back Commission, www.bringneworleansback.org. The commission has been issuing detailed redevelopment plans.

The Brookings Institution, Katrina Issues and the Aftermath Project, Metropolitan Policy Program, 1775 Massachusetts Ave., N.W., Washington, DC 20036; (202) 797-6139; www.brookings.edu/metro/katrina.htm. The think tank provides policy proposals, commentary and statistics.

Center for the Study of Public Health Impacts of Hurricanes, CEBA Building, Suite 3221, Louisiana State University, Baton Rouge, LA 70803; (225) 578-4813; www.publichealth.hurricane.lsu.edu. A research center focusing on disaster prevention and mitigation.

Federal Emergency Management Agency, 500 C St., S.W., Washington, DC 20472; (202) 566-1600; www.fema.gov. The lead federal agency on disaster recovery; provides information on relief program requirements and application deadlines.

Greater New Orleans Community Data Center, www.gnocdc.org. A virtual organization that provides links to the city's most recent social, economic and demographic statistics.

Louisiana Recovery Authority, 525 Florida St., 2nd Floor, Baton Rouge, LA 70801; (225) 382-5502; http://lra.louisiana.gov. The state government's post-disaster reconstruction agency; provides information on the aid flowing to New Orleans.

New Orleans Area Habitat for Humanity, P.O. Box 15052, New Orleans, LA 70175; (504) 861-2077, www.habitat-nola.org. A self-help housing organization building new homes in the city and nearby suburbs.

Savenolamusic, www.savenolamusic.com/index.php. An exhaustive listing of performance bookings and other resources (including medical assistance) for New Orleans musicians, including those forced out of the city.

Urban Land Institute, 1025 Thomas Jefferson St., N.W., Suite 500 West, Washington, DC 20007; (202) 624-7000; www.uli.org. The nonprofit organization for land-use and development professionals is the New Orleans city government's disaster-recovery consultant.

13

Protecting Wetlands

Is the Government Doing Enough?

Jennifer Weeks

Condominiums and shopping centers encroach on the Los Cerritos Wetlands near Long Beach, Calif. The 400-acre site, which once covered 2,400 acres, is considered vital for birds migrating on the Pacific Flyway.

Getty Images/David McNew

From *CQ Researcher*, October 3, 2008.

O n wet spring nights across the Northeastern United States, wood frogs and salamanders go on the march. These amphibians spend most of their lives buried in forest undergrowth, but they need to breed in watery places where no fish will eat their eggs. So they migrate to vernal pools — ponds that form during the wet seasons and range from a few feet to several acres across. If all goes well, their offspring will hatch and grow large enough to breathe air before the pools dry up in summer. Some species, such as fairy shrimp, spend their entire life cycles in the pools, leaving eggs behind that stay dormant through dry months and hatch when the pools reappear a year later.

Vernal pools are wetlands — areas where the soil is always or usually saturated with water and that support plants and animals adapted to moist conditions. Many states protect vernal pools because they provide habitat for rare animals. For example, in Massachusetts it is illegal to dump materials into state-certified vernal pools, install septic systems nearby or cut down more than half of the trees within a 50-foot radius.[1]

Other wetlands play similar roles. Estuaries (mixed salt- and freshwater zones where rivers flow into the sea) are among Earth's most productive ecosystems.

"Shallow marsh channels are important habitat for fish," says Doug Myers, science director of People for Puget Sound, a Seattle conservation group. "Chinook salmon rear their young in estuarine deltas, coves and lagoons in the Northwest. And birds migrating along the Pacific Coast stop to feed along the mud flats."

Many wetlands that are far from coastlines also are important. For example, lakes carved by glaciers across the upper Midwest,

Despite Wetland Gains, Concerns Remain

In the last half-century, the nation has gone from losing nearly half a million acres of wetlands a year to a net annual gain of 32,000 acres a year from 1998-2004. The quality of the new wetland, however, worries many environmentalists. They note, for example, that while there were significant gains in freshwater ponds, crucial intertidal wetlands (mainly deepwater bay bottoms and open ocean) declined by about 4,740 acres a year.

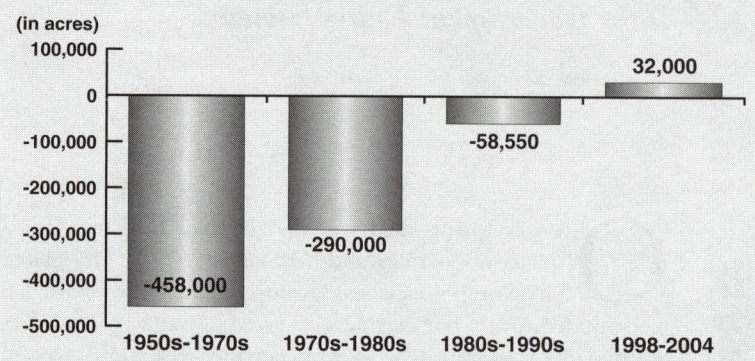

Average Annual Net Wetland Gain/Loss for the Lower 48 States, 1954-2004

Source: T.E. Dahl, "Status and Trends of Wetlands in the Conterminous United States 1998 to 2004," U.S. Fish and Wildlife Service, December 2005

"We see a lot of threats to wetlands around Puget Sound, including urban growth, shoreline development and polluted stormwater runoff from paved areas," says Myers. "It's death by a thousand cuts." Nutrient pollution from farms (excess fertilizer and animal waste) and septic systems washes into lakes and bays nationwide, generating huge algae blooms that deprive aquatic organisms of sunlight and dissolved oxygen.[3]

And many advocates fear that recent U.S. Supreme Court rulings limiting federal jurisdiction over wetlands have made some more vulnerable to development.

Wetland protection affects a range of industries that often excavate or drain land, including commercial and residential construction, agriculture, mining and energy. Under Section 404 of the Clean Water Act, when a project involves dredging or filling in the "waters of the United States" — a category that includes many wetlands — a permit must be obtained from the U.S. Army Corps of Engineers. The Corps then must consult with the Environmental Protection Agency (EPA), which has veto power over permit decisions.

This process can be lengthy and expensive. A 2002 study of 103 permit applications found that the average general permit for lower-impact activities cost $28,915 to prepare and took 313 days to gain approval. Individual permits for higher-impact projects cost $271,596 on average and took more than two years.[4] Developers who proceed without permits face civil penalties of up to $32,500 per day and criminal penalties up to $50,000 per day plus three years in prison.[5]

Many trade groups say they support reasonable wetlands protection but that current standards are too broad and the permitting process too cumbersome. "While [the permits'] environmental purposes are laudable, they do add to the cost and delay the completion of the public and private infrastructure that literally forms the

known as prairie potholes, are critical breeding and nesting areas for millions of ducks, geese and other waterbirds. (*See map, p. 305.*)

Until the 1970s Americans widely regarded wetlands as swampy places that were useless unless they could be drained or filled in. Before settlers arrived, the continental United States contained more than 220 million acres of wetlands. Today less than half of that area (107 million acres) remains.[2] Some of America's most famous and valued wetland areas, such as Florida's Everglades and Louisiana's Gulf Coast, are also its most degraded.

For the past 20 years policymakers have tried to prevent more net losses of wetlands. President George W. Bush raised the bar in 2004, arguing that the United States could achieve net annual increases by creating and restoring more acres than it developed. But environmentalists, outdoor advocates and regulators say that not all wetlands are equal, and that more action is needed to protect and restore high-quality wetlands.

foundation of our nation's economy," Associated General Contractors of America CEO Stephen E. Sandherr told the House Transportation and Infrastructure Committee in July 2007.[6] Contractors, growers and other such groups would like to see the Corps and EPA eliminate or limit federal protection for small, isolated and temporary wetlands.

But environmentalists argue that destroying wetlands could end up costing the country much more, because wetlands provide billions of dollars worth of ecological services that benefit the public. Often referred to as "nature's kidneys," they filter out pollutants from water and trap suspended particles. They also absorb flood waters and release them slowly, like natural sponges. According to one estimate, wetlands cover less than 3 percent of Earth's surface but provide up to 40 percent of annual, renewable ecosystem services such as purifying water and cycling nutrients.[7]

After Hurricane Katrina caused at least $125 billion in damages along Louisiana's Gulf coast in September 2005, several studies indicated the storm surge would have been lower if large swathes of coastal wetlands had not been obliterated by Mississippi River flood-control projects and coastal oil and gas development.[8] In 2007 Louisiana approved a master plan for protecting and restoring its coast that, if fully funded, is expected to cost more than $50 billion and take up to 30 years to complete.[9]

Since the 1980s regulators have used a process known as "mitigation" (preserving, enhancing or creating wetlands to compensate for destroying others) as a tool to balance wetland conservation and development. Initially, owners who wanted to fill in wetlands had to do mitigation projects on the same site or nearby. To make the process more flexible, however, agencies developed mitigation banking, in which developers buy credits from a wetland "bank" (acres restored by a third party) to compensate for acres that they drain or alter.

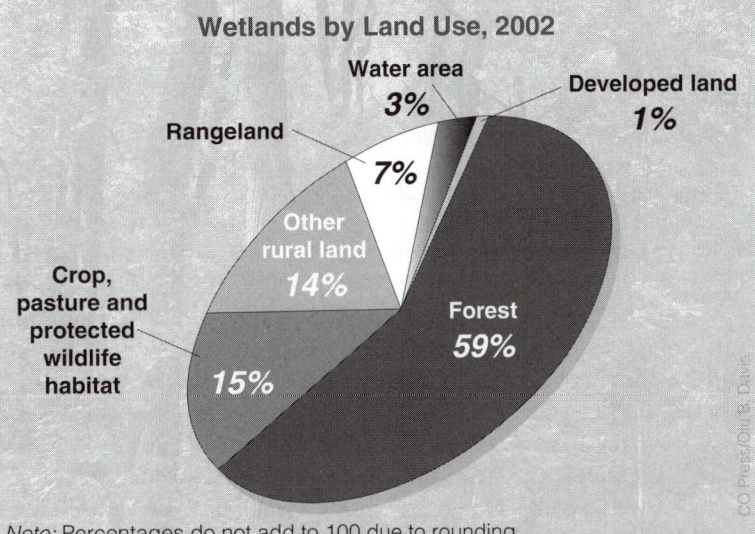

Forests Contain Most of U.S. Wetlands

About 66 million acres — or 59 percent — of the 111 million acres of wetland in the United States are in forests. Another 22 percent are on agricultural and range lands. More than one-third of threatened and endangered species in the U.S. live only in wetlands, and half spend at least part of their lives there. Besides supporting wildlife, wetlands also control pollution and flooding, protect the water supply and provide recreation.

Wetlands by Land Use, 2002

- Water area **3%**
- Developed land **1%**
- Rangeland **7%**
- Other rural land **14%**
- Crop, pasture and protected wildlife habitat **15%**
- Forest **59%**

Note: Percentages do not add to 100 due to rounding.
Source: National Resources Inventory, Natural Resources Conservation Service, 2002

The National Mitigation Banking Association, a trade group, calls mitigation banking "a unique concept . . . that unites sound economic and environmental practices."[10] But skeptics say the process often helps developers rather than maximizing the quality of U.S. wetlands.

"If a developer fills in wetlands for an urban project and restores something 50 miles away, flooding may be caused in the city where the wetlands used to be. There's no net loss of wetlands, but you have a big loss of [ecological] value" says Jon Kusler, associate director of the Association of State Wetland Managers (ASWM).

As scientists, government officials and business leaders debate how to balance wetland protection with development, here are some issues they are considering:

Does the Clean Water Act protect most wetlands?

Like other keystone environmental laws, the 1972 Clean Water Act (CWA) sought to create clear national

Priscilla and Jeff Wilson wait out the flood in St. Charles, Mo. after the Mississippi River inundated the Midwest last June. In 2005, after Hurricane Katrina battered Louisiana's coast, several studies indicated the storm surge would have been lower if coastal wetlands had not been obliterated by Mississippi River flood control projects and coastal oil and gas development.

standards for environmental quality instead of leaving most responsibility to the states.[11] But environmental groups and industry have argued for years over which wetlands fall under federal control. Conservationists say that most wetlands play important ecological roles and should be protected. Businesses counter that federal jurisdiction expanded in the 1980s and '90s to include unimportant wetlands that Congress never intended to regulate. State and local regulators are often caught in the middle.

Initially the Corps of Engineers interpreted the CWA's limits on discharging dredged or fill material into "navigable waters" narrowly, applying them only to bodies such as rivers and canals that could be used for interstate commerce. However, a federal court ruled in 1975 that the law covered all U.S. waters within the scope of Congress' constitutional power to regulate under the Commerce Clause.[12] In response, the Corps rewrote its regulations to also cover possible construction or degradation affecting tributaries of navigable waters, plus wetlands such as prairie potholes, mud flats and sloughs, "which could affect interstate commerce."[13]

The Supreme Court addressed the issue in its 1985 *Riverside Bayview Homes, Inc. v. United States* ruling, which affirmed that Congress could regulate wetlands adjacent to navigable waters. Since water flowed between these systems, the opinion reasoned, activities that harmed the wetlands could also impair the navigable waters.[14]

But in a seminal 2001 case, *Solid Waste Agency of Northern Cook County [SWANCC] v. U.S. Army Corps of Engineers*, the high court held that federal jurisdiction did not cover certain isolated wetlands the Corps had sought to protect because they were used or could be used by migratory birds. (The Corps had said the wetlands were important to interstate commerce because people traveled to view and hunt the birds.)[15] Chief Justice William H. Rehnquist's majority opinion found "no persuasive evidence" that Congress intended to regulate "non-navigable, isolated, intrastate waters." This wording suggested to some observers that other wetlands, regardless of whether they were suitable for birds or not, might fall outside federal protection as well.

"The Rehnquist court took the case intending to write a constitutional decision that limited Congress' power under the Commerce Clause," says Vermont Law School Professor Patrick Parenteau. "They couldn't muster five votes for that position, so they fell back to a vague statutory decision. Ever since, there's been a battle over whether *SWANCC* really announced new, limited principles of constitutional authority."

In the wake of *SWANCC*, many regulators and state courts assumed that small, isolated wetlands lying entirely within one state fell beyond federal protection but that most other types were covered. "People weren't regulating everything they had before, but coverage was still pretty broad," says Kusler of the Association of State Wetland Managers. The Bush administration proposed new guidelines in 2003 that would have narrowed coverage but withdrew them after receiving thousands of critical comments.[16]

Then in 2006 the Supreme Court decided *Rapanos v. United States*, which combined two cases involving tracts in Michigan.[17] One case examined whether the Corps could regulate wetlands next to a man-made ditch that ultimately flowed into navigable waters. The other concerned a wetland that bordered a tributary that ultimately flowed into navigable waters but was separated from the tributary by a four-foot-wide manmade barrier.

In a split verdict (4-1-4), Justice Antonin Scalia and three other justices concluded the Corps had overreached

A Wetlands Glossary

Bog: A wetland ecosystem that is highly acidic and has an accumulation of decomposed plants known as peat.

Carbon sink: A system that absorbs and stores carbon dioxide from the atmosphere. Forests, oceans and wetlands all can act as carbon sinks.

Carbon sequestration: Storing carbon in a natural sink or a geologic reservoir underground.

Dredging: Removing sediment from a channel to make it deep enough for navigation.

Estuary: An environment where land, freshwater and seawater (saline) habitats overlap.

Levee: A raised embankment built to keep a river from overflowing its banks.

Marsh: An environment where terrestrial and aquatic habitats overlap; a wetland dominated by grasses.

Mitigation: Actions that are undertaken to reduce the impact of an activity, such as buying credits from a wetland bank to make up for wetlands that are filled in for development.

Mudflat: A muddy, low-lying strip of ground usually submerged, more or less completely, by the rise of the tide.

Peat: Organic material (leaves, bark, nuts) that has decayed partially. It is dark brown with identifiable plant parts and can be found in peatlands and bogs.

Salt marsh: Flat land flooded by tidal saltwater.

Saltwater intrusion: The invasion of freshwater bodies by denser saltwater.

Swamp: A wetland with trees and shrubs.

Taking: A government action that deprives property owners of their rights, either by claiming the property for public use or by passing regulations making it impossible for them to develop the land.

Watershed: All the water that drains into a particular body of water (stream, pond, river, bay, etc.)

Wetland: Land saturated with water and containing plants and animals adapted to living on, near or in water.

---

in both cases. Scalia argued that "waters of the United States" should include only bodies of water that were relatively permanent, such as streams and lakes and wetlands with a "continuous surface connection" to those waters — but not wetlands that had only intermittent or distant physical connections to U.S. waters. Four other justices took the opposite position, supporting Corps jurisdiction in both cases.

Justice Anthony Kennedy took a middle stance, rejecting the Corps position but with a perspective different from Scalia's. Kennedy proposed a case-by-case approach for determining federal jurisdiction, based on whether wetlands had a "significant nexus" to traditional navigable waters. A wetland met this test if it significantly affected the chemical, biological or physical quality of navigable waters, either alone or in combination with other wetlands.

Given the split verdict, legal doctrine dictated that Kennedy's opinion was the controlling guideline for lower courts because his concurrence provided the fifth vote for vacating lower court decisions that had supported the Corps.

Property-rights advocates praise *Rapanos* for putting overdue limits on federal wetland controls. "The decision told federal regulators that they just can't regulate everything," says Russ Harding, director of the property rights network at Michigan's Mackinac Center for Public Policy and a former state environmental regulator. "It was a good decision, but I would have hoped for a brighter line and more clarity about what is subject to federal authority."

The decision alarmed conservationists, who worry it will worsen ongoing losses of isolated wetlands. "We're very concerned about how many wetlands are losing federal protection," says Scott Yaich, director of conservation operations for Ducks Unlimited, a sportsmen's group that works to protect waterfowl habitat. "EPA and the Corps interpreted *SWANCC* to remove 20 million acres of wetlands from jurisdiction under the Clean Water Act. The Corps' post-*Rapanos* guidance removes up to 60 million acres from federal control."

All sides agree that recent Corps guidance, intended to translate abstruse *Rapanos* terms like "significant nexus" and "relatively permanent waters" into policy, has made the permitting process slower and more cumbersome. According to the guidance, wetlands that meet either the Scalia or Kennedy tests fall under federal jurisdiction. Moreover, Corps field offices across the nation are interpreting the new rules in different ways, says Leah Pilconis, senior counsel at the Associated General Contractors of America. "Not knowing exactly what is required and having decisions made inconsistently wastes time and money in the construction process," she says. "It raises interest costs, makes scheduling harder and delays completion dates."

The AGC and other trade associations want the Corps to narrow its criteria for determining federal jurisdiction and reduce paperwork requirements. Scientists have a broader problem with the current approach: They reject the idea that only some wetlands have a "significant nexus" with waters of the United States.

"Wetlands are all connected," says Joy Zedler, a professor of botany and ecology at the University of Wisconsin, who chaired a 2001 National Academy of Sciences study on wetland restoration. "The Supreme Court is free to make non-science-based decisions, so it can say that wetlands have to be connected above the ground to U.S. waters. But that position doesn't withstand scientific scrutiny, because there are underground connections. We can't project into the future, because we don't know how rainfall patterns will shift and where floodwater patterns will flow. So it makes sense to avoid damaging systems that may be critically connected."

Are federal agencies doing enough to protect wetlands?

In terms of sheer acreage, federal inventories show that the United States has gained more wetlands than it has lost in recent years — a net increase of about 32,000 acres annually between 1998 and 2004.[18] (*See graph, p. 300.*) The increase grew out of a goal President Bush set on Earth Day in 2004 of protecting, improving and restoring or creating 3 million acres or more of wetlands (at least 1 million acres in each category) by 2009. The White House Council on Environmental Quality says the goal has been met ahead of schedule, although Bush's targets do not reflect wetland losses that occurred at the same time.[19]

Critics say development and pollution are still destroying valuable areas. For example, an investigation by *The St. Petersburg Times* found that between 1990 and 2005 Florida lost 84,000 acres of wetlands to development. Moreover, many replacement wetlands that developers were required to create were expensive failures, and the Corps rarely verified information in permit applications or inspected wetlands after permits were approved.[20]

"Peer-reviewed science is supposed to be the determining factor in our permitting process, but it doesn't translate very easily into regulations," says Jason Lauritsen, assistant director of the Audubon Society's Corkscrew Swamp Sanctuary near Naples, Fla. "The broader the scientific gaps are, the more politics can come into play, and decisions tend to favor property owners."

For years wetland advocates and fiscal conservatives have called for reforming the Corps, which they say is too committed to wasteful, large-scale construction projects that often harm the environment.[21] Many past Corps projects, such as Mississippi River flood control levees, have worsened flooding by cutting off water and sediment flows from adjoining floodplains, leaving these areas to dry out and sink. This year EPA vetoed a $220 million Corps proposal to drain 67,000 acres of wetlands along the Yazoo River in Mississippi in order to provide flood control in a sparsely populated rural area.[22]

But critics concede that the Corps is gradually becoming a better environmental steward and is carrying out some valuable restoration projects. For example, in the 1960s when the Corps straightened Florida's winding Kissimmee River — the headwaters of the Everglades — it turned it into a 56-mile canal and drained 30,000 acres of wetlands in the process. Today the Corps is restoring the Kissimmee's meandering course and removing structures that controlled its flow. Although the project is still under way, it has already improved water quality and tripled bird counts around the river. (*See sidebar, p. 312.*)[23]

"The Corps is greener than it was 10 or 15 years ago, although it's hard to say exactly how green," says Kusler of the State Wetland Managers Association. "It came to that role kicking and screaming, but now it ranks restoration goals higher than it used to."

However, he points out, Corps regulations still include many exemptions for activities like draining wetlands, as well as discharges of dredge-and-fill material that occur in the course of ongoing farming, ranching or forestry activities (for example, plowing or maintaining drainage ditches). "The [Clean Water Act's] 404 program still isn't doing an adequate job," Kusler contends.

Expert advisers like the National Research Council say the problem is broader. In the council's view, the

United States does not have a clear, well-focused policy for managing water resources.[24] Many federal and state agencies share responsibility for water issues, and their agendas often conflict. In these situations, the National Academy of Public Administration observed, agencies make separate decisions about individual projects without considering how these steps affect large ecological systems like river basins.[25] Other agencies also shape wetland policy. The U.S. Fish and Wildlife Service (FWS) manages national wildlife refuges and promotes conservation on private lands. As part of the 404 process, FWS prepares "biological opinions" (BiOps) assessing how proposed developments will affect the habitat of endangered or threatened species.

In Florida, the FWS has objected to many proposed wetland development permits. But in 2005 it fired biologist Andrew Eller, who argued the agency was using misleading data to make it look as though the endangered Florida panther — whose habitat is threatened by development — was at a lower risk than it actually was.[26] In response to a legal complaint, FWS corrected its information and reinstated Eller. Now, however, in at least some cases the agency relies on developers to provide data for BiOps.[27]

"The standard set of questions on 404 permit applications was developed by FWS. Applicants fill it out, and we analyze it," says Bill Wilen, a senior biologist with the service's National Wetlands Inventory office. "It saves FWS time and effort by highlighting potential impacts."

Another FWS wetland initiative, conserving land in the prairie pothole region — Iowa, Minnesota, the Dakotas and Montana — is falling short of the agency's goals because land prices are rising. Since 1959 FWS has acquired or protected about 3 million acres of wetlands and grasslands in the area, which provides nesting and breeding habitat and stopover space during migration for

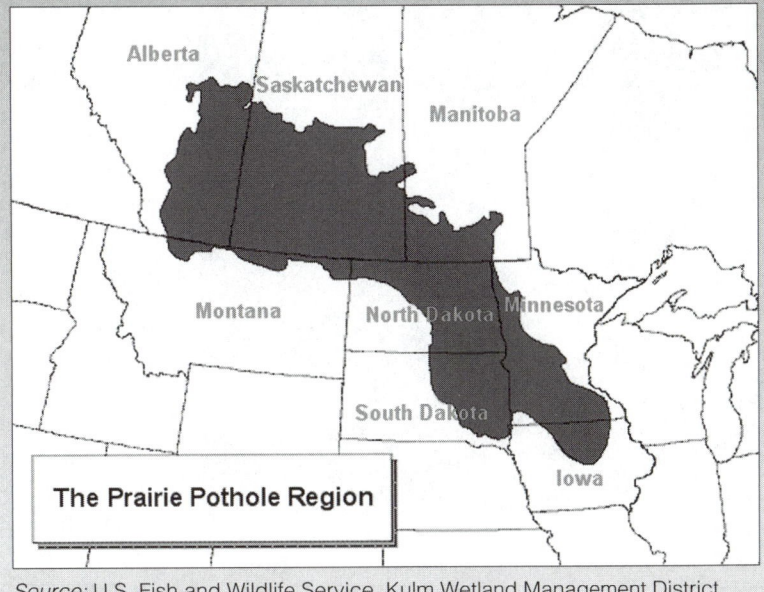

'Duck Factory' Nurtures Waterfowl

The Prairie Pothole Region — also known as the "Duck Factory" of North America — produces more than half the continent's waterfowl. Created by retreating glaciers 12,000 years ago, the 300,000-square-mile region once contained 25 million wetlands, or about 83 sites per square mile — a density unmatched anywhere in North America.

The Prairie Pothole Region

Source: U.S. Fish and Wildlife Service, Kulm Wetland Management District, Kulm, N.D.

hundreds of species of birds. In 2007 the Government Accountability Office (GAO) reported that while FWS was managing these lands effectively, at the current pace it would take the service until 2050 to reach its target of protecting 12 million acres.

Most options for speeding up the process require congressional approval, however. For example, Congress could raise the price of the federal Duck Stamp that hunters must purchase, which has been $15 since 1991. It also could appropriate more money from Treasury's Land and Water Conservation Fund, which helps pay for acquiring land, water and wetlands.[28]

According to biologist Wilen, FWS agrees with GAO's conclusions. "We have very sophisticated models that help us decide where we'd like to purchase land, and we prioritize so we can get the best bang for the buck. FWS wants to get it done, but right now we just don't have the cash to go faster," he says.

Aurora/Getty Images/Peter Essick

Central Florida's once-meandering Kissimmee River is being "unstraightened" as part of the $10 billion Everglades restoration project. The U.S. Army Corps of Engineers channelized the river in 1971 to control periodic flooding, but the project dried out thousands of acres of critical habitat and deprived the Everglades of seasonal water supply. Remnants of the river's winding path can be seen next to a straightened section.

Rising oil and food costs and expanding biofuels production have been driving up land prices, making it harder to protect wetlands.[29] World oil prices are projected to average $116 per barrel in 2008, up from $72 in 2007, triggering price hikes for agricultural commodities because the fertilizer used to grow them is made from fossil fuels.[30] At the same time, the U.S. and other industrialized nations are scaling up production of biofuels made from plants to reduce their reliance on imported oil. Using grain — mostly corn — to make fuel also drives up prices for commodities.

Rising grain prices drive farmers to plant more crops on marginal acres — including land formerly enrolled in the Agriculture Department's Conservation Reserve Program (CRP), which pays farmers to set environmentally sensitive land aside as wildlife habitat. About 34 million acres are protected under the CRP, or just under 10 percent of U.S. cropland. More than 400,000 acres were converted to cropland in North Dakota alone in 2007.[31] "Conservation is in for a long swim against a strong current," said Jim Ringelman, conservation director in the Prairie Pothole Region for Ducks Unlimited.[32]

Does mitigation work?

Since thousands of acres of wetlands are developed each year, the only way to prevent net losses is to restore, improve or create more acres of new wetlands. This process, known as mitigation, has become central to the wetland permitting process. Many experts say that mitigation done correctly can improve the environment and that the process is improving with advances in wetland science. But critics reply that it creates too many easy-to-build, low-value wetlands. To work well, they argue, mitigation should replace not only lost acres but the specific functions of natural wetlands.

In the 1970s and '80s the Corps and EPA required developers to avoid damaging wetland functions, minimize damage or replace these functions onsite or nearby. These conditions also applied to farmers who converted wetlands to cropland after 1985 under the Swampbuster program, which restricts wetland drainage for agriculture.

On-site mitigation makes work harder for builders, who have to work around wetlands, and farmers who cultivate all of their acres. "If their holdings are already farmed, mitigating on site just means trading one wet spot for another," says Rick Robinson, environmental affairs director for the Iowa Farm Bureau Federation (IFBF).

Many field studies in the 1980s and '90s found that mitigation projects required under the 404 program were not meeting their targets, and that some were never finished. According to a 2001 National Research Council report, only 70 to 76 percent of the mitigation required in studies it reviewed was implemented, and half did not meet permit requirements. The committee concluded that "there is a substantial net loss in wetland area from the wetlands permitting program," and that wetlands that were built had low value.[33]

Under pressure to make permitting more flexible, federal and state agencies developed "mitigation banking," in which bank operators create or restore "banks" of wetlands and sell mitigation credits to customers seeking wetland development permits. This approach sought to make permitting more efficient, concentrate more resources on large land parcels and allow regulators to target important wetlands for restoration or improvement.*

Starting in the early 1990s, mitigation banking became an active market. By 2005 the Corps estimated that some 450 mitigation banks were operating across the country, with more planned.[34] Some were run by private companies, others by government agencies with major mitigation responsibilities, such as state transportation departments, or conservation groups. Credit prices ranged from as low as $4,000 per acre in rural areas to $100,000 or more in urban or suburban areas.[35]

"Environmentalists should love mitigation banking," says the Mackinac Institute's Harding. "On-site mitigation isn't very effective because it tends to produce lots of small isolated wetlands that are expensive to create. Banking lets developers move ahead with projects more quickly and creates new viable habitat." In addition, states typically do not allow banks to sell most of their credits until they actually carry out their wetland projects. And bank owners retain long-term responsibility for the health of their wetlands, even after they sell the restoration credits, so they have a financial interest in creating viable wetlands.[36]

To help farmers meet Swampbuster requirements, the Iowa farm bureau created the first mitigation bank in the state in 2002, working with the state Department of Natural Resources (DNR). The bank, located in prairie pothole territory, converted 70 acres of corn and soybean fields into wetlands and has sold most of its available credits for roughly $14,000 apiece.[37]

"It's been going very well," says Robinson. "Agriculture isn't where the big mitigation banking money is, because farmers have smaller environmental impacts than developers and less money to pay, but we've had overwhelming interest from farmers."

But Audubon's Lauritsen sees flaws in the process in Florida. "If you develop a wetland that was wet for three months of the year, mitigation banking doesn't make you replace it with one that is also wet for three months each year. That has an ecological impact on wildlife," he argues. "We need better techniques for recognizing the functions of different types of wetlands and recovering

---

* Mitigation banking is similar to pollution credit programs, which allow industrial polluters to buy unused pollution credits from non-polluters.

what we've lost — especially shallow wetlands, which are the easiest to drain and build on."

Better site selection would help, Lauritsen says. "There's a lot of promise in mitigation banking done the right way," he says. "We have a lot of agricultural property, planted with citrus and row crops, which still has wetland soil and is flooded in the spring before the pumps are turned on. You could restore those properties without spending a lot of money, and produce a lot of dividends."

According to the most recent FWS inventory, there was a net loss of many important types of wetlands between 1998 and 2004, including salt marshes and mangrove forests. They were replaced mainly by freshwater ponds, which increased by almost 700,000 acres (12.6 percent), due mainly to the creation of artificial ponds for purposes such as stormwater control or decorative landscaping. "These ponds are not an equivalent replacement for vegetated wetlands," the FWS notes.[38]

"Ponds are popular because they're easy. If you excavate in a wet place, you'll get plants and animals living there," says the University of Wisconsin's Zedler. "Other types like sedge meadows that are wet in some seasons and dry in others are harder to achieve. But ponds are simple systems, and they don't provide all of the ecological services that we're losing."

Although mitigation can be useful, many wetland advocates say, they see little value in a no-net-loss goal unless the focus shifts from quantity to quality. "Saying that it's OK to trade prairie potholes for stormwater retention basins is like making farmers trade their pickup trucks for compact cars and telling them that they haven't had any net loss of transportation," says Yaich of Ducks Unlimited. "They wouldn't be happy."

BACKGROUND
Overlooked Resources

For most of the nation's history, Americans have viewed wetlands as worthless. Settlers saw wetlands, loosely referred to as mires, fens or swamps, as insect breeding grounds that impeded travel and farming.

Starting in the 1820s, the Army Corps of Engineers dammed and dredged many productive marshes and bottomlands (river flood plains) to improve navigation on U.S. rivers. Under the Swamp Land acts of 1849, 1850 and 1860,

Congress transferred more than 64 million acres categorized as "wet and unfit for cultivation" to 15 states, mostly in the South and Midwest, to allow the land to be drained for flood control and agriculture. Many of the tracts ended up in private hands or were given to railroad companies.[39] Port development in San Francisco, Seattle and other cities led to the diking and filling of coastal marshes.

Contrary to their image, natural wetlands teemed with life. Marshes around the Chesapeake Bay supported fisheries that produced millions of pounds of crabs and oysters yearly in the late 1800s. Prairie potholes — then called sloughs — across the upper Midwest were rich nesting and feeding grounds for birds. *Little House on the Prairie* author Laura Ingalls Wilder, whose family homesteaded in South Dakota in the 1880s, described bird life on a nearby marsh:

"Millions of rustling grass-blades made one murmuring sound, and thousands of wild ducks and geese and herons and cranes and pelicans were talking sharply and brassily in the wind.

All those birds were feeding among the grasses of the sloughs. They rose on flapping wings and settled again, crying news to each other and talking among themselves among the grasses, and eating busily of grass roots and tender water plants and little fishes."[40]

After the Civil War, the Corps took on new responsibility for flood control and regulation of dumping and filling in harbors. In 1899 the Rivers and Harbors Act required developers to obtain a permit from the Corps for any activity that would excavate, discharge material into, or obstruct "navigable waters," including coastal waters, lakes, rivers and streams. The Corps' main focus, however, was construction, not conservation.[41]

States promoted wetland development by creating so-called drainage districts, or local groups with the power to issue bonds, drain land for approved uses and tax all landholders who benefited from this service. Many Midwestern districts installed massive drain-tile systems using underground networks of ceramic pipes that channeled water away from fields to drainage ditches and streams. By 1935, farmers in Illinois had installed enough drain tiles to circle the world six times.[42] "Michigan wouldn't have been settled if it hadn't been drained," says the Mackinac Institute's Harding.

Early Conservation

By the early 20th century, conservation advocates were campaigning to save important natural resources from over-hunting and development. They found a friend in President Theodore Roosevelt, who used his executive power to designate 51 tracts of land in 17 states and territories as National Bird Reservations between 1903 and 1909. Many tracts included islands, lakes, marshes and other wetlands. Thirty-one of these "Roosevelt Reservations" later became units of the National Wildlife Refuge system.[43]

The invention of steam shovels and mechanized earth-moving equipment facilitated carving up landscapes on a bigger scale. In 1928, a year after flooding along the Mississippi River inundated thousands of miles of land from Illinois to the Gulf of Mexico, Congress put the Corps in charge of flood control and navigation along the river's entire length. The Corps began installing levees, stabilizing riverbanks and realigning channels to control flood waters, a program that stretched through the next several decades. It also built a system of 29 locks and dams on the upper Mississippi extending for 670 miles from Minneapolis to St. Louis, to create a nine-foot-deep channel for easy navigation.

These projects profoundly affected wetlands along the river. Levees prevented river waters from spilling over, drying out previously fertile bottomlands. In other places the navigation system raised water levels, putting floodplains under water. In Louisiana levees prevented the Mississippi and its tributaries from flooding and depositing sediments across the delta plain, accelerating erosion along the state's coastline.

Another catastrophic 1928 storm, in Florida, caused massive Lake Okeechobee to flood thousands of surrounding acres, killing some 2,500 people. In response President Herbert Hoover directed the Corps to dike the lake. This cut off freshwater flow from the lake down through the Everglades during rainy seasons, lowering the water table and drying out soils, which spurred further logging and farming on former wetlands.

"The Everglades were dying," wrote journalist Marjorie Stoneman Douglas in her 1947 bestseller, *The Everglades: River of Grass*. "The endless acres of saw grass, brown as an enormous shadow where rain and lake water had once flowed, rustled dry."[44]

Just after Douglas' book was published, President Harry S Truman dedicated a 1.3-million-acre tract as Everglades National Park. But at the same time the

CHRONOLOGY

1890-1900s *Conservationists protect some wetlands, but many are lost.*

1890 Congress gives Army Corps of Engineers control of dredging and filling "navigable waters."

1905 Florida begins draining Everglades for agriculture and development.

1930s-1940s *Wetland conservation efforts expand, along with development.*

1934 Congress authorizes Duck Stamps to fund wetlands conservation.

1936 Agriculture Department begins helping farmers drain wetlands.

1948 After disastrous floods, Congress permits water to be channeled from the Everglades for flood control.

1960s-1980s *Wetland protection expands.*

1969 National Environmental Policy Act requires impact studies for major federal projects, such as dams.

1972 Clean Water Act gives Corps of Engineers responsibility for regulating development in wetlands. . . . Coastal Zone Management Act seeks to protect coast areas.

1973 Endangered Species Act restricts development of wetlands.

1977 President Jimmy Carter orders federal agencies to minimize wetland loss.

1980 Environmental Protection Agency (EPA) embraces concept of saving some wetlands to compensate for destroying others.

1985 Swampbuster program eliminates subsidies for farmers who convert wetlands for agriculture. . . . Supreme Court rules in *U.S. v. Riverside Bayview Homes* that the Corps can regulate wetlands *adjacent* to navigable waters.

1987 National Estuary Program directs EPA to protect important coastal bays.

1988 President George H. W. Bush endorses "no net loss" of wetlands as national policy.

1989 Louisiana sets aside oil revenues for coastal restoration.

1990s-Present *Politicians support wetlands, but property-rights advocates and industry argue federal controls are too broad.*

1990 Congress calls for a plan to restore Louisiana's coastal wetlands.

1995 U.S. House requires government compensation if endangered species or wetlands regulations reduce landowners' property values by more than 20 percent.

2000 Comprehensive Everglades Restoration Plan is launched.

2001 In *SWANCC v. U.S. Army Corps of Engineers*, Supreme Court restricts the Corps' jurisdiction to navigable waters, their tributaries and adjacent wetlands.

2002 Louisiana and the Corps propose a $14 billion coastal restoration plan. Bush administration downscales it drastically.

2004 President George W. Bush pledges to increase overall wetlands acreage annually.

2005 Hurricanes Katrina and Rita destroy some 240 square miles of coastal wetlands in Louisiana and Mississippi.

2006 In divided verdict, the Supreme Court proposes a "significant nexus" test to determine whether isolated wetlands are connected to navigable waters.

2007 President Bush vetoes a $23 billion water bill, which includes funds for Everglades and Louisiana coastal restoration.

2008 Heavy spring rains cause record flooding along the Mississippi River; Hurricanes Gustav and Ivan cause further flooding and property damage along Gulf Coast. . . . Florida announces plans to buy 187,000 acres of the Everglades from U.S. Sugar Corp. for $1.75 billion to aid restoration efforts.

Why Wetlands Matter

They provide valuable "ecosystem services."

Over the past several decades, U.S. laws and regulations have become more protective of wetlands in recognition of the billions of dollars worth of valuable "ecosystem services" they provide by nurturing wildlife, protecting against storms and serving as "nature's kidneys."[1] Depending on a wetland's type and location, these services may include:

Supporting wildlife — Wetlands provide habitat and feeding grounds for animals, birds, fish and shellfish. About three-quarters of the fish and shellfish harvested commercially in the United States depend on coastal estuaries for shelter at some point in their lives, such as spawning or growth before they migrate to open waters.[2] U.S. commercial fisheries generate roughly $25 billion in annual revenues for fishermen, processors and distributors.[3] In April 2008 the Commerce Department declared that the West Coast salmon industry had collapsed because historically low numbers of salmon were returning from the oceans to spawn; scientists said loss of freshwater habitat was a factor.[4]

Many species of shorebirds feed or nest in wetlands, including tidal mudflats, beaches and freshwater marshes. These areas are crucial stops for millions of birds that migrate north and south along the Atlantic and Pacific flyways, including some that travel to Central America or the Caribbean in winter and to Alaska and Canada in summer. Other species that travel up through the central United States depend on flood plains along the lower Mississippi River or prairie potholes in the upper Great Plains.

Cleaning up the water — Plants slow water down as it flows through wetlands, which causes dirt and other particles to settle out and sink to the bottom. Many types of microorganisms in wetlands, such as bacteria and algae, break down dead organisms and wastes. Wetland plants take up excess nutrients, such as nitrogen and phosphorus from farm runoff, that otherwise would contribute to algae blooms and create "dead zones" in the water. So-called constructed (artificial) wetlands are often used to filter and clean polluted water from farms, homes and commercial developments.

Controlling floods — Wetlands are natural sponges that can soak up large quantities of rainwater, storm surge or melting snow, store it and then release it slowly over time. This makes them valuable flood-control systems, especially in urban areas where water runs off quickly from paved surfaces. And coastal wetlands can act as speed bumps that slow incoming storms. Some studies have estimated that four miles of well-vegetated wetlands can reduce storm surge by roughly one foot, although much depends on the type of wetlands and the dimensions of the storm.[5]

Regulating global climate — As plants grow they absorb carbon dioxide (CO_2), the main greenhouse gas that traps heat in the atmosphere and contributes to global climate change. When plants die and decompose, their carbon content is released back into the air. But if plant material is buried in soil — especially cool, wet soils like peat, where decomposition rates are slow — the carbon is stored. Wetlands store large amounts of carbon, but there is great uncertainty about how this process will be affected by climate change. (*See "Current Situation," p. 314.*)

---

[1] Unless otherwise cited, this section is based on Joy B. Zedler and Suzanne Kercher, "Wetland Resources: Status, Trends, Ecosystem Services, and Restorability," *Annual Review of Environment and Resources* (2005), pp. 39-74.

[2] "Habitat Connections: Wetlands, Fisheries and Economics," National Oceanographic and Atmospheric Administration, www.nmfs.noaa.gov/habitat/habitatconservation/publications/habitatconections/habitatconnections.htm.

[3] *Business Wire*, Dec. 5, 2005.

[4] " 'Fishery Failure' Declared for West Coast Salmon Fishery," National Oceanographic and Atmospheric Administration, May 1, 2008.

[5] "Wetlands Break Waves, Quell Surge," LaCoast.gov, www.lacoast.gov/WATERMARKS/2006-03/2protectMainland/; Louisiana Sea Grant Program, "Louisiana Hurricane Resources," www.laseagrant.org/hurricane/archive/wetlands.htm.

Corps was designing the Central & Southern Florida Project — a massive flood control system intended to tame areas around the new park for agriculture and development. Launched in 1948, the project created 1,000 miles of levees, 720 miles of canals and 200 water-control structures to regulate freshwater flows and channel rainy-season runoff out to sea, further drying out the greater Everglades ecosystem.

Other federal agencies also promoted development on wetlands. In 1936 the Agriculture Department started sharing farmers' costs for converting wetlands to cropland. The Civilian Conservation Corps and other Depression-era relief initiatives also put unemployed Americans to work draining wetlands.

To slow wetland losses the U.S. Biological Survey (which later became the Fish and Wildlife Service) in 1934 launched the federal Duck Stamp program. Revenues from the program were used to buy wetlands that were important waterfowl habitat and add them to the National Wildlife Refuge system. Over the next 70 years Duck Stamp sales to hunters financed the purchase or lease of more than 5 million acres.[45]

Exploitation to Protection

By the 1960s economic growth was taking a heavy toll on U.S. water resources. Many rivers, lakes and streams were heavily polluted with industrial discharges. Unrestricted private development was encroaching on scenic coastlines, often in ecologically sensitive areas.

For example, farm fertilizer and phosphate detergent discharges into Lake Erie spawned massive blooms of algae; when the weeds died and decomposed, the process depleted oxygen from the water, leaving the lake so void of fish life that it was widely viewed as biologically dead. In 1963 there was so much industrialization and development around San Francisco Bay that only four of its 276 miles of shoreline were open to the public, and adjoining towns like Berkeley and San Mateo were planning to fill in much of the bay to expand their land areas.[46]

Such developments spurred a new wave of environmentalism and landmark laws including the Clean Water Act of 1972, which created a national permitting system for pollution discharges. Section 404 of the CWA gave the Corps of Engineers authority to regulate dredging and filling in wetlands, subject to oversight by the new Environmental Protection Agency, which had veto power. Congress also passed the Coastal Zone Management Act, which provided federal aid to states that developed comprehensive plans for preserving and restoring their coastlines.

A year later Congress enacted the Endangered Species Act (ESA), which restricted development of areas identified as critical habitat for endangered or threatened species. Section 7 of the act required federal agencies to consult with the Fish and Wildlife Service to ensure that their activities would not jeopardize listed species or damage critical habitat.

While these laws offered new leverage for protecting wetlands, the Agriculture Department and other agencies still supported wetland conversion. President Jimmy Carter, a critic of federal water projects for both their costs and environmental impacts, addressed this conflict in a 1977 executive order that directed all federal agencies to "take action to minimize the destruction, loss or degradation of wetlands, and to preserve and enhance the natural and beneficial values of wetlands in carrying out the agency's responsibilities."[47]

Carter's order eventually led to the Swampbuster program, enacted in the 1985 farm bill. The program made farmers ineligible for federal aid or subsidies if they converted certain types of wetlands to cropland. Like the 404 program, however, Swampbuster allowed mitigation projects to compensate for activities that destroyed wetlands.

Running for president in 1988, George H.W. Bush pledged that his administration would work to achieve "no net loss" of wetlands in the U.S. During his administration (1989-1993) the Agriculture Department expanded the Conservation Reserve Program for preserving environmentally sensitive wetlands. The 1990 farm bill then created a parallel Wetland Reserve Program, which paid farmers for restoring wetland functions to marginal farmlands.

Behind the scenes, however, Vice President Dan Quayle's staff sought to redefine wetlands so that only areas that remained wet year-round received federal protection. This proposal, which was opposed by the EPA and ultimately failed, could have deregulated up to half of U.S. wetlands.[48]

Legal Resistance

Expanding federal controls slowed the net rate of wetland losses significantly in the 1970s and '80s, but some critics said development curbs infringed on landowners' rights by reducing property values. When government committed so-called regulatory takings ("taking" value without actually seizing the property), they argued, it owed owners financial compensation.[49]

Several landowners who initiated lawsuits in the mid-1980s won federal court rulings that wetland regulations were takings, and received monetary damages.[50] In one lawsuit filed by a beachfront developer in South Carolina, the Supreme Court held that government action barring all economic uses of land (assuming that those uses were legal when the property was acquired) automatically constituted a taking.[51] This ruling signaled that if regulators did not make a significant effort to be fair

Complex Plans Aim to Restore Everglades

But politics and funding are still obstacles.

The history of Florida's Everglades echoes the broader story of U.S. wetlands. Long viewed as a swamp, drained and developed for the past century, the Everglades now is only about half as big as it was before World War II, and what's left is severely threatened by water pollution and constant development. However, the area still supports 68 threatened or endangered species of plants, animals and birds, including the Florida panther, wood stork, American crocodile and leatherback turtle.

Indeed, the Everglades is not a swamp but an intricate system of interdependent ecosystems including sawgrass marshes, mangrove forests, tropical hardwood hammocks and the marine environment of Florida Bay. The roughly 6,000-square-mile area is vital to South Florida's water supply.

In 2000 Congress approved the Comprehensive Everglades Restoration Plan (CERP), scheduled to take about 40 years and cost more than $10 billion (up from an initial projected cost of $7.8 billion). The massive rescue operation, which includes 60 individual projects, aims to make more water available for the Everglades by capturing flows that are currently diverted and storing water so it can be released as needed. Some elements of the plan are moving forward, but costs are still rising, and many important elements have been delayed.[1]

Two central problems are hurting the Everglades: It does not receive enough water, and what does flow through is polluted. But making the ecosystem healthy again is more complicated than just opening spigots. Scientists are trying to determine how much water the Everglades needs and how fast it should move.

"The Everglades has a very distinctive land form," explains Greg Noe, an ecologist with the U.S. Geological Survey. "It has elevated ridges and sloughs like the channels in corrugated cardboard, which run north-south and then bend west at the lower end." The long interconnected sloughs, or ditches, contain many fish and small aquatic organisms and are important feeding areas for wading birds. Dense sawgrass grows up to 10 feet high on the ridges.

There was so much sawgrass that writer Marjory Stoneman Douglas famously dubbed the Everglades a "river of grass" in 1947.

As water levels fall, sloughs dry out and become filled with sawgrass. "One big CERP goal is to add enough water back to restore that landscape, and also to improve water quality so that you don't harm the system by putting more water in," says Noe. "No one knows exactly what the right water depths are — if it's too deep you drown everything out, and if it's too shallow the sloughs fill in with sawgrass."

But Noe believes that the CERP research plan can answer these technical questions. "It's the biggest restoration project in the U.S. and probably the most complicated, because so many organizations are involved, but everyone has a vested interest in getting it right," he says. CERP incorporates an approach called adaptive management, in which scientists carry out selected projects, measure results, then refine their next steps based on these findings. "If people weren't willing to learn and change the plan, I'd be worried," says Noe.

Florida has lagged on cleaning up water that flows through the Everglades. After a 1992 legal settlement with the federal government, the Florida legislature passed the Everglades Forever Act in 1994, which required state regulators to ensure that water entering the Everglades would contain no more than 10 parts of phosphorus per billion by 2006 (phosphorus, a nutrient found in agricultural runoff, is one of the main water pollutants in the Everglades), and take other steps to achieve that standard. But in 2003 the state extended the compliance deadline to 2016 in a bill supported by the sugar industry but derided by environmentalists as the "Everglades Whenever" Act.[2]

The state is still struggling to meet minimum national water-quality standards. A May 2007 memo by Major Gen. Don Riley, director of civil works for the U.S. Army Corps of Engineers, asserted that Florida "is not currently meeting [water quality] requirements for water that would flow into [the Lake Okeechobee watershed] and it is not likely to come into compliance for several decades."[3]

to landowners, they risked having their rules struck down in court.

Some observers predicted that these cases would stimulate more antiregulatory claims, but no such wave developed — possibly because federal agencies got the message. "The

'takings revolution' fizzled, primarily because most wetland permits were granted, so there was little to complain about," says Vermont Law School's Parenteau. And mitigation banking, launched in 1990 and expanded under President Clinton, offered developers a new way to offset wetland losses.

But Florida has outdone the federal government on one aspect of Everglades restoration: funding. Although the cleanup costs are supposed to be shared, Florida spent nearly $2.4 billion on Everglades restoration projects from 2000 though 2007 while Congress provided only $360 million. However, the 2007 Water Resources Development Act authorized three important CERP projects with total costs of $1.8 billion, including restoration of more than 150,000 acres of wetlands, and President George W. Bush's fiscal 2009 budget proposal includes $215 million for CERP activities.[4]

Everglades supporters were elated in June when Gov. Charlie Crist, R-Fla., announced a deal to buy out the holdings of U.S. Sugar, one of two major sugar companies in Florida, including 300 square miles of agricultural land south of Lake Okeechobee. Crist's administration said the struggling company would be allowed to farm the land for six more years, after which the state would use it to restore freshwater flow from the lake to the Everglades.

The $1.75 billion sale may not be finalized until sometime in 2009, but skeptics are pointing out that it may benefit the powerful sugar industry as much as it advances Everglades cleanup.[5] Some farmers argue that agriculture is being scapegoated as the root of the Everglades' problems when development is equally at fault.[6]

There's no shortage of new development proposals around the Everglades. In early 2008 Palm Beach County commissioners approved 10,500 acres of new rock mines north of the Everglades, although the state Department of Environmental Protection was still reviewing whether mining would affect local water quality or Everglades restoration.[7] And Miami-Dade County commissioners voted to move the county's "urban development boundary" closer to the Everglades, allowing the Lowe's hardware chain to build a store and offices on 20 acres of wetlands.

"It shoots our credibility," said Miami-Dade Mayor Carlos Alvarez, who pledged to veto the plan.[8]

A September assessment by the National Research Council found that in spite of recent progress, CERP was not moving fast enough. "The project is bogged down in budgeting, planning and procedural matters while the ecosystem that it was created to save is in peril," the council warned.[9]

National Park Service Photo/Rodney Cammauf

Great egrets thrive in Florida's Everglades, along with 68 threatened or endangered species of plants, animals and birds, including the Florida panther and American crocodile.

[1] "South Florida Ecosystem: Some Restoration Progress Has Been Made, but the Effort Faces Significant Delays, Implementation Challenges, and Rising Costs," U.S. Government Accountability Office, Sept. 19, 2007, p. 5; "Cash for Everglades Restoration Dries, Up, The Associated Press, Nov. 21, 2007.

[2] Michael Peltier, "Florida Governor Bush Signs Contentious Everglades Bill," Reuters, May 22, 2003.

[3] Posted online by Public Employees for Environmental Responsibility, www.peer.org/docs/ace/07_14_11_gen_riley_memo.pdf.

[4] Audubon of Florida, "Everglades Report," winter 2008; Daniel Cusick, "Army Corps: Proposed Budget Offers an 'Awkward Kiss on the Cheek' for Everglades," *E&E Report*, Feb. 4, 2008.

[5] Patrik Jonsson, "U.S. Sugar Buyout: Sweet Deal for the Everglades?" *The Christian Science Monitor*, Aug. 20, 2008; Mary Williams Walsh, "Helping the Everglades, or Big Sugar?" *The New York Times*, Sept. 14, 2008, p. BU1.

[6] Jonsson, *op. cit.*

[7] Paul Quinlan and Jennifer Sorentrue, "Miners Get OK to Dig in Western Palm Beach County," *The Palm Beach Post*, April 24, 2008, p. 1B.

[8] "Good News for the Everglades: New Funding and a Mayor's Stand Offer Hope for Florida's Treasure," *Sarasota Herald-Tribune*, May 2, 2008, p. A10.

[9] National Research Council, "Progress Toward Restoring the Everglades," second biennial report, Sept. 29, 2008, http://dels.nas.edu/dels/rpt_briefs/everglades_brief_final.pdf.

But wetland regulation was further complicated by the Supreme Court's 2001 *SWANCC* ruling that Congress could not regulate isolated wetlands based solely on the presence of migratory birds.[52] The ruling effectively deregulated some isolated wetlands, and the language of the majority opinion raised questions about where federal authority stopped. Most state courts, however, continued to define federal jurisdiction quite broadly, and several states passed bills setting up comprehensive state-level protection for wetlands.

President Bush, who had endorsed his father's goal of "no net loss" in 2002, expanded on it in 2004. "Instead of just limiting our losses, we will expand the wetlands of America," Bush said. Critics endorsed the goal but said reaching it would require many steps, including a narrow reading of the *SWANCC* ruling, stricter enforcement of mitigation requirements and more funding for the National Wildlife Refuge system.[53]

The issue was further muddled by the Supreme Court's fragmented *Rapanos* ruling in 2006. Justice Kennedy's proposal for a "significant nexus" test left lower courts to determine case by case whether wetlands were subject to federal jurisdiction. EPA and the Corps issued guidance in 2007 to help regulators, but these standards required additional paperwork that greatly complicated the process of reviewing permit applications.

"Right now the 404 program is probably in as much trouble as it's been in for years," says Yaich of Ducks Unlimited. "The guidance imposed much more difficult tasks in response to Justice Kennedy's opinion, and the system is bogged down. It's the worst of all worlds — we're dealing with applications very inefficiently, including many permits that are perfectly fine, and we're not protecting enough wetlands."

CURRENT SITUATION

Which Waters?

Legislators who are alarmed about wetlands losing federal protection have introduced bills in both houses of Congress to specify which waters are subject to regulation. "By focusing on the phrase 'navigable waters' in its *SWANCC* and *Rapanos* decisions, the Supreme Court muddied the jurisdictional understanding of the CWA," Rep. James L. Oberstar, D-Minn., chairman of the House Transportation Committee, said in introducing the House version of the Clean Water Restoration Act, in 2007.

Oberstar's legislation and its Senate counterpart seek to clarify the issue by replacing the term "navigable waters of the United States" in the Clean Water Act with "waters of the United States." This step, they argue, makes explicit that Congress intended to provide broad protection for water bodies — even non-navigable streams and isolated wetlands — the way the CWA was commonly interpreted prior to the *SWANCC* ruling in 2001.

Many state regulators, as well as environmental and sportsmen's groups, have endorsed the legislation. "Agency guidance issued in 2007 has left in doubt the protection of 'non-navigable' headwater, intermittent and ephemeral streams," a coalition of hunting and fishing groups wrote to Congress in early 2008. "These streams provide valuable habitat in their own right and are critical to downstream water quality and aquatic habitat. Without Clean Water Act protection, these streams are now vulnerable to sewage and industrial pollution as well as dredging and filling."

The concern about non-navigable waters was supported by a March 2008 memo from the EPA's chief enforcement official, who said the *Rapanos* opinion and EPA's guidance for applying the opinion had led the agency to downgrade or avoid pursuing about 500 potential violations of federal wetland law. The House Transportation Committee and the Oversight and Government Reform Committee both are investigating EPA's handling of wetland enforcement cases.

"This sudden reduction in enforcement activity will undermine the implementation of the Clean Water Act and adversely impact EPA's responsibility to protect the nation's waters," Oberstar and Henry A. Waxman, D-Calif., chairman of the Government Reform Committee, told the agency in July.[54]

But opponents, including trade associations, farm bureaus and conservative think tanks, argue that there was wide disagreement about the scope of the CWA before *SWANCC* and that the Clean Water Restoration Act would broaden federal water law far beyond what Congress originally intended. Under the CWRA, many critics say, any puddle or rain gutter could be subject to federal regulation. (*See "At Issue," p. 315.*)

"Expanding the jurisdictional definition could put the Corps in every ditch and grass waterway in Iowa," says Robinson of the Iowa Farm Bureau Federation. "Farmers understand Swampbuster and USDA's wetland protection programs, but bringing in the Corps will make it much more confusing."

The central problem is finding clear principles to justify which waters should be subject to federal versus state oversight. Science offers little help, since researchers say most wetlands are connected ecologically in various ways even if they are physically isolated, so ultimately the debate comes down to warring interpretations of how far Congress can regulate economic activities.

Should Congress pass the Clean Water Restoration Act?

YES Brett Hulsey
Supervisor, Dane County, Wis.

From testimony before U.S. House Transportation
and Infrastructure Committee, April 16, 2008

My county constituents place a high value on the quality of our lakes, streams and drinking water. They want clean, safe water for recreation — for swimming, boating and fishing. They understand that protecting drinking-water sources from pollution makes for better quality water coming out their taps and protects our health and safety at a lower cost. . . .

We have experienced five major floods costing local residents and the county $50 million since 1993. Our citizens want to prevent flood damage in the most environmentally protective and cost-effective ways possible to avoid the costs of repairing homes and infrastructure damaged by flooding. They also want to avoid the costs of cleaning up waters that have been needlessly polluted by others.

We saw the importance of protecting headwater streams and isolated wetlands during the Mississippi River floods of 1993, [which] killed more than 50 and cost at least $16 billion. Our county is at the headwaters of the Yahara River that flows to the Rock River and to the Mississippi, [which] drains 40 percent of the continental United States. After these floods, I worked with [the Federal Emergency Management Agency] and state agencies to purchase more than 10,000 homes and structures and move them out of harm's way. . . .

The [Environmental Protection Agency] estimates that some 20 million acres of wetlands — one-fifth of the remaining wetlands in the lower 48 states — could lose protections based on its interpretation of [the *SWANCC* and *Rapanos* decisions]. This would allow developers to drain wetlands, build new homes that would then be flooded and have to be purchased by local governments and taxpayers. There is a compelling public reason to protect these wetlands and headwater streams from development in the first place. . . .

Some have argued that the Clean Water Restoration Act somehow represents a vast expansion of Clean Water Act protections, but . . . this change in the law was before the *SWANCC* and *Rapanos* decisions. It would restore the law's scope, not expand it.

Some preposterous concerns are that this will mean roadside ditch and gutter regulation. The rain gutter on my house was not regulated by the Clean Water Act before these court decisions, and I am confident that it won't be regulated after the Clean Water Restoration Act is enacted. By the way, my gutters flow to a rain barrel and rain gardens, allowing the water to soak into the ground.

NO Linda C. Runbeck
President, American Property Coalition

From testimony before U.S. House Transportation
and Infrastructure Committee, April 16, 2008

H.R. 2421 has come in through the back door masquerading as a so-called simple clarification of the Clean Water Act when it is not. Rather, this bill has the potential to transform the Clean Water Act into a full-blown national land use control act. In it, federal agencies are given unlimited jurisdictional boundaries to intrude on every activity where Americans are involved with water and land. . . .

The bill would open the door to federal regulation of even insignificant, small depressions of mostly dry land, isolated wetlands, arroyos in the desert, sand flats, ditches and gutters, areas scarcely recognizable as "waters of the U.S." It doesn't end there: this bill would also, for the first time ever, authorize federal regulation of any "activities affecting water." And to be clear, "activities" might have a direct impact or an indirect impact on waters. So, regulated "activities" could take place on a hilltop or a mountaintop 25 miles from water, and the feds would still have the power to bring that activity to an immediate halt. . . .

The bill also offers a convenient scapegoat for Congress to shift the costs (and the blame) associated with water cleanup onto property owners and local governments. At the same time, Congress fails to provide them any meaningful measuring stick, as the bill contains no national water-quality standards. . . . Absent any . . . cost-benefit analyses or effective assessment mechanisms, this bill has the potential to exhaust the resources of individuals and local governments. Finally, after intruding on the freedoms and pocketbooks of millions of Americans, this bill can provide us no assurance that the nation's water quality will be improved. . . .

In conclusion, given the local nature of ditches, gutters, isolated wetlands, small depressions in fields and prairie potholes, the American people deserve something better than a centralized national land use bill imposed on an unsuspecting American public. Congress should take the time to get it right. The right way would be to: 1) establish goals; 2) authorize completion of a comprehensive assessment of the quality of the nation's waters; 3) establish priorities, costs and a realistic timetable for achieving water quality goals; 4) complete the task of bringing the remaining point sources into compliance and 5) allow local governments and local citizens the opportunity to develop local and regional alternatives that will ensure the broadest public support in order to achieve the desired results.

The loss of wetlands habitat where salmon can spawn and rear their young has contributed to the collapse of the West Coast commercial salmon fishery, the Department of Commerce said recently. Historically low numbers of salmon are returning from the ocean to spawn, according to scientists.

"Congress has to say clearly and directly how far it intends to push federal jurisdiction under the Commerce Clause," says Vermont Law School's Parenteau. "Otherwise, we'll never have an end to these arguments."

Louisiana Sinking

Louisiana's coastal marshes are the most threatened wetlands in the United States. Since the 1930s, the state has lost more than 1.2 million acres (1,900 square miles) of coastal habitat due to storms, flood control programs and industrial development. Dams and levees prevent the Mississippi River from flooding and depositing sediments on Louisiana's coastal plain. Thousands of miles of barge access canals, excavated by companies drilling offshore for oil and gas, have sliced through coastal marshes and created channels for saltwater intrusion from the Gulf of Mexico.

About 13 square miles of Louisiana's coastline become open water each year, and in 2005 Hurricanes Katrina and Rita accelerated the process, destroying 240 square miles of wetlands. Federal and state agencies have spent almost $800 million since 1990 on coastal restoration projects, such as reintroducing freshwater to declining marshes, protecting shorelines from erosion and restoring barrier islands.[55] But slowing wetland losses will require much larger-scale efforts.

Coastal scientists say that Katrina and Rita have pushed the situation to a crisis point, and that if the state does not start restoring wetlands faster than it loses them — today five square miles are lost for every one created — within 10 years much of the state's coastline will be permanently gone. Without wetlands to soak up flood waters and help buffer coastal areas, future storms are likely to do even worse damage along the Gulf Coast than recent hurricanes.

"People think we still have 20, 30, 40 years left to get this done. They're not even close," said Kerry St. Pe, director of the Barataria-Terrebonne National Estuary Program. "If we aren't building land I can walk on inside of 10 years, we'll be moving communities."[56]

Scientists began warning in the 1970s that levees and canals were damaging Louisiana's coastline. In 1989 the state created a trust fund with revenues from oil and gas development to pay for restoration projects, and in 1990 Congress authorized federal funding and created a task force to manage the effort. But fishermen, developers and oil and gas companies objected to many projects that hurt their individual economic interests. For example, the state had to fight a two-year legal battle with oyster fishermen who opposed freshwater diversion projects. Ironically, these measures — which siphoned freshwater and sediment from the Mississippi River to rebuild coastal marshes — made many oyster beds more productive.[57]

In 2002 Louisiana and the Corps presented the Bush administration with a 30-year, $14 billion master plan for coastal restoration. The White House cut the plan back to less than $2 billion over a decade. Congress was considering an initial $1.1 billion proposal when hurricanes Rita and Katrina struck in 2005.

The National Research Council, which was then reviewing the scaled-back Louisiana coastal plan, reported in 2006 that while most pieces of the blueprint were sound, a broader plan was needed that showed how the pieces fit together and laid a base for further work. The study also called for better communication with the public about how various projects would affect land use, plus a program to compensate families that had to be moved during restoration.[58]

In late 2007 Congress passed its first water projects authorization bill in eight years, overriding a veto by President Bush, who described the $23 billion legislation as fiscally irresponsible. The bill provided $1.9 billion for Louisiana coastal restoration projects, plus nearly $1 billion for hurricane protection measures. It also created yet another task force to recommend strategies for conserving and restoring the state's coastal ecosystems.[59]

Two more hurricanes, Gustav and Ike, walloped the Gulf Coast in September 2008, causing such massive crop losses from flooding that the state sought $700 million in federal disaster aid specifically for farmers.[60]

"Louisiana sugarcane growers have received agricultural disaster assistance twice over our more than 200 years of production," farmer Wallace Ellender IV told the Senate Agriculture Committee. "The fact that both of those assistance packages were made necessary by intense hurricanes in this decade is a direct result of rampant coastal erosion. Unless we invest in energetic coastal restoration efforts soon, my farm may be a beachfront property in a few short years before slipping quietly beneath the waves."[61]

Wetter or Dryer?

Global climate change is a wild card for wetlands as temperatures rise and U.S. leaders look for ways to reduce atmospheric concentrations of carbon dioxide, the main greenhouse gas (GHG) generated as a result of human activities. GHGs contribute to global warming by trapping heat in the atmosphere and warming Earth's surface. Wetlands are a potential solution, because they absorb large quantities of carbon in plant matter and soils. But climate change could also harm wetlands, either by flooding them or drying them out.[62] Before wetlands can become a solution to climate change, scientists say, we need to know more about how they will be affected by rising temperatures.

Some national and regional policies for reducing GHG emissions allow emitters to "offset," or compensate for, the GHGs they release by paying to grow forests that will pull carbon out of the air. Some wetland advocates would like to see wetlands receive similar treatment. Under such schemes, an electricity producer might receive credit for restoring a specific number of wetland acres where plants and soils would absorb atmospheric carbon to offset some emissions from the company's coal- or gas-fired power plants. The system would be like a mitigation bank, except that instead of selling credits for wetland restoration the offset provider would sell credits for storing carbon.

"Wetlands are one of the better sequestration sources out there. They're equal to or better than forests," says Myers of People for Puget Sound. His organization is identifying

local marshes that were diked and drained for agriculture, where selling carbon sequestration credits could accelerate restoration work and provide additional funding.

But wetland chemistry is complicated. While wetlands store large quantities of carbon, they also emit other greenhouse gases as bacteria break down organic material, and warming may speed these processes up. And as temperatures rise, climate models predict that in many areas rain will fall harder and faster over shorter time periods, so many ecosystems will be subject to extreme wet and dry periods.

More drought could make wetlands less useful as carbon sinks, says U.S. Geological Survey ecologist Greg Noe. "Carbon is very sensitive to drying in wetlands," Noe observes. "For example, peat lands in the Everglades have lost 10 feet of soil over the past 50 years, because as those areas became dryer the soil was exposed to oxygen that sped up the decomposition process."

Overall, however, wetlands are worth studying as carbon sinks, Noe says. "They're not perfect systems because they're very sensitive to changes in hydrology, but they do show a lot of promise," he says. "River systems are one option. There's lots of carbon in them, and it might be fairly easy to restore them — for example, by breaching levees to recreate marshes."

OUTLOOK
Valuing Wetlands

For the past 30 years national policy has declared that wetlands are valuable, but it is still hard to protect individual wetlands when they impede construction projects with dollar values attached.

"We need tools for factoring the value of ecological services into local economies so we can put our money where our mouths are," says the Florida Audubon Society's Lauritsen. "Until people understand the real values that wetlands provide, protecting them will be like putting our fingers in a dike."

Regions that are subject to major floods have the most to gain from restoring wetlands, and some leaders are pressing for action. After Hurricanes Gustav and Ike hit Louisiana in September, Republican Gov. Bobby Jindal said he would draw on state oil and gas revenues for coastal restoration.[63] And after heavy rains caused severe flooding across the Midwest in June, killing 24 people and forcing as many as 40,000 from their homes, some observers argued that more wetlands, not higher levees, were the right strategy for next time.

"No matter how finely tuned our engineering is, Mother Nature did a better job," argued an editorial in Illinois. "The recent floods should prompt a serious push to restore Illinois' lost wetlands — which also soak up pollution — as an alternative to more man-made steel and sand barriers."[64]

Other regions also see wetlands as long-term investments. Federal and state agencies are moving forward with a 50-year program to turn 15,000 acres of former industrial salt ponds around south San Francisco Bay back into tidal marsh. Supporters say the nearly $1 billion project will produce cleaner water, more habitat for wildlife and better flood protection for low-lying, bayside cities like San Jose. "The bay is precious, and tidal wetlands will help make it more resilient," wrote Sen. Dianne Feinstein, D-Calif.[65]

Polls show that Americans support policies to keep rivers, lakes and streams clean and ensure that drinking water is safe. But conservationists will have to convince Americans that all wetlands are valuable, from the Everglades to vernal pools in their own back yards.

"The public wants to protect wetlands, but Americans think about actually wet land, not drainage ditches that hardly ever hold water," says the Mackinac Institute's Harding.

NOTES

1. "Vernal Pool Information," www.massnature.com.

2. T. E. Dahl, "Status and Trends of Wetlands in the Coterminous United States 1998 to 2004," U.S. Fish and Wildlife Service, 2006, p. 57.

3. For background see Mary H. Cooper, "Water Quality," *CQ Researcher*, Nov. 24, 2000, pp. 953-976.

4. David Sunding and David Zilberman, "The Economics of Environmental Regulation by Licensing: An Assessment of Recent Changes to the Wetlands Permitting Process," *Natural Resources Journal*, vol. 42 (2002), pp. 73-76.

5. Testimony of Stephen E. Sandherr, Associated General Contractors of America, before the House Transportation and Infrastructure Committee, July 19, 2007, p. 3.

6. *Ibid.*

7. Joy B. Zedler and Suzanne Kercher, "Wetland Resources: Status, Trends, Ecosystem Services, and Restorability," *Annual Review of Environment and Resources*, vol. 30 (2005), p. 56.

8. Erik Stokstad, "Louisiana's Wetlands Struggle for Survival," *Science*, Nov. 25, 2005, p. 1266. For estimated damages from Katrina, see Axel Graumann, *et al.*, "Hurricane Katrina: A Climatological Perspective," U.S. Department of Commerce, National Oceanographic and Atmospheric Administration, updated August 2006.

9. Louisiana Coastal Protection and Restoration Authority, *Integrated Ecosystem Restoration and Hurricane Protection: Louisiana's Comprehensive Master Plan for a Sustainable Coast* (2007), www.lacpra.org.

10. www.mitigationbanking.org.

11. The CWA was originally titled the Federal Water Pollution Control Act when it was passed in 1972, but became known as the Clean Water Act after it was amended in 1977.

12. *NRDC v. Calloway*, 392 F. Supp. 685 (D.D.C. 1975).

13. 33 C.F.R., section 328.3(a)(iii).

14. 474 U.S. 121 (1985).

15. 531 U.S. 159 (2001).

16. Felicity Barringer, "In Reversal, E.P.A. Won't Narrow Wetlands Protection," *The New York Times*, Dec. 17, 2003, p. A35.

17. 126 S. Ct. 2208 (2006).

18. Dahl, *op. cit.*, p. 46.

19. "Conserving America's Wetlands 2008: Four Years of Partnering Resulted in Accomplishing the President's Goal," Council on Environmental Quality, April 2008.

20. Matthew Waite and Craig Pittman, "Satellite Photographs Show Losses," *St. Petersburg Times*, May 22, 2005, p. 11A; Craig Pittman and Matthew Waite, "They Won't Say No," *St. Petersburg Times*, May 22, 2005, p 1A.

21. For background see David Hosansky, "Reforming the Corps," *CQ Researcher*, May 30, 2003, pp. 497-520.

22. Michael Grunwald, "A Green Day for Bush," *Time*, Feb. 2, 2008; Chris Talbot, "EPA Vetoes Large Flood-Control Plan," The Associated Press, Sept. 3, 2008.

23. Florida Department of Environmental Protection, "Kissimmee River Restoration Continues," June 17, 2005; "Working With Nature: Corps Restoration Projects Benefit People, Communities, and Wildlife," Corps Reform Network, undated, www.corpsreform .org/sitepages/downloads/ProjectsInTheField-Reports/ CRN-pfFS-Pjcts_Restoration.pdf.

24. National Research Council, *New Directions in Water Resources Planning for the U.S. Army Corps of Engineers* (1999), p. 7; "Prioritizing America's Water Resources Investments," National Academy of Public Administration, pp. 115-116.

25. National Academy of Public Administration, *op. cit.*, p. 115. For a study urging the Corps to do more planning in a watershed context, see National Research Council, *Compensating for Wetland Losses Under the Clean Water Act*, 2001.

26. For details see "Campaigns: Florida Panther," Public Employees for Environmental Responsibility, www .peer.org/campaigns/whistleblower/panther/index.php.

27. Ted Williams, "Bait and Switch," *Audubon*, March-April 2008.

28. "Prairie Pothole Region: At the Current Pace of Acquisitions, the U.S. Fish and Wildlife Service Is Unlikely to Achieve Its Habitat Protection Goals for Migratory Birds," U.S. Government Accountability Office, GAO-07-1093, Sept. 2007.

29. For background on biofuels, see Adriel Bettelheim, "Biofuels Boom," *CQ Researcher*, Sept. 29, 2006, pp. 793-816 and Jennifer Weeks, "Buying Green," *CQ Researcher*, Feb. 29, 2008, pp. 193-216.

30. "Short-Term Energy Outlook," U.S. Energy Information Administration, Sept. 9, 2008.

31. Mary Clare Jalonick, "USDA Urges Farmers to Keep Setting Aside Land," The Associated Press, July 29, 2008.

32. "DU Says CRP Losses Astounding," Ducks Unlimited, Jan. 4, 2008, www.ducks.org/news/1456/ DUsaysCRPlossesastou.html.

33. National Research Council, *op. cit.*, pp. 113-121.

34. U.S. Environmental Protection Agency, "Mitigation Banking Factsheet," updated April 18, 2008, www .epa.gov/owow/wetlands/facts/fact16.html.

35. James Salzman and J. B. Ruhl, " 'No Net-Loss' — Instrument Choice in Wetlands Protection," Duke Law School, Science, Technology and Innovation Research Paper Series, Sept. 2005, p. 9; Jessica Wilkinson and Jared Thompson, "2005 Status Report on Compensatory Mitigation in the United States," Environmental Law Institute, 2005, p. 28.

36. National Research Council, *op. cit.*, 2001, pp. 82-92.

37. "Iowa Wetland Mitigation Bank, Inc.," www.ifbf .org/newsissues/environment/Brochure1106.pdf.

38. "Status and Trends of Wetlands in the Coterminous United States 1998 to 2004," U.S. Fish and Wildlife Service, 2005, pp. 44, 74-76.

39. "A Century of Wetland Exploitation," U.S. Geological Survey, Northern Prairie Wildlife Research Center, Aug. 3, 2006.

40. Laura Ingalls Wilder, *By the Shores of Silver Lake* (1971), p. 77.

41. Hosansky, *op. cit.*

42. Alison Carney Brown, "Miles of Tiles," *Chicago Wilderness Magazine*, Spring 2004.

43. William Reffalt, untitled background article for U.S. Fish & Wildlife Service, www.fws.gov/refuges/ centennial/pdf2/pelicanIsland_reffalt.pdf.

44. Marjorie Stoneman Douglas, *The Everglades: River of Grass, 60th anniversary edition* (2007), p. 349.

45. www.fws.gov/duckstamps/Info/Stamps/stampinfo. htm.

46. John Hart, *San Francisco Bay: Portrait of an Estuary* (2003), pp. 33-36.

47. Executive Order 11990, Protection of Wetlands, May 24, 1977, www.epa.gov/owow/wetlands/regs/ eo11990.html.

48. Joseph Alper, "War Over the Wetlands: Ecologists v. the White House," *Science*, Aug. 21, 1992; John H. Cushman Jr., "Quayle, in Last Push for Landowners, Seeks to Relax Wetland Protections," *The New York Times*, Nov. 12, 1992, p. A16.

49. For background see Kenneth Jost, "Property Rights," *CQ Researcher*, June 16, 1995, pp. 513-536. For background on the "takings" ruling, Kenneth Jost, "Hawaii Law Tests 'Regulatory Takings' Doctrine," in "Property Rights," *CQ Researcher*, March 4, 2005, pp. 197-220.

50. *Florida Rock Industries v. United States*, 791 F. 2d 893 (1986), 45 Fed. Cl. 21 (1999); *Loveladies Harbor Inc. v. United States*, 21 Cl.Ct. 153 (1990), 28 F. 3d 1171 (1994).

51. *Lucas v. South Carolina Coastal Council*, 505 US 193 (1992).

52. *Solid Waste Agency of Northern Cook County v. United States Army Corps of Engineers, et al.*, 531 U.S. 159 (2001).

53. Julie M. Sibbing, "Nowhere Near No-Net-Loss," National Wildlife Federation, www.nwf.org/wildlife/pdfs/NowhereNearNoNetLoss.pdf; James Salzman and J.B. Ruhl, "'No Net-Loss' — Instrument of Choice in Wetlands Protection," Duke Law School Science, Technology and Innovation Research Paper Series, Sept. 1, 2005.

54. "Internal EPA Document Shows 500 Enforcement Cases Adversely Affected," U.S. House of Representatives, Committee on Oversight and Government Reform, July 7, 2008, http://oversight.house.gov/story.asp?ID=2065.

55. "Coastal Wetlands: Lessons Learned From Past Efforts in Louisiana Could Help Guide Future Restoration and Protection," U.S. Government Accountability Office, GAO-08-130, Dec. 2007.

56. Bob Marshall, "Last Chance: The Fight to Save a Disappearing Coast," *New Orleans Times-Picayune*, March 4, 2007, p. 1.

57. Jeffrey Meitrodt and Aaron Kuriloff, "Oyster Farmers Initially Backed Project," *New Orleans Times-Picayune*, May 4, 2003, p. 21; Bob Marshall and Mark Schliefstein, "Losing Ground," *New Orleans Times-Picayune*, March 5, 2007, p. 1.

58. "Drawing Louisiana's New Map: Addressing Land Loss in Coastal Louisiana," National Research Council, 2006, pp. 3-12.

59. Bruce Alpert, "Congress Overrides Bush Water Bill Veto," *New Orleans Times-Picayune*, Nov. 8, 2007, p. 2.

60. Jonathan Tilove, "Officials Tell Senate Farmers Need Aid," *New Orleans Times-Picayune*, Sept. 25, 2008, p. 11.

61. Testimony before the Senate Agriculture Committee, Sept. 24, 2008, p. 6.

62. For background see "Wetlands and Global Climate Change," Association of State Wetland Managers, www.aswm.org/science/climate_change/climate_change.htm.

63. "Jindal Calls for Action on Coastal Restoration," WWLTV.com, Sept. 16, 2008.

64. "Take Long View in Assessing Flood Control," *The State Journal-Register*, July 23, 2008, p. 4.

65. Dianne Feinstein, "Bay Restoration at an Exciting Point," *San Jose Mercury News*, Dec. 24, 2007.

BIBLIOGRAPHY

Books

Ernst, Howard R., *Chesapeake Bay Blues: Science, Politics, and the Struggle to Save the Bay, Rowman & Littlefield*, 2003.
A professor of political science at the U.S. Naval Academy shows how development and pollution devastated the nation's largest estuary and how politics slowed clean-up efforts.

Grunwald, Michael, *The Swamp: The Everglades, Florida, and the Politics of Paradise, Simon & Schuster*, 2006.
A *Time* correspondent, who has written extensively about the U.S. Army Corps of Engineers and water development recounts the environmental history of the Everglades and dissects Floridians' relationship with their environment.

Save San Francisco Bay, *Protecting Local Wetlands: A Toolbox For Your Community, Save the Bay*, 2000.
Although it focuses on California, this handbook provides a thorough overview of federal and state controls,

approaches to local wetland regulation and ways tax incentives and other measures can help foster healthy wetlands nationwide.

Articles

"Last Chance: The Fight to Save a Disappearing Coast," *New Orleans Times-Picayune* and Nola.com, March 4-6, 2007, www.nola.com/speced/lastchance/.
A three-part special series warns that many scientists believe the Gulf of Mexico could reach New Orleans' suburbs within a decade unless drastic action is taken to preserve Louisiana's remaining coastal marshes.

Barringer, Felicity, "Death Looms for a Flood-Control Project," *The New York Times*, April 9, 2008, p. A14.
In an unusual exercise of its veto power, the Environmental Protection Agency (EPA) is preparing to veto the Yazoo Pumps, a controversial flood-control project in southern Mississippi that would destroy or damage at least 67,000 acres of wetlands.

Cave, Damien, "Harsh Review of Restoration in Everglades," *The New York Times*, Sept. 30, 2008, p. A18.
A National Research Council report said efforts to rescue the Everglades have failed because of bureaucratic delays, funding shortages and overdevelopment.

Dahl, Thomas, "Beyond No Net Loss: Imagery Aids Wetland Conservation," *Geoworld*, September 2005.
The Fish and Wildlife Service is using high-resolution satellite images and computerized mapping to keep better track of wetland status and trends.

Kay, Jane, "50-Year Plan for Turning South Bay Salt Ponds to Tidal Wetlands," *San Francisco Chronicle*, Dec. 12, 2007, p. A1.
In the largest wetlands restoration on the West Coast, state and federal agencies are launching a 50-year effort to turn salt ponds around San Francisco Bay back into healthy tidal marshes.

Pittman, Craig, and Matthew Waite, "Vanishing Wetlands," *The St. Petersburg Times*, 2005-2006, www.sptimes.com/2006/webspecials06/wetlands/.
An award-winning multi-part investigation finds that faulty permitting and lax oversight are major causes of ongoing wetland losses in Florida.

Tibetts, John H., "Rising Tide: Will Climate Change Drown Coastal Wetlands?" *Coastal Heritage*, winter 2007.
Rising sea levels are already forcing some salt marshes to migrate inland, exposing communities to increased flooding, and climate change is likely to accelerate these effects.

Reports and Studies

"Biodiversity Values of Geographically Isolated Wetlands in the United States," *Natureserve*, Dec. 1, 2005, www.natureserve.org/publications/isolatedwetlands.jsp.
An EPA-funded study by a private conservation organization finds that geographically isolated U.S. wetlands support 86 species of endangered or threatened animals and plants, half of which need isolated wetland habitat to survive.

"Drawing Louisiana's New Map: Addressing Land Loss in Coastal Louisiana," *National Research Council*, 2006.
A peer-reviewed study of coastal restoration efforts proposed by the Corps of Engineers and the state of Louisiana finds that a broader and more integrated plan is needed.

"Prairie Pothole Region: At the Current Pace of Acquisitions, the U.S. Fish and Wildlife Service Is Unlikely to Achieve Its Habitat Protection Goals for Migratory Birds," *U.S. Government Accountability Office*, 2007.
Since 1959, the agency has protected about 3 million acres in the vast region in the northern Great Plains, but it needs to move faster to protect all of the wetlands and grasslands that it has identified as important habitat for migratory birds.

Dahl, T.E., *Status and Trends of Wetlands in the Coterminous United States 1998 to 2004*, U.S. Department of the Interior, Fish and Wildlife Service, 2005.
The most recent federal wetlands inventory finds that the U.S. is now achieving small, annual, net gains in wetlands but that most of the increase is in freshwater ponds.

For More Information

Associated General Contractors of America, 2300 Wilson Blvd., Suite 400, Arlington, VA 22201; (703) 548-3118; www.agc.org. The main trade association for the U.S. commercial construction industry, including highway and municipal projects.

Association of State Wetland Managers, 2 Basin Road, Windham, ME 04062; (207) 892-3399; www.aswm.org. Works to improve wetland regulation and management; open to anyone involved with wetland resources.

Audubon of Florida, 444 Brickell Ave., Suite 850, Miami, FL 33131; (305) 371-6399; www.audubonofflorida.org. State chapter of the National Audubon Society that works to protect and restore ecosystems statewide; operates Corkscrew Swamp Wildlife Sanctuary in Naples, Fla.

Ducks Unlimited, One Waterfowl Way, Memphis, TN 38120; (901) 758-3825; www.ducks.org. A conservation group founded by sportsmen in 1937, during the Dust Bowl, to protect wetlands and other places where waterfowl breed or migrate.

Iowa Farm Bureau Federation, 5400 University Ave., West Des Moines, IA 50266; (515) 225-5400; www.iowafarmbureau.com. Advocates for farmers, farm families and Iowa's rural heritage.

Mackinac Center for Public Policy, 140 West Main St., P.O. Box 568, Midland, MI 48640; (989) 631-0900; www.mackinac.org. A think tank advocating market-oriented solutions to public policy problems in Michigan.

People for Puget Sound, 911 Western Ave., Suite 580, Seattle, WA 58104; (206) 382-7007; www.pugetsound.org. A nonprofit working to protect and restore lands and waters around Puget Sound.

U.S. Army Corps of Engineers, 441 G St., N.W., Washington, DC 20314; (202) 761-0010; www.hq.usace.army.mil. World's largest public engineering, design and construction management agency builds and operates water projects nationwide.

14

Looming Water Crisis

Is the World Running Out of Water?

Peter Behr

AFP/Getty Images/Simon Maina

Kenyan children play in raw sewage in Kibera, Nairobi's largest slum. Each year 1.8 million children — 5,000 a day — die from waterborne illnesses due to a lack of access to sanitation and clean water.

From *CQ Global Researcher*, February 2008.

As 2007 came to a close, the steady drumbeat of headlines about China's worst drought in a half-century affirmed Prime Minister Wen Jiabao's earlier warning that the crisis threatens "the survival of the Chinese nation."[1]

The alarming developments included:

- The drying up of 133 reservoirs in burgeoning Guangdong Province, leaving a quarter of a million people facing water shortages.[2]
- The lowest levels since 1866 on portions of the Yangtze River, restricting barge and ship traffic and reducing hydroelectric output on China's largest river, even as pollution from 9,000 industrial plants along its course jeopardizes drinking water supplies.[3]
- Near-record low levels in vast Lake Poyang, restricting water supplies for 100,000 people.[4]

"My house used to be by the side of the lake," villager Yu Wenchang told the Xinhua News Agency. "Now I have to go over a dozen kilometers away to get to the lake water."[5]

Similar woes are being reported across the globe, as one of the worst decades of drought on record afflicts rich and poor nations alike. While scientists hedge their conclusions about whether long-term climate change is causing the dry spell, many warn that Earth's gradual warming trend unquestionably poses a growing threat to water supplies and food production in arid regions. Already, population growth and economic expansion are straining water supplies in many places, particularly in the poorest nations. But despite an unending series of

Serious Shortages Projected for Many Regions

Water shortages are expected to afflict much of the Earth by 2025, as growing populations use vastly more water for daily life and farming. Areas likely to be hardest hit include China, Western Europe, the United States, Mexico and a wide swath of the globe's midsection from India to North Africa. In the most severe cases, humans are expected to use up to 40 percent of the available water, compared with the current average withdrawal, or use, rate of 10 percent.

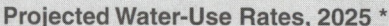

Projected Water-Use Rates, 2025 *

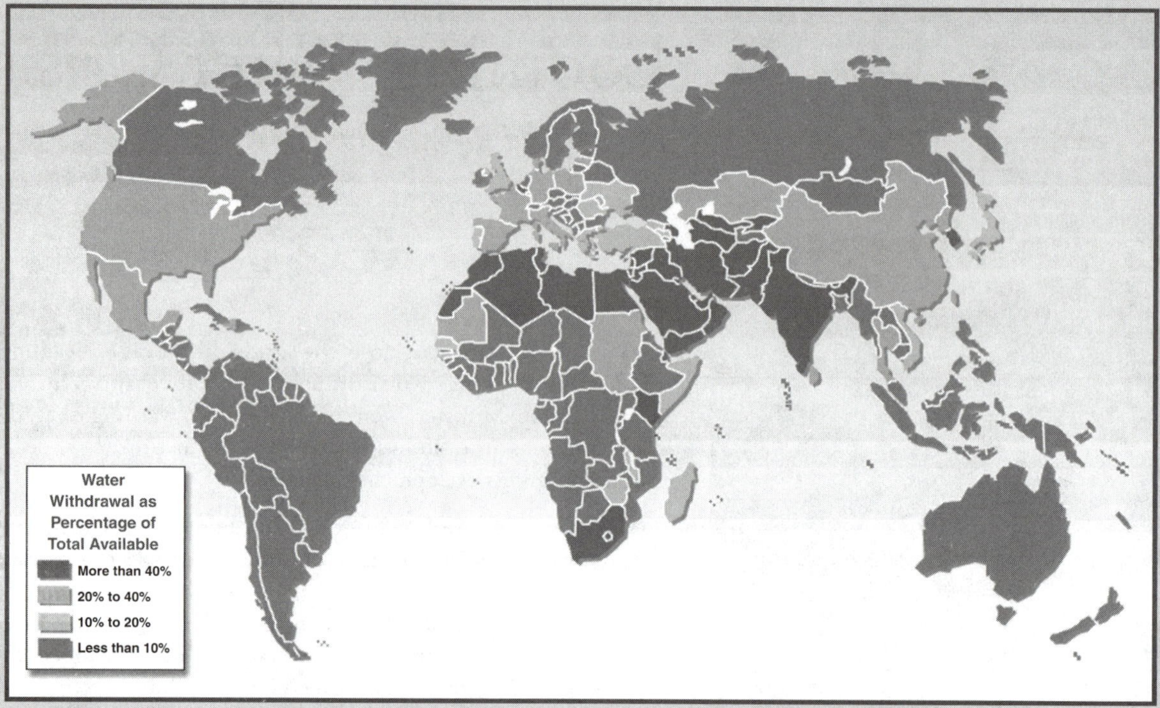

Water Withdrawal as Percentage of Total Available

- More than 40%
- 20% to 40%
- 10% to 20%
- Less than 10%

* Based on data from 1996-2000

Source: World Meteorological Organisation, Global Environment Outlook, U.N. Environment Programme, Earthscan, www.unep.org/dewa/assessments/ecosystems/water/vitalwater/21.htm#21b

international water conferences — attended by thousands of experts — no consensus has emerged on how to make adequate clean water available to all people in affordable, environmentally sustainable ways.[6]

A fifth of the world's population — 1.2 billion people — live in areas experiencing "physical water scarcity," or insufficient supplies for everyone's demands, according to a 2006 study by the International Water Management Institute that draws on the work of 700 scientists and experts. Another 1 billion face "economic scarcity," in which "human capacity or financial resources" cannot provide adequate water, the report found.[7]

While drought and expanding populations visibly affect the world's lakes and rivers, a less-visible problem also threatens water supplies. Accelerated pumping of groundwater for irrigation is depleting underground aquifers faster than they can be refreshed in densely populated areas of North China, India and Mexico. And land and water resources there and beyond are being degraded through erosion, pollution, salination, nutrient depletion and seawater intrusion, according to the institute.

A United Nations task force on water predicted that by 2025, 3 billion people will face "water stress" conditions, lacking enough water to meet all human and environmental needs.[8] By that time, there will be 63 major river basins with populations of at least 10 million, of which 47 are either already water-stressed, will become stressed or will experience a significant deterioration in water supply, according to a separate study by the World Resources Institute incorporating the U.N. data.[9] (*See map, p. 324.*)*

As water depletion accelerates, drought is undermining nature's capacity to replenish this essential resource, punishing the planet's midsection — from eastern Australia and northern China through the Middle East and sub-Saharan Africa to the U.S. Sun Belt, the Great Plains and northern Mexico.

In the United States, chronic alarms over depleted water resources in the Southwestern states have spread to the Southeast. The water level in giant Lake Sidney Lanier outside Atlanta has dropped about a dozen feet in this decade, causing an intense struggle among Georgia and neighboring Alabama and Florida over rights to the lake's diminished flows.[10]

And drought conditions worldwide are likely to worsen as the effects of climate change are felt, many scientists warn.[11] Climate change is expected to expand and intensify drought in traditionally dry regions and disrupt water flows from the world's mountain snowcaps and glaciers.

Finally, a new threat to global water supplies has emerged: terrorism. "The chance that terrorists will strike at water systems is real," said Peter H. Gleick, president of the Pacific Institute for Studies in Development, Environment and Security in Oakland, Calif.[12] Modern public water systems are designed to protect users from biological agents and toxins, but deliberate contamination by terrorists could kill or sicken thousands, he said. Since the Sept. 11, 2001, terrorist attacks most major U.S. cities have sent the federal government confidential reports on the vulnerability of local water supplies, and the Environmental Protection Agency's (EPA) Water Sentinel Initiative is designing a water-contamination warning system.[13]

Perhaps the grimmest long-range prediction on water availability was issued by the Met Office Hadley Centre for Climate Prediction and Research in London. Using

---

* "Water stress" occurs when less than 1,700 cubic meters (448,000 gallons) per person of new fresh water is available annually from rainfall or aquifers for human use, making populations vulnerable to frequent interruptions in water supply.

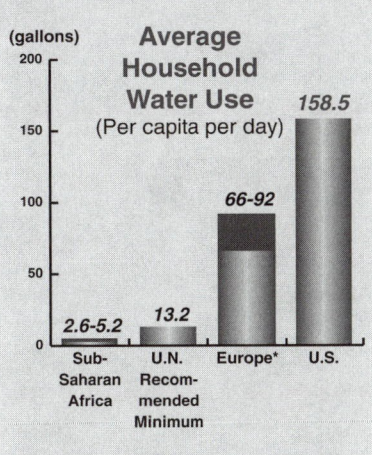

World Water Consumption Varies

The average American uses nearly 160 gallons of water per day for drinking, cooking, bathing and sanitation — more than any other nationality and more than twice the amount used by many Europeans. People in sub-Saharan Africa use only about a quarter of the 13 gallons the United Nations sets as a minimum basic standard.

Average Household Water Use
(Per capita per day)

(gallons)

Region	Gallons
Sub-Saharan Africa	2.6-5.2
U.N. Recommended Minimum	13.2
Europe*	66-92
U.S.	158.5

* Consumption among European countries ranges from 66-92 gallons
Source: World Water Council

---

supercomputer modeling, the center projected that if current trends continue, by this century's end drought will have spread across half the Earth's land surface due to climate change, threatening millions of lives. Moreover, "extreme drought" — which makes traditional agriculture virtually impossible — will affect about a third of the planet, according to the group's November 2006 report.

"Even though (globally) total rainfall will increase as the climate warms, the proportion of land in drought is projected to rise throughout the 21st century," the report said.[14]

"There's almost no aspect of life in the developing countries that these predictions don't undermine — the ability to grow food, the ability to have a safe sanitation system, the availability of water," said Andrew Simms, policy director of the liberal London-based New Economics Foundation.[15] The consequences will be most

Poorest Lag Far Behind in Access

Although progress has been made since 1990, only 37 percent of the residents in sub-Saharan Africa and South Asia had access to sanitation services in 2004. Sub-Saharan Africa lags behind the rest of the world in access to reliable sources of clean water. Meanwhile, more than 90 percent of those living in the industrialized countries, Central and Eastern Europe, Latin America, the Caribbean and the former Soviet republics had access to water in 2004.

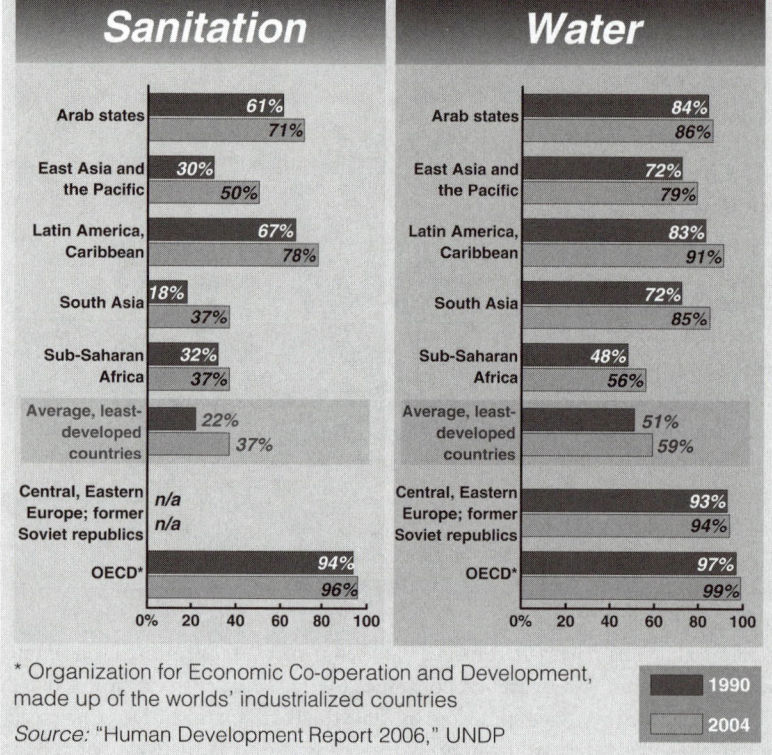

Percentage of Population with Access to:
(1990-2004)

Sanitation

Region	1990	2004
Arab states	61%	71%
East Asia and the Pacific	30%	50%
Latin America, Caribbean	67%	78%
South Asia	18%	37%
Sub-Saharan Africa	32%	37%
Average, least-developed countries	22%	37%
Central, Eastern Europe; former Soviet republics	n/a	n/a
OECD*	94%	96%

Water

Region	1990	2004
Arab states	84%	86%
East Asia and the Pacific	72%	79%
Latin America, Caribbean	83%	91%
South Asia	72%	85%
Sub-Saharan Africa	48%	56%
Average, least-developed countries	51%	59%
Central, Eastern Europe; former Soviet republics	93%	94%
OECD*	97%	99%

* Organization for Economic Co-operation and Development, made up of the worlds' industrialized countries

Source: "Human Development Report 2006," UNDP

to five gallons per person used by the typical person in sub-Saharan Africa. (*See graph, p. 325.*)[16]

But the lack of clean water is not only inconvenient. It can also be deadly. Each year 1.8 million children — 5,000 per day — die from waterborne illnesses such as diarrhea, according to the United Nations. "That's equivalent to 12 full jumbo jets crashing every day," said U.N. water expert Brian Appleton. "If 12 full jumbo jets were crashing every day, the world would want to do something about it — they would want to find out why it was happening."[17]

Policymakers are trying various ways to solve the global water challenge, including contracting with private firms to operate urban water and sanitary systems, adopting new conservation technologies, enacting multination pacts to manage regional watersheds and increasing funds for water projects in the world's poorest regions. Water experts advocate "environmental flow" policies — the release of enough water from dams to sustain the environment of rivers, wetlands and underground aquifers.[18]

And their efforts seem to be paying off — at least in some areas. Between 1990 and 2002, more than 1 billion people in the developing world gained access to fresh water and basic sanitation. But because of population growth, the total number of people still lacking safe water remained more than a billion, and there was no change in the number lacking basic sanitation.[19]

In 2003, the U.N. General Assembly designated the period from 2005 to 2015 as the International Decade for Action on "Water for Life." And the U.N.'s new Millennium Development Goals include a campaign to cut in half by 2015 the proportion of people without sustainable access to safe drinking water and basic

dire for the planet's poorest inhabitants, he added. "For hundreds of millions of people for whom getting through the day is already a struggle, this is going to push them over the precipice."

Access to safe, fresh water separates the well-off — who can treat water as if it were air — from the world's poorest, who hoard it like gold. In the United States, the average consumer uses nearly 160 gallons of water per day, summoned by the twist of a faucet. In much of Africa, women often trudge for hours to and from wells, carrying the two

sanitation — at a cost of more than $10 billion per year.[20] Currently, governments and international agencies like the U.N. and World Bank provide only $4 billion a year in aid for water and sanitation projects.[21]

"We will see these issues play out silently: dry rivers, dead deltas, destocked fisheries, depleted springs and wells," wrote Margaret Carley-Carlson, chairwoman of the Global Water Partnership in Stockholm, and M. S. Swaminathan, president of the Pugwash Conferences on Science and World Affairs in Chennai, India.[22] "We will also see famine; increased and sometimes violent competition for water, especially within states; more migration; and environmental devastation with fires, dust, and new plagues and blights."

Averting that future will require fundamental changes in governmental policies and human practices governing the use, conservation and value of water, experts agree.

As water experts and policymakers discuss how to conserve and protect future water supplies, here are some of the questions they are debating:

Are we running out of water?

Amid the growing alarm about water shortages, water expert Frank Rijsberman offers a contrarian perspective. "The world is far from running out of water," he says. "There is land and human resources and water enough to grow food and provide drinking water for everyone."[23]

The issue is how efficiently water is used, says Rijsberman, former director of the International Water Management Institute in Colombo, Sri Lanka. Every year, about 110,000 cubic kilometers* of rain falls on Earth's surface, of which humans withdraw just over 3 percent — about 3,700 cubic kilometers — from rivers and groundwater to use in cities, industries and farming. About 40,000 cubic kilometers flows into rivers and is absorbed into groundwater, and the rest evaporates.

Much of the water used by humans is returned to watersheds as wastewater, farm runoff or discharges from energy and industrial plants, with only a small fraction used for drinking and cooking.[24] Irrigation claims 70 percent of total water withdrawals, 22 percent is used by industry and the rest goes for homes, personal and municipal uses.[25]

AP Photo/Xinhua, He Fenglun

Dead plants in a parched field attest to the ravages of the worldwide drought in Liujiang, a county of southwest China's Guangxi Zhuang Autonomous Region, in November 2006. Nearly all of the region's 84 counties were affected by the drought, which was caused by unseasonably warm temperatures, according to the Xinhua News Agency.

Water isn't running out everywhere, said Canadian journalist Marq de Villiers, author of *Water: The Fate of Our Most Precious Resource.* "It's only running out in places where it's needed most. It's an allocation, supply and management problem."[26]

It's also a demand problem: Over the past half-century, millions of people have migrated from colder, wetter, northern climates to warmer, drier, southern locales such as the American Southwest or southern France, putting new pressure on those expanding "Sun Belt" communities to build irrigation systems, tap into groundwater supplies or rechannel large amounts of river water.

Experts agree that the world should not be facing an overall water-scarcity crisis. But water supplies in much of Africa, parts of China, southern Europe, northern Mexico and the American Southwest and high plains aren't meeting demand, and climate change may be accelerating the problem, the experts say.[27] The issues

---

* 1 cubic kilometer would cover an area of about 810,000 acres with one foot of water.

Is Access to Clean Water a Human Right?

The question is at the heart of a global debate.

Should all humans have guaranteed access to clean water, or is water an increasingly scarce commodity that should be priced according to its value?

The question stands at the center of a global debate over threats to the world's water resources, as competition for water increases among industry, farming and households. It is also critical in efforts to protect the long-term environmental viability of rivers, lakes and aquifers.

The debate goes back at least to 1992, when an international commission on water and the environment meeting in Ireland issued the "Dublin Principles," which were later adopted by a U.N. panel. The commission concluded: "Water has an economic value . . . and should be recognized as an economic good." Only by recognizing that economic value can water "be properly conserved and allocated to its most important uses."[1]

But the principle also declared it a "basic right of all human beings to have access to clean water and sanitation at an affordable price." Poor households cannot compete with industry for scarce water supplies. Nor could most farmers, who typically receive subsidized prices for irrigation water.

The U.N. Committee on Economic, Social, and Cultural Rights declared in 2002 that all people are entitled to an essential minimum amount of clean water. "Water is fundamental for life and health," it said. "The human right to water is indispensable for leading a healthy life in human dignity."[2]

Canadian activist Maude Barlow says, "You can't really charge for a human right; you can't trade it or deny it to someone because they don't have money." Barlow is co-author of *Blue Gold: The Battle Against Corporate Theft of the World's Water.*[3]

The other side in the debate argues that until water is priced and valued as a scarce resource it will be wasted and billions of dollars required annually to extend water service to the poor and fix leaking water systems will not be forthcoming. Two years before the U.N. declared clean water a human right, the World Water Council — which reflects the views of international lenders and the water-supply industry — called for "full pricing" of water to reflect its "economic, social, environmental and cultural values."[4]

Farmers in dry regions throughout the world get water at preferential rates — or at no charge at all — as a matter of government policy. But if farmers were required to pay the full price for water, they could not compete with industry, which would be willing and able to pay market price.

In industrial countries, 60 percent of the water withdrawn from freshwater sources is used by industry, mainly to generate electricity. The developing world is moving rapidly in the same direction. China's industrial water use, for example, is projected to grow fivefold by 2030.[5]

add up to what the World Commission on Water calls the "gloomy arithmetic of water."[28]

In addition, man has transformed most of the world's great rivers. For example, the Danube — Central Europe's "lifeline" — has been dredged, deepened, straightened, channelized and obstructed by dams and fishing weirs. It is now "a manufactured waterway," says de Villiers, with more than a third of its volume withdrawn for human use, compared to an average of about 10 percent for other rivers.[29]

Pollution is also reducing the world's supply of potable water. In Asia, many rivers "are dead or dying," according to Rijsberman. The Musi River near India's Hyderabad technology center has become "a dwindling black wastewater stream," he writes. "[Y]et the cows that produce the curd and the dairy products for Hyderabad are bathing in that black and stinking water."[30] In China, 265 billion gallons of raw sewage is dumped into the Yangtze River every year.[31]

The depletion and despoiling of the world's reservoirs, rivers and watersheds also contribute to the problem. During the 20th century, more than half the wetlands in parts of Australia, Europe, New Zealand and North America were destroyed by population growth and development. The loss of wetlands increases water runoff, which exacerbates flooding, reduces the replenishment of aquifers and leaves rivers and lakes more vulnerable to pollution.[32]

Aquifers — the immense storehouses of water found beneath the Earth's surface — are the largest and fastest-growing source of irrigation water. Depleting those

"As urban centers and industry increase their demand for water, agriculture is losing out," said the U.N. "Human Development Report 2006."[6]

And the world's poor cannot compete with either farmers or business for water at market prices, said the report. About a third of those without access to clean water live on less than $1 a day. Twice that many live on less than $2 a day. "These figures imply that 660 million people lacking access to [safe] water have, at best, a limited capacity to pay more than a small amount for a connection to water service," the report said. "People might lack water because they are poor, or they might be poor because they lack water." The end result is the same: a limited ability to pay for water.[7]

American water expert Peter H. Gleick calls for a truce in the water rights dispute in favor of problem-solving. Workshops on privatization standards and principles for implementing a human right to water "would be far more likely to produce progress," he writes.[8]

A man protesting the privatization of water in Cochabamba, Bolivia, waves a sign saying "what is ours is ours and it cannot be taken away."

AP Photo/Julie Plasencia

1 "Dublin Statements and Principles," Global Water Partnership; www.gwpforum.org/servlet/PSP?iNodeID=1345.

2 Meena Palaniappan, et al., "Environmental Justice and Water," *The World's Water 2006-2007*, p. 117.

3 Jeff Fleischer, "Interview with Maude Barlow," *Mother Jones*, Jan. 14, 2005, www.motherjones.com/news/qa/2005/01/maude_barlow.html.

4 "Ministerial Declaration of The Hague," World Water Forum, March 22, 2000.

5 Palaniappan, *op. cit.*, p. 125.

6 See "Summary, Human Development Report 2006: Beyond scarcity: Power, poverty and the global water crisis," United Nations Development Programme, p. 17, http://hdr.undp.org/en/media/hdr2006_english_summary.pdf.

7 *Ibid.*, pp. 49-52.

8 Peter Gleick, "Time to Rethink Large International Water Meetings," *The World's Water 2006-2007*, p. 182.

underground rivers will have deleterious effects on the 40 percent of the planet's agricultural output that relies on irrigation from groundwater.[33] Experts say some of that water — which dates back to past ice ages — would take eons to refresh but is being consumed in less than a century.

"Large areas of China, South Asia and the Middle East are now maintaining irrigation through unsustainable mining of groundwater or over-extraction from rivers," said the U.N. "Human Development Report 2006."[34] The problem is widespread in Mexico, India and Russia, as well, although precise data are not available for many countries.[35]

In his seminal 1986 book *Cadillac Desert*, the late Marc Reisner warned about the long-term effects of water policies in the Western United States, including the depletion of the giant Ogallala Aquifer, which runs southward from South Dakota to Texas. It has two distinctions, he wrote, "one of being the largest discrete aquifer in the world, the other of being the fastest-disappearing aquifer in the world."[36]

In the 1930s a farmer on the Great Plains could raise a few gallons per minute from the Ogallala, using a windmill-driven pump. After the New Deal brought electricity to the region and oil and gas discoveries provided plenty of cheap fuel, electric pumps raised 800 gallons per minute.

"All of a sudden, irrigation became very energy- and labor-efficient. You turn on the switch and let it run," says Robert M. Hirsch, associate director for water at

Irrigation Doubled in Developing Nations

The amount of irrigated land more than doubled in developing countries in the past four decades, increasing faster than in the developed world. But the rate of increase for both has slowed in recent years because of heavy draws on groundwater aquifers and competition from industry for water.

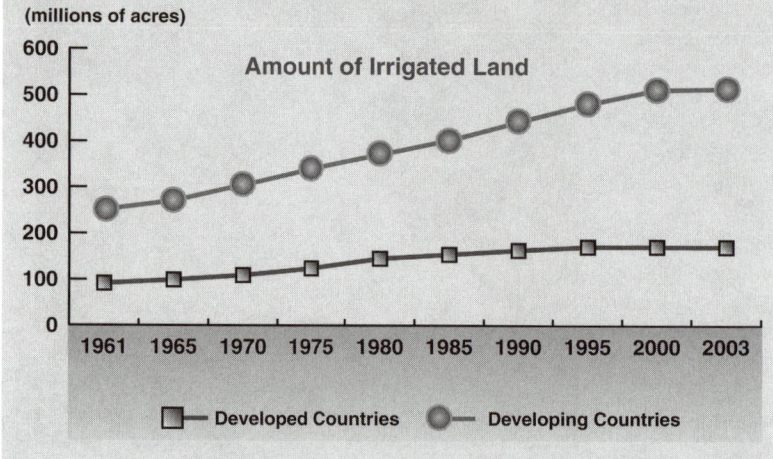

(millions of acres)

Amount of Irrigated Land

Developed Countries — Developing Countries

Source: Peter H. Gleick, et al., "The World's Water: 2006-2007," Pacific Institute, 2006

the U.S. Geological Survey. "There was an explosion of irrigated agriculture, particularly on the high plains, and in California."

In 1937, West Texas had 1,116 irrigation wells. Thirty years later it had 27,983. By 1977, Texas was withdrawing 11 billion gallons of groundwater a day to grow corn, cotton and other crops in what once had been part of the Great American Desert, Reisner wrote.[37]

Now, experts say the Ogallala — a resource that could have lasted hundreds of years — will be virtually depleted within the lifetimes of today's farmers.

Yet during the optimism and opportunism that characterized development of the modern American West, worries about future water supplies evaporated. "What are you going to do with all that water?" the late Felix Sparks, former head of the Colorado Water Conservation Board, asked in the mid-1980s. "When we use it up, we'll just have to get water from somewhere else." But today, "somewhere else" is not an answer, say authors Robin Clarke, editor of climate publications for the United Nations and World Meteorolgal Organization, and environmental author Jannet King. The co-authors of *The Water Atlas* insist water must be considered a finite resource.[38]

Should water be privatized?

In 2000, street fighting broke out between government forces and political activists, rural cocoa farmers and residents of shantytowns on the hilly outskirts of Cochabamba — Bolivia's third-largest city. The dispute was over privatization of the city's water supplies.

The year before, Cochabamba had turned its water and sanitation system over to Aguas del Tunari, a coalition of multinational and Bolivian water and engineering corporations whose biggest stakeholder was Bechtel Corp., based in San Francisco.[39] This was the high-water mark of a global, pro-market movement toward deregulation and privatization of state-owned monopolies in water, electricity and other services.[40] The World Bank and other international lenders had been supporting privatization strategies in hopes that investments and better management by private industry would help bring water and sanitation to more than a billion poor people whose governments couldn't or wouldn't do the job.

But Cochabamba's privatization included a costly dam and pipeline to import more water, which required sharp rate increases starting at 35 percent. Some customers' water bills doubled. Farmers outside the city, who had enjoyed free water, suddenly had to pay. The city erupted in protest, the water company's officials fled and their contract was rescinded.[41] The government reclaimed the water operations, and Cochabamba became a rallying cry against privatization and globalization for the political left.

Elsewhere, however, corporate involvement in water and sanitation system operations has not ceased. Veolia Water, a subsidiary of the French firm Veolia Environment SA — the world's largest water-services firm —signed a $3.8 billion, 30-year contract in 2007 to supply drinking water to 3 million residents of the Chinese river port city of Tianjin. Since 1997, Veolia has signed more than 20 water and sanitation contracts in China, and supplies more than 110 million people in 57 countries worldwide.[42]

These projects, and smaller-scale versions in poorer nations, suggest that while the inflamed debate over water privatization continues, threats of water scarcity and climate change may help accelerate the search for private-sector support.

The percentage of the world's population served at some level by private firms has grown from 5 percent in 1999 to 11 percent — or 707 million people — in 2007, according to *Pinsent Masons Water Yearbook*, a widely consulted summary of private-sector water projects.[43]

Opponents of privatization argue that safe drinking water and adequate sanitation are essential human rights, obligating governments to provide them at affordable rates or free if necessary. "If it's a human need, it can be delivered by the private sector on a for-profit basis. If it's a human right, that's different," says Canadian anti-globalization activist Maude Barlow, co-author of *Blue Gold: The Battle Against Corporate Theft of the World's Water.* "You can't really charge for a human right; you can't trade it or deny it to someone because they don't have money."[44]

Bringing in private firms to run water and sewer operations does not make the services more efficient or affordable, opponents also argue, but forces the poor to pay for corporate profits, shareholder dividends and high executive salaries. "The efficiencies don't happen," asserts Wenonah Hauter, executive director of Food and Water Watch, a Washington anti-globalization group. "The companies simply lay off staff members until they don't have enough people to take care of the infrastructure. And they raise rates. We've seen this all over the world." Last year Hauter's organization issued a study claiming privatized water operations in California, Illinois, Wisconsin and New York charged more for water than comparable publicly owned systems.[45]

Privatization advocates dispute Hauter's claims, and facts to settle the issue are illusive. A 2005 survey by the AEI-Brookings Center for Regulatory Studies found "no systematic empirical evidence comparing public and private water systems in the United States."[46]

A study by the Inter-American Development Bank of water rates in Colombia said prices charged by privatized systems were not significantly different from those charged by public systems.[47] And privatization appears to have improved water quality in urban areas but not in rural communities, said the study. After privatization began, water bills for the poor rose about 10 percent but declined for the wealthy, reflecting a scaling back in government subsidies to poorer consumers. Similar shifts occurred in both privatized and non-privatized cities.[48]

In central cities, water-rate subsidies tend to favor the wealthy and middle classes, who are usually connected to municipal water systems, while the poor often are not, says American journalist Diane Raines Ward, author of *Water Wars: Drought, Flood, Folly, and the Politics of Thirst.* And by keeping water rates artificially low, utilities typically collect only about a third of their actual costs, so they don't raise enough money to expand pipelines to unserved poor neighborhoods, she says.[49]

The rural poor or those living in urban slums often must haul water home from public wells or buy it from independent merchants — delivered by truck or burro — at much higher prices. In Cairo, Egypt, for instance, the poor pay 40 times the real cost of delivery; in Karachi, Pakistan, the figure is 83 times; and in parts of Haiti, 100 times, Ward says.

In the years since Cochabamba galvanized the left against privatizing water, privatization has declined in Latin America and sub-Saharan Africa but increased in Europe and Asia, according to the *Water Yearbook.*[50] The average contract size also has diminished since the 1990s, it said, due to a trend away from mega-contracts with multinational water companies in favor of "local and possibly less contentious contracts."[51]

A U.N.-sponsored analysis cites Chile and parts of Colombia among the successful examples of collaborative water and sanitation services. In Cartagena, Colombia's fifth-largest city, the local government retains control of the pipes and facilities and raises investment capital, but a private firm runs the service. Today, nearly all the city's residents have water in their homes, up from only one-quarter in 1995.[52] Chile's water program offers subsidies to the poorest households, guaranteeing an essential minimum of supply of up to 4,000 gallons per month. Deliveries are monitored to limit cheating, and every household must have a water meter to verify usage.[53]

Experts say the political problems of water privatization cannot be managed without effective government regulation and consumer involvement at all levels. Both elements were missing in Cochabamba but are present in Chile, the U.N. report says.[54]

The outlook is bleak for rancher Andrew Higham's parched land in Gunnedah, in northwestern New South Wales, Australia, in October 2006. Scarce winter rains caused drought across much of the continent last fall and led to severely reduced wheat and barley harvests.

Will water scarcity lead to conflicts?

In 1995 Ismail Serageldin, a World Bank vice president, predicted that "the wars of the next century will be over water."[55]

The reality has been different thus far. "Water resources are rarely the sole source of conflict, and indeed, water is frequently a source of cooperation," writes Gleick, of the Pacific Institute for Studies in Development, Environment and Security, in the new edition of *The World's Water 2006-2007*.[56] The survey of reported conflicts over water in the past 50 years, compiled by Oregon State University researchers, found 37 cases of violence between nations, all but seven in the Middle East.[57]

In 1964, Israel opened its massive National Water Carrier canal to carry water from the Sea of Galilee and the Jordan River to its farms and cities. Syria retaliated to maintain its access to the Jordan by starting two canals to divert Jordan flows for its uses. Skirmishes by military units and raids by the newly established al-Fatah forces escalated until Israeli air strikes halted the diversion projects. By then, Israel and the Arab League were on the road to the Six-Day War of 1967.[58]

"The attacks by Syria, Egypt, and Jordan that eventually followed had many causes, but water remained a priority for both sides," says author Ward.[59]

Still, more than 200 water treaties have been negotiated peacefully over the past half-century. The Partition of India in 1947, for instance, could have led to war between India and newly created Pakistan over control of the mighty Indus River basin. Instead, the two nations were brought together with World Bank support over a perilous decade of negotiations, signing the Indus Water Treaty in 1960. Three rivers were given to Pakistan, and three to India, with a stream of international financial support for dams and canals in both countries. Even when war raged between the two nations in later years, they never attacked water infrastructure.[60]

"Most peoples and even nations are hesitant to deny life's most basic necessity to others," Ward wrote. Two modern exceptions occurred during the Bosnian War (1992-1996), when Serbs "lay waiting to shoot men, women and children arriving at riverbanks or taps around Sarajevo carrying buckets or bottles," and during Saddam Hussein's regime in Iraq, when he diverted the lower waters of the Tigris and Euphrates rivers to destroy the homes and livelihood of the Marsh Arabs.[61]

Except for such instances, cooperation over water resources is common today, even if sometimes grudging and incomplete, says Undala Alam, a professor and specialist in water diplomacy at Britain's Cranfield University. "Turkey was releasing water for Syria and Iraq; the Nile countries are preparing projects jointly to develop the river; the Niger countries have a shared vision for the basin's development, and the Zambezi countries are working within the Southern African Development Community," she notes.[62]

But analysts warn that growing stress on water supplies, coupled with the impact of climate change, will create combustible conditions in the coming years that will undermine collaboration over water.

There is plenty of precedence for the concern, notes Gleick, who describes the history of violence over fresh water as "long and distressing."[63] The latest volume of *The World's Water* lists 22 pages of historical water conflicts — beginning in about 1700 B.C. with the Sumerians' efforts to dam the Tigris River to block retreating rebels.

In the future, climate change is expected to extend and intensify drought in Earth's driest regions and disrupt normal water flows from mountain snowcaps in Europe, North America and Central Asia. "Climate change has the potential to exacerbate tensions over water as precipitation patterns change, declining by as much as 60 percent in some areas," warned a recent report by a panel of retired U.S. generals and admirals convened by CNA, a think tank with longstanding ties to the military. "The potential for escalating tensions, economic disruption and armed conflict is great," said the report, "National Security and the Threat of Climate Change."[64]

On the simplest level, the report said, climate change "has the potential to create sustained natural and humanitarian disasters on a scale far beyond those we see today." Already, it said, Darfur, Ethiopia, Eritrea, Somalia, Angola, Nigeria, Cameroon and Western Sahara have all been hit hard by tensions that can be traced in part to environmental causes.[65] If the drought continues, the report said, more people will leave their homelands, increasing migration pressures within Africa and into Europe.[66]

The impact will be especially acute in the Middle East, where about two-thirds of the inhabitants depend on water sources outside their borders. Water remains a potential flashpoint between the Israelis and Palestinians, who lack established rights to the Jordan River and receive only about 10 percent of the water used by Israel's West Bank settlers.[67] "Only Egypt, Iran and Turkey have abundant fresh water resources," the CNA report said.

The military advisers urged the United States to take a stronger national and international role in stabilizing climate change and to create global partnerships to help less-developed nations confront climate impacts.[68]

Currently, there is only a weak international foundation for water collaboration, according to the U.N. Human Development report. While a 1997 U.N. convention lays out principles for cooperation, only 14 nations have signed it, and it has no workable enforcement mechanism. In 55 years, the International Court of Justice has decided only one case involving international rivers.[69]

It is possible, however, that as the awareness of climate impacts on water supplies deepens, so will the urgency for governments to respond. "Unlike the challenges that we are used to dealing with, these will come upon us extremely slowly, but come they will, and they will be grinding and inexorable," said former Vice Adm. Richard H. Truly, a former astronaut who headed the U.S. National Aeronautics and Space Administration

Mountain Snowpack Is Shrinking

The amount of snow covering the globe's highest mountains has been shrinking over the past half-century, upsetting crucial seasonal water flows that restock rivers, lakes, reservoirs and aquifers. Scientists think short-term climate conditions like El Niño and long-term warming caused by climate change are to blame. By century's end, only 16 percent of New Zealand's current snowpack will remain.

Snowpack Now and Projected in 2100

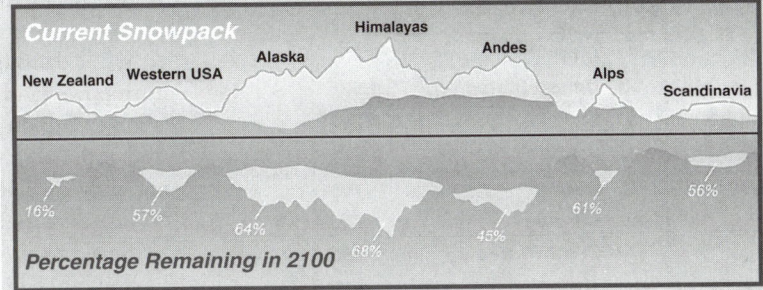

Source: Pacific Northwest National Laboratory, http://picturethis.pnl. gov/picturet.nsf/by+id/ AMER-6PWV.V?opendocument.

(NASA) and served as a CNA consultant.[70] "They will affect every nation, and all simultaneously."

BACKGROUND

Taming Water

The ruins of irrigation canals 8,000 years old have been found in Mesopotamia.[71] Remains of water-storage dams 5,000 years old survive in Egypt and Jordan. Humans have been using waterwheels for milling and threshing since the 1st century B.C., and by 1291 China had completed its Grand Canal running nearly 1,800 kilometers between Beijing and Hangzhou.[72] Water power drove mining, metal drilling, textile and milling industries at the dawn of the Industrial Age.[73] In the United States, the opening of the Niagara Falls hydroelectric power station in 1896 — built by American entrepreneur and inventor George Westinghouse and backed by financier J. P. Morgan and others — inaugurated water's use to generate electric power.[74]

But these early accomplishments were dwarfed in the 20th century by nearly 100 years of massive dam projects that have transformed most of the world's major rivers. Between 1950 and 2000, the number of dams higher than 50 feet increased sevenfold — to more than 41,000

China Leads World in Dam Building

China has three times as many dams as the United States and more than all the next 11 countries combined. Dams typically generate electricity, control flooding and provide water for irrigation.

Countries with the Most Dams

1.	China	22,000
2.	United States	6,575
3.	India	4,291
4.	Japan	2,675
5.	Spain	1,196
6.	Canada	793
7.	South Korea	765
8.	Turkey	625
9.	Brazil	594
10.	France	569
11.	South Africa	539
12.	Mexico	537

Source: Peter H. Gleick, et al., "The World's Water: 2002-2003," Pacific Institute, 2002

structures impounding 14 percent of the world's average river runoff.[75] By 2000, large dams were supplying nearly a fifth of all electrical power worldwide.

Dams also have been critical in the rapid expansion of irrigated farming. "Half of the world's large dams are built exclusively for irrigation, supporting about 12 to 16 percent of world food production, according to the World Commission on Dams."[76]

About 12 percent of large dams were constructed specifically to provide drinking water and sanitation (and a similar percentage were built to control flooding), and many have multiple uses. Whether used for energy, community water, flood control or agriculture, dams have been a key tool of economic growth, according to the commission. Typically, however, the full consequences of such giant projects were not taken into consideration, the commission said. In the past century, the world built, on average, one large dam per day without asking whether it was getting a fair return from the $2 trillion investment, said South African Minister of Education Kader Asmal, who chaired the commission.[77]

The dam-building blitz was enabled by political bias in favor of dams. From the Aswan High Dam in Egypt to the Hoover Dam on the Colorado River, big dams have stood as preeminent symbols of governments' engineering prowess and the use of state power to control devastating floodwaters and feed economic expansion. "Colossal engineering works bestow big contracts and big benefits, divide up waters, hold them fast, channel them away from some and give them to others," says author Ward. "It has always been politics that start the bulldozers moving."[78]

While dams helped expand supplies of drinking water, hydropower and irrigation water, they also attract population expansion that eventually strains the new resources. And until recently, the commission said, policymakers have not fairly considered the damaging impact dams have on downstream rivers and aquifers and the populations that are forced to move to make room for reservoirs.

Resistance to major new dam projects emerged with the rise of the environmental movement in the 1970s, particularly in Europe and the United States, as advocates pointed to the harm caused by dam construction. In the industrial world, "it is now more likely that a dam will be torn down than a new one will go up," says Ward.

But in China, South Asia and South America, dams are "multiplying like mushrooms," she writes.[79] If China's new Three Gorges Dam — the world's largest hydroelectric project — had been built midway through the past century, it might have been considered one of the world's great engineering feats. The main wall of the massive, 60-story structure spanning the Yangtze River was completed in 2006, and by the end of 2008 it is expected to deliver up to 18 million kilowatts per hour — nearly a tenth of the electricity needs of China's surging economy.[80] But in today's perspective, the monumental structure symbolizes the threat of environmental destruction caused by major dam construction.

The gargantuan project's human and environmental costs have alarmed opponents. According to the Chinese government, more than a million riverside residents were forced to move as the water rose behind the dam. The rising water levels have triggered some massive landslides on the riverbanks, and a senior government official warned last September that if such ecological and environmental dangers are not dealt with, "the project could lead to a catastrophe."[81] But more recently, Chinese officials have insisted the project will be operated safely.[82]

CHRONOLOGY

19th Century *The industrial age and urbanization create critical need for municipal water treatment and sanitation services.*

1848 The Public Health Act, followed in 1852 by the Metropolitan Water Act, lead to investments in water treatment and sanitation that dramatically reduce waterborne illnesses in Britain by the end of the century.

1876 Berlin city planner James Hobrecht starts work on drainage system and waterworks that channels sewage to fields as fertilizer. He designs similar systems for Moscow, Cairo and Tokyo.

1900-1980 *Governments around the globe launch major dam construction.*

1902 The Aswan Dam on the Nile River in Egypt is completed to control flooding and regulate water flow for agriculture.

1910 Chlorination begins in the United States. Typhoid fever from polluted drinking water falls from 25 deaths per 100,000 people to almost zero.

1936 Hoover Dam on the Colorado River is opened, fulfilling an agreement among Southwestern states and cities to share the river's flow.

1945 Large-scale groundwater irrigation begins expanding in the Western United States, aided by rural electrification and innovations in pumping and irrigating technology.

1986 Major dam construction has largely stopped in the U.S. but continues in Asia.

1990s *Britain's public utilities are sold to private firms in the late 1980s, triggering a wave of water-system privatization worldwide.*

1994 Construction begins on the Three Gorges Dam on China's Yangtze River, designed to be the largest in the world. More than 1 million people will have to be relocated as the river rises.

2000s *Drought spreads worldwide, heightening concern about climate change's impact on water scarcity. Privatization strategies shift.*

2000 Violent public protests against higher water rates force cancellation of a water-privatization plan in Cochabamba, Bolivia. But privatization continues in China, India and other parts of the world. . . . U.N. adopts the Millennium Development Goals calling for halving the number of people without access to safe water and adequate sanitation by 2015.

2002 China approves massive South-to-North Water Diversion Project, which will eventually link the country's four major rivers to bring water from the south to the arid north.

2005 Group of Eight industrialized nations pledge to double their aid for water, sanitation and other development projects in poorer nations by 2010.

2006 Waterborne-disease epidemics strike Karachi, Lahore and other Pakistani cities, caused by the leakage of sewage and industrial wastes into damaged water-distribution pipelines. . . . U.N. Human Development Report warns that without a major increase in investment, improvements in water and sanitation services will fall far short of the Millennium Development Goals.

2007 Multi-year drought afflicts China, the Horn of Africa, Turkey, Australia, Spain and the U.S. Sun Belt. . . . A director of the Three Gorges Project warns that rising waters behind the dam could cause "water pollution, landslides and other geological disasters," but other officials later say environmental problems will be ameliorated. . . . The Intergovernmental Panel on Climate Change predicts that freshwater resources will decrease in large river basins over the next decade due to drought. . . . Drought prompts several Australian cities to commission new desalination plants. Algeria also has a major plant in construction.

2008 The scarcity of water in key agricultural areas has contributed to soaring world prices for wheat, soybeans, corn, rice and poultry, and the trend is likely to continue this year, say agricultural forecasters.

Empowering Women May Quench Thirst

'Should girls be kept home from school to collect water?'

For millennia, the nomadic Tuareg people have lived by herding, migrating across vast rangelands south of the Sahara Desert to water and graze their animals. But decades of drought are destroying the traditional Tuareg way of life — killing herds, drying up grazing lands and forcing many to settle in villages.

"We used to saddle the camel and put all the nice things on its back and put on our nice clothes and go," Tuareg chief Mohamed Ag Mata told a reporter last year. "We were afraid of nothing."[1]

But the changes, paradoxically, offer hope for a better existence to women and children in the male-dominated Tuareg culture — giving them access to the employment, education and social rights that will give them a greater say in community water policy.

Increasingly, educating and empowering women is seen as an effective way to expand access to clean water across the developing world. Virtually every major international organization dealing with water scarcity is calling for change in women's decision-making roles, including The World Bank, the U.N. Human Development Programme, the World Health Organization, the World Water Forum, the World Commission on Dams and the Stockholm-based Global Water Partnership.

In the developing world, the job of hauling water rests, literally, almost entirely on women's shoulders. A UNICEF study in 23 sub-Saharan countries found that a quarter of women spent 30 minutes to an hour each day collecting and carrying water, and 19 percent spent an hour or more. In Mile Gully, an impoverished rural area of Jamaica, hauling the family's water can take a woman two to five hours a day.[2]

The high incidence of waterborne disease caused by the lack of clean water further burdens women in poor, rural communities, because they are the primary caregivers for the sick. "Should a woman care for a sick child or spend two hours collecting water?" asks the latest U.N. human development report. "Should girls be kept home from school to collect water, freeing time for mothers to grow food or generate income? Or should they be sent to school to gain the skills and assets to escape poverty?"[3]

But despite having to bear the greatest burden caused by a lack of water, women "play no role in the decision making for their communities," said Margaret Mwangi, a specialist in forestry and environmental issues who has worked for UNESCO.[4]

Women's lack of property rights prevents them from having a say in how water is distributed in their provinces. Women own less than 15 percent of the world's land and in many countries cannot legally own property separately from their husbands. "Lacking rights to land, millions of women in South Asia and sub-Saharan Africa are denied formal membership rights to participate in water-user association meetings," according to the U.N. "Human Development Report 2006."[5] And even those who are welcomed at irrigation-association meetings often cannot find the time. "Meetings are on Friday nights. At that time, after cooking for my husband and the kids, I still have a lot of work to do around the house," said a woman in Ecuador. "Even if I go to the meeting, it's only to hear what the men have to say. Men are the ones who talk and discuss."[6]

Unless both water and gender policies are reformed, water scarcity threatens to worsen women's plight, says the Sri Lanka-based International Water Management

Some water experts still advocate new, smaller dams in developing countries to control flooding, store irrigation water and generate electricity. For instance, most of India's rainfall occurs in about 100 hours during the monsoon season. While reservoirs capture some of these torrents, most escape to the sea.[83]

The 4th World Water Forum in Mexico City in 2006 cited Norway as a role model for the value of dams.

"Electricity from hydropower was the key factor in transforming Norway from one of the poorest countries in Europe a century ago to the industrialized and wealthy nation of today," said Anita Utseth, Norway's deputy minister for petroleum and energy.[84]

As Ward notes, "In some places, if no reservoirs are built, poor people will be denied the means to improve their lives."[85]

Institute.[7] Studies recommend a wide range of strategies to strengthen women's roles in gaining access to water and sanitation services, including micro-credit and micro-insurance programs that target women; training programs in rural irrigation and sanitation processes; creating rural women's councils and broadcasting radio programs on women's issues.[8]

But gender traditions can prove hard to change. Along the Bay of Bengal coast, decision-making and financial control over irrigation systems in the Indian state of Andhra Pradesh, has been decentralized, giving more authority to local communities. Nevertheless, only 4 to 5 percent of the women surveyed in two districts believed they could influence decisions in village meetings. "Women, and particularly poor women, rarely participate," the human development report concluded.[9]

Experts say progress for women requires a push from the bottom and pressure from the top. Legislation in Uganda, for instance, requires that all agencies — from national to village levels — include at least 30 percent female representation.

"Affirmative action may not remove cultural barriers," the U.N. report said, "but it does challenge their legitimacy."[10]

That may even be happening among the Tuaregs, says Hadijatou, describing her new life in a village near Timbuktu in Mali. "Before, everything was given to us by the men. When you are given what you need by other people, you are dependent on them. But when you are producing what you need, you depend on nobody. So life is far better now."[11]

Women and girls in poor countries, like these in Pakistan, bear the greatest burden from a lack of potable water.

[1] Richard Harris, "Drought Forces Desert Nomads to Settle Down," National Public Radio, July 2, 2007.

[2] Polioptro Martinez Austria and Paul van Hofwegen, "Synthesis of the 4th World Water Forum," Mexico City, 2006 p. 4, www.worldwaterforum4.org.mx/files/report/SynthesisoftheForum.pdf.

[3] "Human Development Report 2006 — Beyond Scarcity: Power, Poverty and the Global Water Crisis," U.N. Development Programme, 2006, p. 87; http://hdr.undp.org/en/reports/global/hdr2006/.

[4] Margaret Mwangi, "Gender and Drought Hazards in the Rangelands of the Great Horn of Africa," *Women & Environments International Magazine,* Spring 2007, p. 21.

[5] "Human Development Report," *op. cit.*, p. 194.

[6] *Ibid.*

[7] David Molden, ed., "Summary," *Water for Food, Water for Life: A Comprehensive Assessment of Water Management in Agriculture,* International Water Management Institute, p. 10, www.iwmi.cgiar.org/assessment/files_new/synthesis/Summary_SynthesisBook.pdf.

[8] Austria and Hofwegen, *op. cit.*, pp. 43, 63, 96.

[9] "Human Development Report," *op. cit.*, p 193.

[10] *Ibid.*, p. 194.

[11] Harris, *op. cit.*

Regulating Water

Who owns water? What rights do water users have? How should conflicts be resolved?

The globe's oldest recorded societies were formed not only for defense but also to try to control the flow of water in rivers that were crucial to farming. Under Roman law, water resources were the property of the state, which was responsible for their development and protection.

Islamic water law in the parched Middle East followed a similar path — irrigation canals and ditches had to be adequately planned and spaced to prevent infringement on others' water sources.[86]

But ancient codes also recognized that landowners did not have to share well water in times of scarcity, and people living closest to rivers and lakes had first claim on their waters. "The cistern nearest to a water channel is

Imaginechina via AP Images

China's 60-story Three Gorges Dam — the world's largest hydroelectric project — is expected to deliver up to 18 million kilowatts per hour by the end of 2008, nearly a tenth of China's electricity needs. Critics say the Yangtze River structure symbolizes environmental destruction that can be caused by major dam construction. More than a million riverside residents were forced to move as the water rose behind the dam.

filled first, in the interests of peace," said the 12th-century Jewish theologian and philosopher Maimonides.[87]

Eventually, the doctrine of "riparian" rights — giving those living closest to water the first claim on its use — became merged with a "public trust" doctrine, holding that water was a common resource to be managed by the state for the common benefit. One person's use of water could not infringe on a neighbor's reasonable needs. The doctrine was embraced by many countries in Europe — including Britain, France and Spain — which then exported the principle to their colonies abroad.[88]

But in the Western United States, Chile and Mexico, private water rights were recognized, particularly after the 1848 gold rush in the United States. A miner finding a gold seam would claim water from the nearest creek to wash dirt away from precious nuggets. His claim established

a "first-in-time, first-in-use" priority allowing him to take as much as he needed.[89] This "prior appropriation" doctrine was a starter's gun for unchecked diversion and exploitation of water resources to create farms and cities in the arid West.[90]

Of course, in most legal debates about water, individual rights are submerged by political elites, rulers and dominant factions. For instance, Senegalese law provides for a democratic distribution of irrigated lands. But in practice, tribal nobles' descendants still claim the lion's share of the land and allocate rights to powerful outsiders, including military leaders, politicians and judges.[91]

In Central Asia during Soviet rule, for instance, Kyrgyzstan, Tajikistan and Uzbekistan — which abut the Syr Darya and Amu Darya river basins — shared the reservoir and hydropower output from Kyrgyzstan's largest reservoir. Now, as separate states, their cooperation has virtually ended, according to a U.N. report. Kyrgyzstan is holding on to more of its reservoir volume in order to increase its hydropower exports, severely reducing irrigation flows in the other two countries. A constructive dialogue "has been conspicuously absent," according to the U.N. Human Development Report.[92]

Two international treaties — the Helsinki Rules of 1966, adopted by the International Law Association, and articles adopted by the U.N. International Law Commission — specify how cross-border water disputes should be resolved. Rivers that divide nations, according to the treaties — must be considered common resources, not under any one nation's control. They also advocate a policy of "no harm" — each riparian nation has the right to "equitable utilization" of a shared water supply, and a nation's water use should not damage its neighbors' water needs. Prior appropriation claims are not allowed, and countries are called on to share accurate information on water resources.[93]

Before fair water-use policies can be expected, governments must consider the needs of the poor and politically weak, whose water needs are usually greatest, says water expert Sandra Postel, director of the Global Water Policy Project in Massachusetts. That means "adding seats around the table," she says.[94] For example, Ghana successfully expanded its water and sanitation services in recent years after water policy was decentralized, and village and district water councils were formed. The result: improved planning and more reasonable priorities for water funding, according to the U.N.[95]

Misusing Water

In Mumbai's Dharavi slum, which lies between the international airport and the city's financial center, an estimated 1 million Indians live in huts and shanties. With only one toilet for every 1,440 people, gutters overflow with waste in the rainy season, turning the streets into open sewers.[96]

Such unsanitary conditions in developing countries contribute to a plague of diarrhea that not only kills an estimated 1.8 million children across the globe each year but also repeatedly sickens many times that number, leaving them malnourished and vulnerable to other diseases and keeping them from school.[97]

Trachoma, spread by a fly that breeds in human feces, afflicts nearly 6 million people worldwide, causing widespread blindness. The disease "is a passport to poverty," says the U.N.'s "Human Development Report," because it prevents victims from working.[98]

"At the start of the 21st century one in five people living in the developing world — some 1.1 billion people in all — lack access to clean water," and nearly half the developing world has no access to adequate sanitation.[99]

Some of the same conditions existed in Europe and the United States during most of the 19th century, as farm families migrated to vast urban slums. During the summer in 1858, the stench of untreated sewage in the Thames River (called the "Great Stink" by the *London Times*) forced the Parliament to close temporarily.[100] In the 1890s Britain's infant mortality rate was about the same as Nigeria's today.

Water-treatment legislation in mid-19th-century Britain mandated creation of municipal water companies, followed by an expansion of sanitation services after 1880. By 1910, the country's rate of infant mortality had fallen by nearly 40 percent. The critical factor for change, according to some experts, was an extension of voting rights in Britain beyond property-owning classes to those who lacked clean water and sanitation, creating a political constituency for reforms.[101]

But the cost of expanding sanitation services in the developing world today would be immense. A study led by former International Monetary Fund President Michael Camdessus estimates that closing the sanitation services gap could cost $87 billion over the next two decades.[102]

Experts today debate which must come first in the developing world: good governance or solutions to water

AFP/Getty Images/Tony Mwanki

A Masai herdsman in Kenya's Rift Valley tends to a dying sheep in January 2006. Today 850 million people live in areas where adequate food supplies are at risk because of drought — two-thirds of them in South Asia and sub-Saharan Africa, where the impact of climate change on food production is expected to be worst.

and sanitation needs. In *The World's Water 2006-2007*, the authors conclude that "eradicating corruption and political interference and ensuring the participation of all stakeholders will be critical to the successful governance of water."[103] The 1,320-km (820 miles) Rhine River — long called "the sewer of Europe" — was cleaned up after a 1986 industrial fire in Basel, Switzerland, allowed more than 30 tons of pesticides, dyes, mercury and other poisons to spill into the river. Millions of fish were killed, and major cities had to close their municipal water intakes. German Chancellor Angela Merkel, a former environmental minister, has called the "rebirth of the Rhine...one of the great environmental success stories of the century."[104]

But to the east, the blighted Danube testifies to the damage caused by selfish, beggar-thy-neighbor policies by the nations along its 1,770-mile course. Efforts to

Water Schemes Range From Monumental to Zany

Many are costly and controversial.

After wildfires devastated parts of Southern California and dry winds parched the Southwest last summer, New Mexico's Gov. Bill Richardson, a Democratic candidate for president, made a startling proposal.

"States like Wisconsin are awash in water," Richardson told the *Las Vegas Sun*, proposing that water from the Great Lakes be piped to his state. With nearly 20 percent of the world's fresh water, the five vast lakes are an irresistible target to promoters, politicians — and potentially — corporate water suppliers.

"You're going to see increasing pressure to gain access to this supply," said Aaron Packman, a professor of civil and environmental engineering at Northwestern University. "Clearly, it's a case of different regional interests competing for this water."[1]

In 1985, Quebec provincial officials floated a plan to sell Canadian river water to the high plains states. The Great Replenishment and Northern Development Canal (GRAND) envisioned pumping river water from Quebec into a reservoir in Ontario. From there the water could travel by aqueduct to the Great Lakes and then by canal to the American plains. Nothing came of it.

Even grander was the North American Water and Power Alliance in the 1960s, which proposed to dam dozens of north-flowing rivers in Canada's western provinces, channeling their waters into a new reservoir 500 miles long — about the distance from Pittsburgh to Chicago — to irrigate the high plains and refill the Colorado River's flows to California. But the half-trillion-dollar price tag sank the proposal. And its environmental cost would have been "ungraspable," says Canadian journalist Marq de Villiers, author of *Water: The Fate of Our Most Precious Resource.*[2]

The idea still seems to stir anxieties in Canada. An off-hand remark by President George W. Bush in 2001 about the benefits of Canadian water exports to the United States caused a brief uproar, and last year Canada's Liberal Party Leader Stephane Dion accused the government in Ottawa of trying to put the matter back on the U.S.-Canada agenda — a claim both governments denied.[3]

Mega-project dreams still survive in China, however, which is planning a series of canals to carry Yangtze River water thousands of miles to the Yellow River and on to the huge cities of Beijing and Tianjin.[4]

And in 2004, Israel agreed to purchase the equivalent of 35 million gallons of freshwater per day from Turkey's Manavgat River, to be shipped aboard tankers. Turkish water exports to Cyprus and other water-short destinations were

AP Photo/California Dept. of Water Resources/Dale Kolke

The monumental California Aqueduct brings vitally needed water 444 miles from Northern to Southern California farmers and residents.

also under consideration. The agreement was put on hold in 2006 after higher oil prices made tanker transportation uneconomical, according to both countries.[5]

And then there are the slightly zany ideas, such as Calgary entrepreneur James Cran's plan to move water by sea inside floating 5,000-ton plastic bags, or towing Arctic icebergs to distant metropolises.[6]

Most monumental water-moving schemes, however, trigger intense opposition. Gov. Richardson's proposal, for instance, is opposed by eight Great Lakes-area states and two Canadian provinces, and drew a terse, unequivocal "No" from Michigan's Democratic Gov. Jennifer Granholm.[7]

[1] Tim Jones, "Great Lakes key front in water wars," *The Chicago Tribune*, Oct. 28, 2007, www.chicagotribune.com/news/local/chi-water_bdoct28,1,5145249.story.

[2] Marq de Villiers, *Water: The Fate of Our Most Precious Resource* (1999), p. 260.

[3] Launce Rake, "Canadians fearful of U.S. water grab," *Las Vegas Sun*, May 28, 2006. See also Bruce Campion-Smith and Susan Delacourt, "Secret talks underway, Dion claims," *The Toronto Star*, Aug. 18, 2007, p. 18.

[4] Diane Raines Ward, *Water Wars: Drought, Flood, Folly and the Politics of Thirst* (2002), p. 171.

[5] Josef Federman, "Israel, Turkey put landmark water agreement into deep freeze," The Associated Press, April 5, 2006

[6] de Villiers, *op. cit.*, p. 277.

[7] Jones, *op. cit.*

reengineer the river began in the 16th century with projects to steer its annual floods into canals or trap them behind huge dams. Historically, vast amounts of untreated human wastes and toxic industrial effluents were also dumped into the river, a situation that worsened during the Cold War. Soviet-era bosses had no scruples about flushing wastes into rivers, and Moscow pushed Hungarian and Czech governments to divert the Danube into man-made waterways in order to speed Russian barge traffic. Parts of the project were begun, but before it went very far, the Soviet Union collapsed.

In the 1990s, a third of the Danube's flow was being taken for human use — an extraction rate that researchers warned would be unsustainable if the vast region served by the river faced continued growth and a prolonged drought.[105]

Today the Danube nations are working toward the river's recovery, and the European Union has pledged $3.3 billion to help.[106]

Ocean Waters

As a last resort, some wealthy nations and cities facing serious shortages of freshwater — including the Persian Gulf states, Israel, Singapore and a handful of cities in California, Florida and Australia — have turned to desalination of the oceans' limitless resources.

More than 10,000 desalting plants were in operation or contracted for construction in January 2005, with a total capacity of 9.6 billion gallons per day. At present, however, desalination plants have the capability to provide just three one-thousandths of daily global freshwater consumption.[107]

Governments usually subsidize up to a third of the consumer cost for desalinated water because it costs many times more than typical urban water service.[108] Improved technology and engineering dropped average desalination costs from $1.60 per 264 gallons in 1990 to about 60 cents in newer plants by 2002. But construction costs have risen recently due to higher steel prices, and operating costs have climbed sharply as energy prices have risen. (Energy costs account for one-third to more than one-half of the expense of desalinating water.) The safe disposal of the brine residue from desalination remains an environmental issue that is still not well researched, according to "The World's Water" report.[109]

Some experts believe desalination will begin to grow at double-digit rates as water becomes scarce and prices

for conventional water rise.[110] For example, California had 20 desalination plants in the construction pipeline in 2006, which could increase California's desalination capacity 100-fold, providing about 7 percent of the freshwater the state used in 2000.

CURRENT SITUATION
Melting Snows

The deep snowpack covering the world's mountains in winter is a renewable gift of nature — melting in spring to restock rivers, lakes, reservoirs, aquifers and eventually flowing back into the ocean. Then evaporating ocean water turns into snowfall in the mountains, repeating the cycle. But the snowpacks have been shrinking — and melting earlier — over the past half-century, upsetting crucial seasonal water flows.[111]

In parts of the Western United States, for example, the snowpack is down to 40 percent of normal. While short-term climate conditions like El Niño are partly to blame, Earth's predicted warming trend is expected to cause dramatic changes in the future. The U.S. Department of Energy's Pacific Northwest National Laboratory has forecast, for instance, that by century's end South America's Andes Mountains will have lost half of their winter snow cover, and ranges in Europe and the U.S. West nearly half.[112] (*See figure, p. 333.*)

"Our main reservoir is snow, and it's going away," says Phillip Mote, a professor of atmospheric sciences at the University of Washington in Seattle.[113]

The early melting is seen as an indication that climate change is already affecting water scarcity. "Some of what's happening with the early snow melts could be due to variations based on ocean circulation," said Gregg Garfin, project manager of the University of Arizona's Institute for the Study of Planet Earth. "But there's a pretty large fraction that can't be explained that way, and we think that's due to increasing temperatures."[114]

The amount of snow melting into the Colorado River Basin has declined by 10 to 30 percent over the last 30 years, according to Brad Udall, director of the University of Colorado's Western Water Assessment.[115]

Earlier melting has caused unseasonal spring flooding in parts of the West,[116] while a decade of drought has left forests more vulnerable to fires and beetle infestations,

AP Photo/Reed Saxon

Wildfires destroyed hundreds of homes in Malibu, Calif., last October during a severe drought, reigniting the perennial national debate about the folly of building homes in water-scarce areas.

said Tom Swetnam, director of the University of Arizona's Laboratory of Tree-Ring Research. "Lots of people think climate change and the ecological responses are 50 to 100 years away," he said. "But it's not. It's happening now."[117]

In the American Southwest — as in other arid regions of the world — drought is the biggest, most persistent enemy, but scientists are divided over how much of the current drought is due to long-term climate change.

A report by scientists at the Met Office Hadley Centre for Climate Prediction and Research — Britain's weather office — cites evidence that rising emissions of greenhouse gases have exacerbated drought conditions during the past half-century. Greenhouse gases — the carbon dioxide, methane, nitrous oxide and ozone produced from burning fossil fuels — are causing the Earth's temperature to rise by helping to trap the sun's heat, creating a greenhouse effect, according to the Intergovernmental Panel on Climate Change.

"Further research is required," said the Hadley Centre report, noting "the potential seriousness of future climate change impacts if CO_2 emissions continue to increase substantially."[118]

These judgments are still hedged. "It is quite possible that . . . climate change may be having an impact on droughts, not only in the U.S. but around the world," says Michael J. Hayes, director of the National Drought Mitigation Center at the University of Nebraska, Lincoln.

But that's not clear yet. "I don't think we can use what is happening today as an argument for climate change. It should open our eyes to the potential impacts that might occur."

Looking further ahead into the century, scientists warn that drought is likely to persist over longer periods, hitting hardest at the world's most-vulnerable arid regions.[119]

A trend toward extreme weather events, ranging from drought and high temperature to violent storms and flooding, is already evident, according to the National Center for Atmospheric Research.[120] Global warming is likely to fuel even more extreme weather, center researchers said. "There's a two-third's chance there will be a disaster," says Nobel laureate Steven Chu, director of the Lawrence Berkeley National Laboratory, "and that's in the best scenario."[121]

The Southwestern United States and other regions appear headed, by mid-century, to a condition of permanent drought caused by global warming, concluded Columbia University's Lamont-Doherty Earth Observatory, after surveying recent studies. "[G]lobal warming not only causes water shortage through early snow melt, which leads to significant water shortage in the summer over the Southwest, but it also aggregates the problem by reducing precipitation," said Mingfang Ting, senior research scientist at Lamont-Doherty and co-author of the survey.[122]

Wasted Water

Although Atlantans worry that falling levels in Lake Lanier are jeopardizing their drinking water, they might be surprised to learn that up to 18 percent of the city's water is being lost through leaky pipes and wastefulness.[123] In London, the mayor asked the Thames Water company to stanch the 238 million gallons per day being lost through old, leaky water pipes rather than build a costly desalination plant to purify Thames River water. Regulators have since approved the project because of the urgency of the shortages.[124]

U.S. water systems lose an estimated 15 percent to 25 percent of their water through leakage, and older or poorly maintained networks around the world lose more than 40 percent. However, notes American water conservation consultant Amy L. Vickers, water leakage is "chronically underestimated, ignored, or treated as a tired 'Unsolved Mystery,' " by utilities.[125]

Should water be privatized?

YES
Terry L. Anderson
Executive Director, PERC,
Senior Fellow, Hoover Institution

Written for *CQ Global Researcher* February, 2008

"No one washes a rental car" is a truism that suggests that ownership is crucial to stewardship. We also might say, "No one conserves water" for the same reason — too often it's not clear who benefits from conserving water because it's unclear who owns the water. As long as water's cheap, why fix the leaky faucet or switch to an efficient irrigation system?

Making the ownership link is relatively easy, because water is already claimed by someone — either a municipality, individual farmers or a government agency.

In practice, however, claims compete with one another, especially when water is scarce. Miners and farmers on the Western frontier in the 19th century devised the prior-appropriation system, whereby water owners were allowed to resolve conflicts by moving water to higher-valued uses, and trades between farmers have gone on for a century.

The recent drought in the Southeast has raised a red flag about scarcity. The best mechanism for allocating water is to clarify ownership among municipal, agricultural, industrial and environmental users and allow trades. If Atlanta must buy water from lower-valued agricultural users, farmers will have an incentive to save water and sell it, and municipal consumers will face a higher price and thus an incentive to conserve.

Some worry that water markets will put undue burden on the poor while the rich continue enjoying their country club lawns. But the poor could be issued water stamps, akin to food stamps, for buying water. Or suppliers could charge less for minimum amounts of water needed for necessities and increase the price of water for luxuries.

When water rights are allocated through political processes, the poor usually do not get many of the initial rights, forcing them to purchase water if they are to get any. And data from the Chilean water markets suggest that the poor don't fare much better when water is traded on the open market. Perhaps there should be some guaranteed survival quantity of water that is a basic human right.

The problem is not a failure of water markets, but a failure of political allocation, which will not be rectified by preventing water markets from delivering water at a profit to all, regardless of income.

As water scarcity increases in the 21st century, water bureaucracies will bring more conflict, while water markets will foster more cooperation. With this choice, it will be impossible to keep a good water market down.

NO
Wenonah Hauter
Executive Director, Food & Water Watch

Written for *CQ Global Researcher* February, 2008

In the early 1990s, multinational corporations began to view water services as an important, new profit center — especially in the United States, where 85 percent of water utilities are public. With 1.2 billion people in the developing world lacking access to safe drinking water, the corporations lobbied the World Bank to condition its loans for water services on privatization.

Since then, numerous failed ventures have proven that the cost of privatizing water is too high. It was certainly too high for Tanzania, which terminated a 10-year contract with Biwater after two years of poor management left the government short $3.25 million and the poorest citizens of Dar es Salaam without water. Likewise, massive rate hikes and poor management led Bolivia to end a 40-year contract with Bechtel after only a few months. Similar ventures in Argentina, the Philippines, Indonesia, South Africa and the United Kingdom also have proven unworkable.

In the United States, many municipalities have considered privatization to upgrade their aging systems, but the ventures have been plagued by corruption, high rates, poor service and public outrage. Atlanta terminated a 20-year contract with United Water 16 years early due to bungled emergency responses, boil-water alerts, discolored water and billing difficulties. In 2002, a coalition of citizens' organizations in New Orleans defeated what would have been the largest water-privatization initiative in the United States. Meanwhile, residents of Stockton, Calif., sued the city for failing to perform a proper environmental review of the city's water-privatization contract.

Given this abysmal track record, new solutions are necessary to meet water needs. For example, some U.S. cities have cut costs by improving internal management. Phoenix saved $77 million by working with a labor management team to optimize staffing, organize self-directed work teams and utilize new technology. Similarly, San Diego saved $37 million by developing a more cost-conscious management system.

Safeguarding our water systems is a vital public responsibility. Yet, shockingly, the Environmental Protection Agency estimates that each year we fall $22 billion short of our water infrastructure spending needs. To address this funding gap, we must ensure that public utilities can upgrade and maintain their systems without turning to privatization.

At Food & Water Watch, we support a Clean Water Trust Fund to help ensure that the future of America's water lies in publicly accountable management and secure, clean, affordable water for all.

> "If 12 jumbo jets [full of children] were crashing every day, the world would want to do something about it. They would want to find out why it was happening."
>
> — *U.N. water expert Brian Appleton, commenting on the deaths each day of 5,000 children due to lack of access to clean water.*

In coastal cities, vast amounts of rainwater and melting snow are "basically lost," flowing into storm drains that flow out to sea, says the U.S. Geological Survey's Hirsch. "The urban design is to get rid of it as fast as you can: get it off the roof, off the street, into the storm sewers and rush it off into the ocean, never used by anybody." Extravagant water consumption continues in wealthy residential areas and in farming regions where inefficient surface and sprinkler irrigation systems waste up to 25 percent of the water they use.[126] Efficient "drip" irrigation systems — which deliver water directly onto the crops, reducing evaporation to only 5 percent — are used on less than 1 percent of irrigated lands worldwide, largely because of higher equipment costs.[127]

But according to Vickers and other experts, a conservation ethic is beginning to emerge, particularly where water supplies are threatened by drought. For example, aggressive conservation strategies in Boston and Albuquerque, N.M., are reducing systemwide demand by 25 and 18 percent, respectively. "A few other systems, such as New York City, have also realized substantial water savings and wastewater volume reductions that have allowed them to avert major infrastructure expansions," Vickers notes.[128]

In the United States, some states have begun requiring cities to use reclaimed wastewater ("graywater") to irrigate parks and golf courses. Illinois, Florida, California, Arizona and Ohio reported the largest increases. The U.S. Geological Survey estimated that the amount of graywater used more than doubled between the 1970s and 1995.[129]

Water conservation also is expanding in the construction field. In the United States, Canada, Brazil, India and three-dozen other nations, water-saving green architecture for commercial and government buildings is growing in popularity, but the large-scale use of water-conservation practices by water utilities is still "very rare," says Vickers.[130]

Hirsch says policymakers must recognize that rivers and lakes need sustained flows of water to maintain their long-term environmental viability — and their full range of usefulness. Although this movement is "still in its infancy," at least 70 nations have begun programs to conserve or restore water flows in rivers.[131] For example, a $10 billion project in Florida aims to restore the natural flow of the Kissimmee River, and programs in Australia, Israel, Finland, Thailand, South Africa and Zambia would release flood waters from dams to move sediments downstream and expand plant and animal habitats.

"When given a chance, rivers often heal," write the Global Water Policy Project's Postel and Brian Richter, a staff director at the Nature Conservancy, in *Rivers for Life*.[132]

OUTLOOK

Thirst and Hunger

The world's population, now about 6 billion, is likely to jump by more than a third by 2050, reaching nearly 9 billion, according to the U.N.[133] Such a large increase will cause not only thirst but also hunger, says the International Water Management Institute. The average European uses about 13 gallons of water a day for drinking, cooking and sanitation. But the food an individual consumes in a typical day requires 800 to 900 gallons to grow.[134]

"The world needs roughly 70 times more water to produce food than it needs for cities," says Rijsberman, former director of the International Water Management Institute in Sri Lanka.[135]

Since 1950, water withdrawals for human use have tripled and irrigated cropland doubled. Today, despite important increases in farming productivity, 850 million people live in areas where adequate food supplies are at risk — two-thirds of them in South Asia and sub-Saharan Africa, where the impact of climate change on food production is expected to be worst.[136]

The productivity of irrigated cropland has increased dramatically in the past half-century, according to the World Bank. The production of rice and wheat, for instance, increased 100 percent and 160 percent in that period, respectively, with no increase in water use per bushel. "However, in many (river) basins, water productivity remains startlingly low," the bank reports. Without greater agricultural productivity or major shifts in farming locations, the amount of water needed for farming will jump 70 to 90 percent by 2050, according to the assessment.[137]

As food requirements continue to rise, the increase in irrigation has slowed as underground water levels have begun to recede. Farmers also face growing competition for water from industry.[138]

Rijsberman predicts the average price of water used in agriculture worldwide could increase by two to three times in the coming decades, inflating global food prices. In addition, industries and power producers can outbid farmers for scarce water. If irrigated harvests are cut back through a lack of water or because water is diverted to industrial use, world grain prices will rise even more.[139]

Policymakers still must resolve a major question about water pricing: Should it be priced competitively, according to its value, like wheat, rice and other food commodities grown with water? A handful of governments have done just that: Chile allows landowners with water on or under their property to trade water rights to the highest bidders. Mexico, several Australian states and California also have water-trading programs.[140] In Texas, the flamboyant oil trader T. Boone Pickens has created a company, Mesa Water, to buy water from landowners above the Ogallala aquifer, to sell to water-short Texas cities.[141]

But many experts think trading water as a commodity is a non-starter for most governments. "There is no movement in the real world, with elected officials," says U.S. water-law expert Robert Glennon. "Water pricing is the third rail of water politics."

Another option, supported by the World Bank and others, is trading "virtual" water. That occurs when a country with scarce water or poor agricultural land concentrates on developing export goods to earn the money needed to import food from water-rich nations with productive, low-cost food producers. Such trades, which would require a lowering of agricultural trade barriers, could bring down food production costs in water-poor countries and help reduce global water consumption, according to a World Bank report. Wheat grown in India, for example, consumes

AP Photo/Carlos Osorio

National Geographic/Getty Images/James L. Stanfield

Spraying vs. Dripping

Due to evaporation, irrigation systems like this one in Lakefield Township, Mich. (top), waste up to 25 percent of the water they distribute. More expensive drip irrigation systems, like this one in Israel (bottom), lose only about 5 percent to evaporation but are used on less than 1 percent of irrigated lands worldwide.

four times more water than wheat grown in France. By importing maize rather than growing it, Egypt reduces its national water consumption by 5 percent.[142]

But importing "virtual" water also has a downside. "In Morocco, for example, one study showed that while the nation as a whole would benefit from agricultural trade liberalization, those benefits would be concentrated on the urban population; farmers — particularly poor farmers — stood to lose," said a World Bank report.[143] For that reason, critics of expanded international trade oppose the "virtual" approach.

Other advocates call for greater reliance on rain-fed farming. Just over half of the world's food, by value, is produced using rainfall, but this sector — dominated by poor rural farmers — has traditionally been ignored by food producers and governments in favor of major irrigation strategies.

"Upgrading rain-fed areas has high potential both for food production and for poverty alleviation," says the International Water Management Institute. Increasing small-scale rainwater storage with supplemental irrigation and better land management could produce quick output gains in these areas.[144]

If farmers continue to depend on irrigation for 40 percent of their water, producing an acceptable diet for 2.4 billion more people in the next 30 years would require another 20 Nile Rivers or 97 Colorado Rivers, says water expert Postel. "It is not at all clear where this water is to come from."[145]

NOTES

1. Charles C. Mann, "The Rise of Big Water," *Vanity Fair*, May 2007; Reuters, "China drought threatens water supply for millions," March 28, 2007.

2. Xinhua News Agency, "Drought leaves nearly 250,000 short of drinking water in Guangdong," *People's Daily Online*, Dec. 13, 2007; http://english.people.com.cn/90001/90776/6320617.html.

3. Jonathan Watts, "Dry, Polluted, Plagued by Rats: The Crisis in China's Greatest Yangtze River," *The Guardian* (Britain), Jan. 17, 2008; http://chinaview.wordpress.com/category/environment/drought/.

4. Xinhua News Agency, "Climate change blamed as drought hits 100,000 at China's largest freshwater lake," *People's Daily Online*, Dec. 14, 2007; http://english.people.com.cn/90001/90776/6321329.html.

5. Chris O'Brien, "Global Warming Hits China," Forbes.com, Jan. 6, 2008; www.forbes.com/opinions/2008/01/04/poyang-lake-china-oped-cx_cob_0106poyang.html.

6. Peter H. Gleick, "Time to Rethink Large International Water Meetings," *The World's Water 2006-2007*, Island Press, p. 182; www.worldwater.org/.

7. David Molden, ed.; "Summary," *Water for Food, Water for Life: A Comprehensive Assessment of Water Management in Agriculture*, International Water Management Institute, p. 10; www.iwmi.cgiar.org/assessment/files_new/synthesis/Summary_SynthesisBook.pdf.

8. See "Summary, Human Development Report 2006: Beyond scarcity: Power, poverty and the global water crisis," United Nations Development Programme, p. 26, http://hdr.undp.org/en/media/hdr2006_english_summary.pdf.

9. Carmen Revenga, *et al.*, "Executive Summary, Pilot Analysis of Global Ecosystems: Freshwater Systems," World Resources Institute, 2000, pp. 4, 26; www.wri.org/publication/pilot-analysis-global-ecosystems-freshwater-systems.

10. Stacy Shelton, "Lake Lanier hits lowest point since its construction," *The Atlanta-Journal Constitution*, Nov. 19, 2007; www.ajc.com/metro/content/metro/stories/2007/11/19/lanierlowweb_1120.html?cxntlid=homepage_tab_newstab. For background, see Mary H. Cooper, "Water Shortages," *CQ Researcher*, Aug. 1, 2003, pp. 649-672.

11. M. Falkenmark, *et al.*, "On the Verge of a New Water Scarcity: A call for good governance and human ingenuity," Stockholm International Water Institute (SIWI) Policy Brief, 2007, p. 17. For background, see Colin Woodard, "Curbing Climate Change," *CQ Global Researcher*, February 2007, pp. 27-50.

12. "Water and Terrorism," *The World's Water 2006-2007, op. cit.*, p. 1.

13. Environmental Protection Agency, "Water Sentinel Initiative," www.epa.gov/watersecurity/pubs/water_sentinel_factsheet.pdf.

14. Met Office Hadley Centre, "Effects of climate change in developing countries," November 2006, pp. 2-3, www.metoffice.gov.uk/research/hadleycentre/pubs/brochures/COP12.pdf; Michael McCarthy, "The Century of Drought," *The Independent* (London), Oct. 4, 2006, p. 1.

15. McCarthy, *ibid.*, p. 1.

16. World Water Council.

17. Quoted in "Billions without clean water," March 14, 2000, BBC, http://news.bbc.co.uk/2/hi/676064 .stm.

18. David Katz, "Going with the Flow," *The World's Water 2006-2007, op. cit.*, pp. 30-39.

19. Data Table 5, Access to Water Supply and Sanitation by Region, *The World's Water 2006-2007, op. cit.*, p. 258.

20. "Synthesis of the 4th World Water Forum," August 2006, p. 23-24, www.worldwaterforum4.org.mx/ files/report/SynthesisoftheForum.pdf. For background on Millennium Development Goals, see www.un.org/millenniumgoals and "U.N. Fact Sheet on Water and Sanitation," 2006, www.un .org/waterforlifedecade/factsheet.html.

21. "Human Development Report 2006," *op. cit.*, p. 8; http://hdr.undp.org/en/reports/global/hdr2006/.

22. Australian Broadcasting Corp., "Issues in Science and Technology," transcript, Sept. 22, 2007.

23. Frank Rijsberman, Charlotte Fraiture and David Molden, "Water scarcity: the food factor," *Issues in Science and Technology*, June 22, 2007.

24. *Ibid.*

25. Sharon P. Nappier, Robert S. Lawrence, Kellogg J. Schwab, "Dangerous Waters," *Natural History*, November 2007, p. 48.

26. Marq de Villiers, *Water: The Fate of Our Most Precious Resource* (1999), p. 267.

27. "World hit by water shortage," *Birmingham Post*, Aug. 21, 2006, p. 10; http://icbirmingham.icnet-work.co.uk/birminghampost/news/tm_method= full%26objectid=17597105%26siteid=50002-name_page.html.

28. "Water Resources Sector Strategy, Strategic Directions for World Bank Engagement," World Bank, 2004, p. 5, www-wds.worldbank.org/external/ default/WDSContentServer/WDSP/IB/2004/06/ 01/000090341_20040601150257/Rendered/PDF/ 28114.pdf.

29. de Villiers, *op. cit.*, pp. 176-177.

30. Frank R. Rijsberman, "1st Asia-Pacific Water Summit," MaximsNews Network, Oct. 8, 2007; ww.abc.net.au/7.30/content/2006/s1716766.htm.

31. Diane Raines Ward, *Water Wars: Drought, Flood, Folly and the Politics of Thirst* (2002), p. 171.

32. Nappier, *et al.*, *op. cit.*

33. "Human Development Report," *op. cit.*, p. 176. Also see Meena Palaniappan, Emily Lee and Andrea Samulon, "Environmental Justice and Water," *The World's Water 2006-2007, op. cit.*, p. 125.

34. "Human Development Report," *ibid.*

35. Palaniappan, *et al.*, *op. cit.*

36. Marc Reisner, *Cadillac Desert, the American West and its Disappearing Water* (1986), p. 10.

37. *Ibid.*, p. 437.

38. *Ibid.*, pp. 10-11; also see Robin Clarke and Jannet King, *The Water Atlas* (2004).

39. "Approaches to Private Participation in Water Services," World Bank, 2006, p. 213.

40. Daniel Yergin and Joseph Stanislaw, *Commanding Heights: The Battle for the World Economy* (2004).

41. Juan Forero, "Multinational Is Ousted, but Local Ills Persist," *The New York Times*, Dec. 15, 2005, p. 1; also, Public Citizen, "Water Privatization Case Study: Cochabamba, Bolivia," pp. 1-2, www .tradewatch.org/documents/Bolivia_(PDF).PDF; and Bechtel Corp. statement, "Cochabamba and the Aquas del Tunari Consortium," www.bechtel. com/assets/files/PDF/Cochabambafacts0305.pdf.

42. "European environment giant Veolia to increase investment in China to $2.5 billion by 2013," Xinhua News Agency, Nov. 1, 2007.

43. *Pinsent Masons Water Yearbook 2007-08*, p. xii, www.pinsentmasons.com/media/1976627452 .pdf.

44. Quoted in Jeff Fleischer, "Blue Gold: An Interview with Maude Barlow," *Mother Jones*, Jan. 14, 2005, www.motherjones.com/news/qa/2005/01/maude_ barlow.html.

45. "Economic Failures of Private Water Systems," Food & Water Watch, Dec. 2007, www .foodandwaterwatch.org/water/waterprivatization/ usa/Public_vs_Private.pdf.

46. Scott Wallsten and Katrina Kosec, "Public or Private Drinking Water?" AEI-Brookings Joint Center for Regulatory Studies, March 2005, pp. 2, 7;

www.reg-markets.org/publications/abstract
.php?pid=919.

47. Felipe Barrera-Osorio and Mauricio Olivera, "Does Society Win or Lose as a Result of Privatization?" Inter-American Development Bank, Research Network Working Paper #R-525, March 2007, p. 19.

48. *Ibid.*, p. 21.

49. Ward, *op. cit.*, pp. 206-207.

50. *Pinsent Masons Water Yearbook*, *op. cit.*, p. 3.

51. *Ibid.*, p. 5.

52. Paul Constance, "The Day that Water Ran Uphill," *IDB America*, Inter-American Development Bank, Dec. 9, 2007, www.iadb.org/idbamerica/index .cfm?thisid=3909&lanid=1.

53. "Human Development Report," *op. cit.*, p. 92.

54. *Ibid.*, p. 179; Ward, *op. cit.*, p. 210.

55. Malcolm Scully, "The Politics of Running Out of Water," *The Chronicle of Higher Education*, Nov. 17, 2000.

56. Peter H. Gleick, "Environment and Security," *The World's Water 2006-2007*, *op. cit.*, p. 189.

57. "Human Development Report," *op. cit.*, p. 221.

58. Benny Morris, *Righteous Victims* (2001), pp. 303-304.

59. Ward, *op. cit.*, p. 174.

60. *Ibid.*, p. 85.

61. *Ibid.*, p. 192.

62. Undala Alam, letter to the *Financial Times*, April 1, 2006, p. 6. Also see www.transboundarywaters. orst.edu/publications/related_research/Alam1998 .pdf.

63. Gleick, "Environment and Security," *op. cit.*, p. 189.

64. *Security and the Threat of Climate Change* (2007), CNA Corp., p. 3; http://securityandclimate.cna .org/.

65. *Ibid.*, p. 20.

66. *Ibid.*, p. 22.

67. "Human Development Report," *op. cit.*, p. 216; Clarke and King, *op. cit.*, p. 79.

68. *Ibid.*, p. 47.

69. "Human Development Report," *op. cit.*, p. 218.

70. CNA, *op. cit.*, p. 14.

71. "Dams and Development: A New Framework for Decision Making," World Commission on Dams, Nov. 16, 2000, p. 8; www.dams.org/report/wcd_ overview.htm.

72. Xinhua News Agency, "China's Grand Canal Queues for World Heritage Status," July 6, 2004, www.china.org.cn/english/culture/100401.htm.

73. Terry S. Reynolds, *Stronger Than a Hundred Men: A History of the Vertical Water Wheel* (1932), pp. 32, 142.

74. Jill Jonnes, *Empires of Light: Edison, Tesla, Westinghouse, and the Race to Electrify the World* (2004).

75. Revenga, *et al.*, *op. cit.*, p. 12.

76. World Commission on Dams, *op. cit.*, p. 9.

77. *Ibid.*, p. ii.

78. Ward, *op. cit.*, p. 51.

79. *Ibid.*, p. 46.

80. Lin Yang, "China's Three Gorges' Dam Under Fire," *Time*, Oct. 12, 2007, www.time.com/time/ world/article/0,8599,1671000,00.html. Also see Bruce Kennedy, "China's Three Gorges Dam," CNN.com, 2001, www.cnn.com/SPECIALS/ 1999/china.50/asian.superpower/three.gorges/.

81. Jonathan Watts, "Three Georges Dam risk to environment, says China," *The Guardian*, Sept. 27, 2007.

82. Xinhua Financial News, "Chinese Government Fights Back in Defense of Three Gorges Dam," Nov. 27, 2007; Jim Yardley, "China vigorously defends the Three Gorges Dam project," *The International Herald Tribune*, Nov. 28, 2007, p. 3.

83. Revenga, *et al.*, *op. cit.*, p. 28.

84. "Synthesis of the 4th World Water Forum," *op. cit.*

85. Ward, *op. cit.*, p. 47.

86. *Ibid.*, p. 187.

87. de Villiers, *op. cit.*, p. 59. Also see "Islamic Water Management and the Dublin Statement," The International Development Research Center, Canada, www.idrc.ca/en/ev-93949-201-1-DO_TOPIC .html.

88. Katz, *op. cit.*, p. 37.

89. Robert Glennon, *Water Follies: Groundwater Pumping and the Fate of America's Fresh Waters* (2002), p. 16.

90. *Ibid.*, p. 14.

91. "Human Development Report," *op. cit.*, p. 185.

92. *Ibid.*, p. 214.

93. Ward, *op. cit.*, p. 188.

94. Sandra Postel and Brian Richter, *Rivers for Life, Managing Water for People and Nature* (2003), p. 168.

95. "Human Development Report," *op. cit.*, p. 103.

96. *Ibid.*, p. 37.

97. *Ibid.*, p. 42.

98. *Ibid.*, pp. 45-46.

99. *Ibid.*, p. 33.

100. *Ibid.*, p. 29.

101. *Ibid.*, p. 30, citing Frances Bell and Robert Millward, "Public Health Expenditures and Mortality in England and Wales, 1870-1914," pp. 221-249.

102. Palaniappan, *et al.*, *op. cit.*, p. 131, citing the World Water Council, "Financing Water for All," Global Water Partnership, March 2004.

103. *Ibid.*, p. 139.

104. de Villiers, *op. cit.*, p 171.

105. *Ibid.*, pp. 172-177.

106. *Ibid.*, p. 174; "Human Development Report," *op. cit.*, p. 219; "Future Danube Flood Actions Depend On International Cooperation," Commission for the Protection of the Danube, April 21, 2006; www.icpdr.org/icpdr-pages/pr20060421_danube_flood.htm. For background, see Brian Beary, "The New Europe," *CQ Global Researcher*, August, 2007.

107. Peter H. Gleick, Heather Cooley, Gary Wolff, "With a Grain of Salt: An Update on Seawater Desalination," *The World's Water 2006-2007*, *op. cit.*, p. 55.

108. *Ibid.*, pp. 68-70.

109. *Ibid.*, pp. 78-79.

110. *Ibid.*, p. 161. General Electric Co. projects an annual growth rate of 9 to 14 percent, growing from $4.3 billion in annual desalination expenditures in 2005 to $14 billion in 2014.

111. P. W. Mote, *et al.*, "Declining Mountain Snowpack in Western North America," *Bulletin of the American Meteorological Society 86*, January 2005, pp. 49-48.

112. "New Century of Thirst for World's Mountains," Pacific Northwest National Laboratory, May 18, 2006, www.pnl.gov/news/release.asp?id=158.

113. Eric Bontrager, "West will need to revisit water, land management in light of global warming, experts say," *Land Letter*, Sept. 28. 2006; www.eenews.net/ll/ (subscription required).

114. Shaun McKinnon, "Southwest Could Become Dust Bowl, Study Warns," *The Arizona Republic*, April 6, 2007, p. 1; www.azcentral.com/arizonarepublic/news/articles/0406climate-report0406.html.

115. Bontrager, *op. cit.*

116. *Ibid.*

117. Shaun McKinnon, "Snow runoff: What's at Stake," *The Arizona Republic*, Nov. 25, 2007, p. 8; and Stephen Saunders and Maureen Maxwell, "Less Snow, Less Water: Climate Disruption in the West," The Rocky Mountain Climate Organization, September 2005, pp. 2, 9, 19, www.rockymountainclimate.org/website%20pictures/Less%20Snow%20Less%20Water.pdf.

118. "UK Government: Global drought in the 21st century," M2 Presswire, Oct. 26, 2006; www.continuitycentral.com/news02870.htm.

119. "Fourth Assessment Report — Climate Change 2007: Synthesis Report, Summary for Policymakers," Intergovernmental Panel on Climate Change, Nov. 17, 2007, p. 8; www.ipcc.ch/pdf/assessment-report/ar4/syr/ar4_syr_spm.pdf.

120. Claudie Tebaldi, Katharine Hayhoe, Julie M. Arblaster and Gerald A. Meehle, "Going to Extremes," Institute for the Study of Society and Environment, National Center for Atmospheric Research, 2006, p. 22; www.cgd.ucar.edu/ccr/publications/tebaldi_extremes.pdf.

121. Jon Gertner, "The Future is Drying Up," *New York Times Magazine*, Oct. 21, 2007; www.nytimes.com/2007/10/21/magazine/21water-t.html?_r=1&oref=slogin.

122. "New Study Shows Climate Change Likely to Lead to Periods of Extreme Drought in Southwest North America," Lamont-Doherty Earth Observatory, April 6, 2007, www.ldeo.columbia.edu/news-events/new-study-shows-climate-change-likely-lead-periods-extreme-drought-southwest-north-ameri.

123. "A Review of Water Conservation Planning for the Atlanta, Georgia Region, August 2006, prepared for the Florida Department of Environmental Protection," Pacific Institute, p. 23, www.pacinst.org/reports/atlanta/atlanta_analysis.pdf.

124. "Report to the Secretaries of State for Communities and Local Government and Food and Rural Affairs," *The Planning Inspectorate*, Sept. 29, 2006, p. 7-8, www.communities.gov.uk/documents/planningandbuilding/pdf/319931, and www.thameswater.co.uk/UK/region/en_gb/content/News/News_001394.jsp?SECT=Section_Homepage_000431.

125. Amy L. Vickers, "The Future of Water Conservation: Challenges Ahead," The Universities Council on Water Resources (UCOWR), p. 52, www.ucowr.siu.edu/updates/pdf/V114_A8.pdf. Also see Marcia Clemmitt, "Aging Infrastructure," *CQ Researcher*, Sept. 28, 2007, pp. 793-816.

126. Clarke and King, *op. cit.*, p. 87.

127. "Re-engaging in Agricultural Water Management — Challenges and Options," The International Bank for Reconstruction and Development/The World Bank, 2006, p. 3, web.worldbank.org/WBSITE/EXTERNAL/TOPICS/EXTARD/0,,contentMDK:20858509~pagePK:210058~piPK:210062~theSitePK:336682,00.html.

128. Vickers, *op. cit.*, p. 52.

129. Harriet Emerson and Mohamed Lahlou, "Conservation: It's the Future of Water," National Drinking Water Clearinghouse, www.nesc.wvu.edu/ndwc/ndwc_conservarticlesetc.htm/harrietarticle.html.

130. "Fact Sheet," U.S. Green Building Council, www.usgbc.org/DisplayPage.aspx?CMSPageID=222.

131. Katz, *op. cit.*, p. 32.

132. Postel and Richter, *op. cit.*, p. 201.

133. "World Population Prospects," U.N. Department of Economic and Social Affairs, 2006, http://esa.un.org/unpp/.

134. Molden, *op. cit.*, p. 1; *Birmingham Post*, *op. cit.*, p. 10.

135. Quoted in Kerry O'Brien, "Water scarcity 'due to agriculture,'" Australian Broadcasting Corp. Transcripts, Aug. 16, 2006; www.abc.net.au/7.30/content/2006/s1716766.htm.

136. Molden, *op. cit.*, pp. 7-8.

137. *Ibid.*, p. 14.

138. "Re-engaging in Agricultural Water Management," *op. cit.*, p. 38.

139. Rijsberman, *op. cit.*

140. Postel and Richter, *op. cit.*, pp. 112-117.

141. Jim Getz, "Kaufman County won't vote on Pickens' freshwater district: But Roberts County calls election on Pickens' pitch for freshwater district," *The Dallas Morning News*, Sept. 5, 2007.

142. "Re-engaging in Agricultural Water Management," *op. cit.*, p. 102.

143. *Ibid.*, p 103.

144. International Water Management Institute, *op. cit.*, p. 10.

145. de Villiers, *op. cit.*, p 24.

BIBLIOGRAPHY

Books

Clarke, Robin, and Jannet King, *The Water Atlas, The New Press, 2004.*
Editors at the World Meteorological Organization present a visual primer on water scarcity, sanitation shortfalls and climate impact on water resources.

de Villiers, Marq, *Water: The Fate of Our Most Precious Resource, Stoddard Publishing Co.,* 1999.
A Canadian journalist provides a global overview of challenges confronting the world's water supplies.

Glennon, Robert, *Water Follies: Groundwater Pumping and the Fate of America's Fresh Waters, Island Press, 2002.*

An attorney and water-policy expert advocates new policies to preserve Western U.S. aquifers.

Olivera, Oscar, *Cochabamba! Water Rebellion in Bolivia*, South End Press, 2004.

The leader of the Bolivian protest against water privatization gives his side of the conflict.

Postel, Sandra, and Brian Richter, *Rivers for Life, Managing Water for People and Nature*, Island Press, 2003.

Experts at the Global Water Policy Project in Massachusetts (Postel) and The Nature Conservancy (Richter) chronicle the campaign to restore environmental conditions in threatened rivers.

Reisner, Marc, *Cadillac Desert, the American West and Its Disappearing Water*, Penguin Books, 1986.

This award-winning classic by a former Natural Resources Defense Council expert critiques federal land and irrigation policies and their impact on water use in the West.

Ward, Diane Raines, *Water Wars: Drought, Flood, Folly and the Politics of Thirst*, Riverhead Books, 2002.

An environmental writer reviews controversial global policies affecting dams, water treaties and other water-resource issues.

Articles

Mann, Charles C., "The Rise of Big Water," *Vanity Fair*, May 2007.

A correspondent for *Science* and *The Atlantic Monthly* explores the controversy over privatization programs for water and sanitation worldwide.

Reports and Studies

"Approaches to Private Participation in Water Services: A Tool Kit," *The World Bank*, 2006, http://publications .worldbank.org/ecommerce/catalog/product?item_ id=4085442.

The world's major foreign-aid lender provides lessons learned from water-privatization efforts.

"Beyond scarcity: Power, poverty and the global water crisis," *United Nations Development Programme, U.N. Human Development Report* 2006, http://hdr.undp .org/en/reports/global/hdr2006.

This detailed review of worldwide water and sanitation challenges includes case studies of successes and failures.

"Comprehensive Assessment of Water Management in Agriculture: Water for Food, Water for Life," *International Water Management Institute*, 2006, www.fao.org/nr/water/docs/Summary_Synthesis Book.pdf.

A consulting group based in Sri Lanka reports on the impact of water scarcity on global irrigation and food production.

"Dams and Development: A New Framework for Decision Making," *World Commission on Dams*, 2000, www.dams.org/report.

Water experts, educators and government officials assess issues surrounding major dam construction and operations.

"IPCC Fourth Assessment Report," *Intergovernmental Panel on Climate Change*, 2007, www.ipcc.ch/ipccreports/ ar4-syr.htm.

A scientific panel sponsored by the World Meteorological Organization and the United Nations Environment Programme issues its most recent outlook on climate change threats.

"National Security and the Threat of Climate Change," *CNA Corp.*, December 2007, http://securityand climate.cna.org/report/.

A panel of retired U.S. generals and admirals forecasts security issues that will emerge as a result of climate change.

"Synthesis of the 4th World Water Forum, Mexico City," *World Water Council*, 2006, www.worldwater council.org/index.php?id=1386.

An international committee presents a summary of its fourth conference on water-resources issues.

Gleick, Peter H., *et al.*, "The World's Water 2006-2007, The Biennial Report on Freshwater Resources," *The Pacific Institute for Studies in Development, Environment, and Security*, 2006, www.pacinst.org/ publications/worlds_water/2006-2007/index.htm.

The institute's latest review of global water-resource issues includes chronologies of water conflicts and analyses of strategies for sustainable freshwater resource management.

For More Information

The CNA Corp., 4825 Mark Center Drive, Alexandria, VA 22311; (703) 824-2000; www.cna.org. A nonprofit research organization that operates the Center for Naval Analyses and the Institute for Public Research, concentrating on security, defense and other government-policy issues.

Food and Water Watch, 1616 P St., N.W., Suite 300, Washington, DC 20036; (202) 683-2500; www.foodandwaterwatch.org. A liberal research and advocacy organization focused on water resources, food security, sanitation and globalization issues.

Intergovernmental Panel on Climate Change, C/O World Meteorological Organization, 7bis Avenue de la Paix, C.P. 2300, CH-1211 Geneva 2, Switzerland; 41-22-730-8208/84; www.ipcc.ch. Intergovernmental research body.

International Water Management Institute, 127, Sunil Mawatha, Pelawatte, Battaramulla, Colombo, Sri Lanka; 94-11 2880000, 2784080; www.iwmi.cgiar.org. Research group supported by 60 governments, private foundations and international organizations.

The Met Office Hadley Centre, Met Office, FitzRoy Road, Exeter, Devon, EX1 3PB, United Kingdom; 44 (0)1392 885680; www.metoffice.gov.uk/research/hadleycentre. Britain's official center for climate-change research.

Pacific Institute, 654 13th St., Preservation Park, Oakland, CA 94612; (510) 251-1600; www.pacinst.org. A nonpartisan think tank studying development, environment and security issues.

Property and Environment Research Center, 2048 Analysis Dr., Suite A, Bozeman, MT 59718; (406) 587-9591; www.perc.org. A pro-market research and advocacy group.

Public Citizen, 1600 20th St., N.W., Washington, DC 20009; (202) 588-1000; www.citizen.org. A liberal consumer-advocacy group.

Stockholm International Water Institute, Drottninggatan 33, SE — 111 51 Stockholm, Sweden; 46 8 522 139 60; www.siwi.org. A research organization affiliated with the Swedish government.

U.N. Human Development Office, 304 E. 45th St., 12th Floor, New York, NY 10017; (212) 906-3661; hdr.undp.org/en/humandev. Publishes an annual report on health, economic and other social conditions.

U.S. Geological Survey, 12201 Sunrise Valley Dr., Reston, VA 20192; (888) 275-8747; www.usgs.gov. The government's mapping agency and research center on water resources, geology, natural hazards and other physical sciences.

World Bank, 1818 H St., N.W., Washington, DC 20433; (202) 473-1000; www.worldbank.org. Provides technical and financial assistance to developing countries.

World Water Council, Espace Gaymard, 2-4 place d'Arvieux, 13002 Marseille, France; 33 491 994100; www.worldwatercouncil.org. An international research and advocacy group of government and international agency officials, academics and corporate executives; sponsors World Water Forum every three years.

15 Oceans in Crisis

Can the Loss of Ocean Biodiversity Be Halted?

Colin Woodard

A Russian trawler hauls in a netful of red fish on the Grand Banks in the northwest Atlantic Ocean. The world's oceans have lost more than 90 percent of large predatory fish — such as tuna, swordfish and grouper — over the past half-century, prompting fishermen to hunt smaller species. Scientists and environmentalists blame the loss of ocean biodiversity on overfishing, pollution and climate change.

From *CQ Global Researcher*, October 2007.

S all Samba has spent much of his adult life fishing for octopus from his home in Nouadhibou, Mauritania, on Africa's Atlantic coast. Fishing from a wooden canoe, he could bring home 160 pounds on a five-day trip — earning $600 a month in a country where the average wage is only $200. In 2004, he built a home and bought new canoes; times were good.

Not anymore. "You used to be able to catch fish right in the port," the 39-year-old told *The Wall Street Journal* recently. "Now the only thing you can catch is water."[1]

Today Samba and other fishermen must compete with huge industrial trawlers from Russia, China and Spain. But while Samba pulls his catch out of the sea by hand in plastic traps, a single Spanish vessel dragging a massive nylon net catches 260,000 pounds of octopus on a typical 45-day fishing trip.

Some 340 big foreign vessels fish Mauritanian waters because the government recently sold fishing rights to Asian and European nations that have overfished their own territorial waters. Stocks of octopus, which account for half of Mauritania's fish exports, are declining, and Samba has seen his monthly income fall by two-thirds.

Samba's experience is rapidly becoming universal in the world's coastal regions. According to the U.N. Food and Agriculture Organization (FAO), a quarter of the world's commercial fish stocks have been overexploited or depleted, and about half are fully exploited — meaning fishermen are taking as much as can be reliably replenished by the ecosystem.[2] (*See graphic, p. 354.*)

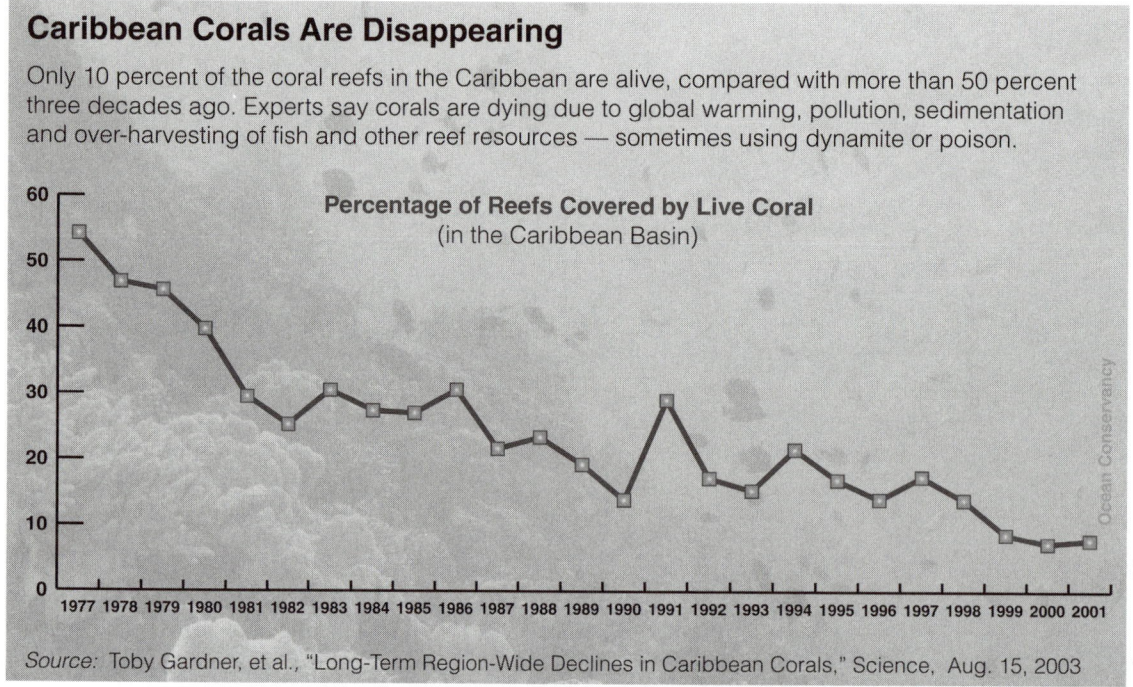

Caribbean Corals Are Disappearing

Only 10 percent of the coral reefs in the Caribbean are alive, compared with more than 50 percent three decades ago. Experts say corals are dying due to global warming, pollution, sedimentation and over-harvesting of fish and other reef resources — sometimes using dynamite or poison.

Percentage of Reefs Covered by Live Coral
(in the Caribbean Basin)

Source: Toby Gardner, et al., "Long-Term Region-Wide Declines in Caribbean Corals," Science, Aug. 15, 2003

Moreover, 90 percent of the world's large, predatory fish have been harvested since 1950, prompting fishermen to progressively move to smaller, less valuable species further down the food chain.[3] The shift has triggered the rapid depletion of marine species previously considered unmarketable — such as dogfish, urchins and basking sharks — which in turn has reduced the food available to the surviving stocks of larger species. Small, lower-valued schooling fish like anchovies now dominate world fishery landings.

"We're eating bait and moving on to jellyfish and plankton," says Daniel Pauly, director of the Fisheries Centre at the University of British Columbia, who predicts future generations will associate seafood not with tuna or cod but with simple, gelatinous creatures. "My kids will tell their children: 'Eat your jellyfish.' "[4]

The decimation of global fisheries is blamed largely on powerful, new technologies that allow fishermen to capture fish faster than the ocean can produce them. Radar, fish finders, satellite tracking and navigation systems, onboard processing plants and flash freezers are put aboard ever faster vessels capable of fishing far from shore for long periods.

In addition, most fishing gear is indiscriminate: The vast nets used by trawlers typically kill huge quantities of unmarketable marine life. Each year 7 million metric tons of seabirds, juvenile fish, sea turtles, dolphins, sharks, crabs, starfish, anemones, sponges and other creatures are caught, killed and discarded by mechanized fishing. On average, this "bycatch" accounts for 8 percent of fishermen's catches; but among shrimp fishermen in the tropics, bycatch represents 56 percent of the haul.[5]

Trawl nets and gear dragged along the sea bottom are said to cause lasting damage to the seafloor habitat and, thus, to the ability of marine ecosystems to sustain themselves. The heavy nets plow away the bottom plants, sponges and corals that animals use for cover, while killing large numbers of the invertebrates they feed on.

In the Gulf of Maine, for instance, the average seafloor section is trawled once a year; on the Georges Bank off Massachusetts, it's plowed three to four times a year. The trawls also create muddy clouds thought to reduce the survival of small fish by clogging their gills.[6] Elliott Norse, president of the Marine Conservation Biology Institute in Bellevue, Wash., calls sea bottom trawling "clear cutting the seafloor." Trawling companies contend there's no proof their activities damage the ocean floor and that trawling actually may benefit seafloor species.

It's not just fish that are in crisis, however. Coral reefs, the foundation of most tropical marine life, are declining at an alarming rate. The latest international assessment found that one-fifth of the world's coral reefs "have been effectively destroyed and show no immediate prospects of recovery," while another 24 percent are "under imminent risk of collapse." Live coral cover on Caribbean reefs has declined by 80 percent over the past 30 years.[7] (*See graph, p. 354.*)

Without corals, tropical oceans would become biological wastelands, because they don't support the growth of phytoplankton, the microscopic plants that form the base of the marine food chain. Reefs are colonies of coral polyps — anemone-like organisms that build limestone shells around themselves. They filter food particles from the water and capture the sun's energy through photosynthetic micro-organisms inside their tissue. Corals support the profusion of fish associated with tropical reefs.[8]

Reefs are being damaged in a variety of ways. Clearing coastal mangroves for development dooms reef creatures that feed there and triggers erosion that smothers the coral polyps under plumes of sand and soil. Overfishing results in the harvesting of increasing numbers of ever-smaller fish, lobsters and conch. Fishermen in the Philippines, Micronesia, Jamaica and Indonesia use dynamite and other explosives to stun and kill marine life over a wide area — a one-time bonanza that destroys the reef. Sewage and fertilizer run-off from towns, resorts, fish farms and golf courses trigger the

Most Fish Stocks Are Overexploited

Three-quarters of the world's fisheries were either fully exploited — at or near their maximum sustainable limits — overexploited or depleted in 2005. Fisheries biologists say the stocks cannot recover quickly and are in danger of further decline.

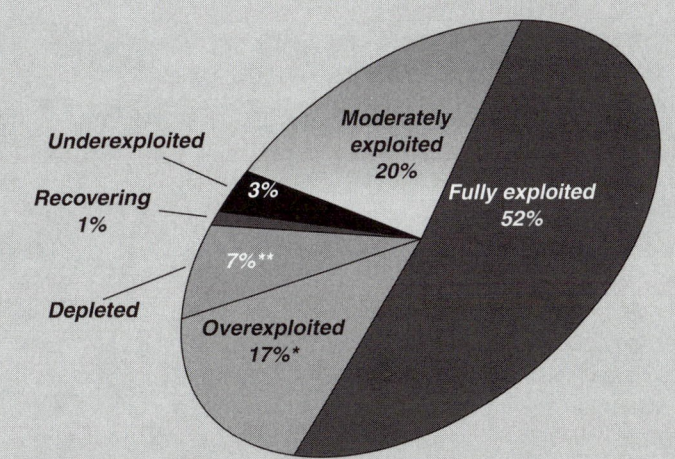

Status of the World's Fish Stocks, 2005

- Underexploited — 3%
- Recovering — 1%
- Depleted — 7%**
- Overexploited — 17%*
- Moderately exploited — 20%
- Fully exploited — 52%

* Exploited beyond the ability of the system to sustain itself over the long term.

** Current catches fall far below historic levels.

China and Peru Catch the Most

China and Peru haul in nearly 27 million tons of fish a year — almost as much as the next eight countries combined.

Amount of fish captured*
(in millions of tons)

World's Top 10 Fishing Countries, 2004

Country	Amount
China	16.9
Peru	9.6
USA	5.0
Chile	4.9
Indonesia	4.8
Japan	4.4
India	3.6
Russia	2.9
Thailand	2.4
Norway	2.5

* Fish caught in the wild, excluding those grown by aquaculture.

Source: "The State of the World Fisheries and Aquaculture 2006," U.N. Food and Agriculture Organization, www.fao.org/docrep/009/A0699e/A0699E04.htm

Beach Litter Can Be Lethal

Nearly 7.7 million pieces of beach litter were collected in 2006 by some 350,000 Ocean Conservancy coastal cleanup volunteers around the world. About two-thirds of the items were food containers and plastic bags; the rest were smoking related. Experts say 1 million seabirds and 100,000 marine mammals and sea turtles die each year after ingesting or becoming entangled in ocean debris.

Top 10 Ocean Debris Items Worldwide

Debris Items	Number of Items	Percent of Total
Cigarette debris	1,901,519	24.7%
Food wrappers, containers	768,115	10.0%
Caps/lids	704,085	9.1%
Bags	691,048	9.0%
Beverage bottles (Plastic) 2 liters or less	570,299	7.4%
Beverage bottles (Glass)	420,800	5.5%
Cups/plates/forks/knives/spoons	353,217	4.6%
Straw/stirrers	349,653	4.5%
Beverage cans	327,494	4.3%
Cigar tips	186,258	2.4%

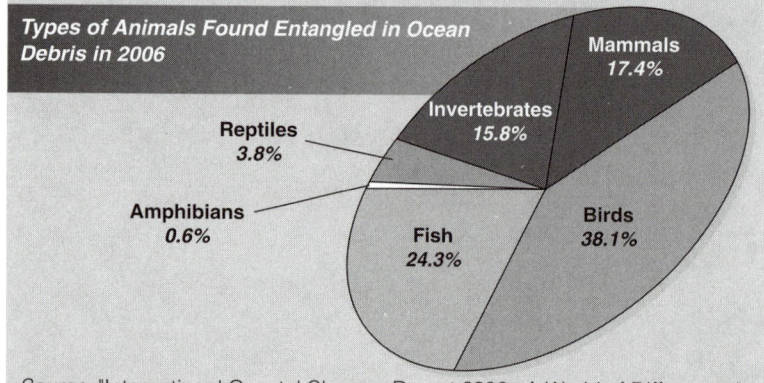

Types of Animals Found Entangled in Ocean Debris in 2006

- Mammals 17.4%
- Invertebrates 15.8%
- Reptiles 3.8%
- Amphibians 0.6%
- Fish 24.3%
- Birds 38.1%

Source: "International Coastal Cleanup Report 2006: A World of Difference," Ocean Conservancy

and other industrial compounds now found in seawater and stored in the animals' fat. Many Inuit have concentrations of certain pesticides in their bodies that exceed safe levels 20-fold. Beached whales often must be treated as hazardous waste because of the high concentrations toxic substances in their bodies.[10] Both wild and farm-raised salmon have also been shown to have potentially significant contaminant levels.[11]

Fertilizers, sewage and other nutrient pollution have triggered massive algal blooms that can strip the ocean of dissolved oxygen, dooming animals that cannot escape the area. Such oxygen-starved "dead zones" have spread from harbors and river mouths to suffocate entire seas. (*See sidebar, p. 360.*) Each summer, fertilizer runoff from 31 states and parts of Canada flows into the Mississippi River and then to the Gulf of Mexico, creating a New Jersey-size dead zone south of New Orleans where few species can survive.[12]

Non-native, or "invasive," species also can damage marine ecosystems.[13] The species are carried around the globe in the ballast tanks of ocean-going vessels, which pump water in and out of the tanks to maintain seaworthiness. This ballast can contain the eggs, larvae or adult forms of hundreds of species, some of which become established in waters that contains no natural predators.

"Once an exotic species is established, trying to remove it is like trying to put the toothpaste back in the tube," says James T. Carlton, professor of marine sciences at Williams College in Massachusetts. In the early 1990s, a comb jelly snuffed out much of the life in the Black Sea (*see p. 360*), while a mutant form of a tropical seaweed, *Caulerpa taxifolia*, has smothered vast stretches of the Mediterranean shore since it was accidentally released into the sea by a Monaco aquarium.[14]

growth of seaweed, kelp and other plants that can smother and eventually kill the reefs. Even far from human activity, reefs are dying from disease and overly warm water temperatures linked to climate change.[9]

Colder waters are affected, too. In the High Arctic, Inuit mothers' breast milk is dangerous to their babies' health because the polar bears, seals, walruses, fish and whales they eat are contaminated by heavy metals, PCBs

Some scientists worry that in many marine ecosystems the more advanced organisms are disappearing while the populations of the most primitive ecosystems are exploding. "Dead zones aren't dead; they are just full of jellyfish and bacteria," notes Jeremy B. C. Jackson, director of the Geosciences Research Division at the Scripps Institution of Oceanography in San Diego, who calls the process "the rise of slime."

In Sweden, summer blooms of *cyanobacteria* turn the surface of the Baltic Sea into a yellow-brown slurry that kills fish, burns people's eyes and makes breathing difficult. Hawaiian condo owners have had to use tractors to remove piles of algae piling up on their beaches, while toxic algal blooms are believed responsible for mass die-offs of sea lions, whales, manatees and dolphins. Red tides — algal blooms that make shellfish poisonous to humans — are 10 times more common than they were 50 years ago, owing in part to increases in sewage and fertilizer run-off. "We're pushing the oceans back to the dawn of evolution, a half-billion years ago when the oceans were ruled by jellyfish and bacteria," says Pauly at the University of British Columbia.[15]

Experts argue that adopting ecosystem-based approaches to regulating human activity on the seas would help ensure the system as a whole is healthy, rather than just focusing on a particular species. Some fishing interests resist such an approach — which would involve creation of marine reserves and other protected areas — but its greatest opponent is public and political apathy.

As scientists and governments try to determine how best to protect the world's oceans, here are some of the questions being debated:

Are humans destroying the oceans?

Yes, according to numerous recent scientific studies including a June 2007 assessment of Europe's seas by 100 scientists from 15 countries.

"In every sea, we found serious damage related to the accelerated pace of coastal development, the way we transport our goods and the way we produce our food on land as well as the sea," said Laurence Mee, director of the Marine Institute at the University of Plymouth (in England), who coordinated the project. "Without a concerted effort to integrate protection of the sea into Europe's development plans, its biodiversity and resources will be lost."[16]

Ocean Conservancy

Plastic bottles, food containers and grocery bags make up a large portion of the refuse that ends up in the ocean and washes ashore. More than 100,000 marine mammals alone are killed each year by either ingesting or becoming entangled in debris.

A four-year analysis released in November 2006 by an international group of ecologists and economists concluded that if current trends continue, every seafood species currently fished will be commercially extinct by 2050. The study found that every species lost increases the speed at which the larger ecosystem unravels.

"Whether we looked at tide pools or studies over the entire world's oceans, we saw the same picture emerging," said the study's lead author, Boris Worm, assistant professor of biology at Dalhousie University in Halifax, Nova Scotia. "I was shocked and disturbed by how consistent these trends are — beyond anything we expected."[17]

Likewise, two independent, bipartisan U.S. commissions — the Pew Oceans Commission and the U.S. Commission on Ocean Policy (USCOP) — concluded in 2003 and 2004, respectively, that pollution, habitat destruction and overfishing are endangering the world's oceans.[18]

"There is overwhelming scientific evidence that our ocean ecosystems are in serious trouble, serious enough that it really is endangering the future of ocean life itself," says Leon Panetta, former chief of staff in the Clinton White House, who chaired the Pew Commission. "The biggest challenge is to get people to pay attention, because if they do, then we can make our case."

"What is the state of our oceans? Unfortunately we have to report to you that the state is not good, and it is getting worse," Admiral James D. Watkins, chair of USCOP told Congress. Furthermore, the harm humans are inflicting on the oceans, the USCOP report concluded, has "serious consequences for the entire planet."[19]

Marine scientists have been aware of the situation for more than a decade. In 1998 — the U.N. International Year of the Ocean — more than 1,600 marine scientists and conservation biologists from 65 nations issued a joint warning that the seas were in peril and that immediate action was needed to prevent further damage.

"Getting scientists to agree on anything is like herding cats, so having 1,600 experts voice their concerns publicly highlights just how seriously the sea is threatened," said Norse, of the Marine Conservation Biology Institute, who organized the effort. "We must change what we're doing now to prevent further irreversible decline."[20]

However, some researchers and fishing industry groups deny there is a problem, claiming the situation is exaggerated by environmentalists to further fundraising opportunities. "Are we running out of fish? No," said Dan Furlong, executive director of the U.S. Mid-Atlantic Fishery Management Council. Furlong cites U.S. National Marine Fisheries Service assessments showing that of the 230 stocks the agency manages, only 44 are known to be overfished, 136 "are not subject to overfishing," while the status of the remaining 50 are unknown. "In other words, the glass is more than half full for those stocks," he says. The public, he says, has been duped by environmentalists who pushed Congress to require that stocks be rebuilt. As a result, he says, "despite significant improvements across a broad range of fisheries, we are cast in the role of doing poorly because we will likely fail to meet . . . the arbitrary, capricious deadline to maximize stocks all at the same time."[21]

Bjorn Lomborg, associate professor of statistics at the University of Aarhus in Denmark, argues in his controversial book *The Skeptical Environmentalist* that while there are problems, the oceans are doing fine.

"The oceans are so incredibly big that our impact on them has been astoundingly insignificant," he argues, citing U.N. data suggesting that in the open oceans, far from land, the U.N. has found the seas to be relatively clean. He acknowledges that fertilizer is creating dead zones in places like the Gulf of Mexico and the Black Sea but says the disruptions are worth it when compared to the improved crop yields.[22]

"Our oceans have not been defiled . . . and although the nutrient influx has increased in many coastal waters like the Gulf of Mexico," he continues. "This does not constitute a major problem — in fact, the benefits generally outweigh the costs."[23]

Critics accuse Lomborg of cherry-picking facts that support his arguments and ignoring evidence to the contrary. For instance, Lomborg's book fails to address the crisis in the fisheries, the decline of the coral reefs, the problems caused by alien species and other issues.

And even some fishermen don't share Lomborg's view. "The combination of modern electronics with large fishing vessels has created a technology too powerful for fish stocks to withstand," said Ted Ames, a fisherman from Stonington, Maine, who won a McArthur Genius Grant for his research into the decline of Gulf of Maine fish stocks.[24]

Is ecosystem-based management the solution?

The destruction of life in the oceans presents humans with perhaps the greatest marine policy challenge in history: figuring out how to manage human activities so they don't damage marine biodiversity, critical habitat and overall ecosystem function. Known as "ecosystem-based management," the approach has wide support, including both USCOP and the Pew Commission.

"You're not going to have any fish to catch — or healthy fishing communities — unless there is a healthy marine ecosystem to provide the fish," says Jane Lubchenco, a professor of marine biology at Oregon State University, a former Pew Commissioner and past president of the American Association for the Advancement of Science. "We need mechanisms to better understand how ocean ecosystems work and how we're changing them if we are going to do a better job managing them."

And many scientists say they don't yet have that understanding.

For the past two years, dozens of scientists in New England and Canada's maritime provinces have been working to develop enough knowledge to undertake ecosystem-based management in the Gulf of Maine by 2010. Scientists working on the Gulf of Maine Census of Marine Life — part of the world's first pilot project for this type of management — are fanning out across the ecosystem examining sea life, ocean currents and the relationship between habitat, predators and prey. A series of ocean buoys is collecting long-term oceanographic data, and other researchers are using sonar technology to map the ocean bottom in unprecedented detail.

"We need to know the big picture of how it happens," says Gerhard Pohle, acting executive director of the Huntsman Marine Science Centre in St. Andrews, New Brunswick, Canada. "If we take one rivet out of the airplane, will it crash? If so, which rivet?"[25]

"We're just beginning to understand how to do the biology on both the super-tiny and the super-large scales," says Lubchenco, who is studying the California Current ecosystem off the U.S. West Coast. "You have to marry oceanography and ecology and genetics and microchemistry in a very interdisciplinary fashion to better understand the processes driving these ecosystems."

But other scientists — many of them government fisheries managers — say sufficient knowledge already exists to start ecosystem-wide management. "Make no mistake, we currently have sufficient scientific information to move forward with an ecosystem-based approach to management," said Andrew Rosenberg, dean of the College of Life Sciences at the University of New Hampshire, a USCOP commissioner and former deputy director of the U.S. National Marine Fisheries Service. "The nation's ocean policy should recognize these principles and seek to integrate management within regional ecosystems."[26]

Some scientists and environmentalists challenge the notion that humans can or should try to manage ecosystems. In the long term, they say, how could one manage a constantly changing ecosystem, when ideas about what is "healthy" or "desirable" are often based on present conditions or a theoretical, idyllic state. Others point out that an ecosystem means different things to different people, making them difficult to adequately define.[27]

Proponents are careful to point out that ecosystem-based management does not seek to manage the ecosystem — which would be scientific hubris in their opinion — but rather human activity affecting the ecosystem. "One of the reasons ecosystem-based management was pooh-poohed for many years was that there was this naïve assumption [that] you just learn everything you need to know about the ecosystem and then you manage it," says Lew Incze, director of the Aquatic Systems Group at the University of Southern Maine in Portland. "Now we know that we will never know everything — you can even have 100 years of good data, but the ocean is always changing.

"The question is," he continues, "what type of knowledge would allow you to pursue the idea?"

The Gulf of Maine Census of Marine Life is attempting to develop a basic framework by testing ideas about what factors control the number of upper-level predators like Atlantic cod or humpback whales; what indicators would best track the health and diversity of the entire system and how currents, tides and natural oceanographic cycles shape life there. "We're just now developing the tools to come to grips with this," says Pohle.

David Benton, executive director of the Marine Conservation Alliance, a coalition of Alaskan fishing interests, says ecosystem-based management is potentially very good for commercial fishermen.

"It's very clear to most of our membership that it is in their long-term interest to make sure that we have healthy oceans and fish stocks and that all the associated components of the ecosystem around those stocks are in good shape," he says. "A lot of these companies are looking at how these fisheries are going to support their business — not two years from now but a decade from now or longer."

Should ocean-floor trawling be restricted?

Concerns about the damage caused by shellfish dredges and trawl nets have prompted many scientists, environmentalists and governmental agencies to call for a ban on trawling where it is likely to cause lasting harm.

A 2002 study by the National Academy of Sciences' National Research Council recommended that the U.S. government reduce the impact and extent of bottom trawling to reduce its impact on undersea life. Trawls scrape away cold-water corals, sponges, plants, sea anemones, starfish and other creatures, the report found, and repeated passes can cause a 93 percent reduction in these and other bottom-dwelling animals.

The Black Sea's Cautionary Tale

Ecosystem collapse shows signs of recovery.

From ancient times, humans have been drawn to the Black Sea, a kidney-shaped basin the size of California nestled between Eastern Europe and Asia Minor. Its anchovy and sturgeon stocks sustained Ancient Greece, medieval Byzantium, the Ottoman Empire and Imperial Russia.

In the 20th century, millions of tourists flocked each summer to its beaches in Turkey and on the "Communist Riviera," which stretched from Bulgaria and Romania to Soviet Russia. They swam, feasted on fish and basked in the sunshine, recuperating from winter months in the factories of Budapest and Birmingham.[1]

Then, with astonishing suddenness, the ecosystem collapsed in the early 1990s due to a combination of fertilizer and sewage pollution runoff, destruction of wetlands and the introduction of an aggressive, non-native, jellyfish-like species. Given the plethora of critical ocean ecosystems now in jeopardy, the Black Sea collapse provides a cautionary tale about the fragility of marine ecosystems, say marine scientists.

"The Black Sea is a microcosm of the environmental problems of the planet," warns Janet Lubchenco, a professor of marine biology at Oregon State University. "Solutions to the Black Sea crisis may enlighten, inform and inspire our global challenges."[2]

Few saw it coming. The Black Sea had been subject to pollution for decades: Industrial wastes, oil spills and radiation from the 1986 Chernobyl nuclear accident had been carried to the sea by its tributaries — apparently without dramatic effect. But it was the buildup of raw sewage and fertilizer runoff — coupled with the accidental introduction of an alien, plankton-devouring species, the comb jelly — that triggered the near-death of the sea.

The sea's largest tributary, the Danube River, drains half the European continent during its 2,000-mile journey from the Black Forest of Switzerland to Romania's Black Sea delta. The last half of that journey winds through Eastern Europe, where for decades every village, town and city flushed its untreated sewage into the river. Starting in the late 1960s, state-owned farms used huge quantities of subsidized chemical fertilizers on their fields, and much of it ran off into the streams feeding the Danube. Hydroelectric projects and navigational canals also damaged or bypassed wetlands that once acted as the river's natural filtering system. And Romania's dictator, Nicolae Ceausescu, waged all-out war on the Danube delta — Europe's greatest wetland — in an ill-conceived attempt to convert it to rice production.[3]

As a result, concentrations of nitrogen and phosphorous nutrients in the Black Sea's ecologically critical northwestern shelf dramatically increased between 1960 and 1980.[4] The nutrients fueled enormous algae blooms in the late 1980s, smothering bottom life by using up the oxygen it needed. As the microscopic plants decomposed, they consumed still more oxygen in vast stretches of the sea, suffocating most other creatures.[5]

Then in 1982, *Mnemiopsis leidyi*, an inch-long comb jelly native to North America, was introduced to the sea in the ballast water of a passing ship. The creature established itself amid the gathering chaos and proceeded to graze the waters clean of survivors. With no natural predators, it ultimately achieved a biomass of 1 billion tons — 10 times the weight of all the fish caught by all the world's fishermen in a year.[6]

"The biomass of other zooplankton dropped sharply, and the catches of commercial fish sharply decreased," noted Yuvenaly P. Zaitsev chief scientist at the Odessa office of the

---

"The more we understand about the ecology of fishes, the more we find that for the animals that live right above the seafloor, the integrity of these seafloors is critical to their survival," said Peter Auster, science director of the National Undersea Research Center at the University of Connecticut and a co-author of the report.[28]

Mark Butler, policy director at the Ecology Action Center in Halifax, Nova Scotia, argues there are other fishing methods that don't damage bottom habitats. "We are talking about protecting the ocean floor, which is often the nursery for young fish. You damage that in a major way, then you perhaps start to impair the health of the fishery itself."[29]

Of particular concern are the effects of trawling on seamounts — underwater mountain havens for life in the deep ocean. A 2006 U.N. study found that many seamount fisheries had been quickly depleted and

Ukrainian National Academy of Science. "*Mnemiopsis* . . . is usually held responsible for much of what happened."[7]

By the early 1990s, total fish landings had fallen to one-seventh of their previous level, and the signature anchovy catch fell by 95 percent. Slicks of ugly, stinking slime drove tourists from the beaches and prompted long closures at the height of summer. Hundreds of bathers became ill and several died from cholera and other infectious diseases that thrived in the algae-choked environment. In 1999 the World Bank estimated the economic damage to the fisheries sector at $300 million a year and $400 million to tourism.[8]

The past five years have seen considerable progress, however, as the European Union — with its strict environmental regulations — expanded to include 10 former communist countries, including Slovakia, Hungary, Romania, Bulgaria and other nations in the Danube's middle and lower basin.[9]

"When these countries joined the EU, they had to adopt new environmental policies and regulations, which has had the benefit of improving the overall water quality situation in the Danube basin," notes Ivan Zavadsky, program director of the Danube/Black Sea Regional Program in Vienna, a joint project of the United Nations and World Bank, which has pumped $70 million into cleanup projects in the region.

New sewage treatment plants have been built in recent years, and many of the most polluting factories and agricultural enterprises collapsed in the early 1990s. As a result, Zavadsky notes, concentrations of phosphorus and nitrogen — the nutrients that ravaged the Black Sea — have dropped 50 percent and 20 percent, respectively, since 1989. Meanwhile, the *Mnemiopsis*' population dropped precipitously after the arrival of the Beroe, another invading comb jelly that feeds exclusively on *Mnemiopsis*. Once the Beroe had eaten all the *Mnemiopsis*, its food source was depleted, so Black Sea populations of both species have now been decimated.[10]

"We're witnessing the first signs of a recovery of the Black Sea ecosystem," says Zavadsky, citing reduced algae blooms and an increase in some bottom plants and animals. "But the situation remains on a knife's edge."

But Janos Zlinszky, the government and public affairs manager of the Regional Environmental Center for Central and Eastern Europe in Szentendre, Hungary, is concerned that many of the gains could be lost if the region's economic recovery outpaces its environmental investments. "Romania and Bulgaria have just joined the EU," he says. "If they decide to focus on intensive agriculture rather than the organic market, we could see great increases in fertilizer and pesticide use."

"There's an extraordinary window of opportunity to take action," says Laurence Mee, director of the Marine Institute at the School of Earth, Ocean and Environmental Sciences at the University of Plymouth, in England. "But it can easily be lost."

[1] Colin Woodard, *Ocean's End: Travels Through Endangered Seas* (2000), pp. 1-25.

[2] From a speech in Trabzon, Turkey, Sept. 20, 1997.

[3] Woodard, *op. cit.*, pp. 13-23.

[4] Amhet Kideys, "Fall and Rise of the Black Sea Ecosystem," *Science*, Aug. 30, 2002, p. 1482.

[5] "Pollution and Problems of the Black Sea," a speech by Radu Mihnea, Romanian Research Institute, in Batumi, Georgia, Sept. 21, 1997.

[6] Kideys, *op. cit.*, p. 1482; Woodard, *op. cit.*, p. 22.

[7] "The Black Sea: Status and Challenges," a speech by Yuvenaly Zaitsev in Novorossiysk, Russia, Sept. 23, 1997.

[8] "Black Sea Transboundary Diagnostic Analysis," Global Environment Facility, August 1997, pp. ii, 15, 123, 125; Woodard, *op. cit.*, p. 22; Emilia Battaglini, "The GEF Strategic Partnership for the Danube/Black Sea," Presentation to World Bank, Bucharest, February 2007.

[9] For background, see Brian Beary, "The New Europe," *CQ Global Researcher*, August 2007.

[10] Kideys, *op. cit.*

estimated that some 95 percent of the ecological damage found on the undersea mountains was due to bottom-trawling. The study prompted New Zealand, the United States and other countries to push for a worldwide ban on bottom trawling on the high seas — international waters located more than 200 nautical miles from dry land. The measure was defeated when Canada, Iceland, Russia and China refused to back it.[30]

The Madrid-based environmental organization Oceana advocates limiting bottom trawlers and dredgers to areas where they already fish, excluding them from areas containing deep sea coral and sponge habitat, two species that recover poorly from trawling disruptions. Although the U.S. Commission on Ocean Policy didn't address the trawling issue specifically, the Pew Commission said it should be excluded wherever it will

Marine Conservation Biology Institute/Elliot A. Norse

More than 7 million metric tons of unwanted sea life — bycatch — is caught in the huge nets of commercial fishermen and discarded, including seabirds, stingrays, juvenile fish, sea turtles, dolphins, sharks, crabs, starfish, anemones, sponges and other creatures. Bycatch often dies before it gets thrown back into the sea. In the tropics, bycatch represents 56 percent of the haul.

reduce biodiversity or alter or destroy "a significant amount of habitat." "Sensitive habitats as well as areas not currently trawled or dredged should be closed to such use immediately," the report said.[31]

Federal fisheries managers in the United States banned bottom trawling from 300,000 square miles of such habitat off the U.S. West Coast. New Zealand, generally regarded as a leader in oceans policy, banned bottom trawling in 2006 in 30 percent of its waters.[32] Rosenberg of the University of New Hampshire contends trawling doesn't need to be universally banned. "You have to manage where trawling occurs and what level of impact we can sustain without reducing the resource productivity."[33]

Meanwhile, the European Union has been criticized for the "cash for access" deals it made with 12 West African states. Under the agreements — which include few, if any, conservation provisions — hundreds of European trawlers are operating in a "fundamentally unsustainable" manner, according to Milan Ilnyckyj, a doctoral student at Oxford University who has studied the problem.[34]

Si'd Ahmed Ould Abeid, president of Mauritania's National Fisheries Federation, said the fisheries agreements with the EU have been "a catastrophe for the fishermen whose catches are down and for the future of the fish in our waters. . . . The fish are just taken from our water, our fishermen lose their lives and we don't gain anything."[35]

Justin Brashares, an assistant professor of environmental science policy at the University of California-Berkeley, argues that the quickest way to increase the production and sustainability of West African domestic fisheries would be to limit the access of the foreign trawlers.

But EU Fisheries Commissioner Joe Borg argues deals such as the one the EU struck with Mauritania would benefit both parties in terms of "jobs, strengthened monitoring and control, conservation of resources in compliance with scientific assessment and environmental protection."[36]

Paul Molyneaux, author of *The Doryman's Reflection*, about his career as a commercial fisherman in Alaska, New Jersey and Maine, says the damage wrought by industrial-scale fishing is so great that it will be years before trawling will be ecologically appropriate in many areas. "In the short term, I think it should be banned," he says. "In many places they have destroyed the ecosystem foundations by dragging, taking too many fish, and disrupting the stock structure. They put everybody else out of business, and then they went out of business themselves."

But trawler owners argue that, far from damaging the environment, their gear actually improves marine productivity by plowing the seafloor and churning up nutrients. "A lot of fishermen feel that they are freshening the bottom, sort of turning over the soil, tending a garden, and that this helps certain species," says Bonnie Brady, executive director of the Long Island Commercial Fishermen's Association.

James Kendall, executive director of the New Bedford (Mass.) Seafood Coalition, argues nobody knows whether scallop dredges harm or hurt the fishery. "Does this activity oxygenate the sediment, release buried nutrients, damage herring-egg beds or adversely affect juvenile fish and scallops?" he asks, adding that more study is needed to answer those questions.[37]

"I am not suggesting that the act of scalloping on the ocean floor does not create an impact upon it, but that it may not be the adverse one so easily assumed," he continues, noting that the best scallop grounds have remained constant for decades, despite intensive dragging.

Some studies from the intensively trawled North Sea support the fishermen's contentions, at least in part. Scientists have observed 35 times as many fish gathered in areas that had recently been trawled compared to adjacent unfished areas, suggesting the fish were attracted to the disturbed bottom to feed. Bottom trawling appears at least partially responsible for increased growth rates in sole and plaice, two North Sea flat fish, presumably because the disturbances promote the growth of small invertebrates they like to eat. A third study suggested that two other North Sea species — gurnards and whiting — were drawn to trawl tracks to feed on tube worms dredged up by the fishing gear.[38]

Furlong, of the Mid-Atlantic Fishery Management Council, contends dragging and dredging can be appropriate in sandy, muddy bottoms like those off New Jersey, Delaware and Maryland. "There's nothing to clear cut down there," he said. "You can't clear cut sand." A 1989 bottom trawling assessment of a sandy area by the Massachusetts Division of Marine Fisheries found no damage to bottom-dwelling lobsters and negligible habitat impacts.[39]

BACKGROUND

Run on the Banks

Fishing has been an important activity since prehistoric times. Fishermen using hand nets, hand lines and open boats may have found the seas teeming, but even then — archaeologists have found — early people depleted seafood resources. Ancient garbage heaps show the size of fish and shellfish often became smaller over time.[40]

The advent of industrialized fishing in the 19th century greatly increased human impact on marine ecosystems. Instead of using baited hooks or traps, fishermen

Greenpeace/©Robert Visser

The Seattle-based factory trawler Northern Eagle can harvest 50-60 metric tons of pollock per day in the Bering Sea. The decimation of global fisheries is blamed largely on powerful new technologies — including radar, fish finders and satellite tracking and navigation systems — as well as onboard processing plants, flash freezers and nets that stretch for miles.

developed gear that could pursue and scoop up fish. In the early 1800s, the development of steam-powered ships allowed fishermen to drag larger net bags across the seafloor. At first it was a clumsy proposition: The bag was held open with wooden beams that often hung up on rocks and other obstructions. In the 1890s, however, British fishermen replaced the beam with a pair of small boards, rigged in such a way that when pulled through water they flew apart like kites, holding the mouth of the net open; a heavy chain kept the net bottom dragging on the seafloor to prevent fish from escaping underneath. The so-called otter trawl was incredibly effective and quickly dominated the North Sea fleet. Starting in 1905, it was deployed in North America.[41]

The destructive potential of trawling was clear as early as 1912, when Congress demanded an investigation of fishermen's claims that it "is such an unduly destructive method that if generally adopted . . . the fishing grounds [will be] quickly rendered unproductive." Investigators recommended that trawls be restricted to a few areas in New England, but their advice was not acted upon.

In the 20th century the scale and power of fishing technology increased enormously. Diesel engines, introduced in the 1920s, were cheaper, safer and more reliable than steam; otter trawls were adapted to trap shrimp, clams, oysters and scallops. Processors invented a way to

CHRONOLOGY

1800s-Early 1900s *Fish stocks decline as fishing becomes more mechanized and new trawling methods are developed.*

1905 The steam-powered otter trawl is deployed in North America, making industrial fishing possible in previously unfished areas.

1920s-1940s *Diesel engines replace steam, triggering an expansion of offshore trawling. U.S. processors develop flash freezing. Norwegian fishermen begin dragging for shrimp.*

1936 New England halibut catch falls to 2 million pounds from 13.5 million in 1902; haddock falls by two-thirds.

1946 International Convention for the Regulation of Whaling is adopted.

1950s *The first factory trawlers come into use, mainly in North Atlantic. Pollution runoff from land-based development begins disrupting global ecosystems.*

1954 A Scottish firm builds the first freezer-equipped "factory" trawler, the *Fairtry*, which is four times the size of conventional trawlers.

1959 Antarctica Treaty is adopted, sparing the southern continent and surrounding oceans from hunting, industrial activity and fishing pressure.

1970s-1980s *Countries extend their territorial seas to prevent foreign overexploitation. Pollution disrupts ocean life. Fisheries decline sharply. Iceland fights "cod war" to extend its territorial waters.*

1972 Congress passes Coastal Zone Management, Clean Water and Marine Mammal Protection acts.

1975 U.N. adopts Convention on International Trade in Endangered Species, which helps reduce cross-border trade in marine animal products.

1977 U.S., Canada, others adopt 200-mile territorial limits. Trawlers move to Africa, Asia and the Caribbean.

1982 U.N. Convention on the Law of the Sea becomes the first international agreement to regulate ocean use. International Whaling Commission bans most commercial whaling beginning in 1986.

1989 Norway restricts cod fishing to protect declining stocks; cod recovers by 1992.

1990s-2000s *Black Sea ecosystem collapses. Coral reefs decline worldwide and climate change, pollution and chronic overfishing appear to be driving oceans into crisis.*

1990 Pollution, overfishing and the introduction of a non-native comb jelly species devastate the Black Sea.

1991 British North Sea cod stocks have declined by more than two-thirds in 10 years.

1992 Canada closes Grand Banks cod fishery; stock stands at 1 percent of 1965 levels.

1994 U.S. closes key New England fisheries; slow recovery begins.

1998 Bleaching destroys 16 percent of the world's coral reefs. Cause is unknown.

2002 European Union (EU) recommends member states adopt integrated coastal zone management.

2003 Pew Oceans Commission urges immediate action to protect the oceans; Canadian study says stocks of large predatory fish have fallen by 90 percent worldwide since 1950.

2004 U.S. Commission on Ocean Policy calls for ecosystem-based response to protecting oceans and coasts.

2006 Iceland breaks whaling ban. . . . Most EU members have adopted integrated coastal zone management plans. . . . Pro-whaling bloc gets whaling ban declared no longer necessary.

2007 Hundreds of marine species — including corals for the first time — are added to the World Conservation Union's "red list" of species facing the risk of extinction.

mass-produce fish fillets — which could be sold fresh, canned or smoked at processing plants — and commercial-scale flash freezing, which eventually led to fish "sticks." In the late 1920s, processors like General Foods began building their own trawler fleets, completing the industrialization of the industry.

But fish stocks could not stand up to the technology. In New England, the halibut catch fell from 13.5 million pounds in 1902 to 2 million in 1936; the haddock catch fell by two-thirds between 1929 and 1936, while winter flounder became so scarce fishermen began targeting the previously spurned yellowtail flounder. By World War II, the yellowtail had been depleted, and near-shore stocks of cod and haddock were driven into commercial extinction.[42]

In 1954, a Scottish whaling firm built the first factory trawler, modeled on the big processing ships that had wiped out Antarctica's whale stocks. *The Fairtry* weighed 2,600 tons, more than four times the size of the conventional trawlers of the day, and was equipped with an onboard processing and freezing plant and nets large enough to swallow the Statue of Liberty. It could operate 24 hours a day for weeks on end, allowing the ships to travel to fisheries thousands of miles from home. The design revolutionized distant-water fishing.

By the 1970s, the Soviet Union was operating more than 700 freezer trawlers, and the two Germanys, Poland, Spain, France and Japan each had dozens more.[43] So-called mid-water trawls were developed to target mackerel, herring and anchovies that lived in medium depths. The ships massed on fishing grounds off Newfoundland, New England, Antarctica and the Bering Sea and mined one fish stock after another into near-oblivion.

In 1977, following Iceland's lead, Canada, the United States and other nations extended their territorial waters from 12 to 200 nautical miles in order to push foreign factory trawlers off their banks and save the fish for themselves. Fish stocks had been damaged, but with proper regulation it was assumed they would recover.

Stocks Crash

After kicking foreign fleets out, the United States, Canada and other nations built their own modern trawler fleets. Though the vessels were much smaller, they carried the latest fish-finding gadgetry and were capable of fishing the offshore banks. Encouraged by government incentives, New England trawlers larger than 125 tons grew by 144 percent between 1976 and 1979, while the number of medium-size trawlers nearly doubled. Other governments offered similar incentives, increasing the size of the world's fishing fleet by 322 percent from 1979 to 1989.[44]

In New England and Canada, the domestic fleets quickly wiped out many stocks, including the cod stocks that had attracted Europeans to colonize the region in the first place. Between 1965 and 1999, New England's haddock catch fell by 95 percent, halibut by 92 percent and cod by 40 percent, prompting managers to close many fishing grounds. On Newfoundland's Grand Banks, the greatest cod fishery in the world was reduced by 98.9 percent in the 30 years leading up to its 1992 closure.

The pain of the closures and other fishing restrictions eroded the economic and cultural foundations of many New England and Canadian communities, and fueled an exodus of young people from Newfoundland. "We are witnessing an entire generation without hope, enthusiasm and access to meaningful, steady employment," noted Michael Temelini, assistant professor of political science at the Memorial University of Newfoundland. "[Our] 500-year-old civilization is disappearing."[45]

Fifteen years after the closure, Newfoundland's cod appear unable to regain their place in the ecosystem, while depleted fish stocks on Georges Bank and in the Gulf of Maine are recovering slowly. Fish plants have closed throughout eastern North America, and large fishing vessels have vanished from harbors whose residents had fished offshore for centuries.[46]

Similar devastation has occurred from the North Sea to the Gulf of Thailand. "Ten years ago, we could catch anything we wanted," said Sophon Loseresakun, a fisherman in Talumphuk, Thailand. "Now we have almost nothing."[47]

Eventually, the large fishing vessels moved on to the developing world, buying access to fishing grounds that once supported small-scale local fishermen. "European and Russian distant-water fishing fleets shrank and their remnants turned south," recalled Carl Safina, president of the Blue Ocean Institute, a marine conservation advocacy group in East Norwich, N.Y., "under-paying their way into the fishing zones of countries too desperate for foreign cash to say no, lest the same bad offer be accepted by a neighboring country and the boats go there instead."[48]

Whaling Nations Want Hunting Ban Lifted

Japan, Iceland and Norway are leading the charge.

Great whales are up against a lot these days: Their food supply has diminished and is laced with PCBs and heavy metals, noise from sonar devices plagues their habitat and entangling fishing nets and passing ships are a constant threat. It's no surprise that most varieties — including blue, fin, humpback, sperm and right — remain on the endangered species list.

But in October 2006 Iceland announced it would resume hunting great whales, breaking the International Whaling Commission's (IWC) 21-year-old global moratorium on commercial whaling.*

Iceland's commercial whalers were permitted to kill nine endangered fin whales — the second-largest species after blue whales — and 30 smaller, more abundant minkes during the year ending Aug. 31, 2007, ostensibly for scientific research. By last November, however, they had already killed seven of the endangered fins, setting off a storm of international criticism.[1]

"It's outside all international norms to hunt an endangered species," says Susan Lieberman, director of the World Wildlife Fund's Global Species Program in Rome. "There is a commercial whaling moratorium in effect, so we're not saying it's fine and dandy to be hunting [the non-endangered] minkes. But targeting fin whales is a far more confrontational and aggressive act."

Whale meat is a delicacy in Iceland, Norway and Japan, particularly with older generations, and whaling nations say hunting and consuming whales is part of their cultural heritage. But critics point out that all three countries have difficulty disposing of whale blubber and other non-meat byproducts, leading conservationists to question why they continue the hunt.

Last November 25 countries — including the United States, Great Britain and Australia — demanded a halt to Iceland's hunt. Critics say it undermines the IWC by directly challenging its moratorium.[2]

"They are testing what the international reaction would be, and I think they've found it has been pretty harsh," says Sue Fisher, trade expert at Britain's Whale and Dolphin Conservation Society. "What they're doing is a violation of the ban."

In fact, the moratorium has been unraveling for years, largely because of Japan's diplomatic maneuvering. It used aid and trade measures to convince a small army of previously disinterested Caribbean and Pacific nations to join the IWC and vote with Japan. As a result, in 2006, the pro-whaling bloc achieved a simple majority and passed a symbolic measure declaring the ban no longer necessary. But the measure fell short of the three-quarters majority needed.

In retaliation, the United Kingdom and other anti-whaling nations have recently recruited five disinterested proxies of their own — Croatia, Cyprus, Ecuador, Greece and Slovenia — to help stave off the pro-whaling bloc.[3]

Norway, which is allowed to legally hunt whales commercially, focused exclusively on minkes, which are about an eighth the mass of fin whales. Operating from small vessels, Norwegian fishermen kill between 600 and 800 minkes each year out of an estimated North Atlantic population of over 170,000.

Norway's leading environmental groups support the hunt, arguing it is a sustainable fishery that produces organic

---

* The 1986 moratorium allowed nations to legally continue whale hunting if they filed official reservations prior to the adoption of the ban. Norway made such a reservation. Iceland and Japan did not, though Iceland tried to claim one after the fact, when it first resumed hunting minkes for "scientific purposes" in 2003. Japan conducts a "scientific" research hunt — also allowed under IWC rules — taking about 900 minkes in the Southern Ocean. Non-whaling nations consider the hunt a violation of the spirit of the treaty. Aboriginal hunters are exempt and permitted to hunt a limited number of whales for cultural and religious purposes.

Today, subsistence fishermen in canoes in Mauritania and other African nations compete with hundreds of government-subsidized Spanish, Russian and Chinese trawlers. West African fish stocks have declined by 50 percent over the past 30 years, and thousands of fishermen have been put out of work.[49] Likewise, South Pacific nations have sold tuna fishing rights to Russian, Chinese and Taiwanese companies, even though the valuable fish is one of their few natural resources.

Other vessels have turned to the high seas, beyond the reach of government, to fish for orange roughy, Patagonian toothfish and other long-lived, slow-to-reproduce species. According to a University of British Columbia study,

meat with fewer inputs than a corporate beef or pork farm. "We use small fishing vessels that consume few inputs and cause almost no pollution — it's very friendly eco-production," says Marius Holm, co-chairman of the Bellona Foundation environmental organization in Oslo. "Our principle is that we should harvest what nature provides, but in a sustainable way regarding the ecosystem as a whole and the specific stocks."

"The hunt we have had along our coast has always been sustainable," says Halvard Johansen, deputy director general of the Norwegian Ministry of Fisheries and Coastal Affairs. "We've been whaling on this coast since the 9th century, and we don't see that big a difference between aboriginal whaling in Alaska, Russia and Greenland and what we do here."

Stefan Asmundsson, Iceland's whaling commissioner, claims his country's hunts are also sustainable, despite targeting an endangered species. "The fin whale stocks being targeted by Iceland are not in any way endangered," he says. "There is no lineage between the stocks in the North Atlantic, which are abundant, and those in the Southern Hemisphere" that were decimated by factory whaling fleets in mid-20th century.

Indeed, many in the West fear a return to those dark days when Norway, Japan and other whaling nations drove many great whales to the brink of extinction to procure industrial oil and pet food. Recovery has been slow. In 2003, a study by Stanford University geneticist Stephen Palumbi suggested that the pre-whaling populations of

Japanese whalers butcher a Baird's beaked whale, a species not in danger of extinction. Despite a 1986 ban on commercial whaling, the International Whaling Commission allows Japan and Norway to hunt whales, and Iceland announced in October 2006 it would resume hunting great whales.

Getty Images/Koichi Kamoshida

North Atlantic humpback, fin and minke whales were far larger than previously thought and won't return to exploitable levels for many decades.[4]

Others say Japan and Iceland are defending whaling out of a sense of national pride rather than economic necessity, since their domestic markets have been unable to absorb the meat from their scientific minke hunts. As whale meat piles up in freezers — 4,400 tons according to Greenpeace — Japan has resorted to introducing it in school lunch programs.

"Almost all those who like whale meat are middle-aged and older," admits Kouji Shingru, owner of the only whale-meat retail shop in Tokyo. "Young people have no experience with eating whale. In fact, my shop is one of the only places where young people have a chance to eat it."[5]

"This is not driven by economics, it's just political, which makes it far more egregious," says Lieberman.

---

[1] Krista Mahr, "Defying global ban, Iceland to resume commercial whaling after almost 2 decades," The Associated Press, Oct. 17, 2006; Colin Woodard, "Thar She Blows," *E Magazine*, January 2007.

[2] Lewis Smith, "Iceland's whaling sinks tourism: Two dozen nations protest hunting," *Calgary Herald*, Nov. 2, 2006.

[3] Micheal McCarthy, "Pro-hunting Japanese seize control of whaling commission," *The Independent* (London), April 17, 2006, p. 2; Richard Lloyd Perry, "Japan may go it alone after defeat over whaling ban," *The Times* (London), June 2, 2007.

[4] Stephen Palumbi and Joe Roman, "Whales before whaling in the North Atlantic," *Science*, July 25, 2003, p. 508.

[5] Greenpeace International press release, Jan. 30, 2007; Leo Lewis, "Giant of the sea used as petfood," *The Times* (London), Feb. 10, 2006.

---

high-seas bottom trawlers receive $152 million a year in subsidies worldwide.

"Eliminating government subsidies would render the fleet economically unviable," said lead author Rashid Sumaila.[50]

"We are vacuuming the ocean of its content," said French environmentalist Jean-Michel Cousteau, son of

the late ocean explorer Jacques Cousteau. "If this continues, there will be nothing left."[51]

Shifting Baselines

Scientists now realize that the damage to the oceans is far worse than previously estimated. New forensic research using fishing logbooks, archaeological evidence and

Great Barrier Reef Marine Park Authority/Paul Marshall

A diver in the Great Barrier Reef Marine Park in Australia photographs masses of bleached staghorn coral, which occurs when sea temperatures rise and kill microbes that give coral its bright colors. Rising sea temperatures and other mostly man-made factors are said to be killing coral reefs at an alarming rate.

genetic tests reveals that ocean life was far more abundant in the pre-industrial era than anyone had assumed.

For instance, after witnessing the destruction of many of Jamaica's coral reefs, Jackson of the Scripps Institution used historical records to determine how the Caribbean might have looked in 1492. "Think about the wildebeests and lions and all that on the plains of Africa," he says. "Well, there was a world in which the biomass of big animals among the reefs was greater than the biomass of the big mammals of the Serengeti plains."[52]

Based on hunting records, adult green sea turtles — now rare — once numbered at least 35 million and may have exceeded 550 million. "Think about that: 35 million 220-pound turtles grazing on crustaceans, sea grass, starfish and mollusks," he says. "The productivity of those reefs must have been fantastic. The whole mind-set of scientists about what is a 'pristine' reef is completely wrong." His research suggests that by wiping out sea turtles — used for food in the 19th century — humans probably triggered the collapse of sea grass beds, which suffer infections when they are not grazed.[53]

Similarly, W. Jeffrey Bolster, a professor of maritime history at the University of New Hampshire, and colleagues used 19th-century logbooks to reconstruct the scale of the cod catch and the average size of the fish.

The results stunned fisheries experts. In 1861 alone, small-boat fishermen from several Maine towns — using small sailboats and baited hooks — caught more fish than all the U.S. and Canadian fishing fleets combined caught in the Gulf of Maine between 1996 and 1999. Today, there are virtually no cod in the area.

"Ask yourself, 'What were all those cod eating?' " Bolster says. "When you think about the copepods and krill, all the way up to the alewives and mackerel that had to be present in the inshore area to feed them, it's flabbergasting.

"The world we have today," he points out, was created by humans trying to "manage" the exploitation of fisheries resources. "In terms of engineered outcomes, it's been a disaster."

Climate Change

Global warming is already affecting polar marine ecosystems. On the Antarctic Peninsula, ice-dependent species like Adelie penguins and Weddell seals have moved southwards, replaced by the Gentoo penguins and elephant seals that prefer open water. Krill, the small marine crustaceans that form the basis of the Antarctic food chain, feed on algae that grow on the underside of winter sea ice. Experts fear less sea ice could mean less krill and, thus, less food to go around.

In the Arctic, reduced ice cover is causing starvation and reproductive failure among polar bears, prompting the United States to propose listing them as a threatened species.[54] Walruses and ringed seals also depend on floating ice as habitat.

Fishermen in Greenland have witnessed considerable changes in the composition of the continent's marine species in recent years. Cold-loving shrimp are becoming rarer on the south and west-central coasts, while cod are becoming more numerous. The fishing season is longer in areas where sea ice is failing to form, but polar bear and seal hunters cannot risk going out on the ice with their sled dogs.

"Hunters and fishermen have passed down detailed information about their environment for generations," says Lene Kielsen Holm, director for environment and sustainable development at the Greenland office of the Inuit Circumpolar Council, which represents the interests of the 160,000 Inuit, the indigenous people of the high arctic. "Now they tell us things are changing so quickly everything they have been taught by their elders is no longer accurate."

Scientists also worry that melting polar glaciers, ice caps and ice sheets could slow ocean circulation. Ocean currents normally act as a conveyor belt, moving warm surface waters toward the poles and cold bottom water from polar areas toward the equator. The release of fresh meltwater alters seawater density, which may slow or even stop circulation, with potentially devastating consequences for human and marine life.

A 2005 study indicated that the Gulf Stream, which keeps northern Europe's climate mild, may have slowed by 30 percent since 1992. "We don't want to say the circulation will shut down, but we are very nervous about our findings," said Harry L. Bryden, a specialist in the role of ocean heat and freshwater currents at the School of Ocean and Earth Science at the National Oceanography Centre in Southampton, England. "They have come as quite a surprise."[55]

Meanwhile, the increase in atmospheric carbon dioxide (CO_2) — one of the major causes of climate change — is making the ocean more acidic, with potentially catastrophic consequences. About 2 billion tons of atmospheric CO_2 ends up in the oceans each year — 10 times the natural rate — and the oceans have become 30 percent more acidic since the Industrial Revolution. That figure is expected to rise to 100 percent to 150 percent by the end of the century.

Increased acidity disrupts the ability of corals and other sea animals to build shells and skeletons. "There's a whole category of organisms that have been around for hundreds of millions of years that are at risk of extinction," says Ken Caldeira, a chemical oceanographer at the Carnegie Institution's Department of Global Ecology at Stanford University. The likely casualties include a range of microscopic creatures at the base of the food chain, including coccolithophores and pteropods; the polyps that build coral reefs; and starfish and sea cucumbers — popular food items for larger creatures. Oysters, scallops, mussels, barnacles and many other creatures may also be affected.

"This is a matter of the utmost importance," said reef expert Ove Hoegh-Guldberg of the University of Queensland in Australia. "I can't really stress it in words enough. It is a do-or-die situation."[56]

Governing the Seas

Historically, the seas were unregulated beyond three nautical miles from land, the effective range of shore-based

The Banggai cardinalfish, native to Indonesia, is among hundreds of marine animals and corals added to the World Conservation Union's 2007 "red list" of species in jeopardy or facing high risk of extinction. The group blames excessive and destructive fishing activities for the loss of ocean biodiversity.

cannon. But in the 20th century, fishery-dependent Iceland — in an effort to protect its fish from foreign fleets — extended its territorial waters first to four then to 12, 50 and, finally, to 200 nautical miles.

Initially, the world protested. Britain dispatched a fleet of warships to protect its trawlers, triggering three bloodless "cod wars" with Iceland's coast guard. Shots were fired, ships rammed and nets cut. Iceland barred British warplanes from landing at the NATO air base in Keflavik. Finally, in 1976, the world backed down, and soon nations around the world had declared their own 200-mile zones.[57]

The 200-mile limit was codified in the 1982 U.N. Convention on the Law of the Sea (UNCLOS), which has since been ratified by 155 nations. The United States — which had extended its own territorial waters to 200 miles in 1977 — has not yet ratified the treaty, but President George W. Bush has said it should be ratified.

Under UNCLOS, governments can regulate fishing and other economic activities within their 200-mile "exclusive economic zones" (EEZ) and are expected to take a precautionary approach in utilizing their EEZs "according to their capabilities." Legal scholars have said the conservation language is so weak as to be useless.

"Just as with bringing up children, a permissive approach to the law of the sea guarantees spoiling," writes John Charles Kunich, associate professor of law at the

Appalachian School of Law in Grundy, Va., and author of *Killing Our Oceans: Dealing with the Mass Extinction of Marine Life.* "It is all too predictable that nations often discover that other pressing needs prevent them . . . from doing anything to protect biodiversity in the oceans."[58]

Nations have cooperated in trying to regulate international exploitation of marine creatures that regularly cross borders through treaty organizations like the International Whaling Commission, the Northwest Atlantic Fisheries Organization and the International Commission for the Conservation of Atlantic Tuna. But the track record of most of these organizations is poor. In most cases, the populations of species they are supposed to protect have declined due to predation by humans. Even when member nations agree to tougher enforcement, unscrupulous vessel owners can simply re-register their ships in a "flag-of-convenience" nation that does not observe the relevant rules.

International cooperation has succeeded, however, in banning drift-net fishing — which indiscriminately kills any fish or mammals that come in contact with the massive nets — and the 1975 Convention on International Trade in Endangered Species helped reduce cross-border trade in hawksbill turtles, Caspian sturgeon roe and many whale products. The 1959 Antarctica Treaty has spared the southern continent and much of the surrounding ocean from continued hunting, industrial activity and fishing pressure.

But with most of the more ecologically productive parts of the ocean located within nations' EEZs, it will likely fall on national governments to protect them.

CURRENT SITUATION

Government Responses

World governments have been slow to address the ocean crisis, often stepping in only after a fishery has collapsed. And governments that have closed fishing grounds have had mixed results. While cod stocks on Canada's Grand Banks have failed to recover, for instance, New England's haddock, flounder and other species are slowly recovering. Scientists say New England stocks can recover completely if policy makers withstand industry pressure to allow more fishing.

Internationally, China, Iceland, Russia and other deep-sea fishing nations blocked a 2006 U.N. effort to ban high-seas bottom trawling. "There were several countries

that really didn't want any controls at all," said U.S. Assistant Secretary of State for Oceans, Environment and Science Claudia McMurray. "We're very disappointed."[59]

Many countries have considered privatizing fisheries by creating individual transferable quotas (ITQs). Under an ITQ system, scientists set quotas on the total allowable catch for a given season, species and fishing ground; shares of the quotas are bought and sold by private entities, and only those holding shares are allowed to fish.

Proponents say that creating "owners" of uncaught fish will encourage responsible stewardship. Opponents say an ITQ system represents a massive transfer of public resources to corporate control.

"Since quotas are bought and sold to the highest bidder, local fishermen — who can't compete with deep-pocketed corporations — are almost inevitably squeezed out," write Pietro Parravano, past president of the Pacific Coast Federation of Fishermen's Associations, and Lee Crockett, formerly of the Marine Fish Conservation Network and now federal fisheries policy director at the Pew Environment Group. "Moreover, because quotas are [initially] set on the number of fish historically caught by individual fishermen, those who tried to allow stocks to replenish by fishing responsibly [are] penalized, while those who fish rapaciously are rewarded."[60]

Others say ITQ rules can be written to prevent the concentration of ownership. Alaska's halibut and sablefish fisheries adopted ITQs in 1995, but the rules limited absentee ownership and consolidation of shares and allowed communities to buy blocks of shares to divvy up among individuals. A decade later, the fishery was safer and greener, according to Linda Behnken, executive director of the Alaska Longline Fishermen's Association.

"From a resource perspective, it's been an unqualified success," she said.[61]

Zoning the Sea

Some governments have tried to zone the ocean bottom just as cities use zoning rules to separate incompatible land uses and to establish parks and preserves. Environmentalists have long advocated a similar approach, as has the World Bank, the U.S. Commission on Ocean Policy and the Pew Oceans Commission. Sea-floor zoning — and establishing marine reserves where certain human activities are prohibited — is also a crucial part of ecosystem-based management.

"It's inevitable that once we developed methods to reach further and further into the sea, we would have to extend the regulatory framework we have on land to the sea," says Callum Roberts, an expert on marine zoning at the University of York in England.

To date, however, less than 2 percent of the oceans are within marine protected areas, and less than 0.2 percent are classified as no-take marine reserves where no disruptive activities are allowed.[62]

The Central American nation of Belize is leading the way on marine protected areas. With the help of the Global Environment Facility — a joint UN/World Bank environmental grant-making agency based in Washington — and scientists from the United States and Britain, Belize has created a surprisingly comprehensive array of fully protected parks, mixed-use reserves and specialized wildlife sanctuaries aimed at protecting biodiversity while enhancing the country's most important industries: fishing and eco-tourism.[63]

One of the reserves, Glover's Reef, a remote atoll 30 miles offshore, has been fully protected and carefully patrolled for nearly a decade. As a result, depleted commercial seafood species have rapidly rebounded: From 1998 to 2003, queen conch populations jumped by 350 percent and spiny lobster 250 percent. Similar results have been observed in New Zealand, where overall ecological productivity has jumped 50 percent in a reserve founded in 1977.[64]

"Right now, it's like we have a few oases in the desert," says Bill Ballantine, a marine biologist and former director of the University of Auckland's Leigh Marine Laboratory, who says the world needs many more.

To be effective, Belize's reserves must be "big enough so that a reasonable number of species can complete their life cycle within its borders, but small enough so the animals inside will produce larvae that wind up outside its borders and seed other fish populations," says Peter Sale, professor emeritus of biological sciences at the University of Windsor, Ontario.[65]

But there are problems, especially in cash-strapped developing countries like Belize. Running the reserves "is an enormously expensive undertaking," says Janet Gibson, former director of Belize's Coastal Zone Management Authority, "and there are really few ways to raise funds apart from charging entrance fees."

In Indonesia, the U.S.-based Nature Conservancy has provided funding for wardens at Komodo National Park,

U.N. Environmental Program/Topham

Wastewater runoff from coastal developments is one of many threats to marine habitats. Each summer fertilizer runoff from 31 states in the United States flows into the Gulf of Mexico via the Mississippi River, creating a huge dead zone south of New Orleans where few species survive.

who have largely driven out the dynamite fishermen who blasted many of the area's reefs to rubble. Researchers have helped the reefs reestablish themselves by piling sandstone and limestone boulders on the sea floor. "Places that were just bare rock and rubble now have great coral growth and are surrounded by fish," says the World Wildlife Fund's senior marine conservation biologist Helen E. Fox, who worked on the project. The technique costs only about $5 per square meter, compared to between $550 and $10,000 to repair corals in the Florida Keys, she says.

In 2006, President Bush created the world's largest fully protected reserve, the 138,000-square-mile Papahanaumokuakea Marine National Monument in the northwestern Hawaiian Islands. The new reserve — 100 times the size of Yosemite National Park and larger than all other U.S. national parks combined — prohibits all exploitative activities except for limited ritualistic fishing by native Hawaiians. Environmentalists and ocean policy advocates widely praised the move, called by Fred Krupp, president of Environmental Defense, "as important as the establishment of Yellowstone."[66]

Some fishermen fear large areas could be declared reserves and closed to fishing. But proponents note that creating a reserve doesn't necessarily preclude fishing; it can, however, restrict fishing by method, times or places.

"What you zone for depends on what you are trying to protect," says Anthony Chatwin, director of the South American marine program at The Nature Conservancy. "Some areas will be reserved to protect marine biodiversity, others purely for fisheries management purposes, but they will be comprehensively put together."

Managing Better?

Some experts have identified examples of sustainable fisheries — those that work within the limits of what marine ecosystems can support. Most include community-based management, in which local communities develop their own rules for how, when and by whom the grounds can be fished.

In the Maine lobster fishery, for instance, catches remain at all-time highs despite an enormous increase in the number of fishermen and traps. Traditionally, lobster-men from each harbor controlled their own piece of the seafloor and defended it from intrusion by anyone without the community's permission. By controlling their own lobster pasture, the fishermen had an incentive to enforce or even enhance conservation laws, according to James Acheson, an anthropologist at the University of Maine. "The whole theory of common property resources like lobster assumes they're bound to be overexploited," he says. "That's nonsense."[67]

Numerous other successful fisheries have similar arrangements, from the coral reefs of Micronesia and Polynesia (where villages control fishing rights to nearby reefs) to the community fishing cooperatives that control inshore grounds in Japan's Ryukyu Islands. They have inspired others to advocate giving fishing communities proprietary rights to the resources they have long relied on in Atlantic Canada and elsewhere.[68]

Molyneaux, the author and former fisherman who received a Guggenheim Fellowship to study sustainable fisheries, points to Chile, where the government has blended privatization with community-based management. Small-scale fishermen are allowed to form unions, which are allocated a slot of ocean bottom. The government sets quotas on commercial species, but the union members decide how to manage the area.

"You don't get sole access to the fish but rather to the sedentary resources: shellfish, seaweed, abalone," says Molyneaux. "It's a form of privatization, but it's community based and intended to keep fishermen in their communities and not moving to shantytowns in the cities."

The unions pay for scientific assessments of the health of their stock but are left to work out the economic strategy for harvesting it. "They figured out how to give people the power to control and promote the resource, a reason for promoting sustainability," he says.

Some fishing gear is clearly less harmful than others. Maine lobstermen fish with baited traps that don't harm juvenile lobsters, oversized lobsters, non-target species or the ocean floor. New Brunswick weir fishermen capture herring in hand-built fish traps, with the rights to use a given location handed down in families. Some Icelandic fishermen combine high-tech with small-scale: fishing from small, locally built boats with hand-baited, computer-tended longlines, sophisticated electronic bottom maps and the capability to sell their catch electronically hours before they ever reach the dock.

Others say conventional gear and management can work, pointing to Alaska, where fisheries managers have prevented overfishing, reduced bycatch and protected habitats. By 2005, the North Pacific Fisheries Management Council — which includes fishing interests, scientists and public officials — had banned bottom trawling in nearly 40 percent of Alaska's federal waters and imposed fishing closures to protect the spawning and nursery grounds of herring, rockfish, crab and other commercial species.

Unlike its New England counterpart, the council never authorized catch quotas above those recommended by its scientific advisers. It also restricted fishing near Stellar sea lion rookeries. Federal managers also banned targeted fishing of key forage species like smelt, capelin and sand lance that feed seabirds and commercial fish.

"People in Alaska had been through some tough times in the past, and they created an ethic that puts protecting the resource first," said Benton of the Marine Conservation Alliance. "People around the world acknowledge Alaska as one of those places where you can look for positive lessons learned."[69]

Saving the Shore

Policy makers are paying considerable attention to calls to develop integrated coastal zone management plans that control human activities throughout an entire watershed and its associated coastline and estuaries.

Should the moratorium on commercial whaling be lifted?

YES
Rune Frøvik
CEO, High North Alliance, Norway

NO
Philippa Brakes
*Senior Biologist, Whale and Dolphin
Conservation Society*

Written for *CQ Global Researcher*, September 2007

Written for *CQ Global Researcher*, September 2007

While fishing continues to enjoy almost universal acceptance as a means of food production, Western urban society has decided unilaterally to shut down whaling with complete disregard for any culture that still practices it.

Each culture has its own culinary idiosyncrasies. For many Asians, dog meat is a delicacy; the French like their frogs, snails and horse meat, and Australians have a taste for kangaroos. And there are just as many taboos — Indians forego the joy of beef-steak, while Jews and Muslims won't touch pork.

Beset with environmental challenges and yet respectful of cultural differences, the world community thankfully embraced Agenda 21's principle of striving for sustainable development — using renewable resources at rates that are within the resources' capacity for renewal.* Yet the West's cultural imperialists would have whales exempted from the sustainable-use principle — placing them above and apart from the animal kingdom to which they obviously belong.

For those who live close to nature, natural resources play vital roles, both nutritional and cultural, in their lives. Thus, coastal people will continue to harvest what nature provides — be it seals, fish, birds . . . or whales. And in the interest of self-preservation, they will strive to do so sustainably.

Sustainable whaling must be managed in accordance with agreed principles, not by launching destructive attacks on those who engage in exactly what we are striving for — sustainable use — just because one's cultural bias finds a particular harvest unpalatable.

In a world where trade depends on the exchange of money, there are commercial aspects to whalers' lives. In Greenland, Iceland, Japan and Norway whale meat is sold in supermarkets, and expensive whale souvenirs are sold to tourists in Alaska. Until whale meat is accepted as currency, whalers must do their shopping the same way as the rest of us — with cash.

Harvesting nature's surplus, including super-abundant whale resources, means biodiversity and habitat do not have to be destroyed and turned into agricultural land. True environmentalists are concerned not with appearances but with practicing the principles that they preach. In so doing, they have either reached the conclusion, or are getting there, that whaling should not only be continued but should even be increased to provide more people with ecological, healthy and nutritious food.

---

* Agenda 21 — adopted by more than 178 governments at the Earth Summit in June 1992 — is a 300-page plan for achieving sustainable development in the 21st century.

The unbridled ravages of commercial whaling — which brought several whale populations to the brink of extinction and significantly depleted many others — should serve as a grave warning to the dangers of the poorly regulated exploitation of marine mammals.

The moratorium was intended to allow whale populations to recover to pre-exploitation levels. Since the moratorium was implemented, however, we have learned what we know and what we don't know about whale populations. We have learned that it's difficult to accurately estimate whale populations and that whales now face new threats from noise and chemical pollution, ship strikes, loss of critical habitat, entanglement in fishing gear and, more recently, challenges due to climate change. All of these threats may influence recovery of whale populations.

Even if the threats to whale populations could be adequately mitigated, many question whether commercial whaling could ever, realistically, be well regulated. The lessons of history — and the burgeoning exploitation of the moratorium's loophole for "scientific" whaling — lead us to conclude that this is unlikely.

Moreover, grave concerns remain as to whether whaling could ever be conducted humanely. Since commercial whaling is conducted for profit, it is argued with good reason that whaling should be held accountable to the same standards for humane slaughter as other animals killed for commercial purposes. It is difficult — even, unpleasant — to imagine a situation in which an animal could escape and be lost during slaughter in an abattoir and be left to die of its injuries. Yet, whales that are injured and escape remain a permanent feature of all whaling practices.

In addition, there are also much broader ethical issues at stake: In the 21st century, many people, even some cultures, no longer view whales as a resource to be exploited but as social beings, with complex lives that should be afforded protection of their interests, not because of their potential value to humankind but because of their own value in and of themselves.

Perhaps rather than asking whether the moratorium should be lifted, the global community should now turn its attention to closing the legal loopholes that permit whaling under objection and whaling for "scientific" purposes, and we should instead ask how we can secure a brighter future for our seaborne cousins so they are protected from commercial hunting permanently.

Three-quarters of the ocean's pollution comes from land-based human activity, and the problem is getting worse. Half of the world's population lives within 62 miles of the coast; in Southeast Asia it's two-thirds. In the United States, 53 percent of the population lives in coastal counties that comprise only 17 percent of the country's landmass. Nine of the world's 10 largest cities are on the coast, and coastal population growth is expected to greatly exceed overall trends.[70] Already, 20th-century development activities have destroyed half of all coastal wetlands.[71]

Reengineering rivers compounds the problem with polluted watersheds. Egypt's Aswan High Dam cut off the flow of nutrients to the Nile Delta, causing the sardine catch to plummet from 18,000 to 600 tons in three years. In Louisiana, decades of levee- and channel-building by the Army Corps of Engineers has transformed the Mississippi River into a ditch that shunts fertilizers and sewage directly into the Gulf of Mexico. And by preventing the river from dropping silt in its delta, the levees are causing the Louisiana bayous to disappear into open water at the rate of 25-35 square miles a year.[72]

"The loss of Louisiana's marshes will incrementally destroy the economy, culture, ecology and infrastructure, not to mention the corresponding tax base of this state and this region," said banker King Milling, chairman of the state-appointed Committee on the Future of Coastal Louisiana.[73]

The U.S. Commission on Ocean Policy and the Pew Oceans Commission have called for integrated, watershed-wide planning in the United States. If implemented, the model might again draw on the experience of Belize, which found that protecting coral reefs required addressing problems far inland.

"To protect the reefs — or any other ecosystem for that matter — you have to take . . . an ecosystem approach," said Gibson, the former head of Belize's Coastal Zone Management Authority (CZMA). "You need to look at pollution in the watersheds, at coastal construction and urban expansion, at fisheries and forest loss, at the effects of tourism and air pollution.

"If there isn't coordination between economic sectors, your efforts to conserve an ecological system are not going to be successful," she continued. The CZMA has coordinated policies governing forestry, fisheries and water quality while sponsoring education programs to show people how rivers, mangroves, cays and reefs interact. Other countries have made advances in creating integrated coastal zone management plans. Australia created a national framework to integrate its state, territorial, regional and local government agencies to manage resources on a river-basin-by-river-basin level.[74] In 2002, the European Union recommended that member states move towards integrated management. A 2007 review found "a positive impact in stimulating progress" but acknowledged it would be a "slow and long-term process." Most member states hadn't adopted national strategies until 2006; six had not done so at all.[75]

OUTLOOK

Out of Mind

The oceans have never gotten the political attention they need, and after the Sept. 11, 2001, terrorist attacks, they seemed to sink even lower on the world's priority list.

"We are moving forward extremely slowly, and in fact we are actually retreating from some of the movement we had toward more concerted international action," says Mee of the University of Plymouth. "There's been concentration on other issues: terrorism, in particular, and security."

Ironically, the urgent attention being focused on climate change has further eclipsed the oceans' problems. "Action by celebrity figures like [former Vice President] Al Gore has managed to put climate change on the agenda and kept it there very effectively," says Mee. "We don't really have many champions for the marine environment. The oceans don't make it onto people's agenda, resulting in the feeling that action can be postponed."

The United States is a case in point. The chairmen of the Pew Oceans Commission and the U.S. Commission on Ocean Policy joined forces to press for implementation of their recommendations, including issuing "report cards" grading governments' progress The U.S. government got a D+ in 2005 and a C- in 2006, reflecting modest progress.

"The improvement is largely attributable to state action and a few notable federal accomplishments," explained Admiral Watkins and Panetta.[76]

States and regional organizations received an A- after 18 took steps to develop comprehensive strategies for protecting marine systems. But there was little progress in most areas. Even modest programs to establish ocean observation systems (which collect basic oceanographic information) or to monitor and protect the endangered North Atlantic right whale have seen drastic funding cuts in the past year. Getting attention for oceans issues will remain challenging due to the lack of public awareness of the problems, and other congressional priorities, such as the Iraq War.

Internationally, even problems that aren't that difficult to solve have been put on the backburner. For instance, many of the disruptions caused by alien species could be prevented if the shipping industry adopted a ballast water-exchange program in which ballast water is pumped to and from sterilized sources rather than into local harbors.

"It costs people money," notes Mee. "It's a tiny marginal cost on transportation, but it requires a greater sense of purpose to push it through."

In the future, the world community is expected to focus more attention on the negative impact China's burgeoning industrialization is having on the world's oceans. According to the World Wildlife Fund, China is now the largest polluter of the Pacific Ocean. Each year China releases about 2.8 billion tons of contaminated water into the Bo Hai — a sea along China's northern coast — and the heavy metal content of Bo Hai bottom mud is now 2,000 times as high as China's official safety standard. In 2006, heavily industrialized Guangdong and Fujian provinces discharged nearly 8.3 billion tons of untreated sewage into the ocean — up 60 percent since 2001. More than 80 percent of the East China Sea — one of the world's largest fisheries — is now rated unsuitable for fishing, and the Chinese prawn catch has plunged 90 percent over the past 15 years.[77]

Bill Wareham, acting director of the Marine Conservation Program at Canada's David Suzuki Foundation, is pessimistic international agencies will cooperate, citing the refusal in 2006 by China, Russia and other deep-sea fishing nations to support the U.N.'s measure to ban trawling.

If the world cannot depend on the U.N. to mandate the protection of fish habitat and to prevent the ongoing decline of high seas fish stocks, "then we are in a very sad state," he said. "The global governance system has failed to move past the stage of denial."[78]

NOTES

1. John W. Miller, "Global fishing trade depletes African waters," *The Wall Street Journal*, July 18, 2007, p. A1.

2. "State of World Fisheries and Aquaculture 2006," Food and Agriculture Organization, 2007.

3. Ransom A. Myers and Bruce Worm, "Rapid Worldwide Depletion of Predatory Fish Communities," *Nature*, May 15, 2003, p. 280.

4. Kenneth R. Weiss, "A primeval tide of toxins," *Los Angeles Times*, July 30, 2006, p. 1.

5. See Kieran Kelleher, "Discards in the world's marine fisheries: An update," Technical Paper 470, Food and Agriculture Organization, 2005, pp. xvi, 38.

6. Eleanor M. Dorsey and Judith Pederson, *Effects of Fishing Gear on the Sea Floor of New England*, Conservation Law Foundation (1998), pp. 1-6.

7. Clive Wilkinson (ed.), *Status of Coral Reefs of the World: 2004, Vol. 1*, Australian Institute for Marine Science, 2004, p. 7.

8. Colin Woodard, *Ocean's End: Travels Through Endangered Seas* (2000), pp. 144-160.

9. *Ibid.*, pp. 44-45, 156; "Research reveals virus link in deaths of reefs," *Evening Herald* [Plymouth, England], May 2, 2007, p. 13.

10. Anne Platt McGinn, "Safeguarding the Health of the Oceans," Worldwatch Institute, 1999, pp. 26-27.

11. For background, see Marcia Clemmitt, "Saving the Oceans," *CQ Researcher*, Nov. 4, 2005, pp. 933-956.

12. For a detailed discussion see Woodard, *op. cit.*, pp. 97-129.

13. For background, see David Hosansky, "Invasive Species," *CQ Researcher*, Oct. 5, 2001, pp. 785-816.

14. Colin Woodard, "Battling killer seaweed," *The Chronicle of Higher Education*, Aug. 2, 2002, p. 14.

15. Kenneth R. Weiss, "Dark tides, ill winds," *Los Angeles Times*, Aug. 1, 2006, p. 1; Weiss, *op. cit.*; Jeremy B. C. Jackson, "Habitat destruction and ecological extinction of marine invertebrates," 2006, http://cbc.amnh.org/symposia/archives/expandingthearc/speakers/transcripts/jackson-text.html; see also Frances M. Van Dolah, "Marine Algal Toxins: Origins, Health Effects,

and Their Increased Occurrence," *Environmental Health Perspectives Supplements*, March 2000, www.ehponline.org/members/2000/suppl-1/133-141 vandolah/vandolah-full.html.

16. "Major study predicts bleak future for Europe's seas," University of Plymouth press release, June 7, 2007.

17. "Current trends project collapse of currently fished seafoods by 2050," National Science Foundation press release, Nov. 2, 2006.

18. Clemmitt, *op. cit.*

19. Testimony of Admiral James D. Watkins before the U.S. Senate Committee on Commerce, Science and Transportation, April 22, 2004, p. xi, http://govinfo.library.unt.edu/oceancommission/newsnotices/prelim_testimony.html.

20. "1,600+ scientists warn that the sea is in peril, call for action now," Marine Conservation Biology Institute press release, Jan. 6, 1998, www.gdrc.org/oceans/troubled.html.

21. Quoted in Clemmitt, *op. cit.* Furlong was citing the "Fish Stocks Sustainability Index" of the National Oceanographic and Atmospheric Administration's Fisheries Service, April 1-June 30, 2007, www.nmfs.noaa.gov/sfa/domes_fish/StatusoFisheries/2006/3rdQuarter/Q3-2006-FSSIDescription.pdf.

22. Bjorn Lomborg, *The Skeptical Environmentalist* (2001), pp. 189, 201, 329.

23. *Ibid.*

24. Edie Clark, "Ted Ames and the Recovery of Maine Fisheries," *Yankee Magazine*, November 2006.

25. Colin Woodard, "Saving Maine," *On Earth*, Summer 2003.

26. Testimony before U.S. House Natural Resources Subcommittee on Fisheries, Wildlife and Oceans, April 26, 2007, www.jointoceancommission.org/images/Rosenberg_testimony_H.R.21_04_26_07.pdf.

27. Wayne A. Morrisey, "Science Policy and Federal Ecosystem-based Management," *Ecological Applications*, August 2006, pp. 717-720; D. S. Slocombe, "Implementing ecosystem-based management," Bioscience, Vol. 43 (1993), pp. 612-622; U.S. Department of Commerce, *The Ecosystem Approach: Vol. I*, June 1995.

28. Kenneth R. Weiss, "Study urges trawling ban in fragile marine habitats," *Los Angeles Times*, March 19, 2002, p. 12; Joe Haberstroh, "The bottom of the trawling matter," *Newsday*, March 31, 2002, p. 31; Jeremy Collie, *et al.*, Effects of Trawling and Dredging on Sea Floor Habitat, National Research Council, March 2002.

29. Glen Whiffen, "Dragging technology hurts: advocate," *St. John's Telegram* [Newfoundland], May 4, 2005, p. A4.

30. U.N. General Assembly, "The Impacts of Fishing on Vulnerable Marine Ecosystems," July 14, 2006, www.un.org/Depts/los/general_assembly/documents/impact_of_fishing.pdf; John Heilprin, "UN ban on bottom trawling fails," *Houston Chronicle*, Nov. 25, 2006, p. 2.

31. "America's Living Oceans: Charting a course for sea change," Pew Oceans Commission, May 2003, p. 47, www.pewtrusts.org/uploadedFiles/wwwpewtrustsorg/Reports/Protecting_ocean_life/env_pew_oceans_final_report.pdf.

32. "NZ to close 30pc of waters to trawling," New Zealand Press Association, Feb. 14, 2006.

33. Jeff Barnard, "Seafloors fished by trawlers hold fewer kinds of fish," The Associated Press, April 18, 2007.

34. Milan Ilnyckyj, "The legality and sustainability of European Union fisheries policy in West Africa," *MIT International Review*, Spring 2007, pp. 33-41, http://web.mit.edu/mitir/2007/spring/fisheries.html.

35. Kim Willsheer, "Mauritanians rue EU fish deal with a catch," *The Guardian*, Feb. 9, 2001.

36. Stephen Castle, "EU Trawlers get fishing rights off Africa for pounds 350m," *The Independent*, July 24, 2006.

37. Haberstroh, *op. cit.*, p. A23; James Kendall, "Scallop dredge fishing," in Dorsey and Pederson, *op. cit.*, pp. 90-93.

38. M. J. Kaiser and B. E. Spencer, "The effects of beam-trawl disturbance on infaunal communities in different habitats," *Journal of Animal Ecology, Vol. 65* (1996), pp. 348-358; A.D. Rijnsdorp and P. I. Van Leewen, "Changes in growth of North Sea plaice

since 1950 in relation to density, eutrophication, beam trawl effort, and temperature," *ICES Journal Marine Science*, Vol. 53 (1996), pp. 1199-1213; R. S. Millner and C. L. Whiting, "Long-term changes in growth and population abundance of sole in North Sea from 1940 to present," *ICES Journal Marine Science*, Vol. 53 (1996), pp. 1185-1195.

39. Haberstroh, *op. cit.*, p. A23. Also see "The impact of bottom trawling on American lobsters off Duxbury Beach, MA," Massachusetts Division of Marine Fisheries, Oct. 1, 1989.

40. For background see Clemmitt, *op. cit.*, p. 946.

41. Colin Woodard, *The Lobster Coast* (2004), pp. 201-207; William Warner, *Distant Water* (1977), pp. 50-53.

42. Woodard, *ibid.*, p. 204.

43. Warner, *op. cit.*, pp. 52-53.

44. Marcus Gee, "Here's a fine kettle of . . . ," *Globe & Mail* [Toronto], May 16, 2003, p. A23; Woodard, *ibid.*, pp. 223-231.

45. Michael Temelini, "The Rock's newfound nationalism," [Toronto] *Globe & Mail*, June 29, 2007, p. A17.

46. For background, see Michael Harris, *Lament for an Ocean* (1998); Woodard, 2004, *op. cit.*, pp. 223-231.

47. "Fishers fear tough catch curbs again after cod-stocks claim," *Aberdeen Press and Journal*, Oct. 23, 2001, p. 19; John McQuaid, "Overfished waters running on empty," *New-Orleans Times-Picayune*, March 24, 1996, p. A39.

48. Carl Safina, "Fishing off the deep end — and back," *Multinational Monitor*, Sept. 1, 2003, p. 8.

49. Anne Platt McGinn, "Rocking the Boat," Worldwatch Institute, June 1998, pp. 43-44.

50. Margaret Munro, "Fuel subsidies keep trawlers 'strip-mining' sea," *Vancouver Sun*, Nov. 17, 2006, p. A3; see also U. R. Sumaila and D. Pauly, (eds.), "Catching more bait: a bottom-up re-estimation of global fisheries subsidies," Fisheries Centre Research Reports 14(6), p. 2. University of British Columbia, www.fisheries. ubc.ca/members/dpauly/chaptersInBooksReports/2006/ExecutiveSummaryCatchingMoreBait.pdf.

51. Patricia J. James, "Cousteau says lack of care impacts sea," *Telegram & Gazette* (Mass.), May 12, 2006, p. B1.

52. The Serengeti — a vast plain stretching from Kenya to northern Tanzania — is famous for its extensive wildlife.

53. Jeremy B. C. Jackson, "What was natural in the coastal oceans?" Proceedings of the National Academy of Sciences, May 8, 2001, pp. 5412-3; Woodard, 2000, *op. cit.*, pp. 160-161.

54. Woodard, *ibid.*, pp. 208-215; Juliet Eilperin, "US wants polar bears listed as threatened," *The Washington Post*, Dec. 27, 2006, p. 1.

55. Fred Pearce, "Failing ocean circulation raises fears of mini ice-age," NewScientist.com news service, Nov. 30, 2005, http://media.newscientist.com/article. ns?id=dn8398.

56. Elizabeth Kolbert, "The darkening sea," *The New Yorker*, Nov. 20, 2006, p. 67; Usha Lee McFarling, "A chemical imbalance," *Los Angeles Times*, Aug. 3, 2006, p. 1.

57. Woodard, 2004, *op. cit.*, pp. 212-213.

58. John Charles Kucinich, *Killing Our Oceans: Dealing with the Mass Extinction of Marine Life* (2006), pp. 56-57.

59. "World Digest," *The Capital* (Annapolis, Md.), Nov. 25, 2006, p. A2.

60. Petro Parravano and Lee Crockett, "Who should own the oceans?" *San Francisco Chronicle*, Sept. 25, 2000.

61. See Clemmitt, *op. cit.*, p. 941.

62. Jane Lubchenco, "Global changes for life in oceans," Conference presentation, *M/S Fram* off Greenland, Sept. 8, 2007; Jon Nevill, "Marine no-take areas: How large should marine protected area networks be?" white paper, Sept. 4, 2006, available from www .onlyoneplanet.com.au.

63. For background, see Rachel S. Cox, "Ecotourism," *CQ Researcher*, Oct. 20, 2006, pp. 865-888.

64. For background see Colin Woodard, "Belizean bonanza," *The Chronicle of Higher Education*, July 2, 2004, http://chronicle.com/subscribe/login?url=/weekly/v50/i43/43a01301.htm.

65. *Ibid.*

66. "U.S Ocean Policy Report Card," Joint Ocean Commission Initiative, February 2007, www

.jointoceancommission.org/images/report-card-06.pdf; Colin Woodard, "Faraway, natural and beautiful and it will stay that way," *Trust*, Fall 2006, pp. 2-11.

67. For a full discussion, see Woodard, *The Lobster Coast, op. cit.*, pp. 267-273.

68. John Cordell, ed., *Sea of Small Boats, Cultural Survival* (1989), pp. 337-367; R.E. Johannes, "Traditional Law of the Sea in Micronesia," *Micronesica*, December 1977, pp. 121-127; Janice Harvey and David Coon, "Beyond the Crisis in the Fisheries: A proposal for community-based ecological fisheries management," Conservation Council of New Brunswick, 1997.

69. Brad Warren, "Conserving Alaska's Oceans," Marine Conservation Alliance, 2006, www.marineconservationalliance.org/news/1359_MCA_Report_for_download.pdf.

70. "Population Trends Along the Coastal United States 1980-2003, National Oceanographic and Atmospheric Administration, March 2005.

71. Peter Weber, "Abandoned Seas: Reversing the Decline of the World's Oceans," Worldwatch Institute, November 1993, pp. 17-24, www.worldwatch.org/node/874; Woodard, 2000, *op. cit.*, p. 45.

72. Woodard, *ibid.*, p. 116.

73. Weber, *op. cit.*, p. 20; Pew Oceans Commission, *op. cit.*, p. 54.

74. "National Cooperative Approach to Integrated Coastal Zone Management," National Resource Management Ministerial Council, 2006, www.environment.gov.au/coasts/publications/framework/pubs/framework.pdf.

75. "Report to the European Parliament and Council: An evaluation of ICZM in Europe," European Commission, June 7, 2007, http://eurlex.europa.eu/LexUriServ/LexUriServ.do?uri=CELEX:52007DC0308:EN:NOT.

76. Leon Pannetta and James Watkins, "State's map for saving the oceans," *The Washington Post*, Feb. 3, 2007, p. A15.

77. See Elizabeth C. Economy, "The Great Leap Backward?" *Foreign Affairs*, September/October 2007, pp. 38-59.

78. James Vassallo, "Canada becoming a 'pariah' over trawling," *Prince Rupert Daily News* (BC), Nov. 28, 2006, p. 2.

BIBLIOGRAPHY
Books

Acheson, James M., *Capturing the Commons: Devising Institutions to Manage the Maine Lobster Industry, University Press of New England,* **2003.**
An anthropologist examines the successes of Maine's lobster fishery and state efforts to incorporate traditional lobster-fishing practices into law.

Barker, Rodney, *And the Waters Turned to Blood, Simon & Schuster,* **1997.**
An investigative journalist chronicles of the rise of a dangerous marine microorganism in the Mid-Atlantic region of the United States and efforts to contain it.

Ellis, Richard, *The Empty Ocean, Island Press,* **2004.**
The author of more than 10 books on the oceans and a research associate at the American Museum of Natural History in New York uses history, anecdote and stunning facts to chronicle humanity's predation on the oceans.

Fujita, Rodney M., *Heal the Ocean: Solutions for Saving Our Seas, New Society Publishers,* **2003.**
A marine ecologist describes successful efforts to confront the problems in the world's oceans.

Meinesz, Alexandre, *Killer Algae: The True Tale of a Biological Invasion, University of Chicago Press,* **1999.**
The scientist who discovered the problem of *Caulerpa taxifolia,* the "killer seaweed" that is taking over the Mediterranean, gives a first-hand account of how bad an invading species can be.

Molyneaux, Paul, *The Doryman's Reflection: A Fisherman's Life, Avalon,* **2005.**
A former commercial fisherman gives a personal account of the collapse of U.S. fisheries, with critical insights into the mindset and values that destroyed a beloved culture.

Warner, William, *Distant Water: The Fate of the North Atlantic Fishermen, Little, Brown,* **1977.**
The classic account of the rise of factory trawlers and the damage they did prior to the advent of 200-mile limits.

Woodard, Colin, *Ocean's End: Travels through Endangered Seas, Basic Books,* **2000.**
The author, a freelance journalist specializing in ocean issues, describes the degradation of the world's oceans.

Articles

Garrison, Virginia, *et al.*, "African and Asian dust: from desert soils to coral reefs," *Bioscience*, May 1, 2003.
Scientists hypothesize that the world's coral reefs may be dying because of dust from African desertification.

Kolbert, Elizabeth, "The Darkening Sea," *The New Yorker*, Nov. 20, 2006.
The author provides a detailed and readable account of what carbon emissions are doing to the ocean through acidification.

Kunzig, Robert, "Twilight of the Cod," *Discover*, April 1995.
Kunzig chronicles the collapse of the New England and Newfoundland cod fisheries in the late 1980s.

Weiss, Kenneth R., *et al.*, "Altered Oceans," *Los Angeles Times*, July 30-Aug. 3, 2006.
In a Pulitzer Prize-winning series, Weiss and others describe the oceans' demise, with emphasis on the "rise of slime."

Reports and Studies

Dorsey, Eleanor, and Judith Pederson (eds.), *Effects of Fishing Gear on the Sea Floor of New England, Conservation Law Foundation*, 1998.
This report catalogs the damage caused by bottom trawlers, as viewed by scientists, environmentalists and fishermen.

Harvey, Janice, and David Coon, "Beyond the Crisis in the Fisheries: A proposal for community-based ecological fisheries management," *Conservation Council of New Brunswick*, 1997.
A groundbreaking report by the Canadian conservation council argues for giving proprietary ownership of fishing resources to the local communities that have relied on them.

***Pew Oceans Commission*, "America's Living Oceans: Charting a Course for Sea Change," May 2003.**
The commission describes the critical state of the world's oceans and recommends an ecosystem-based approach to future ocean management.

***United Nations Food and Agriculture Organization*, "State of the World's Fisheries and Aquaculture 2006," 2007, www.fao.org/docrep/009/A0699e/A0699e00.htm.**
The FAO's latest official report on the state of world fisheries says a quarter of the commercial fish stocks have been over-exploited or depleted and about half are fully exploited.

***U.S. Commission on Ocean Policy*, "An Ocean Blueprint for the 21st Century," 2004.**
The recommendations of a panel established by Congress echo those of the Pew Oceans Commission, while extending analysis to energy, environmental education and the issues afflicting the Great Lakes.

For More Information

Belize Coastal Zone Management Institute, P.O. Box 1884, Belize City, Belize, Central America; +1-501-223-0719; www.coastalzonebelize.org. Coordinates policies that will affect the health of Belize's barrier reef system.

Black Sea Ecosystem Recovery Project, www.undp-drp .org/drp/project_cooperation_BSERP.html. A network of scientists and policy experts sponsored by the U.N. Development Program.

Canadian Department of Fisheries and Oceans, 200 Kent St., 13th Floor, Station 13228, Ottawa, Ontario, Canada K1A 0E6; 613-993-0999; www.dfo-mpo.gc.ca. Manages Canada's fisheries, oceans and marine research.

International Whaling Commission, The Red House, 135 Station Road, Impington, Cambridge, CB24 9NP, United Kingdom; +44-1223-233-971; www.iwcoffice.org. Regulates whaling and the conservation of whales.

Joint Ocean Commission Initiative, c/o Meridian Institute,1920 L St., N.W., Suite 500, Washington, DC 20036-5037; (202) 354-6444; www.jointoceancommission.org. A vehicle for the chairs of the Pew Oceans Commission and U.S. Commission on Ocean Policy to push implementation of their recommendations.

National Fisheries Institute, 7918 Jones Branch Dr., Suite 700, McLean, VA 22102; (703) 752-8880; www.about seafood.com. The main lobbying and advocacy association for commercial fishing and seafood processing industries in the United States.

National Marine Fisheries Service, 1315 East-West Highway, Silver Spring, MD 20910; (301) 713-2239; www.nmfs.noaa.gov. U.S. federal agency responsible for the management of fisheries and international fishing agreements.

Oceana, 2501 M Street, N.W., Suite 300, Washington, DC 20037-1311; (202) 833-3900; www.oceana.org. The world's largest oceans-based environmental group, with branch offices in Europe, South America and the U.S. West Coast.

Ocean Conservancy, 1300 19th St., N.W., Washington, DC 20036; (202) 429-5609; www.oceanconservancy.org. Nonprofit organization promoting healthy and diverse ocean ecosystems and opposing practices that threaten ocean life.

Pew Institute for Ocean Science, 126 East 56th St., New York, NY 10022; (212) 756-0042; www.pewoceanscience.org. A Pew-funded body that conducts, supports, and disseminates scientific information on protecting the world's oceans.

Seaweb, 8401 Colesville Road, Suite 500, Silver Spring, MD 20910; (301) 495-9570; www.seaweb.org. Environmental advocacy group promoting ocean conservation, with branch offices in London and Paris.

The Shark Alliance, Rue Montoyer 39, 1000 Brussels, Belgium; www.sharkalliance.org. A continent-wide coalition of nongovernment organizations working to save Europe's sharks.

University of British Columbia Fisheries Centre, 2202 Main Mall, University of British Columbia, Vancouver, B.C.; Canada V6T 1Z4; 604-822-2731; www.fisheries.ubc. ca. Leading fisheries research institution and home to the scientists who predict the world is facing "seas of slime" and may end up "fishing down the marine food webs."

Biofuels Boom

Can Ethanol Satisfy America's Thirst for Foreign Oil?

Adriel Bettelheim

16

A gas station in Arlington, Va., offers biodiesel and E85 — a blend of 85 percent ethanol and 15 percent gasoline — in May 2006. Concerns over air quality, climate change and U.S. dependence on foreign oil are sparking new interest in ethanol and other agriculture-based alternative fuels. But some economists say it takes more energy to produce ethanol than it delivers, when transportation and other costs are considered.

From *CQ Researcher*,
September 29, 2006.

No doubt few Wall Street investors or members of Congress can locate Edmonds County, S.D., on a map. The sparsely populated area in the north of the state has a population of around 4,000 residents that has been declining for years.

To make matters worse, the most recent corn crop was poor. But that didn't stop Glacial Lakes Energy from coming to town. The company recently raised $95 million in three days to help finance a new processing plant near the tiny town of Mina to convert locally grown corn into ethanol fuel.

"People asked us, 'Why are you going into that area?' So you begin to question yourself," Glacial Lakes' Chairman Jon T. Anderson said at a groundbreaking ceremony in September. But, he said, the potential to be a player in domestic energy production persuaded the company to forge ahead (along with the help of generous federal subsidies). "The optimism is here," he said.[1]

Ethanol plants are springing up across the Midwest, the most visible evidence of a broad effort to increase supplies of renewable fuels. Politicians at the federal and local levels believe renewables, or "biofuels," will gradually reduce U.S. demand for gasoline and other petroleum products.

Enthusiasm for alternative fuels until recently was largely confined to the environmental community and commodities growers. But a number of factors — discontent over the Iraq war, jittery global energy markets, uncertainty over future supplies of crude oil and recent $3 per gallon pump prices — have dramatically changed policymakers' outlook, intensifying efforts to develop a homegrown

Ethanol Produced in 21 States

Ethanol is produced at 128 distillation plants throughout the country. To hold down shipping costs, most of the plans are in the states that grow the most corn.

Number of Ethanol Plants

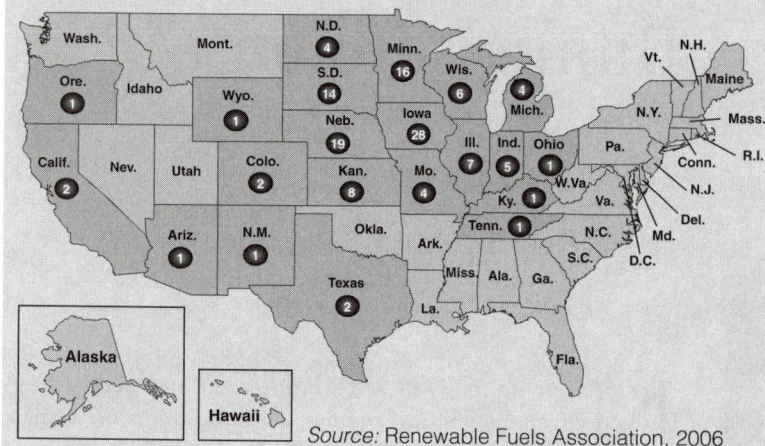

Source: Renewable Fuels Association, 2006

alternative to fossil fuels. Ethanol is on the leading edge, thanks both to the abundance of corn and to more than two decades of federal tax breaks and subsidies to encourage its production. The clean-burning fuel has the added virtue of not emitting carbon dioxide, a "greenhouse" gas implicated in global warming.[2]

In his State of the Union address on Jan. 31, Bush — a former Texas oil wildcatter who has long said that increased domestic oil and gas production will help satisfy the nation's energy needs — hailed ethanol and other renewables as an environmentally friendly tonic that will "make dependence on Middle East oil a thing of the past."[3]

Bush's remarks came after Congress passed an energy bill that ordered refiners to use 7.5 billion gallons of renewable fuels annually by 2012. And with crude oil — which exceeded $70 per barrel this summer — expected to remain above $50 per barrel into the foreseeable future, some farm-state lawmakers are suggesting that the United States should aim to produce 25 percent of its energy needs from farmland and forests by 2025.

"Anyone at a gas pump today knows that we need to act now," says Rep. Gil Gutknecht, R-Minn., one of Congress' most enthusiastic promoters of renewable

fuels. "Support for renewable fuels is good for the environment, cycles more money through our rural economy and reduces our dependence on foreign powers and big oil."

The trend bodes particularly well for Gutknecht and other Corn Belt officials, where 95 percent of the raw material for ethanol is produced. The nation's 128 ethanol distillation plants are concentrated in Iowa, Nebraska, Minnesota and South Dakota, mostly to reduce corn-shipping costs. But the ethanol boom also is drawing in new players, including outside investors who sense the nation is beginning to view agriculture not only as a source of food but also as a long-term provider of energy security.

So far 21 states already have ethanol plants, and with new plants being planned, annual production would increase from today's 4.5 billion gallons to more than 7 billion gallons. (*See map, above, and chart, p. 383.*) By decade's end, some government analysts predict ethanol production will exceed 10 billion gallons — double current levels.[4]

Yet there is considerable skepticism about whether renewable fuels can really reduce the nation's dependence on oil without an accompanying decline in overall energy consumption. If Americans keep consuming more and more energy — commuting longer distances, taking the kids to soccer practice, and so on — even big gains in renewable production won't keep us from having to look abroad.

Many experts think raising fuel-efficiency standards would make a bigger dent than increasing supplies of fuels not everyone wants. Agriculture-based fuels accounted for only six-tenths of a percent of total energy consumption in 2004. Moreover, they have achieved lower-than-expected market penetration over the past quarter-century because of generally low fossil fuel and electricity prices.

Producers continue to rely on generous federal and state subsidies that critics contend are distorting markets and diverting research money from the development of other potential energy sources, such as solar and geothermal. Energy analysts predict it will be difficult to justify continued federal aid for renewable fuels if oil markets stabilize and gas prices fall, providing consumers with cheap and plentiful energy.

Oil prices dipped briefly below $60 in late September for the first time in six months, and natural-gas prices reached their lowest level in more than two years.

"One of the best alternatives to using gasoline is to conserve energy, but you don't get re-elected forcing voters to buy a smaller car," says Kevin Book, senior energy analyst for Friedman Billings Ramsey, an Arlington, Va., investment bank. "Everyone from a farm state loves ethanol. So does everyone with research interests, 35 governors and a substantial majority of the House and Senate. They see this as solving a shortage of refined product."

Ethanol Production to Increase by 50 Percent

Iowa, Nebraska and Illinois produce more than half the ethanol made in the United States. Production will rise by about 50 percent when distillation plants under construction go online.

Ethanol Production Capacity by State, April 2006

State	Currently Operating Million gal/yr	%	Under Construction Million gal/yr	Total Million gal/yr	%
Iowa	1,218	27%	480	1,698	25%
Nebraska	553	12	504	1,057	16
Illinois	724	16	107	831	12
S.D.	585	13	238	823	12
Minn.	536	12	58	594	9
Indiana	102	2	290	392	6
Wis.	188	4	40	228	3
Mich.	50	1	157	207	3
Kansas	167	4	40	207	3
Missouri	110	2	45	155	2
Others	253	6	271	524	8
U.S. Total	**4,486**	**100**	**2,230**	**6,716**	**100**

Note: Percentages do not add to 100 due to rounding.

Source: Congressional Research Service, "Agriculture-Based Renewable Energy Production," May 18, 2006

Others question ethanol's actual energy value as a fuel. Several scientific studies have concluded that — when the costs of growing, harvesting, transporting and processing the crop are thrown into the calculations — it ultimately takes more energy to make ethanol from corn than is derived from burning the fuel. Because ethanol's energy output when burned is only about two-thirds that of gasoline, researchers at the Polytechnic University of New York have estimated the nation's entire corn crop would supply only 3.7 percent of the country's transportation needs. Ethanol-industry backers strenuously dispute the notion that their fuel produces a negative return, saying critics are overstating production costs and making widely varying assumptions about farming practices.[5]

Many energy experts and scientists contend that a more energy-efficient solution is to produce ethanol from switchgrass, wood chips, crop residues or other widely available forms of cellulose, as is the norm in other countries. Advocates of this approach note that Brazil — the world's leading ethanol producer — has met its demand for transportation fuels by using sugar cane.

But there are technological challenges in converting cellulose from trees and grass into sugar to start the ethanol-production process. Committing to another feedstock, or source, instead of corn also would undercut the current boom in corn-based ethanol production and possibly alienate an important political constituency in farm states.

For now, policymakers are straddling the line, continuing strong support for corn-based ethanol while backing research into alternative methods of producing the product and other biofuels. Congress is considering various proposals to increase federally financed research-and-development efforts at government and university labs and to require oil companies to blend more ethanol with their transportation fuels.

With two gas tanks to fill, a Hummer owner turns to biodiesel at a filling station in San Diego, Calif. The station sells alternative fuels in addition to gasoline, but drivers in many states have a hard time finding alternative fuels.

Republicans in Congress are trumpeting their promotion of biofuels in the run-up to the 2006 elections in the hope of bolstering their environmental credentials and demonstrating concern over the reliance on foreign oil.

Meanwhile, the Big Three U.S. automakers have pledged to double production of "flexible fuel" vehicles capable of running on ethanol and other biofuels by 2010. Automakers are poised to benefit from the trend, because companies that produce flexible-fuel vehicles receive extra credit toward meeting federal fuel-efficiency standards for their fleets, regardless of what fuel the vehicles actually burn.

Though ethanol is the only renewable fuel being produced in any significant quantities, other products stand to benefit from the push to expand supplies. One is biodiesel — produced from animal fat or vegetable oil — which works in diesel engines without the need for modifications and is more energy efficient than ethanol. The U.S. Postal Service and the Pentagon, as well as many state governments, are directing their bus and truck fleets to incorporate biodiesel into their fuel base. Country singer Willie Nelson has started a biodiesel-fuel company and is promoting use of "BioWillie" fuel by long-haul truckers. Biodiesel fuel is heavily promoted by soybean growers, who now provide about 90 percent of the raw material for biodiesel.

Energy analysts also suggest that biogas, or methane, can be produced on farms from the decomposition of animal wastes, and that hydrogen could power cars outfitted with special fuel cells.[6] These alternatives, however, are still in early stages of development and deemed years away from large-scale commercial applications.

The push to increase supplies of renewable fuels has overshadowed efforts to tamp down energy demand, such as tightening fuel-efficiency standards for passenger cars. Focusing on the demand side of the equation has merit, in the view of many experts, because the average number of miles driven by every American over age 16 has risen 60 percent — from about 7,500 miles per year in 1970 to about 12,000 in 2004 — a reflection of rising incomes, Americans' tendency to live farther from city centers and consumers' penchant for using sport-utility vehicles, trucks and minivans.

A 2002 study by the National Academy of Sciences concluded that federal fuel-efficiency standards had succeeded in lowering national energy consumption by 2.8 million barrels of oil a day. And the Congressional Budget Office has estimated that raising the standards by a relatively modest 3.8 miles per gallon for cars and light trucks — the classification that includes most SUVs and minivans — would lower the average rate of gas consumption for light trucks by 15 percent and for cars by 12 percent.

But encouraging Americans to buy more fuel-efficient cars is a politically risky proposition, especially since many consumers in recent years took advantage of low-cost financing deals offered by domestic automakers for less fuel-efficient cars. The experts say current efforts to increase fuel supplies are more realistic than prodding drivers to give up their current vehicles and will, over time, still bring a more conservation-centric ethic to policymaking.

"The most important thing for people to realize is the environmental impact of not doing anything, which is global warming," says Joseph Romm, executive director of the Arlington, Va.-based Center for Energy and Climate Solutions and a former energy official in the Clinton administration. "Corn ethanol isn't the endgame, but we need a fuel to replace gasoline that doesn't use so much carbon, and improving the process of conversion on the cellulosic side is a critical task at this point."[7]

As policymakers mull ways to change America's energy-consumption habits and ponder the merits of alternative fuels, here are some questions they are asking:

Can renewable fuels lessen U.S. dependence on foreign oil?

"I believe all Americans want to see a homegrown, renewable fuel play a bigger role in meeting our transportation fuel needs, particularly in light of the recent run-up in gasoline prices we have all endured," said Energy Secretary Samuel W. Bodman during a May appearance in Indianapolis to tout a network of filling stations that dispense E85, a fuel consisting of 85 percent ethanol.

Bodman and many other policymakers sense that Americans are weary of depending on foreign leaders in politically volatile countries to feed their energy needs. Likewise, surging gas and home heating oil prices are intensifying economic anxiety among middle-class consumers, who also are grappling with higher health-care and housing costs. The notion of turning to American farms for price relief is appealing because it would promote energy security and invigorate rural economies.

Efforts to turn that vision into reality are under way in places like the Argonne National Laboratory near Chicago, where the Department of Energy is collaborating on biofuels research with agricultural giant Archer Daniels Midland Corp., the energy conglomerate BP PLC and other businesses. Among the projects is one to design new refineries that can process biomass from crops, grasses and trees and convert it into ethanol and other chemicals at a lower cost than the traditional petroleum-refining process. The Energy Department hopes to use advances in biotechnology to maximize crop yields and optimize the fermentation process that converts plant sugars into ethanol.

But experts say renewable fuels, and ethanol in particular, will have to overcome some significant hurdles to replace imported oil in a meaningful way. Despite the industry's rapid growth, ethanol still accounts for only a small fraction of total U.S. fuel consumption: In 2005, the industry produced 3.9 billion gallons, or approximately 2 percent of national fuel use. Though that share is certain to rise because of federal mandates and subsidies, the product is handicapped by the fact that the fuel is more costly to produce than gasoline — and difficult to obtain outside of the Midwest.[8]

E85, the most aggressively promoted ethanol fuel, is available at more than 850 gas stations. States and agricultural interests are offering loans and other incentives to more station owners to expand its availability. But because cars must be specially engineered to run on the fuel, consumer demand remains relatively low, leaving station operators reluctant to install pumps and underground storage tanks that can cost as much as $200,000. Their ambivalence is partly influenced by oil companies, which are reluctant to support alternative fuels. Ethanol producers rely on the oil companies because they must add their product to gasoline. As a result, at the end of the 2006 summer driving season ethanol fuel could not be found anywhere in the Northeast or New England and was on sale at only a single filling station in California.[9]

"Most of the people who have flexible-fuel vehicles don't have any kind of realistic, practical access [to renewable fuels]," said Don MacKenzie, a vehicles engineer with the Union of Concerned Scientists.[10]

Moving the fuel from the Farm Belt to major coastal population centers is another significant challenge. Producers must ship ethanol in small quantities by train, truck or barge because the compound attracts water molecules that corrode pipelines, posing the risk of groundwater contamination. Though there is talk about building fully dedicated ethanol pipelines, energy companies are taking a wait-and-see approach because the market has not fully developed. Alternatively, they could build processing plants closer to lucrative markets, but that would only be economical if enough corn could be obtained nearby.

"There are costs involved in requiring physical volumes [of fuel] to move where they would otherwise not economically go," notes Lawrence Goldstein, president of the Petroleum Industry Research Foundation, a New York consultancy.

Ethanol's market potential is also heavily influenced by the price of raw material. Many analysts predict the cost of producing ethanol will rise in coming years as more processing plants come online and drive up demand for corn. E85 currently sells for less than regular unleaded gas because the government gives producers a 51-cent tax credit for every gallon they produce, allowing the companies to sell the fuel below cost. The government also insulates domestic producers from overseas competition by levying a 54-cent-per-gallon tariff and a 2.5 percent duty on imported ethanol — policies that keep Brazil's cheaper ethanol off U.S. markets.

Fossil Fuels Dominate Energy Consumption

Renewable-energy sources — including hydroelectric power, wood, waste, ethanol and biodiesel — accounted for only 6 percent of all energy consumed in the United States in 2004. Comparitively, fossil fuels — including oil, coal and natural gas — supplied nearly 90 percent of all energy consumed.

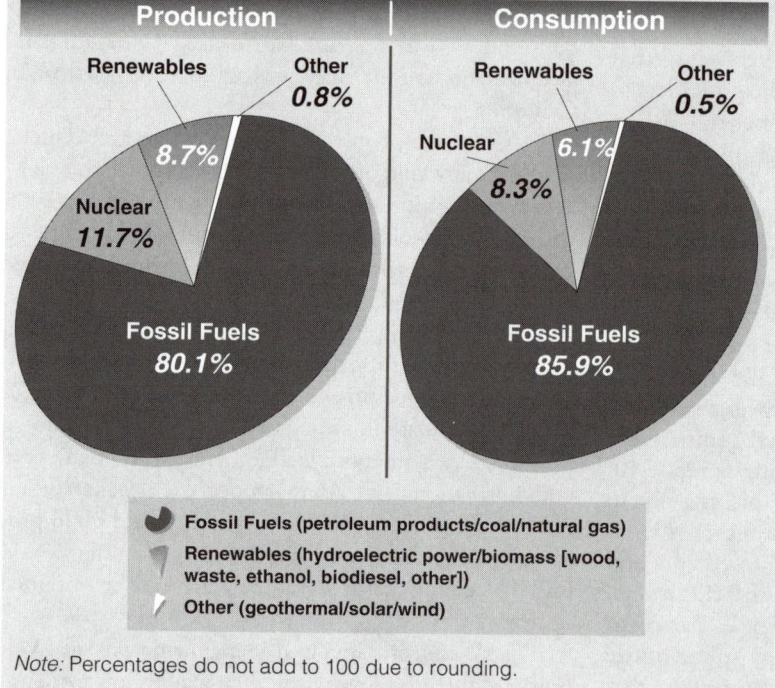

U.S. Energy Production and Consumption, 2004

Production

Renewables — Other **0.8%**

8.7%

Nuclear **11.7%**

Fossil Fuels 80.1%

Consumption

Renewables — Other **0.5%**

Nuclear — **6.1%**

8.3%

Fossil Fuels 85.9%

Fossil Fuels (petroleum products/coal/natural gas)
Renewables (hydroelectric power/biomass [wood, waste, ethanol, biodiesel, other])
Other (geothermal/solar/wind)

Note: Percentages do not add to 100 due to rounding.

Source: Congressional Research Service, "Agriculture-Based Renewable Energy Production," May 18, 2006

But if corn rises above recent levels of $2 per bushel and drives up producers' costs, the fuel might lose its price advantage. That prospect has led some farm-state lawmakers to promote new uses for the fuel, such as mandating that utilities use renewable sources to produce a certain percentage of their electricity.

Even if U.S. energy policies continue to favor renewable fuels, their long-term prospects will be heavily influenced by events overseas. Major oil-producing nations are capable of adjusting production levels to influence the price they receive for crude oil, often to the detriment of alternative fuels. Such was the case in the 1980s, after the Carter administration, responding to spiking crude-oil prices in the mid-1970s, launched a major round of government-funded research to develop conservation technologies and alternative fuels. Middle Eastern members of the Organization of Petroleum Exporting Countries (OPEC) oil cartel, faced with declining demand and more worldwide competition from non-OPEC producers, decided to step up oil production in 1985 and 1986, dramatically lowering the price refiners paid for imported crude. The re-emergence of cheap petroleum weakened political support for alternative fuels just as Ronald Reagan's administration adopted a market-based approach to energy and scaled back subsidies for alternative fuels. Reagan eventually killed the Carter initiative.

A variation of that scenario could play out today if imported oil prices drop further, resulting in a glut of ethanol larger than the levels Congress ordered refiners to blend in their products. Producers and farmers could be crippled by oversupply and unable to recoup their costs.

"There's really no mechanism that would protect this industry from excess supply," says Daniel Welt, a credit analyst for Standard & Poor's Corp. "For an industry to be viable long-term, it should be able to weather the entire commodity cycle, not just the top of the commodity cycle."[11]

Promoters of alternative fuels remain confident that nationwide demand will increase as more ethanol plants begin operations and that the continuation of government incentives will make biodiesel and other alternative fuels economically viable, too.

"The potential for the ethanol industry to continue to build infrastructure and become a substantial volume of our domestic motor-fuels supply is enormous, and if we truly are working toward energy independence, then we must continue moving forward," said Chris Standlee, executive vice president of Abengoa Bioenergy Corp. and vice chair of the Renewable Fuels Association, a Washington, D.C., trade group.[12]

Is corn the best raw material for deriving ethanol?

To understand corn's dominant position in the renewable-fuel industry, one has to first consider its status as the nation's commodity of choice. Modern crop science and genetic engineering have turned today's corn plant into an unusually hearty specimen that grows in a variety of regions. Farmers raised a record 12 billion bushels in 2004, and with even bigger yields forecast, they are finding more and more markets and commercial applications. Corn already is the leading feed grain for cattle and dairy cows, pigs and chickens. Corn sweetener has become a mainstay of sodas, ice cream, canned fruit and other popular foods, and byproducts are used to manufacture textiles, plastics and petroleum products.

Using corn to make fuel has enormous appeal for growers and processors because it gives them a role in debates over energy policy and national security and allows them to make the case that their product is essential to achieving energy independence. "If we were to get serious about renewables, the extent of the demand engulfs anything that agriculture has seen in food and fiber," notes Purdue University economist Wallace Tyner.[13]

The industry's efforts have been helped by the recent decisions of two dozen states to ban MTBE, a rival fuel additive that has been implicated in groundwater pollution. Groups such as the National Corn Growers Association are trying to improve corn's market position through a variety of steps, such as lobbying for requirements that all gasoline sold in the United States contain a 10 percent blend of non-imported renewable fuels by 2010.

"Our nation's farmers are the best in the world at growing corn, which means that we must continually grow existing markets and discover new ones for our product," says Bruce Noel, chairman of the growers association's ethanol committee. "The ethanol market is the single most successful and fastest-growing value-added market for farmers."

But some nagging questions trouble the industry's efforts. Some economists and energy analysts question whether the intensifying push to use corn as a fuel will

Getty Images/Scott Olson

Hybrid corn growing near Freeport, Ill., produces about 4 percent more ethanol than other varieties. A bushel of corn produces about 2.7 gallons of ethanol. Congress this year mandated that refiners use 7.5 billion gallons of renewable fuels annually by 2012.

gradually deplete supplies needed for more traditional uses, potentially driving up food prices. Last year, about 14 percent of the nation's corn went into ethanol production, compared with 11 percent four years ago. This year, the volume of corn for ethanol could rise to 19 percent, according to Department of Agriculture estimates.[14]

There also is a growing body of evidence suggesting that ethanol production consumes more energy than the finished fuel contains, which some critics say points to the need for alternative fuel sources.

"People tend to think of ethanol and see an endless cycle: Corn is used to produce ethanol, ethanol is burned and gives off carbon dioxide and corn uses the carbon dioxide as it grows. But that isn't the case. Fossil fuel actually drives the whole cycle," says University of California-Berkeley engineering Professor Tad Patzek. "Taking grain apart, fermenting it, distilling it and extruding it uses a lot of fossil energy. We are grasping at a solution that is by far the least efficient."[15]

Scientists like Patzek have been debating the costs-benefits of ethanol production for years. For instance, a study by Alexander Farrell — another engineering professor at Patzek's school — reached the opposite conclusion.

And University of Minnesota researchers this summer released a comprehensive analysis of the energy needed to grow corn and soybeans and convert them into biofuels. Writing in the *Proceedings of the National Academies of Sciences*, they concluded that both corn-based ethanol and biodiesel produced from soybeans generate more energy than is needed to produce them. However, while biodiesel from soybeans returns 93 percent more energy than is used to produce it, corn-based ethanol provides only 25 percent more energy.[16]

David Tilman, a coauthor of the study, says ethanol is a good first-generation fuel but eventually could be superceded by commodities that deliver better energy and environmental returns. He points to switchgrass, mixed prairie grasses, woody plants and other cellulose sources that cost less than corn because they can be produced on marginally productive land and require less fertilizer and pesticide. Tilman's findings are echoed by the Union of Concerned Scientists, which estimates corn ethanol reduces greenhouse gas emissions by only 10 to 20 percent per unit of energy delivered, compared to as much as 80 to 90 percent for cellulosic ethanol.

But development of a cellulose-based ethanol industry is years away because of technical challenges in converting the crops into fermentable sugar. Although pilot plants have been established, only a single commercial facility, in Ottawa, Canada, is in operation — using wheat straw. The U.S. Department of Energy estimates using enzymes to break down cellulosic raw material costs 30 to 50 cents per gallon compared to a few cents for corn-based ethanol. If new technology brings cellulosic enzyme costs down to less than 5 cents per gallon, it would have a distinct price advantage over corn-based ethanol. But experts say such breakthroughs may be a decade away.[17]

Meanwhile, officials predict biotechnology advances will continue to improve corn-crop yields, and next-generation processing plants will convert raw materials into fuel more efficiently. Farmers will shift acreage to corn from less profitable crops like soybeans and cotton. And corn growers say because long-term demand for corn as livestock feed is expected to be relatively flat, the net result will be abundant harvests that will satisfy the need for both food and fuel at a reasonable price.

"The increased use of ethanol in our nation's fuel supply is not the singular answer for America's dangerous dependence on foreign oil. However, ethanol is already playing an important role in our nation's overall energy policy and will play an integral part in finding a long-term energy-security solution," says the growers association's Noel.

Should the federal government be doing more to promote the ethanol industry?

President Bush's State of the Union endorsement of renewable fuels and his goal of reducing the nation's need for imported oil by 5 million barrels a day by 2025 have unleashed a variety of new government-sponsored initiatives to promote renewable-energy research and development.

His fiscal 2007 budget request sought $359.2 million for the Department of Energy's Renewable Energy Program — a 30.5 percent increase over 2006 funding levels — and there are indications Congress will meet or exceed the request. The administration also is contributing $160 million over the next three years to build cellulosic biorefineries to make ethanol from corn stalks, wheat straw, switchgrass or other commonly available biomass.

But the far bigger contribution to renewable-energy development comes in the form of tax credits, mandates and subsidies that have been included in energy and farm bills and as amendments to the Clean Air Act for more than a decade. For example, the energy bill Congress passed last year included tax breaks for ethanol, biodiesel, solar, geothermal and other renewable-energy sources totaling $3.4 billion over 10 years.[18]

Such assistance tends to trigger intense debates over the viability of renewable fuels. Critics — including fiscal conservatives and groups opposed to government waste — fear the future of alternative products will be influenced by political considerations instead of market realities and that many of the most heavily subsidized products will never turn a profit or be able to compete head-to-head with fossil fuels. Moreover, the generous taxpayer assistance is benefiting big corporations, not just small refiners and family farmers. Agriculture giant Archer Daniels Midland's earnings for the quarter that ended June 30 more than doubled because of increased demand for crop-based fuels, while its revenues rose 1 percent, to $9.6 billion.

"If ethanol is to succeed as a motor fuel, it will have to be the cheapest ethanol globally available," says Ben Lieberman, a senior economic-policy analyst at the conservative Heritage Foundation. "Consumers would

C H R O N O L O G Y

1900-1960s *Fuel demand surges during the world wars, but renewables can't compete with fossil fuels.*

1908 Ford's Model T becomes the first mass-produced vehicle capable of running on gasoline, ethanol or a combination of the two.

1917-1918 Wartime demand for ethanol surges to 60 million gallons per year.

1919 Prohibition squelches ethanol's commercial viability. In the next decade, oil companies toy with using it to eliminate knocking in engines and raise the octane rating, but turn to lead instead, fearing gas stations will become speakeasies.

1930s The end of Prohibition revives ethanol's place in the market. More than 2,000 gas stations in the Midwest begin selling gasohol, a blend consisting of between 6 percent and 12 percent ethanol.

1941-1945 World War II again drives up demand for fuel, but increased use of ethanol is largely for non-fuel, manufacturing purposes.

1945-1970s Low fuel prices through the 1960s again drive down ethanol's attractiveness as a fuel.

1970s *The Arab oil embargo, the fall of the shah of Iran and increased environmental awareness spark interest in alternative fuels.*

1974 The first legislative effort to promote ethanol as a fuel — the Solar Energy Research, Development and Demonstration Act — leads to widespread research into ways of converting cellulose into fuel.

1975 The government begins to phase out the use of lead as a fuel additive, making ethanol more attractive as a substitute to boost octane.

1979 Amoco Oil Co. begins selling alcohol-blended fuels and is quickly followed by other major oil companies. Congress approves spending some $1 billion on biomass-related projects.

1980s *Congress extends subsidies and tax breaks to spur renewable-fuel production. But market forces discourage widespread use of renewables.*

1984 There are 163 ethanol plants in the United States — a response to tax benefits and government-backed loans approved by Congress the previous four years.

1985-1986 The Organization of Petroleum Exporting Countries (OPEC), responding to lower U.S. demand and competition from non-OPEC oil producers, cuts prices. Ethanol producers, in turn, begin receiving very low prices for their products, despite a 60-cent-per-gallon production credit, and many go out of business. In Denver, ethanol is used for the first time as an oxygenate in the winter to tamp down carbon monoxide emissions.

1987 The Austrian company Gaskoks acquires South African technology and opens the first commercial biodiesel plant.

1990s-Present *States and the federal government mandate that fleet vehicles use more renewable fuels. Tight oil supplies and occasional supply disruptions spur more interest in alternative fuels.*

1998 The ethanol subsidy is extended through 2007, but its size is gradually reduced, from 54-cents-per-gallon to the current 51-cents-per-gallon.

1999-2000 Some states ban use of the fuel additive MTBE because it is showing up in groundwater. The Environmental Protection Agency (EPA) in 2000 recommends the product be phased out nationally.

2004-2005 Violence in the Middle East, a standoff over Iran's nuclear program, rising anti-American sentiment in Venezuela and surging energy demand from China and India raise new concerns about American energy security and the continuity of supplies. Hurricanes Katrina and Rita knock out about 5 million barrels of refining capacity in summer 2005. Congress mandates that refiners use 7.5 billion gallons of renewable fuels annually by 2012.

2006 President George W. Bush promotes renewable fuels and other alternative sources of energy, saying America must be weaned from its appetite for foreign oil.

Drivers Can't Find Enough Ethanol Stations

With great fanfare, Gov. Mitch Daniels announced plans recently to designate the hamlet of Reynolds, Ind., as "BioTown USA" and make it the first community in the United States to meet all its needs with renewable energy.

"We are taking challenges and turning them into opportunities by developing homegrown, local energy production," the first-term Republican governor declared. State officials recruited General Motors to provide free, two-year leases on 20 ethanol-burning cars and generous discounts to locals who purchased flexible-fuel vehicles capable of running on gasoline or E85 — a fuel consisting of 85 percent ethanol. Officials also encouraged the local filling station to install pumps dispensing E85 and biodiesel fuel.[1]

But a year later, the 550 residents of Reynolds are trying to make sense of their unique status. Though residents wound up buying 135 ethanol-burning cars, operators of the filling station balked at the half-million-dollar estimated cost of installing the necessary pumps and decided to sell the business. Drivers determined enough to travel 80 miles to Indianapolis could find ethanol on sale at only two filling stations — but for not much less than regular gas because of a sharp spike in prices for the alternative fuel.

"We need the alternatives to get away from the foreign oil," said insurance agent Gary Dedaker, who owns two flexible-fuel trucks but has not yet been able to use ethanol. "As we get more plants, I think prices will go down."[2]

The experience in Reynolds is being mirrored elsewhere in the Midwest. Though E85 is available at more than 850 service stations nationwide, drivers cannot find enough of it in contiguous locations to make it a viable alternative to gasoline. Those who can often don't buy ethanol-based fuels unless they are significantly cheaper than regular gasoline, because ethanol only delivers three-quarters as much energy per gallon, meaning more frequent fill-ups.[3]

The availability raises serious questions about how much federal and state governments have to spend to create an adequate infrastructure for ethanol. Iowa, the nation's biggest corn producer, this year began giving retailers a 25-cent-per-gallon tax credit for selling E85, and is paying as much as half the cost of installing necessary pumps. In Illinois, Democratic Gov. Rod Blagojevich has proposed spending $30 million to add 900 pumps by 2011. Even if that works, huge gaps remain. Ethanol is unavailable on most of America's two coasts and in New England.

Analysts say motorists frequently don't know enough about the availability of the fuel — and, in some cases, whether their vehicles can burn it — to generate sustained demand. Without steady business, even filling station owners in the heart of the Corn Belt are taking a wait-and-see

benefit if the market, not special-interest politics, decided how much ethanol to use and where it should come from." Lieberman believes Congress should repeal laws that levy tariffs and duties on cheap foreign ethanol instead of continuing to subsidize the domestic ethanol industry.

But ethanol advocates point out that government subsidies for renewable energy comprise only a fraction of the tax breaks and subsidies extended to the fossil fuel industry. Congress in recent years has promoted oil and gas development, including, for example, a provision in the 2004 corporate tax bill that made domestic drilling eligible for a 3-percentage-point reduction in the top tax rate for manufacturing — from 35 percent to 32 percent. And last year's energy bill allowed oil and gas companies to pay lower royalty fees for marginally productive wells and reduced royalty payments for gas wells in shallow

waters in the Gulf of Mexico. It also allowed electric utilities to write off billions of dollars' worth of air-pollution equipment on older power plants and accelerated to 15 years — from 20 years — the depreciation period for property used in the transmission of electricity.[19]

Renewable-fuel proponents say subsidies for the industry are in the national interest because they help create a homegrown industry that over time will insulate Americans from global energy price shocks. Thus Congress and presidential administrations must continue with long-term funding commitments to help their industry compete, they argue.

"As the industry expands outside the traditional Corn Belt, more and more Americans will be able to invest in and realize the benefits of a stronger energy future," says Bob Dinneen, president of the Renewable Fuels Association.

approach, installing pumps when they do largely to support local corn growers. Promotional efforts remain scattershot. In June, Ford Motor Co. and VeraSun Energy, a large ethanol producer, christened 300 miles of interstate between Chicago and St. Louis the "Midwest Ethanol Corridor." Some automakers are giving away $1,000 of free fuel to purchasers of flexible-fuel vehicles.

Part of the problem is timing. Federal and state mandates have prompted refiners in recent years to stop using the chemical MTBE as a fuel additive and instead look to ethanol as a replacement. That drove up demand for the product and raised prices for fuels like E85. Retailers say the result was that ethanol sales tended to rise when gasoline prices crested above $3 per gallon. Below that, customers usually stuck with traditional fossil fuels. During the peak summer driving season, with prices for unleaded regular hovering around $3, ethanol typically was selling for about 40 cents per gallon less, according to spot checks conducted in the Midwest.

Many residents in rural communities in the heartland remain optimistic the home-grown fuel will become commercially viable. In BioTown USA, they are even contemplating other sources of energy production, including burning methane gas from the town's sewer system and nearby hog farms to create electricity for homes and businesses.

"We're addicted to oil," says Charlie Van Voorst, Reynolds' town council president. "It would be nice if we were addicted to ethanol."

AP Photo/John Harrell

Hog farmer William Schroeder of Reynolds, Ind., may sell the waste generated from his 20,000 hogs for use in the "BioTown USA" experiment. Gov. Mitch Daniels wants Reynolds to be the first U.S. community to meet all its needs with renewable energy.

---

[1] For background, see J. K. Wall, "Ethanol Test Town Has . . . No Ethanol," *The Indianapolis Star*, Aug. 27, 2006.

[2] *Ibid.*

[3] See Alexei Barrionuevo, "Fill Up on Corn If You Can," *The New York Times*, Aug. 31, 2006, p. C1.

But some in the Bush administration are struggling with competing impulses to prop up renewable fuels and at the same time subject them to market forces. Energy Secretary Bodman this summer broached the idea of scrapping the 51-cent-per-gallon ethanol production tax credit if the industry grows larger and fuel supplies are plentiful.

"The question to me that I think deserves a discussion is the nature of the subsidy, how long it should stay," Bodman said during a June telephone news conference. "Right now it's geared to stay for another four years through the year 2010. . . . And what happens after that, and what kind of a picture should we be working on? To me those are the key questions and the areas that will, I think, determine the ultimate volumes of ethanol available to our taxpayers."

Though political support for the tax credit is likely to remain strong, Bodman's comments reflect the unease felt in some quarters over how long the government should prop up a growing industry — and what federal policymakers should do if demand for ethanol doesn't match supplies. There is pressure within the energy community to spread the wealth and expand government support for other renewable resources, including wind, solar and geothermal energy.

The popularity of renewable fuels also is triggering a debate over the manner in which Congress awards funding for research into renewable energy. Lawmakers increasingly are "earmarking" funds for specific projects in their states and districts, particularly in the areas of biomass, hydrogen and wind energy research. Because of spending caps, the designations — which usually go to colleges and universities or government labs in home districts — result in corresponding cuts to the size of government grants awarded competitively to researchers

Ethanol Production Grows Rapidly

U.S. ethanol production began after the 1970s energy crises and
rose steadily, sparked by the Energy Tax Act of 1978, which gave
ethanol a partial exemption from the motor fuels excise tax, and the
Clean Air Act Amendments of 1990, which favored ethanol blended
with gasoline. New government incentives are expected to spur
continued production growth through at least 2010.

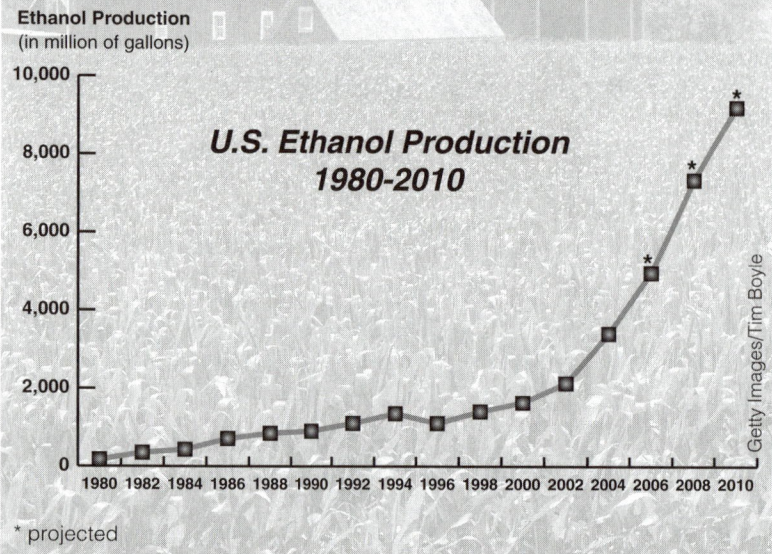

Ethanol Production
(in million of gallons)

*U.S. Ethanol Production
1980-2010*

Getty Images/Tim Boyle

* projected

Sources: Food and Agriculture Policy Institute, University of Missouri, July 2006;
Renewable Fuels Association

from elsewhere in the country.[20] An analysis by the
American Association for the Advancement of Science
(AAAS) found that energy-research earmarks in the fiscal 2006 spending bills more than doubled — to $266
million — over 2005 levels.[21]

"With the fiscal situation unlikely to get better in the
fiscal 2007 budget, congressional appropriators will have
to square demands for earmarked funds against tight
spending targets once again," the AAAS noted. "With
the Bush administration unlikely to expend political
capital against earmarking, the push for earmarking the
R&D budget will not abate in 2007."

BACKGROUND

Alcohol Fuels

The earliest efforts to promote alternative fuels in the
United States did not take place in the Midwest, but in

New Hampshire. Mill owner Samuel
Morey, who was fond of tinkering
with steam engines, developed a rudi-
mentary internal combustion engine
in 1823 that ran on ethanol and tur-
pentine. It soon proved popular with
farmers, who maintained stills on their
land to turn crop waste into lamp oil
and other kinds of fuel for household
use. German engineer Nicholas Otto
developed a more refined version of
Morey's invention in 1860, again using
ethanol as the propellant. By mid-
century, grain alcohol had become a
major illuminating fuel in the United
States.[22]

The Civil War, however, abruptly
put an end to ethanol use. The Union
placed a $2-per-gallon excise tax on
ethanol to pay for war costs. Americans
quickly switched to cheaper kerosene,
leaving ethanol in the shadows for
most of the remainder of the 19th
century. Commercial prospects for the
fuel only began to revive in 1896,
when Henry Ford used pure ethanol
to power his first automobile, called
the quadricycle. A little over a decade
later, Ford began producing the widely
popular Model T, which was a flexible-fuel vehicle, meaning it could run on ethanol, gasoline or a combination
of the two. However, ethanol's market potential from the
beginning of the 20th century on would be influenced
more by U.S. government policies and global events than
by homegrown technologies.

In 1906 Congress decided to lift the excise tax it had
imposed half a century earlier, allowing ethanol to compete
head-to-head with gasoline. The outbreak of World War I
intensified demand for all fuels, prompting ethanol demand
to peak at 50 to 60 million gallons annually. But in 1919,
a year after the war's end, Prohibition put an end to
widespread distribution, leaving gasoline the fuel of choice.
Though some refiners continued to use ethanol to increase
gasoline's octane rating and eliminate engine knocking,
many in the oil industry worried they were turning filling
stations into speakeasies and decided to instead add lead
to motor fuels to boost the octane.

The end of Prohibition and the outbreak of World War II again revived ethanol's fortunes. During the 1930s, more than 2,000 filling stations in the Midwest sold a gasoline blended with 6 to 12 percent ethanol, known as gasohol. Non-fuel wartime manufacturing needs further drove up demand. But the fuel's fortunes took another nosedive at the end of the war, when demand for fuels fell sharply, accompanied by low gasoline prices. From the late 1940s to the late 1970s, virtually no commercial ethanol fuel could be purchased in the United States.

The 1973 Arab oil embargo ushered in a new era for renewable fuels.[23] Energy costs surged in the aftermath of the embargo as the cost of imported crude oil roughly tripled. Making matters worse, federal price controls kept the price of domestic production below market prices. The policy, designed to insulate consumers from some price increases, instead discouraged oil companies from making fuel at home and intensified the nation's reliance on imported oil. The fall of the shah of Iran in 1979 and the Iranian Revolution subsequently reduced the flow of Iranian oil to world markets, creating more supply disruptions and spurring Carter administration efforts to promote conservation, including the first fuel-economy standards.[24] Oil companies, led by Amoco, began selling alcohol-blended fuels, and Congress began supporting research into alternative fuels.

From 1980 to 1984, Congress enacted a series of tax breaks to ethanol producers and blenders and also placed a tariff on imported ethanol. The number of ethanol plants increased to 163 by 1984, and tax writers in the House and Senate increased the ethanol production subsidy to 60 cents per gallon. Officials in Denver, Colo., christened a new use for the product by mandating that ethanol-containing oxygenated fuels be used in wintertime to control carbon monoxide emissions.

But world events again intruded on ethanol's fortunes. Faced with declining market share and revenues, the OPEC oil cartel increased production in the mid-1980s, thus lowering the price of its products. In 1985 and 1986, refining costs for imported oil plunged from $27 per barrel to $14 per barrel, leaving ethanol unable to compete.

And though imported crude prices shot up again during the first Gulf War, OPEC continued to assure long-term demand by boosting production whenever there was a loss of supplies.

Getty Images/Andre Vieira (both)

From Cane to Car

Abundant supplies of sugar cane have made Brazil the world's biggest ethanol producer. This distillation plant is in prosperous São Paulo state (top). Wielding machetes, Brazilian cane cutters take down the last stalks in a field (bottom).

Despite tough market conditions in the 1990s, Washington policymakers continued to support the ethanol industry by requiring that certain car fleets purchase alternative-fuel vehicles, mandating wintertime use of oxygenated fuels and exempting alternative fuels from some excise taxes. The ethanol production tax credit was extended several times, though gradually reduced to the current 51-cents-per-gallon level. Enthusiasm for the fuel extended to states, which began banning the rival fuel additive MTBE over concerns that it was contributing to widespread groundwater contamination.

Biodiesel

Like ethanol, biodiesel's roots extend back to the 19th century. Rudolf Diesel introduced the first diesel engine — an iron

Ethanol Comes With a High Price Tag

Corn-based ethanol produces less energy per gallon and is the most expensive alternative fuel, costing 52 cents more per gallon than gasoline.

Energy and Price Comparisons for Alternative Fuels
(as of February 2006)

Fuel Type	BTUs per gallon*	GEG**	Average Price ($/GEG)
Gasoline	125,071	1.00	$2.23
Ethanol (E85)	90,383	0.72	$2.75
Diesel Fuel	138,690	1.11	$2.31
Biodiesel	138,690	1.11	$2.38
Propane	91,333	0.74	$2.68

* A Btu (British thermal unit) is a measure of the heat content of a fuel and indicates the amount of energy contained in the fuel.

** Gasoline-equivalent gallon (GEG) is the amount of BTUs in a gallon of fuel, compared to the BTUs in a gallon of gasoline.

Source: Congressional Research Service, "Agriculture-Based Renewable Energy Production," May 18, 2006

cylinder with a flywheel in the base — in Germany in 1893, using peanut oil to power the device. He predicted in a 1912 speech that vegetable-oil fuels would become as prevalent as gasoline. But by the 1920s, manufacturers were designing diesel engines to run on lower viscosity fossil fuels, which were cheaper than biofuels.

Interest in biodiesel didn't re-emerge until the late 1970s in South Africa, where chemists processed and refined sunflower oil. The Austrian company Gaskoks acquired the technology and established the first biodiesel pilot plant in 1987. Throughout the 1990s, production gradually expanded through Europe as bus and truck fleets modified their vehicles to run on the fuel and automakers including Renault and Peugeot developed vehicles that could run on diesel fuel blended with up to 30 percent biodiesel. Since 1999, annual U.S. production of the fuel has increased 75-fold — from less than 1 million gallons in 1999 to about 75 million gallons in 2005, made almost entirely from soybeans. The National Biodiesel Board, a trade group, says as of mid-2006 there were 65 companies producing the fuel and another 50 either building or contemplating plants.

Government biodiesel supports are similar to those for ethanol and include a production tax credit of $1 per gallon used in the blending of petroleum-based diesel fuel. Manufacturers producing less than 60 million gallons a year are entitled to a small-producer income tax credit of 10 cents per gallon for the first 15 million gallons. Despite the support, the outlook for continued support for biodiesel is murky; the production tax credit expires in 2008, leaving little time for the industry to develop. In addition, vegetable-oil feedstocks like soybeans, sunflower or rapeseed are less abundant than corn and other sources of ethanol. And biodiesel suffers from a limited ability to substitute for oil imports, even if market conditions warrant it. A hypothetical federal mandate that biodiesel make up 1 percent of current vehicle diesel fuel use would exhaust most available vegetable oils and animal fats and require manufacturers to find an additional 1.3 billion pounds of oil.

"The bottom line is that a small increase in demand for fats and oils for biodiesel production could quickly exhaust available feedstock supplies and push vegetable-oil prices significantly higher due to the low elasticity of demand for vegetable oils in food consumption," the Congressional Research Service concluded in a recent report. "At the same time, it would begin to disturb feed markets."[25]

CURRENT SITUATION

Blocked by 'Pork'

Though the Bush administration and Congress have expressed strong support for renewable fuels, government efforts to spur production are highly contingent on the annual congressional appropriations process. And proposed cuts in fiscal 2007 spending are hampering efforts by the Environmental Protection Agency (EPA) to finalize the rule that actually would expand use of the products in gasoline. On Sept. 7 the EPA officially proposed a rule requiring that 3.71 percent of gasoline demand in 2007 come from renewable sources. In keeping with the goals of last year's energy

Europeans Embrace Biofuels

While the United States is just beginning to view biofuel as a viable alternative to petroleum, Europeans already are embracing ethanol and biodiesel as mainstays at the gas pump. Indeed, the popularity of agriculture-based fuels is forcing European Union (EU) members increasingly to look abroad to satisfy demand for both raw materials and finished product.

With robust economic growth between 1985 and 2004, European demand for transportation fuels rose by nearly 50 percent, forcing governments to import more oil. But two factors prompted governments to seek a clean-burning alternative that could provide some measure of energy security: concerns about possible supply disruptions and Kyoto Protocol mandates to reduce greenhouse-gas emissions.[1]

In 2003, the European Commission set a voluntary goal of deriving at least 2 percent of energy needs from biofuels by the end of 2005 and growing that share by 0.75 percent each year until the end of 2010.

Most of the activity has centered on expanding supplies of biodiesel, which is manufactured primarily from rapeseed oil but also from animal fats and even left-over restaurant grease. Total European rapeseed production this year is projected at 15.3 million tons, with the highest yields coming from Poland and the Baltic states. Oilseed-crushing plants are being built throughout the continent. But agriculture experts say future production is constrained by a lack of suitable land for growing and the high cost of growing and processing raw materials. As a result, Europe is looking abroad for raw materials and a more diverse mix of alternative fuels.[2]

EU nations have built a burgeoning ethanol trade with Pakistan, which in recent years has accounted for 20 percent of Europe's ethanol imports. Other ethanol-exporting countries include Guatemala, Peru, Bolivia, Ecuador, Nicaragua and Panama, as well as South Africa, the Republic of Congo and Egypt. The raw materials, or feedstocks, used to create ethanol run the gamut — from molasses (Pakistan) to sugar cane (Latin America and South Africa) to sugar beets, wheat, corn and rye (Europe).

Trade in biodiesel has not evolved yet because there is no significant production outside of Europe. But to relax pressure on domestic rapeseed-oil production, European biodiesel producers are importing other raw materials, such as palm oil from Malaysia. And because Europe doesn't produce large amounts of soybeans — another biodiesel raw material — it is turning to Brazil, whose crop is desirable because of its high protein and oil content and the country's long growing seasons.

But Europeans are wary of becoming too reliant on overseas markets for their alternative fuels. Researchers are developing new technologies to convert cellulose fibers into ethanol. Royal Dutch Shell and the German biodiesel innovator Choren Industries also are pioneering a gasification process that converts wood or grass into carbon monoxide and hydrogen, then uses catalysts to chemically reassemble the gases into a diesel fuel.

"Second-generation biofuels require further technology development that may take another 10 years or so," said Andre Faijj, an associate professor at Copernicus University at Utrecht University in the Netherlands, who studies energy supplies. "The new generation of technologies emerging will really tip the balance."[3]

---

[1] For background see Mary Cooper, "Global Warming Treaty," *CQ Researcher*, Jan. 26, 2001, pp. 41-64. The treaty, which the U.S. did not ratify, went into force on Feb. 15, 2005.

[2] See "European Union Biofuels Policy and Agriculture: An Overview," Congressional Research Service Report No. RS22404, March 16, 2006.

[3] Quoted in Christopher Knight, "New Alchemy: Grass Into Fuel," *International Herald-Tribune*, Sept. 18, 2006, p. 12.

---

bill, the agency also said it wants to cut petroleum use by 3.9 million gallons by 2012 and correspondingly reduce greenhouse-gas emissions by 14 million tons annually.[26]

House and Senate appropriators, however, refuse to match the administration's request for $11.4 million to implement the regulation, in part because their versions of the fiscal 2007 Interior-Environment spending bill contain hundreds of millions of dollars for earmarked projects directed at their home states and districts. William Wehrum, the EPA's acting chief of air and radiation, says tight budgets have forced the agency to adjust its agenda accordingly, including delaying regulations designed to curtail emissions from locomotive and marine-diesel engines. Though renewable-fuel standards remain high on EPA's to-do list, Wehrum warns, "What we may or may not do in the future depends on what Congress eventually appropriates." Final spending figures are not expected until after the November elections.

Any delays in setting a nationwide target for ethanol use raise concerns within some quarters of the energy industry because they could give rise to a patchwork of state ethanol standards that would complicate oil companies' ability to efficiently deliver fuels. As of mid-2006, six states had set their own standards for blending ethanol with other fuels, and at least 16 others were considering similar moves, according to the Renewable Fuels Association.

Oil companies predict they will encounter bottlenecks and periodic shortages as they try to ship ethanol-blended gasoline to certain regions. The gloomy scenario is reminiscent of the one the industry predicted when it argued against the use of so-called boutique fuels — gasoline blends designed to improve air quality in some parts of the country. However, oil companies say ethanol standards pose a bigger problem because political support for the fuel is intense, and anticipated usage will dwarf that of other alternative fuels.[27]

"If every gallon has to have 5 percent or 10 percent ethanol, that is a problem that absolutely has to be addressed," says Edward Murphy, group director for downstream and industry operations at the American Petroleum Institute, a trade group representing oil companies.

But many are skeptical of the oil companies' claims. The Renewable Fuels Association's Dinneen says blending ethanol with gasoline does not require a special grade of gas from refiners and does not add to the complexity of the fuel-distribution system. State regulators, however, argue that legislatures have a right to set fuel standards, whether to promote cleaner air, local agriculture or both.

New Technologies

While regulators sort out options for renewable-fuel standards, the Big Three automakers are getting on the ethanol bandwagon by accelerating plans to roll out flexible-fuel vehicles. General Motors Corp., Ford Motor Co. and DaimlerChrysler's Chrysler Group jointly announced on June 28 they will double production of cars and trucks capable of running on ethanol blends and other biofuels by 2010. The companies to date have produced about 5 million flexible-fuel vehicles; the commitment would lead to 2 million annually by decade's end. General Motors also has plans to produce hydrogen

fuel cell-powered vehicles as soon as 2011. The company says it will use up to $9 billion freed up as part of a recent corporate restructuring to fund the efforts.[28]

The domestic automakers see flexible-fuel vehicles as a way of enhancing their environmental credentials and competing with Asian rivals, particularly Toyota Motor Corp. and Honda Motor Co., which have capitalized on the burgeoning market for hybrid autos that run on a combination of electric and gas-powered engines. Energy analyst Book notes that flexible-fuel vehicles are considerably cheaper to make than hybrids, which require the use of advanced electronic systems and, usually, an extensive redesign of the vehicle.

"It costs carmakers just a few hundred dollars to turn a regular car into a flexible-fuel vehicle," Book says. "The people who are worried about their energy costs aren't going to pay thousands of dollars extra for a hybrid. For the [maximum] publicity yield, committing to flexible-fuel vehicles is the best bargain."

The car industry isn't alone in adapting technology to promote ethanol. Agriculture companies are beginning to genetically tweak the corn plant so that it can begin to convert itself into the fuel, by adding an enzyme that currently has to be introduced at ethanol-processing plants. The companies also are trying to reduce the amount of lignin in corn, the substance that enables plants to stand upright but which can block conversion of cellulose into ethanol.[29]

Companies such as Monsanto and Pioneer Hi-Bred, a subsidiary of DuPont, say the work represents an extension of ongoing genetic engineering designed to boost agricultural yields and make plants resistant to pests and herbicides. In the case of ethanol, officials say crop science can be used to increase the fermentable starch content of certain corn plants, potentially increasing their production potential 2 percent to 5 percent over other varieties.[30]

Perhaps the most dramatic genetic modification has arisen from research by agriculture giant Syngenta that yielded a technique for coaxing corn into making amylase, an enzyme that breaks down starch into sugar, which is then fermented into ethanol. Syngenta inserted three genes from a microbe called archaea that lives on the sea floor, allowing the corn to make its own amylase. Officials say that because the deep-sea organism lives near hot-water vents, the ethanol plants processing the corn can operate at higher temperatures, increasing efficiency.

Should the government continue to promote ethanol as an alternative to imported oil?

YES — Sen. Richard G. Lugar, R-Ind.
Chairman, Foreign Relations Committee

From speech to the Brookings Institution, March 13, 2006

For decades, the energy debate in this country has pitted so-called pro-oil realists against idealistic advocates of alternative energy. The pro-oil commentators have attempted to discredit alternatives by saying they make up a tiny share of energy consumed and that dependence on oil is a choice of the marketplace. They assert that our government can and should do little to change this. They have implied that those who have bemoaned oil dependency do not understand that every energy alternative comes with its own problems and limitations.

Indeed, advocates of alternative energy must resist the rhetorical temptations to suggest that energy problems are easily solved. They are not. Relieving our dependence on oil in any meaningful way is going to take much greater investments of time, money and political will. There is no silver-bullet solution. . . .

We have entered a different energy era that requires a much different response than in past decades. What is needed is an urgent national campaign led by a succession of presidents and congresses who will ensure that American ingenuity and resources are fully committed to this problem.

We could take our time if this were merely a matter of accomplishing an industrial conversion to more cost-effective technologies. Unfortunately, U.S. dependence on fossil fuels and their growing scarcity worldwide have already created conditions that are threatening our security and prosperity and undermining international stability. In the absence of revolutionary changes in energy policy, we are risking multiple disasters for our country that will constrain living standards, undermine our foreign policy goals and leave us highly vulnerable to the machinations of rogue states. . . .

As alternative fuels become more competitive, oil and gas producers have strong incentive to drop prices to kill the competition. Investors need to know that alternative-energy initiatives will continue to be competitive. A revenue-neutral $35-per-barrel price floor on oil would provide the security investors need. At this price, alternative fuels like cellulosic ethanol, shale and tar sands oil and diesel could still compete with regular gasoline.

Long-term energy security also requires the use of clean energy. As long as we continue to consume fuels that do not burn cleanly or cannot have their damaging gases sequestered, we will continue to pay environmental costs and will remain vulnerable to a climate-change-induced disaster.

NO — Jerry Taylor
Senior Fellow in energy policy and environmental protection, CATO Institute, www.cato.org

When politicians talk about energy independence, the conversation quickly turns to renewable energy. And rightly so. The U.S. consumes a bit beyond 20 million barrels of oil every day, but it produces only about 5 million barrels a day. At present, there is no way to achieve self-sufficiency regardless of how carefully we pinch our gasoline pennies or how aggressively we unleash the domestic oil industry.

Accordingly, if we want to achieve energy independence, it's going to mean giving up oil and moving to something else. Conservatives often talk about nuclear energy as the best prescription for energy independence. Liberals, on the other hand, rhapsodize about the glories of solar and wind power. But no matter how you feel about those technologies, they have virtually no impact on energy independence or the price of gasoline.

We use oil primarily to make transportation fuels and chemicals, whereas we use nuclear, solar and wind power to generate electricity. Until we achieve some fairly arresting breakthroughs in battery-powered technology, most of the alternative fuels we're betting on to break our so-called oil addiction are placebos.

Unfortunately, there is nothing on the horizon that comes close to gasoline as far as cost and performance are concerned. Consider the fact that taxes in Europe put gasoline prices at $5 to $8 per gallon. If alternatives to gasoline had economic merit, they would surely have arisen in Europe.

Ethanol made out of corn is probably the closest thing we have to a domestic alternative to gasoline. But no matter how nice "growing our own fuel" might be in theory, it's uneconomically expensive. Even after 30 years of lavish federal subsidy, ethanol (defined as fuel that is nine parts gasoline and one part ethanol) has only managed to capture a bit more than 3 percent of the automotive-fuels market.

One might think the current run on gasoline prices would have narrowed the cost gap, but one would be wrong. It takes a tremendous amount of energy to grow corn and a lot of energy to distill it into ethanol and get it into the market. Accordingly, rising energy prices have made ethanol more expensive.

Technological breakthroughs in the ethanol business are, of course, possible. And beyond harnessing oil and plants for fuel, we can move cars by compressed natural gas, hydrogen (via fuel cells), coal (by turning the black rock into liquid hydrocarbons) and, of course, with electricity.

For the time being, however, cheap fuel means gasoline. Mandating a switch — given current technology — would increase, not decrease, pump prices.

AP Photo/Dennis Poroy

Singer Willie Nelson inaugurates his first "BioWillie" filling station in San Diego on Feb. 8, 2006. He launched his biodiesel fuel company in 2004 "to do something useful towards eliminating America's dependence on foreign oil, help put the American family farmer back to work and clean up the environment we live in." BioWillie fuel is a blend of 20 percent soybean-based biodiesel fuel and 80 percent commercial diesel.

Similar efforts by Monsanto are aimed at producing a drought-resistant strain of switchgrass that has higher yields and can break down faster in ethanol production. Officials like the long-term potential of switchgrass and other inexpensive types of biomass because they require less fertilizer and irrigation than conventional corn.

Environmentalists increasingly worry, however, that genetically altered corn or soybeans will cross-pollinate in the wild and add undesirable traits to crops intended for food. Margaret Mellon, director of the food and environment program at the Union of Concerned Scientists, questions whether consumers will wind up eating products made from corn with extra enzymes, possibly derived from exotic microbes. Such a scenario took place in 2000, when StarLink corn, a product made by Aventis CropScience

only for livestock use, ended up in human food products, prompting widespread recalls and disrupted exports.

Syngenta dismisses such concerns, saying enzymes like amylase are safe and are found naturally in saliva. But to play it safe, the company is seeking approval of its corn for both human and animal uses in the United States, Europe, South Africa and elsewhere.

OUTLOOK

Environmental Risks?

The debate over long-term use of renewable fuels increasingly involves concerns that expanded production will stretch the nation's agricultural resources thin, pose environmental risks and unleash other unintended side effects.

For instance, recent studies show that even if the entire U.S. corn crop were diverted to ethanol production, it would only provide enough fuel to replace about 12 percent of gasoline demand. Thus, alternative-fuels proponents face a fundamental dilemma: Making the products truly competitive with fossil fuels would require diverting existing crops from food or feed, cutting agricultural exports, finding new raw materials and possibly replacing some low-margin crops that don't play a role in the energy cycle.

"There will be some costs, there is no question about that," said Keith Collins, the Department of Agriculture's chief economist. "But it can be manageable, given the objective of reducing foreign oil imports."[31]

Collins estimates the nation's farmers will have to plant 90 million acres of corn by 2010 in order to fulfill demand for ethanol and livestock feeds and continue to satisfy export markets. He predicts the thirst for ethanol will remain strong as long as crude oil prices remain above $50 per barrel and corn prices do not rise considerably, because subsidies and improving economics of production ensure ethanol will produce a desirable rate of return. In the unlikely event crude prices dip below about $30 per barrel, Collins says there will be no incentive to produce ethanol at levels that exceed the congressionally mandated 7.5-billion gallon renewable-fuel standard.

But sustained demand for ethanol doesn't necessarily guarantee benefits for all sectors of American agriculture. If Collins' estimates about ethanol demand are correct, farmers would have to plant about 10 million acres more of corn than the average planted in 2005 or 2006. They would not undertake such a significant expansion unless corn prices rise to around $3.10 to $3.20 per bushel — near the record high. But those higher prices would likely reduce the attractiveness of American corn on export markets and threaten livestock producers, whose largest single expense is feed costs. Some of those producers, worried about higher operating expenses, already are broaching the idea of a "circuit breaker" mechanism that would temporarily suspend ethanol mandates and incentives if corn supplies get tight, for instance, during a widespread drought.

"We're not throwing a brick through the windshield of the ethanol industry or corn growers," says Kirk Ferrell, vice president of public policy for the National Pork Producers Council. "But we're saying these are concerns we need to look at."[32]

Some producers and their representatives in Congress advocate increasing production by growing corn on farmland that is sitting idle in conservation programs, exempting only the most environmentally sensitive land. The federal Conservation Reserve Program has 36 million acres set aside, and preliminary Agriculture Department estimates conclude between 4.3 million and 7.2 million acres of that amount could be used to grow corn for ethanol or soybeans for biodiesel in a sustainable way. House Agriculture Committee Chairman Robert W. Goodlatte, R-Va., who represents a poultry-growing district, and like-minded lawmakers are expected to explore the prospect when they begin a planned reauthorization of farm programs in 2007.

But placing more acres of corn into production concerns environmentalists, who blame agricultural runoff from Midwestern farms that runs down the Mississippi River for polluting the Gulf of Mexico. The advocacy organization Environmental Working Group says fertilizer-rich agricultural runoff carried into the Gulf has created a "dead zone" of oxygen-robbing algae blooms the size of New Jersey — ranging from 5,000 to 8,000 square miles — that has obliterated all marine life. The group is calling for more careful spending of agriculture subsidies, along with wetland restoration and the planting of more streamside buffers of grass and trees to absorb runoff.

But such concerns sometimes take a back seat in the political race to nurture the ethanol industry. In one sign of the enthusiasm for alternative fuels, the Center for American Progress, a liberal think tank based in Washington, has recommended that the United States produce 25 percent of liquid fuel consumption from renewable resources by 2025, putting it squarely in a camp with Republican farm-state lawmakers like Gutknecht and Goodlatte.

Unlike ethanol, biodiesel poses fewer immediate dilemmas, if only because the industry still is in a nascent state. The industry's long-term viability is highly dependent on the cost of feedstocks; it currently costs about $1.95 to produce a gallon of biodiesel from soybean oil, making it hard to compete with traditional diesel fuel. But government incentives and higher fuel prices are making the industry more profitable, raising more questions about whether agricultural supplies can keep up demand. Agriculture Department economist Collins says biodiesel is expected to account for 2.6 billion pounds, or 13 percent, of total soybean oil use this year — the amount extracted from 229 million bushels of soybeans — or 8 percent of domestic production.

Analysts and politicians predict economic analyses and cost-benefit considerations will play an increasingly prominent role in the next phase of the debate over renewable fuels. Optimistic market-watchers hope the increased popularity of ethanol, biodiesel and other products will place pressure on oil and gas producers to keep their prices low. But most suspect that volatile oil markets will continue to force Congress and future presidents to make tough policy choices in the years ahead.

Violence in the Middle East, anti-American sentiment in Venezuela, nuclear tensions in Iran and political upheaval in Nigeria and other oil-producing regions already have changed the way politicians approach energy policy, and how they view agriculture.

"Energy," says ethanol proponent Sen. Richard Lugar, R-Ind., "is the albatross of U.S. national security."

NOTES

1. See Russ Keen, "Ethanol Plant Digs In," *Aberdeen* (S.D.) *American News*, Sept. 22, 2006, p. A1.

2. For background see Marcia Clemmitt, "Climate Change," *CQ Researcher*, Jan. 27, 2006, pp. 73-96.

3. For background see Jennifer Weeks, "Domestic Energy Development," *CQ Researcher*, Sept. 30, 2005, pp. 809-832; and Mary H. Cooper, "Energy Security," *CQ Researcher*, Feb. 1, 2002, pp. 73-96.

4. For background see John Cochran, "Fuel From the Farm," *CQ Weekly*, Aug. 7, 2006, pp. 2166-2174.

5. See James Jordan and James Powell, "The False Hope of Biofuels," *The Washington Post*, July 2, 2006, p. B7.

6. For background see Mary H. Cooper, "Alternative Fuels," *CQ Researcher*, Feb. 25, 2005, pp. 173-196.

7. See Roel Hammerschlag, "Ethanol's Energy Return on Investment: A Survey of the Literature 1990-present," *Environmental Science and Technology*, Vol. 40, No. 6, pp. 1744-1750.

8. For background see "Agriculture-Based Renewable Energy Production," Congressional Research Service Report RL 32712, May 18, 2006.

9. See Alexei Barrionuevo, "Fill Up on Corn if You Can," *The New York Times*, Aug. 21, 2006, p. C1.

10. Quoted in Josh Goodman, "Pumping Corn," *Governing*, September 2006, pp. 47-49.

11. See "Ethanol Industry Could Face Oversupply, Analysts Say," The Associated Press, June 16, 2006.

12. Testimony before Senate Energy and Natural Resources Committee, June 19, 2006.

13. Quoted in Cochran, *op. cit.*

14. See H. Josef Hebert, "Study: Ethanol Won't Solve Energy Problems," The Associated Press, July 10, 2006.

15. Quoted in Elizabeth Svoboda, "UC Scientist Says Ethanol Uses More Energy Than It Makes," *San Francisco Chronicle*, June 27, 2005, p. A4.

16. See Jason Hill, *et al.*, "Environmental, Economic and Energetic Costs and Benefits of Biodiesel and Ethanol Biofuels," *Proceedings of the National Academy of Science*, Vol. 103, No. 30, July 25, 2006, pp. 11206-11210.

17. See Department of Energy, Energy Efficiency and Renewable Energy Biomass Program, "Cellulase Enzyme Research," www1.eere.energy.gov/biomass/cellulase_enzyme.html.

18. For background see "Renewable Energy: Tax Credit, Budget and Electricity Production Issues," Congressional Research Service Report IB 10041, May 25, 2006.

19. For background see "Petroleum and Ethanol Fuels: Tax Incentives and Related GAO Work," General Accounting Office Report B 286311, Sept. 25, 2000.

20. For background see Marcia Clemmitt, "Pork Barrel Politics" *CQ Researcher*, June 16, 2006, pp. 529-552.

21. See "R&D Earmarks Hit New Record of $2.4 Billion, Up 13 Percent," *R&D Funding Update*, American Association for the Advancement of Science, Jan. 4, 2006, p. 5.

22. Portions of this section adapted from "Energy Kid's Page," Energy Information Administration; Ethanol Timeline available at www. eia.doe.gov/kids/histories/timelines/ethanol.html.

23. For background see R. C. Schroeder, "Arab Oil Money," in *Editorial Research Reports 1974* (Vol. I), available at *CQ Researcher Plus Archive*, CQ Electronic Library, http://library.cqpress.com.

24. For background see D. Teter, "Iran between East and West," in *Editorial Research Reports 1979* (Vol. I); "Auto Research and Regulation," in *Editorial Research Reports 1979* (Vol. I), and M. Leepson, "Synthetic Fuels," in *Editorial Research Reports 1979* (Vol. II); all available at *CQ Researcher Plus Archive*, CQ Electronic Library, http://library.cqpress.com.

25. See "Agriculture-Based Renewable Energy Production," Congressional Research Service Report RL 32712, May 18, 2006, pp. 17-23.

26. See Manu Raju, "Tight Budget Has EPA Hamstrung on Finalizing Renewable Fuels Language," *CQ Today*, Sept. 6, 2006, www.cq.com.

27. See Jeff Tollefson, "Oil Companies Fret About Ethanol Mandates," *CQ Today*, June 19, 2006, www.cq.com.

28. See "Big Three to Make More Biofuels Cars," The Associated Press, June 29, 2006.

29. See Andrew Pollack, "Redesigning Crops to Harvest Fuel," *The New York Times*, Sept. 8, 2006, p. D1.

30. For background see David Hosansky, "Biotech Foods," *CQ Researcher*, March 30, 2001, pp. 249-272.

31. Testimony before Senate Committee on Environment and Public Works, Sept. 6, 2006.

32 Quoted in Cochran, *op. cit.*

BIBLIOGRAPHY

Articles

Brubaker, Harold, "Fresh Energy," *Philadelphia Inquirer*, Aug. 27, 2006, p. E1.
Projects at farms and laboratories across the country to develop ethanol from plants and biomass other than corn are giving experts high hopes for cellulosic ethanol, which has been billed as "just around the corner" since the 1990s.

Cochran, John, "Fuel From the Farm," *CQ Weekly*, Aug. 7, 2006, pp. 2166-2174.
The desire to achieve greater energy independence has bolstered the political prospects of the already influential U.S. corn lobby.

Goodman, Josh, "Pumping Corn," *Governing*, September 2006, pp. 47-49.
Farmers can turn almost any crop into fuel, but the article questions whether they can make any money without government help.

Hill, Jason, *et al.,* "Environmental, Economic and Energetic Costs and Benefits of Biodiesel and Ethanol Biofuels," *Proceedings of the National Academy of Sciences*, July 25, 2006, pp. 11206-11210.
University of Minnesota researchers evaluate whether renewable transportation biofuels yield more energy than the energy invested in their production. The study concludes biodiesel is more energy efficient than ethanol and projects how well existing corn and soybean production would satisfy future demand.

Miller, James P., "Ethanol Fever Cooling Off," *Chicago Tribune*, Aug. 27, 2006, p. C5.
The gold-rush mentality surrounding ethanol is prompting investors to take a harder look at the rush to capitalize on ethanol's promise.

Pollack, Andrew, "Redesigning Crops To Harvest Fuel," *The New York Times*, Sept. 8, 2006, p. C1.
Agricultural scientists are genetically modifying corn and other crops to make it easier to convert them into transportation fuels.

Reel, Monte, "Brazil's Road to Energy Independence," *The Washington Post*, Aug. 20, 2006, p. A1.
Brazil's domestically produced ethanol from sugar cane and even natural gas have supplanted gasoline as preferred transportation fuels.

Reports

"Agriculture-Based Renewable Energy Production," *Congressional Research Service* Report No. RL32712, May 18, 2006, Washington, D.C.
Congress' research arm provides an overview of the history and status of leading, farm-based renewable fuels, with a legislative summary of congressional efforts to promote each product.

"Alternative Fuels and Advanced Technology Vehicles," *Congressional Research Service* Report No. RL33564, July 20, 2006.
Congress' research arm reviews congressional efforts to provide incentives for the development and commercialization of alternative fuels and advanced-technology vehicles.

"Energy Policy: Conceptual Framework and Continuing Issues," *Congressional Research Service* Report No. RL31720, May 11, 2006, Washington, D.C.
The report provides short-term and longer-term policy options in response to rising prices for imported oil and a history of energy policy since the 1970s Arab oil embargo.

"Ethanol: Frequently Asked Questions," *Union of Concerned Scientists*, 2006.
An advocacy group that supports increased use of alternative energy provides a guide to supply-and-demand issues concerning America's most abundant renewable fuel.

"Meeting Energy Demand for the 21st Century," *General Accounting Office* Report GAO-05-414T, March 16, 2005, Washington, D.C.
Plentiful, inexpensive energy has been the backbone of much of America's prosperity. But the GAO says U.S. energy systems are increasingly showing signs of strain and instability.

"Update on Ethanol," *Petroleum Industry Research Foundation*, July 2006.
A nonpartisan research foundation explains why further ethanol-promotion efforts raise costs for consumers and taxpayers.

Lieberman, Ben, "How the Energy Bill Boosted Prices at the Pump," *Heritage Foundation* WebMemo No. 1053, April 28, 2006, www. heritage.org.
A conservative policy analyst asserts that the 2005 energy bill's ethanol mandate had counterproductive consequences for the gasoline market.

For More Information

Alliance of Automobile Manufacturers, 1401 I St., N.W., Suite 900, Washington, DC 20005; (202) 326-5500; www.autoalliance.org. A coalition of nine car and light-truck manufacturers, including the Big Three U.S. automakers, that promotes the companies' efforts at developing alternative-fuel vehicles, hybrids and new fuel cells.

Alliance to Save Energy, 1850 M St., N.W., Suite 600, Washington, DC 20036; (202) 857-0666; www.ase.org. Advocates expanded federal policies to promote energy efficiency.

American Petroleum Institute, 1220 L St., N.W., Washington, DC 20005; (202) 682-8000; www.api.org. The oil and natural gas industry's lobbying arm in Washington, lobbies on fuel standards, climate change and exploration and production issues.

Archer Daniels Midland Co., 4666 Faries Parkway, Decatur, IL 62526; (800) 637-5843; www.admworld.com. The agriculture giant is the biggest domestic ethanol producer.

Environmental Working Group, 1436 U St., N.W., Suite 100, Washington, DC 20009; (202) 667-6982; www.ewg.org. Analyzes government data and scientific studies to expose environmental threats and to find solutions.

National Biodiesel Board, 3337a Emerald Land, Jefferson City, MO 65110; (800) 841-5849; www.biodiesel.org. National trade association representing the biodiesel industry and coordinating body for R&D efforts.

National Corn Growers Association, 122 C St., N.W., Suite 510, Washington, DC 20001; (202) 628-7001; www.ncga.com. Lobbying group that represents corn producers and heavily promotes the use of corn-based ethanol.

Petroleum Industry Research Foundation, 3 Park Ave., 26th floor, New York, NY 10016; (212) 686-6470; www.pirinc.org. Studies energy economics with a special emphasis on oil.

Renewable Fuels Association, 1 Massachusetts Ave., N.W., Suite 820, Washington, DC 20001; (202) 289-3835; www.ethanolrfa.org. The chief lobbying group for the U.S. ethanol industry.

Union of Concerned Scientists, 2 Brattle Square, Cambridge, MA 02238; (617) 547-5552; www.ucsusa.org. Nonprofit of scientists and citizens that promotes environmentally sound policies in energy, global warming and vehicles.

U.S. Department of Energy, Energy Efficiency and Renewable Energy Program, Mail Stop EE-1, Department of Energy, Washington, DC 20585; (202) 586-9220; www1.eere.energy.gov. Promotes much of the government's renewable-energy research, including next-generation vehicles and fuel technologies.

17

Fish Farming

Is It Safe for Humans and the Environment?

Jennifer Weeks

Getty Images/The Christian Science Monitor/John Nordell

Fishermen harvest scallops grown in cages in Massachusetts' Nasketucket Bay. Aquaculture provided an estimated 44 percent of the seafood used for global human consumption in 2005, and experts predict fish farms may soon outproduce wild fisheries. Fish raised on land in tanks or ponds make up 85 percent of both global and U.S. production, but many environmentalists worry the growing use of coastal and offshore operations could foul the seas or allow farmed fish to escape and breed with wild species.

From *CQ Researcher*, July 27, 2007.

t the Portland Fish Exchange, a long warehouse beside Maine's Casco Bay, seafood processors and wholesalers wave their numbers as the auctioneer takes bids on haddock, flounder and other fish fresh off the boat. The exchange handled 30 million pounds of fish per year in the early 1990s, but this year it may sell as little as 5 million pounds. Reasons for the decline include limits on the number of days fishermen can spend at sea and a state ban on selling lobsters accidentally caught in trolling nets.[1]

Fifty miles south and six miles off the coast, the new face of the seafood industry can be seen. Using underwater cages, the University of New Hampshire's Atlantic Marine Aquaculture Center has raised 3,000 pounds of halibut and 15,000 pounds of haddock here since 2004. The project is also demonstrating a method for growing mussels on lines suspended 40 feet below the surface.

"Twenty-five years ago, I was a commercial fisherman in the Gulf of Maine," Richard Langan, director of the university's Open Ocean Aquaculture Project, told a Senate subcommittee in 2006. "One night when I was at the wheel, I looked out the pilothouse window and saw the lights from what must have been at least 50 boats, all doing the same thing as ours — catching as many fish as fast as they could. . . . It was clear to me that New England's commercial fisheries could not sustain that level of exploitation and that there had to be a better way to provide seafood and make a living."[2]

Experts disagree over whether fish farming is providing that better way. But there's no question it is supplying more seafood than

Consumption of Farmed Seafood Is Rising

Aquaculture accounted for nearly half of all seafood eaten worldwide in 2005, compared with slightly more than a third in 2000. During the same period, total consumption of seafood (both farmed and wild) rose to nearly 100 million tons.

Human Consumption of Farm-Raised Seafood
(in millions of tons)

	2000	2001	2002	2003	2004	2005
Total seafood consumption	87.3	89.8	90.0	92.5	95.0	96.5
Aquaculture consumption	32.0	34.2	36.4	38.5	40.9	43.0

Source: "The State of World Fisheries and Aquaculture 2006," Food and Agriculture Organization of the United Nations, 2007

ever. In 2005 aquaculture provided an estimated 44 percent of the seafood used for global human consumption, and experts predict that by 2012 fish farms may out-produce wild fisheries.[3] In the early 1950s fish farms produced less than 1 million tons of seafood per year. By 2004 they were raising 60 million tons of finfish, shellfish and aquatic plants annually worth about $70 billion.

But many environmental and health advocates worry that marine fish farms — especially for large species like salmon, tuna and cod — could foul the oceans. Critics call ocean fish farms "floating feedlots" and say that they have the same potential to become serious pollution sources as large livestock farms.[4]

"We cannot afford to make the same mistakes with ocean agriculture that we have made on land," a task force on marine aquaculture convened by the Woods Hole Oceanographic Institution (WHOI) in Massachusetts warned in a 2007 report. The study concluded that ocean fish farming done properly offered significant health, economic and environmental benefits. Implemented carelessly, however, it could pollute ocean waters, disrupt wild fisheries, introduce exotic species that might become pests and compete with already-stressed wild stocks.[5]

"If you cram enough animals into enclosures at high density, you're going to see pollution. And if you crowd animals together, they're going to be stressed and share their parasites and diseases," says task force member Rebecca Goldburg, a senior scientist with the advocacy group Environmental Defense. "There's plenty of room for aquaculture to learn from the problems of the animal production industry, but we're still figuring out the right system for offshore operations."

Two forces are driving the explosion in aquaculture, known as the Blue Revolution. Many of the world's major wild, or "capture," fisheries have been overharvested and are producing flat or declining yields. Meanwhile, demand for seafood is climbing. Fish is a cheap source of protein in developing countries, and medical experts are telling consumers in industrialized nations to eat more heart-healthy seafood products and less red meat.

Many Americans apparently are following doctors' orders. U.S. per-capita seafood consumption increased by 30 percent from 1980 through 2005, in part because aquaculture made seafood more available and affordable.[6] Most farmed seafood comes from China and other countries whose output dwarfs U.S. production. (*See chart, p. 405.*) The United States imports 80 percent of its seafood for human consumption, including some 2 million tons of farmed products each year. If domestic aquaculture production does not rise, the "seafood trade gap" could grow to 4 million tons per year by 2025, according to the National Oceanographic and Atmospheric Administration (NOAA).[7]

"Globally, aquaculture is growing pretty well, but in the U.S. it's slowing down," says Randy MacMillan, president of the National Aquaculture Association. "Our producers are very efficient and have excellent-quality products, but cheaper imports are flooding the market, and they can't compete. The catfish industry, which is one of our biggest drivers, is taking ponds out of production because of imports from China and Vietnam and economic fraud from mislabeled foreign fish."

In a rare prosecution last year, a seafood trader in Panama City, Fla., was sentenced to four years in prison and fined $1.1 million for selling 1.6 million pounds of Vietnamese basa catfish falsely labeled as more expensive species like bass and grouper.[8]

To meet rising demand for seafood and reduce pressure on wild fisheries, NOAA wants to expand the U.S. aquaculture industry from $1 billion to $5 billion in annual revenues by 2025. The agency has proposed legislation that would allow aquaculture operations in waters under federal control, between three and 200 miles offshore. Marine fish farms currently operate in state waters, which extend three miles offshore along most U.S. coastlines.

China Leads in Aquaculture Production

China raised more than 27 million tons of seafood from 2002-2004 — nearly two-thirds of the 45 million tons of total global aquaculture production. The United States ranked 10th.

Top 10 Aquaculture Producers in 2004

Rank (2004)	Country	No. of tons (2002-2004)	Annual growth
1.	China	27,553,471	5.0%
2.	India	2,225,102	6.3
3.	Vietnam	1,078,755	30.6
4.	Thailand	1,055,579	10.8
5.	Indonesia	940,546	6.9
6.	Bangladesh	823,277	7.8
7.	Japan	698,779	-3.1
8.	Chile	607,481	11.2
9.	Norway	574,194	7.7
10.	United States	545,894	10.4
	Rest of the World	**4,818,443**	**7.3**
	World Total	**45.5 million**	**6.1**

Source: "The State of World Fisheries and Aquaculture 2006," Food and Agriculture Organization of the United Nations, 2007

"The United States accounts for only 1 percent of the global $70 billion per year aquaculture industry," said Commerce Secretary Carlos Gutierrez in March, announcing the offshore legislation. "The U.S. is not in the game, and this bill will help the U.S. compete in this highly profitable industry."

Aquaculture is a diverse business with products ranging from seaweed and tropical aquarium fish to 1,000-pound bluefin tuna. Freshwater fish raised on land in tanks or ponds make up about 85 percent of both global and U.S. production, but saltwater fish are winning a growing share of the market. Two of the most popular types of seafood in the United States, salmon and shrimp, come predominantly from fish farms.

Due to fish migration patterns, breeding seasons, weather and other constraints, good-quality supplies of many wild fish are only available for a few months each year. For example, folk wisdom once held that oysters should only be eaten during months with an "R" (September through April) because warm waters encourage the growth of bacteria in shellfish and because oysters are less flavorful during summer spawning. But worldwide farming has made many types of oysters and other seafood available year-round.

"Farmed products give our menu more stability," says Roger Berkowitz, president of the 35-resturant Legal Sea Foods chain, which also sells many types of wild-caught fish. "You don't always know when wild species will be available."

From a health perspective, more fish is a good thing. Both the U.S. Department of Agriculture and the American Heart Association recommend fish as a source of lean protein and omega-3 fatty acids, which reduce the incidence of cardiovascular disease.[9] Oily fish such as salmon, anchovies and herring are especially good sources of key fatty acids.

Some analysts, however, have raised concerns about pollutants in farmed fish, especially imports. Consumer advocates, U.S. fish farmers, and state officials criticize the Food and Drug Administration (FDA) for

AP Photo/Ric Francis

Hybrid striped bass are netted at the Kent Seatech facility near Palm Springs, Calif. The United States accounts for only 1 percent of the global $70 billion aquaculture industry. To help expand U.S. output, the National Oceanic and Atmospheric Administration has proposed allowing aquaculture operations in offshore federal waters.

inadequately policing imported fish. "We're letting tainted products come into the United States with improper testing," says Barry Costa-Pierce, a professor of fisheries and aquaculture at the University of Rhode Island. "Everybody in the scientific community knows about these issues, but there's no government hammer behind them."

Whether and how to expand U.S. fish farming is part of a broader discussion about the state of the oceans and fisheries. Since 2003 two high-level expert commissions — the government-appointed U.S. Commission on Ocean Policy and the privately funded Pew Oceans Commission — have warned that pollution, overfishing and coastal development pose serious threats to the world's oceans.[10] Congress, states and the Bush administration have taken some steps in response, such as overhauling national policies for managing wild fisheries.

But big-picture ocean aquaculture issues remain unsettled, experts say. "Many new uses are being proposed for the oceans, including offshore wind farms and energy ports," says University of New Hampshire Professor Andrew Rosenberg, a member of the U.S. Commission on Ocean Policy and former deputy director of the National Marine Fisheries Service. "All of these uses require exclusive use of ocean space and raise environmental concerns. We really don't have any consistent management system to decide who gets

to use what piece of the ocean bottom on an exclusive basis."

As lawmakers, scientists and conservationists debate the pros and cons of aquaculture, here are some of the questions they are asking:

Are farmed fish safe to eat?

In the wild, salmon eat tiny shrimp called krill and a variety of other fish. Farmed salmon eat processed feeds that contain fish meal and fish oil from smaller fish like anchovies and herring. Indiana University chemist Ronald Hites and his colleagues identified these feeds as likely culprits in a 2004 study that found higher levels of PCBs, dioxins and other organichlorine pesticides in farmed salmon than in wild salmon. They concluded that salmon farming produced fish containing potentially dangerous concentrations of pollutants because toxins from smaller fish that foraged in polluted waters were concentrated in the feed stocks.[11]

FDA officials replied that the levels of contaminants in farmed salmon did not pose health risks and that farmed salmon was safe to eat.[12] Some producers argued that the study obscured different life histories and feeding habits among wild salmon species, which caused different contaminant levels. They also noted that consumers received much larger doses from meat and dairy products. "No matter how the data [are] calculated and no matter whose PCB values for salmon are used, the amount of PCBs contributed to the diet from farmed or most wild salmon is truly insignificant in the context of overall PCB intake of the average American," Ronald Hardy, director of the University of Idaho's Aquaculture Research Institute, wrote in 2005.[13]

The controversy spurred more research. Several studies indicated that substituting vegetable oil for fish oil in feeds reduced PCB and dioxin levels in farmed fish.[14] A Canadian study found that while farmed salmon generally had higher PCB levels than wild species, all concentrations were at least 50-fold lower than U.S. and Canadian levels of concern, and levels in different types of wild salmon varied widely.[15]

Medical experts stress the bigger health picture. A 2006 article in the *Journal of the American Medical Association* reviewed findings from more than 200 studies and concluded that for most adults, health benefits from eating one or two servings of fish weekly outweighed risks from contaminants. The authors estimated coronary heart disease benefits outweighed cancer risks by up to 370-fold for farmed salmon and by 300-fold to more than 1,000-fold for wild salmon.[16]

"The benefits of fish are well established, while the risks are overblown," said Harvard Medical School Assistant Professor Dariush Mozaffarian, a co-author of the article.[17]

But other problem substances are turning up in imported farmed seafood, much of which comes from countries that allow producers to use drugs and chemicals banned in the United States. One of the most controversial products is farmed shrimp, which has become a large-scale industry in South and Central America and Asia.

Cramming shrimp into ponds makes them vulnerable to diseases and parasites, so shrimp farms in developing countries often use antibiotics, disinfectants and pesticides to keep animals healthy. But certain antibiotics can cause illnesses. For example, some nitrofurans are carcinogenic, and chloramphenicol causes two types of anemia in humans.[18] Others, such as ciprofloxacin, are used in both animal and human medicine, and their overuse threatens human health by creating drug-resistant bacteria that can be passed on to humans in tainted seafood.[19] Fungicides also pose health threats: Malachite green is suspected in genetic mutations, and gentian violet has been linked to mouth cancer.

These additives are banned in the United States, but many have turned up in imported shrimp. According to the advocacy group Food & Water Watch, the FDA rejected 2,817 seafood shipments containing antibiotic residues in 2005 even though it only tested 1.2 percent of all imported seafood.[20] U.S. inspections have detected proscribed antibiotics and fungicides in shrimp from Vietnam, Venezuela, Thailand, Malaysia and Mexico, as well as in Asian catfish, tilapia and eel.[21]

U.S. producers argue their competitors gain an economic edge by raising fish in dirty water and crowded conditions, then dosing them with chemicals to keep them healthy. "The United States has a very stringent regulatory system to review drugs for aquaculture," says the National Aquaculture Association's MacMillan. "That process does not exist in China, Vietnam or some other countries that export seafood here."

Not all imported seafood is tainted. Legal Sea Foods restaurants buy farmed shrimp from sources including Thailand, Vietnam and the Philippines. "I've found over the years that farmed shrimp is a far more consistent product than wild, because people in the U.S. just don't know how to handle shrimp," says company president Berkowitz. "Domestic boats add a lot of chemicals to the product and don't ice it properly, but with farmed shrimp we can dictate the quality that we want."

Legal Sea Foods tests fish at its own in-house laboratory, but most consumers rely on inspections by the FDA.[22] Reports in 2001 and 2004 by the U.S. General Accounting Office (now the Government Accountability Office [GAO]) warned the FDA was not doing enough to improve the safety of imported seafood, mainly because the agency was not putting priority on establishing "equivalence agreements" with seafood-exporting countries. These voluntary agreements document that exporting nations have seafood-safety systems equivalent to U.S. regulations. The GAO also found that the FDA was not quickly reporting problems with imported seafood to port inspectors.[23]

Critics want more oversight of the rising tide of foreign seafood. "About 1 percent of imported seafood is sent to a lab and tested. That's pretty startling considering that seafood causes 18 to 20 percent of food-borne illnesses," says Wenonah Hauter, executive director of Food & Water Watch. "FDA doesn't have the resources or staff to really inspect seafood imports. We hear lots of rhetoric about homeland security, but what about homeland food security?"

FDA officials acknowledge they need more support to police imported food, drugs and other goods. "The world has globalized, and all this stuff is coming in from outside the United States, but the regulations and procedures we have in place really did not contemplate this change," chief medical officer Janet Woodcock said last month.[24]

Taking matters into their own hands, Alabama, Louisiana, and Mississippi — major producers of farm-raised catfish — this year banned Chinese and Vietnamese catfish containing prohibited antibiotics. On June 28 the FDA issued an import alert blocking all imports of Chinese farmed catfish, basa, shrimp, dace (a type of carp) and eel unless they tested negative for nitrofurans, fluoroquinolones, malachite green and gentian violet.[25]

"We're taking this strong step because of current and continuing evidence that certain Chinese aquaculture

Carp Is Top Aquaculture Species

Carp and other members of the cyprinid family, such as barbs and chubs, are by far the most widely cultivated type of fish. Many shellfish and mollusks are also among the top 10 aquaculture species.

Top Ten Aquaculture Species, 2004

Rank	Species	Production (in tons)	Annual Growth (2002-2004)
1	Carps and other cyprinids	16,473,462	4.8%
2	Oysters	4,143,345	3.1
3	Clams, cockles, arkshells	3,705,155	9.1
4	Miscellaneous freshwater fish	3,365,954	-0.3
5	Shrimps, prawns	2,228,421	28.7
6	Salmons, trouts, smelts	1,780,298	5.1
7	Mussels	1,674,224	4.6
8	Tilapias and other cichlids	1,640,471	10.9
9	Scallops, pectens	1,050,080	-2.6
10	Miscellaneous marine mollusks	958,672	-12.4

Source: "The State of World Fisheries and Aquaculture 2006," Food and Agriculture Organization of the United Nations, 2007

products . . . contain illegal substances that are not permitted in seafood sold in the United States," said David Acheson, FDA assistant commissioner for food protection.[26] According to the FDA, contaminant levels in Chinese fish were very low and posed a risk mainly from long-term exposure.

Not all problems stem from imports. In late May melamine, an industrial chemical not authorized in food products, was found in shrimp feed made in Ohio. Earlier this spring, thousands of pets across the United States were killed or sickened by pet foods containing melamine that was traced back to China. The Ohio producer, Tembec, tested its feed ingredients after hearing about the pet food problems. "They just asked themselves, 'I wonder what's in this stuff? I wonder if we have anything in here that shouldn't be in here?' " said a company spokesman.[27]

Is aquaculture polluting the oceans?

Oceans cover almost three-quarters of Earth's surface to an average depth of 2.5 miles. Until recently, few people imagined that human actions could have lasting effects on such vast expanses of water. But recent studies show that overfishing, coastal development, offshore oil drilling and other activities are polluting the seas and damaging marine habitats.[28] Harmful aquaculture practices can make the situation worse.

Marine aquaculture operations raise fish in cages and so-called netpens that allow currents to carry their wastes into the surrounding environment. Discharges of dissolved nutrients, uneaten feed, fish sewage and dead fish cause a form of pollution called eutrophication. Algae and plankton feed on these materials and multiply, then are broken down by bacteria when they die. The decomposition process consumes dissolved oxygen from surrounding water and sediments, making the area less able to support life.

Eutrophication degrades nearby coral reefs and seagrass beds and reduces biodiversity. Some studies have found that surrounding areas recovered quickly when farming stopped, but in other cases impacts persisted several years later.[29] On a local scale, fish farms can be serious pollution sources: An average-size salmon farm with 200,000 fish produces as much fecal matter as a city of 65,000 people.[30]

In its January 2007 report the Woods Hole Marine Aquaculture Task Force concluded that discharges from U.S. fish farms were small compared to other water pollution sources, but it warned that little was known about how well the oceans could absorb these pollutants. Impacts could be much more serious if aquaculture increases, the group warned, especially if fish farms are sited close together.

Furthermore, the United States does not have legal guidelines for ocean water quality as it does for drinking water. "Without federal standards for marine water quality, there's really no way to measure whether marine waters are being polluted by aquaculture," says Goldburg of Environmental Defense. The Clean Water Act requires marine aquaculture farms to apply for discharge permits and employ so-called "best management practices" to limit pollution, but states have broad discretion to define those practices. "EPA and the states need to develop marine water-quality standards so they can measure whether waters are being impaired by all kinds of off-shore development, not just fish farms," Goldburg contends.

Many aquaculture operators say they already are strictly regulated and that marine fish farms will not harm the oceans. "Environmental stewardship is crucial to aquaculture," says MacMillan of the National Aquaculture Association. "Our industry in the United States has only developed in the past 20 years, so we've grown up in a very different environmental and regulatory climate than land-based agriculture. Expectations for us are far more demanding."

The University of New Hampshire's Rosenberg disagrees. "Our environmental standards for aquaculture aren't more stringent than regulations in other countries, they're vaguer," he says. "That's one reason why U.S. production hasn't grown faster — we don't have a clear set of guidelines for how it should be done. We need a policy that recognizes environmental concerns like pollution discharges and the spread of diseases to wild stocks."

Aquaculture can also cause "biological pollution" — interbreeding between wild fish and escaped farm fish. Such genetic mixing produces hybrid offspring that are less well-adapted to survive. A decade-long study in Ireland found that hybrid offspring of wild and farmed salmon had lower survival rates at sea than wild salmon and that 70 percent of second-generation hybrids died within a few weeks of hatching.[31] Similarly, in Norway — where about half a million farmed salmon and sea trout escape each year — hybrid salmon survive and return to rivers for spawning at lower rates than wild fish.[32]

Marine experts worry biological pollution will become more serious as fish farms move offshore, where hurricanes are strong enough to damage oil drilling rigs weighing thousands of tons. "Systems out in the open ocean will be hit by storms, so we have to make sure the biological impacts of escaped fish are as small as possible," says Goldburg. "Unless they can show that escapes pose a very low risk, growers should only produce native fish species from local genotypes that won't cause harm if they mix with wild fish."

Others say the issue is manageable. "Whenever fish escapes happen, it makes headlines," says George Nardi,

Greece's coastline offers ideal conditions for fish farming, one of the country's fastest-growing industries. Greece produces about 60 percent of the European Union's sea bass and sea bream, the most popular species in the Mediterranean region.

AP Photo/Dimitri Messinis

co-founder and chief technology officer at GreatBay Aquaculture in New Hampshire, which is working to commercialize offshore Atlantic cod farming in submersible cages. "The failure gets attention, but no one talks about how many fish are put into tanks and cages every day without any problems. We should put escapes in perspective, learn how to minimize problems and work on the animals that go in so that they don't harm the environment if they do escape."

Some kinds of aquaculture make water cleaner. Bivalve shellfish (species with two hinged shells like oysters, clams and mussels) filter seawater and feed on plankton and suspended particles in the water. By doing so, they control plankton levels and improve water clarity, which helps sunlight penetrate the water and promotes marine plant growth. Mature oysters can filter up to 55 gallons of water per day.[33]

Making more space for shellfish aquaculture can help reduce nutrient overloads that cause algae blooms and eutrophication. "Shellfish are by far the most cost-effective strategy to control pollution," says Woods Hole Oceanographic Institute researcher Hauke Kite-Powell, who is studying shellfish farming for water cleanup at Waquoit Bay in southeastern Massachusetts.[34]

A traditional aquaculture approach called polyculture — growing fish near shellfish and seaweed that feed on fish wastes — is receiving increasing attention from large-scale producers. This makes environmental sense, says

Seafood Safety Information Often Confusing

Study calls for better advice on risks, benefits

Seafood is good for you — unless it's contaminated with mercury, which can cause profound neurological damage — or PCBs, which may cause cancer, say government and private health experts.

But while some farmed fish may have more contaminants than wild fish, chemical levels in both types of fish typically are below government advisory levels, according to government scientists.

With mixed messages like these coming from government agencies and private health groups, it's not surprising there's confusion about how much and what kinds of fish to eat. Health and consumer advocates worry that unclear and conflicting advisories could drive people away from eating the right kinds of seafood. Conversely, some warnings may not keep consumers away from risky species or adequately protect at-risk groups like pregnant women.

For example, in 2004 the Food and Drug Administration (FDA) and the Environmental Protection Agency (EPA) issued a joint advisory warning pregnant women, those who might become pregnant, nursing mothers and young children to avoid shark, swordfish, tilefish and king mackerel — large wild-caught predatory fish that contained high mercury levels. The advisory also recommended limiting consumption of albacore tuna, which contains more mercury than other varieties.[1]

But a survey two years later by the Center for Science in the Public Interest found that only 20 percent of respondents could identify the high-risk fish, and that a comparable number incorrectly thought salmon was high in mercury. The group argued that consumers could not be relied on to remember which fish species were safe to eat and called for mandatory warning notices at seafood counters and on fish packages.[2]

Producers object to mandatory labeling, but California requires retailers to post warnings at seafood counters, and some large grocery chains do so voluntarily at stores nationwide.

Other problems include conflicting state and local warnings — which can recommend different consumption levels of the same species of fish from the same watershed — and getting safety information to ethnic and minority groups that are heavy fish consumers. Some communities have found that personal contact with anglers is a more effective way to raise awareness of risks than simply publishing brochures or posting them on the Internet. Even when warned, however, many people who fish in local waters continue to eat fish.[3]

In any event, Americans are eating less seafood than the levels recommended by the American Heart Association and other health groups, according to a 2006 report from the Institute of Medicine (IOM) of the National Academy of Sciences.[4] Additionally, some of the most widely consumed types, such as salmon and shrimp, contain low amounts of the omega-3 fatty acids that confer important health benefits. The study also found that consumer advice on seafood choices from government agencies and private groups was uncoordinated and fragmented, used inconsistent portion sizes and treated benefits separately from risks.

"We need better work on risk communication," says Malden Nesheim, emeritus professor of nutrition at Cornell University and chair of the study. "Seafood is a good food, and people ought to be consuming it, but there are certain segments of the population that need to be careful, mainly children and pregnant women."

It's not clear whether the relative risks and benefits of eating seafood are understood, Nesheim adds. "We don't have a lot of good data to go by. There's anecdotal evidence that some people stopped eating all fish after the FDA-EPA advisory on mercury was issued, but we can't confirm that."

The IOM study concluded government agencies need to know more about seafood-consumption patterns and levels of nutrients and contaminants in common types of seafood. To help consumers, the IOM urged federal agencies to develop new tools, such as interactive Web-based programs, that users could program with specific information about their ages and risk factors.

"There are health messages that everyone of a certain generation has heard — 'Just Say No' — but like shoes, advice is more helpful if it is sized appropriately and designed appropriately for the intended use," the report observed.[5]

---

[1] "What You Need to Know About Mercury in Fish and Shellfish," Department of Health and Human Services and Environmental Protection Agency, March 2004, www.cfsan.fda.gov/~dms/admehg3.html.

[2] Center for Science in the Public Interest, "Is It High or Is It Low?" July 6, 2006.

[3] Karl Blankenship, "Despite Advisories, Study Finds Many Still Eating Tainted Fish," *Bay Journal*, May 2005; Bill Novak, "Catch of the Day: Good Info," *Capital Times* (Madison, Wis.), Sept. 15, 2006, p. B1.

[4] Institute of Medicine, *Seafood Choices: Balancing Benefits and Risks* (2006).

[5] *Ibid.*, p. 241.

Goldburg: "Recycling nutrients is a foundation of sustainable agriculture. You get another crop, and you cut pollution."

Polyculture is widely used in Asia, but most major Western producers have not adopted the practice yet. Applied on a large scale, it could produce enough fish, shellfish and seaweed to meet growing world demand for seafood over the next several decades, scientists predict.[35] But consumers would have to eat more marine plants and shellfish and fewer of the popular, large carnivorous fish and shrimp that generate aquaculture's worst environmental impacts.

Should the United States commercialize genetically engineered fish?

For $5, hobbyists curious about seafood trends can buy a genetically altered fish at pet stores throughout the United States. The GloFish, the only so-called transgenic fish approved for commercial sale, is produced by injecting a fluorescent protein gene derived from jellyfish and sea anemones into the eggs of zebrafish, a common tropical aquarium species. Mature GloFish, which glow bright green, orange or red, pass fluorescence genes on to their offspring.

Conventional zebrafish are widely used in medical research because they grow quickly, their immune systems are similar to those of humans and their embryos are transparent, so scientists can see early developmental stages clearly. Fluorescent zebrafish technology offers researchers some new options — for example, tinting certain genes or organs to make it easier to watch them develop.[36]

Biotechnology companies are also working on food species. Massachusetts-based Aqua Bounty Technologies is seeking FDA approval for AquAdvantage salmon, which have been genetically modified to grow year-round, not just in summer. The company says AquAdvantage fish will reach market size twice as fast as conventional salmon, saving farmers money on feed and releasing fewer waste products into the oceans.[37]

Researchers worldwide are studying ways to genetically modify many seafood and aquatic plants to make them grow faster, convert feed to body mass more efficiently, resist disease, tolerate cold water or produce useful substances for food, pharmaceuticals and cosmetics. These genetically modified organisms (GMOs) could lower seafood production costs and reduce the need for antibiotics in fish farming. Scientists are also working on products that change color when they detect contaminants in water (the original goal for GloFish) or shellfish engineered to grow without producing proteins that trigger allergic reactions in some consumers.[38]

Many experts worry about health and environmental impacts from transgenic fish. A 2002 National Academy of Sciences study identified several moderately risky substances that might be found in genetically modified (GM) animals, including new proteins that trigger allergies, biologically active substances such as growth hormones and toxic metabolites created through the genetic engineering process.[39]

The report also warned of environmental impacts if GMOs escaped into the wild. "Animals that become feral easily, are highly mobile and have a history of causing extensive community damage" pose the biggest environmental threats, the study concluded.[40] Fish and shellfish fall into this category.

If engineered strains escape from farms in areas where they have no natural predators, they could spread and become invasive. Transgenic fish could also compete with or prey on wild species, especially if they have been altered to grow quickly and eat at higher rates. "GMOs have different properties from conventional species," says the University of New Hampshire's Rosenberg. "They might be conduits for diseases or parasites, so what happens if they escape? Producers may say the odds are 95 percent against escape, but other things work 95 percent of the time too, like condoms, and that's not always good enough."

One way to reduce escape risks is to alter the chromosomes of GMOs so they cannot reproduce in the wild. By subjecting newly fertilized eggs to extreme temperatures, high pressure, or certain chemicals, scientists can produce "triploid" individuals with three sets of chromosomes, which are infertile. Triploidy has been used to reduce escape threats from conventional finfish. But it can be hard to verify that large batches of eggs have been completely sterilized, and a few unaffected eggs in large batches could easily go unnoticed.[41] Another option is to raise finfish stocks that are all male or all female so that escaped fish cannot reproduce in the wild.

Some scientists question whether genetic manipulation adds much value over traditional breeding techniques

CHRONOLOGY

2500 B.C.-Early 1700s *Small-scale aquaculture develops in ancient China, Egypt, Japan.*

1800-1900 *Aquaculture develops in U.S.*

1853 Ohio trout farm artificially fertilizes brook trout eggs.

1871 Congress creates U.S. Fish Commission, which develops a system of federal hatcheries.

1870s-1900s U.S. rivers, lakes and coastal waters stocked with trout and other species.

1900-1960s *Aquaculture becomes professionalized, with support from universities and government.*

1909 First commercial U.S. trout farm established in Idaho.

1910-1930 State and federal researchers develop methods for farming channel catfish.

1938 Mitchell Act funds hatcheries in the Pacific Northwest to replace wild salmon and steelhead spawning grounds blocked or flooded by hydroelectric dams.

1930s-1940s Franklin D. Roosevelt administration supports construction of fish ponds on farms to aid soil and water conservation and generate income.

1940s-1960s Farming of tilapia, shrimp and channel catfish develops in United States.

1970s-1980s *Rising world population helps drive global aquaculture boom. Concerns emerge about water pollution, wild fisheries and contamination in farmed fish.*

1970s U.S. catfish farm acreage hits 40,000 in 1970, up from 400 acres in 1960. Salmon, abalone and mussel farming develop in the United States.

1972 Congress passes Clean Water, Coastal Zone Management and Marine Mammal Protection acts.

1980 National Aquaculture Act promotes U.S. aquaculture, but federal agencies fail to develop a comprehensive system for regulating fish farming. . . . Sturgeon farming begins in California. . . . Massachusetts starts farming quahogs (hard clams).

1989 Alaska bans farming of large ocean fish, such as salmon, in state waters, to protect wild fisheries from escaped farm fish.

1990s-2000s *Restrictions are imposed on aquaculture in response to harmful impacts. U.S. considers fish farms in federal waters.*

1995 U.N. Food and Agriculture Organization adopts code of conduct for responsible fisheries.

1997 Washington state classifies escaped Atlantic salmon from fish farms as a "living pollutant."

2000 An estimated 100,000 salmon escape from Maine fish farm.

2003 Pew Oceans Commission recommends moratorium on new marine finfish farms until Congress legislates standards for sustainable aquaculture. . . . Federal judge rules salmon farms in Maine are violating Clean Water Act.

2004 U.S. Commission on Ocean Policy endorses Pew report, calls for "a coordinated and consistent policy" for aquaculture development. . . . *Science* reports farmed salmon contain higher levels of contaminants than wild salmon.

2005 National Oceanographic and Atmospheric Administration (NOAA) proposes legislation to create regulatory framework for aquaculture in federal waters.

2006 NOAA issues 10-year plan to expand U.S. aquaculture into federal waters.

2007 Alabama, Mississippi and Louisiana ban Chinese catfish after samples are found to contain an antibiotic banned for use in fish by Food and Drug Administration (FDA). . . . FDA halts shipments of five types of Chinese fish for testing.

Proposed Organic-Fish Standards Raise Questions

Use of offshore "netpens" is controversial

Proposed standards for certifying organic aquaculture have raised complex questions about how to define an organic fish. The proposal, developed by a federal working group with strong industry representation, contains several controversial recommendations.

In general, foods that are produced without chemicals, pesticides or genetic alteration are entitled to organic certification from the Department of Agriculture (USDA). To win USDA approval, livestock must be raised on 100 percent organic feed.

Many observers argue that wild fish cannot be certified organic, since there is no way to document what foods they have eaten or chemicals they have been exposed to. This raises the question of whether farmed fish that eat feeds made from wild fish can be certified organic. In response, the working group convened by the USDA's National Organic Standards Board (NOSB) proposed two choices for feed used for organic aquaculture. Option A would allow use of fish meal and fish oil from sustainably managed fisheries, as long as such use did not exceed one pound of wild fish for every pound of aquatic animals cultured, along with scraps from processing of wild seafood for human consumption. Option B would not allow use of fish meal and oil from wild fish.

The working group proposal also would allow species raised in so-called netpens to be certified organic, as long as the pens are sited in areas where effluent discharges will not accumulate to levels that harm the environment. Closed systems, which recirculate water, are also allowed as long as they provide a healthy and high-quality growing environment.

Eager to tap into the booming organic food market, producers generally support the proposed standards, including the less-restrictive feed option A. "Diets of many aquatic animals naturally include other aquatic animals — including crustaceans, other invertebrates and baitfish," Neil Anthony Sims, whose Kona Blue company raises yellowtail in deep waters off Hawaii, wrote in a public-comment Web site. "Inclusion of fish meal and fish oil ensures an efficient, nutritionally complete diet that optimizes fish health," commented U.S. Trout Farmers Association President John Bechtel.[1]

Critics counter that using fish meal and oil is incompatible with the concept of organic production. "[T]he term 'organic' identifies a food product that has been raised under farming practices that are under direct control of the farmer, as well as the requirement that feed inputs to the process itself be organically produced. . . . At present, there is simply no way to raise carnivorous species and be true to the broadly accepted definition of 'organic,' " argued analysts Corey Peet and George Leonard of California's Monterey Bay Aquarium.[2]

Netpens are also a divisive issue. Conservationists say because netpens release untreated wastes to the environment and can spread diseases and parasites to wild stocks, finfish can only be certified organic if they are raised in ponds, tanks or other controlled production systems without direct ocean access. In practice, this approach would rule out raising most large carnivorous fish organically, at least at the outset.

The NOSB has scheduled a public symposium on organic aquaculture on Nov. 27, 2007, in Washington, D.C., to solicit more input on netpens and fish feeds.[3] Meanwhile, other seafood producers also want organic standards. Shellfish farmers say their products exemplify the idea of organic agriculture, since they improve the surrounding environment and require no feed inputs. And Alaska's Republican Sens. Ted Stevens and Lisa Murkowski have pressed for organic standards for wild-caught fish, such as Alaskan salmon, even though an NOSB task force recommended in 2001 against doing so.

"Alaska salmon is as wholesome, if not more, than any other organic product on the market," said Murkowski after she co-sponsored legislation with Stevens in 2003 that directed USDA to allow wild seafood to be certified and labeled as organic.[4]

[1] Included in public comments on the NOSB Aquaculture Working Group interim final report, www.ams.usda.gov/nop/PublicComments/AqaucultureWorkingGroupInterim/PublicCommentsAquaWGInterim.html.

[2] *Ibid.*

[3] 2007 NOSB Organic Aquaculture Symposium Call for Abstracts and Papers, www.ams.usda.gov/nosb/MeetingAgendas/Nov2007/OrganicAquacultureSymposium/CallForAbstractsPapers.html.

[4] The Associated Press, "U.S. Congress Backs Organic Wild Fish Label," April 16, 2003.

that humans have used for centuries to modify plants and animals. Aquaculture is already bringing fish and marine plants under cultivation about 100 times faster than land plants and animals were domesticated, and humans are farming a larger share of known aquatic species than of known land species, even though land agriculture developed some 11,000 years ago.[42]

"We don't need to do gene jockeying with fish," says the University of Rhode Island's Costa-Pierce. "With conventional animal breeding technologies we can get phenomenal gains in growth and other favorable characteristics. I doubt there's a big market for GM fish in North America, so why go down a path of conflict and controversy that could undercut markets for conventional products?"

Many Americans unknowingly eat or use products made from GM crops.[43] In 2006, crops engineered to tolerate herbicides or resist pests accounted for 89 percent of the soybeans planted in the United States, 40 percent of corn and 57 percent of cotton.[44] But surveys show Americans are more comfortable with GM plants than with animals.[45]

"Big corporate producers are very worried about the consumer response to transgenic fish," says Stanford University economist Rosamond Naylor. "Most producers don't want GM fish introduced because they'll run into market constraints in Europe and other places where buyers don't want it." California, Oregon, and Washington state have banned raising GM fish in state waters, and Maryland passed a five-year moratorium in 2001 on releasing GM fish into its coastal waters.

Lower production costs are not a strong argument for commercializing transgenic fish, says Naylor. "Fish are already underpriced in the market because prices don't reflect any of the social costs of production," such as waste discharges or coastal development, she says. "Making fish cheaper through genetic engineering shouldn't be our priority."

Berkowitz would consider putting GM fish on Legal Sea Foods' menu. "If it's deemed safe, we'd have to look at it. It would have to have the same nutritional benefit as wild fish, and I'd want character and flavor profiles before I decided to carry it. But anything that takes the pressure off wild stocks and has the potential to feed more people is good," says Berkowitz. "I don't think people truly understand what genetic engineering means

or that they're [already] consuming a lot of genetically modified produce."

BACKGROUND

Ancient Fish Farmers

Just as humans have farmed the land and domesticated animals for thousands of years, they also have cultivated fish and aquatic plants. More than 2,000 years ago, Chinese rice farmers raised carp as a second "crop" in their rice ponds. Carvings on ancient Egyptian tombs show men harvesting tilapia from ponds. Ancient Romans also bred fish in artificial ponds, called piscinae, for food and commercial sale and as a status symbol.

Most early aquaculture involved freshwater species, since it was easier to control fish in ponds or streams than in ocean waters. Some preindustrial societies, such as Australian aborigines, built elaborate networks of canals with gates and weirs to sort and catch fish. The first ocean fish farms may have been seawater ponds that were built 1,500 to 1,800 years ago in the Hawaiian Islands. These systems had walls made of coral and lava rocks, cemented together with algae, and canals that channeled fish in and out of the ocean through movable grates.[46]

Freshwater aquaculture spread through Europe during the Middle Ages, spurred by Catholic Church doctrine that called for meatless fasting days throughout the year. Monarchs, nobles and monks harvested live fish from streams and stocked them in ponds until they were needed. After water-powered mills appeared around the year 1000, farmers began breeding carp in millponds across Europe.[47]

Rich supplies of fish and shellfish helped to draw European explorers to the New World, but by the 1800s some North American fisheries were already degraded or overharvested. In response, fish culturists began importing and breeding fish to increase supplies. By the 1850s they had learned to propagate artificially, but efforts were too limited to slow the decline of many American fisheries.

In 1871 Spencer Baird, assistant secretary of the Smithsonian Institution, persuaded Congress to create a Commission on Fish and Fisheries, with Baird in charge. The commission was the first U.S. government agency created to conserve a renewable resource. Under Baird the commission built a research laboratory at Woods Hole,

Mass., and launched a broad research program on America's fisheries.

The commission also built a network of fish hatcheries and redistributed salmon, shad, trout, striped bass and other species across the nation. One venture, importing European carp as a cheap protein source for rural communities, proved to be a serious mistake — and an example of the pitfalls of introducing exotic animals to new habitats. Carp spread throughout the continental U.S. and were viewed as pests because they stirred up river and stream bottoms during feeding.

Aquaculture became part of the agricultural extension system in the early 20th century. State and federal researchers developed ways to raise new species like catfish, which local extension offices and land-grant colleges taught to farmers. In 1938, alarmed by the decline of the historic wild salmon and steelhead fisheries on the Columbia River, in the Pacific Northwest, Congress ordered the construction of large-scale hatcheries to boost fish stocks. But hatcheries could not compensate for overfishing and dam construction on the Columbia. From 1960 through 1990, up to 150 million juvenile Chinook salmon were released into the Columbia each year, but the efforts failed to produce sustained increases in harvests.[48]

After World War II the booming postwar economy created growth conditions for aquaculture, giving Americans more time and income for sports (including fishing) and travel (which exposed them to new cuisines and restaurants). Land-based agriculture shifted from small family farms to large-scale production, aided by new machines, synthetic fertilizers and pesticides and animal antibiotics.[49] Similarly, fish farming became more scientific as researchers developed low-cost feeds and standardized procedures for managing ponds and hatcheries.

The Blue Revolution

Starting in the early 1960s, aquaculture grew rapidly in the United States and around the world. Total production, including aquatic plants, rose from about 1 million tons in the early 1950s to almost 60 million tons in 2004. Nearly all the growth occurred in Asia and the Pacific.[50]

Marine experts call the jump to mass production the "Blue Revolution" in a nod to the earlier "Green Revolution" in the 1940s, when private foundations and national governments provided new high-yielding crop

Several miles off the New Hampshire coast, a worker fills a feeding tank that automatically feeds farmed codfish twice a day, powered by solar and wind power. The facility is part of a University of New Hampshire experiment in offshore aquaculture.

AP Photo/Jim Cole

varieties to poor farmers in Asia and Latin America. These crops needed synthetic fertilizers and pesticides, which often caused new problems, such as making insects resistant to pesticides. The Green Revolution thus came to symbolize both the benefits and pitfalls of massive technical intervention in agriculture.

In the United States Southern farmers started building ponds on marginal croplands in the 1950s and stocking them with catfish, a popular and easy-to-raise sport fish with a mild flavor. From the mid-1960s forward the industry became an important job source in Mississippi, Alabama, Louisiana and Arkansas. By 2002 the yearly catfish crop was worth more than $400 million, nearly half the total value of all U.S. aquaculture products.[51]

Aquaculturists also started to raise marine fish and shellfish on both the East and West coasts, including salmon, sturgeon, clams, abalone and mussels. But neither wild fisheries nor the nascent U.S. aquaculture industry could keep up with consumer demand, and U.S. seafood imports rose from $360 million in 1960 to $3.6 billion in 1980.[52]

In the 1980s global aquaculture expanded rapidly, driving prices down for popular seafoods. Shrimp farming grew rapidly in Asia and South America, while commercial salmon farming became established in Norway, Chile, Scotland, Canada and Japan, as well as in Maine and Washington state. Shrimp and salmon, which had been rare delicacies for most Americans a few decades earlier, became year-round mainstays on restaurant menus.

Troubled Waters

As the industry grew, evidence mounted that poorly operated fish farms were spreading disease and competing with wild fisheries. Some of the first alarms came from the Pacific Northwest, where the Interior Department began listing wild salmon runs as endangered in the early 1990s. Competition between hatchery fish and their wild cousins, as well as overfishing and changing ocean conditions, caused Northwest salmon fisheries to collapse starting in the 1970s despite massive government investments in hatcheries.[53]

From 20 to 40 percent of the Atlantic salmon caught in the North Atlantic between 1989 and 1996 were of farmed origin. By 1997, escaped farm salmon were successfully breeding in the wild in the waters off Norway, Ireland, the United Kingdom and eastern North America.[54] Alarmed, Alaska banned finfish farming in state waters in 1989 to protect its wild salmon fishery, although salmon farming continued next door in British Columbia. In 2000 U.S. officials listed Atlantic salmon runs in eight Maine rivers as endangered, partly because of genetic mixing with escaped farm salmon.[55]

Concerns also arose about the potential for fish farms to spread aquatic diseases to wild fisheries. Epidemiological patterns indicated that salmon farms promoted the spread of sea lice, infectious salmon anemia and whirling disease to wild populations in Europe and North America.[56] Shrimp farms were also highly susceptible to disease. For example, white spot syndrome virus wiped out entire aquaculture operations in some parts of Asia and South America and threatened to spread to wild shrimp and other crustaceans via escaped shrimp, flooding, pond discharges or bird predation.[57]

Environmentalists also criticized marine fish farms as serious pollution sources and argued that the problem could grow worse as aquaculture expanded. They focused on waste discharges from ocean pens and cages, including feces, unconsumed fish food, antibiotics and pesticides.

In 2003 a U.S. district court fined two Maine companies for operating salmon farms without Clean Water Act discharge permits and ordered them to suspend operations for two to three years while surrounding areas recovered and to stop stocking European strains of Atlantic salmon. The court also denounced federal and state environmental regulators who had let the farms operate without permits.

"In the absence of any regulatory effort, inertia has reigned supreme, and the entities causing the environmental harm have been given a free pass to continue their heedless despoiling of the environment," wrote Judge Gene Carter.[58]

Consumer demand for seafood kept growing in spite of these debates as Americans sought alternatives to red meat, and researchers touted fish as a good source of lean protein. As debate widened over the risks and benefits of eating seafood, wild as well as farmed, buying fish became complicated. To help consumers and chefs make sustainable choices, ocean advocates and conservation groups published guides that typically endorsed farmed shellfish and vegetarian finfish such as tilapia, but warned users away from salmon and shrimp.

Some health experts worried that these mixed messages, coupled with government warnings about mercury in some species of wild-caught fish, could turn consumers away from seafood altogether.

"An advisory is like a medication," said Joshua T. Cohen, a senior research associate at Harvard University's School of Public Health. "It has a therapeutic effect, but it also has side effects."[59]

Cohen and colleagues calculated that if mercury warnings made people who were not pregnant cut their seafood consumption by one-sixth, risks of heart disease and stroke would rise.

In the early 2000s, two commissions carried out the first broad reviews of U.S. policies related to ocean use and conservation in more than 30 years. The Pew Oceans Commission, funded by the Pew Charitable Trusts, focused on new laws and ways to strengthen existing laws in its 2003 report. The government-funded U.S. Commission on Ocean Policy, which issued its findings in 2004, stressed better coordination between federal agencies and bigger roles for states and communities in managing ocean resources. Both groups, however, found that the oceans were in crisis as a result of overfishing, marine pollution, coastal development and poor coordination between government agencies responsible for managing ocean policies.

CURRENT SITUATION

Offshore Legislation

Congress is considering the National Offshore Aquaculture Act of 2007, which would authorize fish farming in federal waters. The NOAA-sponsored bill directs the secretary of Commerce to develop a process for permitting offshore aquaculture facilities in the U.S. Exclusive Economic Zone, which stretches from three to 200 miles offshore, and to establish environmental requirements for marine fish farms.

"America is at a crossroads," says Michael Rubino, director of NOAA's aquaculture program. "We're importing more than 80 percent of our seafood, and a lot of that is farmed. The choice is between growing some of that domestically or importing an increasing volume. The U.S. has very crowded coastlines, and we value them for other uses, but there's lots of space in federal waters."

Deepwater aquaculture is challenging because currents and storms are stronger, fish are more exposed to predators and it costs more to transport crews and equipment to farm sites. On the positive side, waters are cleaner, ocean currents carry wastes away from fish cages quickly and there are fewer conflicts with other activities such as recreational boaters.

"It's more expensive to farm offshore than to do it right next to the dock in calm water," says University of Alaska economist Gunnar Knapp. "But as more work

Shrimp Is Most Popular U.S. Seafood

Shrimp is the most popular seafood among Americans. Canned tuna is second despite concerns about high mercury levels in some types of tuna.

Per Capita Consumption of Seafood Species by Americans, 2006
(in pounds)

Shrimp	4.40
Canned tuna	2.90
Salmon	2.026
Pollock	1.639
Tilapia	.996
Catfish	.969
Crab	.664
Cod	.505
Clams	.440
Scallops	.305

Source: National Fisheries Institute, www.aboutseafood.com

takes place, the technical challenges of designing cages, feeders and monitoring devices will become less of an obstacle. A lot of pros and cons depend on what kinds of species are farmed, where and how." Because of high costs, offshore producers are likely to concentrate on high-value finfish like cod, halibut and snapper.

Critics say raising more large carnivorous fish will tax supplies of small fish like herring and anchovies used to make fish meal and fish oil, the main ingredients of fish feed. Raising carnivorous species often consumes more protein in the form of fish meal and fish oil than it produces, although the ratio has improved in recent years. Aquaculture already consumes almost half of global fish meal production and three-quarters of fish oil supplies, and most forage fisheries are being fished at or near sustainable harvest levels.[60]

Many observers see the "fish for fish feed" problem as crucial to the future of aquaculture. "The feed nut has got

Extension aquaculture specialist Pat Duncan checks a tank of tilapia at Georgia's Fort Valley State University, where she teaches fish farmers and prospective growers about aquaculture technology and potential commercial markets.

to be cracked," says Goldburg of Environmental Defense. "If you have to catch more fish to put into a farm than you get out at the end, then marine aquaculture is ecologically nonsensical."

NOAA and fish farmers agree that the issue is serious, but they point to new options on the horizon. "These fish are eating other fish anyway, and the conversion ratio is worse in the wild," says Nardi of GreatBay Aquaculture in New Hampshire. "We've made a lot of progress on reducing the amount of fish meal in feed and replacing it with plant protein. Our industry relies on fish meal for feed, so we can't afford to have it run out."

The issue is complicated because fish oil is a major source of omega-3 fatty acids, so not all substitutes have the same nutritional value. "We need more research into alternatives like marine algae," says Rubino. "All fish need protein, but it can come from many places."

Critics also argue that the NOAA legislation does not include strong environmental safeguards for open-ocean fish farming. The bill requires the secretary of Commerce,

working with other agencies, to "identify . . . environmental requirements that apply to offshore aquaculture under existing laws and regulations," including issues such as escapes, disease transmission to wild stocks and impacts on marine ecosystems. The bill also calls on Commerce to "implement such measures as may be necessary to protect the environment," such as limiting or barring sites in certain areas.[61]

"We've learned a huge amount from our experience with salmon, shrimp and catfish, and we have a very sustainable and environmentally responsible aquaculture community in the United States," says Rubino. "We're going to use that same model in federal waters." But many marine experts would like to see more specific requirements.

"The bill should give some direction about where to place offshore aquaculture, based on areas' values for different uses," says Michael Tlusty, research director at the New England Aquarium. "And Commerce is required to monitor offshore aquaculture impacts, but it would be nice to do something with that data." For example, Tlusty points out, the Canadian province of British Columbia requires fish farms to cut back or halt production if impacts exceed certain limits.

Producers say Congress should not legislate prescriptive environmental standards. "If we impose too many conditions, businesses won't be able to invest in that type of production," says National Aquaculture Association President MacMillan. "You can apply conditions to prevent escapes and put bags under cages to capture waste, but that makes it extremely expensive, and we can't see how a company could afford to do that long term."

Strict environmental safeguards would yield more valuable products, argues Stanford economist Naylor. "The United States should raise the bar for aquaculture worldwide. The most sustainable producers out there are doing quite well financially and are trying to raise standards at every turn," Naylor asserts. "It makes sense in any industry. And once you generate demand and scale up production, costs start coming down."

Senior members of Congress have already signaled differences with NOAA. When Sens. Daniel Inouye, D-Hawaii, and Ted Stevens, R-Alaska, introduced the bill at the Bush administration's request, they filed amendments to address environmental risks, require more research on offshore aquaculture and forbid finfish farming in federal waters off Alaska. Inouye announced he would

Will offshore aquaculture benefit U.S. coastal communities?

YES William T. Hogarth
Director, National Marine Fisheries Service, National Oceanic and Atmospheric Administration (NOAA)

Written for *CQ Researcher*, July 2007

Offshore aquaculture will benefit the United States as a whole, from our coastal communities all the way to the heartland. Fish and shellfish farming are integral to global seafood production in the 21st century, and the United States must embrace it or be left behind the rest of the world. Now is not the time to hide behind myths about aquaculture. Over $1 billion of seafood is already farmed in the United States under stringent regulations that protect water quality and ensure aquatic animal health. With a seafood trade deficit of almost $9 billion, the United States must take the initiative to produce more seafood here at home.

One of our best opportunities is in federal waters, three to 200 miles offshore. However, we need the right regulations in place to do that before any permits are issued. That's why the National Offshore Aquaculture Act of 2007 pending in Congress is so important. The current administration bill contains strong environmental requirements, and we are working with Congress to ensure states, councils and a long list of other stakeholders have a role in the development of a new offshore aquaculture industry.

Coastal communities, including fishermen, already play a major role in coastal aquaculture operations in the United States. In fact, aquaculture plays a significant role in many commercial fisheries, including Alaska's, where hatchery-produced salmon make up 20 to 40 percent of the catch annually. And, U.S. fishermen are among those successfully pioneering mussel and finfish farming in the ocean in Hawaii, Puerto Rico and New Hampshire. They are clearly demonstrating that offshore aquaculture is sustainable and safe.

As with any new industry, coastal communities will benefit from the economic "ripple effect" that offshore aquaculture will bring. More seafood production means more jobs, more demand for cold storage, transportation and processing. Businesses, from gas stations to boat repair and maintenance, will benefit. U.S. aquaculture can also provide fresh year-round, reliable product to help meet demand from retailers and consumers.

At NOAA, we are working on new rules to end overfishing in the United States, but even when our wild-capture fisheries are rebuilt and sustainable, they will not produce enough seafood to meet the U.S. appetite for fish and shellfish. Offshore aquaculture will ensure America's place as a global leader in both production of healthy and safe seafood and environmentally responsible seafood farming.

NO Paula Terrel
Fish-farming and water-quality issues coordinator, Alaska Marine Conservation Council *

Written for *CQ Researcher*, July 2007

Coastal communities depend on commercial, recreational and subsistence fishing. But fishing is more than just "earning a living"; it is a way of life. Every new regulation, federal action or market change directly affects coastal communities. Any potential "benefit" from offshore aquaculture must be weighed against the potential social and economic loss to coastal communities and fishing families.

The National Oceanic and Atmospheric Administration (NOAA) argues that offshore aquaculture will result in fewer environmental concerns than those that have plagued coastal fish farming. But the environmental problems associated with near-shore fish farming don't go away just because you move offshore. These risks include escapes of non-native species, ocean pollution, use of chemicals, spread of disease and, more recently, the development of genetically modified fish that will be used as brood stock for farmed species.

NOAA would have us believe that offshore aquaculture will complement wild fisheries. Rather, it is clear that it will compete with existing wild fisheries, especially finfish such as salmon, halibut and cod. Consider:

- Denying fishermen access to their fishing grounds is likely to cause conflicts.
- With offshore aquaculture focusing on carnivorous finfish, such as black cod and halibut, coastal communities will be negatively affected by market confusion about healthy, wild seafood.
- Farming of species that are healthy and are commercially harvested in the wild will compete with, rather than complement, wild fisheries.

NOAA also asserts that offshore aquaculture will provide jobs in coastal communities, but the facts show that:

- The high cost of tending fish far from shore means facilities will likely be automated.
- Mom-and-pop operations will not survive, and operations will be consolidated into a few multinational corporations.
- The United States cannot compete with lower labor costs in other countries.

Offshore aquaculture should not be a substitute for good fisheries management. In places where there are depletions, rebuilding plans and other conservation tools should be used to restore fish populations.

* Terrel and her husband have owned and operated a salmon trawler for 29 years.

Senior scientist Atle Mortensen is studying cod aquaculture at the Norwegian Institute of Fisheries and Aquaculture Research in Tromso. Farmers have perfected salmon aquaculture, but raising the endangered cod is trickier.

also offer a comprehensive bill to address further concerns with NOAA's approach.[62] Inouye and Stevens' actions reflect worries in some coastal communities about the impacts of expanding offshore aquaculture. (*See "At Issue," p. 419.*)

Seafood Safety

Recurring contaminants in imported farmed seafood, along with similar problems in other food sectors, are spurring Congress to pass new laws regulating food safety. China, the source of many tainted food products, appears to be feeling the heat, although it is not clear how quickly Chinese regulators will be able to reform the nation's vast production system, largely made up of smaller farmers.[63]

On May 9, the Senate passed an amendment calling on the FDA to expand seafood inspections and report to Congress on the feasibility of developing a tracer system for all domestic and imported seafood. "It is unacceptable to allow substandard catfish and shrimp, mostly produced in China, to enter the U. S. market when those imported products do not meet the established safety standards that govern our food supply," said Sen. Jeff Sessions, R-Ala., who sponsored the measure.[64]

The bill also included an amendment offered by Sen. Richard J. Durbin, D-Ill., designed to strengthen the nation's food system by creating an early-warning system for food contamination and a registry of adulterated-food cases and requiring companies to maintain records that would help the FDA trace contaminated food. The measure also states the sense of the Senate that the FDA needs more resources and inspectors and that the agency should place priority on negotiating food safety agreements with other countries.

Between 2003 and 2007, however, Congress reduced FDA's budget for inspecting foreign seafood-processing plants from $211,483 to zero.[65] While the program was small, critics say inspecting more foreign plants would help FDA to identify potential risks from imported seafood before shipping. Congress could restore the funding when it considers FDA's budget later this year as part of the fiscal 2008 Agriculture appropriations bill. The FDA, which oversees all food except meat and poultry, has 1,962 inspectors to police nearly 300,000 plants in the United States and abroad.[66]

In late June, just before the FDA banned five types of Chinese farmed fish from entering the United States without testing, regulators in Beijing disclosed they had identified more than 23,000 food-safety violations and closed down 180 food plants in a national crackdown over the previous six months. Problems included use of malachite green in seafood and processing of shark fin with toxic industrial chemicals.[67]

China may be trying to clean up its quality problems, but reforms are likely to come slowly. According to importers and inspectors, most Chinese fish is raised by small family farmers who have to contend with serious industrial water pollution and who know very little about the chemicals they use.[68] And China's poorly organized regulatory system, which is riddled with corruption, gives producers few incentives to meet high standards. As a first step, Sen. Durbin and Rep. Rosa DeLauro, D-Conn., chairwoman of the House Appropriations Subcommittee on Agriculture, have called for negotiating an agreement that would allow FDA inspectors into China.[69]

U.S. consumers who are worried about seafood safety can get some information from country-of-origin labels (COOL), which have been required on fresh and frozen seafood products (but not canned or processed goods) since 2005. The labels also specify whether products are wild-caught or farmed. But many Americans don't read them, says the aquaculture association's MacMillan: "Consumers don't necessarily distinguish between domestically produced fish and fish that's produced abroad or captured in the wild — they buy cheaper fish from countries with lower labor costs. Sometimes that approach comes back to bite them."

University of Alaska economist Knapp agrees that most U.S. consumers know very little about fish, but he says retailers are asking for much more information about seafood products. "Large buyers like Wal-Mart, Safeway and Whole Foods have a very strong incentive only to buy healthful foods. These companies are going to start demanding 100 percent traceability and the ability to audit all along their supply chains," he says. "When markets depend on those conditions, the system will be really reliable."

In fact, Wal-Mart and other large buyers already have adopted standards drafted by the Global Aquaculture Alliance, an industry group, which has set minimum environmental and social conditions for fish farming. While some environmental groups say that industry standards could be stricter, enforcing these codes will help to establish some basic standards for aquaculture, such as cleaning up water discharged from fish farms and ending use of antibiotics.

The new standards are prompting some suppliers, including shrimp farmers in Thailand, to improve their operations and restore environmental damage. For example, Rubicon Resources, a Los Angeles-based supplier of Thai shrimp, has replanted new mangrove swamps to compensate for trees destroyed to make way for its ponds and has standardized treatment of discharged pond water.[70]

OUTLOOK
Seeking Sustainability

As Congress considers authorizing offshore aquaculture or requiring more study, pressure to farm the seas is growing worldwide. Meanwhile, issues such as food-conversion ratios and effluents from fish cages are being considered in the debate over how to conduct large-scale aquaculture without harming the oceans.

Many researchers are developing equipment and methods to minimize environmental impacts. Several companies are patenting rigid spherical cages for ocean finfish farming that are engineered to withstand storms and shark attacks. Researchers are also studying ways to grow shellfish in deep water on submerged lines or platforms.

Another low-impact approach is to adapt marine species to grow in freshwater tanks. Florida's Ocean Boy Farms grows Pacific white saltwater shrimp in low-salinity ponds and uses specially cultivated bacteria to consume shrimp wastes.[71] Other producers are raising game fish like cobia and barramundi at facilities far from the coast in Virginia and Massachusetts.[72]

Using less fish for fish food is a high priority. Some improvements are low-tech. For example, Kona Blue Water Farms, which raises Hawaiian yellowtail in state-controlled deep ocean waters off Hawaii, feeds its fish once a day instead of multiple times so that they devour the food quickly and let very little drift out of their cages. The approach produces one pound of fish from one pound of feed.[73]

Researchers have had trouble finding substitutes for fish meal and fish oil that contain the omega-3 fatty acids and other nutrients that fish need to grow, but some companies are starting to derive these nutrients from sources such as marine algae and polychaete seaworms. In February a Maryland company, Advanced Bionutrition, released a new shrimp feed that completely replaces fish meal and fish oil with nutrients from sustainable sources.

Sustainability is also a social issue, says the University of Rhode Island's Costa-Pierce, who questions whether ocean farming will benefit coastal communities. "It's at a primitive stage of planning, and there's been no discussion of all the other pieces besides production, like hatcheries and transportation," says Costa-Pierce. He is much more enthusiastic about the growth in coastal shellfish farming. "An enormous number of fishermen are fishing part time and raising shellfish part time. That's a very exciting transition because it's an additional enterprise that fits into their lifestyles socially, economically and environmentally."

In the view of the University of Alaska's Knapp, however, aquaculture will benefit fishing communities in the long run by making the economic pie bigger for all fish producers. "Aquaculture is vastly expanding consumer demand for fish," he explains. "It's going to turn people into fish eaters by making fish available and getting them to think about trying it. Farmed salmon can't keep up with demand even though there's three or four times as much salmon in the world now as there was 15 years ago, because they've increased demand so rapidly."

But aquaculture has to be economically sustainable for producers to undertake it. Some experts question whether ocean fish farms in U.S. waters can compete with imported farmed fish. "There's been no hard-nosed economic assessment of the economic viability of cod, haddock and some of the other species that are being tested, and the operations that are making money in Hawaii are in state waters near the shore," says Costa-Pierce.

The economics are especially challenging for companies trying to develop new sustainable approaches, says Nardi of New Hampshire's GreatBay Aquaculture. His company is researching new designs for submersible cages and substitutes for fish meal, and it recirculates water at its dry-land hatchery to minimize discharges.

"We can't do it on our own. We need to team with other people at universities and agencies to get grants and work on these measures until we can see whether they're economically viable" says Nardi. Still, he believes that U.S. aquaculture can and should expand: "If people knew that a big share of their seafood supply is farmed and a growing share will come from farms, they would agree that it makes sense for us to participate in it."

NOTES

1. Clarke Canfield, "Maine Fish Industry, Auction in Jeopardy," The Associated Press, April 21, 2007.

2. Testimony before Senate National Ocean Policy Study Subcommittee, April 6, 2006.

3. United Nations Food and Agriculture Organization, *The State of World Fisheries and Aquaculture 2006* (2007), p. 3; Steven Hedlund, "Farming Closes In on Wild Production," *Seafood Business*, October 2006, p. 1.

4. For background see Jennifer Weeks, "Factory Farms," *CQ Researcher*, Jan. 12, 2007, pp. 25-48.

5. Woods Hole Oceanographic Institute, *Sustainable Marine Aquaculture: Fulfilling the Promise, Managing the Risks* (2007), p. 10, www.whoi.edu. For background see Mary H. Cooper, "Threatened Fisheries," *CQ Researcher*, Aug. 2, 2002, pp. 617-648.

6. National Marine Fisheries Service, *Fisheries of the United States — 2005* (February 2007), p. 74, www.st.nmfs.gov.

7. National Oceanographic and Atmospheric Administration (NOAA), "Quick Stats on Aquaculture," March 12, 2007, www.nmfs.noaa.gov/aquaculture/docs/05_AQ%20Stats.pdf.

8. James Wright, "Fighting Fraud," *Seafood Business*, June 5, 2007; Christian M. Wade and Kevin Begos, "Fishing for Solutions," *Tampa Tribune*, June 23, 2006, p. 1.

9. U.S. Department of Agriculture, "Inside the Pyramid," www.mypyramid.gov/pyramid/meat_why_print.html; American Heart Association, "Fish and Omega-3 Fatty Acids," www.americanheart.org/presenter.jhtml?identifier=4632.

10. For background see Marcia Clemmitt, "Saving the Oceans," *CQ Researcher*, Nov. 4, 2005, pp. 933-956.

11. Ronald A. Hites, *et al.*, "Global Assessment of Organic Contaminants in Farmed Salmon," *Science*, Jan. 9, 2004, pp. 226-229.

12. Eric Pianin, "Toxins Cited in Farmed Salmon," *The Washington Post*, Jan. 9, 2004, p. A1.

13. Ronald W. Hardy, "Contaminants in Salmon: A Follow-Up," *Aquaculture Magazine*, March/April 2005, p. 3.

14. *Ibid.*; "Seafood: Farmed vs. Wild," *Consumer Reports*, January 2005, www.consumerreports.org.

15. M.G. Ikonomou, *et al.*, "Flesh Quality of Market-Size Farmed and Wild British Columbia Salmon," *Environmental Science & Technology*, vol. 41, no. 2 (2007), pp. 437-443.

16. Dariush Mozaffarian and Eric B. Rimm, "Fish Intake, Contaminants, and Human Health: Evaluating the Risks and Benefits," *Journal of the American Medical Association*, vol. 296, no. 15, Oct. 18, 2006, pp. 1885-1895.

17. Suzanne Schlossberg, "Go Fish," *Women's Health*, April 2007.

18. *Merck Veterinary Manual*, www.merckvetmanual.com/mvm/index.jsp.

19. For background, see Adriel Bettelheim, "Drug-Resistant Bacteria," *CQ Researcher*, June 4, 1999, pp. 473-496.

20. *Suspicious Shrimp: The Health Risks of Industrialized Shrimp Production*, Food & Water Watch (December 2006), p. 4.

21. Preston Lauterbach, "Invasion of the Asian Catfish," *Memphis Flyer*, May 31, 2007.

22. For background, see David Hosansky, "Food Safety," *CQ Researcher*, Nov. 1, 2002, pp. 897-920.

23. See U.S. General Accounting Office, *Food Safety: Federal Oversight of Seafood Does Not Sufficiently Protect Consumers*, Jan. 31, 2001, and *Food Safety: FDA's Imported Seafood Safety Program Shows Some Progress, But Further Improvements Are Needed*, Jan. 30, 2004.

24. Robert Cohen, "Lacking Resources, FDA Inspects Less Than 1% of Imports," *San Diego Union-Tribune*, June 13, 2007.

25. Garry Mitchell, "Chinese Catfish Banned in 3 States," The Associated Press, May 16, 2007; Ricardo Alonso-Zaldivar, "FDA Says Chinese Fish Tainted," *Los Angeles Times*, June 29, 2007, p. A1.

26. "FDA Detains Imports of Farm-Raised Chinese Seafood," press release, Food and Drug Administration, June 28, 2007.

27. Andrew Martin, "Melamine From U.S. Put In Feed," *The New York Times*, May 31, 2007.

28. For background, see Clemmitt, *op. cit.*

29. Woods Hole Oceanographic Institute, *op. cit.*

30. Pew Oceans Commission, "America's Living Oceans: Charting A Course for Sea Change," May 2003, p. 77, www.pewoceans.org.

31. James Owen, "Wild-Farm Hybrids Not Reaching Spawning Grounds?" *National Geographic News*, Oct. 28, 2003.

32. World Wildlife Fund, *On the Run: Escaped Farmed Fish in Norwegian Waters* (2005), pp. 6, 22.

33. Puget Sound Action Team, "Shellfish Ecology," July 2003, www.psat.wa.gov/Programs/shellfish/fact_sheets/ecology_web1.pdf.

34. Paul Thacker, "Oysters and Clams Clean Up Dirty Water," *Environmental Science & Technology*, May 15, 2006, pp. 3131-3132.

35. Amir Neori, *et al.*, "The Need for a Balanced Ecosystem Approach to Blue Revolution Aquaculture," *Environment*, April 2007, pp. 41-42.

36. Jason Dean, "Recent Biotechnology Innovation Is a Bit Fishy: A Fluorescent Pet," *The Wall Street Journal*, May 8, 2003; Annie Huang, "Fluorescent Fish Aids Medical Research," The Associated Press, Sept. 1, 2005.

37. Aqua Bounty Technologies, "Our Products," www.aquabounty.com/products.html.

38. Pew Initiative on Food and Biotechnology, *Future Fish: Issues in Science and Regulation of Transgenic Fish* (2003), pp. 6-7, 10, 34.

39. National Research Council, *Animal Biotechnology: Science-Based Concerns* (2002), pp. 68-72.

40. *Ibid.*, p. 10.

41. *Ibid.*, p. 30.

42. Carlos M. Duarte, Nuria Marba and Marianne Holmer, "Rapid Domestication of Marine Species," *Science*, April 20, 2007, pp. 382-383.

43. For background, see David Hosansky, "Biotech Foods," *CQ Researcher*, March 31, 2001, pp. 249-272.

44. U.S. Department of Agriculture, Economic Research Service, "Adoption of Genetically Engineered Crops in the U.S.," July 14, 2006, www.ers.usda.gov/Data/BiotechCrops/adoption.htm.

45. Pew Initiative on Biotechnology, "Public Sentiments About Genetically Modified Food," 2003 and 2005 surveys, http://pewagbiotech.org/research/2006update/.

46. Barry A. Costa-Pierce, "Aquaculture in Ancient Hawaii," *BioScience*, vol. 37, no. 5, May 1987, pp. 320-330.

47. Brian Fagan, *Fish on Friday: Feasting, Fasting, and the Discovery of the New World* (2006), pp. 42-45, 133-141.

48. Jim Lichatowich, *Salmon Without Rivers: A History of the Pacific Salmon Crisis* (1999), pp. 182-190, 199.

49. For background, see Jennifer Weeks, "Factory Farms," *CQ Researcher*, Jan. 12, 2007, pp. 25-48.

50. United Nations Food and Agriculture Organization, *State of World Aquaculture 2006, FAO Fisheries Technical Paper 500* (2006), p. 5.

51. Craig Tucker and Jimmie Avery, "Industry Profile: Pond-Raised Channel Catfish," Mississippi State University, May 2004, www.agecon.msstate.edu/Aquaculture/pubs/Catfish_Industry_Profile.pdf.

52. Nick C. Parker, "History, Status, and Future of Aquaculture in the United States," Alabama Cooperative Extension System, www.aces.edu/dept/fisheries/education/documents/historyofaquaculture.pdf, p. 10.

53. Lichatowich, *op. cit.*

54. Rosamond Naylor, *et al.*, "Fugitive Salmon: Assessing the Risks of Escaped Fish from Net-Pen Aquaculture," *BioScience*, vol. 55, no. 5, May 2005, pp. 427-429.

55. U.S. Fish & Wildlife Service, "Wild Atlantic Salmon in Maine Protected as Endangered Species," news release, Nov. 13, 2000.

56. Naylor, *et al.*, *op. cit.*, p. 431; Martin Krkosek, *et al.*, "Epizootics of Wild Fish Induced By Farm Fish," *Proceedings of the National Academy of Sciences*, vol. 103, no. 42, Oct. 17, 2006.

57. U.S. Department of Agriculture, Animal and Plant Health Inspection Service, "CEI Impact Worksheet: White Spot Disease, Louisiana, USA," May 16, 2007.

58. *United States Public Interest Research Group, et al., v. Atlantic Salmon of Maine, LLC; United States Public Interest Research Group, et al., v. Stolt Sea Farm, Inc.*, 257 F. Supp. 2d 407, May 28, 2003.

59. "Study Finds Government Advisories on Fish Consumption and Mercury May Do More Harm Than Good," Harvard School of Public Health, Oct. 19, 2005; Daniel J. DeNoon, "Benefits of Fish Outweigh Mercury Risk," *WebMD*, Oct. 19, 2005.

60. Woods Hole Oceanographic Institute, *op. cit.*

61. National Offshore Aquaculture Act, H.R. 2010, Sec. 4(a)(4) and 4(a)(5)(B).

62. *Congressional Record*, June 13, 2007, p. S7645.

63. David Barboza, "Food-Safety Crackdown in China," *The New York Times*, June 28, 2007, p. C1.

64. "Senate Adopts Sessions' Amendment to Boost Inspection of Fish and Seafood," press release; www.sessions.senate.gov/pressapp/record.cfm?id=273830.

65. Food & Water Watch, *Import Alert: Government Fails Consumers, Falls Short on Seafood Inspections*, May 2007, p. 3.

66. *Ibid.*, p. 3.

67. Barboza, *op. cit.*

68. Julie Schmidt, "Chinese Fish Crisis Shows Seafood Safety Challenges," *USA Today*, June 28, 2007, p. 1A.

69. "Durbin, DeLauro: Chinese Government Agrees to Toughen Food Safety Standards for Imports," press release, May 9, 2007, www.senate.gov/~durbin/record.cfm?id=273861.

70. Kris Hudson and Wilawan Watcharasakwet, "The New Wal-Mart Effect: Cleaner Thai Shrimp Farms," *The Wall Street Journal*, July 24, 2007, p. B1.

71. See www.oceanboyfarms.com.

72. See www.virginiacobiafarms.biz/VirginiaCobiaFarms, www.australis.us/.

73. Hsiao-Ching Chou, " 'Guilt-Free' Fish Farming Arrives," *Seattle Post-Intelligencer*, Feb. 22, 2006.

BIBLIOGRAPHY

Books

Costa-Pierce, Barry A., ed., *Ecological Aquaculture: The Evolution of the Blue Revolution*, Blackwell, 2002.
A collection of articles by marine scientists highlights lessons about sustainability for today's fish farmers from aquaculture practiced in pre-modern societies.

Lichatowich, Jim, *Salmon Without Rivers: A History of the Pacific Salmon Crisis*, Island Press, 1999.
A fisheries biologist argues that wild salmon populations are dwindling in the Pacific Northwest because human interventions have failed to preserve salmon's habitat.

Molyneaux, Paul, *Swimming in Circles: Aquaculture and the End of Wild Oceans*, Thunder's Mouth Press, 2007.
Contrary to advocates' view that aquaculture can help ease the pressure on wild fisheries, journalist Molyneaux sees fish farming as merely the newest way to exploit the oceans.

***Sourcing Seafood: A Professional's Guide to Procuring Ocean-Friendly Fish and Shellfish*, Seafood Choices Alliance, 2004, www.seafoodchoices.org/resources/documents/SCA%20Directory%20Final.pdf.**
A trade association for the sustainable-seafood industry provides detailed descriptions of many ocean-friendly farmed and wild seafood products.

Articles

Bladholm, Linda, "Down on the (Shrimp) Farm: They're Organic, Planet-Friendly and Florida-Grown," *The Miami Herald*, Feb. 2, 2006.
OceanBoy Farms wants to reshape the shrimp-farming industry by using freshwater tanks instead of coastal ponds.

Greenberg, Paul, "Green to the Gills," *The New York Times Magazine*, June 18, 2006.

Major fish-farming countries like Norway are shaping the future of aquaculture by finding ways to domesticate cod and other wild species.

Lean, Geoffrey, "The GM 99," *The Independent* (London), July 9, 2006, p. 14.
Food giant Unilever is seeking approval in Europe to market ice cream containing an artificial protein copied from fish, but scientists call it a dangerous genetically modified product.

Pierce, Charles P., "The Next Big Fish," *The Boston Globe Magazine*, Nov. 26, 2006, p. 46.
In an illustration of how the seafood industry is globalizing, the barramundi, an Australian game fish, is now being raised in tanks in western Massachusetts and showing up on white-tablecloth U.S. restaurants.

Shumway, Sandra, *et al.*, "Shellfish Aquaculture — In Praise of Sustainable Economies and Environments," *World Aquaculture*, December 2003, pp. 15-17.
An overview of environmental and community benefits produced by shellfish farming.

***U.S. Food and Drug Administration*, "How FDA Regulates Seafood," June 28, 2007, www.fda.gov/ consumer/updates/seafood062807.html.**
The FDA describes how it detected antibiotics and other banned substances in imported seafood.

Reports

Knapp, Gunnar, Cathy A. Roheim and James L. Anderson, *The Great Salmon Run: Competition Between Wild and Farmed Salmon*, World Wildlife Fund, January 2007.

This in-depth look at policy issues related to wild and farmed salmon in North America includes the status of wild stocks, hatchery output, markets, and consumer preferences.

***Import Alert: Government Fails Consumers, Falls Short on Seafood Inspections*, Food & Water Watch, January 2007.**
A consumer watchdog group contends the U.S. Food and Drug Administration is not policing health risks from imported farmed seafood adequately.

***Joint Ocean Commission Initiative*, U.S. Ocean Policy Report Card, 2006, www.jointoceancommission.org/ images/report-card-06.pdf.**
Members of the Pew Oceans Commission and the U.S. Commission on Ocean Policy say the nation's progress toward reforming and improving ocean policy has been uneven and that more funding is needed at all levels of government to support the steps that have been taken.

***Marine Aquaculture Task Force*, Sustainable Marine Aquaculture: Fulfilling the Promise, Managing the Risks, Woods Hole Oceanographic Institute, January 2007.**
A group of experts says ocean fish farming could produce many benefits but also poses significant environmental risks. To make it work, the group calls for the United States to develop a well-structured regulatory system and environmental standards that focus on minimizing potential impacts on the oceans.

***WorldFish Center*, Fish: An Issue for Everyone, revised 2005.**
The nonprofit WorldFish Center, which works to make fish more available for food and income, argues that fish should be a major policy issue on the global agenda.

For More Information

Alaska Marine Conservation Council, P.O. Box 101145, Anchorage, AK 99510; (907) 277-5357; www.akmarine.org. Coalition of fishermen, scientists and conservationists seeking protection and restoration of Alaska's marine environment.

Atlantic Marine Aquaculture Center, University of New Hampshire, 35 Colovos Rd., Durham, NH 03824; (603) 862-3685; amac.unh.edu. Federally funded research center working to stimulate environmentally sustainable offshore ocean aquaculture.

Environmental Defense, 257 Park Ave. South, New York, NY 10010; (212) 505-2100; www.ed.org. National environmental organization conducting scientific and economic analysis of ocean issues.

Food & Water Watch, 1400 16th St., N.W., Suite 225, Washington, DC 20036; (202) 797-6550; www.food andwaterwatch.org. Watchdog group analyzing food safety, agriculture policy, fisheries and water rights.

Kona Blue Water Farms, 1 Keahole Point Rd., Kailua-Kona, HI 96740; (808) 331-1188; www.kona-blue.com. Group of marine biologists and local residents raising Hawaiian yellowtail through environmentally sound practices.

National Aquaculture Association, 111 W. Washington St., Suite 1, Charles Town, WV 25414; (304) 728-2167; www.nationalaquaculture.org. Trade organization for the aquaculture industry, representing both ocean and land-based fish-farming operations.

National Oceanographic and Atmospheric Administration, Aquaculture Program, 1315 East West Highway, Silver Spring, MD 20910; (301) 713-2370; aquaculture.noaa.gov. Manages federal aquaculture activities.

Woods Hole Oceanographic Institution, 266 Woods Hole Rd., Woods Hole, MA 02543; (508) 289-2252; www.whoi .edu. Works to advance ocean science.

Supporting researchers for more than 40 years

Research methods have always been at the core of SAGE's publishing program. Founder Sara Miller McCune published SAGE's first methods book, *Public Policy Evaluation*, in 1970. Soon after, she launched the *Quantitative Applications in the Social Sciences* series—affectionately known as the "little green books."

Always at the forefront of developing and supporting new approaches in methods, SAGE published early groundbreaking texts and journals in the fields of qualitative methods and evaluation.

Today, more than 40 years and two million little green books later, SAGE continues to push the boundaries with a growing list of more than 1,200 research methods books, journals, and reference works across the social, behavioral, and health sciences. Its imprints—Pine Forge Press, home of innovative textbooks in sociology, and Corwin, publisher of PreK–12 resources for teachers and administrators—broaden SAGE's range of offerings in methods. SAGE further extended its impact in 2008 when it acquired CQ Press and its best-selling and highly respected political science research methods list.

From qualitative, quantitative, and mixed methods to evaluation, SAGE is the essential resource for academics and practitioners looking for the latest methods by leading scholars.

For more information, visit **www.sagepub.com**.